ASIAN CANADIAN STUDIES READER

Edited by Roland Sintos Coloma and Gordon Pon

Roland Sintos Coloma and Gordon Pon's *Asian Canadian Studies Reader* brings together essential writings by leading and emerging scholars in the field to explore the vibrancy of the diverse Asian diaspora in Canada. The *Reader* is the perfect textbook for undergraduate courses in Race and Ethnic Studies and the Sociology of Migration.

The volume is organized into four main themes: ethnic, intersectional, comparative, and transnational encounters. It critically engages topics regarding orientalism, settler colonialism, globalization, and nationalism. Each groundbreaking essay challenges our conventional understandings of diversity and multiculturalism by tackling the intricacies of racism and racialization. By capturing the rich diversity within Asian Canadian communities, Coloma and Pon dispel the perceptions of Asians as always immigrants, newcomers, or model minorities. The *Asian Canadian Studies Reader* is the first interdisciplinary collection of essays intended for undergraduate use about Canada's largest racialized minority group.

(Asian Canadian Studies)

ROLAND SINTOS COLOMA is a professor and chair in the Department of Teacher Education at Northern Kentucky University.

GORDON PON is an associate professor in the School of Social Work at Ryerson University.

EDITED BY ROLAND SINTOS COLOMA
AND GORDON PON

Asian Canadian Studies Reader

UNIVERSITY OF TORONTO PRESS
Toronto Buffalo London

Toronto Buffalo London
www.utppublishing.com

ISBN 978-1-4426-3027-7 (cloth) ISBN 978-1-4426-3028-4 (paper)

Asian Canadian Studies Series

Library and Archives Canada Cataloguing in Publication

Asian Canadian studies reader / edited by Roland Sintos Coloma and Gordon Pon.

Includes bibliographical references.
ISBN 978-1-4426-3027-7 (hardcover).–ISBN 978-1-4426-3028-4 (softcover)

1. Asian Canadians. 2. Asians – Canada. 3. Asian Canadians – Ethnic identity. 4. Asian Canadians –Race identity. 5. Asian Canadians – Social conditions. 6. Asian Canadians – Social life and customs. 7. Canada – Ethnic relations. 8. Canada – Race relations. I. Pon, Gordon, editor II. Coloma, Roland Sintos, editor

FC106.A75A74 2017 305.895'071 C2017-901275-4

University of Toronto Press acknowledges the financial assistance to its publishing program of the Canada Council for the Arts and the Ontario Arts Council, an agency of the Government of Ontario.

Canada Council for the Arts Conseil des Arts du Canada

Funded by the Government of Canada Financé par le gouvernement du Canada Canada

Contents

Illustrations

Tables

Acknowledgments

So many people have helped us make the *Asian Canadian Studies Reader* come to fruition. We would like express our deepest gratitude to all the contributors in this *Reader*. Your work has been inspirational and influential in developing the intellectual, political, methodological, and pedagogical landscape of Asian Canadian Studies and in the scholarship on race, gender, class, migration, and transnationalism in Canadian Studies. Your pioneering inquiries and interventions serve as crucial foundations to our growing and exciting fields. Thank you to our graduate assistants – Shawna Carroll, Ken Huynh, Wakako Ishikawa, Laura Kwak, and Neil Ramjewan – for your meticulous diligence and support. Much appreciation goes to Eric Fong, the advisory board of the Asian Canadian Studies book series in the University of Toronto Press, and the anonymous reviewers. We could not have completed this book without the steadfast guidance of Douglas Hildebrand and the technical and marketing assistance of the University of Toronto Press.

We wish to thank the late Dr Roxana Ng, who was a trusted and stalwart colleague, mentor, professor, friend, and inspiring leader, and trailblazer. Her love for and dedication to her students have touched us deeply. She is sorely missed.

We also wish to thank our respective families. Roland thanks his partner James for his love, understanding, and reminders of food, sleep, and laughter. He deeply appreciates his parents, siblings, in-laws, and nieces and nephews in the United States and the Philippines who remind him to visit often and who anchor his and James' transnational family. He is inspired by his fearless cousin Charmaine Sintos and her family, his only relatives in Canada. Dear friends like Robert Diaz, Michael Adia, J.P. Camacho, and Chris Mangrobang make Toronto feel like a second home. While working and living in Canada from 2008 to 2014, he enjoyed the generous welcome, warm friendship, and engaging collaboration of fellow academics, community members, and students in Toronto and beyond. These are life-long ties that will continue in spite of geo-political distance and borders. Gordon would like to thank his wife Doret and daughter Jodie for their loving support and encouragement. He also wishes to thank his siblings Marion, Mona, and Winston for their unconditional love and support of his love for education, books, and reading. And his mother and father for supporting his passion for studying and knowledge seeking.

We also thank the Faculty of Community Services at Ryerson University for their assistance with funding. Lastly, we would like to thank the editors and publishers of the journal articles and book chapters for permission to reproduce parts of previously published materials:

Sedef Arat-Koç. "Whose Transnationalism?: Canada, 'Clash of Civilizations' Discourse, and Arab and Muslim Canadians." In *Transnational Identities and Practices in Canada*, ed. Vic Satzewich and Lloyd Wong, 216–40. Vancouver: University of British Columbia Press, 2006.

Himani Bannerji. "The Paradox of Diversity: The Construction of a Multicultural Canada and 'Women of Color.'" In *The Dark Side of the Nation: Essays on Multiculturalism, Nationalism and Gender*, 15–61. Toronto: Canadian Scholars' Press, 2000.

Lily Cho. "Sweet and Sour: Historical Presence and Diasporic Agency." In *Eating Chinese: Culture on the Menu in Small Town Canada*, 20–43. Toronto: University of Toronto Press, 2010.

Roland Sintos Coloma. "'Too Asian?': On Racism, Paradox, and Ethno-nationalism." *Discourse: Studies in the Cultural Politics of Education* 43 (4) (2013): 579–98.

Eric Fong. "Residential Segregation of Visible Minority Groups in Toronto." In *Inside the Mosaic*, ed. Eric Fong, 51–75. Toronto: University of Toronto Press, 2006.

Richard Fung. "Looking for My Penis: The Eroticized Asian in Gay Video Porn." In *How Do I Look? Queer Film and Video*," ed. Bad Ojbect-Choices, 145–68. Seattle: Bay Press, 1991

Alice Ming Wai Jim. "Redress Express: Chinese Restaurants and the Head Tax Issue in Canadian Art." *Amerasia* 33 (2) (2007): 97–114.

Yasmin Jiwani. "Orientalizing War Talk: Representations of the Gendered Muslim Body Post 9-11 in *The Montreal Gazette*." In *Situating "Race" and Racisms in Space, Time, and Theory*, ed. Jo-Anne Lee and John Lutz, 178–203. Montreal: McGill-Queen's University Press, 2005.

Peter S. Li. "The Racial Subtext in Canada's Immigration Discourse." *Journal of International Migration and Integration* 2 (1) (2001): 77–97.

Roy Miki. "Altered States: Global Currents, the Spectral Nation, and the Production of 'Asian Canadian.'" *Journal of Canadian Studies* 35 (3) (2000): 43–72.

Roxana Ng. "'A Woman Out of Control': Deconstructing Sexism and Racism in the University." *Canadian Journal of Education* 18 (3) (2005): 189–205.

Mona Oikawa. "Cartographies of Violence: Creating Carceral Spaces and Expelling Japanese Canadians from the Nation. In *Cartographies of Violence: Japanese Canadian Women, Memory, and the Subjects of the Internment*, 95–124. Toronto: University of Toronto Press, 2012.

Geraldine Pratt. "Between Homes: Displacement and Belonging for Second-Generation Canadian Youths." *BC Studies* 140 (Winter 2003–4): 41–68.

Sherene Razack. "The Muslims are Coming: The 'Sharia Debate' in Canada." In *Casting Out: The Eviction of Muslims from Western Law and Politics*, by 145–72. Toronto: University of Toronto Press, 2008.

Daiva K. Stasiulis and Abigail B. Bakan. "Marginalized and Dissident Non-Citizens: Foreign Domestic Workers." In *Negotiating Citizenship: Migrant Women in Canada and the Global System*, ed. Daiva K. Stasiulis and Abigail B. Bakan, 86–106. New York: Palgrave Macmillan, 2003.

Sunera Thobani. "Nationals, Citizens, and Others." In *Exalted Subjects: Studies in the Making of Race and Nation in Canada*, 67–102. Toronto: University of Toronto Press, 2010.

Rita Wong. "Decolonizasian: Reading Asian and First Nations Relations in Literature." *Canadian Literature* 199 (Winter 2008): 158–80.

Henry Yu. "Global Migrants and the New Pacific Canada." *International Journal* 64 (2009): 1011–26.

PART ONE

Encountering Asian Canada

1 Asian Canadian Studies Now: Directions and Challenges

GORDON PON, ROLAND SINTOS COLOMA, LAURA J. KWAK, AND KENNETH HUYNH

In this introduction, we discuss the need for Asian[1] Canadian Studies, a brief history of Asian immigration and settlement in Canada, how Asian Canadian resistance has been influenced by Asian American Studies, the challenges faced by proponents of Asian Canadian Studies, and the important insights shared by the contributors to this volume. This book, which has a national focus, serves as a showcase of the rigorous and innovative scholarship on Asians in Canada produced by scholars in wide ranging fields such as sociology, women studies, education, history, geography, literary, and cultural studies. This body of work has been produced by scholars from across Canada and continues to be created despite the lack of institutional support for Asian Canadian Studies and critical studies of race, colonialism, and diaspora in Canadian institutions of higher education.

A Brief History of Asian Immigration to Canada

According to Statistics Canada (2011), Asian Canadians are the largest "visible minority" group in the country, with 4,278,770 people identifying as "Asian" based on the demographic categories of Chinese, South Asian, Filipino, Southeast Asian, West Asian, Korean, Japanese, and multiple categories indicating the combined category of Asian and another group. In 2011 visible minorities (e.g., Asians, Blacks, those from Latin America and the Middle East, etc.) made up 19% of Canada's total population. The top three source countries for migration to Canada within the past decade are all Asian (China, India, and the Philippines). The top 10 visible minority groups in Canada are South Asian (25% of total visible minorities), Chinese (21.1%), Blacks (15.1%), Filipina/os (9.8%), Latin Americans (6%), Arabs (%), Southeast Asians (4.9%), West Asians (3.3%), Koreans (2.5%), and Japanese (1.3%).

The history of immigration and settlement of Asian peoples in Canada, however, presents a harrowing record of nineteenth- and early twentieth-century racism against this racialized group (Backhouse 1999; Roy 1989; Ward 1978). During this time period it was common to read articles in the mainstream press that declared Canada to be a "white man's country" (Adachi 1991; also see Thobani, this volume). Indeed, the first prime minister of Canada, John A. MacDonald, declared in a parliamentary speech that Canada was "a white man's country" (see Dua, this volume). Since the early days of the nation-state, Canada has struggled to balance the need for immigrants with a desire to keep Canada white (Fleras 2010). Galabuzi (2006) notes that Canada's political and economic development is similar to that of other settler societies, involving subordinating Indigenous peoples and developing the capitalist economy as a "foundation for the policies of slavery, marginalization and socio-economic exclusion of racialized immigrants" (75). Thus, while immigrants were needed as a source of labour for the burgeoning hinterland economy and backbreaking toil of jobs such as railway construction (Fleras, 2010), racialized immigrant labourers threatened the whiteness of the nation. During this period the outcome of immigration practices and laws were an interplay of the following factors: ideology, political expediency, international obligations, and the demand of colonial expansionism for cheap labour (Fleras 2010).

The desire for the preservation of a white Canada is evident in Canada's immigration laws. Explicit exclusion based on race was contained in section 38(c) of the Immigration Acts of 1910, 1919, and 1952 (Jakubowski 1997). This section created a class of immigrants who were deemed to be undesirable for admission into Canada (Jakubowski 1997). According to Jakubowski (1997), the Immigration Act of 1910 for the first time explicitly used the term "race" to indicate that some races were "preferred" and others "non-preferred" for admission into Canada as noted in the following Section 38(c) of the Act:

> Any nationality or race of immigrants of any specified class or occupation, by reason of any economic, industrial or other condition temporarily existing in Canada or because such immigrants are deemed unsuitable having regard to climatic, industrial, social, educational, labour ... or because such immigrants are deemed undesirable owing to peculiar customs, habits, modes of life, methods of holding property and because of their probable inability to become readily assimilated or to assume the duties and responsibilities of Canadian citizenship within a reasonable time after their entry.

The Immigration Act of 1910, section 38(c) also created a list of preferred countries (Jakubowski 1997):

> The policy of the Department at the present time is to encourage immigration of farmers, farm labourers, and female domestic servants from the United States, the British Isles, and certain Northern European countries, namely France, Belgium, Holland, Switzerland, Germany, Denmark, Norway, Sweden and Iceland. On the other hand, it is the policy of the Department to do all in its power to keep out of the country ... those belonging to nationalities unlikely to assimilate and who consequently prevent the building up of a united nation of people of similar customs and ideals. (Manpower and Immigration Canada 1974, 9–10)

Fleras (2010) asserts that Blacks and Asians were part of the non-preferred groups and viewed as inherently inferior and unassimilable.

While providing a comprehensive history of Asian groups that have settled in Canada is beyond the scope of this introduction, we do present brief sketches of the immigration history of Canadians of Chinese, Japanese, South Asian and more recently Filipina/o ancestry to highlight the political contexts out of which immigration laws were formulated and the impact of such legislation. We begin with the case of Chinese Canadians. The earliest presence of Chinese people on Turtle Island (the Indigenous name for North America) was in 458 A.D. Griff (1958) writes the following: "In 458 A.D. a group of Buddhist priests travelled to a country they called Fu Shang (the land known as Canada today), 15,000 kilometres to the east of China, which stretched 5,000 kilometres to another ocean" (7). However, Chinese people did not settle permanently until 1788, when 50 artisans accompanied Captain John Meares to Fort Nootka of Vancouver Island (Chan 1983; Wickberg et al. 1982), with many settling in Canada. The next group of Chinese people to arrive in Canada took place in the 1850s. These individuals came mainly from Toisan County in southern China in search of gold in California and British Columbia (Yee 1993). The need for cheap labour to construct the western segments of the Canadian Pacific Railway fuelled the next wave of Chinese settlers in British Columbia from 1881 to 1885. Of the 15,701 Chinese people who entered Canada during this period, about 6,500 were employed as indentured labourers by contractors building the CPR (Li 1988). The indentured Chinese labourers faced considerable racial discrimination and received half of the wages paid to white workers (Yee 1993). Many Chinese men died during the construction of the railway, often perishing because they were assigned the most dangerous tasks such as mountain blasting (Li 1988). Also, with the low rates of pay, many indentured labourers had to work for years to pay off their contractors.

Upon the completion of the CPR in 1885, the first federal anti-Chinese bill was enacted. A fifty-dollar head tax was levied against all Chinese people entering Canada. This law was aimed at curtailing Chinese immigration. As early as 1875, the province of British Columbia passed legislation denying voting rights to the Chinese people. Since provincial voters' lists were used as a qualification, the Chinese people were also excluded from nomination for municipal office, school trustees, jury service, and election to provincial legislatures (Chan 1983; Li 1988). Likewise, since the Chinese people were disenfranchised, they could not enter professions such as law and pharmacy. In 1890 and 1903 bills were enacted that prevented the Chinese people from working underground and performing skilled jobs in the burgeoning mining industries; in 1897 they were prohibited from being hired on public works; and one of the conditions of the sale of Crown timber was that "Asiatics" not be employed (Chan 1983; Li 1988). In addition, in 1900 the head tax was raised to $100, and subsequently increased to $500 in 1903. The nadir of anti-Chinese legislation culminated in the Chinese Immigration Act of 1 July 1923, which was also known as the "Chinese Exclusion Act." The bill represented the most comprehensive policy ever enacted by the Canadian state to restrict the entry of a particular racial group. The Act virtually stopped Chinese immigration to Canada for twenty-four years until its repeal in 1947. The date of 1 July 1923 was termed "Humiliation Day" among the Chinese people in Canada and by their relatives abroad (Chan 1983; Li 1988).

The Chinese Exclusion Act of 1923 prevented many Chinese men from bringing their wives and families to Canada. Therefore, before the end of the Second World War, most of the Chinese in Canada were men. In 1921, out of a total Chinese population of 39,587 there were only 2,424 women in all of Canada (Adilman 1984). Of these women, 1,713 resided in British Columbia, where the population totaled 23,533. Despite their low numbers, Chinese women's labour was indispensable to the survival and economic viability of Chinese families and communities (Adilman 1984; Poy 2013; Women's Book Committee and Chinese Canadian National Council 1992), and they have often been at the unheralded forefront of community activism (J. Lee 2007).

Upon completion of the railway, intense fear, hatred, and demonization of Asian people characterized Canadian society. The Chinese women and men who settled in Canada were, however, far from being passive victims of racism (Women's Book Committee and Chinese Canadian National Council 1992). Many fought back and resisted in myriad ways that ranged from labour organizing to fight unfair wages and treatment (Creese 1987), suing in civil court (Backhouse 1999), to the purchase of firearms following the Vancouver race riot of 1907 (Adachi 1991).

The legislated racism against the Chinese in Canada from 1885 to the early twentieth century was buttressed by popular cultural, political, and social discourses that constructed

Asians, particularly Chinese men, as the "Yellow Peril," which threatened to displace white European immigrants (Lowe 1997). This discourse constructed Chinese men as threatening, conniving, inscrutable, effeminate, filthy, opium smoking, sexual predators who coveted white women (Pon 1996). Asian women, on the other hand, were constituted as dangers to white domination because of their perceived fecundity and lasciviousness, which threatened to produce too many non-white offspring and/or miscegenation (see Dua and Thobani, this volume). Attendant to the emergent Canadian nation-state was the promulgation of what Said (1979) has called "Orientalism," which is the European discourse that constructed the geopolitical space of the Orient as a region of perverseness, backwardness, weakness, femininity, and barbaric crudeness. According to Orientalism, these attributes of the East differentiated the Orient from the Occident, and rendered the Orient befitting for western imperial conquest, as Said explained: "The point here is that the space of the weaker or underdeveloped regions like the Orient was viewed as something inviting French interest, penetration, insemination – in short, colonization" (Said 2007, 52).

In Canada, Orientalism was a discourse that fuelled anti-Asian racism and provided the pathological "Other" against which white settlers could imagine their community as exalted national subjects (see Thobani, this volume). As exalted nationals, their racist exclusionary practices were viewed as safeguarding Canada against the threats to the nation represented by racialized immigrants. Thus, while the burgeoning industries of the emerging nation-state fuelled the demand for cheap Asian labour, Asians were not welcomed within the white national imaginary of who constituted proper Canadians. While the anti-Asian racism in Canada began with a clear targeting of Chinese railway workers, this discrimination extended to Japanese and South Asian immigrants.

Japanese people first settled in Canada in the 1870s, working primarily in the sawmill and salmon fishing industries (Adachi 1991). They, like the Chinese settlers, faced virulent racial discrimination in the form of economic exploitation, being barred from provincial and federal franchise, housing prejudices, and segregation in schools (Henry & Tator 2010). On 7 September 1907, the worst race riot in the history of British Columbia occurred when the right-wing organization called the Asiatic Exclusion League (Ng 2010) organized a protest against Asian immigrants. The crowd swelled to about 5000 when protestors began smashing windows of shops in Vancouver's Chinatown, then about 1000 rioters moved on to the Japanese quarter (Adachi 1991). Adachi describes that "The Japanese met the mob at first with defensive tactics, pelting rocks down from rooftops. But then they sallied forth with sticks, clubs, iron bars, knives and bottles. Crying 'Bonzai' they tore into the mob" (74). The next business day following the riot, the Chinese were reported to be buying revolvers and rounds of ammunition (Adachi 1991). The riot however did not mitigate the virulent racism espoused by the Asiatic Exclusion League, which continued to agitate for total cessation of Asian immigration (Adachi 1991). In 1908 a "Gentleman's Agreement" was struck between the Canadian and Japanese governments that would permit only very few Japanese to enter Canada (Henry & Tator 2010).

The nadir of discrimination against Japanese settlers in Canada occurred in 1942 following the bombing of Pearl Harbor by Japan in 1941, when twenty-three thousand Japanese were sent to relocation and detention camps (Oikawa, this volume). Thirteen thousand and three hundred of these people were in fact born in Canada. Many of the interned men were forced to labour on road construction projects, and women were continually forced to move from camp to camp, camp to farm, farm to domestic service, which involved separation from partners, family members, and friends (see Oikawa, this volume). Void of their human rights, they were stripped of their property, and their businesses and savings were impounded. Oikawa (this volume) notes that a study conducted by Price Waterhouse of Vancouver published in 1986 estimated the total loss for the community at $48 million in 1948 dollars, or $443 million in 1986 dollars.

Both Japanese Canadian men and women resisted the racism of the Internment (see Oikawa, this volume). For example, Japanese Canadian men formed the Nisei Mass Evacuation Group (NMEG), which resisted the governmental order calling for the break-up of families (Miki 1998; 2004; Okazaki 1996; also see Oikawa, this volume), while Japanese Canadian women formed the Nisei Mass Evacuation Women's Group in 1942 to support the interned men and "resist evacuation" (Nunoda 1991; see also Oikawa, this volume).

The South Asians who first settled in Canada in the late nineteenth century also faced intense anti-Asian racism. The first South Asians to arrive in Canada were Sikhs, who settled in British Columbia. We adopt the definition of "South Asians" as advanced by Henry and Tator (2010) as "people who were born or whose ancestors were born in the Indian sub-continent, and include people from India, Pakistan, Sri Lanka, and Bangladesh. It also includes those who have roots in South Asia who migrated to Kenya, Tanzania, Uganda, the Caribbean nations, and other countries" (63). By 1908, there were approximately five thousand South Asians in Canada (Henry & Tator 2010). The racism they faced in Canada included being denied the franchise, and since they were not allowed to vote this precluded them from entering professions such as law, pharmacy, and education, and they were not permitted to sell Crown timber (Henry & Tator 2010).

In 1914 four hundred passengers from India aboard a vessel called the *Komagatu Maru* were denied entry into Canada when it landed in Vancouver. The ship was forced to return to India. Another way in which South Asians were effectively barred from immigrating to Canada was through the Continuous Passage Act, which stipulated that would-be immigrants to Canada must travel continuously from their country of origin to Canada. Because no such vessel existed that could travel continuously from India to Canada without stopping to refuel, this in essence barred Indian people from migrating to Canada.

Today following the September 11 attacks of the World Trade Centre, many South Asians, including dark-skinned persons of Arab or Middle Eastern heritage, particularly those who are or are perceived as Muslim, face acute Islamophobia and anti-Muslim racism (see Arat-Koç and Jiwani, this volume). This discrimination is manifested in hyper-surveillance and racial profiling of South Asians by police and border security officials at airports and border crossings (Thobani 2007). They are also often stereotyped as terrorists and the men as hyperpatriarchal and pre-modern, while the women are viewed as oppressed, meek, and timid (see Arat-Koç, Jiwani, and Thobani, this volume). There is however resistance to the anti-Muslim racism they are facing. For example, Sedef Arat-Koç (see this volume) highlights how activists from these impacted communities are organizing alternative transnationalisms that are trans-ethnic and non-ethnic solidarities, as a way to challenge current national and transnational orders.

According to Fleras (2010), three characteristics defined the early period of immigration when the Chinese, Japanese, and South Asian people began settling in Canada, which are 1) governments were forced to balance competing interests regarding immigration policy: businesses desired a stream of cheap immigrant labour, while organized labour and public sentiment wanted fewer immigrants in Canada because they were seen as depressing wages, fuelling job insecurity, and threatening the living standards of Canadians (Avery 1995; Fleras 2010); 2) governments needed to fulfil economic needs of expanding capitalism such as railway construction; and 3) governments and industries had to fulfil hard labour requirements, or what Fleras calls the "backbreaking toil of taming the wilderness" (252), basically jobs that white Canadians did not want. What is evident is the fact that racialized immigrants were wanted for their labour and were tolerated as long as they quietly toiled away at their jobs (Fleras 2010); however, once the demand for their labour diminished, the state, buttressed by racist labour organizations (Ng 2010), quickly sought to curtail further immigration of racialized people and place restrictions on the civil liberties of those already in Canada, such as denying them the right to vote and from becoming Canadian citizens; denying entry into professions such as law, pharmacy, and education; and preventing access to social welfare programs and services (Thobani 2007).

Fleras (2010) describes a double standard facing immigrants in Canada. On one hand, they are labelled as job stealers, and when unemployed, they are viewed as "free loading parasites" (Fleras, 2010, 244). As such he describes Canadians as "'reluctant hosts' who appear welcoming at times and obstructionist at other times, but whose ambivalence – even hostility – toward certain foreign-born individuals is palpable beneath a folksy veneer of tolerance" (244). Furthermore, this veneer of tolerance is implicated in the quality of life and standard of living in Canada (Fleras 2010). Immigrants are required to offset an aging population and declining birthrate, and "undocumented labour that immigrants and refugees provide is critical to shoring up the middle-class lifestyle that Canadians crave" (Fleras 2010, 243).

The preferred versus non-preferred immigration system would be in place until 1962. In 1962 Canadian immigration policy shifted away from a focus on race, ethnicity, and country of origin to an ostensibly deracialized emphasis on skills, education, and experience (Fleras 2010). In 1967 a point system was introduced in which both "independent and assisted-relative applicants were numerically assessed against the demands of occupation, education, and language expertise" (Fleras 2010, 253). While this colour-blind points system was supposed to be free of racial bias, in reality it continued to favour "class-advantaged male applicants with access to educational credentials in those countries with Canadian embassies for processing applications" (Fleras 2010, 253). Thobani (this volume) points out that immigrant recruiting resources were disproportionately allocated to developed countries in comparison to developing ones. Jakubowski (1997), citing the Law Union of Ontario, describes the following:

> There are five immigration offices in the United Kingdom, but only three in South America, and only five in the whole of Africa, two of which are located in South Africa. The United States has ten offices, but India, with twice the population only has one. (Law Union of Ontario, citied in Jakubowski 1997, 20)

Thobani (this volume) also points out that immigration officers were given discretionary powers to allocate points to applicants for their personal suitability. This resulted in officers disproportionately favouring male applicants as independents over female ones (Thobani, this volume).

The Immigration Act of 1976 signalled another shift in orientation with a declared emphasis on balancing the following: 1) reunifying families, 2) protecting legitimate refugees, 3) enhancing Canada's prosperity and global competitiveness, and 4) preserving Canada's integrity (Fleras 2010). Grace-Edward Galabuzi (2006) asserts that despite the 1960s shift towards the point system, immigrant economic performance has grown worse over the past twenty-five years, signalling a permanent income disparity between racialized immigrant groups and the rest of the Canadian population (Galabuzi 2006). He asserts that these findings reflect barriers to employment or being slotted into low-paying jobs, all of which is being experienced by racialized immigrants. Gender discrimination is also evidenced in the fact that many racialized immigrant women are being "imported into the lower ranks of the health care sector, the textile and garment industry, the service sector and clerical ghettos, and disproportionately subjected to precarious forms of employment" (Galabuzi 2006, 8).

In our post-9/11 world, discourses are emerging that portray Canada as being too lax and thus constituting a haven for terrorists (Fleras 2010). As a result, demands have increased to tighten up the immigration system, including calls for DNA screening, immigration and citizenship testing, and a rigorous deportation system, all of which at times borders on xenophobia (Fleras 2010). For example, the Immigration and Refugee Protection Act of 2002 placed increased emphasis on the security of Canadian society. The Anti-Terrorism Act of 2001, which was passed soon after the events of 9/11, give the police, the RCMP, and CSIS new powers for increased surveillance of persons including protestors and political activists who attend rallies, meetings, and conferences (see Arat-Koç, this volume). One of the most significant implications of this legislation has been "criminalization of dissent," including "the creation of a climate in which even those who are not specifically targeted are still affected and are either silenced or silence themselves" (Sherazee 2002, 20).

Presently, Fleras (2010) asserts that immigration in Canada remains first and foremost self-serving, in that immigrants are vital for the following reasons: 1) offsetting the current effects of an aging population and declining birth rate, 2) increasing the tax paying base to fund costly services and programs, 3) expanding the domestic market, 4) establishing profitable international linkages, and 5) stimulating sustained economic activity through production and consumption (Fleras 2010). There is also the need for "cheap and disposable labour" (Fleras 2010, 252) as evidenced in the temporary agricultural workers (Preibisch & Encalada Grez 2010) and domestic live-in caregivers (see Stasiulis & Bakan, this volume) who are vital to the Canadian economy and standard of living.

A significant source country for women domestic live-in caregivers is the Philippines. Most Filipina/os in Canada have arrived since the 1990s onwards, and now constitute the fourth largest visible minority group (172,000) in Toronto, Ontario (Coloma et al. 2012). The first Filipina/os emigrated to Canada in the 1950s and 1960s and were mostly professionals such as nurses, doctors, and laboratory technicians, who were in demand due to labour shortages (Coloma et al. 2012; Eric 2012). Later in the 1980s many Filipinas entered Canada through the Foreign Domestic Workers Movement program, which in 1992 was replaced with the Live-In Caregiver Program (LCP) (Coloma et al. 2012). Between 1980 to 2001, 12 per cent of Philippine-born arrivals in Canada came under the LCP and 79.6 per cent were women (25,846 out of 32,474) (Coloma et al. 2012). Scholars have argued that foreign domestic workers in Canada face structural discrimination, which makes these women vulnerable to physical abuse, denial of privacy rights, and lacking in fair wages and benefits (see Stasiulis & Bakan, this volume). Coloma et al. (2012) in their book titled *Filipinos in Canada* note that given the relatively recent arrival of Filipina/os in Canada, the "incubation period for cultural and academic production" (12) has been much shorter, which has resulted in scholarship on Filipina/os Canadians being much more recent and emerging.

Not unlike all other Asian Canadian communities, the Filipina/o community has come together to resist the racism directed at their community and created agencies and organizations with mandates committed to social justice. For example, Toronto's Community

Alliance for Social Justice (CASJ) was formed in response to the police shooting in 2004 of a Filipino youth named Jeffrey Reodica (Eric 2012). The CASJ is an organization of Filipino community groups and individuals dedicated to advancing social justice through advocacy, education, and community action (https://casj.wordpress.com/about/). The Migrant Workers Family Resource Centre in Hamilton was formed by a former domestic worker named Josephine Eric (Eric 2012). McElhinny et al. (2012) note that much of the resistance has also been in the form of innovative and strategic collaborations between community-based organizations such as the CASJ and university based academics such as Phillip Kelly; Geraldine Pratt's collaboration with the Philippine Women's Centre in Vancouver; and Sedef Arat-Koç and Fely Villasin's (2001) partnership with INTERCEDE, which is a Toronto-based organization for migrant worker's rights (McElhinny et al. 2012). To be sure, Filipina/o Canadians have organized, resisted, and fought back against the discrimination they face; in this regard, this community is not any different from the countless other Asian immigrants who have settled in Canada and united to resist the perniciousness of racial discrimination and marginalization.

Historically, the critical consciousness, identities, and resistance of Asian Canadian communities were influenced by the Asian American movement of the 1960s and the emergence of Asian American Studies programs in US universities. Anthony Chan (1983) explains that

> Asian America provided a model for Asian Canadian writers. It set the pattern for interests and preoccupations. In particular, Asian American writers brought a new pride to being Asian in white America. Inspired by American works, Asian Canadian writers began to celebrate life in Asian Canada. In time, a trickle of poetry and prose began to emerge from Vancouver to Toronto … more Asian Canadians entered the world of literature, drawing courage from the successes of those who had gone before. (195)

Asian Canadian writers and artists were galvanized by the emerging Asian American consciousness and the Asian American literary movement that was occurring in the 1960s and 70s. Chinese Canadian writers undertook to organize and come together and in April 1978, The Asianadian Resource Workshop was created in Toronto. This collective served as a coordinating centre for Asian Canadian writers, artists, musicians, and educators who were interested in the Asian experience in Canada (Chan 1983). The group initiated the national publication of a community-oriented journal called the *Asianadian: An Asian Canadian Magazine.* This journal provided an important forum for Asian Canadian writers and poets. At the same time, in Vancouver, the Powell Street Review and the Chinese Canadian Writers Workshop published an anthology entitled *Inalienable Rice: A Chinese and Japanese Perspective* (Chu et al. 1979). The Chinese Canadian Writers Workshop included Sean Gunn, Jim Wong Chu, and SKY Lee. Lee's first novel titled *Disappearing Moon Cafe* (Lee 1990) won her the Vancouver Book Award for 1990 and her novel has been studied by numerous scholars of Asian American Studies.

Asian American Studies and the broader Asian American Movement that gave rise to the ethnic studies programs had not only a positive influence on the identities and politics of Asian Canadian writers and artists, but activists as well. One of the most telling moments in the history of Chinese Canadian resistance is the anti-W5 movement. On 30 September 1979 Canadian broadcaster CTV aired a program titled "Campus Giveaway," in which they alleged that 100,000 foreign students were taking spots in professional programs away from white Canadian students (Chan 1983; Fernando 2006). As this was being narrated the camera panned the faces of Chinese students, thus portraying them as foreigners, aliens, and transient sojourners (Chan 1983; Lai 1988; Nipp 1985). The racist nature of the program gave rise to strident activism and street protests in cities such as Toronto that numbered in the thousands. This level of anti-racism activism was unprecedented in the Chinese Canadian community (Chan 1983). Chan (1983) asserts that many of the young Chinese Canadian activists who participated in the activism were undoubtedly inspired by the Asian American movement.

Chan (1983) explains that in 1979 when the CTV aired "Campus Giveaway," Chinese Canadian youth in British Columbia had over time been inspired by the audacity of the Third World strike contingents of Asian American, Black, and Latino students. Chinese Canadian youth were also moved by the nascent and powerful body of Asian American literature by writers such as Maxine Hong Kingston and Frank Chin. Thus Chinese Canadian youth "began their own search for roots and to formulate a new destiny for themselves in Canada" (162). Therefore, when "Campus Giveaway" aired, the Asianadian Resource Workshop and Chinese Canadian students played a central role in the two year anti-W5 movement to demand a public apology from CTV, which the broadcaster eventually provided (Chan 1983; Fernando 2006). Chan notes that the anti-W5 movement was also bolstered by a strong contingent of Chinese Canadians who had emigrated from Hong Kong to Toronto, many of whom had social work backgrounds. While in Hong Kong these activists had participated in the 1971 student demonstrations in support of China's claim against Japan regarding the island of Diao Yutai (Chan 1983). Chan asserts that this background in activism positioned these activists, who were now residing in Toronto, to undertake a robust, strident, and sustained response to the W5 "Campus Giveaway."

The linkages between Asian American Studies and Asian Canadians is thus evident in terms of Chinese Canadian literary works and also in anti-racism activism by groups such as Chinese Canadians. The Asian American movement had a galvanizing and inspiring impact on young Asian Canadians in cities such as Toronto and Vancouver. Today, the links between Asian American Studies and Asian Canadians can be evidenced in the Canadian students who move to the US to study Asian American Studies and the interest that numerous Canadians (students and professors) continue to have in the Asian American Studies conferences, scholarship, and research. Also, Asian American Studies has not been untouched by Asian Canadian literature as evidenced by the numerous Asian American Studies scholars who write about SKY Lee's *Disappearing Moon Cafe* and Joy Kogawa's (1981) *Obasan*. This transnational interest in the work of Lee and Kogawa is not surprising as both Canada and the US share similar sordid modern histories vis-à-vis the indenture of Chinese labourers and internment of Japanese citizens.

Against this backdrop of a brief history of Asian immigration and settlement in Canada, and how Asian Canadian resistance has been positively impacted by Asian American Studies, we now turn our attention to discussing the need for Asian Canadian Studies.

The Need for Asian Canadian Studies Now

Asian Canadian Studies (ACS) as a scholarly area of research and teaching is not yet widely offered in Canadian universities and colleges. At this time, only three universities have academic programs in ACS – Simon Fraser University (established in the 2000s), the University of Toronto (established in 2013), and the University of British Columbia (established in 2014). Simon Fraser University has an undergraduate minor in the Asia-Canada Program where students can focus on the Asian dimension of life in Canada. The University of Toronto and the University of British Columbia have undergraduate minor programs in Asian Canadian Studies. The absence of widespread institutional support for ACS coincides with the lack of academic journals, scholarly associations, and annual conferences that are dedicated to advancing research about Asians in Canada (Ho & Yu 2007; C. Lee 2007).

In 2013 a national organization for Asian Canadian Studies (ACS) was officially launched. The Asian Canadian Studies Network, co-founded by Henry Yu, John Price, and others, is a collective of faculty, students, and community members who envision ACS as a "distinct field of study, research and cultural production for social justice" (http://asiancanadianstudies.ca/). Its mission includes respecting Canada's Indigenous foundations and valuing inclusivity, transnationalism, and transformation. The network promotes networking within and beyond Asian Canadian communities, challenging limited nationalist narratives, emphasizing the trans-Pacific region as a borderless terrain, and valuing participatory research and collective actions for change. Christopher Lee (C. Lee 2007), a member of the ACS Network, argues that Asian Canadian Studies should always remain "a self-reflexive practice that constantly interrogates its own institutional attachments" (4).

When one considers that Asian Canadians are the largest racialized minority group in Canada, it is fitting that ACS programs ought to be instituted throughout the country. This would serve to equitably meet the intellectual and pedagogical needs not only of this diverse population but also of the rest of Canada. As noted earlier, Asian Canadians are the largest "visible minority" group in the country, and the top three source countries for migration to Canada within the past decade are all Asian (Statistics Canada 2011). Consequently, it is incumbent upon Canadian universities and colleges to make curricular and teaching transformations that equitably respond to these changing demographics and realities.

The creation of Asian Canadian Studies programs would, as Christopher Lee (C. Lee 2007, 2) argues, help to "catalyze changes in curriculum, instruction, and research, and stimulate wider dialogue in regards to the legacies and effects of racism and other forms of oppression." Roland Sintos Coloma (2012) argues that the current history curriculum in Canadian secondary and post-secondary schools includes limited depictions of Asian Canadians at best or hardly any mention of them at worst. Mainstream curriculum also tends to avoid the difficult topic of racism. For example, history textbooks that include the experiences of Japanese and Chinese Canadians seldom discuss the linkages between racism, exclusionary laws, and internment. Similarly, Verna St Denis (2011) criticizes the absence of Aboriginal curriculum in the Canadian school system. The establishment of an inclusive and critical Asian Canadian Studies program could address these deficiencies in curriculum and instruction.

Concomitant with the curricular erasure of historical and ongoing anti-Asian racism is the myth that Canada is a multicultural nation that is benevolent and tolerant of racial and cultural differences. There is a prevailing assumption that, because Canada endorses multiculturalism, racism does not exist in the country. However, systemic and structural racism against Asian Canadians – as well as against Aboriginal and other racialized minorities – remains a pressing problem (Carniol 2010; Lavallée & Poole 2010). As noted earlier, following the tragedies on 11 September 2001, racism against Muslim[2] people (and those who are mistaken as Muslims and Arabs) has intensified in the forms of Islamophobia, hyper-surveillance, and racial profiling (see chapters by Arat-Koç, Jiwani, and Razack in this volume). The vicious beating and murder of Reena Virk in British Columbia in 1997 (Jiwani 2010; Lee 2006; Rajiva & Batacharya 2010) and the racially motivated "nipper tipping" assaults on

Asian Canadian fishermen in Ontario in 2007 are two relatively recent and explicit acts of anti-Asian racism. The Live-In Caregiver Program continues to reproduce racism, sexism, classism, and western imperialism through Canada's labour, immigration, and health care policies (Coloma et al. 2012; Stasiulis & Bakan, this volume). Labour market racism continues to marginalize and discriminate against Asian immigrants and Asian Canadians (Das Gupta 1996; Galabuzi 2006; Man 1997, 2007), and media-based racism against Asians is evidenced in the 2010 *Maclean's* magazine article on elite universities being "too Asian" (Coloma, this volume; Cui & Kelly 2012; Heer 2012; Mahtani 2010).

The "Too Asian?" article raises questions about whether or not journalism students are being taught critical perspectives such as anti-racism and about the lack of racial diversity in journalism faculties and in the newsroom. The Eurocentric bias in mainstream curriculum is inseparable from larger problems regarding the under-representation of Indigenous and racialized minority teachers and professors employed in the education system. For example, out of the 436,190 Filipina/os in Canada, there are only eight tenured or tenure-stream professors of Filipino descent in the humanities and social sciences in the entire country (Coloma 2012). The establishment of Asian Canadian Studies does not guarantee the hiring and retention of more racialized minority professors, but it creates an institutional pathway in the academy and a network of scholars who can mentor and guide the next generations of ACS researchers and instructors. These future academics would continue to advance research and curriculum about the oft-ignored issues and communities in Canada.

Despite the absence of institutionally supported ACS programs across the country, there is an impressive body of critical work about Asians in Canada. This includes work by artists, academics, and activists, and is informed by critical perspectives of anti-racism, postcolonialism, Indigenous theories, Marxism, critical race feminism, and others. Asian Canadians have created numerous spaces to advance critical discussions and debates about race and difference. For example, as noted earlier *Asianadian*, a literary magazine, was founded in 1978 by Tony Chan, Cheuk Kwan, and Paul Levine (Ty & Verduyn 2008). The Asian Canadian Writers Workshop produces a magazine called *Ricepaper*, which highlights the diverse cultural works by persons of East Asian, Southeast Asian, and multi-racial Asian descent (Ty & Verduyn 2008). In 2009, Alice Ming Wai Jim convened "Can-Asian, eh? Diaspora, Indigeneity, and the Transpacific," the international annual conference of East Asian and South Asian Councils–Canadian Asian Studies Association (CASA), which took place in Vancouver, British Columbia (Jim 2010). In 2010 the Asian Canadian Theatre Conference was held, which inaugurated a new scholarly field of Asian Canadian theatre and performance studies (Aquino & Knowles 2011). In 2013 the Asian Canadian Studies Network hosted its inaugural meeting in Victoria, British Columbia, entitled "Over the Edge: Forming Asian Canadian Studies," as part of the annual Congress of the Humanities and Social Sciences.

Due to the lack of institutional support, many scholars have sought other avenues to contribute to critical scholarship on race, indigeneity, and diaspora. For instance, the Researchers and Academics of Colour for Equity/Equality (R.A.C.E) collective was founded in 2001, and represents the first cross-Canada network of Indigenous and racialized minority faculty who have shared commitments to promoting critical anti-racist and anti-colonial feminist scholarship (Razack, Smith, & Thobani 2010). Since its inauguration, R.A.C.E. has organized nine annual conferences. Its founding members include Sherene Razack, Sunera Thobani, Sedef Arat-Koç, Yasmin Jiwani, and Enakshi Dua, all of whom have chapters in this volume.

Academics writing, researching, and teaching about Asians in Canada have found important intellectual and pedagogical support in organizations such as R.A.C.E. and the Asian Canadian Studies Network. Yet there is still a crucial need for Asian Canadian Studies programs in universities and colleges to support scholars and students committed to research and teaching on Asians in Canada. Such institutional programs would help facilitate organizing annual conferences, establishing academic journals, advancing research collaborations and dissemination of findings, and building pathways for future generations of scholars and activists.

Finally, there is a need for Asian Canadian Studies to build and strengthen extant linkages between academics and Asian Canadian communities. Many scholars associated with R.A.C.E., for example, are linked to community groups and activism. The Solidarity Committee Against Anti-Asian Racism is a network of activists and academics committed to racial justice and grassroots organizing (see Coloma, this volume). Institutionally supported Asian Canadian Studies would strengthen the activist-scholars' commitment to collaborating with community members in participatory action research (Sin 2007; Wong, Wong, & Fung 2010). This is vital since federal research funding bodies, such as the Social Sciences and Humanities Research Council (SSHRC), require that principal investigators be employed as university professors. Community groups have no access to SSHRC funding without the support of a university faculty member. This is a systemic barrier in the advancement of equitable and inclusive knowledge production, especially if some Asian groups are severely under-represented among the ranks of university faculty members.

Challenges to Asian Canadian Studies

Despite the intellectual, pedagogical, and community need, establishing institutional structures, resources, and support for Asian Canadian Studies faces many challenges. Below we discuss seven barriers. First, Christopher Lee (C. Lee 2007) contends that the absence or "lateness" of Asian Canadian Studies is a result of systemic institutional barriers that point to failures of educational institutions to effectively respond to ethno-racial diversity in general and Asian Canadians in particular. Commenting on the long birth of Asian Canadian literature vis-à-vis its Asian American counterpart, Donald Goellnicht (2000) argues that this protraction is linked in part to an absence in Canada of strident anti-war and Black Power movements. Indeed, Ethnic Studies academic programs were established in United States in the late 1960s with the explicit mandate to critique state policies from anti-racist and anti-imperialist standpoints (Louie & Omatsu 2001; McElhinny et al. 2012; Omatsu 2000; Wei 1993). The lateness of Asian Canadian Studies must be understood within this historical context that differentiates Canada from the United States.

A second barrier contributing to the absence of Asian Canadian Studies in Canada is the federal policy of multiculturalism. This policy constitutes Canada as a benevolent nation that welcomes and celebrates racial and cultural differences, unlike the United States, which is perceived to be assimilationist (Bannerji, see this volume; Haque 2012; St Denis 2011). This notion of multicultural tolerance and benevolence makes it difficult for Canadians to acknowledge Canada's historical and ongoing problems of colonization, racism, and other forms of exclusion and oppression. Advocates for intellectual and pedagogical initiatives such as ACS encounter the hegemonic discourse of the nation-state and its citizens as tolerant and welcoming, which is used to downplay the marginalization of Asian Canadians, Indigenous peoples, and other racialized minorities.

A third factor that obstructs the establishment of ACS is the prevailing discourse of model minority, which asserts that Asians in Canada have largely overcome racial discrimination and have succeeded educationally and materially through hard work, family values, parental upbringing, and other investments in education (Coloma, this volume; Maclear 1994; Pon 2015). The model minority discourse dovetails with the liberal underpinnings of multiculturalism. Together the two discourses function to erase considerations of the educational and socio-cultural needs of Asian Canadians in universities particularly when discussing issues of equity and inclusion. This results in obstructing the establishment of race-conscious research and curriculum programs such as Asian Canadian Studies.

A fourth barrier is what Viet Nguyen (2002) refers to as a disconnect between university professors who teach Asian American Studies and their students. Writing about the US context, he asserts that a significant rupture within Asian American Studies exists between Asian American intellectuals and the majority of Asian American non-academics. Nguyen argues that Asian American intellectuals are "heavily invested in the analysis of their original circumstances and interests of their own production, which are essentially the dialectic between the racist, capitalist exploitation of Asian Americans and the resistance they have posed against such exploitation" (168). But Nguyen contends that many Asian American students do not endorse the same anti-capitalist and anti-racist viewpoints as their professors (see also Pon 2012, 2005). Rather these students see global capitalism as providing a "shared worldview, collective mode of interpretation and common class interest for many – perhaps a majority of – Asian Americans" (168). Such dynamics might enforce the lateness of Asian Canadian Studies.

Similarly, Glenn Omatsu (2000) observes the rise of Asian American neoconservatives who are mostly young professionals and products of the Reagan administration. These arguments by Nguyen (2002) and Omatsu find resonance in Canada with Vivien Lee's (2010) research. She analyses the strident anti-gay marriage activism of Hong Kong–born Chinese Canadians. They opposed the passing of the gay marriage bill in 2005 on the grounds of their Christian beliefs. They championed themselves as protectors of Canada who were safeguarding the nation-state against lesbian, gay, bisexual, and transgendered (LGBT) communities. Such political neo-conservatism signals the ruptures and political heterogeneity that exists within Asian Canada and the oppressions faced by LGBT Asian Canadians (Poon & Ho 2008; Poon & Sin 2008; Wong & Poon 2013). These ruptures and challenges represent important areas for ACS to grapple with.

The neo-conservatism of some Asian Canadians points to what many researchers recognize as the non-singularity of objects of study for Asian Canadian Studies (C. Lee 2007). The complexities and challenges posed by, for example, anti-gay and neoconservative Chinese Canadians, represent the contradictory, competing, contingent, even ambivalent realities and subjectivities that ACS can theorize, research, teach, and address. ACS scholars are well positioned to advance knowledge about these complex subjectivities, especially how markers of difference such as sexual orientation are implicated in oppression that is not outside of globalized, transnational, and colonial discourses that reproduce dominant capitalist hetero-patriarchy. The fact that ACS does not have a single-defining object of study highlights the field's capacity to address a broad range of social, cultural, economic, and political issues.

A fifth barrier to the establishment of ACS is a concern that the field engages in an identity politics that reifies the category of "Asian Canadian." An ongoing criticism points to what seems to be an essentialist and outdated politics of identity that is assumed to be endorsed by ACS. The intellectual and pedagogical goal is not to prematurely declare an object of study for ACS, certainly not one that reifies an essentialized Asian Canadian. Therefore, ACS should not fall prey to an anachronistic identity politics or reduce rich histories and diverse subjectivities to tidy grand narratives (Omi & Takagi 1996). Recall the ACS Network's emphasis on critiquing nationalist narratives and foregrounding a borderless transnationalism.

A sixth dynamic that is a challenge for the development of ACS is the lack of tenured and tenure-stream racialized minority professors in the humanities and social sciences, particularly from South Asian, Vietnamese, and Filipina/o backgrounds, among others. The under-representation of diverse faculty members limits the capacity of a critical mass of professors who could advocate for the institutional support of Asian Canadian Studies.

Finally, a seventh barrier for ACS is the ongoing corporatization of universities (James 2012). Due to cuts in federal funding since the 1990s, universities have become increasingly reliant on professors to bring in research grants as a source of revenue (Polster 2007). Attendant to this trend is the ongoing commercialization and privatization of knowledge production. This means that professors are often encouraged to adopt entrepreneurial approaches and explore ways in which their research can generate revenue. The challenge that the corporatization of higher education poses is that it places the onus on proponents of ACS to prove that such programs would be economically beneficial for universities or, as neo-liberals like to say, constitute "value for money." This neo-liberal logic makes universities less concerned with the public good, and more focussed on fiscal survival and competition between universities (Polster & Newson 2009). In other words, creating ACS programs in the current era needs to confront neo-liberal forces that prioritize corporate influences as opposed to public interest. In this vein, ACS should be careful not to fall prey to corporate pressures that would have the program "used for the education of managers and workers for the new global economy" (C. Lee 2007, 3). The danger for the institutionalization of ACS is that it might become exoticized, commodified, and even celebratory, rather than becoming critical.

Promises and Potential of the *Asian Canadian Studies Reader*

A major benefit of the *Asian Canadian Studies Reader* is its potential ability to establish ACS academic programs in Canadian universities and colleges. The book is structured for teaching use in two ways. First, it can be used as a core textbook in interdisciplinary courses that focus on Asian Canadian Studies, such as "Introduction to Asian Canadian Communities," and in other courses addressing race, migration, and diasporic communities in Canada. Second, it can be adopted as supplementary reading for discipline-based courses in education, English, geography, history, political science, social work, sociology, and women's studies that engage with questions of racial and ethnic diversity.

The *Asian Canadian Studies Reader* is also organized so that it can offer an overarching analytical and teaching framework through the notion of "encounters," which will be further elaborated through the six themes of "encountering Asian Canada," "ethnic encounters," "intersectional encounters," "comparative encounters," "transnational encounters," and "after encounters." In a regular academic term, the book will be able to offer a core set of readings through six thematic parts that can serve as central concepts for teaching, learning, and understanding Asian Canadian lives, cultures, and representations. Hence, as a required or supplementary textbook, the book can provide readings that can be augmented either with discipline-specific articles or with other materials at the discretion of the instructor.

The notion of "encounters" is offered as an interpretative strategy for analysing and reading Asian Canadian Studies because it is capacious for holding in tension the contingent, volatile, contextual, and even precarious meetings/interactions between those racialized as "Asian" and those marked as "Canadian." Concomitantly, the notion of "encounter" captures the richness of possibility, solidarity, and community in these interactions. The strategy of encounter provides the reader with a way to grapple with the highly contested, complex, and socially constructed nature of the category of "Asian Canadian." The notion of "encounters" places right up front before the reader the cruelty of racial categories, but also the very persistent, material, and at times liberating aspects of racialized identities and communities. For instance, bonds of community, solidarity, mutual support, friendship, and pride among Asian Canadians can be forged in response to racial oppression, as evidenced in the formation of the Chinese Canadian National Council in 1980, which was a direct outcome of the anti-W5 movement (Chan 1983; Fernando 2006). These formations, we assert, would not have occurred if not for the nature of the encounters that Chinese Canadians had with white Canadians.

The *Reader* also employs the notion of "encounters" as overarching lenses to view and analyse meetings between not only Asian Canadians and whites, but also Aboriginal peoples, and other racialized minorities. "Encounters" situates the historical and contemporary realities of Asian Canadians as intimately tied with those of other groups. It points to the sites and moments of connections, collisions, contradictions, and even complicities of Asian Canadians in relation to others. In some cases, they result in violence and marginalization implicating racism, sexism, homophobia, classism, and colonialism. In others, they produce sources and possibilities for agency, resistance, and change. These encounters symbolize a crucial component in individuals and groups becoming racialized in Canada. In other words, the construction and treatment of Asian Canadians as racialized minorities do not happen in a vacuum or in isolation; they are always in relation to other groups, both within the cluster of the diverse Asian Canadian communities and outside of them.

The genesis of these invariably contested encounters is captured in "Encountering Asian Canada," which highlights how the formation of the Canadian nation-state is implicated in settler colonialism, white supremacy, and Orientalism (Said 1979). As such, historic and contemporary encounters with Asian Canada inescapably implicate migration and settlement on lands which are procured through colonial conquest and the genocide of Indigenous peoples (Baskin 2011; Cannon & Sunseri 2011; Simpson, James, & Mack 2011; St Denis 2011). The triangulated encounters among Asians, Indigenous peoples, and white settlers signify a foundational contestation that Asian Canadian Studies must continue to confront, particularly vis-à-vis struggles for Indigenous sovereignty and Asian Canadians' position on settler colonialism. The notion of encountering Asian Canada, for example, makes it possible to grasp the ways in which racialized settlers or immigrants in their own claims for national belonging capitalized on state-sanctioned racism against Aboriginal people (see Thobani, this volume), while making possible the uncovering and consideration of historical alliances between Indigenous peoples and Asians in Canada (see Wong, this volume). For example, out of the triangulated encounters between Asians, Whites, and Indigenous peoples, emerge stories of the First People saving settlers, including those from Asia, from death and starvation (see Wong, this volume; Mittelstedt 2014). According to Wong, these dynamics signal the imperatives for a decolonizing, anti-racist, and anti-capitalist alliance across racial, cultural, and gender lines that often emerged out of the encounters with Asian Canada.

"Ethnic Encounters" captures the epistemological and ontological survival and resistance of Asian Canadians to their hailing as "Other." The deadly encounters between white settlers and Indigenous peoples (Lawrence 2003; Lawrence & Dua 2005) implicate the exigencies of global capitalism, western imperialism, and expansionism that interpellated the Asiatic as cheap, exploitable, and available labour for Canadian nation-building projects (Ng 1993). In his framework for addressing the racialized conditions of Asian Canadians, Roland Sintos Coloma (2012) notes that "the pan-ethnic racial categories of 'Asian' and 'Asian Canadian' need to be understood as socio-political constructs that are formed through interpellation and identification that name and bring together a racialized mixture of diverse ethno-national cultural groups" (296). Remarking on the ethno-racial dimensions of diasporic subjectivities, scholars have theorized the strength of Asian Canadian agency as demonstrated in clashes with white supremacy, hetero-patriarchy and hegemonic masculinity, labour market exploitation, poverty, and the ongoing colonization of Indigenous peoples (see chapters by Pratt and Wong in this volume). Reading attentively to ethnic encounters alerts readers not only to the tremendous resilience of Asian Canadians, but also to an ambivalent and difficult implication in colonizing Indigenous lands. In other words, while Asians in Canada fight for citizenship rights, national belonging, and fair wages, we are haunted by the spectre of our own settlement on stolen Indigenous lands (see Wong, this volume).

"Intersectional Encounters" borrows from the work of "primarily feminists of colour" who have shown how racialization is "constituted by other markers of difference, such as gender, sexuality, class, ability, and migration" (Coloma 2012, 297). These critics understand and analyse the interlocking systems of oppression that mark bodies as Asian, woman, and heteronormative, while highlighting Asian Canadian women's resistance to these structural forces (see Dua, this volume). These confrontations with racialized and gendered oppression also demonstrate how sexuality is a central social construct in the colonial project. Thus, while a white male student may accuse a female professor of colour of being a "woman out of control" (see Ng, this volume), post-9/11 accounts of Muslim women as subjugated by Muslim men rely on the sexualisation of women as invariably oppressed by patriarchs (see Jiwani, this volume). The notion of intersectional encounters offers a strategy for interpreting the post- 9/11 resurgence of Orientalism (Said, 1979).

"Comparative Encounters" as an interpretive strategy presents a powerful way for reading Asian Canadian Studies that focuses on the relational aspects of racialized minority groups, particularly how "racial/ethnic groups share similar conditions or shape the conditions of others" (Coloma 2012, 297). Such writings are helpful for comparing the experiences and subjectivities of Asian Canadians with other racialized minority and Indigenous groups. For example, these encounters are important for revealing how women's experiences are linked to political and material ramifications of social relations based on race, class, gender, sexuality, and migration (Stasiulis & Bakan 2005). Comparing these contestations highlights how globalization and the rise of neo-liberalism in settler societies such as Canada differentially impact groups, often relying on discourses that pit one group against the other. These processes are vital to fully grasp how racialization operates transnationally and to configure efficacious responses to complex processes of marginalization. These responses require knowing how and why the formation of "alliances along cross-racial, feminist, and anti-capitalist lines" is vital to decolonization (see Wong, this volume).

"Transnational Encounters" calls attention to scholarship that problematizes the dislocating force of colonialism and contemporary global capitalism that gives rise to rapid international flows of capital, people, knowledge, and culture. These flows have resulted in transnational clashes between the demands of capital and neo-liberalism with human rights and proponents of the Keynesian welfare state (Teeple 2000). Scholars have cautioned against the celebration of transnationalism as triumphant capitalism (Park 2011) and uncritical romanticizing of diaspora (see Cho, this volume). Rather, they focus our attention on a post-9/11 world and the rise in securitization and hyper-surveillance of racialized minority bodies and the gendered practices of global capital (see Jiwani, this volume). These encounters reveal the powerful agency of diasporic subjects and the efficacy of trans-ethnic and non-ethnic solidarities that challenge current national and transnational orders (see Arat-Koç, this volume).

The book concludes with "After Encounters" as a reading strategy to engage with the future conditions, subjectivities, and contestations involving Asian Canadians. Yu (this volume) calls attention to the increasing migration of Asians to Canada as constitutive of a "new Pacific Canada" and gestures to the linguistic elements of such encounters. Concomitant with increasing immigration from Asia to Canada is anti-Asian racism in popular media outlets such as the *Maclean's* "Too Asian?" article (see Coloma, this volume) and the future challenges facing anti-racism activists in configuring inclusive and efficacious responses.

Framed around ways to read and analyse various encounters, the *Asian Canadian Studies Reader* is meant to incite, provoke, and inspire the next generations of students and scholars who can build upon the labour of predecessors and elders. Some of the limitations of the *Reader* is the absence of a focus on the male Asian Canadian experience, religion/spirituality, and ethnicity. While all these areas are important, they are beyond the scope of this collection. We propose that future research in the area of Asian Canadian Studies should examine Asian Canadian men and masculinities, and the role of ethnicity, religion, and spirituality in communities of Asia Canada. These important topics would be particularly promising if examined in relation to encounters within settler colonialism, and ongoing debates in anti-racism, decolonization, and anti-capitalism.

Chapters in the *Reader*

Part I, entitled "Encountering Asian Canada," consists of four chapters that provide foundational lenses to dynamics of race, colonialism, and difference. It begins with Sunera Thobani, who argues that the making of Canadian citizens involves a trichotomous relationship among Aboriginal peoples, preferred white settlers, and non-preferred migrants of colour. The trichotomy analysis foregrounds the contradictions of liberal democracy by proposing that claims for citizenship emerge as central to racialization processes that transform Aboriginal peoples into aliens on their own land, white settlers into exalted citizens, and non-white settlers into perpetual strangers. By tracing the threat of race and the exaltation of white settlers in immigration and citizenship laws and policies, Thobani demystifies the myth of benevolence and innocence in the making of race and nation, and provides the position of non-white settlers as a vector from which to situate and theorize Asian Canada.

Peter Li locate Asian Canadians within mainstream discourses of immigration and multiculturalism that often elide issues of race and racism. He contends that conversations about race can be gleaned from official discourses on immigration. He illustrates this by providing an overview of various documented interactions between agents of law, politics, and jurisprudence and the general public. He asserts that a new form of racism is detectable in official discourses, which serves to reify categories of race and, consequently, racism.

Sherene Razack explores the persistence of modern/pre-modern distinctions and the constructed triangle of the imperilled Muslim woman, the dangerous Muslim man, and the civilized European in debates regarding the application of the Sharia Law to the settlement of family law disputes under the Arbitration Act in the province of Ontario. She provides an intellectual history that demonstrates secularism as a form of governmentality that produces neo-liberal subjects and narratives of morality and modernity as racially charged and fraught with imperialist demands. By examining representations of Muslim women, she asserts that it is often through the language of human rights and gender equality that empire is accomplished and that the Sharia Law debate has elided Muslim women's experiences of racism and patriarchy with mainstream law.

Richard Fung outlines his quest for the Asian penis in white-dominated gay porn. His figurative hunt leads him to examine how Asian men are represented in a number of pornographic films. He asserts that Asian men who consume gay pornography are left to ambivalently look for their own penises because mainstream erotic representations serve to racialize and demasculinize Asian men for the benefit of an intended white audience. He warns that, even with the participation of Asian individuals, if films recycle racist and Orientalizing tropes, then very little is done to alleviate the problematic social and sexual perceptions of Asians.

Part II, entitled "Ethnic Encounters," provides three case studies of Asian Canadian ethnic groups that engage with and complicate Canada's political, socio-cultural, and economic systems. Mona Oikawa presents a spatial analysis that shows how the forced expulsion, displacement, and incarceration of Japanese Canadians during the Second World War are technologies of white settler nation-building. Drawing on interviews with Japanese Canadian women, she shows how these technologies were used to create carceral spaces that demonized racialized and Indigenous peoples. Beginning with the War Measures Act, these racial, gendered, and classed segregations were used to separate Japanese Canadian families and communities, and functioned to pathologize racialized masculinity, while bolstering a white bourgeois heteronormativity. She concludes by calling attention to the Japanese Canadian men and women who bravely resisted the internment.

Alice Ming Wai Jim problematizes the historical mistreatment of the Chinese in Canada and how the Chinese have neither been expediently nor satisfactorily redressed. She analyses several examples of Chinese Canadian art that depict and negotiate with legacies of racial stereotypes and marginalization. Jim contends that the representations of these legacies and the attending documenting of these representations negotiate a politics of recognition in art, an important and ongoing project within and beyond the Chinese Canadian community.

Geraldine Pratt contends that the experiences of Filipino youth trying to make sense of their lives in Canada need to be acknowledged since their recognition benefits both Filipino youth and the society at large. Drawing from focus group interviews in Vancouver, she illustrates the identity formation among Filipino youth as a negotiation between hardship and ambivalence, in regards to their relationship with their immigrant parents, their own racialized experiences in Canada, and their actual experiences in the Philippines. Pratt contends that their narratives illustrate the intertwined historical and ideological conversations that result from imperialism and international migration.

Part III, entitled "Intersectional Encounters," showcases the work of three feminists of colour whose research on the entwined relationship of race, gender, and class captures the complexities of marginalization and resistance. Himani Bannerji argues that the concept of "diversity" must be re-examined, in spite of the fact that it has become common in everyday discourse and national self-definition. She provides a comparative historical overview of how the terms "multiculturalism" and "women of colour" vary in meaning in Canada, the United States, and Britain. She then demonstrates how multiculturalism in Canada operates as an ideology of the state apparatus. She posits that racialized minorities who uncritically accept multiculturalism do so to their detriment since it serves to depoliticize difference. Multiculturalism absolves the state of blame, and under the auspices of this ideology, issues and problems that minorities raise are their own fault.

Roxana Ng utilizes autoethnography to demonstrate how structural racism and sexism operate simultaneously to marginalize certain voices in the academy. Drawing from an incident in which a white male graduate student lodged a complaint against her, she illustrates how those who work in dominant institutions serve to perpetuate prevailing values and norms. To counter this dynamic, Ng proposes an anti-racist and feminist approach in situations of conflict, which she uses to analyse and make sense of her experience.

Yasmin Jiwani illustrates how reductive tropes that frame racialized and gendered Muslim bodies continue to have currency. Using Edward Said's concept of Orientalism as a framework of analysis, she analyses stories in *The Montreal Gazette* that appeared following the horrors of 11 September 2001. She shows how the mainstream press subscribes to and perpetuates stereotypical notions of the subjugated Muslim women and the crazed Muslim men. She notes that such depictions persisted in *The Gazette* even though it has a sizable Muslim readership.

Part IV, entitled "Comparative Encounters," highlights historical and ongoing connections between Asian Canadians and Aboriginal peoples and other racialized minorities as well as connections among various Asian Canadian groups. Rita Wong explores what happens if Asian Canadians position Indigenous peoples' struggles, instead of normalized whiteness, as the main reference point through which it comes to articulate their racialized subjectivities. Drawing on literary works, such as *Disappearing Moon Cafe*, *Exile and the Heart*, *Burning Vision*, and *Yin Chin*, Wong points to immigrant complicity in the colonization of land as well as the possibility of making decolonizing alliances. She suggests that fiction offers a speculative space to imagine ways for dialogue and interaction to spark deeper understanding of Asian-Aboriginal interrelatedness.

Ena Dua examines debates in the late 1800s on whether to allow female migration from China, Japan, and India to Canada in order to reveal how regulations of Asian immigrants' sexuality was integral to the construction of race and nation. She notes that initial fears of miscegenation led to the exclusion of Asian women to prevent the settlement of Asian men, but later gave way to the inclusion of Asian women to prevent mixed race relations. By analysing legislations through the notion of "exclusion through inclusion," Dua demonstrates that the history of female Asian migration has been part of Canada's practices of exclusion.

Daiva Stasiulis and Abigail Bakan compare the experiences of Caribbean and Filipina domestic workers in Canada. They argue that immigrants seeking citizenship rights through the migration process are under considerable pressure due to severe restrictions on permanent citizenship. They reconceptualize the notion of citizenship as a negotiated relationship existing within social, political, and economic relations of collective conflict, which are shaped by gendered, racial, class, and internationally based state hierarchies. Stasiulis and

Bakan emphasize the transformative power and agency of highly exploited migrant women who negotiate their citizenship at both national and international levels.

Eric Fong draws on census data for Toronto to compare residential segregation patterns between racialized minority groups and European immigrant groups. His findings reveal that increases in socio-economic status are generally correlated to decreases in residential segregation for racialized minorities. However, the social integration of South Asians and Blacks is negatively impacted by social distance factors, such as racial preferences or social desirability. Fong's chapter is a significant piece because it brings to bear how South Asians and Blacks are rated lower on social desirability scales in comparison to whites and South East Asians. This article thus forces a grappling with the saliency of skin colour as a potential factor in racial preferences. In this way by comparing different racial groups, Fong calls attention to how the construction and treatment of various groups of Asian Canadians do not happen in a vacuum or in isolation; rather, they are always socially constructed in relation to other groups including Blacks. This is a vital contribution to the collection because it highlights that skin colour matters and reminds readers that anti-Asian racism cannot be fully understood without considerations of anti-Black racism.

Part V, entitled "Transnational Encounters," underscores the utility and relevance of transnationalism as a unit of analysis and as an interpretive framework in Asian Canadian Studies. Lily Cho focuses on strategies for reading and detecting differences in agency between migrants and native-born individuals in transnational colonial contexts. She makes distinctions between postcolonial theories of agency advanced by Homi Bhabha and diasporic forms of agency that can be detected in small-town Chinese restaurants in Canada. Remarking on the popular dish "sweet and sour pork," she notes how diasporic resistance against racism and colonialism requires no identifiable heroine or large-scale rebellion, but relies on subtle subterfuge attendant to fluency in Cantonese. For Cho, reading agency in diaspora requires careful attention to such historical agency.

Roy Miki embraces the "post" as a sign of an altered state in which the future is fraught with uncertainties but also possibilities of resistance and novel collective formations. Miki articulates a contradiction in the production of Asian Canadian subjectivities in which discourses of globalization abound, while still haunted by the spectre of a nation unable to escape reactionary and anti-Asian nationalism. On one hand, national discourses, which are rooted in colonialism and white supremacy, continue to view Asian Canadians as "foreigners" or "aliens" in the nation. On the other hand, Asian Canadians signify vast global commercial markets that are coveted by corporations and capitalists. Miki contends that this contradictory subject positioning allows Asian Canadians, particularly artists and writers, to articulate resistance to Enlightenment binaries and hegemonic power relations, while fashioning new collective formations. The task for readers is to be keenly alert to these critical vocabularies and the imaginings of an alternate nation.

Sedef Arat-Koç challenges the common celebratory view of transnationalism as the free movement of people around the world by detailing the ways in which Arabs and Muslims have been depicted, treated, and regulated in the post-9/11 era. She examines how transnationalism is reconfiguring Canadian identity and its boundaries, alongside changes to national technologies such as borders, immigration, justice, and the military. She concludes by focussing on alternative transnationalisms, the trans-ethnic and non-ethnic solidarities that are developing to challenge current national and transnational orders.

Part VI, entitled "After Encounters," offers new frameworks to teach and engage with Asian Canadian Studies. Henry Yu proposes that trans-Pacific migrations have transformed in the last twenty-five years, resulting in the emergence of a globally connected Pacific Canada. He refers to Pacific Canada as a perspective on Canada's past, present, and future that highlights the ways in which the nation has been shaped by its engagement with the Pacific rather than the Atlantic world. Pacific Canada refers to economic, social, cultural, and political connections, including the increasing prevalence of circular global migration flows and the creation of highly mobile, well-educated, and financially secure immigrants. He argues that the delayed entry of Asian Canadians into formal electoral politics may have profound consequences for their political engagement.

Laura Kwak presents a provocative vision for Asian Canadian Studies that involves actively pursuing an integrated political and scholarly focus on four interconnected areas: relational racialization, settler colonialism, Asian Canadian politics, and Asian Canadian feminisms. Relational racialization highlights the heterogeneity of Asian Canadian communities and how they are positioned as victims of racism and complicit in ongoing imperial projects. In confronting settler colonialism, Kwak asserts that Indigenous knowledge provides alternative ways for Asians in Canada to understand their role and participation in a settler colonial state. She argues that Asian Canadian politics remains understudied, and pushes for the expansion of the definition of politics to include the work of artists, scholars, and activists. Finally, she advances the potential for Asian Canadian feminisms to create spaces to learn, share, and support scholarship and activism.

Roland Sintos Coloma contends that the 2010 *Maclean's* article titled "Too Asian?" reveals the paradoxical position of Asians in Canada as both wanted and unwanted. The controversial article asserts that many white youths are no longer applying to elite universities because these institutions are becoming overpopulated by Asian and Asian Canadian students. Coloma notes that the community activism in response to the article was reliant on a strategic form of identification called ethno-nationalism, that is, a claim that Asian Canadians are "real Canadians" as well. He suggests, however, that ethno-nationalism is reliant on a disavowal of the foreign-national, the physical and symbolic marker of their Asianness or otherness, which places limits on pan-Asian solidarity.

Conclusion

We hope that this *Reader* may serve to advance the establishment of Asian Canadian Studies in post-secondary institutions across Canada. The impressive body of critical work included in this volume has emerged in the absence of established Asian Canadian Studies programs. We note the challenges facing the institutional establishment of Asian Canadian Studies. Our aspirations are that this collection might attract more people to the scholarly work on Asians in Canada and inspire greater collective efforts to create Asian Canadian Studies now.

NOTES

1 Our use of the term "Asian" is in keeping with Coloma (2012, 595) who states that the term designates

> the heterogeneous, dynamic, and socio-politically constructed grouping of peoples, cultures, materials, and ideas that derive from East Asian, South Asian, Southeast Asian, and West

Asian backgrounds. It is, admittedly, geographically regional and broadly continental in its articulation. It is attentive to the local and global histories, legacies, and continuations of imperialisms, colonialisms, wars, and conflicts over sovereignties, nationalisms, and territorialities. My use of the term "Asian," especially in the Canadian context, moves away from the dominant emphasis on East Asia and on the peoples and cultures of Chinese, Japanese, and Korean ancestry. Its conventional use often excludes other Asian ethnic groups, such as Indians and Filipina/os.

2 Our use of the term "Muslim" is in line with how Sedef Arat-Koç (this volume) notes that it encompasses many ethnocultural and linguistic groups the majority of whom are neither Arab or Middle Eastern, but are Indonesian, Malaysian, Filipino, Sudanese, Indian, or Chinese.

REFERENCES

Adachi, Ken. 1991. *The Enemy that Never Was: A History of Japanese Canadians*. Toronto: McClelland & Stewart.

Adilman, Tamara. 1984. "Preliminary Sketches of Chinese Women and Work in British Columbia 1858-1950." In *Not Just Pin Money*, ed. B.K. Lathan and R.J. Pazdro, 53–78. Victoria: Camosun College.

Aquino, Nina L., and Ric Knowles, eds. 2011. *Asian Canadian Theatre: New Essays on Canadian Theatre*. Toronto: Playwrights Canada Press.

Arat-Koç, Sedef, and Fely Villasin. 2001. *Caregivers Break the Silence: A Participatory Action Research on the Abuse and Violence, Including the Impact of Family Separation Experienced by Women in the Live-in Caregiver Program*. Toronto: INTERCEDE.

Avery, Donald. 1995. *Reluctant Hosts: Canada's Response to Immigrant Workers, 1896–1994*. Toronto: McClelland and Stewart.

Backhouse, Constance. 1999. *Colour-Coded: A Legal History of Racism in Canada*. Toronto: University of Toronto Press.

Baskin, Cyndy. 2011. *Strong Helper's Teachings: The Value of Indigenous Knowledges in the Helping Professions*. Toronto: Canadian Scholars' Press.

Cannon, Martin J., and Sunseri, L., eds. 2011. *Racism, Colonialism, and Indigeneity in Canada: A Reader*. Don Mills, ON: Oxford University Press.

Chan, Anthony. 1983. *Gold Mountain*. Vancouver: Gold Star.

Chu, Garrick, Sean Gunn, Paul Yee, Ken Shikaze, Linda Uyehara Hoffman, and Rick Shiomi, eds. 1979. *Inalienable Rice: A Chinese and Japanese Canadian Anthology*. Vancouver: Powell Street Review & Asian Canadian Writers Workshop.

Coloma, Roland Sintos. 2012. "Abject Beings: Filipina/os in Canadian Historical Narrations." In *Filipinos in Canada: Disturbing Invisibility*, ed. R.S. Coloma, B. McElhinny, E. Tungohan, J.P.C. Catungal, and L.M. Davidson, 284–304. Toronto: University of Toronto Press.

Coloma, R.S., B. McElhinny, E. Tungohan, J.P.C. Catungal, and L.M. Davidson, eds. 2012. *Filipinos in Canada: Disturbing Invisibility*. Toronto: University of Toronto Press.

Carniol, Ben. 2010. *Case Critical: Social Services and Social Justice in Canada*. 6th Edition. Toronto: Between the Lines Press.

Creese, Gillian. 1987. "Organizing Against Racism in the Workplace: Chinese Workers in Vancouver before the Second World War." *Canadian Ethnic Studies* 9 (3): 35–46.

Cui, Dan, and Jennifer Kelly. 2012. "Ruling Through Discourse: The Experience of Chinese Canadian Youth." In *"Too Asian?": Racism, Privilege, and Post-Secondary Education*, ed. R.J. Gilmour, D. Bhandar, J. Heer, and M.C.K. Ma, 83–94. Toronto: Between the Lines.

Das Gupta, Tania. 1996. *Racism and Paid Work*. Toronto: Garamond Press.

Eric, Josephine. 2012. "The Rites of Passage of Filipinas in Canada: Two Migration Cohorts." In *Filipinos in Canada: Disturbing Invisibility*, ed. R.S. Coloma, B. McElhinny, E. Tungohan, J.P.C. Catungal, and L.M. Davidson, 123–41. Toronto: University of Toronto Press.

Fernando, Shanti. 2006. *Race and the City: Chinese Canadian and Chinese American Political Mobilization*. Vancouver: University of British Columbia Press.

Fleras, Augie. 2010. *Unequal Relations: An Introduction to Race, Ethnic, and Aboriginal Dynamics in Canada*. 6th ed. Toronto: Pearson Canada.

Galabuzi, Grace-Edward. 2006. *Canada's Economic Apartheid: The Social Exclusion of Racialized Groups in the New Century*. Toronto: Canadian Scholars' Press.

Goellnicht, Donald. 2000. "A Long Labour: The Protracted Birth of Asian Canadian Literature." *Essays on Canadian Writing* 72:1–44.

Griff, Harold. 1958. *British Columbia: The People's Early Story*. Vancouver: Tribune Publishing Company.

Haque, Eve. 2012. *Multiculturalism within a Bilingual Framework: Language, Race, and Belonging in Canada*. Toronto: University of Toronto Press.

Heer, Jeet. 2012. "Introduction." In *"Too Asian?": Racism, Privilege, and Post-Secondary Education*, ed. R.J. Gilmour, D. Bhandar, J. Heer, and M.C.K. Ma, 1–13. Toronto: Between the Lines.

Henry, Frances, and Carol Tator. 2010. *The Colour of Democracy: Racism in Canadian Society*. 4th ed. Toronto: Nelson Education.

Ho, Rob, and Henry Yu. 2007. "Teaching Asian Canada: Beyond the Parallel." *Amerasia* 33 (2): 87–96. http://dx.doi.org/10.17953/amer.33.2.r672435873098486.

Jakubowski, Lisa Marie. 1997. *Immigration and the Legalization of Racism*. Halifax: Fernwood.

James, Carl E. 2012. "Strategies of Engagement: How Racialized Faculty Negotiate the University System." *Canadian Ethnic Studies* 44 (1): 133–52. http://dx.doi.org/10.1353/ces.2012.0007.

Jim, Alice M.W. 2010. Conference Report: 2009 CASA Conference of EAC and SAC/Rapport do la Conférence de l'Asie de l'est (CAE) et Conseil de l'Asie du sud (CAS). *CASA Bulletin de l'ACEA* 1, no. 1: 3–6.

Jiwani, Yasmin. 2010. "Erasing Race: The Story of Reena Virk." In *Reena Virk: Critical Perspectives on a Canadian Murder*, ed. M. Rajiva and S. Batacharya, 82–121. Toronto: Canadian Scholars' Press.

Kogawa, Joy. 1981. *Obasan*. Toronto: Leter & Orpen Dennys.

Lai, David C.Y. 1988. *Chinatown: Towns Within Cities in Canada*. Vancouver: University of British Columbia Press.

Lavallée, Lynn, and Jennifer Poole. 2010. "Beyond Recovery: Colonization, Health and Healing for Indigenous People in Canada." *International Journal of Mental Health and Addiction* 8 (2): 271–81. http://dx.doi.org/10.1007/s11469-009-9239-8.

Lawrence, Bonita. 2003. "Gender, Race, and the Regulation of Native Identity in Canada and the United States: An Overview." *Hypatia* 18 (2): 3–31. http://dx.doi.org/10.1111/j.1527-2001.2003.tb00799.x.

Lawrence, Bonita, and Enakshi Dua. 2005. "Decolonizing Antiracism." *Social Justice (San Francisco, Calif.)* 32 (4): 120–43.

Lee, Christopher. 2007. "The Lateness of Asian Canadian Studies." *Amerasia* 33 (2): 1–18. http://dx.doi.org/10.17953/amer.33.2.c8053m5q76215018.

Lee, Jo-Anne. 2006. "Issues in Constituting Asian-Canadian Feminisms." In *Asian Women: Interconnections*, ed. T. Hellwig and S. Thobani, 21–46. Toronto: Women's Press.

Lee, Jo-Anne. 2007. "Gender, Ethnicity, and Hybrid Forms of Community-Based Urban Activism in Vancouver, 1957–1978." *Gender, Place and Culture* 14 (4): 381–407. http://dx.doi.org/10.1080/09663690701439702.

Lee, S.K.Y. 1990. *Disappearing Moon Cafe*. Vancouver: Douglas & McIntyre.

Lee, Vivian. 2010. *"I'm not homophobic, I'm Chinese": Hong Kong Canadian Discourses of Heterosexuality, Marriage Debates, 2002–2006*. Doctoral dissertation. Toronto: York University.

Li, Peter. S. 1988. *The Chinese in Canada*. Toronto: Oxford University Press.

Louie, Steve, and Glenn Omatsu, eds. 2001. *Asian Americans: The Movement and the Moment*. Los Angeles: UCLA Asian American Studies Press.

Lowe, Lisa. 1997. *Immigrant Acts: On Asian American Cultural Politics*. Durham: Duke University Press.

Maclear, Kyo. 1994, July. "The Myth of the 'Model Minority': Rethinking the Education of Asian Canadians." *Our Schools/Our Selves* 5, no. 3: 54–76.

Mahtani, Minelle. 2010. "Canadian Media: It's Time to Cover the Uncovered." *Globe and Mail*. http://www.theglobeandmail.com/opinion/canadian-media-its-time-to-cover-the-undercovered/article1314521/. Downloaded 6 June 2013.

Man, Guida. 1997. "Women's Work is Never Done: Social Organization of Work and the Experience of Women in Middle-Class Hong Kong Chinese Immigrant Families in Canada." *Gender Research* 2:183–226.

Man, Guida. 2007. "Racialization of Gender, Work, and Transnational Migration: The Experience of Chinese Immigrant Women in Canada." In *Race and Racism in 21st Century Canada*, ed. S.P. Hier and B.S. Bolaria, 235–52. Peterborough: Broadview Press.

Manpower and Immigration Canada. 1974. *The Immigration Program*. Ottawa: Information Canada.

McElhinny, Bonnie, and Lisa Davidson M., Catungal, John P.C., Tungohan, Ethel, and Coloma, Roland Sintos. 2012. "Spectres of (In)visibility: Filipina/o Labour, Culture, and Youth in Canada." In *Filipinos in Canada: Disturbing Invisibility*, edited by R.S. Coloma, B. McElhinny, E. Tungohan, J.P.C. Catungal, and L.M. Davidson, 284–304. Toronto: University of Toronto Press.

Miki, Roy. 1998. *Broken Entries: Race, Subjectivity, Writing*. Toronto: The Mercury Press.

Miki, Roy. 2004. *Redress: Inside the Japanese Canadian Call for Justice*. Vancouver: Raincoast Books.

Mittelstedt, Meg. 2014. 13 Oct.. "Touring BC's 'Hidden' History Shared by Chinese and Indigenous People." *The Tyee*. https://thetyee.ca/News/2014/10/13/Shared-Chinese-Indigenous-History/.

Ng, Roxana. 1993. "Racism, Sexism, and Nation Building in Canada." In *Race, Identity, and Representation in Education*, ed. C. McCarthy and W. Crichlow, 50–9. New York: Routledge.

Ng, Winnie. 2010. *Racing Solidarity, Remaking Labour: Labour Renewal from a Decolonizing and Anti-Racism Perspective*. Doctoral dissertation. Toronto: University of Toronto.

Nguyen, V.T. 2002. *Race and Resistance: Literature and Politics in Asian America*. New York: Oxford University Press. http://dx.doi.org/10.1093/acprof:oso/9780195146998.001.0001.

Nipp, Dora. 1985. "The Chinese in Toronto." In *Gathering Place: Peoples and Neighbourhoods of Toronto*, ed. R.F. Harney, 147–75. Toronto: Multicultural Society of Ontario.

Nunoda, Peter. 1991. *A Community in Transition and Conflict: The Japanese Canadians, 1935–1951*. Doctoral dissertation. Winnipeg: University of Manitoba.

Okazaki, Robert K. 1996. *The Nisei Mass Evacuation Group and P.O.W. Camp 101*. Trans. Jean Okazaki and Curtis Okazaki. Scarborough, ON: Self-published.

Omatsu, Glenn. 2000. "The 'Four Prisons' and the Movements of Liberation: Asian American Activism from 1960s to the 1990s." In *Asian American Studies*, ed. J.Y.S. Wu and M. Song, 64–196. Piscataway, NJ: Rutgers University Press.

Omi, Michael, and Dana Y. Takagi. 1996. "Situating Asian Americans in the Political Discourse on Affirmative Action." *Representations (Berkeley, Calif.)* 55 (Summer): 155–62. http://dx.doi.org/10.2307/3043744.

Park, Hijin. 2011. "Migrants, Minorities and Economies: Transnational Feminism and the Asian/Canadian Woman Subject." *Asian Journal of Women's Studies* 17 (4): 7–38. http://dx.doi.org/10.1080/12259276.2011.11666115.

Polster, Claire. 2007. "The Nature and Implications of the Growing Importance of Research Grants to Canadian Universities and Academics." *Higher Education* 53 (5): 599–622. http://dx.doi.org/10.1007/s10734-005-1118-z.

Polster, Claire, and Janice Newson. 2009. *Open for Business? What's Wrong with Corporatizing our Universities? Plenty!* Canadian Centre for Policy Alternatives. https://www.policyalternatives.ca/publications/monitor/open-business.

Pon, Gordon. 2005. "Anti-Racism in the Cosmopolis: Race, Class, and Gender in the Lives of Elite Chinese Canadian Women." *Social Justice (San Francisco, Calif.)* 32 (4): 161–79.

Pon, Gordon. 2012. "Queering Asian Masculinities and Transnationalism: Implications for Anti-Oppression and Consciousness-Raising." In *Troubled Masculinities: Reimagining Urban Men*, ed. K. Moffatt, 93–108. Toronto: University of Toronto Press.

Pon, Gordon. 2015. ""Importing the Asian 'Model Minority' Discourse into Canada: Implications for Social Work and Education." In *Killing the Model Minority Stereotype: Asian American Counter-Stories and Complicity*, ed. N. Hartlep, 83–95. Charlotte, NC: Information Age Publishing, Inc.

Pon, Madge. 1996. "'Like a Chinese Puzzle': The Construction of Chinese Masculinity in Jack Canuck." In *Gender and History in Canada*, ed. Joy Parr and Mark Rosenfeld, 88–100. Toronto: Copp Clark Ltd.

Poon, Maurice K.L, and Peter T. Ho. 2008. "Negotiating Social Stigma Among Gay Asian Men." *Sexualities* 11 (1–2): 245–68. http://dx.doi.org/10.1177/1363460707085472.

Poon, Maurice K.L., and Rick Sin. 2008. "'Without Power Analysis, There Won't Be Any Equality': Interrogating the Idea of Love in Asian/Caucasian Gay Relationships." *Gay & Lesbian Issues and Psychology Review* 4 (3): 198–200.

Poy, Vivienne. 2013. *Passage to Promise Land: Voices of Chinese Immigrant Women in Canada.* Montreal: McGill-Queen's University Press.

Preibisch, Kerry L., and Evelyn Encalada Grez. 2010. "The Other Side of *El Otro Lado*: Mexican Migrant Women and Labor Flexibility in Canadian Agriculture." *Signs (Chicago, Ill.)* 35 (2): 289–316. http://dx.doi.org/10.1086/605483.

Rajiva, Mythili, and Sheila Batacharya, eds. 2010. *Reena Virk: Critical Perspectives on a Canadian Murder*. Toronto: Canadian Scholars' Press.

Razack, Sherene, Malinda Smith, and Sunera Thobani, eds. 2010. *States of Race: Critical Race Feminism for the 21st Century*. Toronto: Between the Lines Press.

Roy, Patricia. 1989. *A White Man's Province: British Columbia Politicians and Chinese/Japanese Immigrants 1858–1914*. Vancouver: University of British Columbia Press.

Said, Edward. 1979. *Orientalism*. London: Penguin.

Said, Edward. 2007. "Latent and Manifest Orientalism." In *Race and Racialization: Essential Readings*, ed. T. Das Gupta, C.E. James, R.C.A. Maaka, G.-E. Galabuzi, and C. Anderson, 45–55. Toronto: Canadian Scholars' Press.

Sherazee, Amina. 2002. "Criminalizing Dissent: Secret Trials, Racial Profiling and the Enemy Within." Paper presented at *Race, Racism and Empire: The Local and the Global Conference*, Toronto: York University, 29 April–1May.

Sin, Rick. 2007. "Community Action Research: Lessons from the Chinese Communities in Montreal." In *Doing Anti-Oppressive Practice: Building Transformative Politicized Social Work*, ed. D. Baines, 160–75. Halifax: Fernwood.

Simpson, Jennifer, Carl E. James, and Johnny Mack. 2011. "Multiculturalism, Colonialism, and Racialization: Conceptual Starting Points." *Review of Education, Pedagogy & Cultural Studies* 33 (4): 285–305. http://dx.doi.org/10.1080/10714413.2011.597637.

Statistics Canada. 2011. *2011 National Household Survey: Data Tables: Visible Minority (15), Generation Status (4), Age Groups (10) and Sex (3) for the Population in Private Households of Canada, Provinces and Territories, Census Metropolitan Areas and Census Agglomeration*. Ottawa: Government of Canada.

Stasiulis, Daiva K., and Abigail B. Bakan 2005. *Negotiating Citizenship: Migrant Women in Canada and the Global System*. Toronto: University of Toronto Press.

St Denis, Verna. 2011. "'Silencing Aboriginal Curricular Content and Perspectives Through Multiculturalism: 'There are Other Children Here'." *Review of Education, Pedagogy & Cultural Studies* 33:306–17. http://dx.doi.org/10.1080/10714413.2011.597638.

Thobani, Sunera. 2007. *Exalted Subjects: Studies in the Making of Race and Nation in Canada*. Toronto: University of Toronto Press.

Teeple, Gary. 2000. *Globalization and the Decline of Social Reform into the Twenty-First Century*. Aurora, ON: Garamond.

Ty, Eleanor, and Christyl Verduyn, eds. 2008. *Asian Canadian Writing: Beyond Autoethnography*. Waterloo: Wilfrid Laurier University Press.

Ward, Peter W. 1978. *White Canada Forever: Popular Attitudes and Public Policy Towards Orientals in British Columbia*. Montreal: McGill Queen's University Press.

Wei, William. 1993. *The Asian American Movement*. Philadelphia: Temple University Press.

Wickberg, Edgar, Henry Conn, Ronald J. Conn, Graham Johnson, and William E. Willmott, eds. 1982. *From China to Canada: A History of the Chinese Communities in Canada*. Toronto: McClelland & Stewart.

Women's Book Committee and Chinese Canadian National Council. 1992. *Jin Guo: Voices of Chinese Canadian Women*. Toronto: Women's Press.

Wong, Josephine P., and Maurice K.L. Poon. 2013. "Challenging Homophobia and Heterosexism through Storytelling and Critical Dialogue among Hong Kong Chinese Immigrant Parents in Toronto." *Culture, Health & Sexuality* 15 (1): 15–28. http://dx.doi.org/10.1080/13691058.2012.738310.

Wong, Yuk-lin Renita, Josephine, P. Wong, and Kenneth P. Fung. 2010. "Mental Health Promotion Through Empowerment and Community Capacity Building Among East and South East Asian Immigrant and Refugee Women." *Canadian Issues* Summer, 108–13.

Yee, Paul. 1993. *Saltwater City*. Vancouver: Douglas & McIntyre.

2 Nationals, Citizens, and Others

SUNERA THOBANI

The Rights of Citizens

I begin this chapter on Canadian citizenship by troubling the work of feminist philosopher and political theorist Seyla Benhabib, who tackles the contentious issues of international human rights, national sovereignty and citizenship, as well as the challenges presented to these by global migrations in her recent Seeley Lectures at Cambridge University.[1] I contend that she too readily accepts the principle that self-governing political communities of citizens in powerful countries should have the right to decide on the fate of relatively powerless Others. Her reluctance to challenge the power relations between citizens and their Others, I believe, forecloses the possibility of ethical relations between them. Notwithstanding her commitment to "democratic iterations," Benhabib's conceptualization of citizenship is based largely on an "internal" discussion within the political community, with strangers cast largely as supplicants dependent on the responsibly exercised largesse of nationals. Rather than examining citizenship from the perspectives of those denied this status, including indigenous peoples, immigrants and migrants, it is largely the experience of those included within this institution that remains at the centre of her conceptualization of the institution. She also downplays the fact that the crisis of migration, now as in the past, is largely a problem of controlling persons-of-colour-on-the-move, of regulating those who refuse to remain where they are said to belong.

Citizenship has, of course, long served as the signifier par excellence of membership in the nation-state; this status is much valorized in master narratives of nationhood, including that of the Canadian nation. This institution is universally accepted as reflecting the height of the political evolution of the human being as a modern subject, with clearly delineated rights and entitlements.[2] The claims of nationals to a legitimate and unassailable membership within the political community are rooted in their historical access to this institution. For previously excluded groups, these claims are also cherished, considered the result of their struggles to make the institution more inclusive.

Drawing upon Immanuel Kant's notion of "cosmopolitan right" and Hannah Arendt's reflections on statelessness and the individual's "right to have rights," Benhabib argues that a profound contradiction is to be found between the paradigm of universal human rights and the rights of sovereign democratic societies to shape the boundaries that define their respective political communities. Kant's conception of cosmopolitan right addressed the vexing question of the moral and legal relations of individuals who cross borders to the states whose jurisdiction they enter. Benhabib reads Kant's concept of this right as defining "a novel domain situated between the law of specific polities on one hand and customary international law on the other hand."[3] Cosmopolitan right extends "a right of temporary sojourn" to foreigners, a right which arises from "a special contract of beneficence" that accrues to all human beings "by virtue of their common possession ... of the surface of the earth," so long as the recognition of this right does no harm to the receiving society.[4] Benhabib argues that such a right should also include permanent residence, not only temporary sojourn, under particular circumstances. Moreover, this right should be grounded in a recognition of the universality of human rights and not in the "beneficence" of receiving societies, as Kant would have it.

The question of statelessness was a key concern for Hannah Arendt in the wake of the devastating consequences of the imposition of this condition upon Jews and other minorities in Europe with the rise of fascism, and Benhabib is especially attentive to this concern. For Arendt, totalitarianism's "disregard for human life and the eventual treatment of human beings as 'superfluous' entities began ... when millions of human beings were rendered 'stateless' and denied the 'right to have rights.'"[5] Although Arendt criticized the "weaknesses" of the nation-state system and highlighted the moral obligation that endows every individual with the "right to have rights," she remained "sceptical" about "all ideals of a world government."[6] Benhabib argues that because the condition of statelessness abrogates all human rights, it is too serious an issue to be treated as only a question of sovereign privilege.

For her part, Benhabib makes a case for the principles of "moral universalism" and "cosmopolitan federalism" to uphold the recognition of the "rights of others."[7] Arguing that citizenship and the granting of the right of permanent residence "ought not to be viewed as unilateral acts of self-determination" since access to this status has serious consequences for "other entities in the world community," she advocates "just membership" and "just distribution" as a way out of the conundrum of reconciling universal human rights with the principle of sovereignty. The "others" whose rights are the particular concern of Benhabib's deliberations are variously defined as "aliens," 'strangers," "immigrants," "asylum seekers," and "refugees." Benhabib recognizes the paradox in this situation where citizens with rights decide upon the extent of the rights to be granted to others, pointing out that this paradox "can never be completely eliminated." Despite this being the case, she argues that the impact of these decisions can – and should – be mitigated: "We can render the distinctions between 'citizens' and 'aliens,' 'us' and 'them,' fluid – and negotiable through democratic iterations."[8] The notion that moral and ethical obligations are owed by the community of citizens to these Others permeates Benhabib's reasoning, as does a commitment to the "cosmopolitan solidarity which increasingly brings all human beings, by virtue of their humanity alone, under the net of universal rights."[9]

Although Benhabib's call for a more ethical and internationally accountable recognition of the rights of Others is to be lauded, her formulation of the problem renders invisible the reality that this "problem" is today, as it has been at least for the previous few centuries, mainly a problem of race. It is the racialization of persons-on-the-move that is central to their ontologization as aliens by exalted citizens, who claim inalienable rights for themselves while helping to destroy those of Others. The crisis of immigration into the west is a racial crisis, for it threatens the erosion of white supremacy by the potential enfranchisement of aliens. In the modern era, with brief periods of exception for Jews, the Irish and Eastern Europeans, white populations have generally been able to travel as and where they please.[10]

The aliens who present themselves at the Canadian borders today come from countries that are among the most coveted sites for the operations of Canadian corporations. Many of these countries are also the destinations of the high-flying trade missions led by a dizzying array of prime ministers and trade ministers. It might well be asked, then, what makes a Chinese woman, who sews a shirt in a Chinese factory that sells for three dollars on the streets of Vancouver, a 'stranger" when she presents herself at the Canadian border as a migrant? Is not the relationship between the nation of consuming citizens and this woman – and with the countless others like her whose lives are spent making the products that clothe, feed, nurture, and sustain these citizens – an intimate one?

The meaning of the status of the sojourner, or the degree of hospitality extended to all persons-on-the-move, cannot be conflated. For example, while seasonal migrant workers from Mexico are deemed a perennial problem in the United States, and domestic workers are regulated through live-in requirements in Canada, corporate and trade executives, finance and development experts, among others, cross borders with ease and frequency. The latter are courted by the most lucrative employment contracts, tax exemptions, and housing and living allowances, all of which characterize the lives of expatriates in the countries of the global South. Indeed, a whole system of international institutions promoting trade and development has been organized, including through the International Monetary Fund, the World Bank, and the World Trade Organization, to facilitate precisely their right to global travel and cosmopolitan hospitality as they make the planet the site of their entrepreneurial ventures.

Citizenship in a Settler Society

The limitations of Benhabib's naturalizing assumptions of citizenship entitlement and alien incursions are perhaps nowhere as obvious as in the case of settler societies-cum-liberal democracies such as Canada.[11] In this case, the political community of citizens is a community based in the legal negation of Aboriginal sovereignty, with Aboriginal peoples today among the strangers and aliens who seek to defend their rights from the incursions of citizens. All non-Aboriginal populations have historically become nationals or Others through processes of migration. However, the unequal conditions organizing these migrations have been such that different rights have been allowed these populations and their descendants. The question of migration and citizenship are thus deeply entwined in national formation, with immigration policies organizing access to formal citizenship.

The central contradiction of Canadian citizenship, deeply rooted in its earliest stages of development, is that the citizenship rights of settlers, nationals, and immigrants remain based in the institution of white supremacy. Citizenship originated in the dispossession of Aboriginal peoples and was denied for almost a century to most people of colour or, if allowed, only erratically and as a matter of exception. Here, the category citizen did not emerge through some internal process within a natural community, with regrettable consequences for outsiders. Citizenship emerged as integral to the very processes that transformed insiders (Aboriginal peoples) into aliens in their own territories, while simultaneously transforming outsiders (colonizers, settlers, migrants) into exalted insiders (Canadian citizens). The category "citizen," born from the genocidal violence of colonization, exists in a dialectical relation with its Other, the "Indian," for whom the emergence of this citizenship was deadly, not emancipatory.

The institution of citizenship was key to the processes of settlement, economic development, and nation-building. It organized and normalized colonial dispossession through the granting of individual rights of domicile and land ownership to nationals, even as it gave concrete meaning to the category Indian, primarily as lack, including the lack of "the right to have rights." With these rights invested in the institution of citizenship, the institution itself became inseparable from the forced internal migrations of Aboriginal peoples onto reserves and the destruction of their communities as sovereign entities.

Access to formal citizenship for all non-Aboriginal populations was organized through migration or by birth within the nation's borders. If a major condition for the founding of the nation-state was the acquisition of national territory, no less important was the recruitment of a national population, for which the state turned primarily to European source countries. Immigration policy became central to the process of generating a national population and regulating its access to resources. From Confederation until the 1960s and 1970s, immigration and naturalization legislation distinguished first British and French, and later, other Europeans, as "preferred races" for integration into the nation.[12] This exaltation positioned Europeans as the "true" subjects of the nation. For over a century after Confederation, the state therefore organized and solidified white racial identity as *political* (citizen) identity. The nation's racial identity, as well as its legal citizenship, thus became fused as white.[13]

The western scientific theories of white racial superiority popular during this period, instituted in state practices, saturated the hallowed institution of citizenship. It is ironic that even as the nation was imagined to be a homogenous entity in its foundational moment, free of the contaminating influence of the Native cultures that preceded it and of the polluting presence of Black and Asian peoples, the specific legislations enacted by the state demonstrate elite recognition that this was not indeed the case. The Indian Act and the various immigration and citizenship legislation attest to the presence of various Others, even as they simultaneously testify to the commitment to expel them from nationality.

Relatively disenfranchised groups among national subjects, including women and the working class, challenged state and elite power to increase their own access to citizenship. Unevenly endowed as their rights were, however, these groups made common cause with the elite and the state in curtailing the access of non-European populations to the same rights. Here, another aspect of citizenship becomes evident: citizenship serves as a status that mobilizes national subjects, classed and gendered as they may be themselves, in defence of the institution against the claims of those designated as undeserving outsiders.

The unequal conditions under which respective phases of migration into Canada have been organized have had long-lasting consequences for access to citizenship. Non-preferred races were no longer overtly designated as such after the 1960s, and they acquired increased access to citizenship. However, their de facto unequal rights have been maintained through their ideological designation as immigrants, newcomers, new Canadians, and visible minorities, even after they acquire de jure status as citizens. The category immigrant undermines the very notion of the nation as a homogenous entity, as well as of the nation as a nonracial entity.[14] It reveals the heterogeneous nature of the population by drawing attention to the presence of racial Others within the nation's psychosocial and physical space. However, the racialized category immigrant also paradoxically helps sustain the myth of the nation as homogenous, by constructing as perpetual strangers those to whom the category is assigned, even when they are second or third generation Canadian born citizens, as is the case with the contemporary use of the term "immigrant communities."

As racially excluded immigrants sought to expand the institution of citizenship to accommodate their own demands for inclusion, they left largely unchallenged the role of this institution in the dispossession of Aboriginal peoples. The extension of citizenship rights to these racialized immigrants thus resulted in their qualified integration into the political community, but at the cost of fostering their complicity in the colonial domination of Aboriginal peoples.

The increased migrations of those previously designated non-preferred races after the liberalization of immigration and citizenship legislation in the 1970s meant the nation once again faced the spectre of non-whites emerging as a significant demographic and cultural force, with their growing economic and political power eclipsing the white domination of national institutions. These fears have not diminished with time. The notion that the liberalization of immigration and citizenship legislation since the 1970s somehow brought to an end the historical racialization of the nation will be contested in the following sections.

Citizenship Rights and Rites

Although citizenship was of concern to the ancient Greeks, the advent of modernity brought about a profound reconceptualization of the human subject and its relation to sovereign power. Cast in the modern figure of the citizen, the status of this subject became inextricably linked with the individualist and rationalist ethos, as well as with the notions of equality, fairness, and just treatment at the heart of liberal political theory. Although citizenship is a complex and deeply contested construct, it has been enthusiastically welcomed as an emancipatory measure by those included within its orbit, and desperately struggled for by those excluded from its entitlements.

Feminists have argued that the liberal concept of the citizen is deeply masculinist, hiding the sexual contract that underpins the social contract of citizens within a common brotherhood.[15] They have pointed out that while citizenship is located within the public sphere, it is in the private sphere that male domination of women is organized. This domination subsequently shapes women's rights within the public sphere.

The status of citizen exalts the national subject as an equal among its compatriot, thus upholding the chimera of its equality despite its experience of deeply entrenched socio-economic inequalities. It also enables the shaping of individual subjectivity in a manner that underscores this mythic equality, however unrealized this equality might remain in practice. The hailing of the subject-as-citizen enables it to experience itself as beyond the whims and mercies of a tyrannical sovereign, safe from arbitrary infractions. Instead, this subject experiences itself as the anchor of an enlightened sovereign power and, hence, as an *empowered* subject itself. The wide array of 'social customs" and "conventional acts" through which these individuals enact and realize their citizenship as *empowered subjects* are therefore as relevant as the legal rights incorporated within the status.[16] In this section, I characterize these practices as rituals and rites, which sustain the citizenship of nationals in their daily encounters with each other, and with outsiders.

Rituals and rites are most often associated with the realm of the sacred, but a number of social theorists have made a convincing case that ritual, and in particular the "interaction ritual," remains the "basic social event."[17] Rituals lie at the heart of social life, sustaining social bonds among members of the community through their repeated performance. Among the rituals and rites of citizenship can be included the affective recitations of national anthems; the raising of flags; the public pledges and oaths of allegiance to the sovereign; and the celebrations of national holidays and the parades, plays, firework displays, street parties, family dinners, and so on, that mark these. The political practices associated with elections, referendums, voting, and so on, are also ritualistic enactments of citizenship. Such rituals and rites are clearly integral to producing the forms of affiliation that are central to civic integration; they become the sites where members of the collective perform their own belonging and recognize that of their compatriots.

The rites and rituals of citizenship, however, can – and do – assume other more overtly malevolent expressions. Among the rites that have also inducted individuals into the national political communities in North America are the ritualized forms of "national" violence, such as the lynching of Black men in the southern United States, the painting of swastikas on synagogues, and the "Paki-bashing" by ultranationalists; the raping of women in situations of war and conflict; the burning of crosses; the pulling off of Muslim women's headscarves; the organized riots and mob violence enacted upon the bodies of Chinese and other aliens. Such rites also include the highly ritualized erasures of the presence of minorities in national historiography and the markers of national accomplishments, as well as the more banal liturgies recited against their presence (why don't they speak English? do they have to wear turbans?; and so on). The exclusion of racial minorities from housing, employment, access to loans, the repeated questioning about where they are really from, the repeated insistence that they provide documents to prove their legality add to the repertoire of these bonding rituals among nationals.

Such banal practices tend to be treated as isolated, unrelated, and based largely in individual ignorance and certainly not meant to offend. This sort of approach hides their highly repetitive, historic, and ritualized occurrence, as well as the widespread social tolerance – if not explicit sanction – they enjoy. Identifying these practices as rites of citizenship directs attention to their important function in reinforcing notions of legitimate belonging, in reinforcing the incontestability of the citizenship of nationals as they enact their insider status. Rites have symbolic value as well as concrete outcomes, and they signify the limits of the acceptable. Most importantly, they demonstrate who has power and who is prohibited from exercising such power.

Making Canadian Citizens

The colonizing migrations of European settlers created overseas populations to govern and develop colonies in the interests of European powers, and were intended to be a permanent affair in white settler societies.[18] Immigration policies across the British Empire were intimately linked to this imperial goal:[19] "All the British colonies of settlement – Canada, Australia, New Zealand and South Africa – were from the first deeply committed to the dream of becoming outposts of the 'British race.'"

The development of Canada as a self-governing territory, with its own political institutions and population base, was built upon its close ties to Britain and its privileged white status.[20] The political autonomy that the new state acquired through the British North America Act (1867) enabled it to further consolidate colonial relations and expand westwards. Until almost the mid-twentieth century, the actual legal status of "Canadians" was that of British subjects with domicile in Canada: immigration and naturalization legislation organized access to this legal status.[21] The creation of a distinct Canadian citizenship was to wait until 1947, when the first Citizenship Act was legislated.

During this period, Aboriginal peoples were relegated to an infantilized status as wards of the state under the Indian Act.[22] All aspects of Aboriginal people's lives were controlled, including where they could reside, where they could travel, and what work they could do.[23] With settlement eroding the economic base of Aboriginal societies, it consequently undermined the power of Aboriginal nations to determine their political systems, the conditions and forms of membership within their political communities, and the attendant forms of social relations.

The extension of citizenship to Aboriginal communities was tied to the goal of encouraging private ownership of land by Aboriginal peoples as individuals. It sought to destroy their collective ownership of these lands, hence making them available to Europeans.[24] Moreover, Native women were barred from participation in the colonial forms of governance imposed upon their societies, including the band council system, which eroded the political power they had previously enjoyed.[25]

Citizenship, as the quintessential hallmark of liberal democracy, was thus racialized from its very importation into the country; Aboriginal peoples were granted no democratic space or extension of rights and entitlements within the national political institutions that came to govern their lives.[26] Indigenous forms of sociopolitical systems, their organization of the rights, entitlements, obligations, and responsibilities which bound the members of these communities together, were simply deemed non-existent, and irrelevant by the state.

Settlers were recruited with offers of "free land and easy wealth as inducements," as well as with other forms of social and financial supports.[27] Certainly not all emigrants from Britain and France had access to such incentives, their class, gender, and sexuality gave rise to inequalities in such access. However, their classification as preferred races and, hence, as *future citizens*, provided them with significant opportunities for land ownership and upward socio-economic mobility. While conflicting gender and class interests within these communities were reproduced subsequent to their migration, their integration into the nation as preferred races suppressed these material divisions within the framework of an otherwise – and equally material – shared racial interest in the new social order.

In addition to the role of state policy, however, it is important to note that white supremacy had to be established on the ground across the country. Cycles of racial conflict, and racial accommodation, occurred within the dynamic and changing milieu of the emerging settler society, in which social norms, values, and political structures were in their early stages of development. However, they did not shift so far as to include Asian and Black, or any other non-white migrant group. Benedict Anderson's formulation of the nation as shaped by elites in the form of "official nationalism," as well as by the "popular nationalism" of other classes, is pertinent to the experience of Canadian nation-building.[28] The "official nationalism" of the state expressed most strongly in the Indian Act and the immigration and citizenship policies, interacted with the "popular nationalism" of its white subjects, who actively enacted the dispossession of Native peoples on the ground, as they did the exclusion of "non-preferred" races from access to land, mobility, and employment. The popular racism these subjects articulated forged a common interest among them *as nationals* through their exclusion of outsiders.

The active participation of British and French women in nation-building has been found to have been of vital importance: "the appearance of white women was coterminous with white settlement and brought both a sharp rise in racist sentiment and heightened class-consciousness within fur-trade society."[29] During the nineteenth and early twentieth centuries, the organizations established by Canadian women largely shared the goal of Canadian men to "Keep Canada White." Trades unions were likewise extremely hostile to the presence of nonpreferred races, whom they defined as taking jobs away from white workers.[30] By constructing Asian workers as an economic threat to their own well-being, white workers could mobilize campaigns against the former's immigration and employment; their trades unions used such campaigns to strengthen and consolidate their own membership base and political muscle, particularly in provinces like British Columbia.[31]

Lisa Lowe has noted that Orientalist constructs abounded within American national culture during this period, and that these were central to the denial of citizenship rights to Asian immigrants until the mid-twentieth century.[32] In Peter Ward's study of anti-Asian racism in British Columbia (from the mid-nineteenth to the mid-twentieth century), he analysed how the white citizens of the province remained committed to the preservation of their racial identity. With few exceptions, politicians, writers, media commentators, clergy, and trade unionists mobilized for this political goal at the provincial and federal levels. Having relegated Aboriginal populations to the margins, Ward points out that the target for the white population's racist and nativist sentiments were the Asians, "a dynamic, growing segment in west coast society."[33]

As they imposed such representations onto the unwanted migrants, these subjects exalted themselves as clean, orderly, lawful, healthy, and civilized, and hence worthy of citizenship. Most nationals publicly performed the rites and rituals of citizenship to promote the emerging racial hierarchy and to enhance their access to political and economic power through the disenfranchisement of Others. Among such rites were the routine harassment of migrants; the active petitioning of provincial and federal governments to curb Asian and Black immigration; organized forays into Asian neighbourhoods and attacks on Asians; the burning down of their camps, homes, and shops; boycotts of the businesses of whites who employed Asians; and the segregation of non-white children from their own in order to pass their racial privileges onto subsequent generations.[34]

As noted above, the legal status of Canadians until the mid-twentieth century was that of British and French subjects. The first Canadian Citizenship Act was legislated after the end of the Second World War. The Citizenship Act created three classes of citizens: natural born, naturalized, and those granted citizenship by virtue of a certificate of citizenship.[35] It also specified particular grounds, including disloyalty and treason, for the revocation of citizenship and the deportation of certain classes of citizens.[36]

The first Citizenship Act thus distinguished between classes of citizens even *after* they acquired this legal status, ensuring that citizenship status was not to be unconditional for all citizens. The new Citizenship Act maintained a right of the state to impose a condition of statelessness upon immigrant citizens, thus allowing their immigrant status to permeate their citizenship even after they became naturalized, distinguishing them from the real citizens whose status could not be revoked. In institutionalizing the deportation clause, the new Citizenship Act allowed the use of this clause to curtail the access of specific groups to full citizenship, such as the right to political activism and access to public assistance.[37]

The Act allowed independent access to citizenship for Canadian women, stipulating they would not lose this status upon marriage to a non-citizen. This was in stark contrast to the political treatment of Aboriginal women who lost their Indian status (and political membership in their community) upon marriage to non-Aboriginal men. The Act also allowed non-citizen women to become eligible for citizenship through marriage to a Canadian citizen and, in this way, extended these women's access to citizenship. However, given the racialized immigration policies and the rampant fears of miscegenation that marked the period, few women of the non-preferred races would have been able to benefit from this increased access to citizenship.

Section 10 of the Act allowed the minister of immigration to grant certificates of citizenship, and also stipulated (unequal) eligibility criteria on the basis of linguistic proficiency.

For applicants fluent in either English or French, the period of domicile required was five years. For applicants who spoke neither of these languages, domicile was defined as a period of 20 years. Then, as now, non-European working-class immigrants, particularly women, would have been the least likely to have fluency in these languages. As non-preferred races, these immigrants already encountered significant barriers to enter and reside in the country. Now, the Act stipulated that they were required to meet the longest residency requirement for citizenship eligibility. Racialized immigration policies regulating access to formal citizenship were to remain in effect for close to three decades following the introduction of the Act.

Contesting Nationality?

Although the earliest arrival of Black and Asian migrants can be traced to the pre-Confederation period, the racism they encountered in the national commitment to "Keep Canada White" greatly curtailed this migration.[38] Even when their labour was recognized as necessary for economic development, these migrants were reviled and cast in the figure of the inassimilable and degenerate stranger. As was the case in other settler societies, like the United States,[39] racial classifications were legislated in Canada to restrict the immigration of non-preferred races: the Chinese Immigration Act of 1885, the Exclusion Act of 1923, the Continuous Passage Requirement of 1908, various head taxes, and the institutionalization of race in the 1910 Immigration Act were among some of the more notorious pieces of legislation.[40] Migrants from Africa, Asia, and the Caribbean – a part of the British Empire in which they had the status of British subjects – were denied the same mobility rights as white subjects through such policies.[41] Even when these migrants managed to enter the country, racialized legal exclusions applied to them whether *they were naturalized citizens or not*, as they did to their descendants, whether *they were Canadian-born or not*.[42] As discussed above, immigration and nationalization legislation enacted from Confederation until the mid-twentieth century secured the emergence of the white population as a majority.[43]

Black slaves and migrants, among the earliest undesired communities to migrate to Canada, were subjected to treatment that was in contrast to that of whites.[44] Despite being considered political allies in defending British interests against American expansion, Black peoples were given access to land on the basis of a "license of occupation," and not on the basis of ownership.[45] The refusal to grant them ownership, in tandem with the other racist practices discussed above, sent a clear message to this community: "American negroes were not welcome and were not encouraged to come; and, although no law was passed to exclude them, careful administrative procedures ensured that their applications would be rejected."[46] Although most Black people in the United States were "too poor and disadvantaged to contemplate migration," racial slavery in Canada and Black migration from the US had established Black communities in the country. But without "the necessary reinforcements," their numbers did not increase.[47] In fact, they actually declined.[48]

The building of the railway, a central plank in the National Economic Policy, was indispensable to the settlement of the western provinces and to the expansion of the national market economy. Chinese (and later South Asian) men were recruited to build this, and so critical was the labour they provided that without it, the building of the railways would have been "indefinitely postponed."[49] After the project was completed, however, the Chinese migrants were defined as a threat to society and "virtually every evil was blamed upon them."[50]

The subsequent Chinese Immigration Act of 1885 imposed a head tax on Chinese immigrants to curtail their entry.[51] The Exclusion Act in 1923 sought to prevent all Chinese immigration, with the consequence that less than 50 Chinese immigrants were permitted to enter the country between 1923 and 1947.[52] Similar legislation was also enacted to curtail South Asian and Japanese immigration, among them the Continuous Passage requirement introduced in 1908.[53] In the year after its introduction, only six South Asian immigrants entered the country; in the year prior to its introduction, these immigrants had numbered 2,500.[54] The 1910 Immigration Act legislated prohibitions on the grounds of race and became the "principal instrument" for the "Keep Canada White" policies. This Act remained in effect for the next 50 years,[55] during which time immigration from Europe was actively solicited. In the first decade of the twentieth century, immigration accounted for 44 per cent of the growth in the population.[56] The restrictions on non-white immigration ensured that the majority of this growth remained white.

The policies promoting European immigration were gendered, tailored to meet the special campaigns that recruited women. Likewise, the policies restricting non-European immigration were also gendered, with women being particularly defined for exclusion: if white women were to be the "mothers" of the nation, non-white women were said to herald its doom. Few women from China and South Asia were allowed to immigrate prior to the 1960s. Single Black women were allowed entry as domestic workers, but only on the condition that their families not accompany them.[57] As will be discussed more fully in the next chapter, women of the nonpreferred races were constituted as morally degenerate, sexually depraved, and endowed with a fecundity more animalistic than human. Keeping them out of the country was considered a special priority of immigration policies.

Yet, despite the intense discrimination these migrants encountered, they persisted in their attempts to enter the country. They used legal means when they could and resorted to extra-legal means when compelled to do so. They mobilized their budding communities against racist policies in Canada and within the British Empire; they lobbied for family reunification and for the right of illegal immigrants to remain in the country.[58] They also organized to gain access to Canadian citizenship.

Even when these migrants did acquire it, their citizenship remained a tenuous affair. The experience of Japanese-Canadians provides the definitive example, illustrating the ever-present threat to racial minorities of a state of exception to their precarious access to equality in the regime of citizenship. Japanese-Canadians were given greater access to immigration than other Asians as a result of Canadian state support for the alliance between the British and Japanese states.[59] However, their relatively greater access to citizenship did not protect them from becoming defined as an enemy race and having their citizenship suspended in a moment defined as a national crisis.[60] The internment of this community, and the suspension of their rights, separated families and destroyed an economically vibrant community. The suspension was to remain in effect for seven years, as their racial identity was deemed more significant than their citizen status or their remarkable contributions to the nation's economy.

The role of white citizens in mobilizing for the eviction and internment of Japanese-Canadians was critical and has been defined as 'spontaneous" and "widespread."[61] In the virulent eruption of this racism, state and nation worked in concert to contain a racial enemy within the citizenry, as they had done before. The internment was still in effect at the time of the introduction of the first Citizenship Act, and it was referred to by Members of Parliament from British Columbia who asked for reassurance that the Act's introduction would not allow Japanese-Canadians to return to the province. Reassuring them it would not, Paul Martin Sr. agreed to an amendment upholding the Order in Council for the internment.[62]

Although victims themselves of European domination and colonizing processes in their countries of origin, non-preferred races were to contribute to the marginalization of Aboriginal populations as they sought greater inclusion in the colonial society, oblivious – or even hostile – to Aboriginal presence. Many of the immigrants who became party to the marginalization of Aboriginal peoples had themselves been coerced into migration, whether under conditions of enslavement, as was the case with Black migrants, or under conditions of indentureship, as was the case with many Chinese and South Asian migrants.

The political struggles that migrant populations waged to gain equal access to citizenship, and to economic and social institutions, focused their attention more intently on the forms of power and the institutions serving the interests of nationals. The relocation of Native communities onto reserves furthered the geographical contiguity of these migrants with white nationals and further distanced them from Native communities. Consequently, the more these migrants sought proximity to nationals, the more they furthered their own social and political distance from Native communities. Their descendants, many oblivious to their own histories of racialized exclusions, are all the more readily amenable to reproducing this distance.

Liberalizing Citizenship

Canadian society underwent significant transformation in the 1960s and 1970s, a period of liberalization that brought about shifts in the organization of processes of racialization. Among the key policy changes during this period were the elimination of overtly racial classifications in immigration policies, increased access to Canadian citizenship for previously excluded groups, and the adoption of state multiculturalism. Aboriginal peoples also acquired access to education and the courts, as well as to the franchise. Many of the restrictions on their mobility were also removed. In this section, I focus on some of the most significant changes to immigration and citizenship policies.

The Immigration Regulations of 1962 emphasized the labour market needs of the country. The point system introduced in 1967 reflected this and focused on the education, profession, occupation, language, and skill levels of prospective immigrants, as well as on their family ties to Canada.[63] Popularly defined as instituting a non-discriminatory immigration program, the point system was subsequently entrenched in the Immigration Act, 1976–77.[64] Immigration for permanent settlement became organized mainly through the independent and family immigrant classes, as well as through the refugee protection program.[65]

Citizenship legislation was also revised during this period and the "preferential treatment" of British subjects was removed.[66] Inequalities in the residency requirements for citizenship eligibility (20 years for residents who did not speak English or French) were also removed.[67] These changes greatly expanded access to citizenship for all immigrants admitted for permanent settlement, including those previously designated non-preferred races. Effectively ending the official "Keep Canada White" policies of an earlier era, these changes became widely defined as reflecting a period of innovation.[68] Subsequently, the Canadian immigration program has come to be defined as among the most humanitarian and compassionate in the world. These liberalized immigration policies, the source of considerable national pride, have come to sustain contemporary exaltations of Canadian nationality as the most generous and humane in the world.

The result of the changes to immigration and citizenship policies have been significant. Whereas 90 per cent of all immigrants prior to 1961 were European-born, they came to represent only 25 per cent between 1981 and 1991, during which six out of the 10 largest source countries were in Asia.[69] A number of scholars have pointed out that while the point system made a commitment in principle to end race and sex discrimination, it did not do so in effect. First, resources for immigrant recruitment and processing are allocated unequally, favouring developed countries over developing ones. Second, immigration officers have discretionary powers to allocate points to applicants for their personal suitability and independent status. The allocation of these points reflects the biases of the officers, who have disproportionately favoured male applicants as independents over female applicants.

The liberalization of immigration policy undoubtedly reflected a growing awareness among nationals of the damaging effects of overt racial distinctions in state policy. But with Aboriginal populations having been decimated and displaced onto reserves, immigration was the primary source of population growth. The increased presence of immigrants in the country became an unavoidable necessity, as was the case in the other hypercapitalist countries also experiencing labour shortages. As a result of the pressures on Canada to present itself as the destination of choice for immigration, and of the political organizing of migrants for access to citizenship, the liberalization of citizenship became unavoidable. Here, I wish to highlight three aspects of the changes to immigration and citizenship legislation that maintained the earlier racialized constructs of nation, nationals, and citizenship.

In the absence of a just resolution to the challenge of Aboriginal sovereignty, Canadian citizenship remained rooted within the colonial dynamic and continued to be a means to further the cultural and political elimination of Aboriginality. The drive to extend citizenship to Aboriginal peoples remained tied to the objective of "bleeding" them off from their nations, and to regulate their integration into the Canadian mainstream, primarily as individuals with no special claims arising from their historical relationship to the land. In other words, citizenship remained the "final solution" to the Indian problem no less so in the present than was the case in the past.[70]

Further, the deployment of citizenship to confer an (abstract) "equality" on all subjects, including Aboriginal peoples, enabled it to construct Aboriginal peoples in the national imagination as ingrates who demanded preferential treatment and special rights, over and above what was a fair entitlement of all other citizens. In their rejection of assimilation into the mainstream, Aboriginal people were all the more readily constructed as demanding more than their fair share, and hence, as discriminating *against* Canadian citizens, placing them at a disadvantage.[71] More sympathetic nationals have come to regard Aboriginal peoples' conflictual relationship to citizenship as mainly a conflict between their ethnic and cultural identity on the one hand, and their civic and political identity on the other. In other words, they approach Aboriginal struggles as primarily cultural and ethnic, and not as political struggles.

Increased access to de jure citizenship for non-Canadian-born individuals continued to be organized primarily through the unequal conditions of their immigration after the liberalization, as had been the case previously. The unequal conditions of entry for the family class, for example, which required a sponsor to undertake financial responsibility for their dependents, denied these dependents equal entitlements to social programs even after they acquired legal citizenship. Further, the immigration policies that regulated the entry of domestic workers trapped them into a near-complete dependency on their employers by the stipulation that they live-in at their place of employment for a period of two years. The regulation of migrants as temporary workers, on the other hand, prohibited their subsequent access to citizenship. These unequal conditions that organized migration continued to organize a multitiered citizenship, which became instituted through the specific regulations of the immigration program.

Sponsorship regulations, for example, denied sponsored immigrants and their families equal access to the social rights of citizenship. Whereas those immigrants who did not speak English and French were required to prove residency for 20 years before they could acquire citizenship and its social entitlements prior to the liberalization of these policies, the liberalized sponsorship regulations stipulated unequal access to social entitlements for *all* sponsored immigrants for the duration of their sponsorship, even after their acquisition of citizenship (which has required shorter residency periods than the sponsorship regulation). These regulations have had particularly serious consequences for immigrant women.

The role of citizenship in institutionalizing the dispossession of Aboriginal peoples' resources, the inequalities sponsorship regulations organize within the body politic, and the maintenance of the deportation clause contribute to the enduring symbolic attachment of citizenship to whiteness. Despite these serious limitations, the liberalization of citizenship has enabled representations of the nation-state as being a liberal democracy in essence rather than a colonial settler society. Racial identity (white, officially British and French) is repeatedly reinscribed as the authentic and trustworthy marker of citizenship in daily life. Nationality and citizenship coexist in an overlapping manner, so that some citizens can claim nationality while others are denied such claims, even when they share the legal status of citizenship.

The symbolic association of citizenship with whiteness can be regularly witnessed in seemingly innocent rites, such as routine questioning of immigrants about where they are really from; in the not so innocent exhortation to immigrants to go back to where they came from; and in the "reasonable" demand that they produce identity papers and proof of residence when they attempt to access health, education, and social services. Such rites of citizenship, even when couched in the form of polite requests to prove legality, reflect the common-sense knowledge shared among nationals that strangers need to prove their legality before they should be allowed to access their rights. The expansion of citizenship to include people of colour has undoubtedly brought about significant changes in their status and rights, an important one being the right of family reunification. However, citizenship has failed to be the panacea many had dreamed it to be.

Moreover, before the events of 11 September 2001, the London bombings of 7 July 2005, and the global effects of the US-led "war on terror," Canadians might well have considered the processes of outright exclusion from citizenship, such as those experienced by Japanese Canadians, as isolated and aberrant, a shameful moment in the nation's past which is best relegated to the historical archives. In the wake of these events, however, it is clear that these familiar (and tested) processes can be applied to Muslims or any other non-preferred group, resulting in the suspension of their citizenship rights and in their being presented as a threat to the nation in moments of crisis.

Canadian citizenship was integrative and inclusive for European immigrants until well into the twentieth century. It organized their membership in the nation and gave them formal legal rights and entitlements. As such, citizenship was an institution that expanded their political participation and enhanced their exalted status as modern subjects. Yet, simultaneously, it also became an exclusionary mechanism, producing Indians and immigrants as racial strangers. Citizenship symbolized the drive towards greater equality in the historical "march of progress."[72] Benhabib, for her part, also furthers such an understanding of citizenship, naturalizing the right of citizens to have rights, and presenting as equally natural their inclination to protect these from the encroachments of outsiders. Contrary to such formulations, Canadian citizenship emerged with the clear intention to produce racial divisions among the populations within the territorial bounds of the nation-state, divisions which remain significant to this day and which continue the project of all racial states to produce national/racial homogeneity in the face of actual heterogeneity.

NOTES

1 Benhabib 2004.
2 Menzies, Adamoski, and Chunn (2002) identify three major paradigms of citizenship: civic republicanism, which defines the citizen as a responsible and active participant in the public sphere and governance; liberal individualism, which defines citizenship as a status, such that "requirements from the state do not extend beyond "freedom and security"; and neo-liberalism, informed by Marshall's conception of social and welfare citizenship. See R. Menzies, R. Adamoski, and D. Chunn 2002, 11–42.
3 Benhabib (2004, 25) draws on the analysis of Katrin Flikschuh, who discussed Kant's recognition of three interrelated but distinct rights: rights of persons and the state; rights between states: and rights between persons and foreign states.
4 This right particularly cannot be denied to strangers who face "destruction." Kant's notion of this right has "become incorporated into the Geneva Convention on the Status of Refugees as the principle of "non-refoulement." ibid., 35.
5 Ibid., 50. Arendt traced the source of totalitarianism to European colonization of Africa.
6 Ibid., 61.
7 Ibid., 2.
8 Ibid., 19–21.
9 Ibid., 21.
10 During the nineteenth century, "race" had a different meaning than it was to assume during the twentieth century. So, for example, the Irish, the Jews, the Polish, the Hungarians, and so on were all defined as racially inferior to the British and French, and their immigration to North America was not looked upon favourably. However, during the twentieth century, these other European groups were integrated into the racialized category "white" in Canada (Bannerji, 2000).
11 Whether the assumptions underpinning Benhabib's theory of citizenship and universal human rights can be unproblematically applied to any liberal democracy is a question beyond the scope of this study.
12 See Jakubowski 1997, 11–12. See also Stasiulis and Jhappan 1995; Bolaria and Li 1988; Ward 2002.
13 As Mamdani (2001, 22) has noted: "If your inclusion or exclusion from a regime of rights or entitlements is based on your race or ethnicity, as defined by law, then this becomes a central defining fact for you the individual and your group. From this point of view, both race and ethnicity need to be understood as political – and not cultural, or even biological – identities."

14 See Bannerji 2000.
15 Pateman 1988.
16 A right is defined as "a moral or legal entitlement to have or do something" in the *Oxford English Dictionary*, 2nd ed. A rite is defined as "a body of customary observances characteristic of a Church or a part of it ... a social custom, practice, or conventional act" (1989, 1516).
17 Drawing upon the theories of Durkheim, Coffman, and Collins, Bellah (2003, 31–44) defines the secular ritual at the heart of social interactions: "In this process of ritual interaction the members of the group, through their shared experience, feel a sense of membership, however fleeting, with a sense of boundary between those sharing the experience and all those outside it; they feel some sense of moral obligation to each other, which is symbolized by whatever they focused on during the interaction; and finally, they are charged with what Collins calls emotional energy but which he identifies with what Durkheim called moral force. Since, according to Collins, all of social life consists of strings of such ritual interactions, then ritual becomes the most fundamental category for the understanding of social action."
18 See Anderson 1983.
19 For example, the Empire Settlement Act of 1922 committed Britain to work with Dominion governments and private agencies to develop emigration and settlement programs into those colonies. See Carrothers 1929; Hawkins 1989; Peterson 1975.
20 The race of the ruling elite was the basis upon which Canada acquired its independence from the British state: "the 'gifts' of liberal democratic government and relative political autonomy so that (Canada) might develop within a shared framework of civilization and moral and material standards. Hence, although Canada (and the other so-called 'white dominions') shared with the so-called 'dependent colonies' a peripheral position in the international political economy prior to the twentieth century, as a cultural, social and political entity, it was a chip off the metropolitan block" (Stasiulis and Jhappan 1995, 97). See also Hawkins 1989.
21 Examining the development of Canadian citizenship, Carty and Ward (1986) have pointed out that "most policies encouraging migration reflected the assumption that northwestern Europeans and Americans of like descent made the best prospective citizens" (1986, 68).
22 Dyck 1991, 3.
23 Carter 1993, 32.
24 See Lawrence 1999.
25 Aboriginal women acquired enfranchisement in the 1960s (see Maracle 1993).
26 At the time of Confederation, the legal status of "Canadian citizens" was that of British subjects with domicile in Canada (Carty and Ward 1986; Ungerleider 1992). The "Canadian" population was 60 per cent British and 30 per cent French. Kalbach 1990, 18). The ruling elite, of course, came from these two "races."
27 Such supports included access to "cheap" land, financial grants, assisted passages and assistance with settlement and employment. See Green 1995; Hawkins 1989; Parr 1987; Vibert 1996; Dyck 1991.
28 Anderson 1983.
29 Stasiulis and Jhappan 1995.
30 Buchignani and Indra 1985.
31 Bolaria and Li 1988; Ward 2002.
32 Lisa Lowe 1998.
33 Ward 2002, 92.
34 For discussion of the anti-Asian campaigns, see ibid.; Bolaria and Li 1988.

35 These three classes are defined as follows:

(i) natural-born citizens, including children born outside the country with Canadian fathers and children born out of "wedlock" to Canadian mothers (CCA 1947, Sections 4 and 5).
(ii) naturalized citizens: British subjects with Canadian domicile, "domicile" being defined as five years residence; women married to Canadian citizens; British subjects admitted into Canada for permanent residence (ibid., Section 9).
(iii) citizens granted a citizenship Certificate by the Minister by virtue of the following: coming of age at 18 years and filing an intention to become citizens; spouses of, and resident with, Canadian citizens or British subjects (ibid., Section 10).

36 "The Governor in Council may order that any person other than a naturalborn Canadian citizen shall cease to be a Canadian citizen if, upon a report from the Minister, he is satisfied that the said person either: (a) has, during any war in which Canada is or has been engaged, unlawfully traded or communicated with the enemy or with a subject of an enemy state or has been engaged in or associated with any business which to his knowledge is carried on in such manner as to assist the enemy in such war ... (d) if out of Canada, has shown himself by act or speech to be disaffected or disloyal to His Majesty, or, if in Canada, has been convicted of treason or sedition by a court of competent jurisdiction" (section 21 (1)).

37 Roberts 1988.

38 Some Black people were brought to Canada as slaves, and others came as Loyalists and pioneers as early as the seventeenth century (Bolaria and Li 1988). The first Chinese migrants to come to Canada are recorded to have arrived in 1858. See Li 1998, 3.

39 See Lowe 1998.

40 See Hawkins 1989; Ungerleider 1992; Stasiulis and Jhappan 1995; Jakubowski 1997; Bolaria and Li 1988.

41 Gordon 1985; Women, Immigration and Nationality Group (WING), 1985; Potts 1990; Mazumdar 1984.

42 Bolaria and Li 1988; Buchignani and Indra 1985.

43 For example, the Chinese population in British Columbia fluctuated from being about 15 per cent to 40 per cent of the population in the 1860s (Ward 2002, 14). The Chinese were about 17.1 per cent of the population in 1870, but by 1921 they had been reduced to 5.1 per cent of the population. In 1901, Asians in the province were 10.9 per cent of the total population. However, by 1941, they had been reduced to 5.2 per cent of the population (ibid., 170–1).

44 By 1759, there were over 1,000 Black slaves in New France and by 1767 there were 104 in Nova Scotia. In 1783, Loyalists brought 2,000 more Black slaves into the country (Bolaria and Li 1988, 166). The Royal Commission on Bilingualism and Biculturalism noted the following about the history of Black migration: "Negroes came to new France and to the Provinces of British North America in the l8th century chiefly as slaves. In the 19th century, they formed sizable settlements as freedmen and fugitives in the Maritimes, in southwestern Ontario, and in Victoria. Many returned to the United States in the 1860s, during and after the Civil War. The 1871 census figure of 21,500 for Canada probably represents a drop in the negro population from an earlier period. The 1881, 1901, and 1911 censuses record further declines" (Palmer 1975). See also Kilian 1978.

45 Bolaria and Li 1988, 168.

46 Palmer 1975.

47 Hawkins 1989.

48 The construction of the railway led to 17,000 Chinese workers being recruited between 1876 and 1884 (Adilman 1984, 55). See also Mazumdar 1984; Jakubowski 1997.
49 See Porter 1966. The labour of Chinese men was so critical to building this railway and the risks of this work so great that the 1970 Report on Bilingualism and Biculturalism stated, "It has been said that a Chinese is buried beneath every mile of track of the railway through the mountains of British Columbia" (Palmer 1975, 6).
50 Bolaria and Li 1988, 86.
51 The head tax was initially set at $10 and steadily increased over the years to $50 between 1896 and 1900; $100 for the next three years; and $500 from 1904 to 1923. See Hawkins 1989; Adilman 1984; Ungerleider 1992.
52 See Hawkins 1989; Ungerleider 1992. In addition to reducing the immigration of the Chinese, the head tax was also a lucrative source of revenue for the state. Between 1886 and 1924, special registrations required of Chinese immigrants and the head tax brought in revenues amounting to $22.5 million (Bolaria and Li 1988, 90).
53 This legislation required immigrants to travel from the country of origin to Canada in an uninterrupted journey. At that time, only one steamship company offered continuous passage to Canada, and this company was persuaded by the state to discontinue selling tickets (Buchignani and Indra 1985; Mazumdar 1984; Adhopia 1993). Tickets were not sold even to those South Asians who were already settled in Canada and were visiting the country of their origin.
54 Ungerleider 1992, 9. In 1910, a $200 head tax on South Asians was introduced.
55 Hawkins 1989; Jakubowski 1997.
56 Ungerleider 1992, 9.
57 Adhopia 1993; Buchignani and Indra 1985; Adilman 1984; Doman 1984.
58 Chinese and South Asian immigrants organized campaigns against the various head taxes and the Chinese Exclusion Act. See Adhopia 1993; Buchignani and Indra 1985.
59 This situation changed in 1908 when immigration from Japan was made subject to a "Gentlemen's Agreement," which allowed only returning Japanese immigrants and their families, along with their employees, to enter the country. This agreement lasted until 1940.
60 In 1942, 22,000 Japanese-Canadian women, men, and children in British Columbia were given twenty-four hours to vacate their homes. Branded as "enemy aliens," their businesses, houses, and other belongings were confiscated by the state. Seventy-five per cent of them had been born in Canada and were "citizens" by birth and by domicile. But this status was not sufficient to prevent 4,000 of them from being deported to Japan.
61 See Ward 2002, 158–9.
62 Demirjian, Gray, and Wright 1996.
63 The Immigration Act 1976–77, contained a specific non-discrimination clause on the following grounds: "to ensure that any person who seeks admission to Canada on either a permanent or temporary basis is subject to standards of admission that do not discriminate on the grounds of race, national or ethnic origin, colour, religion or sex" (section 3(f)).
64 As the name indicates, immigrants were to be assessed on the allocation of points for their skills and the educational and occupational qualifications they possessed. Additionally, family members of immigrants and citizens were also allowed to immigrate.
65 The Act defined these categories as follows: (1) the family class, based upon the reunification of immediate family members of citizens and landed immigrants; and assisted relatives who did not have enough points to qualify under the independent category, but who were nominated by a relative in Canada for sponsorship; (2) independent applicants, whose eligibility was to be determined through the point system, with points being allocated on the basis of their

skills (this class included assisted relatives), and (3) refugees, who feared persecution and met the United Nations definition of "convention refugees." Additional categories under which immigration was also organized were the Non-Immigrant Employment Authorization Program (NIEAP), introduced in 1973, and the domestic worker category. The NIEAP allowed workers to enter the country on temporary work permits. See Sharma 1997; Bolaria 1992; Stasiulis 1997.

66 Brodie 2002. The most salient change (for the purpose of this study) was that the residency requirement for eligibility to citizenship was reduced to three years, and the twenty-year residency requirement for applicants who did not speak English or French was eliminated (Demirjian, Gray, and Wright 1996).

67 Demirjian, Gray, and Wright 1996.

68 Green and Green 1997; Hawkins 1989.

69 Abu-Laban 1998; Das Gupta, 1995; Ng 1998; Ng and Strout 1977. Between 1951 and 1957, 91.39 per cent of immigration recruitment expenses went to "developed" countries, and between 1962 and 1969, 78.2 per cent went to the same. Likewise, there were five immigration offices in the United Kingdom and ten in the United States in 1981, compared with one in India and one for the entire continent of Africa (Jakubowski 1997, 18–20).

70 See Green 1995; Lawrence 1999.

71 See Bateman 1997 for a discussion of such public attitudes in Canada and the United States.

72 Marshall 1992. Most contemporary discussions take Marshall's theorization of citizenship, rooted in liberal political theory, as their point of departure.

REFERENCES

Abu-Laban, Yasmeen. 1998. "Keeping "Em Out: Gender, Race and Class Biases in Canadian Immigration Policy." In *Painting the Maple: Essays on Race, Gender and the Construction of Canada*, ed. Joan Anderson, Avigail Eisenberg, Sherril Grace, and Veronica Strong-Boag, 69–82. Vancouver: University of British Columbia Press.

Adhopia, Ajit. 1993. *The Hindus of Canada*. New Delhi: Inderlekh Publications.

Adilman, Tamara. 1984. "A Preliminary Sketch of Chinese Women and Work in British Columbia 1858-1950." In *Not Just Pin Money*, edited by Latham and Pazdro, 53–78. Victoria: Camosun College.

Anderson, Benedict. 1983. *Imagined Communities: Reflections on the Origin and Spread of Nationalism*. London: Verso.

Bannerji, Himani. 2000. *The Dark Side of the Nation: Essays on Multiculturalism, Nationalism and Gender*. Toronto: Women's Press.

Bateman, Rebecca. 1997. "Comparative Thoughts on the Politics of Aboriginal Assimilation." *BC Studies* (114): 59–83.

Bellah, Robert N. 2003. "The Ritual Roots of Society and Culture." In *Handbook of the Sociology of Religion*, ed. Michele Dillon, 31–44. Cambridge: Cambridge University Press. http://dx.doi.org/10.1017/CBO9780511807961.003.

Benhabib, Seyla. 2004. *The Rights of Others: Aliens, Residents and Citizens*. Cambridge: Cambridge University Press. http://dx.doi.org/10.1017/CBO9780511790799.

Bolaria, B. Singh. 1992. "From Immigrant Settlers to Migrant Transients: Foreign Professionals in Canada." In *Deconstructing a Nation: Immigration, Multiculturalism and Racism in '90s Canada*, ed. Vic Satzewich, 211–28. Halifax: Fernwood.

Bolaria, B. Singh, and Peter S. Li. 1988. *Racial Oppression in Canada*. Toronto: Garamond.

British North American Act. 1867. http://www.justice.gc.ca/eng/rp-pr/csj-sjc/constitution/lawreg-loireg/p1t11.html.

Brodie, Janine. 2002. "Three Stories of Canadian Citizenship." In *Contesting Canadian Citizenship*, ed. Robert Adamoski, Dorothy E. Chunn, and Robert Menzies, 43–65. Peterborough: Broadview Press.

Buchignani, Norman, and Doreen M. Indra. 1985. *Continuous Journey: A Social History of South Asians in Canada*. Toronto: McClelland and Stewart.

Canadian Citizenship Act (CCA). 1947.

Carrothers, William A. 1929. *Emigration from the British Isles*. London: P.S. King and Son.

Carter, Sarah. 1993. "Categories and Terrains of Exclusion: Constructing the 'Indian Woman' in the Early Settlement Era in Western Canada." *Great Plains Quarterly* 13 (3): 147–61.

Carty, R. Kenneth, and Peter Ward. 1986. "The Making of a Canadian Political Citizenship." In *National Politics and Community in Canada*, edited by R. Kenneth Carty and Peter Ward, 65–79. Vancouver: University of British Columbia Press.

Das Gupta, Tania. 1995. "Families of Native Peoples, Immigrants, and People of Colour." In *Canadian Families: Diversity, Conflict and Change*, ed. Nancy Mandell and Anne Duffy, 141–174. Toronto: Harcourt Brace.

Demirjian, Annie, Douglas Gray, and David Wright. 1996. *The 1947 Canadian Citizenship Act: Issues and Significance, Prepared for Citizenship and Immigration Canada*. Ottawa: Consulting and Audit Canada.

Doman, Mahinder Kaur. 1984. "A Note on Asian Indian Women in British Columbia 1900-1935." In *Not Just Pin Money: Selected Essays on the History of Women's Work in British Columbia*, ed. Barbara K. Latham and Roberta J. Pazdro, 99–104. Victoria: Camosun College.

Dyck, Noel. 1991. *What Is the Indian "Problem": Tutelage and Resistance in Canadian Indian Administration*. St. John's: Memorial University of Newfoundland.

Gordon, Paul. 1985. *Policing Immigration: Britain's Internal Controls*. London: Pluto Press.

Green, Joyce. 1995. "Towards a Détente with History: Confronting Canada's Colonial Legacy." *International Journal of Canadian Studies* 12:85–105.

Green, Alan G., and David A. Green. 1997. "The Economic Goals of Canada's Immigration Policy, Past and Present." Paper presented at the British Columbia Centre for Excellence on Immigration, Vancouver, British Columbia.

Hawkins, Freda. 1989. *Critical Years in Immigration: Canada and Australia Compared*. Montreal: McGill-Queen's University Press.

Jakubowski, Lisa Marie. 1997. *Immigration and the Legalization of Racism*. Halifax: Fernwood Publishing.

Kalbach, Warren E. 1990. "A Demographic Overview of Racial and Ethnic Groups in Canada." In *Race and Ethnic Relations in Canada*, ed. Peter Li, 18–47. Toronto: Oxford University Press.

Kilian, Crawford. 1978. *Go Do Something Beautiful: The Black Pioneers of British Columbia*. Vancouver: Douglas and McIntyre.

Lawrence, Bonita. 1999. *"Real" Indians and Others: Mixed-Race Urban Native People, the Indian Act, and the Rebuilding of Indigenous Nations*. PhD dissertation, University of Toronto.

Li, Peter. 1998. *The Chinese in Canada*. Toronto: Oxford University Press.

Lowe, Lisa. 1998. *Immigrant Acts: On Asian American Cultural Politics*. Durham, NC: Duke University Press.

Mamdani, Mahmood. 2001. *When Victims Become Killers*. Princeton, New Jersey: Princeton University Press.

Maracle, Lee. 1993. "Racism, Sexism and Patriarchy." In *Returning the Gaze: Essays on Racism, Feminism and Politics*, ed. Himani Bannerji, 148–158. Toronto: Sister Vision Press.

Marshall, Thomas H. 1992. "Citizenship and Social Class." In *Citizenship and Social Class*, ed. Thomas H. Marshall and Tom Bottomore, 3–51. London: Pluto Press.
Mazumdar, Sucheta. 1984. "Colonial Impact and Punjabi Emigration to the United States." In *Labor Immigration under Capitalism: Asian Workers in the United States Before World War II*, ed. Lucie Cheng and Edna Bonacich, 316–36. Berkeley: University of California Press.
Menzies, Robert, Robert Adamoski, and Dorothy Chunn. 2002. "Rethinking the Citizen in Canadian Social History." In *Contesting Canadian Citizenship: Historical Readings*, ed. Robert Adamoski, Dorothy Chunn, and Robert Menzies, 11–42. Peterborough, ON: Broadview Press.
Ng, Roxana. 1998. "Gendering Policy Research on Immigration." In *Gendering Immigration: Integration Policy Research Workshop Proceedings and a Selective Review of Policy Research Literature 1987–1996*, 13–22. Ottawa: Status of Women Canada.
Ng, Roxana, and Janet Strout. 1977. *Services for Immigrant Women: Report and Evaluation of a Series of Four Workshops Conducted in the Summer, 1977*. Vancouver: Women's Research Centre.
Oxford English Dictionary. 1989. 2nd ed. 20 vols. Oxford: Oxford University Press. Also available at http://www.oed.com/.
Palmer, Howard, ed. 1975. *Immigration and the Rise of Multiculturalism*. Vancouver: Copp Clark Pub.
Parr, Joy. 1987. "The Skilled Emigrant and Her Kin: Gender, Culture, and Labour Recruitment." *Canadian Historical Review* 68 (4): 529–51. http://dx.doi.org/10.3138/CHR-068-04-02.
Pateman, Carol. 1988. *The Sexual Contract*. Cambridge: Polity Press.
Peterson, William. 1975. "Canada's Immigration: The Ideological Background." In *Immigration and the Rise of Multiculturalism*, ed. Howard Palmer, 22–33. Toronto: Copp Clark.
Porter, John. 1966. *The Vertical Mosaic*. Toronto: University of Toronto Press.
Potts, Lydia. 1990. *The World Labour Market: A History of Migration*. London: Zed Books.
Roberts, Barbara. 1988. *Whence They Came: Deportation from Canada 1900–1935*. Ottawa: University of Ottawa Press.
Sharma, Nandita. 1997. "Cheap Myths and Bonded Lives: Freedom and Citizenship in Canadian Society." *Beyond Law* 6, no. 17: 35–62.
Stasiulis, Daiva. 1997. "The Political Economy of Race, Ethnicity and Migration." In *Understanding Canada: Building the New Political Economy*, ed. Wallace Clement, 141–171. Montreal: McGill-Queen's University Press.
Stasiulis, Daiva, and Radha Jhappan. 1995. "The Fractious Politics of a Settler Society: Canada." In *Unsettling Settler Societies: Articulations of Gender, Race, Ethnicity and Class*, ed. Daiva Stasiulis and Nira Yuval-Davis, 95–131. London: Sage Publications Ltd. http://dx.doi.org/10.4135/9781446222225.n4.
Ungerleider, Charles. 1992. "Immigration, Multiculturalism, and Citizenship: The Development of the Canadian Social Justice Infrastructure." *Canadian Ethnic Studies* 24 (3): 7–22.
Vibert, Elizabeth. 1996. "Real Men Hunt Buffalo: Masculinity, Race and Class in British Fur Traders' Narratives." *Gender & History* 8 (1): 4–21. http://dx.doi.org/10.1111/j.1468-0424.1996.tb00221.x.
Ward, Peter. 2002. *White Canada Forever: Popular Attitudes and Public Policy toward Orientals in British Columbia*. Montreal: McGill-Queen's University Press.
WING (Women, Immigration, and Nationality Group). 1985. *Worlds Apart: Women under Immigration and Nationality Law*. London and Sydney: Pluto Press.

3 The Racial Subtext in Canada's Immigration Discourse[1]

PETER S. LI

In this article, I examine the articulation of race in Canada's immigration discourse and argue that racial messages are often articulated subtly in a democratic society such that their nature, form, and effect are elusive. The use of a racial subtext, that is, the hiding of racial signification in a benign discourse and conveying it in coded language, represents a sophisticated way of articulating "race" in a democratic society that makes such articulation socially acceptable. The analysis also illustrates how a public policy debate can, perhaps unwittingly, contribute to divisions of socially constructed "racial" groups by giving credence to racial assumptions that are camouflaged in what appears to be neutral language of a public discourse.

Although the articulation of racism in a democratic society can be elusive, racism is essentially a social feature that recognizes the social significance of classifying people into immutable racial groups based on real or imagined congenital features. The term *racialization* is often used to highlight the social process of attributing social significance to phenotypical features of people and designating those so signified as "racial" (Li 1998; Miles 1989; Satzewich 1998). One result of racialization is to provide a normative coherence for people to organize and to interpret at least some of their experiences. At the more extreme level, racialization can easily provide grounds for unequal treatment, as well as a rationale for justifying inequality.

There is an apparent contradiction between the premise of racialization and the tenet of democracy, as the former implies the signification of primordial features, whereas the latter negates it and regards all human beings as equals. To address this paradox, Henry, Tator, Mattis, and Rees (2000) coin the term *democratic racism* to highlight how racism can be justified in a democratic society in racial myths and stereotypes without requiring its followers to denounce the principles of democracy. In practice, as Li (1994) argues, the significance of race in a democratic society can be articulated in codified language that sanctifies what otherwise would be unholy racial messages and transforms them into noble concerns of citizens that become acceptable and even appealing to majority members. In other words, racist discourse assumes a gentle appearance in order to claim its legitimacy in a democratic society. More succinctly, Zong (1997) adopts the term *new racism* to highlight its oblique and covert nature from its conventional blatant manifestation.

In this article, I adopt the notion of a *discourse* to study Canada's immigration debate. The deconstruction of the discourse reveals a hidden racial subtext. The racial messages of the subtext are articulated unambiguously, although the subtext itself tends to be opaque. Uncovering the racial subtext requires deconstructing the vocabulary, the assumptions, and the rationale of the discourse.

Racism and Racial Discourse

There is little doubt that racism involves an ideology that advocates a hierarchy of superiority premised upon what are believed to be genetically and culturally constituted "races," although academics disagree over whether social practice and structural inequality should be included in the concept (Banton 1977; Bonilla-Silva 1997; Henry et al. 2000; Li 1999; Miles 1989; Satzewich 1998). Thus racism presupposes the signification of "race" as congenital and logical grounds for categorizing people into naturally constituted immutable groups. Because there is no scientific basis that can justify using superficial features such as skin colour to construct a defensible "racial" taxonomy, racial signification must be socially constructed (Bolaria and Li 1988; Miles 1989; Rex 1983).

Racism can be articulated in an elusive and covert manner in a democratic society precisely because the construction of race is not scientifically grounded, and the absence of a scientific standard provides flexibility in racial signification. Thus it is not so much the fundamental nature of racism that has changed under liberal democracy as how racial messages are articulated and race is constructed that gives the impression that racism has taken on a new form.

The mutational appearance of racism makes it difficult to detect in a democratic society. In particular, the traditional approach to study racism as blatantly expressed individual prejudice is ill equipped to track the changing forms of racism, as old measurement tools can easily become obsolete when race is articulated covertly and subtly.[2]

Bonilla-Silva (1997) is critical of the idealist perspective of racism that confines racism to the realm of social psychology. In this tradition, racism is viewed as individual prejudiced attitudes that collectively reflect the level of racism in society. Standard questions like those used in the Bogardus Social Distance Scale (Bogardus 1925, 1968) have been repeatedly adopted in opinion polls to gauge a country's level of racism, which is assumed to be static (Owen, Eisner, and McFaul 1981). Typically, such measurements yield results that show racism declines over time (Bonilla-Silva 1997). In reality the articulation of race and racism may have changed, and survey questions that at one time might have detected respondents' blatant racist dispositions may at another time fail to capture those respondents who hold such beliefs but are reluctant to express them to a pollster because of heightened awareness that explicit racial remarks are politically and socially inopportune. In short, as the political climate changes and racial discourse assumes an opaque appearance, respondents may learn to verbalize racial tolerance and to adopt a benign language to articulate racial messages without appearing racist to themselves and to others.

Attitudinal surveys of racial prejudice may be an acceptable way to study racism if prejudice is the only form of racism and if it is unchanged over time. In reality, as Wellman (1977) describes it, racism is "*a* culturally sanctioned, rational response to struggles over scarce resources" (35). Therefore, as the structural position of subordinate groups changes or as racial dominance softens, the racial thinking of the dominant whites also changes accordingly to accommodate the new realities. For this reason, racism cannot be studied merely as enduring prejudiced ideas of individuals, but must be located in the narratives and everyday experiences of people (Essed 1991).

It is in its ability to tackle the subtle articulation of race and racism that discourse analysis proves to be useful (Mills 1997; Tator, Henry, and Mattis 1998). One way to conceptualize discourse is to regard it as a domain of language use in the process of knowledge construction, which involves common terminologies, accepted assumptions, and a well-versed rationale that are adopted to make sense of social practices and social phenomena (Foucault 1972). A discourse implies abiding by what Foucault calls "the rules of some discursive policy" and applying "the rules of exclusion" (216, 224). In particular, critical discourse analysts stress unravelling unequal power relations that are embedded in language and text with a view to changing social outcomes (Caldas-Coulthard, and Coulthard 1996; Mills 1997; van Dijk 1993). A discourse analysis of race does not imply reducing racism to only ideas engaged in a language. It is recognition of the inadequacy of studying racism as pertaining only to a formal set of beliefs that upholds a racial hierarchy premised on congenital differences of people. After all, it is precisely this explicit version of racism that most citizens of a democratic society have little hesitation in rejecting, because such a formal ideology is too blatantly contradictory to the fundamental values of democracy. Even racial supremacists, who are relatively small in number in most democratic societies, tend to adopt a more sophisticated language to cover their racist stance in order to win wider public support and to avoid legal prosecutions (Li 1995). A racial discourse implies constructing the language, the terminology, and the rules, as well as setting the limits on how racial practices are to be represented and understood; in turn it means using the defined language and the constructed knowledge to make sense of events and to influence future outcomes.

To study racial discourses involves accepting racism as an everyday phenomenon that is manifested in a benign version, often without the label of racism. This version is communicated in coded language so that on appearance it is not race or racism at stake, but in essence it carries a message about unbridgeable differences of people premised upon values, traditions, and ways of life subsumed under skin colour or other superficial features. The users of this codified language sometimes are not aware that they are engaged in a racist discourse as they themselves tend to be convinced by its rhetoric, and they truly believe that they share the democratic values and therefore cannot be branded as racists. From their vantage point, to do so amounts to using a heavy-handed label like racism to silence them, when in fact they believe they are expressing their legitimate views as citizens of a democratic society.

Racial Subtext in Canada's Immigration Discourse

Canada's immigration discourse is an outgrowth of the government's interest in involving the public in major policy decisions in recent years, although there has always been sustained public interest in and media attention on immigration. However, it would be incorrect to assume that the discourse represents the government's position, although the official stance on various aspects of immigration forms a part of the discourse. Participants in the discourse include politicians, government officials, academics, community groups, and individual citizens, and their views are often articulated in public opinions, discussions, debates, prevailing viewpoints, academic writings, and media reports about issues of immigration.

The importance of public consultation to the government was underscored by Sergio Marchi, the then Minister of Citizenship and Immigration, in the House of Commons in 1994: "Consultation will always be the hallmark of how this government decides its policy" (Citizenship and Immigration Canada [CIC] 1994a). On another occasion Marchi (1994) expanded on this point as follows:

> Government in general has to do a better job of listening to the views of groups which are directly involved with specific policy areas ... In immigration, this means listening to school

> boards, health associations, municipalities, labour, police, community service groups, and individual Canadians ... If immigration is truly to be about nation building, then all Canadians must have a part in shaping the future. (3)

No doubt the government considers public consultation as an indispensable component in formulating a major policy like immigration. Many methods, including opinion polls, town hall meetings, conferences, and expert consultations, have been used to seek the informed consent and cooperation of citizens and interest groups, broadly referred to as stakeholders. In this atmosphere, individual citizens and interest groups have the unmistakable impression that they are exercising their democratic rights in expressing their views about the desirability or undesirability of immigration and how the policy should be framed.

Canada's immigration discourse does not necessarily imply a consensus; in fact, there are many conflicting views about various topics of immigration. But the discourse has clearly adopted certain language styles, terminologies, assumptions, and indeed a rationale for articulating issues of immigration. One such issue is the question of *diversity.*

There is a prevailing view in Canada's immigration discourse that changes in immigration policy since the 1960s have produced a pattern of immigration that results in large numbers of immigrants from "non-traditional" sources of Asia and Africa to Canada, and that the sudden growth of non-white immigrants has posed a challenge for Canada to respond to diversity. Specifically, increased diversity has produced tensions in major cities where immigrants tend to concentrate, based on both real and alleged differences between long-time residents of Canada and immigrants from different cultural backgrounds. Typical examples cited include the undue demands placed on the school system as a result of large numbers of immigrant children not speaking the official languages, the social segregation and urban congestion created by the development of ethno-specific immigrant malls and concentrated ethnic businesses, and confrontations in established neighbourhoods where the heritage and traditional values of Canada are deemed to have been undermined by new immigrants' disregard of architectural preservation and environmental protection. It does not matter whether some or all of these problems are caused by diversity, but as long as some citizens hold such views and see their lives being adversely affected, the government feels obligated to take into account citizens' concerns and their readiness to accept diversity in setting future policy.

The above viewpoint is routinely echoed in public meetings and government discussion papers. For example, a discussion paper produced by Employment and Immigration Canada (1989) and intended to "stimulate an informed and frank debate" has this to say.

> More and more in public discussions of immigration issues people are drawing attention to the fact that Canada's immigration is coming increasingly from "non-traditional" parts of the world. Thirty years ago, more than 80 per cent of Canada's immigrants came from Europe or countries of European heritage, whereas 70 per cent now come from Asia, Africa, and Latin America, with 43 per cent coming from Asia alone ... As a result, many Canadians are concerned that the country is in danger of losing a sense of national identity ... Unfortunately, some of the opposition to immigration which has been expressed in Canada is rooted in racism and we must vigilantly ensure that this destructive force does not spread. People's fears must be confronted and misinformation must be dispelled ... Yet it would be wrong to dismiss most Canadians' concerns on these grounds. Many Canadians, who have always been proud of Canada's humanitarian and tolerant traditions, are also feeling uneasy. (8–9)

Other problems of diversity have been identified such as its adverse effects on the large urban centres, which are "experiencing adjustment strains as their social services and schools endeavour to meet the diverse needs of these concentrated numbers of new immigrants" (11).

The above viewpoint, its language, and its logic are rather revealing. First, terms such as *diverse* or *diversity* have been used as surrogates to refer to *non-white* immigrants. Second, the "problem of diversity" has been presented as being triggered by large numbers of immigrants from non-traditional source countries, mainly those from Asia and Africa. This line of argument is increasingly evident in government discussion papers on immigration throughout the 1990s. For example, in a discussion document circulated by CIC (1994b), it repeats under the heading of "Immigration and Diversity" the fact that large numbers of immigrants now come from Asia and concludes that "while there may be increasing concerns about the number of immigrants coming to Canada, there is evidence to suggest that these concerns are linked as much to issues of unemployment and the economy as they are to issues of diversity" (10). In other words, not only is the "problem of diversity" caused by large numbers of non-white immigrants concentrated in urban centres, but citizens' concerns over too many immigrants are really prompted by their uneasiness over non-whites as much as by issues pertaining to unemployment and the economy. Thus citizens' concerns over diversity have been elevated to the same magnitude and seriousness as concerns over the economy and jobs. Over time, as the concept of diversity is repeatedly used in immigration discourse in the above context, it becomes a coded word to designate non-white immigrants and the problems they have brought to urban Canada, as well as the grounds for citizens' concerns.[3]

Third, the message of citizens' concerns over diversity is unmistakable about how a sudden increase in diversity over a short period can create tensions and divisions, because diversity is cast as different from, if not opposed to, Canadian values and traditions. More specifically, the concerns are premised upon the presumed truism that, unlike native born Canadians or European immigrants who came earlier, the recent third-world type of non-white immigrants bring with them different values and behaviours that are incompatible with those in traditional Canada, and their large concentrated presence in Canada's cities undermines Canada's unity. In reality the view about diversity causing divisiveness is not based on solid scientific findings, but premised on the mere fact that non-white immigrants have a different skin colour and look different from European Canadians and on the rhetoric that immigrants must respect core Canadian values. Thus it remains a yet-to-be-proven claim that non-white immigrants possess such different cultural beliefs that they would undermine Canadian values, traditions, and institutions. Yet in the immigration discourse the linkage between diversity and fragmentation is unmistakable. For example, this message is reiterated in another report (CIC 1994c) as follows:

> A number of Canadians expressed concerns about the impact which immigration and citizenship policies are having upon the values and traditions that form the foundation of Canadian society. This is not to say that Canadians are becoming intolerant. In fact, when describing the most cherished characteristics of their society, Canadians usually mentioned tolerance among the first. Many people agreed with the Standing Committee on Citizenship and Immigration which reported that "*Diversity is one of Canada's great strengths ...*" But they are also worried that their country is becoming fragmented, that it is becoming a loose collection of parts each pursuing its own agenda, rather than a cohesive entity striving for the collective good of Canada. (10, emphasis in original)

Fourth, the message on "the problem of diversity" is always presented as legitimate concerns of Canadians who support the "humanitarian and tolerant traditions" and are proud of Canada's diversity, but who nevertheless worry about Canada losing its national identity because of too many immigrants from different cultures and origins. In short, the message makes it clear that racism is unacceptable to Canada, and Canadians remain tolerant and are not being racists when they voice their concerns over too much diversity. This is accomplished by reiterating Canada's long-standing position of tolerance and anti-racism every time Canadians pass judgment on the social worth of immigrants' race or colour.

Concerns over "the problem of diversity" are often justified on the grounds that long-time Canadians are experiencing too rapid social changes within too short a time that are caused by too many non-traditional immigrants. Obviously, what constitutes "too many," "too rapid," and "too short" requires a normative assessment. There is no doubt that the immigration patterns of the 1980s and 1990s have changed the racial composition of immigrants. However, similar concerns over too many non-white immigrants and the atmosphere of unease that they created were expressed in the 1970s even before the arrival of large numbers of immigrants from non-traditional source countries.[4] It would appear that it is the constructed image of hordes of immigrants of a different race or colour that has been seen as challenging the cultural complacency of Canada and its implied cohesiveness.

There are also other coded messages in the immigration discourse. In general, the discourse uses public concerns of immigration as pretexts to justify policy changes. Because the public concerns arise from reactions to immigration trends, and because such trends indicate a surge of non-white immigrants to Canada, the concerns are by implication attributable to non-white immigrants and their differences. For example, a report (Employment and Immigration Canada 1989) indicates that some Canadians "*are* uneasy or unsure about immigration's impact" and that "close to one fifth of Canadians are quite opposed to many aspects of Canada's immigration program and an even greater number just do not know how many, or what kinds of immigrants, Canada should encourage in the next decade" (8). Typical concerns of a more specific nature have to do with Canadians "losing a sense of national identity," Canadian society "changing too fast," and the need to preserve Canada's "core national values" (9). A CIC (1994a) report follows a similar approach to cite Canadians' worries about personal safety and about fiscal burdens due to some immigrant sponsors failing to honour their financial obligations (11–12).[5] Taken together, the coded messages tend to attribute Canadians' increased concerns over immigration to the social problems "caused" by recent immigrants and their differences. Thus the solution to these social problems – from weakening national values to overburdening the health care system – lies in better control of the immigration system and of the composition of immigrants.

The "Race" Question in Public Polls and Media Reports

The racial message of the immigration discourse is further formalized and legitimized in opinion polls about immigration and in media reporting of these results. Government departments frequently use public opinions to obtain citizens' views regarding social issues and policy support.[6] In discussions and consultations about immigration, the government is interested in finding out from Canadians the level of immigration and the type of immigrants that are acceptable to them. The media and polling companies also support public opinion surveys about immigration because the topic is sensational, controversial, and newsworthy.

It is in seeking Canadians' views on diversity in opinion polls that the racial subtext of the immigration discourse becomes most apparent. Certain standard questions have been routinely used in such polls as means to gauge what is often referred to as the tolerance level of Canadians towards diversity. For example, in a national immigration survey conducted in January 2000 by Ekos Research Associates for the federal government, the following question was asked: "Forgetting about the overall number of immigrants coming to Canada, of those who come would you say there are too many, too few or the right amount who are members of visible minorities?" (6). The same question was also used in polls conducted in December 1999, July 1999, December 1998, April 1998, November 1997, November 1996, November 1995, November 1994, and February 1994. A news report on the survey written by reporter Nahlah Ayed and released by Canadian Press on March 10, 2000, was widely printed in several major newspapers (e.g., *Globe and Mail* 2000 and *Vancouver Sun* 2000). The report revealed that 27% of the respondents in the 2000 survey indicated that there were "too many" visible minority immigrants, compared with 25% who said so in 1999 and 22% in 1998. The *Vancouver Sun* used the headline "survey finds less tolerance for immigrants" to highlight the story. It becomes clear that the view of a numeric minority on visible minority immigrants being too numerous is elevated to the level of Canadians' tolerance of diversity, and the minute change of percentage of this segment over time (from 25% to 27%) is given the scientific stature of revealing "Canadians becoming less tolerant."

A clear racial message can be ascertained in how the survey question is framed and interpreted, even though the words *race or non-white* are not used. First, the wording of the question indicates that pollsters and interest groups funding the survey can legitimately ask the general public to consider race as a factor in immigration and to assess the social worth of non-whites in terms of whether there are too many or too few of them, provided a term like *race* or *colour* is avoided. The term *visible minorities* replaces a racially charged term such as *coloured people*, but the people framing the question as well as the respondents answering it are clear about what the term *visible minorities* means. Another phrase that has been used in polls to substitute for *coloured people* is "people who are different from most Canadians." Pollsters sometimes use this codified phrase to ask respondents to indicate whether they think such people should be kept out of Canada. The attractiveness of a term like visible minorities is that its softer appearance and its being used in the Employment Act (Statutes of Canada 1986) make it a convenient label that can be innocently adopted to discuss the social worthiness of race and non-whites without running the risk of being branded racist. Most Canadians would probably find it objectionable if asked to express an opinion about whether there are too many or too few non-whites in a situation in which they are a participant such as a school, a corporation, or a social occasion, in part because this is too blatantly racist, and in part because the principle of racial equality is clearly defined in the Charter and Canadian tradition.[7] Yet when the question about visible minorities is asked in a public poll, it appears to be much more acceptable, and indeed neutral, as a tool to find out how far Canadians are prepared to accept non-whites or "coloured races." In short, opinion polls sanctify the racial phenomenon that Canadians should find it meaningful to evaluate the "coloured" segment of the population as too many or too few purely on the basis of race.[8] The way the colour question is camouflaged in opinion polls reifies the notion of race by legitimizing the right of Canadians to pass judgments on newcomers based on their superficial features. Furthermore, Canadians' opinions on immigrants' race are not seen as a social problem that has to be addressed; rather, it is presented as a democratic choice of citizens regarding how many diverse elements in Canadian society they are prepared to tolerate.

There is further evidence to suggest that pollsters and interest groups actively pursue the question about opinions regarding immigrants' race in opinion surveys, and then present such opinions as citizens' intolerance of diversity or their "cultural insecurity" that should be taken into account in policy formulation. For example, in an immigration consulting meeting organized by Citizenship and Immigration Canada in Montebello, Quebec on March 6–7, 1994, results of a public opinion survey conducted by Ekos Research Associates were presented, and it was reported that

> Growing intolerance appears to have a racial dimension [since] 87% of respondents who believe that too many immigrants are drawn from visible minorities also believe that immigration levels are too high ... [and that] Canadians are concerned about a "slipping away of our values" and a loss of Canadian identity. (Public Policy Forum 1994)[9]

Shortly after this, an article in the *Globe and Mail* on March 28 referred to the finding in the Ekos survey that showed "most Canadians believe there are too many immigrants, especially from visible minorities," and used it to explain how "cultural insecurity" amid change fuels resentment among a majority of Canadians towards Asian, African and Arab migrants." It is clear from the prevailing interpretation that respondents' opinions on race are not considered racist in the immigration consultation circle, but rather are regarded as Canadians' genuine expression of "growing intolerance" or "cultural insecurity" based on a legitimate concern that too many non-whites would render Canadian values "slipping away." Furthermore, the message is clear that Canadians' reservations over too many immigrants is misunderstood when in fact they are concerned only about too many non-white immigrants and not immigrants per se.[10] Thus the racial message in the immigration discourse is covered up as non-racist and indeed elevated to the level of noble concerns by citizens who only want to protect Canada's ideological tradition and the national unity.

The fact that the racial message in the immigration discourse is typically regarded as the legitimate concerns of citizens also implies that polling results have a substantial influence on the outcomes of the immigration debate. Lucienne Robillard, the then Minister of Citizenship and Immigration, made this point clear when she announced in 1996 the government's intention not to increase the immigration level because "the Canadian population is divided, according the last poll we had" (Peirol 1996). Often Canadians' reservations over admitting more immigrants and their opinions regarding too many non-white immigrants are treated by the media as an indication of a public backlash and not a problem of Canadian society that has to be addressed (Peirol 1996).[11] The term *backlash* implies a public disapproval of a policy direction that produces a widely perceived undesirable social change.

The Reification of Race in Academic Research

The construction of the racial subtext in the immigration discourse has been facilitated by a long academic tradition that studies how respondents in opinion surveys place different values on people of different race or origin. In this tradition, prejudiced attitudes of individuals are treated as if they are free-floating ideas without a material base (Bonilla-Silva 1997; Wellman 1977), and the scientific inquiry is further reduced to the empirical question of explaining why some individuals are prejudiced and others are not. Academics have developed various concepts to describe prejudiced attitudes, and in so doing often make them appear natural and legitimate, and therefore less offensive. For example, the notion of "social distance" is widely adopted in attitudinal surveys to capture the degree to which respondents are prepared to accept members of a different race as a close kin, fellow club members, neighbours, co-workers, or citizens (Bogardus 1925, 1968; Owen et al. 1981). This notion and similar constructs have been used in several major attitudinal surveys in Canada (Berry and Kalin 1995; Berry, Kalin, and Taylor 1977; Kalin and Berry 1996).

A question on social distance was used in the 2000 survey conducted by Ekos Research Associates and commissioned by Citizenship and Immigration Canada. In the survey, respondents were asked to indicate how they felt about someone from a given country moving into their neighbourhood. The results, presented as a measurement of social distance, show that respondents were more positive towards those from the UK and France than those from China, Jamaica, or Somalia; furthermore, the results were compared with similar findings in a 1992 survey (Ekos Research Associates 2000). A national survey conducted by the Angus Reid Group (1991) and commissioned by Multiculturalism and Citizenship Canada also included a similar question that presented respondents with a list of selected ethnocultural groups and asked them to indicate how comfortable they were with members of each group, ranging from "not at all comfortable with" to "very comfortable."[12] The results, described as "*comfort* levels," show that those of European origin had a higher comfort rating than those of non-white origin – Chinese, Black, Muslim, Arab, Indo-Pakistani, and Sikh (51).

This type of research is sometimes justified on the grounds that the normative hierarchy of racial groups unravelled in attitudinal surveys actually reflects the status hierarchy of racial groups in society, and that documenting racist attitudes is one necessary step towards eliminating them. In reality, this type of research accepts the premise that race is a valid scientific construct and supports its continuous usage as a meaningful concept by systematically asking respondents to place value judgments on people based on colour. In his critique of research that reifies race, Miles (1982) argues that such research gives primacy to race as if it were an active agent in and of itself, when in fact race is a consequence of social construction. At the very least, social scientists have been insensitive in systematically encouraging the articulation of racial differences by conditioning respondents to choose preferences based on race, origin, or skin colour, and then by attributing a pseudoscientific label such as comfort level or social distance to beautify and legitimize such choices. Over time, as these questions on racial preferences are repeatedly asked by academics in studies, the legitimacy of asking such questions is engraved in the minds of people in that their frequent recurrence in survey questionnaires becomes ipso facto a justification of their social merit and scientific validity. When these academic tools are increasingly popularized in opinion polls and in the immigration discourse, the public articulation of racial preferences itself and the means by which such preferences are articulated also become entrenched and institutionalized.

Conclusion

A democratic society like Canada has a legal framework to uphold the democratic principles of equality and non-discrimination. This is evident in the Canadian Charter of Rights and Freedoms, the Multiculturalism Act, and the Employment Equity Act. At the same time, Canadian society has also recognized the social significance of race in its everyday life. In short, although a society like Canada has formally censured the blatant form of racism and racial discrimination, it tolerates and at times promotes a softer version that maintains racial distinctions as natural and as immutable differences of people. Thus a codified version of racist discourse is being propagated, and people accept this type of discourse as legitimate and not racist. Ironically, it is the readiness of most people to reject the more extreme position of racism that makes the softer version so much more palatable and natural.

This article suggests that there is a racial subtext in Canada's immigration discourse. The discourse develops a vocabulary, adopts certain assumptions, and endorses a rationale to advance a framework of understanding the "diversity problem" in immigration. In such a framework, codified concepts such as *diversity* are used to substitute for *non-white immigrants,* especially those from Asia or Africa. The notion of diversity has become a meaningful concept in the immigration discourse. It provides a simplistic but convenient explanation as to why some Canadians oppose a higher level of immigration. The dominant and widely accepted explanation is that Canadians are afraid of losing their traditions and values when they are confronted with too much diversity within too short a time. Hence Canadians' opposition to more immigrants, especially visible minority immigrants, is not premised upon racism, but based on concerns about national unity and social cohesion. In short, typical Canadians are seen as under siege by too much diversity, and they are worried that Canada's heritage and cultural cohesion are being washed away by too many immigrants who are too different from them. Thus in the immigration discourse the discussion of race or skin colour is central but codified, and the discourse often reiterates Canada's support of tolerance and opposition to racism in order to justify how citizens' concerns over diversity are noble and not racist.

An aspect of Canada's immigration discourse involves constructing the problem of diversity in opinion polls and media reports. In such a construction, Canadians are systematically asked to indicate whether they think that there are too many visible minority immigrants, and in doing so are in fact placing a social value on race. Thus a coded language is used to cover up a blatant discussion of skin colour. The discourse reifies race by recognizing the legitimacy of evaluating superficial physical differences of people, and by casting non-white immigrants and Canadians as opposites based on socially constructed immutable differences. Over time the discourse makes it socially acceptable to consider immigrants on racial grounds; in turn, physical and cultural characteristics of non-white immigrants become socially significant, because they represent convenient markers by which they can be distinguished and problematized.

In the immigration discourse, racial messages expressed in opinion polls are sanctified in that they are seen as citizens' democratic choices and legitimate concerns. The discourse provides a rationale to justify such views. As these views are repeatedly sought in opinion polls, they assume a legitimate and indeed a respectable position in the immigration discourse. In time the discourse mitigates racial messages and makes them respectable.

The construction of a racial subtext in the immigration discourse has also been facilitated by the academic tradition that develops many of the tools and concepts that enable the race question to be asked subtly in opinion polls without making it appear offensive. In effect, such academic research reifies race by encouraging the public to evaluate the desirability of people based on skin colour and by covering up such race-based evaluations with pseudo-scientific constructs.[13]

The stakeholders of the immigration discourse – academic, journalists, pollsters, policy-makers, and individual citizens – participate in the construction of a racial subtext that ultimately transforms the racial messages into "valid concerns" and "scientific findings," and transforms what would otherwise be unacceptable racially based opinions into acceptable voices in a legitimate public debate. Over time a vicious circle is formed: as the race problem is constructed, racial differences become self-evident grounds of "social fragmentation" and "racial tension," and the concern over race assumes a valid voice that is taken seriously and righteously in policy consideration. In the final analysis, it is the discourse itself, and not superficial racial differences of immigrants and Canadians, that fragments Canada and its people.

The above analysis has policy implications. First, it suggests that it is unnecessary, and indeed divisive, to justify immigration policy changes with immigrant-induced social problems that are generalized to non-white immigrants. Changes so premised are defensive at best. In addition to casting immigrants and native-born Canadians in opposition, they inevitably lead to tighter control and more regulation as natural solutions to the "immigration problem." Second, social policy development and academic research must respect the principles of racial equality and non-discrimination guaranteed in the Canadian Charter by abandoning the use of racial subtext in the construction of knowledge and policy perspective. Third, immigration policy development can contribute to developing a harmonious society based on respect of differences by dispelling racial stereotypes and cultural myths.

NOTES

1 A version of this paper was presented at a plenary session of the Fifth International Metropolis Conference, November 13–17, 2000, Vancouver.

2 Wellman (1977) makes the same point about the changing manifestation of racism in the US and its elusive appearance as follows: "It has become increasingly obvious in recent years that many American attitudes about racist issues are not expressed in obvious ways, do not reflect hostility, and are not always misjudgments of the problems. These kinds of attitudes, however, cannot be detected or adequately interpreted as long as racial feelings are conceptualized as prejudice" (6).

3 In June and July 1994, the Democracy Education Network (1994) organized 58 study circles in six Canadian cities as a part of the federal government's consultation on the immigration policy. Its summary report states that one of the four concerns expressed by participants has to do with "integration and settlement" and "the dilemmas of diversity" (2).

4 A case in point can be found in Toronto's experience in the late 1970s when the city witnessed several incidents of non-whites being pushed off subway platforms and hit by incoming trains. These events were so racially charged that the provincial government appointed the Ontario Task Force on Human Relations to investigate. In its report, the Task Force wrote:

> With what appeared to some as unseemly haste, large numbers of black, brown and yellow skinned people suddenly appeared on the streets, the buses, and in public places. Some English-speaking residents who had not perceived the extent to which Toronto had become a multicultural entity, now discovered that they lived in a multi-racial community, and indeed, were now members of a minority themselves. Needless to say, they had difficulty adjusting to the cultural shock ... These factors, and many less discernable [sic] have created an atmosphere in which overt violence is perceived to be less unacceptable by the hoodlum element which perpetrates the crimes against the visible minority. (Pitman 1977, 38)

At that time the number of visible minorities in Canada was relatively small, as they made up only 6.3% of Canada's population in 1986 and 11.2% in 1996 (Statistics Canada 1998). The Toronto case illustrates how the notion of excessively large numbers of non-white immigrants in the immigration debate is often normatively constructed.

5 For further evidence of the immigration discourse and the messages delivered, see Citizenship and Immigration Canada 1994b, 1994c, 1994d; Employment and Immigration Canada 1989, 1990.

6 Government-funded opinion polls are routinely conducted, but the results are not always released publicly. For example, in an internal report written for Citizenship and Immigration Canada, the author states that the report is based on surveys collected by Ekos in November 1996, Environics in December 1996, and Angus Reid in February 1997, which include "questions asked specifically on behalf of CIC (Citizenship and Immigration)" (Palmer 1997, 1). In a news story reported by the *Toronto Star* on August 19, 1996, the paper said it had to use the Access to Information Act in order to obtain results of a public opinion poll on immigration commissioned by the federal government.

7 Section 15 of the Canadian Charter of Rights and Freedoms states:

> Every individual is equal before and under the law and has the right to the equal protection and equal benefit of the law without discrimination and, in particular, without discrimination based on race, national or ethnic origin, colour, religion, sex, age or mental or physical disability. (Statutes of Canada 1982, c. 11)

8 It is sometimes pointed out that Canada has a right to choose its immigrants, and that Canadians have a say in exercising this right. Advocates of immigration restriction also point out that Canadians do experience problems caused by immigrants coming from a different background; an often cited problem has to do with public schools being overwhelmed by immigrant children who do not speak the official languages, which results in non-immigrant parents worrying about declining educational quality (Globe and Mail 1994). My argument is not about whether Canada has a right to choose its immigrants or whether there are problems of adjustment for immigrants and Canadian society. The simple fact remains that the Charter guarantees the equality of rights and non-discrimination for all, and the choice of preferred immigrants cannot be based on race or colour in violation of the Charter, just as immigrant selection cannot be based on gender. In asking respondents to indicate their "racial preference" of immigrants and in giving a "racial preference" as the answer, Canadians are in fact using race or colour as a criterion in choosing their preferred immigrants.

9 Michael Valpy, a well-known columnist, was sympathetic to the dominant interpretation of cultural insecurity in the immigration discourse. He wrote:

> Ekos found that opposition to high immigration levels does not rest primarily on economic insecurity – the traditional blue-collar fears of immigrants-are-taking-our-jobs. Rather it rests most of all on cultural insecurity. The cultural fear is a product of resurging anxieties – particularly anglophone anxieties – about eroding Canadian identity. It is about the lack of sufficient Canadian homogeneous tribalness to form national consensuses on public policy direction (Valpy 1994).

Some readers expressed different views, but these opposition voices were ineffective in influencing the dominant perspective in the immigration discourse. For example, a reader wrote:

> I expected Canadians to regard freedom, honesty, hard work, personal accountability and tolerance as their most cherished values. I am not aware of any immigrant group not subscribing to these ideals. However, I am definitely aware of the millions who cheat on taxes, engage in UT and welfare fraud, expect 42 weeks government handout after 10 weeks employment, indulge in cross-border shopping with false customs declarations ... and intolerant to and unwilling to respect the culture of aboriginals (the "true" Canadians), and these millions are mostly members of Mr. Valpy's "old Canada." (Hill 1994)

Such opposition voices are largely ignored in the immigration discourse.

10 The corollary of this argument is that some Canadians are concerned over too many non-white immigrants and that they would probably not have said that there were too many immigrants if these immigrants were white.

11 Alan Li, President of the Chinese-Canadian National Council, argued for the need to regard negative public opinions on immigration as a social problem in itself: "Unless the government takes a more proactive stance on immigration, public perceptions will not change. These are misconceptions that the government hasn't taken steps to correct" (Peirol 1996).

12 The wording of the question is as follows: "I would like you to think of recent immigrants to Canada. These are persons who were born and raised outside of Canada. How comfortable would you feel being around individuals from the following groups of immigrants ... How about ..." (Angus Reid Group 1991).

13 Some may argue that the academic tradition of studying individual racist attitudes using tools such as the social-distance scale is necessary in order to understand and to combat racism. In reality, findings of such research are seldom used to combat racism; rather, they are often represented by pseudo-scientific labels such as "social distance" or "discomfort levels" to camouflage the racist nature and indeed to justify racial concerns. These survey tools are also so overused that they have conditioned respondents to accept the legitimacy of passing judgements on others based on race or colour. The point is not to condemn survey tools in studying racism or racist behaviours. However, academics must take a more objective stance by calling racist behaviours racist and not use some other fancy terms. As well, they must conduct research with a clear view that racist behaviours are constitutionally and morally unacceptable and with the objective of exposing and disallowing racist practices. A good example of such a critical approach is the work of Henry (1989) and Henry and Ginsberg (1985).

REFERENCES

Angus Reid Group. 1991. *Multiculturalism and Canadians: Attitude study 1991*. Submitted to Multiculturalism and Citizenship Canada.

Banton, Michael. 1977. *The Idea of Race*. London: Tavistock.

Berry, John W., and Rudolph Kalin. 1995. "Multicultural and Ethnic Attitudes in Canada: An Overview of the 1991 National Survey." *Canadian Journal of Behavioural Science* 27 (3): 301–20. http://dx.doi.org/10.1037/0008-400X.27.3.301.

Berry, John W., Rudolph Kalin, and Donald M. Taylor. 1977. *Multiculturalism and Ethnic Attitudes in Canada*. Ottawa: Minister of Supply and Services.

Bogardus, Emory S. 1925. "Measuring Social Distances." *Journal of Applied Sociology* 9:299–308.

Bogardus, Emory S. 1968. "Comparing Racial Distance in Ethiopia, South Africa, and the United States." *Sociology and Social Research* 52:149–56.

Bolaria, B. Singh, and S. Peter Li. 1988. *Racial Oppression in Canada.* 2nd ed. Toronto: Garamond Press.
Bonilla-Silva, Eduardo. 1997. "Rethinking Racism: Toward a Structural Interpretation." *American Sociological Review* 62 (3): 465–80. http://dx.doi.org/10.2307/2657316.
Caldas-Coulthard, Carmen R., and Malcolm Coulthard, eds. 1996. *Texts and Practices: Readings in Critical Discourse Analysis.* London: Routledge.
Canada. Statistics Canada. 1998. *The Daily.* February 17.
Canada Act, Statutes of Canada. 1982, C:11.
Citizenship and Immigration Canada. House of Commons. 1994a. *Speaking Notes for the Honourable Sergio Marchi, P.C., M.P, Minister of Citizenship and Immigration Tabling of the Strategy and the Immigration and Citizenship Plan.* [Ottawa, ON].
Citizenship and Immigration Canada. House of Commons. 1994b. *Canada and Immigration: A Discussion Paper.* [Ottawa, ON].
Citizenship and Immigration Canada. House of Commons. 1994c. Minister of Supply and Services. *Into the 21st Century: A Strategy for Immigration and Citizenship.* [Ottawa, ON].
Citizenship and Immigration Canada. House of Commons. 1994d. Minister of Supply and Services. *Immigration Consultations Report.* [Ottawa, ON].
Democracy Education Network. 1994. "Talking About Immigration: The Study Circles of the Future of Immigration Policy".
Ekos Research Associates. 2000. "National Immigration Survey." Presentation to the Hon. Elinor Caplan, P.C.M.R, Minister of Citizenship and Immigration.
Employment and Immigration Canada. Minister of Supply and Services. 1990. *Report on the Consultations on Immigration for 1991–1995.* [Ottawa, ON].
Employment and Immigration Canada. Minister of Supply and Services. 1989. *Immigration to Canada: Issues for Discussion. IM 061/11/89.* [Ottawa, ON].
Employment Equity Act, Statutes of Canada. 1986, C. 31.
Essed, Philomena. 1991. *Understanding Everyday Racism.* Newbury Park, CA: Sage.
Foucault, Michel. 1972. *The Archaeology of Knowledge and the Discourse on Language.* New York: Pantheon Books.
Globe and Mail. 1994. "How Many Immigrants Should Canada Admit?" February 4.
Henry, Francis. 1989. *Who Gets the Work in 1989?* Ottawa: Economic Council of Canada.
Henry, Francis, and Effie Ginsberg. 1985. *Who Gets the Work? A Test of Racial Discrimination in Employment.* Toronto: Social Planning Council of Metro Toronto and the Urban Alliance on Race Relations.
Henry, Frances, Carol Tator, Winston Mattis, and Tim Rees. 2000. *The Colour of Democracy: Racism in Canadian Society.* Toronto: Harcourt Canada.
Hill, Rod. 1994. "Canadian Values." *Globe and Mail,* March 22.
Toronto Star. 1996, August 19. "Immigration Levels Concern About 60%."
Kalin, Rudolph, and John W. Berry. 1996. "Interethnic Attitudes in Canada: Ethnocentrism, Consensual Hierarchy and Reciprocity." *Canadian Journal of Behavioural Science* 28 (4): 253–61. http://dx.doi.org/10.1037/0008-400X.28.4.253.
Li, Peter S. 1994. "Unneighbourly Houses or Unwelcome Chinese: The Social Construction of Race in the Battle Over 'Monster Homes' in Vancouver, Canada." *International Journal of Comparative Race and Ethnic Studies* 1 (1): 14–33.
Li, Peter S. 1995. "Racial Supremacism Under Social Democracy." *Canadian Ethnic Studies* 27 (1): 1–17.
Li, Peter S. 1998. "The Market Value and Social Value of Race." In *Racism and Social Inequality in Canada*, ed. Vic Satzewich, 115–130. Toronto: Thompson Educational Publishing.

Li, Peter S. 1999. "Race and Ethnicity." In *Race and Ethnic Relations in Canada*, ed. Peter S. Li, 3–20. Toronto: Oxford University Press.

Marchi, Sergio. 1994. "Speaking Points for an Address by the Honourable Sergio Marchi, Minister of Citizenship and Immigration." Presentation at the Canada 2005 Conference, Ottawa, September 12.

Miles, Robert. 1982. *Racism and Migrant Labour*. London: Routledge & Kegan Paul.

Miles, Robert. 1989. *Racism*. London: Routledge.

Mills, Sara. 1997. *Discourse*. London: Routledge.

Owen, Carolyn A., Howard C. Eisner, and Thomas R. McFaul. 1981. "A Half-Century of Social Distance Research: National Replication of the Bogardus Studies." *Sociology and Social Research* 66:80–99.

Palmer, Douglas L. 1997. *"Canadians' Attitudes Towards Immigration: November and December 1996, and February 1997 Surveys." Report Prepared for Program Support, Strategic Policy, Planning and Research Branch, Citizenship and Immigration Canada*. Ottawa: CIC.

Peirol, Paulette. 1996. "Immigration Levels Reflect Backlash." *Globe and Mail*, October 30.

Pitman, Walter. 1977. "Now is Not Too Late." Report Submitted to the Council of Metropolitan Toronto by Task Force on Human Relations.

Globe and Mail. 2000, March 11. "Poll Shows Opposition to Minorities Rising."

Public Policy Forum. 1994. *Developing a Ten-Year Strategic Framework for Canadian Citizenship and Immigration Policy and Programs: Finding the Right Consultative Process*. Ottawa: Public Policy Forum.

Rex, John. 1983. *Race Relations in Sociological Theory*. London: Routledge.

Satzewich, Vic. 1998. "Race, Racism and Racialization: Contested Concepts." In *Racism and Social Inequality in Canada*, ed. Vic Satzewich, 25–45. Toronto: Thompson Educational Publishing.

Tator, Carol, Frances Henry, and Winston Mattis. 1998. *Challenging Racism in the Arts: Case Studies of Controversy and Conflict*. Toronto: University of Toronto Press.

Vancouver Sun. 2000, March 11. "Survey Finds Less Tolerance for Immigrants."

Valpy, Michael. 1994. "Streets a Fear of Losing the Old Canada." *Globe and Mail*, March 11.

van Dijk, Teun A. 1993. "Principles of Critical Discourse Analysis." *Discourse & Society* 4 (2): 249–83. http://dx.doi.org/10.1177/0957926593004002006.

Wellman, David T. 1977. *Portraits of White Racism*. Cambridge, UK: Cambridge University Press.

Zong, Li. 1997. "New Racism, Cultural Diversity and the Search for a National Identity." In *The Battle Over Multiculturalism: Does it Help or Hinder Canadian Unity?* ed. Andrew Cardozo and Louis Musto, 115–26. Ottawa: Pearson-Shoyama Institute.

4 The Muslims Are Coming: The "Sharia Debate" in Canada

SHERENE H. RAZACK

What politics are promoted by the notion that the world is *not* divided into modern and non-modern, into West and non-West?

Talal Asad[1]

Entry Point: Dead Bodies and Dead Subjects

In June 2004 I attended a keynote lecture in Toronto on honour killings in Europe by Unni Wikan, a Norwegian anthropologist who specializes in Muslim cultures. I was interested in Wikan because she had had an impact on the debates concerning Muslim women in Norway. Professor Wikan was introduced as someone who had rescued people in great need, particularly young Muslim girls. I learned that she had just received a free-speech award for showing great courage in working for social justice. Her courage in this case was in daring to speak up against Muslim cultures and on the evils of both multiculturalism and a too-soft approach to immigrants.

Wikan's presentation began with Power Point slides of the funeral of Fadime Sahindal, a Kurdish woman murdered by her father (an immigrant to Sweden) when she decided to leave home to live with a non-Kurdish man. Sahindal received a state funeral in Sweden, broadcast live on Swedish television. She had expressed a wish to be buried in a church, and Wikan showed slides of the bishop, who called her a martyr, and the six women who carried her coffin, a practice Wikan speculated that the Muslim men in her community agreed to "probably because they realised they didn't have a choice."[2] The keynote presentation continued with many pictures of the beautiful Sahindal, her long, curly hair flowing. There were even pictures of her grave.

Throughout this somewhat macabre visual journey, I wondered why Fadime Sahindal's dead body had to be so prominently displayed for the benefit of the three hundred or so, mostly white, Western academics attending a conference of the Jean Piaget Society. My discomfort reached an apex in the question period that followed, when members of the audience, some of the women on the verge of tears and with voices quivering with anger, expressed their outrage at the barbarous Muslim men to whom Wikan often referred. A palpable warmth and white group solidarity suffused the audience as they collectively contemplated what might be done to save the Muslim woman and to keep the "dangerous" Muslim man in line. I was reminded of the regenerative properties of unveiling the Muslim woman, that is to say, of its power to give birth to the European.

On this June morning, the productive power of the ideas of the imperilled Muslim woman and the "dangerous" Muslim man, ideas that instal the civilized European and enable practices of surveillance and regulation, was not the only thing to worry about. Fadime Sahindal was murdered by her father. How do we keep her murder in mind at the same time that we remember what it can mean to those who are anxious to draw a line in the sand between barbaric Muslims and civilized Europeans? As I have written elsewhere, strategies to confront violence against women, of the kind Fadime Sahindal died from, fail if they mostly work to instal the colour line between modern white subjects and pre-modern non-white subjects, between those who help and those who require assistance. Strategies born of such evangelical impulses seldom undermine the structures and practices that both give rise to and sustain violence against women for the simple reason that such structures are not even acknowledged. If the violence Sahindal experienced is thought to come out of her culture, pure and simple, then there is little chance to confront the multiplicity of factors that have produced and sustained it.[3]

The eternal triangle of the imperilled Muslim woman, the "dangerous" Muslim man, and the civilized European is fully in evidence in the context that is the topic of this chapter: Canadian feminist and state responses to the prospect of the introduction of Sharia law as an option for Muslims settling disputes in family law. In the French-speaking province of Quebec, faith-based legal options in the realm of family law have been rejected outright. In the English-speaking province of Ontario an option had long existed through the *Arbitration Act* (1991) that enabled individuals to hire third parties to privately adjudicate their conflicts using any agreed-upon rules or laws.[4] This option was mostly used to settle commercial disputes, although Jewish groups had used it in matters of divorce. When a Muslim group proposed to use the *Arbitration Act* to settle disputes in the family-law arena using Islamic principles (which they described as the application of Sharia law), feminists expressed a vociferous opposition to faith-based arbitration. Despite feminist protest, and following an inquiry, the government initially found no compelling reason to deny faith-based arbitration in the settlement of family disputes to Muslims while Jews and indeed all other groups retained the right under the *Arbitration Act*. However, a few short months later, after intense public debate, the government reversed its position, announcing on 11 September 2005 that it intended to introduce legislation that would eliminate all faith-based arbitration.[5] The debate about faith-based arbitration in Ontario, a public discussion that took place for most of 2004–5, is the focus of this chapter.

As this debate progressed, I was sometimes asked by concerned Muslim feminists if I had anything useful to contribute to the "Sharia debate," as faith-based arbitration came to be called. Like the women who approached me, I worried deeply about the rise in fundamentalism worldwide and felt sure that Sharia law through the *Arbitration Act* was not a good idea for women. At the same time, I had grave misgivings about how feminists had so far responded to the threat of Sharia, reinstalling the modernity/pre-modernity distinction apparently without hesitation. I considered it risky for feminists to work with ideas of the secular over the religious, the modern and the pre-modern, in short with strategies that deployed the three figures I had come to know so well from the European context. Such constructs fit so neatly into the contemporary Western project to mark Muslims as suspect bodies and to limit their citizenship rights that it seemed to me that a considerable amount of caution was in order. On the other hand, it also seemed likely that those feminists who took an anti-Sharia position did so out of the conviction that Muslim women were at risk of losing their rights under faith-based arbitration, particularly if conservative Muslim interpretations of women's rights in Islam were to prevail. Feminists were concerned that private dispute mechanisms were unlikely to operate in women's interests and that Muslim women could be pressured into accepting faith-based arbitration. The "Sharia debate" highlighted the fact that Muslim women were caught between the proverbial rock (a state likely to use their rights as a means to police Muslim populations) and a hard place (patriarchal and conservative religious forces within their own communities).

I argue below that in their concern to curtail conservative and patriarchal forces within the Muslim community, Canadian feminists (both Muslim and non-Muslim) used frameworks that installed a secular/religious divide that functions as a colour line, marking the difference between the white, modern, enlightened West and people of colour, in particular, Muslims. This colour line is an especially pernicious one in a *post-9/11* world when, in the name of anti-terrorism, Western states have won support for a variety of punitive and stigmatizing measures against Muslims and other groups of colour. Such measures are often defended as civilizing measures, necessary in order to bring democracy, human rights, and women's rights to Muslim countries. I suggest that feminist responses have helped to sustain a form of governmentality, one in which the productive power of the imperilled Muslim woman functions to keep in line Muslim communities at the same time that it defuses more radical feminist and anti-racist critique of conservative religious forces. Drawing from Talal Asad's idea that secularism is one way in which the modern state secures its own power and actively produces the citizen whose loyalty is first and foremost to the state, I explore below how ideas about women's rights and secularism are part of the neoliberal management of racial-minority populations who are scripted as pre-modern and requiring considerable regulation and surveillance. Secularism as a policy regulating the conduct of citizens requires and produces a normative citizen who is unconnected to community, a figure who achieves definition only in comparison to racial Others, the latter presumed to be trapped in the pre-modern by virtue of their particularist tendencies.

We are in a historical moment in which feminism can be easily annexed to the project of empire. As I and others have shown, it is often through the language of human rights and gender equality that empire is accomplished today.[6] The West is understood as culturally committed to the values of the Enlightenment, while the non-West remains incompletely modern at best, or hostile to modernity at worst. Within this conceptual framework, one often described as a clash of civilizations, it is the duty of modern peoples to bring pre-modern peoples in line. When the occupation of Afghanistan by American forces can be justified as necessary in order to save Afghan women from the Taliban, feminists must necessarily pay attention to how their demands serve the interests of imperialism and white supremacy. As Inderpal Grewal has persuasively argued, human-rights discourses, including those regarding women's rights as human rights, are productive discourses. They instal "free subjects who can save those suffering from human rights abuses" and sustain "rescue from culture" as the main rationality.[7] What do discourses of rescue erase and what do they produce?

Such considerable legal and social interest in Muslims may seem at first blush obvious if one accepts that the "war on terror" has brought with it an intensification of race thinking and the marking of the "culturally different" as aliens outside the polity. It may also seem obvious when viewed as part of the ongoing management of racial populations, especially if one considers that Muslims constitute a majority of Europe's immigrants. In Canada, however, Muslims do not constitute the largest group of migrants. The sensation, therefore, that the civilized world is being overrun by Muslims derives less from the actual numbers and more from a circulating global narrative of the "war on terror." This is nowhere more evident than when, in February 2007, the small town of Hérouxville, Quebec, a town with no foreign-born or Muslim residents at all, felt compelled to announce that it prohibits the stoning of women. As the town's city councillors explained to the Muslim women who met with them to discuss the need for such a formal declaration, they were worried that a Sharia law might be implemented provincially. For these councillors, it was necessary to act quickly, pre-empting the threat before it materialized.[8] If, as I suggest, these are moral panics over Muslims even where there are none, we must in the end return to the productive function of the three figures who people the pages of the newspapers: the "dangerous" Muslim man, the imperilled Muslim woman, and the civilized European.

1. The "Sharia Debate" in Ontario: "From Britannia to Sharia"

The Ontario "Sharia debate" began life as a moral panic. That is to say, a small event came to stand in for a crisis of giant proportions, one on to which was projected social anxieties about Muslim bodies. Parenthetically, it is noteworthy that such media-orchestrated panics are traceable in every Western country since 2001. For example, widespread condemnation of bodies marked as "Muslim," and heightened support for punitive measures against them, followed the media-foregrounded gang rape of a white Australian woman by Lebanese males in Sydney, Australia. As Binoy Kampmark has shown, the rape case became a point of departure for public commentary on the dangers of multiculturalism and on the evil Islam posed for the West, in spite of the fact that the rapists were Christians.[9] We can see the same kind of media spectacle around the banning of the hijab in various countries, notably France, a context to which many Canadian social commentators referred when discussing faith-based arbitration. In each of these "panics," Muslim women's bodies become the ground on which nations and citizens are established as civilized and modern, while Muslims and immigrants remain trapped in the pre-modern, a process not unlike the one I described with respect to Fadime Sahindal. The polarization successfully pre-empts examining how the state and its institutions are implicated both in the marginalization of communities of colour and in the oppression of women. Not insignificantly, media panics also afford an opportunity for the race pleasure Anthony Farley describes as a pleasure in one's own superiority and the other's abjection.

In late November of 2003, Syed Mumtaz Ali, a retired lawyer, announced to the media that a new organization, the Islamic Institute of Civil Justice, had been established. The organization planned to apply Islamic principles of family and inheritance law to resolve family law and inheritance disputes within the Muslim community in Canada, services he described as the application of Sharia law. (Sharia Law is not a codified set of laws but rather a framework for interpreting laws based on the Qu'ran and the Hadith.) The *Arbitration Act* already permitted the resolution of private disputes in this way and had done so for a decade, but Ali's announcement created the impression that something had changed in law that now made it easier to apply Sharia. The panic that ensued, from the fear that Sharia law (with its associated images of women being stoned to death) had now come to Canadian shores, was of such a magnitude that the federal government, pressed to set up an inquiry into the *Arbitration Act,* was ultimately obliged to clarify that it had not changed the law and that it had not collaborated with the newly formed Islamic Institute.[10]

The tracks for making Syed Ali's announcement into a moral panic were well worn. Headlines on the barbarism of Sharia itself were appearing as early as 2001, and media reports of the story of Amina Lawal, the Nigerian woman sentenced to death by stoning, prepared the ground for the now familiar theme of a "Clash of Civilizations" between Islam and the West. The events of September 11, 2001 simply escalated the clash. The November 2003 headlines on Sharia that announced the Islamic Institute's plans alerted Canadians that they were on the brink of their own fateful encounter between Islam and the West, a swift descent from the ideals of the British Empire to a barbaric multicultural present, in short, from "Britannia to Sharia."[11] The headlines warned of "legal apartheid,"[12] and suggested ominously that "religious law undermines loyalty to Canada."[13] Sharia was above all "un-Canadian."[14]

Canadian feminists believed there was a great deal to fear from Mumtaz Ali and his small group. The Canadian Council of Muslim Women met with the government to discuss their concerns. An International Campaign Against Sharia, headed by a Canadian of Iranian origin, was formed. Various feminist organizations, among them the Women's Legal Education and Action Fund (LEAF), the National Association of Women and the Law (NAWL), the Metropolitan Toronto Action Committee on Violence Against Women (METRAC), and the National Council of University Women, added their voices to the general feminist alarm. Feminist lobbying succeeded to the extent that the Ontario government responded by appointing a Member of Parliament, Marion Boyd, a long-time feminist who was well respected by feminists in the mainstream anti-violence movement, to explore the "use of private arbitration to resolve family and inheritance cases, and the impact that using arbitration may have on vulnerable people."[15] Boyd met with over 50 individuals and organizations from July to September 2004, releasing a report that left feminists dismayed by her recommendation that the *Arbitration Act* remain unchanged. Boyd also concluded that the safeguards recommended by feminists worried about vulnerable Muslim women were not necessary.

Canadian Feminist Positions

The figure of the imperilled Muslim woman stood at the core of feminist responses to the idea of faith-based arbitration advanced by Ali and the Islamic Institute. As they sought to make clear to the government, extremely vulnerable and at risk in family and community, Muslim women were best protected by the state, a protection achieved through the absolute separation of religion and law. The Canadian Council of Muslim Women, for example, armed with statistics from the 2001 census, declared that even though Muslim women were among the most highly educated in the country, they tended to work part-time and in low-paying jobs. Quoting statistics indicating that fewer separated Muslim women sought divorce than did separated women in the Canadian population, and that marriage breakdown for Muslim women between the ages of 18 and 24 is higher than for other women of the same age group, the Council opined that these patterns could be attributed to higher than usual "cultural and economic pressures."[16] Muslim women may in fact be persuaded to agree to arbitration under pressure, and the *Arbitration Act* did not contain safeguards to protect them from their families and communities. Rejecting outright any position that would involve strengthening women's position *within* faith-based arbitration (the government had proposed education materials informing women of their rights under religious and family law), the Council insisted that since there was no consensus about Sharia, and no accountability for how it was interpreted, conservative and patriarchal interpretations were likely to prevail. The answer, then, had to lie in secular law. Without it, women would be left at the mercy of their communities.[17]

If secularism offered women shelter from community, however, then the state became women's chief protector, an entity conceptualized as a neutral power, uncontaminated by conflicting loyalties to kin or community, and offering equal protection to all its citizens regardless of race or gender. Feminists appealed to the state on the basis of its universalism. The Canadian Council of Muslim Women received strong support from the international group Women Living Under Muslim Laws. Echoing the sentiment that family and community were dangerous places for women, and that a fully secular state was women's best protector, WLUML warned that the proposal on the part of the Islamic Institute amounted to "the political manipulation of culture and identity." Such moves were global, suggested WLUML, and had already jeopardized women's autonomy in France and the United Kingdom. WLUML described the European situation as

> an unholy alliance between some progressives and the fundamentalists who then sought to take advantage of state policies of multiculturalism and the realities of continuing racial discrimination to demand special rights for the "Muslim community." But these special rights inevitably involve anti-women practices and highly regressive interpretations of Islam. They also unquestioningly presume that all migrants from Muslim contexts identify with "Muslim."[18]

Concluding that "any victory for conservative forces among communities in Europe and North America will in this globalized world automatically reinforce fundamentalist groups in Muslim countries and elsewhere," and reminding Canadians that giving power to conservative movements will not address the problems Muslim communities have in Europe and North America, the organization stated its views boldly: "Obscurantist men" cannot speak for Muslim women.[19] Linking the rise in fundamentalism elsewhere to the Canadian situation both provided Mumtaz Ali and his small group with a profile and power they did not seem to possess and sustained the idea that the state remained beyond reproach as the protector of women. If the community could be kept from contaminating the state through such policies as multiculturalism, then women's rights would remain secure.

In installing an opposition between multiculturalism and women's rights, WLUML repeats an argument that has raged in Western feminist circles for some time. Its academic form, for instance, is discernable in the positions taken by Susan Moller Okin, that multiculturalism is bad for women, and by her critics, who suggest that once feminism is put in opposition to multiculturalism, racism quickly pervades what becomes efforts to save non-Western women from their cultures. Many scholars have pointed out these dilemmas and suggested the issues are more complicated than the simple assertion that multiculturalism is good or bad.[20] As Floya Anthias suggests, to navigate between the poles of feminism and multiculturalism two things must be borne in mind: relationships between dominant and subordinate groups and "the need to attack this unequal relationship at national and global levels" and similar relationships of inequality within groups.[21] Key to keeping these things in mind is remembering that women are agents with multilayered identities who need to resist class exploitation and racial domination and be free from violence and gender inequality. Anthias stresses that we must avoid homogenizing and totalizing cultures, just as we must avoid treating gender as a unitary category that stands apart from all other things. Further, all "practices that serve to subordinate and oppress are to be attacked and these practices are tied to a range of structural processes which include the State apparatus, the socio-legal framework and the dominance of Western capitalist and cultural forms.[22] Similarly, in *Dislocating Culture,* Uma Narayan has argued that feminists must "insist that there are many ways to inhabit nations and cultures critically and creatively," pushing for a more historical and political understanding of tradition.[23]

Following the line of argument expressed by WLUML, some Canadian feminists opposed to faith-based arbitration articulated a fervent belief in secularism and a commitment to the position that multiculturalism was bad for women. For instance, they spoke glowingly of the French context, where the hijab, or headscarf, was recently banned in schools. (The presence of French-speaking feminists in some of the more vocal feminist organizations may have accounted for the multiple references to the French context.) Secularism in France was represented as historical progress, the triumph of universalism over class and religious conflict. In a research report for the Canadian Council of Muslim Women, Pascale Fournier wrote admiringly of the French decision to ban the hijab and connected it to France's revolutionary tradition.

> The most important feature of current French politics is its neo-republican discourse of French identity, in which membership in the national community involves an absolute commitment to the Republic and to its core values of égalité (equality) and laicité (the separation of state and religion). This republican model was forged in the context of the 1789 French Revolution, as a direct reaction to the historical French struggle against its own monarchy, ruling aristocracy and religious establishment.[24]

Sharing this faith in secularism, the National Association of Women and the Law elaborated that if faith-based arbitration were allowed, "freely chosen" arbitrators will be the new judges of women, imposing their own principles as the law of the land. While arbitrators chosen by Muslim communities could not be trusted, judges were deemed a better option for women. In view of the likelihood that judges would be of European origin, NAWL proposed cultural-sensitivity training to augment the latter's capacity to protect Muslim women from their cultures and communities.

Only one feminist organization, the Women's Legal Education and Action Fund (LEAF), initially supported the use of religious principles when they do not conflict with Canadian law. LEAF acknowledged that the use of arbitration was attractive because it was an alternate and cheaper form of dispute resolution. Further, they noted that some Muslim women were in favour of using Sharia. Believing that there was contemporary "negative stereotyping of Muslims," but seeking as well to heed women who were concerned about conservative religious influences, the organization recommended that a number of safeguards be built into the *Arbitration Act* to protect women from being coerced into arbitration. LEAF later reversed its position, announcing that it now believed that the government should prohibit the use of the *Arbitration Act* to protect women from being coerced into settling their disputes in accordance with religious law. It is possible that this reversal emerged from the realization that the government refused to consider building in safeguards into the act.[25] On the whole, then, although Canadian feminist organizations did not all adopt the dramatic tones of Homa Arjomand of the International Campaign to End Sharia that Sharia was a "barbaric act" and that permitting the use of the *Arbitration Act* to settle family law disputes would "escalate all the slavish obligations of the wife towards the husband under the Islamic Laws and ancient traditions," feminist organizations remained opposed categorically to religious legal options.

Feminist rejection of faith-based arbitration left no room to stand for women seeking to live a faith-based life, a schism that was clearly in evidence at a community forum to discuss Sharia. At a public meeting sponsored by Arjomand and the International Campaign to

End Sharia, a group of young veiled women from a Somali youth group repeatedly asked questions relating to the need for religious tolerance, arguing that their Muslim faith and their Muslim youth group was a refuge from the racism they experienced in high school. Speaking of teacher and principal surveillance, police surveillance, and the media demonizing of Muslims, the young women argued that Sharia would be more applicable in their lives should they choose to use it for family issues. Most of their remarks were dismissed by the speakers on the platform on the basis that the young women did not know how fundamentalism operated. Dismissed as naive, and told that they had been coerced into wearing the veil, some of the young women chose to leave the meeting.[26]

It is not surprising that at least initially the government refused to endorse a staunch secularist position. To do so would have meant, in the first instance, treating Muslims differently from other groups, most notably Jews. The Boyd report also quickly zeroed in on the weaknesses in feminist arguments, exploiting these to defend its position that faith-based arbitration should continue. Noting that feminists and others appeared to be misinformed as to the extent to which such arbitrations could contravene Canadian law, the report made clear that if the principal objection to faith-based arbitration had to do with the specific vulnerabilities of Muslim women, then one option was to educate this group about their religious and secular options (the former suggestion was roundly rejected by the Canadian Council of Muslim Women). Responding to the repeated feminist argument that family and community were particularly perilous places for Muslim women, and for women at risk of domestic violence in particular, the Boyd report quotes a critical feminist scholar, Liisa Hajjar, who holds that a more complex assessment of women's lives was "an important rejoinder to cultural stereotypes that Muslim women are uniquely or exceptionally vulnerable.[27] Rebuking feminists in this way for offering an overly simplistic analysis of vulnerable women and dangerous men, the Boyd report also suggested that opposing minority rights (under multiculturalism) to individual rights was an equally simplistic way of describing what was at issue.[28] Thus, feminist criticisms, including important arguments for inserting safeguards into the *Arbitration Act*, were, in the end, dismissed.

The government's reversal of its position in support of faith-based arbitration came several months after the Boyd report. The reversal was greeted in the press by an even more solidly entrenched set of dualisms involving the secular progressive West and brutal Islam. Journalists such as the *Toronto Star's* Rosie DiManno reminded Canadians that the "time has come for Canadians to be weaned off the teat of multiculturalism as a primary source of sustenance and self-identity." Adding that we should not be labelled racist for "daring to champion the secular over the infantalizing religious," she noted that the government's move is clearly aimed at "circumscribing Islamic authority."[29] Others were more subtle, defending the women who had opposed Sharia as women who were in a position to know its dangers.[30] Only Haroon Siddiqui, a journalist at the *Toronto Star*, suggested what the long-term impact of the decision to abolish faith-based arbitration might be, writing that the government had "bought into fear-mongering that Muslim barbarians are knocking on the gates of Ontario" and was "engendering an atmosphere of fear and mutual hostility."[31]

2. Towards Rupturing the Dichotomy

When gender is placed in opposition to culture, and women's status becomes linked to the triumph of the individual over the group, two categories of women are brought into existence: those who have successfully made it out of community and culture and others who are to be assisted into modernity. We are, once again, on the emotional terrain I introduced with the Unni Wikan story, where community stands in the way of women's entrance into modernity, and where civilized Europeans must discipline non-Europeans in order to secure the modern state.

Women who tell a narrative of rescue can forget their own class position and histories and secure their own innocence, a politics many scholars have shown. For example, in her critique of the liberal feminist internationalism of Martha Nussbaum, Sangeeta Ray draws on an article by Anupama Rao on elite Indian feminist responses to Dalit women.[32] Upper-caste feminists understood patriarchy in Dalit women's lives in a way that enabled them to inhabit a non-caste position, Rao showed. The forgetting of their own caste dominance was enabled by an exclusive focus on what Dalit men did to Dalit women. Understanding the complex ways in which Dalit women's oppression is structured requires more critical self-reflection than is evident in Nussbaum and other liberals, Ray argues, and it will require something other than positivist methodology, in which we simply ask Indian women how they feel and either take the words at face value (as Nussbaum does when she asks Indian feminists and Dalit women how they feel) or accuse them of false consciousness or immaturity, as Arjomand does. Addressing the same issues as Ray, Carol Quillen commented:

> If we really want to further the cause of justice, we need to understand how discursive and material structures – race, capitalism, nation-states, orientalism, family, and liberalism itself – shape our very emergence as differentiated "human" by establishing and then occluding hierarchical relations among us. We need, in other words, a view of the human that focuses on the social and psychological processes of self-formation in a context that acknowledges, as Chow states, how we can be "at the mercy" of broad ideological and social structures that in many ways "speak and act" us.[33]

What do these "discursive and material structures" look like in the context of the Canadian Sharia debate and how were feminists at the mercy of "broad ideological and social structures," as Chow suggests? Certainly ideological and social structures "speak" us as though we are autonomous individuals who simply contract with each other. If, as Inderpal Grewal reminds us, feminist activism constructs a variety of gendered subjects,[34] how might feminists have avoided being drawn into the framework of superior, secular women, saving their less-enlightened and more-imperilled sisters from religion and community, and still responded to the dangers at hand? Finally, what should feminist politics look like in the Canadian context given the dangers of both white supremacy and patriarchy and the exigencies of a post-9/11 world as they operate in the West?

Feminists who have considered the discursive and material structures operating in the lives of women who find themselves confronting the forces of Muslim fundamentalism in the Middle East (or, more properly, Islamization) have sometimes concluded that women do indeed need to turn to the state as arbiter and to stake their claims on universalist ground, as Canadian feminists did. For example, attempting to move beyond the tradition-modernity divide and to pay attention to the ways that ideological and social structures "speak" us, Amina Jamal explores how Pakistani feminists in the late 1980s and 1990s resorted to liberal notions of citizenship and gender-neutral notions about rights and the universalism of the public sphere to defend women's rights within a context of an intense Islamization and a corresponding oppression of women.[35] Jamal argues that the perils of liberalism notwithstanding, for Pakistani women confronted by the Islamic state's proposal to change the laws of evidence so that two male witnesses would be required for every crime, or the government's disregard for the murders of women accused of sullying the honour of their communities, it made eminent political sense to insist that the state act as a neutral arbiter over various tribal customs and that it respect fundamental human rights. Simultaneously, women's groups also argued their position from within Islam, maintaining that the proposed law of evidence, for example, was both discriminatory and anti-Islam. It is, however, principally in their appeal to the idea of a "transcendent citizen-subject" that Jamal finds the counter-hegemonic potential of Pakistani feminist strategies against the evidence rule and the state's tepid response to "honour" killings.[36] She identifies one central rhetorical strategy of Pakistani feminists, whereby rather than stress that women were particularly vulnerable, they stressed women's rights as citizens, underlining that what was at issue was the meaning of citizenship itself.

Jamal is very careful to assess the social and political context of feminist activism that makes Pakistani feminist political choices comprehensible. She notes, for instance, the rising power during this period of religious parties, which stepped in to fill the void left by the mainstream parties' oscillation between a pro-US position, with its promises of membership in the world community, and an anti-imperialist position that often translates locally as pro-Islamic militancy. Allied sometimes to the military government of General Musharraf, and sometimes opposing it, the religious parties' strength, coupled with Musharraf's attention to US security concerns at the expense of democratization, have been bad news for women's rights. Reminding us that Islamists are not fundamentalists with a fixed set of beliefs but rather individuals engaged in a political project with a particular vision, and noting their practice of deriding critics as "Westernized" and as "Westernized women" disloyal to the nation, Jamal suggests that we understand the feminist struggle in Pakistan as one between two competing versions of modernity, and between two competing sections of the middle class. Feminists, she maintains, simply had no other choice but to frame their responses in liberal terms, and we must understand their appropriation of modernity as a strategy. Their approach was not without its perils. To argue, as Pakistani feminists did, for the separation of religion and state was to engage in a battle over the meaning of secularism. As in the Canadian context, where Mumtaz Ali and the Islamic Council insisted that the only true Muslim was one who opted for Sharia law, Pakistani feminists found themselves having to defend themselves as still pro-Islam, and insisting that there were other ways of being Muslim. The call for secularism can mean many things, Jamal insists, including a separation of religion and state or a regulation of religious options within the state. In choosing the options they did, Pakistani feminists simply calculated the odds, understanding what they were up against as the eviction of women from citizenship.

I want to suggest that, differently from the Pakistani context, the appeal to the idea of a transcendent citizen subject carries with it some risks that are specific to the local and global context of white nations in the post-9/11 world. As Jamal herself sees, Pakistani feminists opposing Islamic law do so from a context where such laws affect everyone. Canadian feminists rejecting faith-based arbitration do so in a white settler state, one anxious to control its minority populations and to gain membership in the fraternity of white nations. Being tough on Muslims, as many European scholars have observed, is one significant way in which contemporary Western governments secure both their own domestic base (through appealing to the right and consolidating the idea that there is one white national culture) and their international stature (through appearing to be active participants of the "war on terror"). To consider the material and discursive structures in our own context, Canadian feminists had to be worried by the growing resonance of the idea of a clash of civilizations and the intense regulation in the West of those scripted on the Muslim side of the divide. When feminist strategies unhesitatingly invoked the idea that Islam and Muslim men were intrinsically threatening, and a secular state was the only way to safeguard women's rights, they provided grist for an already powerful mill: as the antithesis of Western civilization, Muslim populations in the West have to be watched and regulated, a surveillance that begins at the border. The companion idea installed by the notion that a secular state provides the best protection is the idea that the normative citizen is one without group-based loyalties, a figure for whom communitarian identities are best kept at home. This "unbiased liberal subject," as Gokariksel and Mitchell argue, is extremely important for neoliberal state formation and economic development, effects Canadian feminists needed to consider more seriously than was evident during the "Sharia debate" in Ontario.[37] That the unbiased liberal subject achieves definition through comparison to the racialized subject (viewed as communitarian, hence biased) should give us greater pause when we invoke the idea of a free-floating citizen.

Secularism as a Form of Governmentality

In the West, feminist faith in the state and in secularism sits uneasily alongside current legislative and policy moves to restrict the rights of immigrants and racial minorities in the name of anti-terrorism and the protection of Western civilization as secular and modern. As discussed in chapter 1, the *Anti-Terrorism Act,* with its suspension of fundamental rights, for instance, has created a perilous situation for Muslims or those who are taken to be Muslims, a situation often defended as the West's need to protect itself from a barbaric Islam. For another instance, the use of security certificates (discussed in chapter 1) under the *Immigration and Refugee Protection Act* to detain Muslim men who are not citizens, and to deport them after a secret trial in which they are not allowed to hear the evidence against them, suggests that the post-9/11 era has not offered much evidence of Western states' commitment to universalism. How might we reconcile the actions of a state prepared to deprive Muslims of the right of habeas corpus and to hold them in solitary confinement for years without due process with the same state's protection of Muslim women from the men of their communities?

The state's central conceptual tool in suspending the rights of those suspected of involvement in terrorism or considered to have the potential to be terrorists has been the idea that Islam breeds a particular pre-modern subject, one who possesses a violent hatred of the West and who is not committed to the rule of law, respect for human rights and women's rights, or democracy.[38] The Western subject, in contrast, is one who has progressed into modernity, a progression marked principally by his entrance into the secular, the religious leanings of leaders such as George W. Bush notwithstanding. Thus, one might begin to delineate the conditions under which Canadian feminists engaged in the debate over faith-based arbitration by considering how modern states secure their power through the idea of secularism.

Secularism is popularly understood in the way that the philosopher Charles Taylor describes its origins. As Talal Asad discusses in his book *Formations of the Secular,* Taylor argues that the modern state has to make citizenship the primary principle of identity because this is the only way that it can transcend the conflicts that emerge from different identities. But secularism does not simply provide peace and toleration, as Taylor imagines.

Secularism secures the power of the state as neutral arbiter. For Taylor, the state resolves the quarrels among different groups through persuasion and negotiation. Asad sees a less benign state that exercises force to guarantee the social arrangements it wants. At its inception in Europe, secularism as political doctrine guaranteed the peace between warring religious factions by shifting the site of violence from within Europe to outside of it. Secularism's triumph as political doctrine is closely connected to colonialism and to the rise of a system of capitalist nation-states. Of all the things that secularism can mean, it has not always meant tolerance. Those who do not fit the public personality of the state are simply defined as religious minorities and find themselves in a defensive position. Asad's arguments suggest that we examine what contemporary notions of secularism secure for Western states and that we abandon the romantic idea that secularism simply represents progress from the pre-modern to the modern.

Asad's comments on the hijab affair in France are perhaps most pertinent here.[39] As in the Sharia debate in Ontario, the vast majority of French intellectuals of both the left and the right felt that "the secular character of the Republic is under threat because of Islam, which they see as being symbolized by the headscarf." In France the secular character of the Republic is captured in the concept of *laicité* which most people trace to the end of the nineteenth century. Asad reminds us of its earlier foundation. In the sixteenth-century wars of religion, European Christian states adopted the principle that the religion of the ruler is the religion of the state. What is significant here is that a political principle replaced a religious one and "transcendent power and authority were now given to the state to decide not only on who was deserving of religious tolerance but on what precisely religious tolerance was." In Europe we then see French Protestants getting the right to practise their religion in Catholic France at the same time that Spain is expelling its Muslim converts. By the time of the French revolution, when religion comes largely to mean personal belief and the church simply appears as a rival for political power, there is bitter conflict between church and state, a conflict that the state wins in the name of the revolution's ideals of humanity and progress.

Public schools at the end of the nineteenth century became a way in which the state schooled its citizens to take on their new role as secular citizens without conflicting loyalties. A significant amount of France's imperial conquests took place at this time. "Anti-clerical schooling at home, unequal agreements with the Church, and imperial expansion abroad were the pillars on which *laicité* was established under the Third Republic." Asad advances the interesting argument that today in France the sixteenth-century political rule (that the religion of the ruler is the religion of the state) is still the operating principle, and what continues to be significant is "not the maintenance or interdiction of a particular religion by the state ... but the installation of a single power drawn from a single source and facing a single political task: the worldly care of its population regardless of its beliefs." The state takes it upon itself to determine signs of religion's presence (rather than who is and is not of the religion of the ruler), and in this way manages various populations through its activities, populations marked as "religious" *for one reason or another.* One way to regulate Muslim populations in France is to mark them formally as populations that must be forcibly brought into the modern through secularism. So seductive is this vision of a modern people civilizing a pre-modern one that few have considered what else has been achieved by the banning of headscarves and how the power of the state and its management of a subordinate population is manifested in the French context.

I would offer the French rather than the Pakistani situation as the one that Canadian feminists should consider for lessons in how secularism operates as the management of the conduct of racialized immigrant populations in the West today. As Asad clarifies, the "headscarf worn by Muslim women was held to be a religious sign conflicting with the state's secular personality."[40] The Stasi commission appointed to investigate headscarves in schooling interpreted the wearing of headscarves as the "will to display" Muslim identity.[41] Since the state was owed exclusive loyalty in the public sphere, the wearing of headscarves had to be banned. Both the interpretation of what the headscarf means to its wearers and the state's decision to insist that citizens have a public identity that is exclusive must be understood within a context of profound suspicion of Muslims.

Asad concludes that important questions were not asked about the state's reasons for finding the headscarf in schools incompatible with the practice of French citizenship. First, everyone who lives in France is not equal before the law. A number of Muslims from France's former colonies live, work, and pay taxes in France but do not enjoy full citizenship rights. A focus on the veil as a practice antithetical to citizenship marks Muslims as undeserving of full citizenship rights (as incompletely modern peoples) and it obscures the legitimate grievances that French Muslims have concerning their unequal treatment. Second, the French state is ceding some of its national autonomy to the European Union as a result of the exigencies of a global economy. The control of migrant populations is a central aspect of these largely hidden manoeuvres, as is the installation of a citizen subject who is autonomous and without group loyalties or claims. Finally, the circulation of media images and narratives across borders profoundly shape "the direction of fears, longings, resentments towards peoples and places."[42] These factors suggest that we are a long way from the uncomplicated idea of a majority of citizens deciding that the social contract requires the banning of the wearing of headscarfs. If these unasked questions were engaged with, we would have to consider how the public sphere might be negotiated creatively given citizens' transnational loyalties and the fact that they do not live their lives in a strict separation of politics and religion, nor are they autonomous subjects freely contracting with each other.

Why is it important to deconstruct the secular and inquire into its productive function? Here again, Asad is clear that the important point is to ask what the secular/religious, modernity/pre-modernity distinction secures.

> Modernity is a *project – or* rather, a series of interlinked projects – that certain people in power seek to achieve. The project aims at institutionalizing a number of (sometimes conflicting, often evolving) principles: constitutionalism, moral autonomy, democracy, human rights, civil equality, industry, consumerism, freedom of the market - and secularism. It employs proliferating technologies (of production, warfare, travel, entertainment, medicine) that generate new experiences of space and time, of cruelty and health, of consumption and knowledge. The notion that these experiences constitute "disenchantment" – implying a direct access to reality, a stripping away of myth, magic, and the sacred – is a salient feature of the modern epoch.[43]

The categories of secular and religious are the "terms on which modern living is required to take place, and nonmodern peoples are invited to assess their adequacy. For representations of "the secular" and the "religious" in modern and modernizing states mediate people's identities, help shape their sensibilities, and guarantee their experiences."[44] As Étienne Balibar has shown,

> individuality itself is always an institution, it has to be represented and acknowledged, which can be reached only if the individual is released from strict membership or a "fusion" within

> his (her) Gemeinschaft, thus becoming able to adopt various social roles, to "play on several memberships: or to "shift identity" in order to perform different social functions, while remaining a member of a superior community or a "subject." It has problematic prerequisites, however, because it is connected with the imposition of normality, a normal or standard way of life and a set of beliefs (a "dominant" practical ideology), which has to be maintained for successive generations, at least for the overwhelming majority, or the "mainstream: across class and other barriers.[45]

The implications of taking these ideas seriously are, I believe, that feminists can no longer simplistically assume that the secular is a haven for women, and religion a dangerous place. Lest the point about how the power of the state is mediated be missed, it should be abundantly clear that a reversal strategy, where religion is safe for women and the state is not, would interrupt neither empire nor patriarchy. Instead, keeping a steady eye on their productive function, we, as feminists, would have to consider what we achieve and what we sustain by our strategies as they feed into the state's personality and its particular version of the secular and the religious, as well as into the specific patriarchies of Muslims and non-Muslims in Canada. We should remember that patriarchies themselves are not only cultural practices but systems interlocked with capitalism and white supremacy.[46] Finally, we need to keep our eye on the transnational effects of our strategies, something those against faith-based arbitration understood clearly but only in the context of the spread of fundamentalisms and not in the context of a global white supremacy manifesting as the American bid for empire. Canadian feminists did not consider fundamentalism's mirror image, the spread of the idea that a family of white nations must wage war on terror and religion through the institution of Western law and secularism.

The Neoliberal Subject

Gokariksel and Mitchell have usefully clarified how secularism produces the neoliberal subject. Understanding global neoliberalism as "a political philosophy of governance that upholds an active achievement of a *laissez-faire* economic system," they note:

> The concept of neo-liberal governance concerns the ways in which individual "subjects" are regulated and disciplined through various institutions and processes in society so that they come to understand their own positions and personhood in ways that are compatible with neoliberal trends towards individual autonomy and entrepreneurship and away from a more social understanding of the world and of the relationship between the state and its citizens.[47]

The idea of a monocultural, secular state works to consolidate who is understood to be the ideal citizen. Since the ideal citizen is an individual without any sort of group-based identity, a non-citizen is someone who remains trapped within group-based identities. The terrible danger of the autonomous individual as citizen is the closing down of the possibility of acknowledging group-based harm, as well as group-based privilege. If, as Lauren Berlant has shown, property, privacy, and individuality become "the only ground for the true practice of nationhood" and the ideal citizen is unanchored in history and concrete social relations, then specific harms such as colonialism and racism cannot be acknowledged. Conversely, the specific entitlements enjoyed by colonizers (in this case, the right to be seen as normative citizens) become invisible.[48] Reparations or strategies designed for specific groups come to seem like "catering to the unique sensitivity of a small group" and not as part of an answer to a highly structured inequality.[49] It is this logic that enables so many to easily dismiss Black-focused schools and affirmative action as encouraging narrow tribal identities rather than the redressing of contemporary and historical injustice. Why don't we all just assimilate is the plaintive response to historical injustice increasingly heard whenever racial minorities press their claims for justice.

The call for assimilation and the idea that the nation must be a single, unified, homogeneous body is one that is highly compatible with a white-supremacist agenda and with the surveillance of Muslims. The Stasi commission, as Ezekiel observed, believed that the "concern with oneness prevails over all expression of difference, perceived as a threat."[50] If Muslims are unassimilable, then the state is justified in keeping them out or limiting their citizenship rights. Monoculture readily collapses into anti-immigrant sentiment, as Sivanandan argues, referring to the British context. Assimilationist discourses are not only the basis to anti-immigrant positions but are eminently productive for the "war on terror." Multiculturalism, the argument goes, "has been instrumental in breeding terrorists by steeping them in their own culture and so alienating them from British society."[51] The best anti-terrorist move, then, is to forcibly integrate citizens, a logic that conveniently ignores the role that injustice, military occupations, and racism play in producing terrorists.

As Liz Fekete documents, the citizen subject without ties to community is the conceptual underpinning for a number of repressive measures across Europe:

> Assimilation is being forced through by the adoption of a number of measures, which include the recasting of citizenship laws according to security considerations; the introduction of compulsory language and civics tests for citizenship applicants; codes of conduct for the trustees of mosques; [and] a cultural code of conduct for Muslim girls and women who, in some areas of Europe, will be forbidden to wear the hijab in state institutions.[52]

It is impossible, Fekete concludes, to divorce the current debate on a single, unified national culture from the "war on terror." Fekete asks where the ban on the headscarf will end, noting that in France the government is considering extending its ban to other public spaces and producing in the process a stigmatized and humiliated Muslim population. The French public has already understood the banning of the hijab as licence to do just that, as Ezekiel reports. Although the ban applies to schools, Muslim women wearing headscarfs have found themselves being prevented from doing a wide number of things (working, volunteering, receiving medical services, registering for a marriage, etc.) as citizens take it into their own hands to manage public space, as Ghassan Hage insightfully shows for the Australian context as well.[53] The banning of the hijab made clear who rightfully belongs in public space. The banning of faith-based arbitration in Ontario, coming as it did with all the attendant discourses about modernity and pre-modernity and the normative citizen as someone without ties to community, may well have the same effect.

In Canada, it was quickly evident that the categories of the secular and the religious as oppositions were enabled by, and simultaneously productive of, the idea of a world of civilized Canadians at risk from Muslim terrorists and unassimilable immigrants. Sharia law became an issue of the importation of immigrants' feudal and pre-modern values into a civilized land. Quebec's international-relations minister expressed this view succinctly: "We must rework the social contract (for immigrants) so that the people, Muslims who want to come to Quebec and who do not respect women's rights, or rights, whatever they may be, in our civil code, at that moment, then they stay in their country and do not come to Quebec, because it's unacceptable."[54]

The real threat, however, lay not with the importation of feudal values but, more directly, in the presence of dangerous Muslims. A journalist spelled out these connections in a popular women's magazine by writing about Mumtaz Syed Ali that the retired Toronto lawyer was "linked to a "self-described fundamentalist" who is the cleric at a mosque attended by the grandparents of a young man who has admitted his connections to Al Qaeda."[55] Terrorist by association (and a long one at that), to stop Syed Mumtaz Ali and the Islamic Institute was to take on terrorism itself. Ariane Brunet of the human-rights organization Rights and Democracy chided Canadians that a civilized nation with a well-known commitment to peace could not possibly tolerate Sharia: "Here is Canada, the peacemaker, the mediator. We have an image here. And here we're adopting the Sharia law."[56] In Canada the state seeks to show its membership in the family of civilized nations through its participation in "anti-terrorism" activities. Through peacekeeping, as I have argued elsewhere, Canada secures its reputation as a nation that is not implicated in the crises that befall the Third World. Rather, our role is simply one of mediator, assisting the Third World out of the morass into which it has mysteriously fallen. Feminist narratives about saving Muslim women through the imposition of secularism rely on the same omissions that underpin the national narrative of a peacekeeping nation. That is, they obscure how the state manages its minority populations and produces neoliberal subjects, sustaining the very conditions in which fundamentalisms thrive – conditions of social and economic marginality.

To avoid sustaining the colour line between tribal Muslims and a modern state, feminists must complicate the simple frames available for understanding how and where patriarchy operates. While for Nobel Prize-winner Shirin Ebadi it may be understandable to consider secularism the only appropriate response to the idea of Islamic tribunals,[57] from the perspective of a state where fundamentalists have *not* achieved anything like the power they achieved in Iran or Pakistan, and in view of the state's compelling interest in marking Muslims and indeed all Third World immigrants as pre-modern and confined to the realm of the culturally marked, perhaps the best response to Syed Ali and his small group might well have been to flood the market with alternative stories of culture, rather than to grant the conservative religious narrative the legitimacy it won by feminists opposing it outright in the name of secularism. It is by no means evident that this strategy would have ruptured the secular/religious, modern/pre-modern divide, but an equal possibility exists that by re-inscribing so completely these dualisms, feminist gains were made at too great an expense.

Conclusion

Azizah Al-Hibri once warned: "If Western feminists are now vying for control of the lives of immigrant women by justifying coercive state action, then, these women have not learned the lessons of history, be it colonialism, imperialism or even fascism.[58] Making another related point, Abdullahi An-Na'im noted that a human-rights strategy based on gender alone is disastrous. Such a strategy inevitably depends upon, even as it sustains, the idea that "unmarked" cultures and people (dominant groups are thought to have values while subordinate groups have culture) are already in the modern, while "marked" groups remain in pre-modernity. As An-Na'im put it, the minority culture is required to clean up its gender act, while the majority culture can take all the time it wants. The argument for gender inequality, he insisted, has to be made within culture, and the polarity of gender versus culture has to be undermined. What might Canadian feminists have done to mitigate the power of the state to use feminist concerns to stigmatize and police Muslims and to produce the normative citizen as unconnected to community? How could arguments for gender equality have been made within culture rather than in opposition to it?

The "Sharia law" debate quickly developed into a spectacle. Those advocating the use of Sharia garnered attention, which only grew as more feminists came on board to denounce them. Here we might consider strategy. Knowing that a full-scale moral panic is entirely likely given today's geopolitics, did feminist groups sufficiently consider the conditions of communication as they immediately embraced the position of the secular over the religious? I wonder what would have been the outcome had Muslim feminists in particular, regardless of their own misgivings, expended more energy on the question, what is needed to safeguard faith-based arbitration for women? The Council of Muslim Women did in fact consider this question, inviting those in favour of faith-based arbitration to a discussion. In the end, however, the dangers posed by faith-based arbitration were considered too great to risk pursuing faith-based alternatives. This was perhaps a strategic error. It might have been possible to get more safeguards within the *Arbitration Act* to protect Muslim women who use it, or who are coerced into using it, although the government seemed unwilling to consider this option, as the Boyd report demonstrated. At the very least, the circulation of ideas about alternative ways to be Muslim might have tempered the production of the neoliberal subject as citizen.

It is easy in hindsight to see how there could have been more discussion about the racist dangers present in a modernity/pre-modernity distinction. For example, there could have been a feminist conference on what post-9/11 conditions have meant for Muslim communities. In other words, could the power of conservative Muslims have been diffused through rhetorical strategies that emphasized that there were other ways of being Muslim? And other dangers? To point out that Syed Mumtaz Ali and his new organization had not consulted widely in Muslim communities and to emphasize his group's limited base of support might not have worked as a strategy, however, given the dominant group's investment in the idea that Muslims are an undifferentiated pre-modern people. As Sivanandan and Ezekiel both point out, Western states have been willing to foster separatist religious enclaves providing such groups restrict their claims to culture. In Britain, the anti-racist basis to multiculturalism (responding to specific group claims of injustice) lost ground as the state became willing to respond more to cultural demands for separate spaces than to demands that required redistribution.[59] In France, the French government concurred with the creation of the French Muslim Council, made up of representatives of mosques: the larger the mosque (measured in square footage), the greater the number of representatives, a regulation that facilitated the domination of mosques funded by the Gulf states. Muslim women have little chance of being heard either within community or outside of it as conservative men become the legitimized representatives of community.[60] Finally, in Canada, the Ontario government has resisted the demand for Black-focused schools, a measure intended to counter the drop-out rate of African Canadians, a national commitment to multiculturalism notwithstanding. Under these conditions, it would not have been easy for Muslim women to contest the meaning of what it means to be a Muslim and a citizen of a modern state. If feminists had few tools with which to confront the strategies of governance in neoliberal and white-supremacist states, however, at the very least we could have refrained from deliberately invoking the spectre of a clash of civilizations and the necessity of keeping pre-modern peoples in line.

I do not have answers for negotiating the currents of contemporary neoliberalism and empire, only suggested strategies to interrupt the powerful deployment of the imperilled Muslim woman as the means to draw a colour line between the modern and the pre-modern. My suggestions concern subjecting the state to as much scrutiny as we do conservative religious groups. Where I run aground, however, is in the perception of risk. Many of my good friends breathed a sigh of relief when Premier McGuinty announced the end of faith-based arbitration. These are friends who know the power of fundamentalism and how much it oppresses women. They are women who insist that Sharia always works in favour of men and that for it to work otherwise requires considerable resources that Canadian Muslim women do not have. Making equality arguments within Islam certainly requires a long-term strategy. As things stand, Canadian Muslim communities will continue to use Islamic principles informally and women remain unprotected in this arena. However, should a woman be able to turn to common law, something that requires resources and a willingness to live without community, the possibility exists that she may be able to secure her rights under Western law. But here too, we must note that Muslim women's experiences of Canadian law have not been entirely positive and that our secular state is a racist state, complete with patriarchal and racist judges. At the end of the day, something positive may have been achieved in that the plans of a small conservative religious faction may have been upset, but it has been achieved through reinforcing some rather terrible dualisms (women's rights versus multiculturalism; West versus Muslims; enlightened Western feminists versus imperilled Muslim women) that, in a post-9/11 era, has tremendous utility for states seeking to regulate Muslim populations. Was it worth it? Only time will tell, but my guess is that the way is paved, if it was not before, for the kinds of laws we are seeing in Europe, which are enacted in the name of protecting Muslim women but are thinly disguised methods of putting Muslim populations under heavy surveillance while relieving the state of scrutiny about its practices towards both Muslims and all women. As in the narratives of rescue with which I began, it seems likely that Muslim women won some protection, but only at the cost of increasing anti-Muslim/anti-immigrant racism and consolidating the idea of civilized Europeans. When the "war on terror" in the West requires imperilled Muslim women and dangerous Muslim men as a central part of its conceptual apparatus, we become obligated as anti-imperial feminists to pursue anti-patriarchal strategies within, rather than outside, our communities, the difficulties of doing so notwithstanding.

NOTES

1 Asad 2003, 17.
2 Wikan 2004.
3 Razack 2004b.
4 *Arbitration Act* 1991, c. 17.
5 Yelaja and Benzie 2005.
6 Razack 2004a; Rajagopal 2003; Grewal 1999.
7 Grewal 2005, 152.
8 Moore 2007. Also, Muslim Women of the Hidaya Association 2007.
9 Kampmark 2003.
10 Boyd 2004
11 Warren 2003.

12 Elgert 2003, A19.
13 Harkirpal Singh 2003, A23.
14 Harris 2003, A15
15 Boyd 2004, 5.
16 Canadian Council of Muslim Women n.d.
17 Ibid.
18 Women Living Under Muslim Laws 2005.
19 Ibid.
20 For example, Leti Volpp has responded to Susan Moller Okin's polemical essay in which Okin argues that multiculturalism is bad for women (an argument that relies upon the case example of forced marriages, among other practices). Okin's position reinstals the West as superior in a number of ways, Volpp points out. First, the West is represented as more advanced and less patriarchal than Muslim societies, and the immigrant/Muslim woman is represented as a victim of her culture and devoid of agency in contrast to her freer Western sister. Second, the free, autonomous Western woman and her oppressed Third World sister who is mired in tradition "elides the level of violence intrinsic to the United States." Third World cultures are essentialized and static and feminist liberation means a life somehow lived outside of culture, or at least outside Third World culture. Within such dichotomies, it is difficult to understand the forces that influence cultural practices and identifying practices that would strengthen women's contestations within culture. Volpp 2001, 1181. See also Honig 1999.
21 Anthias 2002, 275.
22 Ibid. 285.
23 Narayan 1997, 33.
24 Pascale Fournier for the Canadian Council of Muslim Women 2004.
25 Women's LEAF 2004. LEAF's revised position was contained in a press release and letter to Michael Bryant, the then attorney general. Women's LEAF 2005 on file with author.
26 Public Meeting 2004.
27 Boyd 2004, 100.
28 Ibid. 89.
29 DiManno 2005.
30 Hurst 2005.
31 Siddiqui 2005.
32 Ray 2003.
33 Quillen 2001,138.
34 Grewal 2005, 27.
35 Jamal 2005.
36 Ibid. 75–6.
37 Gokariksel and Mitchell 2005.
38 See Razack 2006, on which chapter 1 is based.
39 Asad 2004; also reproduced in part as Asad 2005.
40 Asad 2004.
41 Ibid.
42 Ibid.
43 Asad 2003, 13.
44 Ibid. 14.
45 Balibar 1995.
46 I am grateful to Sedef Arat-Koç for reminding me of this point.

47 Gokariksel and Mitchell 2005, 149.
48 Berlant 1997, 192.
49 Delgado and Stefancic 1996, 773.
50 Ezekiel 2005, 233.
51 Sivanandan 2006, 3.
52 Fekete 2004, 4.
53 Ezekiel 2005, 231; Hage 2000.
54 De Sousa 2005.
55 Armstrong 2004.
56 Brunet 2005.
57 Peritz 2005.
58 Al-Hibri 1999, 45.
59 Sivanandan 2006, 3.
60 Ezekiel 2005, 233.

REFERENCES

Al-Hibri, Azizah. 1999. "Is Western Patriarchal Feminism Good for Third World/Minority Women?" In *Is Multiculturalism Bad for Women?* ed. Joshua Cohen, Matthew Howard, and Martha C. Nussbaum, 41–6. Princeton: Princeton University Press.

Anthias, Floya. 2002. "Beyond Feminism and Multiculturalism." *Women's Studies International Forum* 25 (3): 275–86. http://dx.doi.org/10.1016/S0277-5395(02)00259-5.

Arbitration Act. 1991. S.O. c. 17.

Armstrong, Sally. 2004. "Criminal Justice. Commentary." *Chatelaine* 77 (11): 152–7.

Asad, Talal. 2005. "Reflections on Laicité and the Public Sphere." *Items and Issues* 5, no. 3, Social Science Research Council. http://www.ssrc.org/publications/items/v5n5/refelctions2.html.

Asad, Talal. 2004. "Reflections on Laicité and the Public Sphere." Keynote address at the Beirut Conference on Public Spheres, October 22–24. https://www.scribd.com/document/36116973/Talal-Asad-Reflections-on-Secularism-and-the-Public-Sphere.

Asad, Talal. 2003. *Formations of the Secular*. Stanford: Stanford University Press.

Balibar, Étienne. 1995. "Ambiguous Universality." *Differences: A Journal of Feminist Cultural Studies* 7 (1): 48–74.

Berlant, Lauren. 1997. *The Queen of America Goes to Washington City*. Durham: Duke University Press.

Boyd, Marion. 2004. "Dispute Resolution in Family Law: Protecting Choice, Promoting Inclusion." *Ministry of Attorney General*, http://www.attorneygeneral.jus.gov.on.ca/english/about/pubs/boyd/executivesummary.pdf.

Brunet, Ariane. 2005. "Canada: Women Criticize Sharia." *Gazette Montreal*, April 15

Canadian Council of Muslim Women. n.d. "An Open Letter to Premier Dalton McGuinty and Attorney General Michael Bryant," http://beta.ccmw.com/wp-content/uploads/2013/04/CCMW-Open-Letter-to-Premier-Dalton-McGuinty-and-Attorney-General-Michael-Bryant-January-2005.pdf.

De Sousa, Mike. 2005. "Keep Islamic Law out of Canada, Quebec Politicians Urge." *Montreal Gazette*, March 11, A1.

Delgado, Richard, and Jean Stefancic. 1996. "Cosmopolitan Inside Out: International Norms and the Struggle for Civil Rights and Local Justice." *Connecticut Law Review* 27 (3): 773–88.

DiManno, Rosie. 2005. "Sharia Solution a Fair One, and Not Racist." *Toronto Star*, September 16, A2.

Elgert, Ken. 2003. "Islamic Law a Step Toward Legal Apartheid." *Edmonton Journal,* December 4, A19.

Ezekiel, Judith. 2005. "Magritte Meets Maghreb: This Is Not a Veil." *Australian Feminist Studies* 20 (47): 231–43. http://dx.doi.org/10.1080/08164640500090400.

Fekete, Liz. 2004. "Anti-Muslim Racism and the European Security State." *Race & Class* 46 (1): 3–29. http://dx.doi.org/10.1177/0306396804045512.

Gokariksel, Banu, and Katharyne Mitchell. 2005. "Veiling, Secularism, and the Neo-liberal Subject: National Narratives and Supranational Desires in Turkey and France." *Global Networks* 5 (2): 147–65. http://dx.doi.org/10.1111/j.1471-0374.2005.00112.x.

Grewal, Inderpal. 2005. *Transnational America: Feminisms, Diasporas, Neoliberalisms.* Durham, London: Duke University Press. http://dx.doi.org/10.1215/9780822386544.

Grewal, Inderpal. 1999. "Women's Rights as Human Rights: Feminist Practices, Global Feminism and Human Rights Regimes in Transnationality." *Citizenship Studies* 3 (3): 337–54. http://dx.doi.org/10.1080/13621029908420719.

Hage, Ghassan. 2000. *White Nation: Fantasies of White Supremacy in a Multicultural Society.* New York, London: Routledge.

Harkirpal Singh, Sara. 2003. "Religious Law Undermines Loyalty to Canada." *Vancouver Sun,* December 10, A23.

Harris, Ghammim. 2003. "Sharia Is Not a Law by Canadian Standards." *Vancouver Sun,* December 15, A15.

Honig, Bonnie. 1999. "My Culture Made Me Do It': Response to Okin." In *Is Multiculturalism Bad for Women?* ed. Joshua Cohen, Matthew Howard, and Martha C. Nussbaum, 35–40. Princeton, NJ: Princeton University Press.

Hurst, Lynda. 2005. "Distortions and Red Herrings." *Toronto Star,* September 17, A6.

Jamal, Amina. 2005. "Transnational Feminism as Critical Practice: A Reading of Feminist Discourses in Pakistan." *Meridians (Middletown, Conn.)* 5 (2): 57–82. http://dx.doi.org/10.2979/MER.2005.5.2.57.

Kampmark, Binoy. 2003. "Islam, Women and Australia's Cultural Discourse of Terror." *Hecate* 29 (1): 86–105.

Moore, Dene. 2007. "Muslims Visit Quebec Town." *Toronto Star,* February 12.

Muslim Women of the Hidaya Association. 2007. Email communication, February 12, m_hayder@hotmail.com.

Narayan, Uma. 1997. *Dislocating Cultures: Identities, Traditions, and Third World Feminism.* New York: Routledge.

Fournier, Pascale, and the Canadian Council of Muslim Women. 2004. "The Reception of Muslim Family Law in Western Liberal States." http://archive.ccmw.com/documents/PositionPapers/pascale_paper.pdf.

Peritz, Ingrid. 2005. "Ebadi Decries Islamic Law for Canada." *Globe and Mail,* June 14, A7.

Public Meeting. 2004. "International Campaign Against Sharia Courts in Canada." Held at Oriole Community Centre, 2975 Don Mills Rd., Toronto, June 26.

Quillen, Carol. 2001. "Reply to Chow and Nussbaum." *Signs (Chicago, Ill.)* 27 (1): 136–8. http://dx.doi.org/10.1086/495674.

Rajagopal, Balakrishnan. 2003. *International Law from Below: Development, Social Movements and Third World Resistance.* Cambridge, New York: Cambridge University Press. http://dx.doi.org/10.1017/CBO9780511494079.

Ray, Sangeeta. 2003. "Against Earnestness: The Place of Performance in Feminist Theory." *Journal of Practical Feminist Philosophy* 3 (1): 68–79. http://dx.doi.org/10.5840/studpracphil2003314.

Razack, Sherene H. 2004a. *Dark Threats and White Knights: The Somalia Affair, Peacekeeping, and the New Imperialism*. Toronto: University of Toronto Press.

Razack, Sherene H. 2004b. "Imperilled Muslim Women, Dangerous Muslim Men and Civilised Europeans: Legal and Social Responses to Forced Marriages." *Feminist Legal Studies* 12 (2): 129–74. http://dx.doi.org/10.1023/B:FEST.0000043305.66172.92.

Razack, Sherene. 2006. "'Your Client Has a Profile': Race and Security in Canada." Working paper, Court Challenges Program.

Siddiqui, Haroon. 2005. "Sharia Is Gone but Fear and Hostility Remain." *Toronto Star*, September 15, A25.

Sivanandan, A. 2006. "Race, Terror and Civil Society." *Race & Class* 47 (3): 1–8. http://dx.doi.org/10.1177/0306396806061083.

Volpp, Leti. 2001. "Feminism versus Multiculturalism." *Columbia Law Review* 101 (5): 1181–1218. http://dx.doi.org/10.2307/1123774.

Warren, David. 2003. "Multiculturalism—from Britannia to Sharia." *National Post*, December 8, A14.

Wikan, Unni. 2004. "Honour Killings and the Problem of Justice in Modern-day Europe." Paper presented at the conference Social Development, Social Inequalities and Social Justice, Jean Piaget Society, Toronto, Ontario, June 4.

Women's Legal Education and Action Fund. 2005. "Revised Position in Response to Marion Boyd's Report on the Use of the Ontario Arbitration Act for Religious Arbitration of Family Law."

Women's Legal Education and Actual Fund (LEAF). 2004. "Submission to Marion Boyd in Relation to Her Review of the *Arbitration Act*." September 17, http://archive.ccmw.com/activities/act_arb_submission_marionboyd.html.

Women Living Under Muslim Laws. 2005. "Call for Action: Support Canadian Women's Struggle against Sharia Courts." April 7, http://www.wluml.org/action/canada-support-canadian-womens-struggle-against-sharia-courts.

Yelaja, Prithi, and Robert Benzie. 2005. "McGuinty: No Sharia Law." *Toronto Star*, September 12, A1.

5 Looking for My Penis: The Eroticized Asian in Gay Video Porn

RICHARD FUNG

> Several scientists have begun to examine the relation between personality and human reproductive behaviour from a gene-based evolutionary perspective ... In this vein we reported a study of racial difference in sexual restraint such that Orientals > whites > blacks. Restraint was indexed in numerous ways, having in common a lowered allocation of bodily energy to sexual functioning. We found the same racial pattern occurred on gamete production (dizygotic birthing frequency per 100: Mongoloids, 4; Caucasoids, 8; Negroids, 16), intercourse frequencies (premarital, marital, extramarital), developmental precocity (age at first intercourse, age at first pregnancy, number of pregnancies), primary sexual characteristics (size of penis, vagina, testis, ovaries), secondary sexual characteristics (salient voice, muscularity, buttocks, breasts), and biologic control of behaviour (periodicity of sexual response, predictability of life of life history from onset of puberty), as well as in androgen levels and sexual attitudes.

This passage from the *Journal of Research in Personality* was written by University of Western Ontario psychologist Philippe Rushton (with Anthony Bogaert), who enjoys considerable controversy in Canadian academic circles and in the popular media. His thesis, articulated throughout his work, appropriates biological studies of the continuum of reproductive strategies of oysters through to chimpanzees and posits that degree of "sexuality" – interpreted as penis and vagina size, frequency of intercourse, buttock and lip size – correlates positively with criminality and sociopathic behaviour and inversely with intelligence, health, and longevity. Rushton sees race as the determining factor and places East Asians (Rushton uses the word Orientals) on one end of the spectrum and blacks on the other. Since whites fall squarely in the middle, the position of perfect balance, there is no need for analysis, and they remain free of scrutiny.

Notwithstanding its profound scientific shortcomings, Rushton's work serves as an excellent articulation of a dominant discourse on race and sexuality in Western society – a system of ideas and reciprocal practices that originated in Europe simultaneously with (some argue as a conscious justification for)[1] colonial expansion and slavery. In the nineteenth century these ideas took on a scientific gloss with social Darwinism and eugenics. Now they reappear, somewhat altered, in psychology journals from the likes of Rushton. It is important to add that these ideas have also permeated the global popular consciousness. Anyone who has been exposed to Western television or advertising images, which is much of the world, will have absorbed this particular constellation of stereotyping and racial hierarchy. In Trinidad in the 1960s, on the outer reaches of the empire, everyone in my schoolyard was thoroughly versed in these "truths" about the races.

Historically, most organizing against racism has concentrated on fighting discrimination that stems from the intelligence-social behaviour variable assumed by Rushton's scale. Discrimination based on perceived intellectual ability does, after all, have direct ramifications in terms of education and employment, and therefore for survival. Until recently, issues of gender and sexuality remained a low priority for those who claimed to speak for the communities.[2] But antiracist strategies that fail to subvert the race-gender status quo are of seriously limited value. Racism cannot be narrowly defined in terms of race hatred. Race is a factor in even our most intimate relationships.

The contemporary construction of race and sex as exemplified by Rushton has endowed black people, both men and women, with a threatening hypersexuality. Asians, on the other hand, are collectively seen as undersexed.[3] But here I want to make some crucial distinctions. First, in North America stereotyping has focused almost exclusively on what recent colonial language designates as "Orientals" – that is East and Southeast Asian peoples – as opposed to the "Orientalism" discussed by Edward Said (1978), which concerns the Middle East. This current, popular usage is based more on a perception of similar physical features – black hair, "slanted" eyes, high cheek bones, and so on – than through a reference to common cultural traits. South Asians, people whose backgrounds are in the Indian subcontinent and Sri Lanka, hardly figure at all in North American popular representations, and those few images are ostensibly devoid of sexual connotation.[4]

Second, within the totalizing stereotype of the "Oriental," there are competing and sometimes contradictory sexual associations based on nationality. So, for example, a person could be seen as Japanese and somewhat kinky, or Filipino and "available." The very same person could also be seen as "Oriental" and therefore sexless. In addition, the racial hierarchy revamped by Rushton is itself in tension with an earlier and only partially eclipsed depiction of all Asians as having an undisciplined and dangerous libido. I am referring to the writings of the early European explorers and missionaries, but also to antimiscegenation laws and such specific legislation as the 1912 Saskatchewan law that barred white women from employment in Chinese-owned businesses.

Finally, East Asian women figure differently from men both in reality and in representation. In "Lotus Blossoms Don't Bleed," Renee Tajima (1984) points out that in Hollywood films:

> There are two basic types: the Lotus Blossom Baby (a.k.a. China Doll, Geisha Girl, shy Polynesian beauty, et al.) and the Dragon Lady (Fu Manchu's various female relations, prostitutes, devious madames) ... Asian women in film are, for the most part, passive figures who exist to serve men – as love interests for white men (re: Lotus Blossoms) or as partners in crime for men of their own kind (re: Dragon Ladies). (28)

Further:

> Dutiful creatures that they are, Asian women are often assigned the task of expendability in a situation of illicit love. ... Noticeably lacking is the portrayal of love relationships between Asian women and Asian men, particularly as lead characters. (29)

Because of their supposed passivity and sexual compliance, Asian women have been fetishized in dominant representation, and there is a large and growing body of literature by Asian women on the oppressiveness of these images. Asian men, however – at least since

Sessue Hayakawa, who made a Hollywood career in the 1920s of representing the Asian man as sexual threat[5] – have been consigned to one of two categories: the egghead/wimp, or – in what may be analogous to the lotus blossom-dragon lady dichotomy – the kung fu master/ninja/samurai. He is sometimes dangerous, sometimes friendly, but almost always characterized by a desexualized Zen asceticism. So whereas, as Fanon tells us, "the Negro is eclipsed. He is turned into a penis. He is a penis,"[6] the Asian man is defined by a striking absence down there. And if Asian men have no sexuality, how can we have homosexuality?

Even as recently as the early 1980s, I remember having to prove my queer credentials before being admitted with other Asian men into a Toronto gay club. I do not believe it was a question of a colour barrier. Rather, my friends and I felt that the doorman was genuinely unsure about our sexual orientation. We also felt that had we been white and dressed similarly, our entrance would have been automatic.[7]

Although a motto for the lesbian and gay movements has been "we are everywhere," Asians are largely absent from the images produced by both the political and the commercial sectors of the mainstream gay and lesbian communities. From the earliest articulation of the Asian gay and lesbian movements, a principal concern has therefore been visibility. In political organizing, the demand for a voice, or rather the demand to be heard, has largely been responded to by the problematic practice of "minority" representation on panels and boards.[8] But since racism is a question of power and not of numbers, this strategy has often led to a dead-end tokenistic integration, failing to address the real imbalances.

Creating a space for Asian gay and lesbian representation has meant among other things, deepening an understanding of what is at stake for Asians in coming out publicly.[9] As is the case for many other people of colour and especially immigrants, our families and our ethnic communities are a rare source of affirmation in a racist society. In coming out, we risk (or feel that we risk) losing this support, though the ever-growing organizations of lesbian and gay Asians have worked against this process of cultural exile. In my own experience, the existence of a gay Asian community broke down the cultural schizophrenia in which I related on the one hand to a heterosexual family that affirmed my ethnic culture and on the other to a gay community that was predominantly white. Knowing that there was support also helped me come out to my family and further bridge the gap.

If we look at commercial gay sexual representation, it appears that the antiracist movements have had little impact: the images of men and male beauty are still of white men and white male beauty. These are the standards against which we compare both ourselves and often our brothers – Asian, black, native, and Latino.[10] Although other people's rejection (or fetishization) of us according to the established racial hierarchies may be experienced as oppressive, we are not necessarily moved to scrutinize our own desire and its relationship to the hegemonic image of the white man.[11]

In my lifelong vocation of looking for my penis, trying to fill in the visual void, I have come across only a handful of primary and secondary references to Asian male sexuality in North American representation. Even in my own video work, the stress has been on deconstructing sexual representation and only marginally on creating erotica. So I was very excited at the discovery of a Vietnamese American working in gay porn.

Having acted in six videotapes, Sum Yung Mahn is perhaps the only Asian to qualify as a gay porn "star." Variously known as Brad Troung or Sam or Sum Yung Mahn, he has worked for a number of different production studios. All of the tapes in which he appears are distributed through International Wavelength, a San Francisco-based mail order company whose catalogue entries feature Asians in American, Thai, and Japanese productions.

According to the owner of International Wavelength, about 90 per cent of the Asian tapes are bought by white men, and the remaining 10 per cent are purchased by Asians. But the number of Asian buyers is growing.

In examining Sum Yung Mahn's work, it is important to recognize the different strategies used for fitting an Asian actor into the traditionally white world of gay porn and how the terms of entry are determined by the perceived demands of an intended audience. Three tapes, each geared towards a specific erotic interest, illustrate these strategies.

Below the Belt (1985), directed by Philip St. John, California Dream Machine Productions), like most porn tapes, has an episodic structure. All the sequences involve the students and sensei of an all-male karate dojo. The authenticity of the setting is proclaimed with the opening shots of a gym full of gi-clad, serious-faced young men going through their weapons exercises. Each of the main actors is introduced in turn; with the exception of the teacher, who has dark hair, all fit into the current porn conventions of Aryan, blond, shaved, good looks.[12] Moreover, since Sum Yung Mahn is not even listed in the opening credits, we can surmise that this tape is not targeted to an audience with any particular erotic interest in Asian men. Most gay video porn exclusively uses white actors; those tapes having the least bit of racial integration are pitched to the specialty market through outlets such as International Wavelength.[13] This visual apartheid stems, I assume, from an erroneous perception that the sexual appetites of gay men are exclusive and unchangeable.

A karate dojo offers a rich opportunity to introduce Asian actors. One might imagine it as the gay orientalist's dream project. But given the intended audience for this video, the erotic appeal of the dojo, except for the costumes and a few misplaced props (Taiwanese and Korean flags for a Japanese art form?) are completely appropriated into a white world.

The tape's action occurs in a gym, in the students' apartments, and in a garden. The one scene with Sum Yung Mahn is a dream sequence. Two students, Robbie and Stevie, are sitting in a locker room. Robbie confesses that he has been having strange dreams about Greg, their teacher. Cut to the dream sequence, which is coded by clouds of green smoke. Robbie is wearing a red headband with black markings suggesting script (if indeed they belong to an Asian language, they are not the Japanese or Chinese characters that one would expect). He is trapped in an elaborate snare. Enter a character in a black ninja mask, wielding a nanchaku. Robbie narrates: "I knew this evil samurai would kill me." The masked figure is menacingly running the nanchaku chain under Robbie's genitals when Greg, the teacher, appears and disposes of him. Robbie explains to Stevie in the locker room: "I knew that I owed him my life, and I knew I had to please him [long pause] in any way that he wanted." During that pause we cut back to the dream. Amid more puffs of smoke, Greg, carrying a man in his arms, approaches a low platform. Although Greg's back is towards the camera, we can see that the man is wearing the red headband that identifies him as Robbie. As Greg lays him down, we see that Robbie has "turned Japanese"! It's Sum Yung Mahn.

Greg fucks Sum Yung Mahn, who is always face down.

The scene constructs anal intercourse for the Asian Robbie as an act of submission, not of pleasure: unlike other scenes of anal intercourse in the tape, for example, there is no dubbed dialogue on the order of "Oh yeah ... fuck me harder!" but merely ambiguous groans. Without coming, Greg leaves. A group of (white) men wearing Japanese outfits encircle the platform, and Asian Robbie, or "the Oriental boy," as he is listed in the final credits, turns to lie on his back. He sucks a cock, licks someone's balls. The other men come all over his body; he comes. The final shot of the sequence zooms in to a close-up of Sum Yung Mahn's headband, which dissolves to a similar close-up of Robbie wearing the same headband, emphasizing that the two actors represent one character.

We now cut back to the locker room. Robbie's story has made Stevie horny. He reaches into Robbie's pants, pulls out his penis, and sex follows. In his Asian manifestation, Robbie is fucked and sucks others off (Greek passive/French active/ bottom). His passivity is pronounced, and he is never shown other than prone. As a white man, his role is completely reversed: he is at first sucked off by Stevie, and then he fucks him (Greek active/French passive/top). Neither of Robbie's manifestations veers from his prescribed role.

To a greater extent than most other gay porn tapes, *Below the Belt* is directly about power. The hierarchical dojo setting is milked for its evocation of dominance and submission. With the exception of one very romantic sequence midway through the tape, most of the actors stick to their defined roles of top or bottom. Sex, especially anal sex, as punishment is a recurrent image. In this genre of gay pornography, the role-playing in the dream sequence is perfectly apt. What is significant, however, is how race figures into the equation. In a tape that appropriates emblems of Asian power (karate), the only place for a real Asian actor is as a caricature of passivity. Sum Yung Mahn does not portray an Asian, but rather the literalization of a metaphor, so that by being passive, Robbie actually becomes "Oriental." At a more practical level, the device of the dream also allows the producers to introduce an element of the mysterious, the exotic, without disrupting the racial status quo of the rest of the tape. Even in the dream sequence, Sum Yung Mahn is at the centre of the frame as spectacle, having minimal physical involvement with the men around him. Although the sequence ends with his climax, he exists for the pleasure of others.

Richard Dyer (1985), writing about gay porn, states that:

> although the pleasure of anal sex (i.e., of being anally fucked) is represented, the narrative is never organized around the desire to be fucked, but around the desire to ejaculate (whether or not following from anal intercourse). Thus, although at a level of public representation gay men may be thought of as deviant and disruptive of masculine norms because we assert the pleasure of being fucked and the eroticism of the anus, in our pornography this takes a back seat. (28)

Although Tom Waugh's amendment to this argument – that anal pleasure is represented in individual sequence[14] – also holds true for *Below the Belt*, as a whole the power of the penis and the pleasure of ejaculation are clearly the narrative's organizing principles. As with the vast majority of North American tapes featuring Asians, the problem is not the representation of anal pleasure, per se, but rather that the narratives privilege the penis while always assigning the Asian the role of bottom; Asian and anus are conflated. In the case of Sum Yung Mahn, being fucked may well be his personal sexual preference. But the fact remains that there are very few occasions in North American video porn in which an Asian fucks a white man, so few, in fact, that International Wavelength promotes the tape *Studio X* (1986) with the blurb "Sum Yung Mahn makes history as the first Asian who fucks a non-Asian."[15]

Although I agree with Waugh that in gay as opposed to straight porn "the spectator's positions in relation to the representations are open and in flux," this observation applies only when all the participants are white. Race introduces another dimension that may serve to close down some of this mobility. This is not to suggest that the experience of gay men of colour with this kind of sexual representation is the same as that of heterosexual women with regard to the gendered gaze of straight porn. For one thing, Asian gay men are men. We can therefore physically experience the pleasures depicted on the screen, since we too have erections and ejaculations and can experience anal penetration. A shifting identification may occur despite the racially defined roles, and most gay Asian men in North America are used to obtaining pleasure from all-white pornography. This, of course, goes hand in hand with many problems of self-image and sexual identity. Still, I have been struck by the unanimity with which gay Asian men I have met, from all over this continent as well as from Asia, immediately identify and resist these representations. Whenever I mention the topic of Asian actors in American porn, the first question I am asked is whether the Asian is simply shown getting fucked.

Asian Knights (1985, directed by Ed Sung. William Richhe Productions), the second tape I want to consider, has an Asian producer-director and a predominantly Asian cast. In its first scenario, two Asian men, Brad and Rick, are seeing a white psychiatrist because they are unable to have sex with each other:

> RICK: We never have sex with other Asians. We usually have sex with Caucasian guys.
> COUNSELOR: Have you had the opportunity to have sex together?
> RICK: Yes, a coupla times, but we never get going.

Homophobia, like other forms of oppression, is seldom dealt with in gay video porn. With the exception of safe sex tapes that attempt a rare blend of the pedagogical with the pornographic, social or political issues are not generally associated with the erotic. It is therefore unusual to see one of the favoured discussion topics for gay Asian consciousness-raising groups employed as a sex fantasy in *Asian Knights*. The desexualized image of Asian men that I have described has seriously affected our relationships with one another, and often gay Asian men find it difficult to see each other beyond the terms of platonic friendship or competition, to consider other Asian men as lovers.

True to the conventions of porn, minimal counseling from the psychiatrist convinces Rick and Brad to shed their clothes. Immediately sprouting erections, they proceed to have sex. But what appears to be an assertion of gay Asian desire is quickly derailed. As Brad and Rick make love on the couch, the camera cross-cuts to the psychiatrist looking on from an armchair. The rhetoric of the editing suggests that we are observing the two Asian men from his point of view. Soon the white man takes off his clothes and joins in. He immediately takes up a position at the centre of the action – and at the centre of the frame. What appeared to be a "conversion fantasy" for gay Asian desire was merely a ruse. Brad and Rick's temporary mutual absorption really occurs to establish the superior sexual draw of the white psychiatrist, a stand-in for the white male viewer who is the real sexual subject of the tape. And the question of Asian-Asian desire, though presented as the main narrative force of the sequence, is deflected, or rather reframed from a white perspective.

Sex between the two Asian men in this sequence can be related somewhat to heterosexual sex in some gay porn films, such as those produced by the Gage brothers. In *Heatstroke* (1982), for example, sex with a woman is used to establish the authenticity of the straight man who is about to be seduced into gay sex. It dramatizes the significance of the conversion from the sanctioned object of desire, underscoring the power of the gay man to incite desire in his socially defined superior. It is also tied up with the fantasies of (female) virginity and conquest in Judeo-Christian and other patriarchal societies. The therapy-session sequence of *Asian Knights* also suggests parallels to representations of lesbians in straight porn, representations that are not meant to eroticize women loving women, but rather to titillate and empower the sexual ego of the heterosexual male viewer.

Asian Knights is organized to sell representations of Asians to white men. Unlike Sum Yung Mahn in *Below the Belt*, the actors are therefore more expressive and sexually assertive, as often the seducers as the seduced. But though the roles shift during the predominantly oral sex, the Asians remain passive in anal intercourse, except that they are now shown to want it! How much this assertion of agency represents a step forward remains a question.

Even in the one sequence of *Asian Knights* in which the Asian actor fucks the white man, the scenario privileges the pleasure of the white man over that of the Asian. The sequence begins with the Asian reading a magazine. When the white man (played by porn star Eric Stryker) returns home from a hard day at the office, the waiting Asian asks how his day went, undresses him (even taking off his socks), and proceeds to massage his back.[16] The Asian man acts the role of the mythologized geisha or "the good wife" as fantasized in the mail-order bride business. And, in fact, the "house boy" is one of the most persistent white fantasies about Asian men. The fantasy is also a reality in many Asian countries where economic imperialism gives foreigners, whatever their race, the pick of handsome men in financial need. The accompanying cultural imperialism grants status to those Asians with white lovers. White men who for various reasons, especially age, are deemed unattractive in their own countries suddenly find themselves elevated and desired.

From the opening shot of painted lotus blossoms on a screen to the shot of a Japanese garden that separates the episodes, from the Chinese pop music to the chinoiserie in the apartment, there is a conscious attempt in *Asian Knights* to evoke a particular atmosphere.[17] Self-conscious "Oriental" signifiers are part and parcel of a colonial fantasy – and reality – that empowers one kind of gay man over another. Though I have known Asian men in dependent relations with older, wealthier white men, as an erotic fantasy the house boy scenario tends to work one way. I know of no scenarios of Asian men and white house boys. It is not the representation of the fantasy that offends, or even the fantasy itself, rather the uniformity with which these narratives reappear and the uncomfortable relationship they have to real social conditions.

International Skin (1985, directed by William Richhe, N'wayvo Richhe Productions), as its name suggests, features a Latino, a black man, Sum Yung Mahn, and a number of white actors. Unlike the other tapes I have discussed, there are no "Oriental" devices. And although Sum Yung Mahn and all the men of colour are inevitably fucked (without reciprocating), there is mutual sexual engagement between the white and nonwhite characters.

In this tape Sum Yung Mahn is Brad, a film student making a movie for his class. Brad is the narrator, and the film begins with a self-reflexive "head and shoulders" shot of Sum Yung Mahn explaining the scenario. The film we are watching supposedly represents Brad's point of view. But here again the tape is not targeted to black, Asian, or Latino men; though Brad introduces all of these men as his friends, no two men of colour ever meet on screen. Men of colour are not invited to participate in the internationalism that is being sold, except through identification with white characters. This tape illustrates how an agenda of integration becomes problematic if it frames the issue solely in terms of black-white, Asian-white mixing: it perpetuates a system of white-centeredness.

The gay Asian viewer is not constructed as sexual subject in any of this work – not on the screen, not as a viewer. I may find Sum Yung Mahn attractive, I may desire his body, but I am always aware that he is not meant for me. I may lust after Eric Stryker and imagine myself as the Asian who is having sex with him, but the role the Asian plays in the scene with him is demeaning. It is not that there is anything wrong with the image of servitude, per se, but rather that it is one of the few fantasy scenarios in which we figure, and we are always in the role of servant.

Are there then no pleasures for an Asian viewer? The answer to this question is extremely complex. There is first of all no essential Asian viewer. The race of the person viewing says nothing about how race figures in his or her own desires. Uni-racial white representations in porn may not in themselves present a problem in addressing many gay Asian men's desires. But the issue is not simply that porn may deny pleasures to some gay Asian men. We also need to examine what role the pleasure of porn plays in securing a consensus about race and desirability that ultimately works to our disadvantage.

Though the sequences I have focused on in the preceding examples are those in which the discourses about Asian sexuality are most clearly articulated, they do not define the totality of depiction in these tapes. Much of the time the actors merely reproduce or attempt to reproduce the conventions of pornography. The fact that, with the exception of Sum Yung Mahn, they rarely succeed – because of their body type, because Midwestern-cowboy porn dialect with Vietnamese intonation is just a bit incongruous, because they groan or gyrate just a bit too much – more than anything brings home the relative rigidity of the genre's codes. There is little seamlessness here. There are times, however, when the actors appear neither as simulated whites nor as symbolic others. There are several moments in *International Skin*, for example, in which the focus shifts from the genitals to hands caressing a body; these moments feel to me more "genuine." I do not mean this in the sense of an essential Asian sexuality, but rather a moment is captured in which the actor stops pretending. He does not stop acting, but he stops pretending to be a white porn star. I find myself focusing on moments like these, in which the racist ideology of the text seems to be temporarily suspended or rather eclipsed by the erotic power of the moment.

In "Pornography and the Doubleness of Sex for Women," Joanna Russ (1986) writes:

> Sex is ecstatic, autonomous and lovely for women. Sex is violent, dangerous and unpleasant for women. I don't mean a dichotomy (i.e., two kinds or women or even two kinds or sex) but rather a continuum in which no one's experience is wholly positive or negative. (39)

Gay Asian men are men and therefore not normally victims of the rape, incest, or other sexual harassment to which Russ is referring. However, there is a kind of doubleness, of ambivalence, in the way that Asian men experience contemporary North American gay communities. The "ghetto," the mainstream gay movement, can be a place of freedom and sexual identity. But it is also a site of racial, cultural, and sexual alienation sometimes more pronounced than that in straight society. For me sex is a source of pleasure, but also a site of humiliation and pain. Released from the social constraints against expressing overt racism in public, the intimacy of sex can provide my (non-Asian) partner an opening for letting me know my place – sometimes literally, as when after we come, he turns over and asks where I come from.[18] Most gay Asian men I know have similar experiences.

This is just one reality that differentiates the experiences and therefore the political priorities of gay Asians and, I think, other gay men of colour from those of white men. For one thing we cannot afford to take a libertarian approach. Porn can be an active agent in representing and reproducing a sex-race status quo. We cannot attain a healthy alliance without coming to terms with these differences.

The barriers that impede pornography from providing representations of Asian men that are erotic and politically palatable (as opposed to correct) are similar to those that inhibit the Asian documentary, the Asian feature, the Asian experimental film and videotape. We are seen as too peripheral, not commercially viable – not the general audience. *Looking for Langston* (1988), which is the first film I have seen that affirms rather than appropriates the sexuality of black gay men, was produced under exceptional economic circumstances that freed it from the constraints of the marketplace.[19] Should we call for an independent gay Asian pornography? Perhaps I am, in a utopian sort of way, though I feel that the problems in North America's porn conventions are manifold and go beyond the question of race. There is such a limited vision of what constitutes the erotic.

In Canada, the major debate about race and representation has shifted from an emphasis on the image to a discussion of appropriation and control of production and distribution – who gets to produce the work. But as we have seen in the case of *Asian Knights*, the race of the producer is no automatic guarantee of "consciousness" about these issues or of a different product. Much depends on who is constructed as the audience for the work. In any case, it is not surprising that under capitalism, finding my penis may ultimately be a matter of dollars and cents.

Discussion

AUDIENCE MEMBER: You made a comment about perceived distinctions between Chinese and Japanese sexuality. I have no idea what you mean.

RICHARD FUNG: In the West, there are specific sexual ambiences associated with the different Asian nationalities, sometimes based on cultural artifacts, sometimes on mere conjecture. These discourses exist simultaneously, even though in conflict with, totalizing notions of "Oriental" sexuality. Japanese male sexuality has come to be identified with strength, virility, perhaps a certain kinkiness, as signified for example by the clothing and gestures in *Below the Belt*. Japanese sexuality is seen as more "potent" than Chinese sexuality, which is generally represented as more passive and languorous. At the same time, there is the cliché that "all Orientals look alike." So in this paradox of the invisibility of difference lies the fascination. If he can ascertain where I'm from, he feels that he knows what he can expect from me. In response to this query about "ethnic origins," a friend of mine answers, "Where would you like me to be from?" I like this response because it gently confronts the question while maintaining the erotic possibilities of the moment.

SIMON WATNEY: I wanted to point out that the first film you showed, *Below the Belt*, presents us with a classic anxiety dream image. In it there is someone whose identity is that of a top man, but that identity is established in relation to a competing identity that allows him to enjoy sexual passivity, which is represented as a racial identity. It's as if he were in racial drag. I thought this film was extraordinary. Under what other conditions are Caucasian men invited to fantasize ourselves as racially other? And it seems to me that the only condition that would allow the visibility of that fantasy to be acted out in this way is the prior anxiety about a desired role, about top and bottom positions. This film is incredibly transparent and unconscious about how it construes or confuses sexual role-playing in relation to race. And the thrust of it all seems to be the construction of the Asian body as a kind of conciliatory pseudoheterosexuality for the white "top," who has anus envy, as it were.

FUNG: I completely agree. This film says too much for its own good by making this racist agenda so clear.

RAY NAVARRO: I think your presentation was really important, and it parallels research I'm doing with regard to the image of Latino men in gay male porn. I wondered if you might comment a bit more, however, about the class relations you find within this kind of work. For example, I've found a consistent theme running throughout gay white male porn of Latino men represented as either campesino or criminal. That is, it focuses less on body type – masculine, slight, or whatever – than on signifiers of class. It appears to be a class fantasy collapsed with a race fantasy, and in a way it parallels the actual power relations between the Latino stars and the producers and distributors, most of whom are white.

FUNG: There are ways in which your comments can also apply to Asians. Unlike whites and blacks, most Asians featured in gay erotica are younger men. Since youth generally implies less economical power, class-race hierarchies appear in most of the work. In the tapes I've been looking at, the occupations of the white actors are usually specified, while those of the Asians are not. The white actors are assigned fantasy appeal based on profession, whereas for the Asians, the sexual cachet of race is deemed sufficient. In *Asian Knights* there are also sequences in which the characters' lack of "work" carries connotations of the house-wife or, more particularly, the house boy.

There is at least one other way to look at this discrepancy. The lack of a specified occupation may be taken to suggest that the Asian actor is the subject of the fantasy, a surrogate for the Asian viewer, and therefore does not need to be coded with specific attributes.

TOM WAUGH: I think your comparison of the way the Asian male body is used in gay white porn to the way lesbianism is employed in heterosexual pornography is very interesting. You also suggested that racial markers in gay porn tend to close down its potential for openness and flux in identifications. Do you think we can take it further and say that racial markers in gay porn replicate, or function in the same way as, gender markers do in heterosexual pornography?

FUNG: What, in fact, I intended to say with my comparison of the use of lesbians in heterosexual porn and that of Asian male bodies in white gay male porn was that they're similar but also very different. I think that certain comparisons of gender with race are appropriate, but there are also profound differences. The fact that Asian gay men are men means that, as viewers, our responses to this work are grounded in our gender and the way gender functions in this society. Lesbians are women, with all that that entails. I suspect that although most Asian gay men experience ambivalence with white gay porn, the issues for women in relation to heterosexual pornography are more fundamental.

WAUGH: The same rigidity of roles seems to be present in most situations.

FUNG: Yes, that's true. If you notice the way the Asian body is spoken of in Rushton's work, the terms he uses are otherwise used when speaking of women. But it is too easy to discredit these arguments. I have tried instead to show how Rushton's conclusions are commensurate with the assumptions everywhere present in education and popular thought.

AUDIENCE MEMBER: I'm going to play devil's advocate. Don't you think gay Asian men who are interested in watching gay porn involving Asian actors will get a hold of the racially unmarked porn that is produced in Thailand or Japan? And if your answer is yes, then why should a white producer of gay porn go to the trouble of making tapes that cater to a relatively small gay Asian market? This is about dollars and cents. It seems obvious that the industry will cater to the white man's fantasy.

FUNG: On the last point I partially agree. That's why I'm calling for an independent porn in which the gay Asian man is producer, actor, and intended viewer. I say this somewhat half-heartedly, because personally I am not very interested in producing porn, though I do want to continue working with sexually explicit material. But I also feel that one cannot assume, as the porn industry apparently does, that the desires of even white men are so fixed and exclusive. Regarding the first part of your question, however, I must insist that Asian Americans and Asian Canadians are Americans and Canadians. I myself am a fourth-generation Trinidadian and have only a tenuous link with Chinese culture and aesthetics, except for what I have consciously searched after and learned. I purposely chose not to talk about Japanese or Thai productions because they come from cultural contexts about which I am incapable of commenting. In addition, the fact that porn from those countries is sometimes unmarked racially does not mean that it speaks to my experience or desires, my own culture of sexuality.

ISAAC JULIEN: With regard to race representation or racial signifiers in the context of porn, your presentation elaborated a problem that came up in some of the safe sex tapes that were shown earlier. In them one could see a kind of trope that traces a circular pattern – a repetition that leads a black or Asian spectator to a specific realm of fantasy. I wonder if you could talk a bit more about the role of fantasy, or the fantasy one sees in porn tapes produced predominantly by white producers. I see a fixing of different black subjects in recognizable stereotypes rather than a more dialectical representation of black identities, where a number of options or fantasy positions would be made available.

FUNG: Your last film, *Looking for Langston*, is one of the few films I know of that has placed the sexuality of the black gay subject at its center. As I said earlier, my own work, especially *Chinese Characters [1986]*, is more concerned with pulling apart the tropes you refer to than in constructing an alternative erotics. At the same time, I feel that this latter task is imperative and I hope that it is taken up more. It is in this context that I think the current attack on the National Endowment for the Arts and arts funding in the United States supports the racist status quo. If it succeeds, it effectively squelches the possibility of articulating counterhegemonic views of sexuality. Just before I left Toronto, I attended an event called "Cum Talk," organized by two people from Gay Asians Toronto and from Khush, the group for South Asian lesbians and gay men. We looked at porn and talked about the images people had of us, the role of "bottom" that we are constantly cast in. Then we spoke of what actually happened when we had sex with white men. What became clear was that we don't play out that role and are very rarely asked to. So there is a discrepancy between the ideology of sexuality and its practice, between sexual representation and sexual reality.

GREG BORDOWITZ: When Jean Carlomusto and I began working on the porn project at Gay Men's Health Crisis, we had big ideas of challenging many of the roles and positionings involved in the dominant industry. But as I've worked more with porn, I find that it's really not an efficient arena in which to make such challenges. There is some room to question assumptions, but there are not many ways to challenge the codes of porn, except to question the conditions of production, which was an important point raised at the end of your talk. It seems to me that the only real way to picture more possibilities is, again, to create self-determining groups, make resources available for people of color and lesbians and other groups so that they can produce porn for themselves.

FUNG: I only partly agree with you, because I think, so far as is possible, we have to take responsibility for the kinds of images we create, or re-create. *Asian Knights* had a Chinese producer, after all. But, yes, of course, the crucial thing is to activate more voices, which would establish the conditions for something else to happen. The liberal response to racism is that we need to integrate everyone – people should all become coffee-colored, or everyone should have sex with everyone else. But such an account doesn't often account for the specificity of our desires. I have seen very little porn produced from such an integrationist mentality that actually affirms my desire. It's so easy to find my fantasies appropriated for the pleasures of a white viewer. In that sense, porn is most useful for revealing relationships of power.

JOSÉ ARROYO: You've been talking critically about a certain kind of colonial imagery. Isaac's film *Looking for Langston* contains not only a deconstruction of this imagery in its critique of the Mapplethorpe photographs, but also a new construction of black desire. What kind of strategies do you see for a similar reconstructing of erotic Asian imagery?

FUNG: One of the first things that needs to be done is to construct Asians as viewing subjects. My first videotape, *Orientations [1984]*, had that as a primary goal. I thought of Asians as sexual subjects, but also as viewing subjects to whom the work should be geared. Many of us, whether we're watching news or pornography or looking at advertising, see that the image or message is not really being directed at us. For example, the sexism and heterosexism of a disk jockey's attitudes become obvious when he or she says. "When you and your girlfriend go out tonight. ..." Even though that's meant to address a general audience, it's clear that this audience is presumed not to have any women (not to mention lesbians!) in it. The general audience, as I analyse him, is white, male, heterosexual, middle-class, and centre-right politically. So we have to understand this presumption first, to see that only very specific people are being addressed. When I make my videotapes, I know that I am addressing Asians. That means that I can take certain things for granted and introduce other things in a completely different context. But there are still other questions of audience. When we make outreach films directed at the straight community – the "general public" – in an effort to make lesbian and gay issues visible, we often sacrifice many of the themes that are important to how we express our sexualities: drag, issues of promiscuity, and so on. But when I made a tape for a gay audience, I talked about those same issues very differently. For one thing, I talked about those issues. And I tried to image them in ways that were very different from the way the dominant media image them. In *Orientations* I had one guy talk about park and washroom sex – about being a slut, basically – in a park at midday with front lighting. He talked very straightforwardly about it, which is only to say that there are many possibilities for doing this. I think, however, that to talk about gay Asian desire is very difficult, because we need to swim through so much muck to get to it. It is very difficult (if even desirable) to do in purely positive terms, and I think it's necessary to do a lot of deconstruction along the way. I have no ready-made strategies; I feel it's a hit-and-miss sort of project.

LEI CHOU: I want to bring back the issue of class. One of the gay Asian stereotypes that you mentioned was the Asian house boy. The reality is that many of these people are immigrants: English is a second language for them, and they are thus economically disenfranchised through being socially and culturally displaced. So when you talk about finding the Asian penis in pornography, how will this project work for such people, since pornography is basically white and middle-class, what kind of tool is it? Who really is your target audience?

FUNG: If I understand your question correctly, you are asking about the prognosis for new and different representations within commercial porn. And I don't think that prognosis is very good: changes will probably happen very slowly. At the same time, I think that pornography is an especially important site of struggle precisely for those Asians who are, as you say, economically and socially at a disadvantage. For those who are most isolated, whether in families or rural areas, print pornography is often the first introduction to gay sexuality – before, for example, the gay and lesbian press or gay Asian support groups. But this porn provides mixed messages: it affirms gay identity articulated almost exclusively as white. Whether we like it or not, mainstream gay porn is more available to most gay Asian men than any independent work you or I might produce. That is why pornography is a subject of such concern for me.

NOTES

1 See Williams 1966.

2 Feminists of colour have long pointed out that racism is phrased differently for men and women. Nevertheless, since it is usually heterosexual (and often middle-class) males whose voices are validated by the power structure, it is their interests that are taken up as "representing" the communities. See Smith 1982, 162.

3 The mainstream "leadership" within Asian communities often colludes with the myth of the model minority and the reassuring desexualization of Asian people.

4 In Britain, however, more race-sex stereotypes of South Asians exist. Led by artists such as Pratibha Parnar, Sunil Gupta, and Hanif Kureishi, there is also growing and already significant body of work by South Asians themselves that takes up questions of sexuality.

5 See Gong 1982–83, 37–41.

6 Fanon 1970, 120. For a reconsideration of this statement in the light of contemporary black gay issues, see Mercer 1988, 141.

7 I do not think this could happen in today's Toronto, which now has the second-largest Chinese community on the continent. Perhaps it would not have happened in San Francisco. But I still believe that there is an onus on gay Asians and other gay people of colour to prove our homosexuality.

8 The term "minority" is misleading. Racism is not a matter of numbers but of power. This is especially clear in situations where people of colour constitute actual majorities, as in most former European colonies. At the same time, I feel that none of the current terms is really satisfactory and that too much time spent on the politics of "naming" can in the end be divisionary.

9 To organize effectively with lesbian and gay Asians, we must reject self-righteous condemnation of "closetedness" and see coming out more as a process or a goal, rather than as a prerequisite for participation in the movement.

10 Racism is available to be used by anyone. The conclusion that – because racism = power + prejudice – only white people can be racist is Eurocentric and simply wrong. Individuals have varying degrees and different sources of power, depending on the given moment in a shifting context. This does not contradict the fact, in contemporary North American society, racism is generally organized around white supremacy.

11 From simple observation, I feel safe in saying that most gay Asian men in North America hold white men as their idealized sexual partners. However, I am not trying to construct an argument for determinism, and there of outstanding problems that are not problems that are not easily answered by current analyses of power. What of the experience of Asians who are attracted to men of colour, including other Asians? What about white men who prefer Asians sexually? How and to what extent is desire articulated in terms of race as opposed to body type or other attributes? To what extent is sexual attraction exclusive or changeable? These questions are all politically loaded, as they parallel and impact the debates between essentialists and social constructionists on the nature of homosexuality itself. They are also emotionally charged, in that sexual choice involving race has been a basis for moral judgment.

12 See Dyer 1986. In his chapter on Marilyn Monroe, Dyer writes extensively on the relationship between blondness, whiteness, and desirability.

13 Print porn is somewhat more racially integrated, as are the new safe sex tapes – by the Gay Men's Health Crisis, for example – produced in a political and pedagogical rather than commercial context.

14 Waugh 1985, 31.
15 International Wavelength News 2 1991.
16 It seems to me that the undressing here is organized around the pleasure of the white man being served. This is contrast to the undressing scenes in, say James Bond films, in which the narrative is organized around undressing as an act of revealing the woman's body, an indicator of sexual conquest.
17 Interestingly, the gay video porn from Japan and Thailand that I have seen has none of this Oriental coding. Asianness is not taken up as a sign but is taken for granted as a setting for the narrative.
18 Though this is a common enough question in our postcolonial, urban environments, when asked of Asians, it often reveals two agendas: first, the assumption that all Asians are newly arrived immigrants and, second, a fascination with difference and sameness. Although we (Asians) all supposedly look alike, there are specific characteristics and stereotypes associated with each particular ethnic group. The inability to tell us apart underlies the inscrutability attributed to Asians. The "inscrutability" took on sadly ridiculous proportions when during World War II the Chinese were issued badges so that white Canadians could distinguish them from "the enemy."
19 For more on the origins of the black film and video workshops in Britain, see Pines 1988, 26.

REFERENCES

Asian Knights. 1985. Directed by Ed Sung. William Richhe Productions.
Below the Belt. 1985. Directed by Philip St John. California Dream Machine Productions.
Chinese Characters. 1986. Directed by Richard Fung.
Dyer, Richard. 1985. "Male Gay Porn: Coming to Terms." *Jump Cut* 30:27–9.
Dyer, Richard. 1986. *Heavenly Bodies: Film Stars and Society*. New York: St. Martin's.
Fanon, Frantz. 1970. *Black Skin, White Masks*. London: Paladin.
Gong, Stephen. 1982–83. "Zen Warrior of the Celluloid (Silent) Years: The Art of Sessue Hayakawa." *Bridge* 8 (Winter): 37–41.
Heatstroke. 1982. Directed by Tim Kincaid. Gagefilm Productions.
International Skin. 1985. Directed by William Richhe. N'wayvo Richhe Productions.
International Wavelength News 2 (Jan. 1991).
Looking for Langston. 1988. Directed by Issac Julien. U.K.; Sankofa Film and Video.
Mercer, Kobena. 1988. "Imaging the Black Man's Sex." In *Photography/Politics: Two*, edited by Pat Holland, Jo Spence, and Simon Watney, 141. London: Comedia/Methuen, 1987. Reprinted in *Male Order: Unwrapping Masculinity*, edited by Rowena Chapman and Jonathan Rutherford. London: Lawrence and Wishart.
Orientations. 1984. Directed by Richard Fung.
Pines, Jim. 1988. "The Cultural Context of Black British Cinema." In *Blackframes: Critical Perspectives on Black Independent Cinema*, ed. Mybe B. Cham and Claire Andrade-Watkins, 26–30. Cambridge: MIT Press.
Rushton, J. Phillipe, and Anthony F. Bogaert. 1988. "Race versus Social Class Difference in Sexual Behaviour: A Follow up Test of the r/K Dimension." *Journal of Research in Personality* 22 (3): 259–72. http://dx.doi.org/10.1016/0092-6566(88)90029-3.
Russ, Joanna. 1986. "Pornography and the Doubleness of Sex for Women." *Jump Cut* 32:38–41.
Said, Edward. 1978. *Orientalism*. London: Routledge and Kegan Paul.

Smith, Barbara. 1982. "Toward a Black Feminist Criticism." In *All the Women Are White, All the Blacks Are Men, But Some of Us Are Brave: Black Women's Studies*, ed. Gloria T. Hall, Patricia B. Scott, and Barbara Smith, 157–75. Old Westbury, NY: Feminist Press.

Studio X. 1986. International Wavelength.

Tajima, Renee. 1984. "Lotus Blossoms Don't Bleed: Images of Asian Women." In *Anthologies of Asian American Film and Video*, ed. Renee Tajima, 28–33. New York: Third World Newsreel.

Waugh, Tom. 1985. "Men's Pornography, Gay vs. Straight." *Jump Cut* 30:30–5.

Williams, Eric. 1966. *Capitalism and Slavery*. New York: Capricorn.

PART TWO

Ethnic Encounters

6 Cartographies of Violence: Creating Carceral Spaces and Expelling Japanese Canadians from the Nation

MONA OIKAWA

Introduction

This abridged chapter is from a book that analyses the testimonies of 21 Japanese Canadian women, 11 of whom were expelled from their homes on the west coast of Canada by the federal government in the 1940s and 10 of whom are daughters of the women expelled. Based on the emphases of the 11 women expelled on the descriptions of the places from which people were removed and to which they were sent, I argue that a spatial analysis is critical to an analysis of the Internment of Japanese Canadians.[1] This chapter commences such an analysis.

The Colonial Technologies of Expulsion, Forced Displacement, and Spatial Segregation

I begin this chapter by acknowledging that "unmapping"[2] Canada to find the cartography of the Internment requires acknowledging another map that has been rendered invisible – that of Indigenous nations on whose territories Canada was founded. The unmapping of Canada that this book advocates, therefore, begins by recognizing the making of Canada through colonialism and the use of colonial technologies against Indigenous peoples by the settler nation of Canada. Hence, the unmapping of the sites of the Internment must recognize the colonial cartographies of violence through which Canada was founded and the expulsion and forced displacement of Indigenous peoples.

The technologies[3] used against Indigenous peoples and authorized by the use of settler-state law, including the Indian Act,[4] such as expulsion, forced displacement, incarceration, segregation, dispossession, separation, destruction of families and communities, denigration of languages other than English and French, the role of the Christian churches in destroying traditional spiritual practices and numerous other methods have been implemented and practised for centuries. Settler control of Indigenous nations established techniques that could be adapted for the policing of immigrants and the eventual formulation and administration of the Internment. While the settler practices used against Indigenous peoples were clearly intended as acts of genocide and the practices of the Internment were initially intended to achieve the expulsion of all Japanese Canadians from Canada, they must be seen as relational. Colonial technologies are foundational to the making of Canada and the "spatial organization of domination."[5] Although I would not conflate the processes of settler colonialism and the Internment, I would stress that it is essential to see them as linked.

The technologies of expulsion and forced displacement that were used against Indigenous peoples and Japanese Canadians and the use of space to create differential entitlements to power are, I argue, Canadian technologies of white settler nation-building. Honed through colonization and the establishment of reserves for status Indians, the technologies of expulsion and forced displacement created carceral spaces that settlers used to signify racial and Indigenous difference in relation to white bourgeois areas. This technique of expelling and displacing the first inhabitants from their territories materially and symbolically made the nation of Canada. In the 1940s the technologies of expulsion and displacement, authorized through the War Measures Act, were implemented against Japanese Canadians through the establishment of the 100-mile coastal radius. This Act was used to remove them from the BC coastal area, enforce their incarceration in different sites from British Columbia to central Canada, and eventually force their dispersal to destinations east of the province.

Hence, the distracting periodizing signpost that directs us to look at the war with Japan as the ultimate cause of the Internment also promotes Canada's innocence. The Internment, I argue, is not only connected to Canada's war with Japan but also is an extension of the efforts of white settlers to secure the territories taken from Indigenous peoples.[6] Rather than conceptualizing the Internment as being related solely to the war in the Pacific, I would suggest that our temporal and geographic gaze be adjusted to see it as reflecting the battle for white bourgeois settler supremacy that was variously and differently waged against Indigenous peoples, people of Japanese ancestry, and other racialized and marginalized groups living in Canada.

Understanding that spaces and subjects are produced in relation to each other underlines the importance of Edward Said's notion of analysing histories as "contrapuntal"[7] through their intertwining and overlapping. A contrapuntal understanding of histories of subordination that illustrates how these histories interlock with each other in the building of a settler nation requires acknowledging that, prior to the 1940s, Indigenous peoples were dispossessed and forced to live in carceral spaces of exclusion and marginalization, that is, places such as reserves and residential schools, and Canada itself.

The expulsion of Japanese Canadians from the restricted area occurred shortly after the finalization of the building of the reserve system in British Columbia.[8] The colonial and racial construction of the nation becomes even clearer when we unmap the first sites considered by the federal government for the incarceration of Japanese Canadians – residential schools and reserves across the country inhabited by Indigenous peoples.[9] In imagining the Canadian settler nation and its citizens, state officials also relationally imagined those who were considered extraneous to both. Their colonial and racial imagination conceptualized that Indigenous peoples could share carceral and Indigenous spaces with a group constructed as racially foreign, or that Japanese Canadians could be used to again displace Indigenous peoples through their own forced displacement.[10] In addition, the use of the permit system to control and monitor the movement of Japanese Canadians between internment sites and during the dispersal is reminiscent of the pass system developed to restrict and control the movement of Indigenous peoples.[11] The use of forced displacement and the spatialization of exclusion as tools of nation-building deployed against Japanese Canadians were simultaneously used again against Indigenous peoples. In Canada, the federal government used the War Measures Act to expel Japanese Canadians from the West Coast and the members of the Stoney Point reserve from their land in southern Ontario;[12] the United States used Executive Order 9066 to expel 120,000 Japanese Americans from the West Coast and to remove the Aleuts from their land in Alaska.[13] While the reason for the expulsion of Indigenous communities given by settler governments was because their territories were needed for "military installations,"[14] and thus their existence was constructed as standing in the way of securing the nation, and the reason given for Japanese Canadians' expulsion was because they were deemed a threat to national security, these examples of the application of Canadian and US law clarify against whom emergency legislation was applied for wholesale expulsion during the state-defined emergency of the 1940s and whose lives were heralded as in need of protection. Clearly, the settler state drew on colonial technologies in its construction of relational spaces and relational subjects.

Hence my unmapping must begin by acknowledging that the Canadian nation has been forged through the removal of Indigenous peoples from their territories and the enforcement of their racialized segregation, practices that were foundational to the creation of racial categorization as practised in Canada. The history of racialization for Japanese Canadians in Canada must therefore acknowledge the pre-establishment of the racial categories of "Indian" and "white" that were violently procured and maintained through the practices of colonialism both past and present. Moreover, as Japanese Canadians, we must examine our own material and social positions, living on the land of Indigenous peoples and in relation to them;[15] we must examine the current practices of a settler and "racial state"[16] that divides and positions us relationally, practices in which we participate and from which we differently benefit.

Spatializing the Narrative of the Internment

Politicians and citizens who supported the expulsion of Japanese Canadians established the zones of racial exclusion by legislating the 100-mile restricted area and creating numerous carceral sites. They argued that the expulsion of Japanese Canadians was necessary to the security of Canadians. Such an argument obscures the social relations and the racial violence of the expulsion and has been soundly debunked by Ann Sunahara[17] and others. For years, however, this argument of national security masked who was actually being threatened and by whom. While Japanese Canadians committed no violence against Canadians, violence was done to them by the Canadian government and others participating in the Internment causing long-term effects. These effects are difficult to see, and hence to name, unless we actually visualize and render visible the material spaces to which people were forced to move and the people who were moved into those spaces.

Power was disseminated through "multiple separations, individualizing distributions, and organization in depth of surveillance and control."[18] The creation of the Internment as a multiply spatialized incarceration hinders our very ability to see these spaces as carceral and so facilitates our forgetting of the effects the Internment produced. The women's testimonies provide a verbal unmapping of the places of incarceration and illustrate some of the ways in which the very heterogeneity of these material and social spaces affect what is remembered and named.

"Spatializing the historical narrative"[19] enables us to conceptualize history as not solely about a linear march through time, but also about space. What this spatial analysis renders visible is how discourses of power are both produced through and produce these sites. Edward Soja refers to spatial analysis as an "interpretive geography," a way of recognizing "spatiality as simultaneously ... a social product (or outcome) and a shaping force (or medium) in social life."[20] This methodological approach enables an understanding of how social domination can be disguised and normalized. Keeping in mind that over 22,000 people were removed from their homes on the Canadian West Coast and incarcerated in different and separate locations, we can begin to understand how spaces organize different forms of surveillance and how "discipline proceeds from the distribution of individuals in space."[21]

Identities were made through these contrapuntal, relational spaces. Both Japanese Canadians and white Canadians were relationally made through spatial expulsion, the establishment of carceral sites in six Canadian provinces, and the dispersal of Japanese Canadians. The ability of white bourgeois subjects to displace people based on the perceived "race" of those they wished to expel served to secure their own whiteness and spaces of entitlement. Power necessarily enforced and normalized this social and spatial arrangement. The violence of these processes and their exclusionary discourses and practices, including racism, sexism, heteronormativity, economic exploitation, and ableism, were compounded and obscured by spatial separations and segregation.

Audrey Kobayashi uses a spatial analysis to describe the imposed "placelessness" of Japanese Canadians. Kobayashi situates the denial of geographic rights, a "right to place," within the Canadian state, wherein concentrated power is used to control space. She names racism as the "mechanism through which the power to deny geographic rights is released, and the ideological channel through which the contest of spatial control is negotiated."[22] Kobayashi enumerates three ways, all of which were applied to Japanese Canadians, in which geographic rights can be denied or limited:

> one, *exclusion*, by which certain groups are denied spatial access to designated places, either entire countries or parts of countries; two, *restriction* of the freedom of movement from one place to another, or of the presence of designated persons in specific places and times; three, *expulsion*, whereby designated groups are removed from a place and subsequently excluded and restricted.[23]

As Kobayashi states, "spatial discrimination" was imposed upon Japanese Canadians, particularly between the years 1941 and 1949. However, she emphasizes that the spatial exclusions that transpired during this period were but a "logical extension" of a 50-year history in which geographic rights were denied through a "social context of racism."[24]

Social exclusions in British Columbia were made through the law. For example, Indigenous peoples and Asian Canadians could not vote in municipal, provincial, and federal elections. Banned from the voting lists, they were by default excluded from holding public office and from becoming lawyers, pharmacists, architects, and chartered accountants.[25] A white citizenry strove to eliminate the sea changes that were occurring as Japanese Canadians became more economically able to move into other areas of Vancouver and the province and began organizing to fight for the vote and the rights of citizenship.[26] As Kobayashi states: "the dominant notion that Asians should keep their place both geographically in ethnic ghettos and socially became stronger as Japanese-Canadian citizens attempted to secure a place beyond these realms."[27]

The Second World War presented an opportunity to ascribe to people of Japanese ancestry the mark of disloyalty and thus the pretext for their removal from the coastal area, away from the space claimed by white bourgeois citizens. Dispossessing Japanese Canadians of property and other possessions, and discounting the citizenship of even those who were born in Canada, were moves that normalized their disentitlement to the rights of citizenship; their statelessness was used to identify them as belonging to the nation of the "enemy."

White bourgeois men easily imagined and rationalized that Japanese Canadians should live in restricted spaces of incarceration and servitude. Japanese Canadians were thus barred from the 100-mile restricted coastal area and from the imagined white collective space of the Canadian nation.

Creating a Nationless People

Canada's entry into the Second World War provided the pretext for placing greater and greater spatial restrictions on all people of Japanese ancestry living in the country. The Canadian federal cabinet used the War Measures Act to authorize the wholesale expulsion of Japanese Canadians.[28] More than 40 Orders-in-Council were applied to "persons of the Japanese race" regarding detention, incarceration, movement, dispossession, housing, employment, dispersal, loyalty, citizenship and other matters.[29] Orders-in-Council issued by the federal government clearly specified where and when they could travel. For example, on 8 December 1941, all fishing boats were impounded and the waters were declared out of bounds. Order-in-Council P.C. 365, issued on 16 January 1942, designated the 100-mile "protected area" from the Pacific Ocean to the Cascade Mountains and from the Yukon to the US border.[30] Order-in-council P.C.1486, issued on 24 February 1942, allowed the minister of justice to control the movements of all people of Japanese ancestry in these "protected areas."[31]

A dusk-to-dawn curfew imposed on all people of Japanese descent on 28 February 1942 limited their access to public places and to one another, thus curtailing their ability to gather in groups and to work outside of daylight hours.[32] Community infrastructures supporting communication and intracommunal relations were hastily dismantled and rendered illegal by the federal government. Japanese-language schools and the three vernacular newspapers published in Vancouver were closed.[33] Community gatherings were forbidden and churches were not permitted to hold services, except in the case of funerals.[34] Curfews and prohibitions placed upon communal gatherings were the first steps towards spatially separating friends and family members in separate carceral sites in far-flung regions.

Haru, who lived in Vancouver in what she called a "Japanese community," was forced to leave her home with her family when she was 18. When describing the curfew, she underlined the spatial limitations invoked through the law. From dusk to dawn Japanese Canadians became prisoners in their own homes. Haru situated herself in relation to Chinese Canadians.

HARU: We had a curfew. You heard about the curfew? We couldn't go out after ten o'clock ..., the Chinese could go but they all wore badges.
MO: What did the badge say?
HARU: They're not Japanese.[35]

Historically banned from the rights of Canadian citizenship, both Japanese Canadians and Chinese Canadians tried to prove their loyalty to Canada. The badge worn by Chinese Canadians that identified them as "Chinese" was an attempt to secure their safety in and access to public space after the curfew. While marking an association with China, one of the allied countries during the war, the badge also marked their own racial exclusion from Canadian citizenship. However, this self-marking procured spatial access and socially divided them from Japanese Canadians.

Haru also situated herself in relation to Italian Canadians and German Canadians, contextualizing the war's chronology and the fact that Canada was at war with several countries. She wondered why the treatment of other groups at war with Canada was different: "But I couldn't understand because the war was with Italy and Germany, too. And yet they never went through that. Japan was the last to get into the war."

Sunahara has pointed out that while German Canadian and Italian Canadian leaders of organizations were detained, the federal government "resisted demands in 1940 by the Great War Veterans Association to intern all German and Italian aliens."[36] However, 597 Italian Canadian men were interned at the Petawawa prisoner-of-war camp.[37] The RCMP also monitored the Italian Canadian community in Toronto and some people "stopped speaking Italian and anglicized their names.[38] According to Reg Whitaker and Gregory S. Kealey, "847 pro-Germans were interned (out of a potential population base of more than a half-million), with most released by late 1944 or early 1945."[39] Twelve women of German descent were incarcerated in Kingston Penitentiary.[40]

Haru's testimony drew my attention to the differential treatment of these three Canadian groups, linked to the Axis powers during the war. Race and ethnicity as perceived within Canada and their penalties or privileges were therefore differently lived by differently racialized and ethnicized people during the 1940s. Race, ethnicity, and whiteness had to be re-imagined by the federal government and its officials in determining the status and fate of each racialized or ethnicized group. As differences were imagined and discursively operationalized, racialized and ethnicized communities were placed in a relational hierarchy in Canada, allowing most Italian Canadians and German Canadians to maintain spatial toeholds of varying sizes in the nation. All Japanese Canadians (both citizens and Japanese nationals), however, were racialized as one group and one enemy, and, as a group, they were expelled from the coastal area.

S. was 12 when her family was forced to leave Vancouver. She had lived in a predominantly white area of the city and had close associations with white neighbours and Japanese Canadians, most of the latter living "downtown." When I asked her what she remembered about her parents being told to leave Vancouver, she began by describing how she learned about the government's actions. She then discussed the curfew and the support her family extended to their friends to ensure a way of being together during the early days of upheaval and uncertainty:

> I'm not sure exactly how it happened. I know there was a great deal of talk. Friends would come over. And we would hear all the news of what's happening downtown and I can't remember the exact time that they were told or how it affected them. Well, I know they were quite upset at the time. But it always involved other friends who were going through worse circumstances than ours ... We had more people staying over at our house because we lived far away from the downtown area. They would come to visit us and they'd stay beyond the curfew time. So, we'd have people staying at our house. Just to get back home the next day.[41]

Evelyn, who was 11, remembered that her first encounter with the notion of war was when England declared war on Germany. She bought "war savings stamps" and "bugged" her parents for the 25 cents to purchase them. She remembered that when Canada declared war on Japan, the curfew was imposed and one of her neighbours "got caught" for being outside after dusk.[42]

May lived with the stress of fearing punishment for breaking the curfew. At the time, she was 13 and lived in a predominantly white neighbourhood. She recalled one occasion when she was late: "I remember seeing a policeman and being just slightly panicked, wondering, well, like was I going to go to jail or what was going to happen." However, because she was "in the middle" of a group of neighbourhood white children, "he just simply turned a blind eye. Because he was a neighbourhood policeman."[43]

The fear of being caught outside after the curfew was also expressed by Shizuye Takashima who lived in Vancouver and recalled hurrying home with her sister after seeing a movie. Takashima's (1971) book, *A Child in Prison Camp*, conveys the profound anxieties she observed and felt as a child and the day-by-day erosion of their lives as the restrictions were imposed. In this instance, a man threatened to call the police when he saw the two young girls and told them to "Get off *our* streets!"[44]

Dispossession

Part of the process of creating a "placeless" and hence "nationless" people was to dispossess them. This ensured that they would not have homes to return to if they were ever able to return to BC and served as a deterrent to their return to the coastal area. Ownership of property is one of the defining criterion of the liberal subject;[45] those who dispossessed Japanese Canadians and claimed their property ensured their own security of place in the nation. This confiscation of property denied Japanese Canadians the material and symbolic right to owning a piece of the settler nation and sealed their fate in 1942 as landless, propertyless, and homeless. Thus, dispossession and displacement go hand-in-hand in the legislation that aimed to control Japanese Canadians, evict them from the Canadian nation, and deny their citizenship. Some of this legislation and how it was experienced by particular women is outlined in this section.

White citizens were appointed by the federal government to oversee the expulsion of Japanese Canadians from British Columbia. Order-in-Council P.C. 288 established a three-man Japanese Fishing Vessels Disposal Committee under the Department of Fisheries that was responsible for the disposal of fishers' boats.[46] On 8 December 1941, 1,200 fishing boats were impounded and placed under the control of this committee.[47] All of the men whose boats were confiscated were Canadian citizens.[48] On 4 March 1942, Order-in-Council P.C. 1665 was proclaimed and gave to the British Columbia Security Commission (BCSC) the right to

> [r]equire by order any person of the Japanese race, in any protected area in British Columbia, to remain at his place of residence or to leave his place of residence and to proceed to any other place within or without the protected area at such time and in such manner as the Commission may prescribe in such order, or to order the detention of any such person, and any such order may be enforced by any person nominated by the Commission to do so.[49]

P.C. 1665 then enabled the establishment of the Custodian of Enemy Property in Vancouver, the responsibility for which came under the Department of the Secretary of State. All Japanese Canadian property, including "Real Estate, personal effects, business and farms,"[50] was placed under the "control and management"[51] of the Custodian and later sold without the permission of its owners.

Motor vehicles, radios, and cameras were confiscated by the Custodian. Families were allowed to take only 150 pounds of baggage per adult and 75 pounds per child over 12 with a maximum allowance of 1,000 pounds per family, which meant they had to leave behind possessions that were often looted or destroyed. Thus dispossession began well before the issuance of Order-in-Council P.C. 469 on 19 January 1943, which allowed the Custodian to liquidate all property under his control.

As Sunahara revealed, among the beneficiaries of this confiscated property were veterans of the Second World War. On 23 June 1943, 769 farms owned by Japanese Canadians and $43,000 worth of income accrued after the owners were expelled were given to the Veterans' Land Act Board.[52] While the farms were slated for use by veterans,[53] no Japanese Canadian veteran was included in this reward for patriotism.[54] The dispossession of Japanese Canadians thus enabled other citizens to own and belong to the nation, in this instance as reward for military service. Furthermore, there were racial limits to the rewards for participating in nationalism and proving one's loyalty to Canada through military service; despite their service, Japanese Canadian veterans of the First World War were incarcerated and dispossessed. My grandmother lost her home and farm acreage in the Fraser Valley when they were confiscated by the Custodian, and my father and his younger brother Robert, both veterans of the Second World War, were not rewarded with farms. In fact, my father never again saw the home he and his brothers bought for my grandmother; rather, along with all Japanese Canadians, my father was legally prevented from returning to the "restricted area" of the West Coast until 1949.

The women interviewed reminded me that gender and a woman's relationship to property must be considered when discussing the dispossession of Japanese Canadians. Relationships to property are gendered and gender affects what people report as their losses. As many women did not own titles to boats or property, they may not report these items as being lost or confiscated even if these possessions were owned by fathers or partners; as such, gender and the often subordinate position of women in relation to familial property and the invisibility of their labour in procuring that property is also connected to class in these memories and constructions of ownership.[55] As Peter Nunoda revealed, in 1931 approximately two-thirds of Japanese Canadians were working class, 18 per cent of whom were designated as "unskilled."[56] Many of these people did not own property.[57] Not owning property is always constructed in relation to those who do and this relationship affects the ways in which people talk about the material losses they suffered. There is always a consciousness that other people might have lost more, in material terms, especially on the part of those who owned little in the pre-Internment period. Given a context wherein the focus of dispossession has largely rested on the material tangibility of loss as opposed to potentiality (e.g., future income), those who did not possess according to these criteria may also tend to minimize their losses.[58] Much of material value was lost in the massive confiscation of everything other than the "one bag" that most people were allowed to take with them. A study conducted by Price Waterhouse of Vancouver published in 1986 estimated the total loss for Japanese Canadians expelled at $48 million in 1948 dollars, or $443 million in 1986 dollars.[59] Importantly, this study did include a calculation of the income that was lost. However, the researchers deemed it inappropriate to include a figure for "lost education" or "non-pecuniary" losses. Also, the accounting firm did not estimate those losses attributable to the "dispersal." What the women reported as *their* losses, however, were losses often less tangible than property, hence these "effects" have not been counted.

Haru recalled that "what little furniture we had, we had to sell it for next to nothing." Kazuko, who was 17 when her family was forced to move, remarked that they were allowed to carry one bag per person:

> The Mounties came and said that we're going, "Here's a notice." And we opened the notice and it said, "You have to leave this place in twenty-four hours. And just one baggage to a person." So we didn't have much time at all. Because this wasn't expected.[60]

Kazuko, however, was also conscious of the position of her parents and added: "so that was, mostly for my parents; that was really sad. You know, everything, you lost."

These "adult" reports are to be contrasted to that of a woman who was a child at the time of the expulsion. Margaret, who lived in Richmond, was forced to move to Manitoba to a sugar beet farm when she was 12. She told me the only thing she could remember about leaving her home was that they were ordered to leave their dog:

> The only thing that we, the kids, remember was our dog. We couldn't take our dog. So we had to give our dog away. Of course, our dog came back the day before we left. So we did end up bringing it to Manitoba. We didn't know what else to do.[61]

Some of the women who were children at the time of the expulsion situate themselves within a childhood memory, less encumbered by what they report as the hardships of their elders. Yet when they did discuss their elders' losses, there was often a profound grief, reflective of the enormity of the loss. This age-specific, self-situated experience may not be understood by those who hear these testimonies. We may expect the adult to report what an adult might have experienced over 50 years ago. We might not recognize that memories from childhood and the language in which they are expressed may be different from those who were adults at the time, nor recognize that some parents might have attempted to shield children from their own struggles and pain.

The ability to take something cherished with her was an important memory for Margaret. Yet, when she described her family's losses, she articulated them in relation to those who were older, who lost "their" possessions. As Margaret stated:

> We were only allowed to take one baggage each. So, my grandmother had a lot of heirloom things. The government said, "You have to move, you have to leave everything. It'll only be a matter of a year and a half, two years tops. Leave everything and you're only allowed one baggage." We had this woodshed which locked. So my grandmother put everything in there, locked it up, hoping, you know, within a couple of years to come back and claim it all. But when my brother went back after the war, they had smashed in the windows, taken, smashed everything that they could smash and took whatever was valuable. So, we had nothing left. I think that was the hardest part for my grandmother. 'Cause it was all family things that she had left. That was very hard for her. Well, that's war. Yeah. I think a lot of people went through that, anyways, you know. It's not just us.

It is important to notice here that Margaret described her grandmother's losses as "family things." They symbolize a relationship to others. As well, she situated herself within a context of "war" where others also suffered losses. The relationships conveyed here spanned time and space, connecting people across national boundaries through history and family.

Yoshiko, who was only five when she was forced to move from Vancouver, could not remember leaving the city.[62] She knew her parents owned a car and that "very few people at that time owned cars." The way their losses have manifested themselves for her is through her knowledge that they no longer have things that she remembered being a part of her familial surroundings before they were forced to move from Vancouver. The evidence of these possessions is materialized through the photographs they have retained from this period. She stated: "We have pictures of us, our home in Vancouver before we moved. You know, those shelves of dolls, Japanese dolls? And things on the walls. We don't have any of that."

S., who was 12 at the time her family was forced to leave Vancouver, described the process of dispossession in this way: "We always thought we would go back. So, I can remember my mother packing boxes, which we left with the neighbours, thinking we would claim them. All our good Japanese things. And things we just didn't want to take." In contrast to Yoshiko's experience, however, S.'s family did eventually retrieve the possessions they had entrusted to their neighbour.

Esther, who was three years of age at the time, did not remember the home she left in New Westminster. Her parents lived in a float house and had not bought any property. She commented, "Perhaps it was just as well they didn't. Because it was confiscated anyways, right?" In contrast to Yoshiko's family, Esther's did not own a car. She reported that her "father had a fishing boat. And my two oldest brothers had a fishing boat." Her family left their other possessions in the float house and asked a "Polish man" to look after them.[63]

Evelyn, who was 11 at the time of the expulsion, recalled her father trying to reassure the children that leaving Vancouver would be "like a holiday." Her father's business contact bought his boat from him. Evelyn described this loss of her father's boat in relation to the loss sustained by other fishers: "Yes. We were lucky. You see most of the people's boats were confiscated. But they bought my father's boat." But she also told me that they had to sell their furniture to the neighbour "for next to nothing." She remembered one possession, in particular, that was very difficult to give up – her father's violin. Evelyn underscored this by saying, "He did seem sad. He, I think, gave it to the neighbour's daughter."

May's father had died just before Canada's declaration of war against Japan. She was 14 when she, her mother, and sister were moved to Hastings Park in June 1942. She described how they were dispossessed and moved to their first site of incarceration, all in one day:

> So I finished my school year in June and then we sold all our furniture and stuff. By then my father was dead, you see. So there was a Japanese man, maybe there was more than one, who together with a, I think he was an auctioneer, a *hakujin* auctioneer. ... We got word that there were these people available who would come and give you a price for everything in your house and they just simply came and moved it out on a certain day. And on that day then we went into Hastings Park, so that we could be moved out from there. It was the Manning Pool. And by this time my mother was very sick. She was extremely sick. She had done some housework after my dad died because she needed some money.

In May's family, dispossession included the theft of money from a private insurance plan that her father had paid for by skipping lunches. Upon his death, a white lawyer had approached her mother and she asked his advice on what to do with the insurance policy money. This is what happened:

> When the evacuation notice came, mother went to talk to [the lawyer] and he had said, "they're going to tell you to use your own money up, you know, before you can go on welfare. So maybe if I hold this, because you are certainly going to need some monies over and above welfare." So this is what we did, we went out and bought things like blankets and things that would be needed for warmth, and we spent some of that money. But then we left the rest of the money with him. Unfortunately what we did not know was that he was an alcoholic. And so he never seemed to have the money to send us after we got in the camps. Those were some of the kinds of things that feel bad to me. Heck, if that was going to happen, why didn't Daddy just go and eat lunch, you know. I mean he would have been better off to have eaten, you know.

Connecting the Places of the Internment

Other places of incarceration are forgotten when the Internment is reduced to "camps" in British Columbia.[64] The geographic and social distinctions among the Internment sites are effaced through the unitary word "camp." This collapsing of spaces in the collective memory of the Internment is part of the production of its forgetting. Spatially conflating the incarceration and displacement of over 22,000 people to the (sometimes) admitted sites of amorphous camps is a function of the denial of the spatial scope of the incarcerations and dispersal. Like the rendition of the Internment as a temporal moment, a "sad chapter" or "page" of past Canadian history, the singularity of space obfuscates the extent and materiality of the violence that destroyed communal and familial relations through incarceration, dispersal, and deportation. What is also obscured through such monolithic representations are the ways in which different spaces produced heterogeneous gendered subjects.

We may not be aware, therefore, of the differences between the camps, their topographies, and the ways in which divisions were created within and between each site. For example, a BCSC report described the Sandon camp as being located "high in the hills north-west of Kaslo and east of New Denver," and could be "reached by a narrow, winding, steeply graded road ... difficult to negotiate in the winter."[65] The annual snowfall for Sandon was 20 feet and the town had two to three hours a day of sunlight in the winter.[66] When I visited this site near the middle of October 1992 as part of an organized community tour, the town and environs were snow-covered. The bus driver admitted that driving on the sole access road was risky. A participant on the tour who had been incarcerated in Sandon told me it was referred to as the "hell hole."

There were other carceral sites: Hastings Park in Vancouver (which for many was the first place of incarceration); the five so-called self-support camps; the various road camps to which men were sent (17 at the Yellow-Blue River Highway Project that traversed the border of BC and Alberta, seven at the Hope-Princeton Highway Project in BC, seven at the Revelstoke-Sicamous Highway Project in BC, and six at the Schreiber-Jackfish Highway Project in Ontario)[67] and that were operated by the Department of Mines and Resources; the prisoner-of-war (POW) camps in Angler and Petawawa, Ontario, and Kananaskis-Seebe, Alberta, operated by the Department of National Defence to which some of the men were sent; Neys Hostel in northern Ontario; and other hostels in Saskatchewan, Manitoba, Quebec, and southern Ontario. There were the sites of forced labour on sugar beet and other farms on the Prairies and in Ontario. There were domestic service and other jobs that women and men were forced to accept "east of the Rockies" in Quebec, Ontario, and Manitoba in the face of unemployment in the camps, destitution, or the threat of deportation to Japan when the repatriation survey was conducted.[68] There were industrial projects in Ontario and in Westwold and Taylor Lake, BC.[69] The most geographically distant site was Japan, the country from which Canada barred the return of Japanese Canadians who were there when war was declared and the country to which 3,964 people were forced to move through the coercive signing of the repatriation survey.[70]

The RCMP and the BC Provincial Police enforced the policies of the BCSC. As people were moved to different carceral sites, "permanent detachments" of the RCMP were set up at each of them.[71] "[T]he movement of all individual Japanese was controlled through a system of Permits rigorously enforced,"[72] issued by the RCMP or the BC Provincial Police. Roadblocks were established at the "necessary places."[73] The BCSC underlined that "it is not deemed desirable that the Japanese shall be permitted to wander at will throughout the country."[74]

The remoteness of most of the Internment sites made the conditions of each site less visible to the politicians who envisioned and ordered the expulsions. Thus they protected *themselves* from witnessing the actions they had legislated and the harmful effects they caused.[75] The distribution of Japanese Canadians across multiple sites and provinces divided people into smaller groupings that were less visible than one large group of 22,000 people and ensured that any attempts to organize resistance could be contained. The spatial separations allowed the federal government to make relational identities for the incarceration sites and relational site-specific identities for the people interned. This physical and discursive relational mapping obfuscated the carceral nature of the places of the Internment.

In addition, the use of euphemistic language distanced the government and its administrators from the effects of their actions and left a semantic legacy with which we continue to struggle. For example, Lieutenant-Colonel of National Defence R.H. Webb used the term "family system"[76] to describe the BC interior camps; this term obfuscates the fact that many men were forced to work and live outside of the camps, away from their families. His terminology suggests a particular notion of family that excludes the non-nuclear family and other forms of intimate relationships, including a network of relatives, lovers, and friends. It renders invisible the many women, men, and children who were "missing" and "missed" in the different sites, as they were separated over time and space, some never to be reunited. The word "family" itself was a euphemism used by the government and its administrators to (mis)identify sites such as sugar beet farms and the "self-support" camps as places where families were kept together. Hence the violence of forced separations, the destruction of families, and their effects were forgotten.

Families, however, as they were constituted in the Japanese Canadian community, were forever changed or destroyed. For example, Evelyn was moved to Lillooet, a "self-support" camp, and was separated from her maternal grandparents who were moved to the Lemon Creek camp. Aya, who was married at the time, was moved to Greenwood and Tashme and reported that her mother and brothers were moved to a sugar beet farm in Manitoba.

The women I interviewed articulated their connections to different places and the people incarcerated therein. Haru, who was incarcerated in a BC interior camp, reported to me that she knew that life in the "self-support" camps was difficult because one of her relatives had lived there. It is this very awareness of the hardships inherent in each place that affects a survivor's ability to name her own experience as uniquely difficult. This memory of entire communities being expelled and how one constructs oneself in relationship to them is something that I refer to as "memory of community."

Women were moved from place to place, sometimes from camp to camp, camp to farm, farm to domestic service, and all combinations of overseen movement and control to places unknown, and often separated from partners and various family members and friends in this continual displacement. All of this occurred after the initial traumatic removal from their homes. Although historians of the Internment have struggled to name the processes of expulsion, the term "second uprooting"[77] used to describe what is sometimes referred to as the "dispersal" from the interior camps does not quite capture the number of movements that transpired after 1941.

Each description of each place gave me but a glimpse of life differently lived by each woman and the material and psychological challenges of those places. Each departure, including the one from "home," to unknown confinement and restriction, from familiar geography to changing landscapes and climates, was a leaving of cherished people and all the people who had surrounded them, a weeding through again of ever-diminishing possessions, and was replete with the accumulation of loss.

Racializing Masculinity: Road Camps and Prisoner-of-War Camps

Racializing discourses depicted Japanese Canadian men as Other in relation to a normative white bourgeois masculinity. The government mobilized a particular notion of racialized masculinity to produce the road camps through Order-in-Council P.C. 1271 issued on 13 February 1942. Men who were not Canadian citizens were the first to be expelled from the restricted area. This expulsion of men who were Japanese nationals, as well as the creation of the POW camps as a site for men who were "prisoners of war" (although both Japanese nationals and Japanese Canadian citizens were incarcerated there), depended upon the heightened image of a demonized and racialized masculinity, that of the "enemy" or "alien," constructed to legitimate their incarceration. The spectre of the "disloyal Japanese," hinged upon the Orientalist notion of their Otherness and had to be made tangible to white Canadians on a continual basis, and the notion of disloyalty was discursively used to defend the construction of the incarceration sites. Ironically, at the same time that these men were constructed as the enemy and a threat to national security, the federal, British Columbia, Alberta, and Ontario governments assigned many of them to highway construction and other projects that were critical to securing spatial access for their citizens and to serving the interests of a capitalist economy in the building of the nation.

The classic notion of Jeremy Bentham's panopticon, described by Foucault as being built around a "tower" in which the guard is able to "see constantly and to recognize [prisoners] immediately,"[78] is a fitting description of the surveillance used at the Angler POW camp with its guard towers and barbed wire. In addition, Japanese Canadian men incarcerated there had to wear uniforms with red circles sewn onto the back that "provided a target for camp guards."[79] This use of the red symbol, a "spectacle of identity,"[80] connoted the national identity of the Japanese "enemy." Hence, the BCSC masculinized and racialized the 750 men incarcerated in the Petawawa and Angler POW camps as "those Japanese known to be dangerous, or to have the slightest subversive tendencies and, therefore, considered to be a potential menace."[81]

The demonization of Japanese Canadian men and their spatial separation were critical to the government's legitimization of the Internment and forwarded its notion that Japanese men were inherently dangerous and essentially different from white men. In using the POW camps, the government also created another category of people it called "internees," and it then used this distinction to categorize other sites of incarceration as other (less severe) than "internment."[82] As Sunahara has demonstrated, the government was also careful in describing those born in Canada (even though they were in POW camps) as "not interned," since only "aliens" could be legally interned according to the Geneva Convention.[83] The POW camps were used to produce notions of racialized men as enemies and a threat to the nation while disguising their Canadian citizenship status.

Despite the lack of guard towers in other incarceration sites, all Japanese Canadians in these places were not free to leave and were monitored and controlled through site-specific techniques. What Foucault called a "panoptic system" – in which those who monitor and discipline demonstrate "a certain power, and for that reason ... also act as the vehicle for transmitting a wider power"[84] – was actualized across the sites of incarceration. Through P.C. 1271, 1,700 male Japanese nationals were moved to road-camp sites, two-thirds were married and had on average two or three children.[85] Men who were Canadian-born and able-bodied were soon to follow, with a total of 2,150 being sent to road camps in Ontario and in British Columbia.[86] Many of the men sent to the BC interior camps were forced to do hard labour outside the camp, sometimes returning on the weekends.[87]

Approximately 2,900 men were removed from their families in 1942. Over 7,000 women, 15 years of age and older, were then moved to various incarceration sites. Over 8,000 children under the age of 15 (approximately 3,500 girls and 4,600 boys) had to be cared for in these sites.[88] As is shown in the next section, males over the age of 13 were separated from women and children in the Hastings Park site. It was thus assumed by the government that women would care for the children, those who were not "able-bodied," and the elderly not only in Hastings Park but also in the camps to which they were eventually sent. The gendered presumption – the women must provide this care – was mobilized by the white officials and administrators and materialized through the separation of men from the sites in which these activities took place. While the government, at times, might have rendered women invisible – as in the case of a 1942 government report where "women and children were listed in the same category"[89] – gender was always critical in the operationalization of the Internment. Although some of the Internment literature alludes to the patriarchal practices of Japanese, Japanese Canadian, or Japanese American men, there has been little analysis of how male-domination and gender-specific roles were promulgated through the actions of the white politicians, public servants, Internment administrators, and other participants in this process.

It is important to also note that a category of physical ability and its correlates "not able-bodied" and "physically unfit'[90] were reinforced through the Internment, and forged through government discourses and spatial separations. In this process, some of the men who were sent to the BC interior camps were deemed not able to undertake the hard, physical labour required in the road camps and thus were characterized as "not able-bodied." While many of the men and women deemed not able by the government had, in fact, been very able in their jobs and related responsibilities before the expulsion, their relegation to the interior camps reinforced their new identities as "not able-bodied." Hence, these gendered divisions of work and space that were enforced through spatial separations also assigned hegemonic notions of ability, further marking bodies already pathologized through racial exclusion within a spatially distinguishable hierarchical grid of identity categories.[91] Separating men who could not labour in the road camps from the men who could discursively emasculated the former by designating them "dependants" in this spatialized hierarchical arrangement.

Just as the removal of men constructed Japanese Canadians in relation to a white hegemonic able-bodied masculinity, so too did it produce a white hegemonic able-bodied femininity. The separation of racialized women from their partners, lovers, children, parents, siblings, extended family, friends, and neighbours and their forced removal from their homes relationally constructed the privilege of white families and communities who were assured of their entitlement to occupy the coastal area and their homes. While the removal of many Japanese Canadian men from their families ensured that the women would assume the childcare functions prescribed in hegemonic white male-dominated family structures, Japanese Canadian women's gendered subject position was not unitarily similar to that of white women. White women, although differently located in terms of their own class and ethnicized positions, benefited from the bolstering of whiteness secured by the racial exclusions of the Internment.[92]

As has been documented by Sunahara and others, many of the men forced into POW camps were those who protested their separation from their families through the expulsion process.[93] In particular, the Nisei Mass Evacuation Group (NMEG) is cited as an example of resistance to the governmental order calling for the break-up of families.[94] While the resistance of these men to the expulsion and separation of their families is undeniably significant and must be recognized, it is important to note that their actions are often the sole examples of "resistance" signalled in Internment narratives. As Nunoda has pointed out, little is known about the Nisei Mass Evacuation Women's Group, formed in April 1942 to support the interned men and "resist evacuation";[95] indeed, there is little mention in the literature or in community commemorative representations of women's individual and organized "resistance." For example, the actions of Mrs. Tanaka-Goto, who refused the orders to leave her home in 1942 and who was incarcerated in Oakalla prison before being sent to the Greenwood camp, have largely remained unacknowledged.[96] Other than Muriel Kitagawa, very few women (and men for that matter) have been depicted as resisting during the Internment.

Hastings Park

When the Order-in-Council to remove Japanese Canadians was enacted, the first communities to be expelled were those in "outlying" coastal areas.[97] Many of the people who did not live in Vancouver at the time were first incarcerated on the grounds of Hastings Park in the Pacific National Exhibition (P.N.E.) buildings; the racialized space and the racialized subjects within were therefore highly visible in the most inhabited city of British Columbia. Women and children were placed in the Livestock Building and the men were kept in the Forum Building. Conceptualized by the BCSC as a place to hold at least 4,000 people at a time, Hasting Park was used to confine 8,000 people in total who were sent there before they were moved to other carceral sites.[98] The buildings of the P.N.E., ordinarily used to display livestock and agricultural and manufacturing products, were expropriated by the Department of National Defence and quickly emptied of their usual exhibits. Sunahara describes Hastings Park as "a holding pen for human beings ... converted from animal to human shelter in only seven days ... the ever-present stink of animals and the maggots and the dirt ... encrusted the buildings in Hastings Park."[99] Sunahara's description must be contrasted to a BCSC report that describes it as "[a]t all times ... kept scrupulously clean."[100] The report also states, "Many valuable lessons in food values were learned by the Japanese during their stay in Hastings Park and while they were there every effort was made to educate them to the correct standard of proper diet. Sanitary and laundry conveniences and all the more simple accoutrements of *modern civilization* were installed."[101] The notion of modern Western "civilization" was critical to the construction of the Internment. Just as in the colonial project, in which the colonized must be shown to be "uncivilized" and "backward," white officials continually referred to the need to "civilize" or "Canadianize" Japanese Canadians.

Meyda Yeğenoğlu delineates how temporality is used to legitimate the violence of colonialism by rendering the colonial project as one which seeks to modernize and raise to the "advanced" moment of the colonist the "backward" and "primitive" Other.[102] I would extend her analysis to spatial as well as temporal constructions of domination and superiority. Spatially segregating them in livestock buildings and other uninhabitable environments created the uncivilized spaces needed as proof of "Japanese backwardness." In this way, white administrators created colonies to be conquered "within" their nation; colonies to which they could travel and from which they could leave, and over which they ultimately maintained control.

Confining Japanese Canadians to dehumanized spaces relationally produced the humanity of the white subjects outside of these spaces and the white employees who inhabited them not by force but by "choice." The white subject relationally secured for itself the notion of being "civilized," and the continual repetition of the civilizing/Canadianizing discourse was essential to "the dissimulation of the violence"[103] and its material and discursive effects.

Kazuko's interview shed light on what was deemed to be "modern civilization" by the BCSC. They also reveal what "valuable lessons in food values" were imparted:

> The first place where we went was Hastings Park, with lots of other people. You know, you just sleep on the floor and ... the sugar was rationed, so even when you got porridge, the sugar was not even a teaspoonful. And milk didn't even cover the porridge. Porridge was like a paste. You know, because it was so many people to cook for. And then also we had to help with the dishes afterwards, which is natural. But the meals were, oh gosh, I'm telling you, were like, you wouldn't even feed it to a dog. It was just terrible. So we were very happy to get out of there.

Haru described her memories of Hastings Park in this way:

> The men were taken first to Hastings Park. My father and my mother, then even in Hastings Park we couldn't stay together. The men were all in one building and the women and children were in another building. That was an experience. And then once you're there, it's like a prison. There was a gate, you couldn't go out. You had to get a special permit to go into Vancouver if you wanted to go and do some business. And so our lives were: you slept in a horse building or manufacturer's building where they had bunks. And they gave you blankets that you could put a rope on to make a partition. And it was very hard because there were hundreds of people there and you didn't know who they were. They came from all over Vancouver and Vancouver Island. They were total strangers. Regardless of how hot, how rainy, we had to go to another building to stand in line for hours to get our food, for breakfasts, lunch, and supper. And we all got a tin plate. I can remember that. It was so hot one day. By the time you got there, you just thought you were going to pass out, just to get your supper.

According to Sunahara, in Hastings Park married men "were prohibited from entering the building housing their wives and young children."[104] I would argue that the confinement of men and of boys over 13 years of age to the Forum Building and their separation from women and girls normalized white masculinity by pathologizing the racialized male. This age and gendered distinction marked these male children as necessitating spatial segregation. This determination of the age of 13 was linked to a construction of an Orientalized heterosexuality and masculinity, delimiting spatial contact and heterosexual sexual relations between males and females by imposing upon all males around the age of puberty and older physical separation from females. Hence the construction of the "enemy" entailed the interlocking of a racialized masculinity and heterosexuality. This action bolstered and normalized a white bourgeois heteronormativity by entitling white subjects to "family," heterosexual sexual relations, and "community," which reinforced white masculine and heterosexual hegemony.[105] Moreover, by separating partners and determining if or when they would be reunited, the federal government controlled for years relationships, including sexual ones, and the spaces in which relating and sexuality could be expressed.

Muriel Kitagawa's writings provide an account of women contesting the treatment of Japanese Canadians incarcerated in Hastings Park. Kitagawa learned of a woman's protest to a white nurse after finding maggots in the Livestock Building. According to Kitagawa, the nurse responded, "Well, there's worms in the garden aren't there?"[106] Kitagawa's friends, Eiko and Fumi, publicly challenged the nurse, who was known to call people "filthy Japs."[107] Eiko also protested the actions of a white RCMP officer who hit women when they congregated at the entrance to their "cage," while they were awaiting news about the men who were refusing to go to the road camp in Schreiber, Ontario. As Kitagawa reports, Eiko "raked him with fighting words."[108]

Forrest La Violette, who witnessed the conditions in Hastings Park, described how the anger of those confined "became converted into demands upon the Security Commission for improvement."[109] Some of these demands were articulated in a petition dated 19 June 1942, which was addressed to the representative of the International Red Cross in Montreal. This petition included the following demands:

> the emancipation from unnecessary restrictions, the rights of the democratic nation, freedom of speech ... sympathetic understanding of an oppressed people, differential treatment for Japanese nationals and Canadian citizens, appointment of a medical officer for Hastings Park, and the return from work camps of the husbands of expectant mothers.[110]

In contrast to Kitagawa, in describing the attempts of some Japanese Canadians to organize and protest in Hastings Park, La Violette demeaned their demands and compared them to Japanese Americans who had been labelled as exhibiting a "demandatory psychology" by the American internment-camp administrators.[111]

Haru emphasized that in Hastings Park "there were hundreds of people and you didn't know who they were." May also felt isolated when she was confined in Hastings Park with her mother and sister. She knew none of the other people there, and her sense of isolation was reinforced by a memory shared by her sister-in-law decades later at the funeral of her mother-in-law. May's sister-in-law (whom she did not know during the Internment) confessed this recollection to her:

> She said, "You know, May, I've been meaning to tell you because I think I've had a little bit of a guilty conscience. When you were in Hastings Park, I remember you and your sister and your mother sitting in the shade of a building in the afternoons. And you would be sitting there listening to a portable record player. We used to run past you and call [you] names."

May said that hearing about this incident reinforced her sense "that it was not just me ... internally feeling out of place ... I must have looked out of place." The expulsion resulted in the ejection of Japanese Canadians from home and nation. Being "out of place" was a material and social condition to which they would be subjected for years to come.

May's sharing of her sister-in-law's memory, confided to her years after their detention in Hastings Park, illustrates that memories of the Internment, and reflections upon these memories, are continually being built across time and space. Internment survivors, especially those who enter Japanese Canadian spaces, may encounter those they knew before and/or during the Internment; some of these reunions are taking place more than 60 years after the Internment. How do people live with the anticipation and materialization of such meetings, I wonder, filled as they may be with narratives of years together and separated, evoking memories of why and how they were separated and the pain of those evocations? And by contrast, how do they wrestle with the absences of those who are never to be seen again?

Conclusion

Japanese Canadian male and female identities were re-made spatially through the Internment in relation to white gendered and heterosexual identities. Spatial and social entitlement for white subjects was secured through the social and spatial disentitlement of racialized Others. The Nisei Mass Evacuation Group (NMEG) called attention to the fact that Japanese Canadians were "British subjects by birth" and to the inherent contradictions between the "civil rights of any ordinary Canadian" and the practices to which Japanese Canadians were being subjected. In a letter to the chairman of the BCSC, members of the NMEG made it clear just how well they understood that being able to live in a family was supposed to be a right of Canadian citizenship and a right that Japanese Canadians were being denied,

> ... we think it totally unnecessary that our last remaining freedom should be taken from us – the freedom to live with our families. We were taught in our Canadian schools that we should always cherish freedom and do our utmost for the protection of women and children. We can now fully appreciate what that meant. We were also taught in our churches that the unity of family is sacred and must be regarded as a God-given human right and should be cherished as life itself.[112]

Hence, the NMEG and others mentioned above named these processes of relational subject formation between Japanese Canadians and their white incarcerators in their many acts of resistance. In naming the liberal principles upon which Canadian citizenship was supposed to be based, they were well aware that their entitlement to these principles had been negated because they were constructed as an enemy "race." Moreover, their appeals to liberal values and to those who constructed themselves as liberal subjects went unaddressed and the men of the NMEG were eventually sent to POW camps. The women, from whom they were spatially separated, were left to care for the children, the elders, and those deemed not able-bodied.

NOTES

1 For examples of theorizing the racialization of space in the production of Canada, see McKittrick and Woods 2007; Nelson 2008; Razack 2002; Teelucksingh 2006. For an example of the relational

construction of Indigenous peoples and Chinese Canadians in British Columbia, see Mawani 2009.

2 Phillips 1997, 143.

3 The term "technology" is borrowed from Foucault 1995, 30.

4 Canada 1876. This version of the Act was in effect during the Internment.

5 Hartman 1997, 69.

6 For an analysis of Canada as a "settler society," see, for example, Stasiulis and Yuval-Davis 1995, 1–38. See also Lawrence 2004 and 2002.

7 I am using Edward Said's notion of contrapuntal analysis here. As Said (1994) states, "We must be able to think through and interpret together experiences that are discrepant, each with a particular agenda and pace of development, its own internal formations, its internal coherence and system of external relationships, all of them co-existing and interacting with others" (32).

8 According to Richard Colebrook Harris (2002), by the early 1900s, "more than 1,500 small reserves [were] scattered" across British Columbia (265).

9 Oikawa 2006.

10 The federal government considered moving some Japanese Canadians to the Muncey Reserve in Ontario, for example. They also considered moving the children from residential schools and then moving Japanese Canadians into those schools. See Oikawa (2006). The U.S. government built two of the camps to incarcerate Japanese Americans on two different reservations. See Drinnon 1987, xxiii.

11 In citing historian F. Laurie Barron, Dickason (1997) refers to the pass system as a "form of selectively applied administrative tyranny," (289); note omitted. See also Lawrence 2004, 35. Ikebuchi Ketchell (2009) describes Japanese Canadians forced to work on sugar beet farms as requiring by the BCSC "a permit to travel more than ten miles from where they lived, making social surveillance unproblematic, thus guaranteeing that Japanese Canadians were never outside of this civic gaze" (33).

12 Sunahara 1996, 8.

13 Berreman (1964) describes the forced displacement of Aleuts and the military presence in the Aleutian village of Nikolski in a laudatory fashion, illustrating how the violence of expulsion is forgotten through a discourse of progress: "More recent but effective accultural influences have been the presence of the military and other outside personnel in and around the village since 1957; a period of wartime removal to a good sized town and education outside increased communication with the outside world ... and greatly expanded the opportunities to acquire and use a cash income in and out of the village" (232). Loo (1993) reports that the U.S. government offered $12,000 to each Aleut survivor as reparation for their forced displacement (100).

14 Sunahara 1996, 18.

15 On this point, see Lawrence and Dua 2005, 120–43, and Oikawa 2006.

16 Goldberg 2002.

17 Sunahara 1981.

18 Foucault 1995, 198.

19 Soja 1989, 1.

20 Ibid., 7.

21 Foucault 1995, 141.

22 Kobayashi 1989, 70.

23 Ibid.; emphasis in the original.

24 Ibid.

25 National Association of Japanese Canadians n.d., 2. See also Adachi 1976, 52–3.

26 See Adachi's (1976) description of the Japanese Canadian Citizens League's organizing drive and efforts to win the franchise in 1936 (160–4), and Miki's (2004) analysis of their actions (30–7).
27 Kobayashi 1989, 74. See also La Violette's (1948) description of Vancouver Alderman Halford Wilson's proposal in early 1941 (before the bombing of Pearl Harbor) that Japanese Canadians be segregated into a ghetto. He further states, "A by-law was drafted for the purpose of requiring Orientals to live in "their recognized localities." (27n51).
28 Canada 1914. For a description of the use of the War Measures Act during the First and Second World Wars, see Sunahara 1996, 7–22.
29 Kobayashi 1990, 456.
30 Adachi 1976, 209.
31 Ibid., 216.
32 Ibid., 232.
33 Ibid., 200.
34 Watada 1996, 107.
35 Haru [pseud.], interview by author, November 23, 1995. All subsequent quotes by Haru are taken from this interview. See Choy's (1995) description of the relationship between Chinese Canadians and Japanese Canadians in Vancouver as the war in Asia began and "the tin buttons pinned on our lapels that had the Chinese flag proudly stamped on them ... I also had one that said: I AM CHINESE" (219). See also Sunahara 1981, 68, and Ikebuchi Ketchell's (2009) newspaper citation regarding Chinese Canadians in Manitoba who wore "victory buttons" with the word "Chinese ... plainly on the button." Ikebuchi Ketchell argues that the buttons indicate the "ever-vigilant surveillance of Japanese Canadians" (30).
36 Sunahara 1996, 17.
37 Maria De Angelis (1996) describes the incarceration of Italian Canadian men (25). She adds that men were also incarcerated at three other internment camps: one at St Helen's Island in Quebec and two in Fredericton, New Brunswick. She states that the total number of men incarcerated is unknown.
38 Iacovetta 1992, 144.
39 Whitaker and Kealey 2000, 137.
40 McBride 2000, 156.
41 S. [pseud.], interview by author, August 16, 1995. All subsequent quotes by S. are taken from this interview.
42 Evelyn [pseud.], interview by author, August 26, 1995. All subsequent quotes by Evelyn are taken from this interview.
43 May [pseud.], interview by author, March 24, 1992. All subsequent quotes by May are taken from this interview.
44 Takashima 1971, n.p.; emphasis added.
45 Ian McKay 2009, 376.
46 Canada, British Columbia Security Commission 1942, 3. See also Adachi 1976, 209.
47 NAJC n.d., 2.
48 Sunahara 1981, 28.
49 Order-in-Council, P.C. 1665, March 4, 1942, quoted in Kobayashi 1990, 457.
50 Canada, British Columbia Security Commission 1942, 3. See also Adachi 1976, 218. Often the names of white people involved in the Internment and dispersal are not mentioned in the literature and are thus forgotten. The Custodian of Enemy Property was Glen McPherson (Miki 2004, 142).
51 Adachi 1976, 233.

52 See Sunahara 1981, 107–8, for a description of the legislative processes surrounding the confiscation of property through the Veterans' Land Act.

53 Sunahara 1981, 107.

54 Zennosuke Inouye, a veteran of the First World War, purchased land in Surrey, British Columbia, on September 20, 1919 through the Soldier Settlement Act, 1910. Considered a "soldier settler: he was given special consideration by the federal government and was able to return to his property on December 20, 1948. Inouye was not given a house through this special consideration; he was merely allowed to keep the house that he owned before the expulsion. According to Neary (2004), Inouye "was the only dispossessed Japanese-Canadian veteran to get his land back" (446). Neary adds that Inouye's house was "destroyed by fire on February 19, 1949. The building had been insured for only $300 by the custodian ..." (447, note omitted).

55 The description of men as owners of property is also reproduced in narratives of the Internment. For example, Miki (2004) writes of Masue Tagashira who, with her husband, "resettled outside the 'protected area' in Revelstoke, and from there, for many years, her husband tried to prevent the sale of *his* assets" (251, emphasis added).

56 Nunoda 1991, 58.

57 Ibid., 59.

58 See Nunoda's (1991) discussion of the 1947 Co-operative Committee on Japanese Canadians' (CCJC) fight for compensation for losses sustained by Japanese Canadians. Nunoda contends that initially the CCJC advocated fighting for lost income as well as property losses. This demand was eventually dropped. Nunoda argues that by dropping the claim for lost income, "the CCJC was already predisposed to ignoring a large segment of working class claims" (287).

59 National Association of Japanese Canadians, 1985, 1.

60 Kazuko [pseud.], interview by author, October 19, 1995. All subsequent quotes by Kazuko are taken from this interview.

61 Margaret [pseud.], interview by author, June 20, 1995. All subsequent quotes by Margaret are taken from this interview. I would suspect that few people were allowed to take their family pets with them and I believe this was permitted in Margaret's family's case because they were sent to a sugar beet farm.

62 Yoshiko [pseud.], interview by author, December 22, 1994. All subsequent quotes by Yoshiko are taken from this interview. Yoshiko also described not being able to remember the pre-Internment period.

63 Esther [pseud.], interview by author, August 17, 1995.

64 See, for example, critic Christopher Hume's (1996) review of Andrew Danson's photographic exhibit *Face Kao: Portraits of Japanese Canadians Interned during World War II* (66). Hume states, "In 1941 ... Pearl Harbor had just been attacked and if you were a Canadian of Japanese descent, you suddenly found yourself in a prison camp." In addition, Hume states, "4,000 Japanese Canadians [were] forced into exile." See also Rochon (2010) who states, "Japanese-Canadians on the West Coast were placed in internment camps: in "Devoted to Driving 'A Nail of Gold.'"

65 Canada, BCSC 1942, 20.

66 Watada 1996, 115.

67 Shimizu 1993.

68 See, Oikawa, 1986, chapter 2.

69 Canada, BCSC 1942, 28.

70 Ibid., 68.

71 Ibid., 16.

72 Ibid., 7.
73 Ibid., 16.
74 Ibid.
75 For a discussion of the distantiated processes of expelling racialized people from the nation, see Goldberg 1993, 81, 98, 137.
76 Library and Archives Canada (LAC), Records of the British Columbia Security Commission, RG 36/27, vol. 22, file 800, "Slocan: General 1942–1943, 1945–1948," R.H. Webb to Austin Taylor, 29 March 1942, 2; emphasis added.
77 Sunahara (1981) uses this term to describe the specific events of 1946 and the pressure exerted by the government to force people to leave the camps. She is not alone in the use of this term to describe the process of leaving the camps.
78 Foucault 1995, 200.
79 Adachi 1976, photo caption, n.p.
80 Gilroy 1997, 305.
81 Canada, BCSC 1942, 2. The number cited is from Canada Department of Labour 1944, 5. It is important to note that numbers may differ in different government reports. This reflects the constant movement of people between places at different moments of officials counting them.
82 According to Sunahara (1981), 296 Issei men and 470 Nisei men were interned in prisoner-of-war camps (70).
83 Sunahara 1981, 66.
84 Foucault 1980, 72.
85 Adachi 1976, 232.
86 Canada, Department of Labour 1944, 5.
87 Yoshiko stated that men left Slocan to work in logging camps and returned on the weekends.
88 Numbers are calculated from the 1941 census. Canada, Dominion Bureau of Statistics, 1946, 164.
89 The numbers show that 9,389 "males" and 14,091 "women and children" were accounted for. Note that the total was 23,480, 16 of whom were citizens of the United States. LAC, Records of the British Columbia Security Commission. RG 36/27, vol.1, file "Distribution of Japanese," "Memorandum Covering Japanese Movement Pacific Coast," 18 July 1942.
90 Canada, Department of Labour 1944, 18.
91 For an analysis of the relationship between space and constructions of disability, see Kitchin 1998, 343–56.
92 See Perry's (2001) analysis of the historical construction of a white Canadian citizenry that functioned to consolidate the white identities of women from different class and ethnic backgrounds.
93 See Sunahara 1981, especially 66–70. See also Takeo Ujo Nakano's account of being incarcerated at the Angler POW camp in Nakano with Nakano (1980), and Okazaki (1996).
94 See, for example, Okazaki 1996, 67–71; Miki's (1998) description (19–20, 190–1), and Miki 2004, 57–66.
95 Nunoda 1991, 98.
96 For a description of Tanaka-Goto, see Ayukawa 1995, 116.
97 Canada, BCSC 1942, 5.
98 Canada, Department of Labour 1944, 5.
99 Sunahara, *The Politics of Racism*, 55.
100 Canada, BCSC, *Removal*, 8.
101 Ibid.; emphasis added.

102 Yeğenoğlu 1998, 96.
103 Ibid., 94.
104 Sunahara 1981, 57.
105 See Lowe 1991, 11, for her analysis of Asian masculinity and its construction as "different" from Anglo- and Euro-American white masculinity; and also Eng's (1997) extension of Lowe's analysis in his argument that Asian masculinity is excluded from definitions of "normative heterosexuality" (40).
106 Kitagawa 1985, 116.
107 Ibid.
108 Ibid.
109 La Violette 1948, 65.
110 Ibid., 67.
111 Ibid., 65n23.
112 NMEG to Austin Taylor, 15 April 1942, quoted in Okazaki 1996, Appendices, A107.

REFERENCES

Adachi, Ken. 1976. *The Enemy That Never Was: A History of the Japanese Canadians*. Toronto: McClelland and Stewart.

Ayukawa, Midge. 1995. "Good Wives and Wise Mothers." *BC Studies* 105–6:103–18.

Berreman, Gerald D. 1964. "Aleut Reference Group Alienation, Mobility, and Acculturation." *American Anthropologist* 66 (2): 231–50. http://dx.doi.org/10.1525/aa.1964.66.2.02a00010.

Canada. 1876. *An Act to Amend and Consolidate the Laws Respecting Indians*, R.S.C. c. 18, ss. 1–100.

Canada, British Columbia Security Commission. 1942. *Removal of Japanese from Protected Areas: Report of the British Columbia Security Commission*. Vancouver: BCSC.

Canada, Department of Labour. 1944. *Report of the Department of Labour on the Administration of Japanese Affairs in Canada, 1942–1946*. Ottawa: Department of Labour.

Canada, Dominion Bureau of Statistics. 1946. *Eighth Census of Canada 1941*, vol. 3. Ottawa: Edmond Cloutier.

Canada. 1914. *Statutes of Canada*, Geo.V, c.2.

Choy, Wayson. 1995. *Jade Peony*. Vancouver: Douglas and McIntyre.

De Angelis, Maria. 1996. "Testimonies: Internment, Racism and Injustice in Canada." In *In Justice: Canada, Minorities, and Human Rights*, ed. Roy Miki and Scott McFarlane, 23–6. Winnipeg: National Association of Japanese Canadians.

Dickason, Olive Patricia. 1997. *Canada's First Nations: A History of Founding Peoples from Earliest Times*. 2nd ed. Toronto: Oxford University Press.

Drinnon, Richard. 1987. *Keeper of Concentration Camps: Dillon S. Myer and American Racism*. Berkeley: University of California Press.

Eng, David. 1997. "Out Here and Over There: Queerness and Diaspora in Asian American Studies." *Social Text* 52/53: 31–52. http://dx.doi.org/10.2307/466733.

Foucault, Michel. 1995. *Discipline and Punish: The Birth of the Prison*. Trans. Alan Sheridan. New York: Vintage Books.

Foucault, Michel. 1980. *Power/Knowledge: Selected Interviews and Other Writings, 1972–1977*. Ed. Colin Gordon. Trans. Colin Gordon, Leo Marshall, John Mcpham, and Kate Soper. New York: Pantheon.

Gilroy, Paul. 1997. "Diaspora and the Detours of Identity." In *Identity and Difference*, edited by Kathryn Woodward, 301–46. London: Sage in association with the Open University.
Goldberg, David. 2002. *The Racial State*. Malden, MA: Blackwell.
Goldberg, David.1993. *Racist Culture: Philosophy and the Politics of Meaning*. Oxford: Blackwell.
Harris, Richard Colebrook. 2002. *Making Native Space: Colonialism, Resistance, and Reserves in British Columbia*. Vancouver: University of British Columbia Press.
Hartman, Saidiya V. 1997. *Scenes of Subjection: Terror, Slavery, and Self-Making in Nineteenth-Century America*. New York: Oxford University Press.
Hume, Christopher. 1996. "Facing the Enemy that Never Was." *Toronto Star*, April 11.
Iacovetta, Franca. 1992. *Such Hardworking People: Italian Immigrants in Postwar Toronto*. Montreal: McGill-Queen's University Press.
Ikebuchi Ketchell, Shelly. 2009. "'Carceral Ambivalence: Japanese Canadian 'Internment' and the Sugar Beet Programme During WWII." *Surveillance & Society* 7 (1): 21–35.
Kitagawa, Muriel. 1985. *This Is My Own: Letters to Wes and Other Writings on Japanese Canadians, 1941–1948*. Ed. Roy Miki. Vancouver: Talonbooks.
Kitchin, Rob. 1998. "'Out of Place,' 'Knowing One's Place': Space, Power and the Exclusion of Disabled People." *Disability & Society* 13 (3): 343–56. http://dx.doi.org/10.1080/09687599826678.
Kobayashi, Audrey. 1990. "Racism and Law in Canada: A Geographical Perspective." *Urban Geography* 11 (5): 447–73. http://dx.doi.org/10.2747/0272-3638.11.5.447.
Kobayashi, Audrey. 1989. "The Historical Context for Japanese-Canadian Uprooting." In *Social Change and Space: Indigenous Nations and Ethnic Communities in Canada and Finland*, ed. Ludger Müller-Wille, 69–82. Montreal: Northern Studies Program, McGill University.
La Violette, Forrest. 1948. *The Canadian Japanese and World War II*. Toronto: University of Toronto Press.
Lawrence, Bonita. 2004. *"Real" Indians and Others: Mixed-Blood Urban Native Peoples and Indigenous Nationhood*. Vancouver: University of British Columbia Press.
Lawrence, Bonita. 2002. "Rewriting Histories of the Land: Colonization and Indigenous Resistance in Eastern Canada." In *Race, Space, and the Law: Unmapping a White Settler Society*, ed. Sherene H. Razack, 21–46. Toronto: Between the Lines.
Lawrence, Bonita, and Enakshi Dua. 2005. "Decolonizing Anti-racism." *Social Justice* 32:120–43.
Loo, Chalsa. 1993. "An Integrative-Sequential Treatment Model for Posttraumatic Stress Disorder: A Case Study of the Japanese American Internment and Redress." *Clinical Psychology Review* 13 (2): 89–117. http://dx.doi.org/10.1016/0272-7358(93)90036-L.
Lowe, Lisa. 1991. *Immigrant Acts: On Asian American Cultural Politics*. Durham, NC: Duke University Press.
Mawani, Renisa. 2009. *Colonial Proximities: Cross Racial Encounters and Juridical Truths in British Columbia, 1871–1921*. Vancouver: University of British Columbia Press.
McBride, Michelle. 2000. "The Curious Case of Female Internees." In *Enemies Within: Italian and Other Internees in Canada and Abroad*, ed. Franca Iacovetta, Roberto Perin, and Angelo Principe, 148–70. Toronto: University of Toronto Press.
McKay, Ian. 2009. "Canada as a Long Liberal Revolution: On Writing the History of Actually Existing Canadian Liberalisms, 1840s–1940s." In *Liberalism and Hegemony: Debating the Canadian Liberal Revolution*, ed. Jean-François Constant and Michel Ducharme, 347–452. Toronto: University of Toronto Press.
McKittrick, Katherine, and Clyde Woods, eds. 2007. *Black Geographies and the Politics of Place*. Toronto: Between the Lines.

Miki, Roy. 2004. *Redress: Inside the Japanese Canadian Call for Justice*. Vancouver: Raincoast Books.

Miki, Roy. 1998. *Broken Entries: Race, Subjectivity, Writing*. Toronto: The Mercury Press.

Nakano, Takeo Ujo with Leatrice Nakano. 1980. *Within the Barbed Wire Fence*. Toronto: University of Toronto Press.

National Association of Japanese Canadians. 1985. *Economic Losses of Japanese Canadians after 1941*. Winnipeg: National Association of Japanese Canadians.

Neary, Peter. 2004. "Zennosuke Inouye's Land: A Canadian Veterans Affairs Dilemma." *Canadian Historical Review* 85 (3): 423–50. http://dx.doi.org/10.3138/CHR.85.3.423.

Nelson, Jennifer J. 2008. *Razing Africville: A Geography of Racism*. Toronto: University of Toronto Press.

Nunoda, Peter. 1991. "*A Community in Transition and Conflict: The Japanese Canadians, 1935–1951*." PhD dissertation, University of Manitoba.

Oikawa, Mona. 2006. "Re-Mapping Histories Site by Site: Connecting the Internment of Japanese Canadians to the Colonization of Aboriginal Peoples in Canada." In *Aboriginal Connections to Race, Environment and Traditions*, ed. Rick Riewe and Jill Oakes, 17–26. Winnipeg: Aboriginal Issues Press, University of Manitoba.

Oikawa, Mona. 1986. "'Driven to Scatter Far and Wide': The Forced Resettlement of Japanese Canadians to Southern Ontario, 1944–1949." MA thesis, University of Toronto.

Okazaki, Robert K. 1996. *The Nisei Mass Evacuation Group and P.O.W. Camp '101.'* Trans. Jean Okazaki and Curtis Okazaki. Scarborough, ON: Self-published.

Perry, Adele. 2001. *On the Edge of Empire: Gender, Race, and the Making of British Columbia, 1849–1871*. Toronto: University of Toronto Press.

Phillips, Richard. 1997. *Mapping Men and Empire: A Geography of Adventure*. New York: Routledge.

Razack, Sherene H., ed. 2002. *Race, Space, and the Law: Unmapping a White Settler Society*. Toronto: Between the Lines.

Rochon, Lisa. 2010. "Devoted to Driving 'A Nail of Gold.'" *Globe and Mail*, April 17, R7.

Said, Edward. 1994. *Culture and Imperialism*. New York: Vintage Books.

Shimizu, Yon. 1993. *The Exiles: An Archival History of the World War II Japanese Road Camps in British Columbia and Ontario*. Wallaceburg, ON: Shimizu Consulting and Publishing.

Soja, Edward. 1989. *Postmodern Geographies: The Reassertion of Space in Critical Social Theory*. London: Verso.

Stasiulis, Daiva, and Nira Yuval-Davis. 1995. "Introduction: Beyond Dichotomies – Gender, Race, Ethnicity and Class in Settler Societies." In *Unsettling Settler Societies: Articulations of Gender, Race, Ethnicity and Class*, ed. Daiva Stasiulis and Nira Yuval-Davis, 1–38. Thousand Oaks, CA: Sage. http://dx.doi.org/10.4135/9781446222225.n1.

Sunahara, Ann. 1996. "Legislative Roots of Injustice: The Abuse of Emergency Law in Canada: Is It Inevitable?" In *In Justice: Canada, Minorities, and Human Rights*, ed. Roy Miki and Scott McFarlane, 158–70. Winnipeg: National Association of Japanese Canadians.

Sunahara, Ann. 1981. *The Politics of Racism: The Uprooting of Japanese Canadians during the Second World War*. Toronto: James Lorimer.

Takashima, Shizuye. 1971. *A Child in Prison Camp*. Montreal: Tundra Books.

Teelucksingh, Cheryl, ed. 2006. *Claiming Space: Racialization in Canadian Cities*. Waterloo, ON: Wilfrid Laurier University Press.

Watada, Terry. 1996. *Bukkyo Tozen: A History of Jodo Shinshu Buddhism in Canada, 1905–1995*. Toronto: HpF Press and the Toronto Buddhist Church.

Whitaker, Reg, and Gregory S. Kealey. 2000. "A War on Ethnicity? The RCMP and Internment." In *Enemies Within: Italian and Other Internees in Canada and Abroad*, ed. Franca Iacovetta, Roberto Perin, and Angelo Principe, 128–47. Toronto: University of Toronto Press.

Yeğenoğlu, Meyda. 1998. *Colonial Fantasies: Towards a Feminist Reading of Orientalism*. Cambridge: Cambridge University Press. http://dx.doi.org/10.1017/CBO9780511583445.

7 Redress Express: Chinese Restaurants and the Head Tax Issue in Canadian Art

ALICE MING WAI JIM

Race, to go

What side of John A. MacDonald's tracks you on anyways?
How fast you think this train is going to go?[1]

Last summer I came across a most remarkable prefixed rubric via Canada's national newspaper *The Globe and Mail.* "All aboard the Redress Express," the headliner read.[2] The media had coined this name for the cross-country train ride to Ottawa by Chinese head tax payers and their families to hear Prime Minister Stephen Harper deliver a long overdue apology on June 22, 2006. "On behalf of all Canadians and the Government of Canada, we offer a full apology to Chinese Canadians for the head tax and express our deepest sorrow for the subsequent exclusion of Chinese immigrants. ...To give substantive meaning to today's apology, the government of Canada will offer symbolic payments to living head taxpayers and living spouses of deceased payers."[3]

The Redress Express, publicized less than a week before the announcement, served as another kind of symbolic act. It was a palpable, visual way of making the connection between what Harper called "the most important nation building exercise in Canadian history – the construction of the Canadian Pacific Railway" and the contribution of early Chinese immigrants to this enterprise despite "the stigma and exclusion" experienced by them.[4] The "redress train" however did not figure in the newspaper article. Featured was a photograph of one of the few surviving head tax payers, 95-year-old James Marr from Edmonton, holding the ceremonial "Last Spike" as he arrived in Toronto's Union Station, one of the train's cross-country stops. To close the books on the head tax, the passengers of the Redress Express would be placing this iron spike on the wall of the Railway Committee Room in Parliament where the decision was made to build the national railway over 120 years ago.[5]

Upon reading the headline, three points had immediately struck me about the term "Redress Express." First, the redress movement could hardly be described as speedy – judiciously timed, perhaps, but not speedy. Redress by definition is never Express. Certainly not if you are 101 years old and have been bumping around for five days on a train to hear a highly televised apology.[6] To get to this point, the Chinese head tax redress campaign spanned over two decades (almost as long as the ban on Chinese immigration), weathered two different governments (first a Liberal politics of commemoration and then a Conservative politics of reconciliation), and initiated the organization of over a dozen Chinese Canadian community lobby groups.[7]

Second, "Redress Express" seemed to roll off the tongue ever so smugly as the name for an ethnic restaurant that could only be opened for business in what legal scholar Roy Brooks has called the "Age of Apology."[8] The suggestively gastronomic name brought to mind the recent growing scholarship on prefixed terms such as reparation, redress, and reconciliation in movement discourses as well as Asian Canadian critical discourse.[9] To pursue the mixed metaphor as a possible name for a fast food joint thus might bring out a recent serving up of hyphenated Canadian culture carried out with a certain expediency. With the apology and its accompanying pledges satisfying the goal of symbolic redress for the head tax issue as "the latest installment of victim politics, Canadian-style," as one admonishing national affairs columnist wrote,[10] it could be said the "race card" for Chinese Canadians has been served. Doled out then as the main dish at the hypothetical Redress Express – as an over-stuffed signifier for all the cafés, diners, fast-food chains, take-outs, and restaurants run by any of the ethnocultural communities in Canada seeking redress – would be the symbolic implications of reparation politics. Go back over, for example, what is at stake with simply ordering "Chinese, to go" in today's multicultural age of consumption given that "the political climate for recognition-seeking movements is becoming increasingly unfavorable."[11]

Third, from the PM's apology on behalf of Canadians, for which he received a standing ovation, to the repeated reproduction of certain head tax certificates circulated until they became nothing more than a generic, anonymous Chinese face, the political rhetoric and media images generated by the redress begged the question if the prevailing representations circulating around the head tax movement were any different from the pervasive images of the Asian Other, positive and negative, typically produced and consumed in North American society. In fact, the recent media events have placed a key emphasis on the ways in which redress has been and is being expressed primarily in public discourse. By contrast, this essay explores its expression in the visual arts.

It has been months now since I saw that headline but I am still grappling with the meaning of "Redress Express" – as appeal, journey, and possible destination – principally in relation to some specific examples of Chinese Canadian art. Two main bodies of works are under consideration, those that incorporate quite evidently the redress issue in some fashion or other, and those that deal with the Chinese restaurant as a key signifier of Chinese culture as well as a significant site of redress activity in and of itself. What follows is an explorative probing into the contexts of and possible connections among this otherwise small but diverse sampling of works by six Canadian artists of Chinese descent. Broadly speaking, this essay attempts to lay out a preliminary course for a reconsideration of artworks which have been produced from the early 1990s to present, alongside critical discourses on identity politics, within the same twenty-year period of the head tax redress, and hopes to explore the implications of these convergences for future theoretical and practical directions.[12]

"I Don't Need This to Tell Me Who I Am"[13]

The most consistent kinds of faces seen throughout the redress movement have been the faces of either very young Chinese men on yellow, faded head tax certificates with tattered corners or the few very elderly surviving head tax payers and their spouses captured by the media on their way to Ottawa. In contemporary art, these two types of images, separated by at least a generation, have appeared much more sparingly and rarely together.[14] Vancouver-based artist Sharyn Yuen's *John Chinaman* (1991) is an early example that focuses on the head tax issue as well as the long-term intergenerational effects of the prohibitive immigration laws (Figure 7.1).[15]

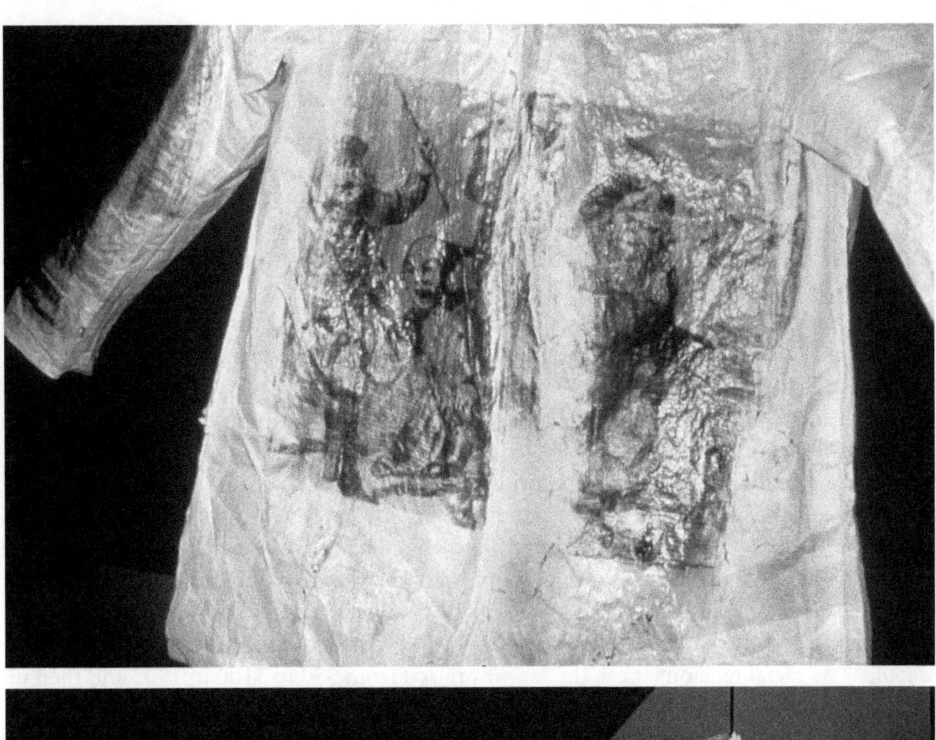

Figure 7.1 *John Chinaman*, 1991, by Sharyn Yuen

Dedicated to the Chinese workers who completed the railway and then had to face the head tax, Yuen's installation consists of 11 life-size white handmade paper suit jackets. On the front and back of each jacket are photo transfers of several head tax certificates alongside pages and statistics from the Chinese Immigration Act. The first major influx of Chinese into Canada was between 1881 and 1884 when 15,700 Chinese workers were recruited to undertake the most dangerous and labour-intensive work required to complete the Canadian Pacific Railway. With its use of both paper and white, elements associated with death in Chinese culture, *John Chinaman* is a haunting commemoration of the estimated 1,000 Chinese workers who died working on the transcontinental line.[16]

The idea for the piece emerged from discussions with the artist's father who, born in Canada in 1911, experienced direct racism growing up in British Columbia during the head tax years. This close connection is impersonalized however by the work's title, *John Chinaman*, which stresses the generic English name ascribed to Chinese men.[17] Used in the language of the immigration acts, the stereotype of the Chinaman, as "subservient and dangerously suspect" at the same time, is firmly located within a "Western, imperial discourse that legislated the category of Chinese identity."[18] In 1885, the Canadian government passed the Chinese Immigration Act that introduced the head tax. The avowed purpose of the tax was to discourage Chinese immigration, pacifying the fears and anxieties in primarily Western Canada concerning the Yellow Peril, the perceived threat in the Western imaginary of hordes of invading Asians taking jobs and other means of livelihood away from white people.[19] As racial tensions grew, the tax was raised from $50 to $100 in 1900 and then up to $500 in 1903.[20] Head tax certificates were issued to confirm that the immigrants had paid the tax, making these papers "confirmation of existence and identity" for over 81,000 Chinese in Canada at one time.[21] Yuen's 11 paper jackets thus not only suggest the literal incorporation of the identification papers as if it were a second skin, but also is on another structural level, a way in which the Chinese Canadian subject is redressed.

As a consequence of the 62-year period of legislated activity under racist federal policies, many families were kept apart for years and the formation of a viable early Chinese Canadian community was prevented. The first Chinese communities in Canada were constituted by primarily "bachelor societies." The head tax and then the outright ban on immigration prevented the Chinese, most of whom were men, from bringing their wives and children over to join them in Canada.[22] With the government also refusing to pay for return passage, the Chinese who could not afford the trip home had little choice but to remain and find work in mining and logging camps, restaurants, laundries, canneries, grocery stores, or on farms. These were essentially the only kinds of businesses where Chinese could be employed since, until the passage of the Canadian Citizenship Act of 1947 (the same year the Exclusion Act was repealed), Chinese were denied the right to vote or to gain membership required for professional occupations. Despite these hardships, evidence of community building in and among the bachelor societies indicate that, contrary to the popular stereotype of the Chinese as "eternal immigrants" or "sojourners" with no indigenous contributions or ties (and expected to return to China once the railway was completed), many Chinese once arrived, intended to stay and settle in Canada.[23]

The way of life in these early Chinese Canadian bachelor societies is the subject of Montreal-based artist Mary Sui Yee Wong's *Well Wishers II* (1995) (Figure 7.2).[24] The installation suggests both a Chinese laundry (one of the few places Chinese were allowed to work) and a domestic setting through its use of various washer room props and an archival photograph taken in 1900 of the founders of the Chinese Empire Reform Association.

Figure 7.2 *Well Wishers II*, 1995, by Mary Sui Yee Wong

More specifically, *Well Wishers II* brings forward a contemplation of the political nature of the Chinese social body in early Canada.

Established in 1899, the Empire Reform Association was made up on mostly older more prosperous Chinese Canadian merchants who supported the modernization of China.[25] Although not all Chinese sought refuge in keeping abreast of happenings in their homeland, as "a choice between participation or isolation" and given the wider pattern of anti-Asian sentiments fostered in Canadian politics, public policy, and Canadian society in general at the time, many bachelor workers inevitably took a keen interest in the politics of China.[26] Being involved kept them in touch with their families and ancestral home, relieved the boredom of the dead-end jobs to which they were relegated and enabled new social networks to be formed.[27] It is precisely this active and organized level of political, and to an extent, social involvement that is visually amplified in Wong's installation in the way the composite photograph of individual portraits of 43 Chinese men is reproduced in multiple to cover one entire wall. The only other things on the wall are three small white facecloths and five metal drinking cups that hang in orderly rows. In the foreground, 11 large porcelain washbasins filled with clear water are arranged in a two-tiered circular format.

According to the artist, "all the objects in this work relate to the Chinese notion of face which teaches the importance of maintaining integrity when confronting one's enemies. One must keep face, have face, and save face."[28] The appearance of so many faces and the notion of face itself are particularly evocative in past and present contexts. In early twentieth-century North America, Chinese faces signified, at best, simply cheap and dispensable labour; and at its worst, Yellow Peril.

Within a 15-year period, the exhibition in the 1990s of Yuen and Wong's works in cultural centers, galleries, and museums contrasts strikingly with the very public exposure of one particular work featuring an image of a head tax certificate shown in 2006 as part of an ongoing series of photographs titled *I Am Who I Am* by Vancouver-based artist Gu Xiong (Figure 7.3). Started in 2001, *I Am Who I Am* is a series of portraits of Chinese Canadians with quotes from them superimposed on their photographs in Mandarin, French, and English. As part of the series, Gu reproduced a head tax certificate belonging to his friend's father who came to Canada at 14 years of age. The head tax image was one of 25 photos from the project's first instalment in Montreal's Chinatown in 2001 as a La Mois de la Photo commissioned work.[29] Featured in the other portraits, such as one of a Chinese man with the text "I opened a laundry and a restaurant," are present-day and historical figures important to the development of Chinese Canadian communities usually in connection to the cities, and ideally to their Chinatowns, in which the project is shown. For example, the 2003 instalment in Panama surveyed key figures in that city's Chinatown. In both Montreal and Panama, the artist was able to realize his intended installation of the work in full public view as banners strung from lampposts across the streets in Chinatown. Remarkably however, there has been little support to present this project in Vancouver's Chinatown, Canada's largest and oldest. It was not until the artist was invited to participate in the 2006 World Urban Festival, launched as the official arts and cultural festival for the World Urban Forum, that Vancouver audiences were able to see this piece.

The prominent placement of the image of the head tax certificate, finally, at the entrance of the festival grounds, could be seen as long overdue – for both artist and issue, but also, more divisively, as either serendipitous or opportunistic, with the wide media coverage and, more significantly, the dates of the festival running from June 21 to 25, 2006. On the second day of the festival, the government presented its apology to Chinese Canadians for "the

Figure 7.3 *I Am Who I Am*, 2001, by Gu Xiong

Figure 7.4 *Orientally Yours: A Division of Gold Mountain Restaurant*, 2007, by Karen Tam

shameful policies of our past." Here it would seem that the media attention on the surviving head tax payers, and the apology, not only gave face to those appearing in the head tax certificates long displayed more as anonymous historical documents, but also played up the desirability of images of these private documents for public consumption as now something more palatable. Although circulated widely in other venues nationally and internationally, Gu's *I Am Who I Am* project, despite its identify-affirming title, was not able to impart its local currency until the historical moment of redress was in effect achieved on a highly mediatized level.

Redress Express

> The problem with race as special event is that like all specials – lunch special, special of the day, flavour of the month – they are, by definition, not the staple, not the norm. On the other hand, without such events, the issue may never be raised at all.
>
> Richard Fung, "Conference Calls: Race as Special Event"[30]

A work that conjures up multiple references to Redress Express is the recent series of Chinese restaurant installations by Montreal artist Karen Tam (Figure 7.4).[31] It travels, adapts, and serves informative tidbits on Chinese food culture, and by extension, the history of Chinese settlement in Canada. More specifically, it attempts to expose the cultural underpinnings and ethnic stereotypes that define family-owned Chinese restaurants in Canada as well as the evolution of Chinese Canadian cuisine. It has been seen on numerous occasions outside of that curious May programming slot: Asian Heritage Month.

The project has been presented in over a dozen cities across Canada since Tam developed the idea for her M.F.A. thesis exhibition at the Art Institute of Chicago in 2002. In each city, the artist recreates a site-specific Chinese restaurant, complete with its own name – Restaurant Montagne d'Or/Gold Mountain Restaurant in Montreal, Shangri-la Café in Toronto, House of Wong in Windsor, Ontario, and so on. Tam's restaurants, give or take a few elements, are typically decorated with ornate gates at the entrance, red and gold lanterns hung from the ceiling, signage in "Chinatown" or "Chopstick" fonts, and custom-made paper placements and plasticized menus that rest on tables arranged as expected in a real eating establishment. The artist achieves the kitschy yet familiar dated interiors mostly by gathering furniture and décor elements such as porcelain Buddhas and fake plants from local secondhand stores, or by borrowing them from local Chinese restaurateurs who she interviews as part of the research for the installation. In the more elaborate installations, a backroom rudimentarily stocked with enough equipment and foodstuff – rice bags recounting the Chinese contribution to building the railway and 50-pound bags of MSG – depicting the back kitchen of a Chinese restaurant is also open to visitors. The end result is a setting that not only envelops visitors but also enables them to enter into and experience a restaurant in ways not normally accessible to them. "With an installation, you walk through the space in which the work takes place."[32] The only anomaly is that no food is served, although visitors are free to bring in their own meals, which they do.

In both conceptualization and execution of her restaurant installation, Tam draws from her experience of growing up and working in her father's restaurant in Montreal. The focus on not so much the Chinese café variations that serve "Canadian and Chinese cuisine" which were the first kinds of restaurants the Chinese established primarily in small towns in Western Canada, but rather the later specialized "authentic" Chinese restaurant businesses set up by the Chinese communities in larger cities and usually clustered around Chinatowns that are now increasingly being replaced by chain outlets and fusion eateries and "fading from the scene."[33]

It is precisely because of the impossibility of recreating an authentic Chinese origin for her restaurants (the artist is keenly aware of this) that establishes the project as a productive site of investigation into the implications of changing notions of "authenticity" and consuming the Other. An important strategy lies in the menus Tam designs. Rather than indicating the set meals on offer, the menus are a pretext to access Chinese Canadian history; they contain information on how popular so-called Chinese dishes in North American restaurants such as chow mein, chop suey, and egg rolls only came to be during the first wave of Chinese immigration to the West Coast in the 1850s. On the side, the history of some typical racial slurs is explained. According to cultural critic Lily Cho, in naming dishes as Chinese, "the menu textualizes Chineseness, providing a medium through which Chineseness can be reproduced and disseminated" as stereotypes that "are actually serving back to power" the projections of dominant culture.[34] These projections are in fact the major source of play in Tam's work. Part of the installation is a video work, titled *Plum Sauce*, which shows her father preparing standardized hybrid Chinese Canadian dishes such as egg rolls, wonton, and almond cookies for Western consumption, revealing that plum sauce is actually made with pumpkin sauce in Canada. The cooking sequence is interrupted by interviews with current and former restaurant owners of the host city, which provides further awareness "of the history of these restaurants and of the restaurant workers themselves. As a customer, you never know what life is like inside the restaurant."[35]

Recent studies on Chinese restaurants in Canada in a number of academic fields have broadened understandings of the migration and settlement experience of Chinese Canadians as well as the construction of race in connection to food culture. Owing to the history of Chinese settlement in Canada, it was common for children in the Chinese community to work in the family restaurant, grocery story or laundry. However, as author Day's Lee writes in Tam's catalogue, "The restaurant was not just a business. It was a part of a larger community. That sense of community among the Chinese grew out of necessity. Fear of the 'yellow peril' ... was beginning to fade, but every so often, children or adults opened the door to the restaurant and yell 'Go back home to China!'"[36] Obviously a site of cultural exchange, the Chinese restaurant since the nineteenth century also served as an ethnic resource for immigrant communities, providing a sense of kinship, a link to China, a location for trade, and a means to self-employment for owners. These conditions have changed with further waves of Cantonese immigration in the 1960s and then in the 1980s, in anticipation of the Hong Kong handover, but the Chinese restaurant remains a central image of Chinese Canadian life and an iconic institution in diasporic communities in general.

The basis for Tam's project is similar to an earlier project by Vancouver-based artist Kira Wu called *Fuel, Food & Longings* (2001), which, playing on the usual "Gas, Food, and Lodgings," aims to construct an environment in a gallery describing Chinese restaurants and their kitchens existing, in contrast to Tam, in non-urban contexts (Figure 7.5). Wu's video installation incorporates an online web cast video feed from her brother's small town diner/café in Alberta (all three of the artist's brothers own such diners in the Canadian Prairies), inviting visitors to the gallery "to experience the reversal of exotic, cultural spaces" as they watch real-time behind-the-scenes action in a Chinese back kitchen. Both Wu's and Tam's projects enact a double displacement of the expectations for Chinese food, first in the way that it is not served, and second, in the double take upon realizing that the display is in fact not a restaurant in operation but an art project that has intentionally taken over the premises of one to turn it inside out. If consumption substitutes for experience of the Other and the political implications of that process, as much as it is a way to connect with cultural memory, here, either will connect to the fact that these are in themselves overlapping experiences deliberately manufactured for real restaurant customers and visitors to the installation alike. The projected restaurant activity thus takes on symbolic functions, not only for broader questions of ethnic relations, but also for the emergence of immigrant communities in the global context.

Montreal artist Shelly Low's *Self Serve* (2006) shares this exploration of the commodification, manufacturing, and serving up of culture through a series of self-portraits in which the artist holds up "Chinese-motif" porcelain soup spoons and restaurant plates that hide her face and gestures towards stereotypical signifiers of Asian physiognomy (slanted eyes and round facial features) and Chineseness (Chinoiserie and "China Dolls") (Figure 7.6). The refusal to show her face also serves to challenge both the images we hang on to that perpetuate notions of the Other as well as how the Chinese subject substantiates a sense of Self within a self-conscious projection and representation of the ethnic or exotic "other." Like Tam, Low also deploys the discursive power of the custom-made menu to draw out historical memory. In *Roi des nouilles (Noodle King)* (2006), three portraits taken as if they were mug shots, full frontal, and right and left profiles, are printed directly on assembled Chinese take-out menus collected from around the city (Figure 7.7). They feature the artist as the "noodle queen" donning blocks of uncooked Ramen noodles as headdress suggestive of colonial English white wigs. For another project, personal stories and statistics about

Figure 7.5 *Fuel, Food & Longings*, 2001, by Kira Wu

Figure 7.6 *Self Serve*, 2006, by Shelly Low

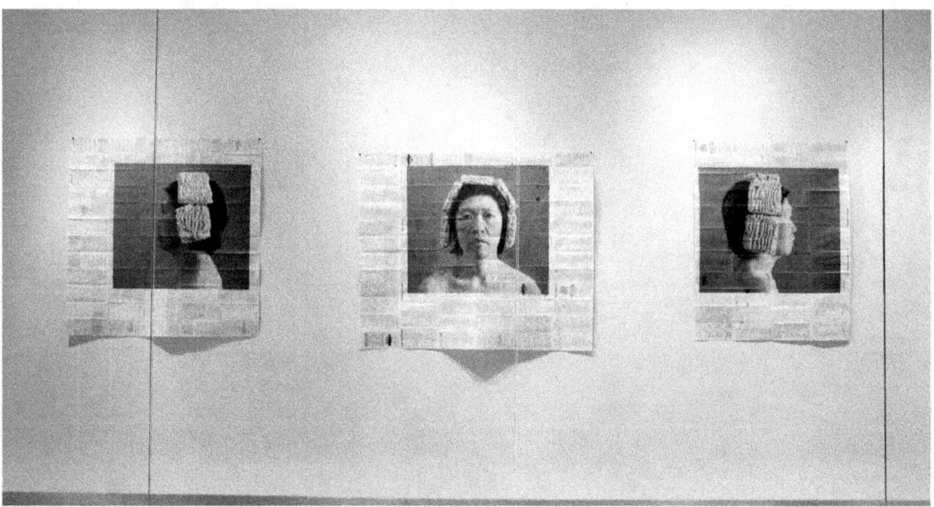

Figure 7.7 *Roi des nouilles (Noodle King)*, 2006, by Shelly Low

Chinese restaurants (the artist's parents owned a hybrid Polynesian/Chinese restaurant during the late 1970s and 1980s) and, more biting, about the Chinese head tax (Ottawa only issued the redress payments four months after the apology) are included on a take-out menu designed by the artist and intended for door-to-door distribution to reach audiences outside of the gallery context.

In closing with Low's self-portraits, a historical loop has been made back to the connection between the photo-identification of Chinese faces and the Chinese restaurant as both signifier and cultural institution that comes closer to an understanding what Redress Express might possibly serve. "Redress Express" as a critical project (exhibition, symposia, text) is an attempt to enable complex narrations in transit to take place in order to examine the redress issue and the Chinese restaurant as they relate to art, identity, and geography. An obvious connection between the six artworks surveyed is their contextualization within the development of early Chinese Canadian history. This historicization, however, does not presume that the Chinese Canadian experience is only to be located in the redress issue or the Chinese restaurant alone, or that there are not important stories from communities in close proximity which can be told in parallel or in relation. Rather, it is to acknowledge the Chinese restaurant as a relatively iconic institution that constitutes the first interface to Chinese culture for many Canadians, non-Chinese and Canadian-born Chinese alike, and to hope an examination of this phenomenon in tandem with the head tax issue in contemporary art will enable a redress of broader social implications for Chinese Canadian history. Given the current chapter of Asian Canadian art history is itself at an important point of transition in light of the shifting terrain and currency of recognition politics, further work is also required to locate the Chinese restaurant and the head tax issue within this and future chapters and confront issues that concern the current politics of race, representation and recognition in Canadian art as a whole.

The call for redress has long been the bookend of Asian Canadian critiques of Canada's racist past. The recent victory and its inevitable effects on the current politics of reparation and representation in this country however present yet another call: to ensure an ongoing, rigorous treatment that this issue demands in order to close a chapter, yes, but not foreclose building on the lessons learned in writing the next. With the host of 2007 anniversaries of historical dates significant to Asian Canadian communities recently celebrated, this provision of critical texts in contemporary discourse and practice becomes all the more imperative.

NOTES

1 Wah 1999, 259–260, last two lines. The Chinese head tax was established in 1885 under the Conservative government of Sir John A. Macdonald and was imposed until 1923 when the Chinese Immigration Act was amended. The Chinese Exclusion Act, as it was known since then, banned Chinese immigration until its repeal in 1947. This twenty-four-year ban resulted in a period during which only sixteen Chinese were admitted (exceptions were made for diplomats, clergymen, teachers, actors, merchants and tourists).

2 Bonoguore 2006.

3 No mention was made of compensation also sought in the redress campaign (based on a "one certificate, one payment" principle) for children and descendants of head tax payers (about 4,000 certificates are registered). Considering over 81,000 Chinese paid the head tax between 1885 and 1923 amounting to a total of $23 million, the *ex-gratia* payment of $20,000 to each of the handful of surviving head tax payers (only 29 are known to be still alive) or their widows (approximately another 250 or so) is obviously a symbolic sum. The wording of the apology is all the more ironic given Canada's express policy during the exclusion period was to reduce the Chinese population in Canada to keep Canada "white" even though Chinese labour was still essential to completing major unfinished parts of the railway.

4 The Chinese were the only immigrants who had to pay a head tax in the history of Canada. There are of course other overlapping histories of racial injustices in this country. This essay focuses on the Chinese-Canadian experience. Remarkably, in what appears as a seemingly

overreaching policy goal, the government also announced in the same address the establishment of a $34 million "national recognition" program "to help finance community projects aimed at acknowledging the impact of past wartime measures and immigration restrictions on ethno-cultural communities," such as the internment during the Second and First World Wars of Ukrainian, Italian, German, and Japanese Canadians, and the exclusion of Jewish and Indian immigrants. $2.5 million of the fund is allocated for a specific head tax history project.

5 For most of the now elderly head taxpayers, this and the apology were probably the only official ceremonies they had been allowed to attend involving the railway they and their ancestors helped build. Chinese workers were excluded from the photo-op ceremonies on November 7, 1885, marking the completion of the railway at Craigellachie, B.C. where dignitaries were each given a commemorative iron spike. The "Last Spike," one of these iron pegs, was donated to the Chinese Canadian redress cause for its Last Spike Campaign in 2003 by Yukon author Pierre Berton.

6 By my calculations, five first-class airplane tickets could have gotten most of the nineteen passengers to Ottawa in less than five hours. My accounting is prompted by a sentiment briefly expressed by Karin Lee of the B.C. Coalition of Head Tax Payers, in Mulgrew 2006.

7 The head tax redress campaign began in 1984 with the Mack case. Already in progress since the 1970s was the redress movement for the internment of Japanese Canadians during World War Two, which would result in the Redress Agreement on Sept. 22, 1988. For an insider's account, see Miki 2005.

8 Brooks 1999.

9 For examples, see, in the political sciences, James 2004; in Asian Canadian studies, Cho 2002.

10 Simpson 2006.

11 James 2004, 898.

12 This is part of a larger research project I am working on that aims to study the relationship between the politics of recognition in Canada and current directions in contemporary art by Asian Canadians.

13 A line from "Half-Past," a poem by Clara Ho (n.d.), about an elderly head tax payer's sentiment towards the head tax certificate. Published on the Chinese Canadian National Council website.

14 This is in contrast to, for example, representations in film, notably Karen Cho's documentary *In the Shadow of Gold Mountain* (National Film Board of Canada, 2004).

15 Shown as part of the ground breaking 1991 exhibition "Self Not Whole: Cultural Identity & Chinese-Canadian Artists in Vancouver" curated by Henry Tsang and Lorraine Chan for the Chinese Cultural Center in Vancouver. For "Artist Statement," see Tsang 1991, 60–61.

16 The number of deaths has been updated from the modest estimate of 600, equaling approximately four lives lost for every mile of track that was laid, initially provided by Andrew Onderdunk, the outside American labour broker contracted by the government to "recruit" Chinese workers through an informal system of indentured labour that paid their passage from China to the work camps on the Fraser River of British Columbia, making, as Cho notes, the amount of the head tax in many ways irrelevant as a deterrent to immigrants. Cho 2002, 73.

17 "Chinaman," perhaps a misfired transliteration of how Chinese refer to themselves (*zhongguoren*), was considered less derogatory than the term "coolie" or "chink."

18 Cho's (2002) incisive essay discusses the deep ambivalences of official government discourses on Chinese identity in the immigration acts, locating current misreadings of the head tax project between two contradictory narratives: the "dependency on Chinese labour and discriminatory restrictive measures placed on Chinese immigration" (67–68, 70). Another compelling work that evokes the ambivalent construction of the Chinaman stereotype is Paul Wong's video installation *Chinaman's Peak: Walking the Mountain* (1992). Referencing the history of Chinese railway workers in Canada, the video begins by asking who the "Chinaman" was. Gagnon 2000, 168.

19 A clear manifestation of Yellow Peril mania was demonstrated in Vancouver's Anti-Asian riots of 1907. Yet as the exhibition "Yellow Peril: Reconsidered" underscored, "'Yellow Peril' is redefined and identified as ever present insidious new forms." Gagnon 1990, 16. Projects such as Jamelie Hassan's *The Hong-Kong, for Dave and Lucy* (1984), which chronicles the closing of the artists' friends' Chinese restaurant in London, Ontario, after it was destroyed by vandalism, attest to the contemporary persistence of and necessary vigilance towards this racial epithet and its very dangerous manifestations. See artist pages in Fischer 1999, 120–121.

20 $500 in 1903 is about the equivalent of $20,000 today, although with compound interest, the estimate is between $200,000 to $300,000.

21 Ho, n.d.

22 For an account of the experiences of wives and children of bachelor workers, see Sugiman 1992.

23 The isolation experienced by these men and the cultural construction of the sojourner is examined in another work by Sharyn Yuen, *Sojourner* (1992), an installation comprised of six glass plates that stand upright on the floor as if they were tombstones. Each of the panels is sandblasted with a different text and image – "Voice," "Cultivate," "Isolate," "Cultivate," "Tremor and Voice," "Reverie" and "Silence." These statements, in addition to providing a historical context, give voice to the Chinese-Canadian experience past and present. For a more extended discussion of this work and Yuen's *John Chinaman*, see Gagnon 2000, 130–133. Playing on the term Yellow Peril, Ho Tam's first video work, *The Yellow Pages* (1994) also provides a cultural primer, but from A to Z and in a satirical manner, on the Asian experience in North American and beyond.

24 Shown at the Montreal McCord Museum of Canadian History in December 1995–February 1996, as part of "A Rare Flower: A Century of Cantonese Opera," curated by Rosa Ho and Elizabeth Johnson.

25 Active between 1899 and 1911, the Empire Reform Association supported a constitutional monarchy in China, as opposed to the co-existing Chinese Freemasons who supported armed revolution. Wickberg, Con, Con, Johnson, Wickberg, & Willmott, 1982, 74–75, 104.

26 Yee 1988, 47. For example, "because the federal franchise was based on provincial voter's lists, and because most Chinese Canadians lived on the West Coast, the B.C. law preventing persons of Chinese descent from voting or standing for office in provincial elections effectively disenfranchised most Chinese Canadians until 1947." James 2004, 889.

27 Chan 1983, 137.

28 Wong 1995.

29 Notably, this work also deals with Quebec's language laws, specifically Bill 101, titled *Charte de la langue française*, originally passed in 1977, that requires all public signage in the province to be in French although translations in English and other languages are allowed provided they are half the size. Li 2007, 198.

30 Quoted in Gagnon 2000, 69.

31 There are of course numerous other earlier examples in the visual arts, as well as film and video, that explore the Chinese(-Canadian) café, diner or restaurant, too many to mention here.

32 Tam, cited in Lee 2006, 39.

33 Lee 2006, 40.

34 Cho 2006, 51–52. Tam's menus could be said to function as counter-texts similar to how Cho's reads Fred Wah's *Diamond Grill* menu.

35 Tam, cited in Lee 2006, 40. Notably, one version also included Cheuk Kwan's video series *Chinese Restaurants* (2005).

36 Lee 2006, 39.

REFERENCES

Bonoguore, Tenille. 2006. "All Aboard the Redress Express: Next Stop, an Apology in Ottawa." *Globe and Mail*, June 21, A7.

Brooks, Roy L. 1999. "The Age of Apology." In *When Sorry Isn't Enough: The Controversy over Apologies and Reparations for Human Injustice*, ed. Roy L. Brooks, 3–11. New York: New York University Press.

Chan, Anthony B. 1983. *Gold Mountain: The Chinese in the New World*. Vancouver: New Star Books.

Cho, Lily. 2006. "On Eating Chinese: Diasporic Agency and the Chinese Canadian Restaurant Menu." In *Reading Chinese Transnationalisms: Society, Literature, Film*, ed. Maria N. Ng and Philip Holden, 51–52. Hong Kong: Hong Kong University Press.

Cho, Lily. 2002. "Rereading Head Tax Racism: Redress, Stereotype and Anti-Racist Critical Practice." *Essays on Canadian Writing* 75:62–84.

Fischer, Barbara, ed. 1999. *Foodculture: Tasting Identities and Geographies in Art*. Toronto: YYZ Books.

Gagnon, Monika Kin. 2000. *Other Conundrums: Race, Culture, and Canadian Art*. Vancouver: Arsenal Press.

Gagnon, Monika Kin. 1990. "Belonging in Exclusion." In *Yellow Peril: Reconsidered*, ed. Paul Wong, 13–16. Vancouver: On Edge.

Ho, Clara. n.d. "Half-Past." http://www.ccnc.ca/redress/stories.html.

James, Matt. 2004. "Recognition, Redistribution and Redress: The Case of the 'Chinese Head Tax.'" *Canadian Journal of Political Science* 37 (4): 883–902.

Lee, Day. 2006. "Memories of a Chinese-Canadian Restaurant." In *Karen Tam: Gold Mountain Restaurant [Restaurant Montagne d'Or]*, edited by Sonia Pelletier, 37–41. *Montréal, arts interculturels* (MAI).

Li, Xiaoping. 2007. "*Interview with Gu Xiong.*" *Voices Rising: Asian Canadian Cultural Activism*. Vancouver: University of British Columbia Press.

Miki, Roy. 2005. *Redress: Inside the Japanese Canadian Call for Justice*. Vancouver: Raincoast Books.

Mulgrew, Ian. 2006. "Head-Tax Foes Trek to Ottawa for Apology." *National Post*, June 19.

Simpson, Jeffrey. 2006. "The Latest Installment of Victim Politics, Canadian-Style." *Globe and Mail*, June 22.

Sugiman, Momoye, ed. 1992. *Jin Guo: Voices of Chinese Canadian Women*. Toronto: Women's Press.

Tsang, Henry. 1991. "Artist Statement." In *Self Not Whole: Cultural Identity & Chinese-Canadian Artists in Vancouver*, ed. Henry Tsang, 60–61. Vancouver: Chinese Cultural Centre.

Wah, Fred. 1999. "Race, to Go." In *Swallowing Clouds: An Anthology of Chinese-Canadian Poetry*, ed. Andy Quan and Jim Wong-Chu, 259–260. Vancouver: Arsenal Pulp Press.

Wickberg, Edgar, ed. Con, Henry, Con, Ronald J., Johnson, Graham, Wickberg, and Willmott, William, E. 1982. *From China to Canada: A History of the Chinese Communities in Canada*. Toronto: McClelland & Stewart.

Wong, Mary Sui Yee. 1995. "Artist Statement." McCord Museum of Canadian History, Montreal.

Yee, Paul. 1988. *Salt Water City: An Illustrated History of the Chinese in Vancouver*. Toronto: Douglas and McIntyre.

8 Between Homes: Displacement and Belonging for Second-Generation Filipino-Canadian Youths

GERALDINE PRATT IN COLLABORATION WITH THE UGNAYAN NG KABATAANG PILIPINO SA CANADA / FILIPINO-CANADIAN YOUTH ALLIANCE

In the spring of 2000, the Ugnayan ng Kabataang Filipino sa Canada/ Filipino-Canadian Youth Alliance (UKPC/FCYA) in Vancouver began to write a play in order to enact their community's experiences in Vancouver. The play begins in the Philippines, with Rosa graduating from university with a summa cum laude nursing degree. Her mother is a laundrywoman, and her father was recently laid off. Experiencing difficulties obtaining work in the Philippines, Rosa takes what she believes to be a promising nursing job in Canada. The recruitment agency has tricked her, and she soon finds herself working as a nanny in a White, middle-class Canadian home. Ashamed, Rosa continues to tell her family in the Philippines that she is working as a nurse in Canada. When Rosa sponsors the migration of her brother and sister to Canada three years later, her secret is soon revealed. Most of the rest of the play takes place in their Vancouver apartment, where Rosa speaks of the difficulties of being a Filipina migrant in Canada as well as her concerns about and frustrations with her younger siblings' efforts to succeed here. Her siblings are showing the effects of their own forced migration; her brother is "flipping hamburgers" at a fast food restaurant while he makes plans to attend a community college. Her younger sister is coping with the violent racism within her high school. When Rosa appeals to her younger brother and sister, citing her own sacrifices, her younger sister replies, "Nobody even asked me if I wanted to come. I had friends in the Philippines no matter who I was ... I want to go home."[1]

The UKPC/FCYA is organized by second- and first-generation immigrant youths; within the core group of organizers, half were in fact born in Canada.[2] And yet they chose to narrate their community's experiences in Canada from the vantage point of the very recent immigrant, shown first bidding farewell to relatives and friends at the Manila airport and then struggling during their first years in Canada. Why does this place and moment loom so large within the imaginations of these second-generation Filipino-Canadian youths? It is because those moments of departure and struggle still reverberate throughout their lives, and they continue to feel displaced – not quite at home – in their country of birth. The play is part of their struggle against a type of forgetfulness, "a corrosive forgetting, codified as assimilation" (Muñoz 1995, 78), and an effort to recover a home in the Philippines in order to achieve a sense of belonging.

We have conducted focus groups with a small number (26) of first- and second-generation Filipino youths in order to hear their stories of dislocation and home-making.[3] This paper documents this process and, thus, should not be looked at as standing apart from the play written and performed by the UKPC but, rather, as another example of UKPC'S organising work.[4] Given this, we rely heavily on direct quotation.

If it is important for Filipino-Canadian youths to tell these stories, then it is also important for all Canadians to hear them. The Filipino community in Vancouver is large; excluding those born in the United Kingdom, in 1996 it was the third largest immigrant community (Hiebert 1999a). Echoing a similar academic silence about the Filipino community in the United States, there is very little known about this community in Vancouver.[5] In the US, some have speculated that this is because assimilation into the American mainstream has been fast and successful, prepared by a history of American colonialism in the Philippines: "the Filipino ... sets foot on the US continent – she, her body, and sensibility – has been prepared by the thoroughly Americanized culture of the homeland" (San Juan 1991, 118, qtd. in Espiritu and Wolf 2001).[6] And yet studies of second-generation youths in the United States suggest a more complex process that shows both a strong resistance to assimilation and the costs of their parents' migration; in particular, high levels of educational success are matched by a rejection of an American identity, relatively low rates of self-esteem, high rates of depression, and persistent thoughts of suicide, particularly among young women.[7]

San Juan (2000) argues that the assimilationist explanation for Americans' scholarly neglect of Filipinos is not only wrong but that it also betrays a reluctance to examine a peculiarly American brand of empire that was first worked out in the Philippines during the 1898 to 1946 occupation. He insists that the "Americanization" of Filipino culture(s) – including the lives of Filipinos living in the United States – must be read within a history of American imperial expansion: "Filipinos [living in the United States] cannot concentrate solely on what is happening within the physical borders of this nation-state; this border has tentacles extending to the Philippines, even though the [military] bases are gone" (12). Canada is not equivalent to the United States, of course, but the forced migration of Filipinos living in Canada must be read within the same history of dislocation, uneven economic development, and political struggle. An itinerary for such an exploration was traced in a phrase that reoccurred during the focus groups: "Made in the Philippines, born in Canada." It is a phrase literally and jokingly used to refer to children who were conceived in the Philippines before their parents immigrated and were then born in Canada, but it carries other meanings as well. It is a phrase that stakes geographical claims and points to how Canadian birth and citizenship are persistently renegotiated in relation to the Philippines. Filipino youths are negotiating multiple homelands in an effort to belong.

This paper, then, sits awkwardly within discussions of domestic space precisely because it is a provocation, a refusal and reversal of conventional understandings of home as a bounded, protective space. Filipino-Canadian youths certainly express a yearning to be at home. But home is an ideal – a desire that leads them away from Vancouver to the Philippines. Home-making is a process of venturing out and gathering together loose threads of biography scattered in Canada and the Philippines in order to unify one's life story and to find the resources to rebel against alienating experiences of racialization. This is a process that is important to all Canadians, and it is something that has the potential to change Canada, as a multicultural home, profoundly.

Hauntings of Dislocation

Most Filipino migration to Canada has occurred since the late 1960s, after Canadian immigration practices were shifted from explicitly racial criteria to a point system geared to employment needs. Through the late 1960s and 1970s, many nurses were recruited to

Canada (almost one in four nurses admitted to Canada during this period came from the Philippines [Chen 1998]). They were followed in the mid-1970s by large numbers of garment workers and by family members who could now enter through new family reunification policies. From the mid-1980s onward nurses were no longer sought, and increasing numbers of women were admitted to Canada as live-in domestic workers. Between 1990 and 1994, for instance, almost 42 per cent of Filipinos who became landed immigrants entered Canada through what is now called the Live-in Caregiver Program (McKay and Philippine Women Centre 2002). Even this sketchy history suggests that a considerable amount of migration to Canada from the Philippines has been initiated by women. In metropolitan Vancouver in 1991, for instance, there were 15,315 employed Filipinas and just 5,525 employed Filipino men (Hiebert 1999b). This is a very different pattern of settlement from that displayed not only by other Asian immigrants to Canada but also by Filipino immigrants to the United States.

Other patterns are more familiar. Filipinos are sometimes represented by the Canadian state as "model minorities": hardworking and economically productive. In a Statistics Canada (2001, 5) profile on "Visible Minorities in Canada," for instance, Filipinos are distinguished for their relatively low rates of unemployment and poverty. With "just ... 24% of Filipinos ... living with low incomes," Filipinos are represented as being "[a]t the other end of the scale" from "Blacks, Koreans and Southeast Asians," roughly half of whom have low incomes. That one-quarter of Filipinos have low incomes (surely a high percentage on some other scale!) tells another familiar immigrant story – one of deskilling and poor income returns on educational investments. Though the proportion of Filipinos with a university degree exceeds that for the Canadian-born population, average individual incomes for Filipinos are lower (McKay and Philippine Women Centre 2002). In 1991, in the Vancouver Census Metropolitan Area, the return on "educational capital" was less for Filipinas than for women of British origin or even for the female labour force as a whole (Hiebert 1999b). Compared to all other groups of women in the Vancouver CMA, Filipinas were clustered in the narrowest range of occupations, including nursing, lower-level "medical other," clerical, housekeeping, and childcare. Compared to all other men in Vancouver, Filipino men experienced the third highest rate of occupational segregation and were clustered in some of the same occupations as were Filipina women, including clerical, janitorial, and factory work (Hiebert 1999b).[8]

These broad statistics begin to describe some of the labour market experiences of Filipino immigrants to Canada – those of the parents of the Filipino youths who participated in our study. It is important to recognize that parents' experiences of dislocation and relocation touch the lives of their children. Hirsch (1999) coins the term "postmemory" to describe the impact of parents' memories of trauma on their childrens' lives. Postmemories are "experiences that they 'remember' only as the stories and images with which they grew up, but that are so powerful, so monumental, as to constitute memories in their own right" (8). "Postmemory is a powerful and very particular form of memory precisely because its connection to its object or source is mediated not through recollection but through an imaginative investment and creation" (Hirsch 1997, 22). Sugg (2003) extends this argument to the children of exiles from Cuba, conceiving postmemories of the wounds of exile as a "generational legacy" that causes children to identify intensely with both these wounds and with Cuba as a homeland.

In keeping with Sugg's notion of postmemory, Filipino youths heard stories of their parents' struggles with racism and deskilling in Canada. Charlene recounts: "I think I heard more from my dad that he didn't like it very much ... He [said] that he experienced a little bit of depression, or maybe a lot, for the first year ... [He] said it was really cold, not just weather-wise but, you know, nobody talks to you, nobody really helps you out ... it was hard for him to adjust to that." Clara remembers: "I think that it was easier for me than for my parents." Her mother "would come home and she would say something about what a co-worker said to her. She was really offended ... So I remember things like that. It was easier for me at school" (Focus Group 6, 4 April 2001). Even though these youths are "second-generation" immigrants, they lived their parents' adjustments first-hand – their stories of their first years of arrival as well as their stories of daily experiences and frustrations at work. Clara assesses her own experiences in relation to those of her parents. We might ask what it means for a child to weigh her parents' difficulties against her own. It is a burden of sorts.

The "cascade" of trauma from one generation to the next may also work through silences and evasions. Rather than being affected by stories "so powerful, so monumental," sometimes it is the absence of such stories that generates a search for family memories, a search whose purpose is to piece together a coherent family narrative and to reclaim lost status. May tells of her parents and aunts, who immigrated in the 1970s:

> I didn't care too much about my parents' experience until much later in my life, about six or seven years ago ... [My parents and aunts] were mostly professionals when they came. I think that this is a common experience for many of us who [were born here or] came over at a young age. You go through twenty years from the '70s to '90s. Integration. Growing up here. Hearing very little about your parents' experiences unless you really probe ... I didn't know where my parents were from until I started asking. (Focus Group 10, 26 August 2001)

Charlene spoke of scrutinizing family pictures as a way of assessing and collecting concrete evidence of her parents' experience of migration: "[My mother] said that it was okay, that at least she had a big support system [when she first arrived in the 1970s]. Because I do look at pictures of her [when she first arrived in Canada] and ... [she is] always with a bunch of other nurses." Monica commented, "I know my mom worked in an office [in the Philippines] because there's pictures. Like really old pictures, with her answering the phone and things like this. And I know that she went to business college because she has this business college ring." Of her father, she said, "he didn't really tell me what his jobs were [in the Philippines]." Indeed, she was continuously frustrated by his reluctance to elaborate on his reasons for leaving the Philippines (Focus Group 4, 31 March 2001). Hirsch (1997, 22) argues that photographs are a particularly potent source of postmemory because they are "perched on the edge between memory and postmemory": they both bring back the past and provide visual evidence of its irretrievability, teetering poignantly between memory and forgetting. As children's eyes wander across photographs, and as they listen to stories relating to a time before they were born, they learn things about their parents and the Philippines that allow them to reassess their own (and their parents') worth. They work with these images and stories in creative ways to forge a new sense of self in the present out of the resources of the past. For example, they learn that the father they know as a school maintenance worker was also a mechanical engineer; a Zamboni driver was a teacher; and a security guard a civil engineer. They thus get a concrete measure of their parents' deskilling.[9] Recovering their parents' lives in the Philippines can be one way of seeing both their parents and themselves in a new light.

Homelessness

Photographs entered into the focus group narratives in another way: as documentary evidence that these youths can never belong in White Canadian society. Reflecting on her eight years of ice skating, Melissa said, "It's funny, because you had these group pictures of who is in your class. Da, da, da, da, who's chocolate sprinkle? And we're just looking back. And, it's like, alriiiighty then." Of her 12 years of ballet, Ethel said, "Who do you see in ballet? Not Filipinos. Try to fit in there. White tights and everything" (Focus Group 2, 15 March 2001). Youths spoke of the many ways in which they are haunted by this sense of exclusion in their daily lives, this sense of never really belonging. These stories move around what is now a common argument in cultural studies: legal citizenship is not equivalent to cultural citizenship, and racialized immigrants are perpetually produced as cultural outsiders. In Lowe's (1996a, 6) words, "the Asian immigrant - at odds with the cultural, racial, and linguistic forms of the [American] nation - emerges in a site that defers and displaces the temporality of assimilation." Many of the youths' stories have a familiar ring, and it is this very familiarity - even banality - that demands that they be repeated.[10]

Youths spoke of the many ways that White Canadians insist upon their perpetually immigrant status. Teachers treat grade-school children born in Canada as small ambassadors of "their" nation, which is assumed to be the Philippines. As May told it:

> I remember growing up, [when I was] in elementary school. This is when Aquino went through People Power. Or when the people ousted Marcos and Aquino came into power. It was big international news. I remember sitting at my desk and my teacher asking me about it. I was eight years old then. I don't really care. Why would she expect that I would have an opinion about it? Even in university, one of my TAs told me that I understood and spoke English really well. You are the authority on people of colour issues. (Focus Group 10, 26 August 2001)

Another common experience involves having their Canadian birthright explicitly denied by White Canadians. The following is representative of a conversation that came up again and again in at least five of the focus groups.

> MONICA: "Where are you from?" "Vancouver, Winnipeg, okay." Like you know, it's still not the answer they are looking for.
>
> CHARLENE: Like, *[I answer:]* "Montreal." "No really." "What do you want, like *[I'm from]* Maple Ridge?" *[Laughter]*
>
> MONICA: Well, I got into almost an argument with one of my clients. This was like a few years back. She was born in Grace Hospital in Winnipeg, and I thought I was also born in Grace Hospital. But then I found out later when I told my mom this story that I'm not. But anyway, I go, "Oh, I was also born in that hospital." And she goes, "Oh, you mean the name, not Winnipeg." And I go, "Yeah, I was born in Winnipeg's Grace Hospital." She just assumed that I meant the hospital, like I was born in Grace Hospital Philippines or something. "No, you know, in that hospital in Winnipeg." We almost had an argument about it. I was more hot-tempered *[then]*. I'm like, "What are you talking about? I WAS BORN IN GRACE HOSPITAL!" *[Laughter]* (Focus Group 4, 31 March 2001)

This assumption was naturalized in an amusing but telling way when Vicki was doing her practicum as a student teacher:

> What's funny is the school I am in is predominantly Caucasian or White ... We were talking about rocks. And where they come from and stuff. And all of a sudden, the hand goes up. "Well, where do you come from?" And automatically ... oh, okay, these are little kids. And usually if someone came up to me, say another White person, [I'd say] "Well, I was born here, so I am Canadian." And then they are, like, "Oh." And then they take offence to it. Then I say [to the kids], "Well, my parents are from the Philippines. But I was born here. I am Filipino." So the kids were amazed. "Oh, so you are Filipino." And they would say, "My mom went to the Philippines!" And all these hands go up. "My mom's nanny or my nanny is a Filipino." (Focus Group 6, 4 April 2001)

What these statements indicate is that identifying as Filipino or with the Philippines is not just a choice: it emerges out of a process of being continuously read as a recently arrived outsider.[11] As Ong (1996) notes, immigrants do not arrive as "ready-made ethnics." Ethnic identification involves a sense of belonging that emerges in relation to a complex weave of state and non-state, institutionalized and everyday, cultural practices and is imposed by everyday experiences of racial exclusion. This is captured in a vivid way in Maricel's account of eating lunch at work. The conversation turns around her use of a knife (which plays on the "knife edge" of interest in cultural plurality and in casting Filipinos as primitive).

> MARICEL: Because it's funny, I prepare my food at work. There's this big guy at work. He's lived in Vancouver all of his life. He says, "You just don't use a knife, do you?" he goes, "Let me wash a knife." I would say, "No, no, it's okay." And then someone else in the staff room who has known me for ages goes, "Oh, she doesn't use a knife." He said, "What do you mean? She is eating meat." They said, "No, you don't understand. It is not in her culture. She doesn't know how to use a knife." He said, "Are you serious?" I said, "Yeah, actually I don't really know how to eat with a knife."... He said, "I want to see this." So, he's watching me eat my meat and rice with spoon and fork. He goes, "Incredible! I just don't get it." And then I have to explain this thing about knives and make up a story about how it's in our culture how we are forbidden to have knives.
>
> MONICA: Great, you're contributing to the mis-education of this man! (Focus Group 6, 4 April 2001)

We thus witnessed the invention of a cultural story in an effort to save face.

Another type of seemingly multicultural inclusion can be extremely isolating: this is sexualisation and exoticization. Young women were very familiar with being objectified as "Asian woman" and were particularly wary of men who had learned a few phrases of Tagalog. Youths had the impression that courses taught in Vancouver in Tagalog are used by White men who are involved (or wanting to be involved) with Filipina women. According to Charlene,

> A lot of people assume that I am fifteen or sixteen. When the older White men start talking to me in a subtle, but sexual, way it's really disgusting ... I think that what disturbs me also is when White men, or men from other nationalities, start talking to you, hitting on you, in Tagalog. They know that! They know how to do that

to you in Tagalog ... When they walk down the street, and say, "Oh, maganda! [beautiful]" "How do you know that?! Get away from me!" ... Earlier this year, I went out to this store to pick up some lunch. This guy opened the door and let me out. I thanked him. He started to follow me. He said to me, "Oh, are you Filipino?" I thought: "Oh, here we go. Leave me alone." [May interjects: "You know it's bad when they ask that."] I'm clutching my lunch. I'm waiting for the light to turn. I just wanted to walk right then. Eventually he started to tell me that he stayed in Manila for a bit. "Oh, that's nice." He said, "You women are so beautiful." I started walking away really fast and said, "Okay, bye." I turned and walked the other direction from where my office was to get away from this guy. I walked for 10 minutes just to make sure I lost him. (Focus Group 10, August 26, 2001)

Even a story on mail-order brides, written by one youth, Sean, as part of his coursework in a publishing program at Langara College, was reworked to sexualise Asian women (Parlan 2001). He intended his article to be a hard-hitting critique of the economic relations that lead women to market themselves as brides. It was, however, edited to reflect the perspectives of men who shop for mail-order brides. Much space is given to detailing the process of ordering a bride, and relatively little is given to accounts of women's experiences and their collective resistance. The cover really tells the whole story (see Figure 8.1): the article (which Sean had entitled "Mail-Order Brides") is billed as: "Veiled Propositions: The Story of Mail-Order Brides" and is situated alongside an image of a naked Filipina woman whose downcast and side-long gaze suggests nothing of the active opposition with which Scan was concerned.

Filipino men are not immune to this process of stereotypical sexualisation. As Carlo and Charlene told it:

CARLO: In a lot of magazines *[you see the question,]* "Are Asian men sexy?" I guess they are becoming more visible.

CHARLENE: In the last few months, I've noticed a lot of Asian magazines directed toward the Asian community have been doing these articles about Asian men ... A funny thing happened where this reporter from the *Toronto Star* called me for an interview ... I thought she would have wanted to talk about our organizing work in Ugnayan. Then she says, "I'm doing this article on Asian men. I noticed that Asian men are not really noticed. Asian women are more in the forefront of articles on Asian people. I just wanted to know if you thought Asian men were attractive or sexy."

CARLO: The King and I, man ... It's a trendy thing ... Before it was trendy to have a gay friend, especially if you are living in the West End. Now, it's the multicultural.[12] (Focus Group 10, 26 August 2001)

If seemingly more benign than sexism, exoticism breeds just as much isolation and alienation.

One way of fighting against this isolation/alienation is to identify strongly and positively with Filipino culture. At one of the focus groups, a participant who had moved to Vancouver in 1981, when she was two years old, asked two women who were born in Canada: "Do you think that not being born in the Philippines makes you look for those Filipino roots more? I'm thinking, because I was born in the Philippines, I don't have the strong urge to actively search for those connections" (Focus Group 4, 31 March 2001). This is an interesting question, situating, as it does, an intense identification with Filipino culture in personal histories of exclusion within Canada. In May's words: "[We identify as Filipinos] because

Figure 8.1 Sexualising Filipinas. Front cover of *Pacific Rim Magazine*, vol. 2, no. 3, 2001

we are forced to in our daily experience ... it was to defend ourselves ... emotionally and mentally. [We were] arming ourselves to go to school" (Focus Group 10, 26 August 2001).

Charlene also described how her experiences of racism within Canada led her to embrace a Filipino identity:

> I see myself as more Filipino. Because at least I know myself, at least I have a better sense of who I am as a Filipino. No matter what, they'll always assume that I was not born here anyway. I was born and raised here, I can speak both official languages. I can speak French better than I can speak Tagalog or Illongo. Which I wish it wasn't that way all of the time. But, like, that's how it is usually. Like once when I was in high school, there was this incident. This girl had just moved from the Philippines. I was in the tenth grade or eleventh grade, and she was in the eighth grade. She didn't know anybody, so I talked to her right away. And my friends noticed and they said, "Why are you talking to her?" I was, like, "Well, she's Filipino, and she just came here and she doesn't know anybody. I don't want her to feel alone in school." "Oh, you're so different from all of them." "Well, what do you mean?" "You know, all of THEM." And they were pointing to all of the Chinese students on the other side of the cafeteria. "Oh, you are not like all of the black-haired people." Then I figure, what if I wasn't born here or if I never, if I was not put in a group with them when I first came to Maple Ridge? I don't think I would have known them. I'm the only person of colour that they frequently talk to. And if that is what Canadian means, if that's the Canadian attitude, then I don't like that. I'm more confident saying that I'm more Filipino. (Focus Group 4, 31 March 2001)

Ethel described a similar process of consciously self-identifying as Filipino:

> That's how I used to think. I'm Canadian. Then I started changing my mind: "I'm Filipino." But anyway, right now I see myself as Filipino and I have absolutely no problem saying that. There was a time when I used to have that problem that I'm Filipino ... I feel a deeper connection to my roots that I did not have before. I still identify myself as Filipino-Canadian because I have been here all my life. But I connect more strongly with my Filipino identity than my Canadian identity. I don't know if I have ... Most of my friends are Filipino ... I don't really have ... or maybe at work ... actually I don't really have any friends at work. [Laughter] My friends where I used to work, they were ... well, my closest friend was Filipino. You know? That's how I identify myself the most. (Focus Group 2, 15 March 2001)

This is a process of identification that is both imposed and struggled for. In one focus group, Eda, a 15-year-old who immigrated to Canada in 1996 at the age of ten, denied the authenticity of this identification when he stated flatly that "100 per cent Filipino is made in the Philippines" (Focus Group 5). Eda's statement produced a strong reaction from the four Canadian-born Filipinos in the group, who argued that Filipino refers, in large part, to "where I choose to learn my heritage." This nicely states Grossberg's (2000, 154) claim that "belonging is a matter less of identity than of identification, of involvement and investment, of the line of connecting and binding different events together."

When Filipino youth assert that their identification emerges from "where they choose to learn their heritage," their spatial claim is more than metaphorical. Filipino youths are not only stitching together moments of past and present but also different places. To continue with Grossberg, "to belong – in a different mode – ... is also to belong to a different time-space" (ibid.).

Going to the Philippines

Ong (1996) has criticized the ways in which the Latino Cultural Studies Working Group (Flores and Benmayor 1997) has deployed the concept of cultural citizenship; that is, as a set of cultural practices that demand both the right to a distinctive social space for Latino Americans in the United States and a sense of belonging within the nation. She argues that this notion of cultural citizenship gives the erroneous impression that cultural identification is self-made. For Ong, ideas of belonging and not belonging are produced within complex fields of cultural and economic power. She compares the production of Hong Kong immigrants and Cambodian refugees in the United States: because of their different economic positions, the former, she argues, undergo a process of whitening, while the latter undergo a process of darkening. She details how both groups manipulate and negotiate these positions but are unable to stand outside the process of subjectification imposed by the dominant, White American society. Siu (2001) notes that both of these approaches (Ong's and the one she criticizes) are limited by the same presumption that subject formation takes place within the borders of a single nation-state. It may be that groups attain a capacity for self-production by literally moving outside the nation-state. This is one way of understanding the significance of the Philippines for Filipino-Canadian youths.

Wolf (2002) writes about the "emotional transnationalism" of second generation Filipino-American youths in San Diego. While parents maintain relationships that directly link the United States and the Philippines, their children maintain the links "at the level of emotion, ideologies, and conflicting cultural codes" (350). The youths who participated in our focus groups certainly held these sentiments: "When I think of the Philippines or see the flag or see a Filipino sticker on their car, it brings this joy. I know it's a bit sappy" (Charlene, Focus Group 10, 26 August 2001). But they have also made actual trips to the Philippines, which functioned as what Sugg (2003) refers to – in reference to Cuban-Americans – as "therapeutic returns."[13] Sugg notes that "the journey itself [to Cuba] does seem to be necessary to this process of working through ... [a] multiple (as opposed to [a] dual) sense of belonging." Filipino-Canadian youths describe the journey to the Philippines as a journey to a space of belonging. Anthony, a 24-year-old born at Vancouver General Hospital, described his year studying at a college in the Philippines as "the happiest time of my life." Junior, a 21-year-old born and raised in Montreal, said simply: "I loved the Philippines" (Focus Group 7, 5 April 2001).

Melissa and Monica described in some detail the comfort of feeling at home in the Philippines:

MELISSA: I went back to the Philippines throughout my life. When I was older I went to the Philippines ... it was the same thing: *[the recognition]* that everyone's Filipino. It was just weird ... So when you get a taste of that, and when you get back, it's like, "Hold up, I'm different" ... To hang out with my mom's side of the family, which of course is Filipino, it just feels like home. You get used to this spoon and fork, eating with your hands, whatever.

MONICA: I have been back to the Philippines three times and it is totally different everywhere you look. It is true. It is all Filipinos. It is such a surreal experience because you are used to looking and seeing all Caucasians or whatever ... It's not even about superficial cultural things, but sometimes it is. If you are going to ask for Balut or if you are going to ask for Taho or something like that, they are not going to look at you and say, "What the hell is that?" (Focus Group 2, 15, March 2001)

In an anthology of writings by young Filipino-Canadians produced by the UKPC/FCYA (2000), Cherrie June Emnance writes:

> If I could only have one wish come true, I would wish to be *home*.
>
> I was born and raised here in Canada for 22 years now. Everything that I have learned, accomplished, and experienced revolves here. My usual group of friends I hang out with, the usual day of activities I'm used to, and even the stressful life I lead in school and work belongs here in Canada. But I've come to the realization that I'm missing one thing in my life ... the feeling of "home." I know, it sounds strange that I've lived here all my life and yet I still say that I'm missing the feeling of my "home," but it's true.
>
> I miss the sound of jeepnies beeping for way, roosters crowing in the morning, and even the smell of the thick air. I miss being able to appreciate the simple gifts of life and knowing that when I am "home," who I really am is all that matters to the people I am surrounded by. I can go "home" for two weeks out of three whole years, and still feel like I've never left. It's the greatest feeling knowing that I have family who make me feel like they've never left my side, like we've never been apart. I miss the feeling of knowing I belong with my family at "home" and being able to express myself freely about how I really feel, rather than being somebody I'm not.
>
> If I could only have one wish come true that would make me genuinely happy, I would wish to be "home" in the Philippines.

A parent of one of the focus group participants told me that Filipino parents like to send their youths back to the Philippines for an extended period of time so that they can develop a more realistic impression of this place called home. Listening to Filipino-Canadian youths, one can hear the efforts of parents to manage this return: "Like, [my parents] would tell us [about] life in the Philippines and how it's not easy... I know it's a hard life in the Philippines. For the people there, they have to work all the time. And it's not easy to go to school even ... You have more options here" (Carlo, Focus Group 3, 30 March 2001). Monica expressed the same feeling: "Especially the first time we went to the Philippines when I was nine [my parents said] 'The way your cousins live in the Philippines, that is how we would have lived. So you should be happy and thankful'" (Focus Group 2, 15 March 2001). Anthony, like all of his brothers, was sent back to the Philippines for one year of Bible college, and he tells of his mother's efforts to control the length and long-term repercussions of this "therapeutic return." There is a struggle between Anthony and his mother about the meaning of the Philippines as a home – as a repository for cultural values as opposed to a place of domicile.

> We planned it before, but it was a decision with my mom. But when I was in the Philippines, I really loved it there and didn't want to come back here. But my mom said no, I have to come back. What would I have done there? I would have tried to get a job. And it probably would have been really hard. She was afraid that I was going to settle down with a girl there or something. She sent my dad to the Philippines to pick me up. I was there for one month longer the first time, one month longer than my brother. My brother had gone to the States. I was travelling through the Philippines and [then] my dad came back [to the Philippines to retrieve me]. I remember having discussions with my mom. I never planned to stay there. But sometimes ... just to scare her ... Basically I felt like I was forced back by my mom. (Focus Group 7, 5 April 2001)

Anthony, who has a degree in information technology from the British Columbia Institute of Technology, continued to entertain fantasies of a permanent return to the Philippines but only at the age of retirement. He imagined returning as a fisher.

It would be wrong to simplify these youths' experiences of the Philippines to fantasies and desires for a home and for belonging or to Anthony's kind of nostalgic (future) return as rural fisher.[14] Their impressions of the Philippines are seasoned by their parents' commentary, by a critique of the Philippines government's responsibility for their parents' forced migration, and by an understanding that life can be very hard there. Asked whether he could actually see himself living the life of a fisher, Anthony equivocated: "No, not really ... their life is probably not that simple."

For many it is not the Philippine nation that is sought as home; rather, it is a concrete history of struggle that allows them to re-imagine themselves. This home is a community of resistance, and it is a type of home that can be brought back to Canada and used to reconfigure Vancouver as home. May expressed this notion of the Philippines as home:

> It is a sentiment for the people. It is not a sentiment for the [nation-state]. It could be for the family who brought you here. Or for your grandmother who raised us. When we look back at our history, we try to look back at the people's history. When we learn about that, there is really a strong connection to the Filipino people that we never learn about in Canada. They hardly learn about that in their textbooks in the Philippines. So many years of being colonized and living in poverty. What we really appreciate when we go back is how people really struggle ... Collectively, you can really see how people resisted their oppression ... Especially for people who grew up not feeling proud about being Filipino. We found something to be proud of and it is incredible. Your self-identification also changes ... I don't think it is a romantic sentiment. We also know there are struggles within the Philippines. (Focus Group 10, 26 August 2001)

Uncovering this specific, material history of a real, not just an imaginary, place becomes an important means of establishing self-worth. In a poem published in the Ugnayan ng Kabataang Filipino sa Canada/Filipino Canadian Youth Alliance anthology (UKPC/FCYA 2000, 25), Christine Mangosing expresses not only a sense of plural identification but also the fact that a recovery of her Filipino "roots" strengthens her resistance to racism and daily feelings of dislocation in Canada.

> I have dark almond shaped eyes
> emphasized with a slant
> I have naturally black hair
> but chemically enhanced
> I have a question in mind that I can't seem to decide
> if I'm too light or too dark, or if my nose is too wide
> I speak confidently in a voice strongly disguised
> with words spoken by whom we were colonized
> And this same voice that once fumbled with my native tongue
> knows not the words of the anthem that should be rightfully sung.
> Blood of the Spanish and the Chinese flow through my veins
> and Western cultural influence dictates my ways
> For I was raised beneath a North American sun
> Lacking knowledge of the country where my life begun.
> But now I find, as I strive to revive
> the ROOTS I have once denied
> Genuine pride in the Filipino that's me
> and greater insight into my identity

So here I stand, reverberating my RHYMES
with the intention to share through my words
How I've struggled to reach the point where being
Filipino and Canadian merge
And in gaining knowledge of my Filipino people's past and present reality
I strengthen my RESISTANCE
to oppressive racial persistence
and find my place in global society.

Returning to Canada

Christine's reference to global society may not be quite specific enough in that it misses the very concrete connections that are being forged between particular geographies and histories. The UKPC/FCYA now sees its struggle in Canada as part of the struggle in the Philippines. Crossing national boundaries has brought its struggle against racism in Canada into a larger history of resistance. This alters the geographical reach of the activities of the UKPC/FCYA to include struggles within the Philippines (e.g., an extended Oust Estrada campaign).[15] On the face of it, it may seem odd that Canadian-born citizens who have made a few periodic visits to the Philippines should work so hard on a campaign in another country. But such a campaign is seen to be part of their history in Canada. Feeling the effect of their parents' forced migration from the Philippines within their daily lives, they understand the political and economic relations within the Philippines to be part of not only their history but also their daily existence.[16]

And it is not simply that the geographical reach of the UKPC/FCYA has expanded: members learn directly from community organizing traditions in the Philippines. Every year the UKPC/FCYA now sends youths to the Philippines to learn from organizations there. Representations to the Philippines from youth groups from North America have increased substantially in recent years and have attracted the interest of organizations in the Philippines.[17] The theatre project with which we began is, in fact, an outgrowth of one such visit; the project was directly shaped through a guide to doing theatre among the masses – a guide that was brought to Canada from the Philippines. But, significantly, the theatre project was a synthesis of experiences undergone in both Canada and the Philippines. The play was partially centred around a confrontation between Filipino and White youths at Vancouver Technical Secondary School in 1999, a confrontation that led to a Filipino student being slashed. Despite documentation of the existence of graffiti such as "All Flips Must Die," testimonies from girls that rocks had been thrown at them when trying to board the bus, the fact that 25 Filipino youths were refusing to go to school because they feared for their safety, and representations from Filipino parents, the UKPC/FCYA was frustrated by the reluctance of the Vancouver School Board to publicly name the problems at the school as racist. The play is an application of a community-organizing technique learned in the Philippines, and its purpose is to give voice to the sense of despair and frustration felt by Filipino-Canadian youths in Canada. In other words, if the methodology is Filipino, the content is distinctly Canadian.

And how might such cultural practices enter into a process of revisioning Canada as a home? In contrast to the Philippines as a repository of sentiment and a political space from which to draw strength and learn specific oppositional tactics, Canada was typically represented as a liberal state from which to claim rights – not a particularly "home-like" image.

As Carlo, put it: "When you are saying you are Canadian, it is like a defence mechanism. [In reaction to] when people think you can't speak English, or whatever. 'Where are you from?''Well, I'm Canadian. I know as much about it as you do, of this country or whatever. I am just as smart as you are.' It is just someone assuming things about you and you want to prove them wrong."

Charlene continued:

> That is how I use the fact I was born here ... I let them know I have just as much of a right to be here ... I was born here and I use that to assert myself as an individual here ... for our community, we use that [in the following way:] "Because you brought us here because you want our labour. Give us what we deserve." When I see Canadian people who are waving the Canadian flag, I feel detached on a certain level regarding patriotism. (Focus Group 10, 26 August 2001)

But the types of mappings that they are practising in their daily lives in Canada – as they fold the history of the Philippines into their mundane existence and insist on the continuities and connections (not just the discontinuities and ruptures) between Canada and the Philippines – also exceed this liberal reading of the state as a guarantor of rights. This has some implications for re-imagining multiculturalism.

Re-imagining Multicultural Canada

Multiculturalism is tied up with Canadian nationalism in important and complex ways. Mitchell (2001, 57) argues that it is "doubly inscribed: it is inherently nationalist in purpose and orientation, and it is also clearly based on a proceduralist model of liberalism that privileges British philosophy and culture as the nationalist norm."[18] Multiculturalism is thus Canadian and Anglo. Following Taylor (1994), Mitchell argues that federal multiculturalism is based on a proceduralist model of liberalism, which is inherently individualist and which envisions encompassing an endlessly expanding number of groups through the type of rights discourse deployed by Carlo and Charlene. But Carlo and Charlene also understand that access to rights in Canada is unequal (Razack 1998), and UKPC/FCYA argues that, if ethnic groups are simply "tolerated" in relation to the cultural norm (Hage 1998), then multiculturalism reinforces the cultural hegemony of Anglo-Canadians.

As Mitchell argues, immigrant groups do not necessarily embrace the fundamental principle of individualism that underlies the federalist multicultural model. She develops this argument in relation to affluent Chinese immigrant parents who, in Richmond, British Columbia, have entered into a conversation with Canadian parents about the goals and ideals of their children's education. Chinese immigrant parents have been strong supporters of "traditional" schools in Richmond, arguing that these schools teach an ethical code that will equip their children for a competitive global society. They see this as more important than focusing on creativity and the child's rights to individuality. Mitchell argues that this debate throws the idea of "an implicitly 'national' education program in question" (68) as Chinese immigrant parents frame the needs of their children in terms of global rather than national citizenship. Assessing the progressive potential of these parents' actions, Mitchell asks the following questions:

> Rather than through the "generous" inclusion of outside groups into a hegemonic nation-state project, how can the project itself be reformulated from the "bottom up"? How can

multiculturalism be given teeth through a reconstitution of the project "from below"? How can national responsibilities articulate with global ones and vice versa?

These are large questions, and they point towards a different model of multiculturalism than that which celebrates a pluralistic blending of the diversity of cultures within Canada. Mitchell notes that the political demands of the Richmond Chinese Canadian parents are not necessarily progressive because they have the potential to "leapfrog from [the nation-state] directly into the netherworld of global capitalism" (71). The political and cultural activities of Filipino-Canadian youths suggest a different, mediating, geographical imagination in relation to multiculturalism – one that works between the nation-state and the "netherworld of global capitalism." This entails tracing the specific histories of connection between Canada and other nations. This geography of connectivity poses multiculturalism as a process of articulation rather than of pluralism, and it ruptures the national boundedness of the multicultural project in Canada. To be fully multicultural, Canadians must appreciate the specificity of connections and the complexity of identifications and attachments held by many Canadian citizens. This offers a way of re-imagining Canada, not just Filipino youths.

An important irony to note in relation to Charlene's and Carlo's disavowal of attachment to Canada is that they nonetheless exercise their civic duty of public participation, likely more fully than do the majority of Canadians, through their activities at the UKPC/FCYA. Operating in what Holston (1995) has called "the spaces of insurgent citizenship,"[19] the youth alliance introduces new ideas and new practices that potentially change the meaning of Canada as a home. By bringing organizing traditions from the Philippines to Canada, the UKPC/FCYA blurs some of the distinctiveness of national boundaries. In quite another context, Mike Davis (2000, 144) has argued that the large Mexican/Central American working class in Los Angeles "may yet reshape the American labor movement"; "new wave campaigns have overwhelmed employers with an innovative tactical repertoire that has included guerrilla theatre and film [and] public art" (147), some of which has been imported from other national contexts (Houston and Pulido 2002). "To be Latino in the United States," argues Davis (2000, 15) "is ... to participate in a unique process of cultural syncretism that may become a transformative template for the whole society." Without resorting to Davis's hyperbole, we want to suggest that second-generation Filipino-Canadians' efforts to find a home in Canada may also hold the promise of transforming it, not only by tracing ongoing histories of connection between the Philippines and Canada but also by transforming the practice of politics and contemporary claims to belonging within Canada.[20]

A close study of the identification of Filipino-Canadian youths also suggests fresh ways of conceiving identity formation. Žižek (2002) has recently complained that postcolonial and multicultural studies share a tendency to conceive of identity formation among postcolonial subjects and racialized minorities strictly in the terms set by the dominant society. Minoritized subjects are granted the right to narrate stories of victimization, but, "at the end of the day, we learn that the root of postcolonial exploitation is [the dominant group's] intolerance towards the Other, and, furthermore, that this intolerance itself is rooted in our intolerance towards the 'Stranger in Ourselves,' in our inability to confront what we repressed in and of ourselves" (Žižek, 545). Academic stories about identification continuously circle around and back to the stories of the dominant.

Filipino youths are narrating more than their victimization, and their process of identity-formation exceeds the tight, recursive circuit of identification between colonized and colonizer. And while their identification as Filipino emerges in relation to processes of exclusion within Canada, it is not contained by them: it involves a specific engagement with the reverberating effects of imperialism across the generations. Although many second-generation Filipino-Canadian youths are not exactly "at home in the world," their world exceeds Canada in ways that they are successfully mobilizing in order to claim belonging.

NOTES

1 The young woman who first played this part has indeed returned to the Philippines. The play has been performed a number of times, including at the Kalayaan Centre in May 2000, in Winnipeg for the Filipino-Canadian National Consultative Forum in August 2000, at the Asian Connections conference at the University of British Columbia in November 2000, during Asian Heritage Month in May 2001, and at the National Forum for Filipino Nurses in December 2001.

2 In 1993 the Montreal Coalition of Filipino Students was organized. In that same year, the Canadian Youth Network for Asian Pacific Solidarity (CYNAPS) and the British Columbia Committee for Human Rights in the Philippines sponsored a national speaking tour featuring a member from the League of Filipino Students (LFS), a student organization based in the Philippines. During the tour, this representative of LFS met with MCFS and other politically conscious Filipino youths across Canada. In the summer of 1994, Filipino youths from Winnipeg, Toronto, Montreal, and Vancouver met in St-Hilaire, Quebec, for a national consultation, where they passed a resolution to begin local youth organizations in their respective cities. One woman attending from Vancouver was involved with the Philippine Women Centre (PWC), and she and several other young women involved with the PWC already felt that they needed a separate group in which to address their distinctive issues. With the help of the PWC, they organized the UKPC/FCYA in the summer of 1995. The first issues with which they dealt were those of identity (e.g., Who are we? Are we Filipino or Canadian?), racism, and their own unfamiliarity with Filipino history. In 1996 UKPC/FCYA organized a province wide consultation (entitled "As We Begin to Understand Our Roots") attended by forty to fifty youths, during which they began to explore the history of the Philippines and their families' histories of migration.

3 We conducted ten focus groups from spring to fall 2001. The focus groups varied in size, from four to six people, and there was some overlap as some individuals participated more than once. A total of twenty-six youths, between the ages of fourteen and twenty-eight, participated. Since the sample was assembled through social networks, we cannot claim any representativeness for the views expressed. For a project similar in intent and methodology, see Strobel (1997).

4 As a middle-aged, White Canadian academic, in a number of ways Pratt has an ambiguous relationship to this group. This project is framed within her collaboration with the UKPC'S parent organization, the Philippine Women Centre (see Pratt in collaboration with the Philippine Women Centre 1998, 1999). For the present study, Pratt was present at only two of the focus groups, and in all cases the groups were facilitated by UKPC members. Pratt drafted her first analysis on the basis of transcribed records. This became a point of discussion with the UKPC and ultimately led to the mutually agreed upon final draft.

5 A number of US scholars note the oddity of this silence given that Filipinos constitute the largest Asian-origin immigrant group in the United States (Bonus 2000; Espiritu 1994; Espiritu and Wolf 2001; Okamura 1998; San Juan 2000). In the Canadian case, Anita Beltran Chen's (1998) socio-demographic work is the most comprehensive nation-wide study of Filipino-Canadians,

but, being based on research conducted in the 1970s and 1980s, it is now quite dated. In Canada, there is a vast literature on the Live-in Caregiver Program (e.g., Arat-Koç 1989, 1990, 1992; Bakan and Stasiulis 1994, 1995, 1997; Daenzer 1993; Pratt 1997, 1999; Stasiulis and Bakan 2001; Stiell and England 1997) but very little on the broader community, including Canadian-born Filipinos.

6 Rosaldo has argued that this disinterest on the part of American academics extends to the Philippines because it is considered "too Westernized," with "no culture" of its own (Rosaldo 1988, 78, qtd. in Espiritu 1994).

7 The figures are startling. Drawing upon interviews with 808 Filipino youths in San Diego, conducted as part of a longitudinal study (Children of Immigrants Longitudinal Study), Espiritu and Wolf (2001) report that, in 1992, 59 per cent of the sample identified as Filipino-American and 31 per cent as Filipino. Only 5 per cent identified as American. Only three years later, drawing upon essentially the same sample of youths, 55 per cent now identified as Filipino and 37 per cent as Filipino-American. Half of those who identified as Filipino-American in 1992 now identified as Filipino. Resistance to assimilation is also noted by Bonus (2000) and Okamura (1998). Surveys of teens in San Diego high schools indicate that Filipina female students report high levels of suicidal ideation (46 per cent) and alarming rates of reported actual suicide attempts (23 per cent) – the highest of any ethnic group surveyed (cited in Espiritu and Wolf 2001, 178).

8 For comparable analyses of Toronto, see Lo et al. (2000) and Ornstein (2000).

9 These examples are drawn directly from the focus groups. The sample of second-generation youths is too small to draw meaningful generalizations, but there are some suggestive patterns. All of the mothers had paid employment and experienced relatively little downward occupational mobility, principally because six of the twelve could practise their profession of nursing when they immigrated to Canada. (The situation has now changed, and many professional nurses from the Philippines now enter Canada through the Live-in Caregiver Program. The process of deskilling is thus now a greater problem.) The situation was a little different for their fathers, half of whom experienced downward occupational mobility (of the type already described) or retired after immigrating to Canada.

10 These stories strike a chord with those of other diasporic communities. Catherine Sugg (2003), for example, writes of the "suspended migration" of second-generation Cuban-Americans who are caught between cultural memories of a Cuban homeland and life in the United States.

11 Espiritu (1994) also notes the primary significance of experiences of racism for second-generation Filipino American youths' identification as Filipino. In the Canadian context, Elaine Chang (1994), writing about her experiences growing up as a Korean-Canadian, makes the explicit and eloquent argument that her capacity to construct her identity has always been conditioned by how she was read. The persistent construction of Asians as outsiders within the nation has been conceived of as part of the process through which the culturally dominant create the nation as home – in other words, as part of a home-making project on the part of White Canadians (Anderson 1991).

12 For a discussion of the exoticization of Black culture in mainstream popular culture (e.g., Nike, rap music), especially influential among White, middle-class male youths, see Sernhede (2000).

13 These therapeutic returns can work very differently, depending on the circumstances of the group in question. Studying Mexican-American teenaged girls living in Los Angeles, Melissa Hyams (2002) describes how visits to relatives in Mexico strengthen their identification with the United States. The visits confirm their national and personal superiority and modernity as measured against the "backwardness" of their Mexican relatives. As one young woman put it:

"Same hair, different hairstyle." The Filipino youths with whom we spoke tended not to operate within such a polarized frame of modernity and underdevelopment, and visits to the Philippines were seen as rich opportunities for rethinking their own identities and political strategy.

14 This should not imply that Filipino-Canadian youths' dreams of return are always nostalgic: two of the Canadian-born members of the Youth Alliance are living in the Philippines on a permanent basis.

15 The UKPC'S first campaign on the impacts of systemic racism on Filipino-Canadian youths was a response to the attack on sixteen youths of colour, mainly Filipino, in Squamish, BC, in 1998. This was followed by a conflict at Vancouver Technical Secondary School in Vancouver in 1999. At this time, the group also began to try to understand how multiculturalism mediates and displaces diagnoses of racism. A second campaign began in 1999 to commemorate the centennial of the Filipino-American War, and it has continued and intensified as the Philippines becomes the "second front" of the US-led war on terrorism. Aside from these initiatives, the organization has participated in other international campaigns, including the Oust Estrada campaign.

16 There are interesting parallels to an argument that Lisa Lowe makes regarding the way in which some Korean-Americans interpreted the Los Angeles uprising in April 1992, particularly the interpretation offered by the Korean-American documentary film *Sa-I-Gu*. The title, which means 4.29, or April 29, embeds the Los Angeles uprising firmly within Korean national history because it follows "after the manner of naming other events in Korean history –3.1 (sam-il) for March 1, 1919, when massive protests against Japanese colonial rule began in Korea; 6.25 (yooki-o) or June 25, 1950, when the Korean War began; and 4.19 (sa-il-ku), or April 19, 1960, when the first student movement in the world to overthrow a government began in South Korea. The ironic similarity between 4.19 and 4.29 does not escape most Korean Americans" (Kim 1993, 216). Lowe (1996b, 423) argues that this allusion to Korean nationalism through the naming of the film is "not a direct transference of Korean nationalism but a discontinuous rearticulation of it that includes the crucial consideration of the racialization of Korean immigrants in the United States as workers of color." This subtle mapping of continuities and discontinuities, which involves a partial folding of one geography into another, is an act of translation and articulation that respects the particularities of history and geography.

17 This comment was made by the national vice-chair of ANAKBAYAN (the national comprehensive youth organization in the Philippines) when visiting Canada in July 2001 to attend the first national conference of Filipino-Canadian youths, which was held in Toronto. Roughly ninety youths attended from across Canada.

18 Mitchell is drawing on the analysis of Charles Taylor (1994), which interprets the conflicts over the Meech Lake Accord as, in part, a clash between two different variants of liberalism.

19 It is important not to romanticize these spaces, especially when they are created through exclusion from formal politics. Bonus (2000) describes patterns of political activity in Southern California that seem familiar in the Vancouver context: low visibility of Filipino participation in legislative politics but high participation in community politics, and an insistence on rights to monocultural organizing (as opposed to pan-Asian-American or pluralist multiculturalism).

20 Another aspect of this involves considering the specificity of Filipino- Canadian identification. In this sense, Strobel's (1996, 43) comment that there is an emerging theme among second-generation Filipino Americans – "We are all Filipinos, everywhere, anytime" – bears examination. Without explicit comparative work, our observations are speculative, but we note the large proportion of women community activists and leaders in Vancouver, the politicization of many domestic workers while enrolled in the Live-In Caregiver Program, and the possibility

of a different process of articulation across racialized groups in Canada as compared, for example, to the United States, reflecting different histories of racialization and state regulation.

REFERENCES

Anderson, Kay J. 1991. *Vancouver's Chinatown: Racial Discourse in Canada, 1875–1980*. Montreal, Kingston: McGill-Queen's University Press.

Arat-Koç, Sedef. 1989. "In the Privacy of Our Own Home: Foreign Domestic Workers as Solution to the Crisis in the Domestic Sphere in Canada." *Studies in Political Economy* 28 (1): 33–58. http://dx.doi.org/10.1080/19187033.1989.11675524.

Arat-Koç, Sedef. 1990. "Importing Housewives: Non-citizen Domestic Workers and the Crisis of the Domestic Sphere in Canada." In *Through the Kitchen Window: The Politics of Home and Family*, ed. S. Arat-Koç, M. Luxton, and H. Rosenberg, 81–103. Toronto: Garamond.

Arat-Koç, Sedef. 1992. "Immigration Policies, Migrant Domestic Workers and Definition of Citizenship in Canada." In *Deconstructing a Nation: Immigration, Multiculturalism and Racism in '90s Canada*, ed. V. Satzewich, 229–42. Halifax: Fernwood.

Bakan, Abigail, and Daiva Stasiulis. 1994. "Foreign Domestic Worker Policy in Canada and the Social Boundaries of Modern Citizenship." *Science and Society* 58:7–33.

Bakan, Abigail, and Daiva Stasiulis. 1995. "Making the Match: Domestic Placement Agencies and the Racialization of Women's Household Work." *Signs (Chicago, Ill.)* 20 (2): 303–35. http://dx.doi.org/10.1086/494976.

Bakan, Abigail, and Daiva Stasiulis, eds. 1997. *Not One of the Family: Foreign Domestic Workers in Canada*. Toronto: University of Toronto Press.

Bonus, Rick. 2000. *Locating Filipino Americans: Ethnicity and the Cultural Politics of Space*. Philadelphia: Temple University Press.

Chang, Elaine K. 1994. "A Not-So-New Spelling of My Name: Notes Toward (and Against) a Politics of Equivocation." In *Displacements: Cultural Identities in Question*, ed. A. Bammer, 251–66. Bloomington: Indiana University Press.

Chen, Anita B. 1998. *From Sunbelt to Snowbelt: Filipinos in Canada*. Calgary: Canadian Ethnic Studies Association.

Daenzer, Patricia. 1993. *Regulating Class Privilege: Immigrant Servants in Canada, 1940s–1990s*. Toronto: Canadian Scholars" Press.

Davis, Mike. 2000. *Magical Urbanism: Latinos Reinvent the US Big City*. London: Verso.

Espiritu, Ye. L. 1994. "The Intersection of Race, Ethnicity, and Class: The Multiple Identities of Second-Generation Filipinos." *Identities (Yverdon)* 1 (2-3): 249–73. http://dx.doi.org/10.1080/1070289X.1994.9962507.

Espiritu, Ye L., and Diane L. Wolf. 2001. "The Paradox of Assimilation: Children of Filipino Immigrants in San Diego." In *Ethnicities: Children of Immigrants in America*, ed. R.G. Rumbaut and A. Portes, 157–86. Berkeley: University of California Press.

Flores, William V., and Rina Benmayor. 1997. *Latino Cultural Citizenship: Claiming Identity, Space and Rights*. Boston: Beacon.

Grossberg, Lawrence. 2000. "History, Imagination and the Politics of Belonging." In *Without Guarantees: In Honour of Stuart Hall*, ed. P. Gilroy, L. Grossberg, and A. McRobbie, 148–64. London: Verso.

Hage, Ghassan. 1998. *White Nation: Fantasies of White Supremacy in a Multicultural Society*. Sydney: Pluto.

Hiebert, Daniel. 1999a. "Immigration and the Changing Social Geography of Greater Vancouver." *BC Studies* 121:35–82.

Hiebert, Daniel. 1999b. "Local Geographies of Labor Market Segmentation: Montreal, Toronto, and Vancouver, 1991." *Economic Geography* 75 (4): 339–69. http://dx.doi.org/10.2307/144476.

Hirsch, Marianne. 1997. *Family Frames: Photography, Narrative and Postmemory*. Cambridge, MA: Harvard University Press.

Hirsch, Marianne. 1999. "Projected Memory: Holocaust Photographs in Personal and Public Fantasy." In *Acts of Memory: Cultural Recall in the Present*, ed. M. Ball, J. Crewe, and L. Spitzer, 2–23. Hanover: University Press of New England.

Holston, James. 1995. "Spaces of Insurgent Citizenship." *Planning Theory* 13:35–52.

Houston, Donna, and Laura Pulido. 2002. "The Work of Performativity: Staging Social Justice at the University of Southern California." *Environment and Planning. D, Society & Space* 20 (4): 401–24. http://dx.doi.org/10.1068/d344.

Hyams, Melissa. 2002. "'Over There' and 'Back Then': An Odyssey in National Subjectivity." *Environment and Planning. D, Society & Space* 20 (4): 459–76. http://dx.doi.org/10.1068/d331.

Kim, Elaine. 1993. "Home Is Where the Han Is: A Korean American Perspective on the Los Angeles Upheavals." In *Reading Rodney King, Reading Urban Uprisings*, ed. R. Gooding-Williams, 215–35. New York: Routledge.

Lo, Lucia, Valerie Preston, Shuguang Wang, Katherine Reil, Edward Harvey, and Bobby Siu. 2000. "Immigrants' Economic Status in Toronto: Rethinking Settlement and Integration Strategies." *CERIS Working Paper* 15.

Lowe, Lisa. 1996a. *Immigrant Acts: On Asian American Cultural Politics*. Durham: Duke University Press.

Lowe, Lisa. 1996b. "Imagining Los Angeles in the Production of Multiculturalism." In *Mapping Multiculturalism*, ed. A. Gordon and C. Newfield, 413–23. Minneapolis: University of Minnesota Press.

McKay, Deirdre, and the Philippine Women Centre. 2002. "Filipina Identities: Geographies of Social Integration/Exclusion in the Canadian Metropolis." *Working Paper of Vancouver Centre of Excellence: Immigration*.

Mitchell, Katharyne. 2001. "Education for Democratic Citizenship: Transnationalism, Multiculturalism, and the Limits of Liberalism." *Harvard Educational Review* 71 (1): 51–78. http://dx.doi.org/10.17763/haer.71.1.h16p5h8236321451.

Muñoz, José E. 1995. "No es Facil: Notes on the Negotiation of Cubanidad and Exilic Memory in Carmelita Tropicana's 'Milk of Amnesia.'" *Drama Review* 39 (3): 76–82. http://dx.doi.org/10.2307/1146465.

Okamura, Jonathan Y. 1998. *Imagining the Filipino American Diaspora: Transnational Relations, Identities, and Communities*. New York, London: Garland.

Ong, Aihwa. 1996. "Cultural Citizenship as Subject-Making: Immigrants Negotiate Racial and Cultural Boundaries in the United States." *Current Anthropology* 37 (5): 737–51. http://dx.doi.org/10.1086/204560.

Ornstein, Michael. 2000. *Ethno-Racial Inequality in the City of Toronto: An Analysis of the 1996 Census*. Toronto: City of Toronto and CERIS.

Parlan, Sean. 2001. "Mail-Order Brides." *Pacific Rim Magazine* 2:18–20.

Pratt, Geraldine. 1997. "Stereotypes and Ambivalence: Nanny Agents' Stereotypes of Domestic Workers in Vancouver, BC." *Gender, Place and Culture* 4:159–77. http://dx.doi.org/10.1080/09663699725413.

Pratt, Geraldine. 1999. "From Registered Nurse to Registered Nanny: Discursive Geographies of Filipina Domestic Workers in Vancouver, BC." *Economic Geography* 75 (3): 215–36. http://dx.doi.org/10.2307/144575.

Pratt, Geraldine in collaboration with the Philippine Women Centre. 1998. "Inscribing Domestic Work on Filipina Bodies." In *Places through the Body*, edited by H. Nast and S. Pile, 283–304. London and New York: Routledge.

Pratt, Geraldine in collaboration with the Philippine Women Centre. 1999. "Is This Really Canada? Domestic Workers" Experiences in Vancouver, BC." In *Gender, Migration and Domestic Service*, edited by J. Momsen, 23–42. London and New York: Routledge.

Razack, Sherene. 1998. *Looking White People in the Eye: Gender, Race, and Culture in Courtrooms and Classrooms*. Toronto: University of Toronto Press.

Rosaldo, Renato. 1988. "Ideology, Place, and People without Culture." *Cultural Anthropology* 3 (1): 77–87. http://dx.doi.org/10.1525/can.1988.3.1.02a00070.

San Juan, Epifanio Jr. 1991. "Mapping the Boundaries: The Filipino Writer in the USA." *Journal of Ethnic Studies* 19:117–31.

San Juan, Epifanio Jr. 2000. *After Postcolonialism: Remapping Philippines-United States Confrontations*. Lanham: Rowman and Littlefield.

Schecter, Tanya. 1997. *Race, Class, Women and the State: The Case of Domestic Labour*. Montreal: Black Rose.

Sernhede, Ove. 2000. "Exoticism and Death as a Modern Taboo: Gangsta Rap and the Search for Intensity." In *Without Guarantees: In Honour of Stuart Hall*, ed. P. Gilroy, L. Grossberg, and A. McRobbie, 302–17. London: Verso.

Siu, Lok. 2001. "Diasporic Cultural Citizenship: Chineseness and Belonging in Central America and Panama." *Social Text* 69: 7–28. http://dx.doi.org/10.1215/01642472-19-4_69-7.

Stasiulis, Daiva, and Abigail B. Bakan. 2001. "Negotiating the Citizenship Divide: Foreign Domestic Worker Policy and Legal Jurisprudence." In *Women's Legal Strategies in Canada: A Friendly Assessment*, ed. R. Jhappan, 237–94. Toronto: University of Toronto Press.

Statistics Canada. 2001. *Visible Minorities in Canada: Canadian Centre for Justice Statistics Profile Series*. http://www.statcan.gc.ca/pub/85f0033m/85f0033m2001009-eng.pdf

Stiell, Bernadette, and Kim England. 1997. "Domestic Distinctions: Constructing Difference among Paid Domestic Workers in Toronto." *Gender, Place and Culture* 4 (3): 339–60. http://dx.doi.org/10.1080/09663699725387.

Strobel, Leny M. 1996. "'Born-Again Filipino': Filipino American Identity and Asian Panethnicity." *Amerasia Journal* 22 (2): 31–53. http://dx.doi.org/10.17953/amer.22.2.v7841w4h7881hk04.

Strobel, Leny M. 1997. "Coming Full Circle: Narratives of Decolonization among Post-1965 Filipino Americans." In *Filipino Americans: Transformation and Identity*, ed. M. Root, 62–79. Thousand Oaks: Sage. http://dx.doi.org/10.4135/9781452243177.n5.

Sugg, Catherine. 2003. "Suspended Migrations: Sexuality and Cultural Memory in Achy Obejas and Carmelita Tropicana." *Environment and Planning. D, Society & Space* 21:461–77. http://dx.doi.org/10.1068/d366.

Taylor, Charles. 1994. *Multiculturalism: Examining the Politics of Recognition*. Princeton: Princeton University Press.

Ugnayan ng Kabataang Filipino sa Canada/ Filipino-Canadian Youth Alliance. 2000. *Our Heroes, Our Heritage, Our Struggle: An Anthology of Written and Visual Works by Young Filipino-Canadians*. Available from Kalayaan Centre, 451 Powell Street, Vancouver, BC, VOA 107.

Wolf, Diane L. 2002. "Family Secrets: Transnational Struggles among Children of Filipino Immigrants." In *Filipinos in Global Migrations: At Home in the World?* ed. F.V. Aguilar, Jr., 347–9. Quezon City, Philippines: Philippine Migration Research Network.
Žižek, Slavoj. 2002. "A Plea for Leninist Intolerance." *Critical Inquiry* 28 (2): 542–66. http://dx.doi.org/10.1086/449051.

PART THREE

Intersectional Encounters

9 The Paradox of Diversity: The Construction of a Multicultural Canada and "Women of Color"[1]

HIMANI BANNERJI

"Women of color", diversity, difference, and multiculturalism – concepts and discourses explored in this chapter – are now very familiar despite their relatively recent appearance on the stage of politics and theory. This chapter particularly explores and critiques the uses of multicultural discourse, especially as it rests on the notion of diversity in Canada where I have lived long enough to study its emergence, and experienced the effects of its deployment in politics and our everyday life. I begin by noting that the discourse of multiculturalism as used in Canada and the US needs to be differentiated in one major respect. Whereas multiculturalism is a state initiated enterprise in Canada, with a legal and a governing apparatus consisting of legislation and official policies with appropriate administrative bureaus, in the US that is not the case. This is not surprising because the historical and political conjunctures in Canada, with regard to state formation and national identity and its post-1950s image of itself as a "mosaic" society (Porter 1965), are coherent with such an ideological elaboration by the state. The US on the other hand, with its war of independence from Britain, has been known for its longstanding and strong nationalism, its assimilationist or melting pot political culture, with a general drive to Americanize the cultures within its national boundary while also actively seeking an international cultural hegemony. This imperative directing ethnic cultures inside and outside of the US to succumb to American culture, together with the fact that construction of "race" more than (racialized) ethnicity has directed class formation in the US from the eras of slavery and industrialization until recently, when ethnicity of the Hispanic or Asian population is much in view, give multiculturalism in the US a more complex and ambiguous character than in Canada. There, one can speak of multiculturalism from above or from below, whereas in Canada the case is somewhat different, since it is state initiated.

My impressions regarding multiculturalism in the US come from reading both critical and creative literature, and from anthologies such as *Mapping Multiculturalism* (Gordon & Newfield 1996), *Multiculturalism: A Critical Reader* (Goldberg 1994) and *Revolutionary Multiculturalism: Pedagogies of Dissent in the New Millennium* (McLaren 1997), to name some of the more important ones. These representative collections, along with others, point to an increasing use of culturalist/ethnicist discourses (often racialized) by the US corporate and governmental sectors, while also indicating the lack of state-sponsored and centralized legal forms of multiculturalism. The anthologies speak to a basic contradiction. They disclose how governing in the US continues to use an assimilationist universalism deployed through a language of liberal pluralism and citizenship, while also proliferating and relying on a language of racialized ethnicity of social and cultural alienness.

Gordon and Newfield (1996)'s introduction to *Mapping Multiculturalism* weighs out the pros and cons of multicultural discourses, which they note arrived in the early 1990s. They point out the discourse's potential (under certain circumstances) for providing "a major framework for analyzing intergroup relations in the United States" (1), and its ability to confront racism and connect to "race relations" which are in need of major changes. Seen thus, multiculturalism becomes the heir to the deceased civil rights movement, and helps to disclose what Omi and Winant call "dispersed projects" of racism (3). But the perceived downside to multiculturalism was that in the 1980s it "replaced the emphasis on race and racism with an emphasis on cultural diversity ... and allowed the aura of free play to suggest a creative power to racial groups that lacked political and economic power" (3). This is one defining aspect of what I call the Paradox of Diversity – how the concept of diversity simultaneously allows for an elision of actual social relations, while reifying concrete cultural description, and through this process obscures any understanding of difference as construction of power. This is evidenced in how Gordon and Newfield do not mention, but imply, that this "aura of free play," this culturalization of politics, hides the hard realities of profit and class making in the US, and also establishes the centrality of an American culture by simultaneously designating other cultures as both autonomous and subcultures. A scathing criticism of multiculturalism as a tool for corporate America, both in terms of internal diversity management and international capitalism or globalization, features prominently in the essays. One of the strongest of these is the piece by Angela Davis.

Davis' (1996) attempt to link social and economic relations of a racialized US (international) capitalism to a critique of multiculturalism is partially offset by those who seek to use it for the creation of a coalitional subject, especially in the feminine. Here, the concept of cultural hybridity, construed as integral to multiculturalism, gives it a populist or a radical face, as for example, in Alarcón's (1996) conjugated subjects. For Alarcón, and others such as Sandoval or Wallace, multiculturalism with its possibilities for cultural hybridity becomes a freeing discourse for subject construction which goes beyond the masculinized rhetoric of cultural nationalism or the fixity of a national identity (Sandoval 1991). For Wallace (1994), as for Carby (1998) in *Race Men*, this is a conscious politics signalling a paradigm of multiple determinations and incommensurability.[2] This is where notions such as "border" identity, a new public sphere and so on, become central.[3] For McLaren (1997, 13–14) multiculturalism can be revolutionary by giving him "a sense of atopy, indeterminacy, liminalities, out of overlapping cultural identifications and social practices," while Anzaldúa (1990) speaks to a multicultural subject and the importance of "making face" and "making soul."

It is interesting to note the relative absence of enthusiasm for multiculturalism among those critics who hold a political economic perspective and see it as an ideology for local and global capitalism and cross-border domination by the US economy. Gomez-Peña (1996, 66), speaking about Mexican immigrants to the US rendered into "illegal aliens," illustrates how neoliberalism "under the banner of diversity," and thus of multiculturalism, renders "service to capital accumulation" (McLaren 1997, 8). In the same critical vein, Parenti (1996) characterizes the US as fascist, and speaks to the use of a multicultural discourse to create identities which McLaren terms (1997, 8) as forms of "ideological trafficking between nationality and ethnicity." Cruz (1996) speaks of multiculturalism's role in negotiating between global capitalism and the fiscal crisis of the state. This radical political economy perspective emphasizing exploitation, dispossession, and survival, takes the issues of multiculturalism and diversity beyond questions of conscious identity such as culture and ideology, or of a paradigm of homogeneity and heterogeneity as used by Goldberg (1994), or of ethical imperatives with respect to the "other."

The use of the discourse of multiculturalism in Britain is, as in the US, a complicated and voluntary affair. Unlike Canada, the British state has not put forward definitive legislation on this basis. The Black British use of multiculturalism, which has been both anticolonial and cultural in terms of political identities and agencies, came out of an anti-racist and anti-empire struggle mounted from a class perspective. Notions of hybridity, openness and fluidity of identities, rather than strong state or ethnic nationalism, characterize a multiculturalist approach that has marked "Black" politics in Britain. Anti-racist politics in Britain has largely developed under the umbrella of Black and class politics. The notion "Black," disarticulated from a biologistic connotation, has codified an oppositional political stance, and this is what Julia Sudbury, for example in *Other Kinds of Dreams* (1998), speaks to as she develops her thesis on Black womanist politics of coalition in Britain. She tells us that, avoiding the British government's divisive naming of local non-white population as "Black" and "Asian," women of the third world in Britain have called themselves "Black." The term "Black," therefore, is not a correlate of being African in this usage.[4]

The centrality of the dominant English culture, with its colonial self-importance dating back from the days of the empire, has not yielded to any talk of adjustment under the pressure of "other" cultures, though the large presence of immigrants from South Asia and the Caribbean has made some difference in literary and everyday cultural life – in novels, cinema, music, or food habits, for example. In an official sense, the state of Britain and its political ideology do not respond to diversity by gestures of inclusivity, but rather continue the "Englishness" that the era of the empire has created. Stuart Hall, Erol Lawrence, and Paul Gilroy have all spoken extensively to this phenomenon, stressing the racist practices and cultural commonsense of the English national imaginary in books such as *The Empire Strikes Back* (Centre for Contemporary Cultural Studies 1982) while the journal *Race and Class*, edited from London by A. Shivanandan, or his book *A Different Hunger* (Shivanandan 1982), speak to the racist imperialist capitalism of Britain and its highly racialized class formation.

Non-white women's politics in Britain also encompasses the paradox of diversity as evidenced in intergroup politics, for example between African, Caribbean, Indian, and Bangladeshi women, as well as politics between them, white women's movements and the state. New Black women's politics, more womanist than feminist, moved away from the earlier, mainly white, women's liberation movement, to one where there was sought, if not always realized, a cohesion of different women. The politics of grassroots non-white women's activism which Sudbury records and analyzes has a strong anti-racist component, and also a greater attachment to prevalent politics and political culture of the third world countries from which the women come.

This seems to have created a few important responses speaking to problems and divisiveness among non-white women themselves. Amina Mama (Anthias, Yuval-Davis, & Cain 1992) has seen this type of womanist Black women's politics as a facade for identity/authenticity politics, while Pratibha Parmar (1990) has spoken to both the divides and points of identity among women. Others have spoken of the resentment among Asian women, who seem to feel that in spite of politicization of the term "Black," it has meant African leadership in anti-racist women's struggles (Modood 1990). On the other side, there has also been a resentment among Afrocentric women who question the move away from Africa as a point of departure for anti-racist politics, and resent the extension of this term to include others (see Sudbury 1998, 129–131). A very different take on all of this has been put forward by those who, excited by the notion of a postmodern, hybrid (feminine) subject of multiple and shifting subject positions, have approached questions of political subjectivity and agency from a radical multicultural position, similar to those in the US (Anthias, Yuval-Davis & Cain 1992; Bhabnani & Phoenix 1994; Brah 1996).

This discussion on the variations of the themes of multiculturalism and "women of color" should make it evident to what extent they are dependent on context and location in terms of whether they serve the status quo or the opposition. Particularly in the US, feminists have variously named themselves as women of colour, Black women or third world women – often interchangeably – and wrote and organized towards the forging of a social politics in connection with coalition building towards social democracy, radical democracy and a multiculturalist, anti-imperialist feminism. Mohanty, Russo, and Torres (1991) and Alexander and Mohanty (1997) give us powerful versions of a radical, or even revolutionary, use of this term. Such unselfconsciousness is possible because of the radicalization of the term "women of color" by anthologies such as *Third World Women and the Politics of Feminism* (Mohanty, Russo & Torres 1991). The introduction of this book directly signals the radical political use of this term, by equating "women of color" with third-world women as a mode for creating a "viable oppositional alliance" (Mohanty et al. 1991, 7). Mohanty, in her essay "Under Western Eyes," also makes it clear that "woman" is not a found meaning, but is a social subject and agent, a constructed category, and this construction takes place "in a variety of political contexts" (65). This same oppositional anti-racist position is clarified in Ann Russo's "Race, Identity and Feminist Struggles: We Cannot Live Without our Lives" (Mohanty et al. 1991). She too does not problematize the category "women of color", but connects it to anti-racist feminist organizing. The same oppositional use is further developed in *Feminist Genealogies, Colonial Legacies, Democratic Futures* (Alexander & Mohanty 1997). Here, the woman subject-agent is again called "woman of color" or third world woman, with "aim(s) to provide a comparative, relational and historically based conception of feminism, one that differs markedly from the liberal pluralist understanding of feminism. ..." (Alexander & Mohanty 1997, xvi). This political-theoretical position which redeems the term "woman of color" from liberal pluralism is expressed by Moya in explicating and building on Cherrie Moraga's stance in *This Bridge Called My Back* (Anzaldúa & Moraga 1983). Moya (with Moraga) rids the notion of its cultural pluralism by associating it with non-white, third world women's "flesh and blood experiences" (Moraga's expression) in the US, and by extension, other western capitalist democracies (Alexander & Mohanty 1997, 23). In her own articulation of a "theory in the flesh", Moraga "emphasizes the materiality of the body by conceptualizing 'flesh' as the site on or with which the woman of colour experiences the painful material effects of living in a particular social location" (Alexander & Mohanty 1997, 145). Thus, Moya builds out of Moraga a realist theory of identity, distinct from identity as projected by cultural nationalism, under the name of "women of color". It speaks to the forging of an oppositional/coalitional identity, to becoming, rather than being born as a "woman of color", as a process of an anti-imperialist political conscientization takes place among feminists.

This discussion on "women of color" is incomplete without a reference to Patricia Hill Collins (1990), who has tried to create an epistemology of resistance, while also speaking of Black or Afrocentric identities. Her theorization of Black feminist thought is one of specialized knowledge created in rejection of and opposition to the claim to universality of standard European academic knowledge. She argues that "At the core of Black feminist thought lie theories created by African-American women which clarify a Black women's standpoint – in essence, an interpretation of Black women's experiences and ideas by those who participate in them" (1990, 15). This position vindicates nonacademic knowledge as experts' knowledge, thus reclaiming Black women's intellectual tradition, generated from their everyday ideas. In this way, Black women – "mothers, teachers, church members, and cultural creators" – become intellectuals (1990, 15). To a large extent her radicalization of the term "Black women" signals to the strand of British anti-racist activism written about by Sudbury (1998). Though still interested in Afro-centrism, Collins seeks to void that notion of its cultural nationalist and particularist context, thus leaving us with an interesting text full of tensions between a general ethical politics and a strong emphasis on the African diaspora's history of domination and resistance.

Angela Davis (1996, 41) contends that multiculturalist discourse has been coopted as a tool for "diversity management". The most salient aspect of this context is that multiculturalism is a state-sanctioned, state-organized ideological affair in Canada. Not just in Orwell's ideologically constructed communist dystopia, but in actual mundane granting/funding, in electoral policies and outcomes, in ethnic cultural fairs and religious celebrations, in court legal defences, this particular variant of multiculturalism organizes the socio-cultural, legal-economic space of Canada.

Canada: Constructing "The Woman of Color" Through Multiculturalism and Diversity

People who are not familiar with North American political and cultural, especially feminist, language are often puzzled and repelled by the expression "woman of color." I know this because this expression has become a part of my ordinary vocabulary in recent years, and often when I have used it in India, my interlocutors, even feminist ones, looked puzzled or annoyed. Most reminded me that I had reverted to a racist, segregational language of apartheid and the American South – a "colored woman." Even when I tried to insist on the difference between these two expressions, these women were reluctant to relinquish this association. Their reaction reminded me of a time during my early years in Canada during the early '70s, when I learned and evolved my anti-racist feminist politics without this word anywhere in sight. At some point it traveled to us from below the 49th parallel, and found a congenial home on our tongue.

The Indian women's response was similar to my own long years of reluctance to use this notion for any purpose of social analysis and critique. In the past I used the notion "non-white" for the purpose of creating an anti-racist critique, maintaining that in the context of analysing racialized social organization and relations, what needs to be stressed is the non-whiteness of this woman social subject of oppression. The expression "woman of color" has crept up on me, especially when I am speaking in common language in my daily interchange with other non-white women who are doing anti-racist work in Canada. They use it, as do their US counterparts, as a term of alterity, or even of opposition to the status quo in spite of the statist nature of this concept in Canada, as do I. The question is, how or why did this happen? What necessities or circumstances drew me into this orbit?

I remember that one of the earliest occasions when I heard this expression was when I was invited to read poetry in a cultural festival which was called "Rainbow Women: Multicultural Women in Concert." It was organized by Faith Nolan, now a well-known Black

Canadian singer. I was struck by the notion of rainbow women, which, I was told, had to do with my being a "woman of color" and bringing this colour to join others in a rainbow combination. I was not taken by this exercise. I found "woman of color" to be both a coy and an offensive notion and, like many others, thought of the expression "colored." I did not want to call myself this. Nor did I feel convinced of the capacity for resistance attributed to this notion, which encoded a multicultural unity, cherishing diversity, through promulgating a generic or homogenizing term which would cover all non-white "others", mostly those who were not Black. It is also significant that most of the time this term does not refer to Black women, or those of the First Nations. I was quite determined not to use it, but as the '80s rolled by "woman of color" was Canadianized. And here I am using it every once in a while, for the purpose of intelligibility, to keep in step with my fellow anti-racist feminists!

So what discursive revolution, paradigm shift, occurred in Canada during the '80s and the '90s which could have been hospitable to, or indeed embraced, this "woman of color"? In my view, there are two broad political areas which need to be problematized. One could be called, following Louis Althusser (1971), the ideological apparatuses of the state, including its political and civil administration; and the other, the civil society (Gramsci 1971), the everyday world of common social relations, values and practices of culture and power. We may begin first by speaking of the state, not because it was the first to name us as political agents in terms of being "women of color". It did not, as the term had a US origin. But it provided the political culture for accepting, using and naturalizing a colour-based notion of subjectivity and agency, which in continuity with Canada's colonial formation, came to dominate the cultural politics of Canada's "other" women. Canadians have been living in a historical and current environment of political colour coding, even, or mainly, when forging a liberal democratic politics for the country as a whole.

To clarify my claim I draw attention to the entry of official multiculturalism onto the Canadian political stage. The open door policy of immigration, especially attributed to the Liberal party and its charismatic leader, Pierre Trudeau, throughout the 1960s and '70s, had brought many "people of color", other "races," into the country.[5] The reason for this was the expectation of capitalist industrial growth in Canada and the aspiration to the creation of a liberal democratic nationhood. The former British colonies in particular provided cheap labour, both skilled and unskilled, as well as the democratic grounds for converging "otherness". Unlike the radical alternative political-cultural activists, the Canadian state was careful not to directly use the notion of colour in the way it designated the newcomers. But colour was translated into the language of visibility. The new Canadian social and political subject was appellated "visible minority," stressing both the features of being non-white and therefore visible in a way whites are not, and of being politically minor players. It is at this time, at the urging of the National Directorate of Women and the Secretary of State, that non-white women made a niche for themselves in the mainstream politics by creating a representational organization, the National Coalition of Visible Minority Women.[6]

The suitability of "woman of color" for Canadian political culture was such that no one did then, or does now, speak about the absurdity of calling white women colourless or invisible. This status of "visible minority" was not felt by a large number of women to be problematic or compromising, since they shared political values with the mainstream. Minor as their part was, set apart by their visibility, which was also the only ground of their political eligibility, they were content. This popular feminist term actually relied for its political meaning and vitality upon the mainstream analogue and the same discourse of multiculturalism pertaining to "visible minority" women embedded in both state and society for its existential environment. With no interest in class politics, and no real analysis of or resistance to racialization or ethnicization, chiefly preoccupied with bureaucratic representation or inclusion for a very limited power sharing within the status quo, these political terminologies became current usages. "Visible minority" women translated well into "women of color", and that became the name chosen by alternative politics of Canada. This practice followed the US, and it solved the problem of finding a name for building coalition among all women. It vaguely and pleasantly gestured to "race" as colour and, of course, to gender/patriarchy by evoking woman. But the concept of "race" lost its hard edges of criticality, class disappeared entirely, and colour gave a feeling of brightness, brilliance, or vividness, of a celebration of a difference which was disconnected from social relations of power – hence, "rainbow women".

Common sense of skin and colour, particularly in the colonial context, is old. Bodies – skin, facial features, height, build, and so forth – had been morally and politically signified for centuries in North America and Europe (see Gilman 1986). Reducing Africans to "negroes" was an ideological and semantic normalcy for centuries in European and English languages. The "yellow peril" had resulted in the dispersion of the Japanese people into concentration camps. Colour, ethnicity, and bodies had long been conflated with moral/cultural ontologies. It is not an exaggeration to say that it was within the context and content of these practices, meanings and political possibilities that the liberal multicultural construction of "woman of color" took place. Moreover, the word "color" became an associational and connotative path to diverse histories and cultures of the nations of "other" women. They themselves summoned it to convey their colourfulness through it, thereby quickly slipping into the cultural discourse of tradition versus modernity. Their colour signalled traditional cultures, in a constellation of invented traditions.[7] Culturally integrated colour was thus seemingly divested of its racist undertones, and lost its location in power relations. This erasure indicates the epistemological possibilities of the notion of multicultural diversity. If this desocialized and ahistorical notion of diversity were not a naturalized form of political culture and discourse in Canada, and in the West as a whole, such a coinage or neologism would not have been so easily adopted by women who see themselves as practitioners of politics of opposition. The formal equality of liberal pluralism encoded by diversity also helped to allay anxieties and suspicions.

Some may object that I am making a mountain out of a mole hill by focusing so much on one single political and cultural expression. Does a name, it may be asked, make so much difference? Would not a rose by any other name smell as sweet? If we had instead called ourselves non-white women, for example, what different political task would we have accomplished? My answer to these anticipated objections or questions would be that the language with which we build or express our political agency has to be taken very seriously. An expression in that context, even when it seems innocuous and solitary, has to be treated as a bit of ideology, and as a part of a broader ideological semantics called discourse. Thus, we have to treat "woman of color" as a name for a particular type of political agency and examine its ability to disclose our lives and experiences as lived within an organization of social relations of power. It is only then that we can attend to the political direction to which this agency points us. Treated thus, we can safely say that the notion "woman of color" does not direct us to examine crucial social relations within which we live, to histories and forms of consciousness of power that mark our presence in the US or Canada. Instead this, as a naturalized reworking of the term "colored women," performs an ideological accommodation of "race," while erasing class. Also, in equating our political identities with a racialized cultural construction, a second level of reality is created which is far from the actualities of our lives. Yet these social actualities are the realities that need to be addressed daily and changed through our politics. If at least, in the course of our anti-racist feminist politics, we call ourselves non-white women, we can gesture towards white privilege. The use of a negative prefix automatically raises issues and questions. But a substitution through the language of diversity and colour distracts us from what actually happens to us in our raced and gendered class existence and culturalizes our politics. In other words, it depoliticizes us.[8]

Since the responsibility for this depoliticization falls upon the epistemology and ideology of diversity, the cornerstone of a pluralist liberal politics and its legitimation, we need to explore critically the workings of the concept of diversity. Official multiculturalism, which has also become the politics of Canadian civil society, our daily political commonsense, cannot be challenged otherwise. If resistance politics develops from below, from civil society, and if that realm itself is saturated with a historical and official political culture of domination, then that politics of resistance itself can become a part of the state's ideological apparatus. The dangers inherent in constructing a multicultural Canada, with a reified and racialized political agency called "woman of color", calls for a critique of the epistemology and ideology of diversity. The next section of this chapter, therefore, engages in this critique.

The Name of the Rose, or What Difference Does It Make What I Call It

Diversity has become a commonplace word in our political and cultural world. This seems to have happened in the last decade or so. So much so that even businesses have adapted their talk about profit and productivity to the language of diversity, while governments and public institutions set up bureaucracies in its name. Organizations have been created merging notions of community with diversity – speaking to ethnocultural pluralities and collective cultural identities. We also have critical feminist anthologies of the politics of diversity[9], while political theorists have used the term in their communitarian and liberal ways (Elliott & Fleras 1992; Kymlicka 1995; Taylor 1992, 1993; Trudeau 1968).

This discourse of diversity is a fusion of a cultural classification with politics. That is, our empirically being from various countries, with our particular looks, languages and cultures, has become an occasion for interpreting, constructing and ascribing differences with connotations of power relations. In this political deployment, the notion of diversity escapes from its denotative function and dictionary meaning and emerges as a value-free, power neutral indicator of difference and multiplicity.

The two ways in which the neutral appearance of the notion of diversity becomes a useful ideology to practices of power are quite simple. On the one hand, the use of such a concept with a reference to simple multiplicity allows the reading of all social and cultural forms or differences in terms of descriptive plurality. On the other, in its relationship to description, it introduces the need to put in or retain a concrete particular content for each of these seemingly neutral differences. The social relations of power that create the difference implied in sexist-racism, for example, just drop out of sight, and social being becomes a matter of a cultural essence (Bannerji 1991). This is its paradox – that the concept of diversity simultaneously allows for an emptying out of actual social relations and suggests a concreteness of cultural description, and through this process obscures any understanding of difference as construction of power. Thus, there is a construction of a collective cultural essence and a conflation between this, or what we are culturally supposed to be, and what we are ascribed with, in the context of social organization of inequality. We cannot then make a distinction between racist stereotypes and ordinary historical/cultural differences of everyday life and practices of people from different parts of the world. Cultural traits that come, let us say, from different parts of the third-world, are used to both create and eclipse racism, and we are discouraged from reading them in terms of relations and symbolic forms of power. The result is also an erasure of class and patriarchy among the immigrant multi-cultures of "others", as they too fall within this paradox of essentialization and multiplicity signified by cultural diversity of official multiculturalism. In fact, it is this uncritical, de-materialized, seemingly depoliticized reading of culture through which culture becomes a political tool, an ideology of power which is expressed in racist-sexist or heterosexist differences. The discourse of diversity, as a complex systemically interpretive language of governing, cannot be read as an innocent pluralism.[10]

The ideological nature of this language of diversity is evident from its frequent use and efficacy in the public and official, that is, institutional realms. Its function has been to provide a conceptual apparatus in keeping with needs which the presence of heterogeneous peoples and cultures has created in the Canadian state and public sphere. This has both offset and, thus, stabilized the Canadian national imaginary[11] and its manifestation as the state apparatus, which is built on core assumptions of cultural and political homogeneity of a Canadianness. This language of diversity is a coping mechanism for dealing with an actually conflicting heterogeneity, seeking to incorporate it into an ideological binary which is predicated upon the existence of a homogeneous national, that is, a Canadian cultural self with its multiple and different "others" (see Bannerji 1997). These multiple "other" cultural presences in Canada, interpreted as a threat to national culture which called for a coping, and therefore an incorporating and interpretive mechanism, produced the situation summed up as the challenge of multiculturalism. This has compelled administrative, political and ideological innovations which will help to maintain the status quo. This is where the discourse of diversity has been of crucial importance because this new language of ruling and administration protects ideologies and practices already in place. It is postulated upon pluralist premises of a liberal democratic state, which Canada aspires to be, but also adds specific dimensions of legitimation to particular administrative functions.[12]

The usefulness of the discourse of diversity as a device for managing public or social relations and spaces, of serving as a form of moral regulation of happy coexistence, is obvious. The Canadian government and other public institutions, the media, and the ideological projection of the Canadian nation (and its unity) are marked by this discourse. In the universities, both in pedagogic and administrative spheres, this language is prominent. It is the staple discourse of arts and community projects, conditioning their working agendas as well as the politics of the funding bodies. In the workplace, diversity sensitization or training has largely displaced talk about and/or resistance to racism and sexism. Even law appeals to diversity in using cultural and religious defences, suppressing contradictions and violences of patriarchy, for example, while fulfilling the state's pluralist obligations (see Volpp 1994).

The discourse of diversity has also inscribed our social movements – the women's movement or the trade union movement, for example – where again it helps to obscure deeper/structural relations of power, such as of racism and sexism or racist heterosexism,[13] both among women and the working class, and reduces the problem of social justice into questions of curry and turban. Many years ago Elizabeth Spelman (1988) wrote a book criticizing North American liberal/bourgeois feminism for its Eurocentrism. This critique of essentialism and Eurocentrism (Bannerji 1991) developed into a critique of an ideological and identity stance known as whiteness (Frankenberg 1993; Stoler 1995). Roman (1993, 72) states:

> ... to say that white is a color does not rescue the concept of "race" from similar forms of empty pluralism and dangerous relativism invoked by the larger essentialist discourse of "race." Try as I might to recognize whiteness as a structural power relation that confers cultural and economic privileges, the phrase, spoken declaratively by the racially privileged, can also become a form of white defensiveness.

But of more immediate importance for us are the critiques made by Black and third world feminists, such as Collins, Mohanty, and Alexander, regarding the politically exclusionary, debilitating and epistemologically occlusive effects of such theorization as conducted within the academy. Alexander and Mohanty (1997) especially take to task women's studies within US academies. They were, they stated, neither "the right color," nor gender, nor nationality, in terms of self-definition of the US Academy, and by extension of the women's studies establishment (xiv). As they put it: "Our experience makes sense only in analogy to African-American women" (xiv). The authors in this anthology also question the political and epistemological impact that postmodernism is having within women's studies. As Alexander and Mohanty put it: "... localized questions of experience, identity, culture, and history, which enable us to understand specific processes of domination and subordination, are often dismissed by postmodern theories as reiteration of cultural 'essences,' or unified stable identity" (xvii). These current critiques were anticipated as early as 1982 by Hazel Carby (1982).

This discourse of diversity in its comprehensive ideological and political form is materialized and extended as the discourse of multiculturalism, with its linguistic constellation of "visible minority", "women of color", and so on. Cultural sensitivity towards and tolerance of "others" are two behavioural imperatives of this multicultural politics, both at the level of state and society. The all-pervasive presence of diversity in our public discourse has created a situation where even those who are not entirely comfortable with its discursive constellation use it in its various guises in an unconscious submission to what is around, and for reasons of intelligibility. Being effective with funding proposals means translating our needs and concerns into the discourses of multiculturalism. This means speaking in the language of "cultural communities" and their diversities, of ethnicities and "women of color" and "visible minorities" – both male and female. Otherwise, our funders or the state do not hear us.

So, it would seem that there is much invested in the fact of naming, in the words we use to express our socio-political understandings, because they are more than just words, they are ideological concepts. They imply intentions and political and organizational practices. Calling people by different names, in different political contexts, has always produced significantly different results. These names are, after all, not just names to call people by, but rather codes for political subjectivities and agencies. Naming ourselves in terms of class, for example as the proletariat, assuming class as the basis of our political identity, would imply a different political ideology, practice and goal, than if we constructed our political agency with names such as "women/people of color" or "visible minorities". Contrary to Shakespeare's assertion that a rose by any other name would smell as sweet, we see that not to be the case in political-ideological matters. In politics, the essence of the flower lies in the name by which it is called. In fact, it is the naming that decides what flower we have at hand. To say this is to say explicitly that discourse is more than a linguistic manoeuvre. It is a matter of putting in words, mediating, and organizing social relations of ruling, of meanings organized through power. It is best to remind ourselves of the title of Dionne Brand's poetry book, *No Language is Neutral* (Brand 1990).

The Essence of the Name, or What Is to Be Gained by Calling Something Diversity

In order to understand how the concept of diversity works ideologically, we have to feed into it the notion of difference constructed through social relations of power and read it in terms of the binaries of homogeneity and heterogeneity already referred to in our discussion on multiculturalism. It does not require much effort to realize that diversity is not equal to multiplied sameness, rather it presumes a distinct difference in each instance. But this makes us ask, distinctly different from what? The answer is from each other and from whatever it is that is homogeneous – which is an identified and multiplied sameness, serving as the distinguishing element at the core in relation to which difference is primarily measured. The difference that produces heterogeneity suggests otherness in relation to that core, and in social politics this otherness is more than an existential, ontological fact. It is a socially constructed otherness or heterogeneity, its difference signifying both social value and power. It is not just another cultural self, floating non-relationally in a sociohistorical vacuum. In the historical context of the creation of Canada, of its growth into an uneasy amalgam of a white settler colony with liberal democracy, the definitions and relations between a national self and its "other", between homogeneity and heterogeneity, sameness and diversity, become deeply power ridden.[14] From the days of colonial capitalism to the present-day global imperialism, there has emerged an ideologically homogeneous identity dubbed Canadian, whose nation and state Canada is supposed to be.

The core community is synthesized into a national "we", and it decides on the terms of multiculturalism and the degree to which multicultural "others" should be tolerated or accommodated. This "we" is an essentialized version of a colonial European turned into Canadian and the subject or the agent of Canadian nationalism. But the identity of the Canadian "we" does not reside in language, religion or other aspects of culture, but rather in the European/North American physical origin – in the body and the colour of skin. Colour of skin is elevated here beyond its contingent status and becomes an essential quality called "whiteness", and this becomes the ideological signifier of a unified non-diversity.[15] The "others" outside of this moral and cultural "whiteness" are targets for either assimilation or tolerance. These diverse or multicultural elements, who are also called newcomers, introducing notions of territoriality and politicized time, create accommodational difficulties for white Canadians, both at the level of the civil society, culture and economy, and also for the ruling practices of the state. An ideological coping mechanism becomes urgent in view of a substantial third world immigration allowed by Canada through the 1960s up to recent years (see Elliott & Fleras 1992). This new practical and discursive/ideological venture, or an extension of what Althusser has called an ideological state apparatus, indicates both the crisis and its management. After all, the importation of Chinese or South Asian migrant labour, or the legally restricted presence of the Japanese since the last century, did not pose the same problems which the newly arrived immigrants do (see Bolaria & Li 1988). As landed residents or apprentice citizens, or as actual citizens of Canada, they cannot be left in the same limbo of legal and political non-personhood as their predecessors were until the 1950s. Yet, they are not authentic Canadians in the ideological sense, in their physical identity, and culture. What is more, so-called authentic Canadians are unhappy with their presence, even though they enhance Canada's economic growth. But they, among other third-world immigrants, are here, and this calls for the creation of an ideology and apparatus of multiculturalism (with its discourse of a special kind of plurality called diversity) as strategies of containment and management.

We began to hear of the notion of "diversity" from the time of allowing citizenship to the previously indentured Chinese and South Asians, and from the time of Canada's open door policy in relation to its plans for capitalist growth. The metaphor of Canadian society as the vertical mosaic is an early intimation of the complexities of evolution of a political ideology involving otherness in a liberal democratic context. The open door policy not only allowed but actively pursued immigration from ex-colonized third-world countries. Along with that came political refugees. This is when diversity came to be seen as really diverse, in spite of the fact that many came from French and English speaking countries, many were Christians, and a large number had more than a passing acquaintance with cultures of Europe and North America.

The Canadian state had to deal with a labour importation policy which was primarily meant to create a working class, but not "guest workers" as in Germany. This involved resistance from white Canadians, from the so-called Canadian worker. It also had to contain the mobility drives of immigrants who were otherwise compliant, but wanted to get a secure economic niche in the country's labour and consumer markets. In the very early 1980s, Prime Minister Pierre Trudeau enunciated his multicultural policy, and a discourse of nation, community, and diversity began to be cobbled together. It began as a state or an official/institutional discourse, and involved the translation of issues of social and economic injustice into issues of culture (see Kymlicka 1995). Multiculturalism was therefore not a demand from below, but an ideological elaboration from above, in which the third-world immigrants found themselves. This was an apparatus which rearranged questions of social justice, unemployment, and racism, into issues of cultural diversity and focused on symbols of religion, on so-called tradition. Thus, immigrants were ethnicized, culturalized and mapped into traditional/ethnic communities. Gradually a political and administrative framework came into being where structural inequalities could be less seen or spoken about. Anti-racism and class politics could not keep pace with constantly proliferating ideological state or institutional apparatuses which identified people in terms of their cultural identity, and converted or conflated racist ascriptions of difference within the Canadian space into the power neutral notion of diversity. Politics in Canada were reshaped and routed through this culturalization or ethnicization, and a politics of identity was constructed which the immigrants themselves embraced as the only venue for social and political agency.

Now the state and the media were projecting to the world at large that what the incoming third-world population of Canada primarily wanted was the same religious, linguistic, and cultural life they had in their countries of origin. They were frozen into being seen as traditional cultures and thus socially conservative. They were bringing down the standards of Canadian modernity and criminalizing the country. The problem for the Canadian state and society then became one of considering what or how much they could retain in Canada of their previous cultures without compromising the national character. The fact that their demands came in many types, and the most important ones pertained to discrimination by the state and the economy which threatened employment possibilities, family reunification for refugees, facilities for women, and so forth, became political non-issues.

Since the 1960s, political developments took place in Canada which show the twists and turns in the relationship between third-world immigrants and the state.[16] With the poor development of left politics in the country and the growth of multicultural ideology, all political consciousness regarding third-world immigrants has been multiculturalized. According to this story of neo-colonialism, the problems of exploitation, racism, and discrimination, never gain much credibility or publicity with the Canadian state, the public, or the media. This reality is what the cultural language and politics of diversity obscures, displaces, and erases. It is obvious that the third world or non-white immigrants are not the beneficiaries of the discourse of diversity.

The state of Canada wants its differentiated inferior citizens to speak in the state's own language of multicultural identity, of ethnicity and community. This is mainly the language of representation permitted to them. Ethnic or racialized cultural community, not political community organized on the basis of class, gender, and racialization, is what the state is willing to acknowledge in their case. Continuous struggles involving issues of "race" and class have created something called "race relations" in some institutions, which, if it becomes anti-racist in any real way, is de-scaled or defunded. Human Rights Commissions which treat cases individually, with no proper powers of enforcement, often act as pawns of the state and capital, while adjudicating very few cases and ruling rarely in favour of the complainant. By simultaneously blocking the politico-social process of racialization from view while organizing people as raced ethnicities, the state of multiculturalism seeks to obscure issues of class and patriarchy as actionable, and therefore the possibility of discovering intercommunity commonalities – for example, between third-world immigrants and aboriginal peoples, or among the different strands of working classes – diminishes considerably.

Multiculturalism as an official practice and discourse has worked actively to create the notion and practices of insulated communities. Under its political guidance and funding, a political-social space was organized. Politically constructed homogenized communities, with their increasingly fundamentalist boundaries of cultures, traditions, and religions, emerged from where there were immigrants from different parts of the world with different cultures and values. They developed leaders or spokespersons, usually men, who liaised with the state on their behalf, and their organizational behaviour fulfilled the expectations of the Canadian state. New political agents and constituencies thus came to life, as people sought to be politically active in these new cultural identity terms. So they became interpellated by the state under certain religious and ethnically named agencies. What is more, this new cultural politics, leaving out problems of class and patriarchy, appealed to the conservative elements in the immigrant population, since religion could be made to overdetermine these uncomfortable actualities, and concentrated on the so-called culture and morality of the community. Official multiculturalism, which gave the conservative male self-styled representatives carte blanche to do this, also empowered the same male leaders as patriarchs and enhanced their sexism and masculinism. In the name of culture and god, within the high walls of community and ethnicity, women and children could be dominated and acted against violently because the religions or culture and tradition of "others" supposedly sanctioned this oppression and brutality. And, as politically and ideologically constituted homogenized cultural essences which are typed as traditional, such as Muslim or Sikh or Hindu communities, violence against women could go on without any significant or effective state intervention.

For these newly-constructed communities, their ethnic self-appellations, born of their long familiarity with colonial and imperialist discourse, were perfectly in keeping with colonial-racist stereotypes used by the Canadian state and culture. It was and is not noted either by the multicultural state or by its clients, the so-called communities, that back in their so-called home countries, in whose names their multiculture is fabricated, the contestation that is going on bears little resemblance to these monolithic identities that they project in Canada. Being real countries, lived historical political spaces, these countries were and are going through many political and social struggles, changing their forms, none of which were in the position to be petrified into immutable cultural identities.[17] The genealogies of these reified cultural identities which are mobilized in Canada are entirely colonial, though they are being constantly re-worked in the modern context of state formation and capital's transformation. A simple binary of cultural stereotyping of tradition and modernity stands for India and Canada, respectively. The problem of multiculturalism, then, is how much tradition can be accommodated by Canadian modernity without affecting in any real way the overall political and cultural hegemony of Europeans. It is also assumed by both the state and the media, as well as the male representatives of the "communities", that Indians or South Asians are essentially traditional and as such patriarchy is congenial to their cultural identity, while class conflict is a modern or non-traditional aberration.

The result of this convergence between the Canadian state and conservative male representatives or community agents has been very distressing for women in particular. The gap is immense between the multicultural paradigm and the actuality of a migrant citizen's life in Canada. Among multiculturalists of both the communitarian and the liberal persuasion Canada is a nation space which contains different "races" and ethnicities, and this presence demands either a "politics of recognition" (Taylor 1992) or a modified set of individual and group rights. But for both groups this diversity of "others" or difference between Canadian self and "other" has no political dimension. It speaks to nothing like class formation or class struggle, the existence of active and deep racism, or of a social organization entailing racialized class production of gender. The history of colonization is also not brought to bear on the notions of diversity and difference. So, the answer to my original question "what is to be gained from a discourse of diversity and its politics of multiculturalism?" – lies in just what has actually happened in Canadian politics and its theorization, what I have been describing so far, namely in the erasure and occlusion of social relations of power and ruling. This diversified reification of cultures and culturalization of politics allows for both the practice and occlusion of heterosexism and racism of a narrow bourgeois nationalism. This means the maintenance of a status quo of domination, whereby many hard socio-political questions and basic structural changes may now be avoided. People can be blamed for bringing on their own misfortunes, while rule of capital and class can continue their violence of racism, sexism, and homophobia.

Conclusion

Diversity discourse makes it impossible to understand or name systemic and cultural racism, and its implication in gender and class. It is derived from and is in keeping with a language of plurality that has existed in liberal democracy. It relies on reading the notion of difference in a socially abstract manner, which also wipes away its location in history, thus obscuring capitalist colonialism and slavery. By obscuring or deflecting from historical and present power relations, perceptions, and systematized ideologies, the deployment of diversity reduces to and manages difference as ethnic cultural issues. It then becomes a matter of coexistence of value-free, power-neutral plurality, of cultural differences where modernity and tradition, so-called white and Black cultures, supposedly hold the same value. Differences or diversities are then seen as inherent, as ontological or essential cultural traits of the individuals of particular cultural communities, rather than as racist ascriptions or stereotypes. This is not dissonant with colonial anthropology's way of assigning non-European cultures a special, hyphenated and bracketed status.[18]

When concreteness or embodiment is thus ideologically depoliticized and dehistoricized by its articulation to the discourse of diversity, we are presented with many ontological cultural particularities which serve as markers of ethnicity and group boundaries. Since these ethnic communities are conceived as discrete entities, and there is no recognition of a core cultural-power group, a dispersion effect is introduced through the discourse of diversity which occludes its own presumption of otherness, of being diverse, and which is predicated upon a homogeneous Canadian identity. It is with regard to this that diversity is measured, and hides its assumptions of homogeneity under the cover of a value and power neutral heterogeneity. Thus, it banishes from view a process of homogenization or essentialization which underpins the project of liberal pluralism. Ultimately then, the discourse of diversity is an ideology. It has its own political imperatives in what is called multiculturalism elaborated within the precincts of the state. It translates out into different political possibilities within the framework of capitalism and bourgeois democracy, and both communitarian liberals and liberals for individual rights may find it congenial to their own goals. Politics of recognition, an ideology of tolerance, advocacy of limited group rights, may all result from adopting the discourse of diversity, but what difference they would actually make to those peoples' lives which are objects of multicultural politics, is another story.

This conceptual feat of emptying out difference of its actual political and cultural content, and thus presenting it as neutral diversity, can only be done by relying on the wholly artificial separation of the public and the private – as parallels of the political and the personal. It is possible because the concept of diversity is much more hospitable to an abstract notion of plurality than that of difference, which instantly summons questions of comparison to "others" with regard to whom any difference is postulated. A socialization, and therefore politicization, of this concept of difference is far more likely than diversity to lend itself to content saturated with social relations of class, gender, "race," sexuality, and so on. This makes difference a much better heuristic device, if not exactly an analytical concept, for understanding situations which both imply and call for politics. I am content to call myself an anti-racist and Marxist feminist. It is a distinctly political and socially grounded cultural identity. It does not rely solely on the culture of community at birth, but also speaks to what we have become as political subjects and agents in our own adult political and cultural efforts. This striving for a political self-definition, a self-conscious anti-oppression task of historical recovery, is not a matter of essentialized cultural diversities, but rather, as Paula Moya says (Alexander & Mohanty 1997, 141), it involves an act of "deconstruction of difference." With class, "race", gender, and sexuality seen as components of this difference, we admit of both solidarities and relations of opposition. We can unite, as coalition is a basic prerequisite of organizing for change, with others inhabiting similar socio-cultural locations, and see that unity in political terms. This seeing of common social conditions produced through oppressive relations, rather than an essentialized version of cultures, is an act and task of political conscientization.

This same question of political naming or agency has been discussed by many feminists, both white and non-white. For Alexander and Mohanty (1997), the answer lies in democracy, but not of the capitalist liberal type. They evolve the notion of feminist democracy, but feminist distinct from radical feminism. They speak to a "transborder, transnational participatory democracy" which resists hegemonic democracy of our times, and to "universal citizenship," to "anticapitalist, anticolonial feminist democracy" in a very similar way to my proposal (xxix–xxxi). This is not radical democracy without class, class struggle, or anti-imperialism. Thus, it is different from the projects for new social movements as enunciated by Laclau and Mouffe (1985) and their followers, who believe that they can make democracy real without fighting racialized, gendered, local, national, and global capitalism. Mohanty and Alexander eschew cultural relativism encouraged by multiculturalism from above, and seek a redefinition of justice. They want to see a "critical application of feminist praxis in global contexts" which insists on "responsibility, accountability, engagement, and solidarity," and advance in their anthology "a paradigm of decolonization which stresses power, history, memory, relational analysis, justice (not just representation), and ethics as the issues central to [their] analysis of globalization" (Alexander & Mohanty 1997, xix). I would say this is a proposal which we should support as the most extensively liberatory one.

NOTES

1 This is a reworked version of a paper given at Southeastern Women's Studies Association Annual Conference, Athens, Georgia, in April 1997.

2 Wallace is aware of the problems associated with multiculturalism, but supports it from a psychoanalytic perspective involving many aspects of self formation.

3 See in this context McLaren's (1997) introduction, but also Connolly (1995).

4 Regarding the term "Black women" in political usage, see Sudbury (1998, 20).

5 For a history of immigration in Canada, see Law Union of Ontario (1981).

6 See Brand & Carty (1993); also Ng (1993). For an uncritical liberal view, see Government of Canada (1986).

7 On invention of tradition see Hobsbawm & Ranger (1984); also Mani (1989), and Ismail & Jeganathan (1995).

8 On culturalizing politics, see Benjamin (1969).

9 For an example of feminist anthologies using "diversity" in the title, see Hamilton (1986), especially the introduction.

10 For the ground of a theoretical critique of diversity, see Roman (1993).

11 On the Canadian national imaginary, see Bannerji (1996).

12 For diversity language in administration, see Davis (1996) on the language of corporate multiculturalism.

13 For homophobia and racist heterosexism in cultural nationalism or ethnic communitarianism, see, in the U.S. context, Collins (1998) and Carby (1998), to name two texts. In the Canadian context, very little has been written about this phenomenon, probably due to the deeply social and economic involvement of the so called communities in the state's policies of multiculturalism. See Dua & Robertson (1999), and Bannerji (1999).

14 On the racialized nature of Canada's political economy as a white settler colony, and its attempts to install itself as a liberal democracy, see Bolaria & Li (1988).

15 On reading the skin as whiteness, as an ideological/political construction, see Frankenberg (1993).

16 For example, the change in immigration policy from the "family reunification" program to a primarily skills based one shifts the demography of Canada. It brings a kind of immigrant, perhaps from Eastern Europe, who does not pose the problem of "race."
17 See Butalia & Sarkar (1997). The essays in this anthology show the intensity of the political struggle between secular, left feminist forces and the Hindu right.
18 For examples of colonial anthropology, see Radcliffe-Brown (1965); Evans-Pritchard (1965); also for post-modernist, radical versions, see Geertz (1988) or Comaroff & Comaroff (1991).

REFERENCES

Alarcón, Norma. 1996. "Conjugating Subjects in the Age of Multiculturalism." In *Mapping Multiculturalism*, ed. Avery Gordon and Christopher Newfield, 40–48. Minneapolis, MN: University of Minnesota Press.

Alexander, Jacqui, and Chandra Mohanty, eds. 1997. *Feminist Genealogies, Colonial Legacies, Democratic Futures*. London, New York: Routledge.

Althusser, Louis. 1971. *Lenin and Philosophy. Translated by Ben Brewster*. London: Verso.

Anthias, Floya, Nira Yuval-Davis, and Harriet Cain, eds. 1992. *Racialized Boundaries*. London, New York: Routledge.

Anzaldúa, Gloria, ed. 1990. *Making Face, Making Soul/Haciendo Caras: Creative and Critical Perspectives by Women of Color*. San Francisco: An Aunt Lute Foundations Book.

Anzaldúa, Gloria, and Cherrie Moraga, eds. 1983. *This Bridge Called My Back: Writings by Radical Women of Color*. New York: Kitchen Table Women of Color Press.

Bannerji, Himani. 1991. "But Who Speaks for us?" In *Unsettling Relations: The University as a Site of Feminist Struggles*, ed. Himani Bannerji, Linda Carty, Kari Dehli, Susan Heald, and Kate McKenna, 67–108. Toronto: Women's Press.

Bannerji, Himani. 1996. "On the Dark Side of the Nation: Politics of Multiculturalism and the State in Canada." *Journal of Canadian Studies. Revue d'Etudes Canadiennes* 31 (3): 103–28.

Bannerji, Himani. 1997. "Geography Lessons: On Being an Insider/Outsider to the Canadian Nation." In *Dangerous Territories: Struggles for Difference and Equality in Education*, ed. Leslie Roman and Linda Eyre, 23–42. New York, London: Routledge.

Bannerji, Himani. 1999. "A Question of Silence: Reflections on Violence Against Women in Communities of Color." In *Scratching the Surface: Canadian Anti-Racist Feminist Thought*, ed. Enakshi Dua and Angela Robertson, 261–277. London: The Women's Press.

Benjamin, Walter. 1969. "The Work of Art in the Age of Mechanical Reproduction." In *Illuminations*, ed. Hannah Arendt, trans. Harry Zohn., 217–252. New York: Schocken Books.

Bhabnani, Kumkum, and Ann Phoenix, eds. 1994. *Shifting Identities, Shifting Racisms*. London: Sage.

Brah, Avtar. 1996. *Cartographies of Diaspora: Contesting Identities*. London, New York: Routledge.

Bolaria, B. Singh, and Peter S. Li. 1988. *Racial Oppression in Canada*. Toronto: Garamond Press.

Brand, Dionne. 1990. *No Language is Neutral*. Toronto: McClelland & Stewart.

Brand, Dionne, and Linda Carty. 1993. "Visible Minority Women: A Creation of the Colonial State." In *Returning the Gaze: Essays on Racism, Feminism and Politics*, ed. Himani Bannerji, 207–222. Toronto: Sister Vision Press.

Butalia, Urvashi, and Tanika Sarkar, eds. 1997. *Women of the Hindu Right*. New Delhi: Kali for Women.

Carby, Hazel V. 1982. "White Women Listen! Black Feminism and the Boundaries of Sisterhood." In *Centre for Contemporary Cultural Studies: The Empire Strikes Back*, 212–235. London: Hutchinson.

Carby, Hazel V. 1998. *Race Men*. Cambridge, MA: Harvard University Press.
Centre for Contemporary Cultural Studies. 1982. *The Empire Strikes Back*. London: Hutchinson.
Collins, Patricia Hill. 1990. *Black Feminist Thought: Knowledge, Consciousness and the Politics of Empowerment*. London: HarperCollins.
Collins, Patricia Hill. 1998. *Fighting Words: Black Women and the Search for Justice*. Minneapolis, MN: University of Minnesota Press.
Comaroff, Jean, and John Comaroff. 1991. *Of Revelation and Revolution*. Chicago: University of Chicago Press. http://dx.doi.org/10.7208/chicago/9780226114477.001.0001.
Connolly, William. 1995. *The Ethos of Pluralization*. Minneapolis, MN: University of Minnesota Press.
Cruz, Jon. 1996. "From Farce to Tragedy: Reflections on the Reification of Race at Century's End." In *Mapping Multiculturalism*, ed. Avery Gordon and Christopher Newfield, 19–39. Minneapolis, MN: University of Minnesota Press.
Davis, Angela Y. 1996. "Gender, Class and Multiculturalism: Rethinking "Race" Politics." In *Mapping Multiculturalism*, ed. Avery Gordon and Christopher Newfield, 40–48. Minneapolis, MN: University of Minnesota Press.
Dua, Ena, and Angela Robertson, eds. 1999. *Scratching the Surface*. Toronto: Women's Press.
Elliott, Jean L., and Augie Fleras. 1992. *Multiculturalism in Canada: The Challenge of Diversity*. Toronto: Nelson.
Evans-Pritchard, Edward E. 1965. *Theories of Primitive Religion*. Oxford: Clarendon Press.
Frankenberg, Ruth. 1993. *White Women, Race Matters: The Social Construction of Whiteness*. Minneapolis, MN: University of Minnesota Press.
Geertz, Clifford. 1988. *Works and Lives: The Anthropologist as Author*. Stanford, CA: Stanford University Press.
Gilman, Sander. 1986. "Black Bodies, White Bodies: Toward an Iconography of Female Sexuality in Late Nineteenth Century Art, Medicine and Literature." In *"Race," Writing, and Difference*, ed. Henry Louis Gates, Jr., 223–261. Chicago: University of Chicago Press. http://dx.doi.org/10.1086/448327.
Goldberg, David T., ed. 1994. *Multiculturalism: A Critical Reader*. Oxford, England: Blackwell.
Gomez-Peña, Guillermo. 1996. *The New World Border*. San Francisco: City Lights Books.
Gordon, Avery, and Christopher Newfield, eds. 1996. *Mapping Multiculturalism*. Minneapolis, MN: University of Minnesota Press.
Government of Canada. 1986. *Equality Now: Report of the Special Committee on Visible Minorities*. Ottawa, Canada: House of Commons.
Gramsci, Antonio. 1971. "State and Civil Society." In *Selections from the Prison Notebooks*, ed. and trans. Quentin Hoare and Geoffrey Smith, 210–276. New York: International Publishers.
Hamilton, Roberta, ed. 1986. *The Politics of Diversity*. Boston: Beacon Press.
Hobsbawm, Eric, and Terence Ranger, eds. 1984. *The Invention of Tradition*. Cambridge, UK: Cambridge University Press.
Ismail, Qadri, and Pradeep Jeganathan, eds. 1995. *Unmaking the Nation: The Politics of Identity and History in Modern Sri Lanka*. Colombo, Sri Lanka: Social Scientists' Association.
Kymlicka, Will. 1995. *Multicultural Citizenship: A Liberal Theory of Minority Rights*. Oxford, UK: Clarendon Press.
Laclau, Ernest, and Chantal Mouffe. 1985. *Hegemony and Socialist Strategy: Towards a Radical Democratic Politics*. London: Verso.
Law Union of Ontario. 1981. *The Immigrants Handbook*. Montreal: Black Rose Books.

Mani, Lata. 1989. "Contentious Traditions: The Debate on Sati in Colonial India." In *Recasting Women: Essays in Indian Colonial History*, ed. Kumkum Sangari and Sudesh Vaid, 88–126. New Brunswick, NJ: Rutgers University Press.

McLaren, Peter, ed. 1997. *Revolutionary Multiculturalism: Pedagogies of Dissent in the New Millennium*. Boulder, CO: Westview Press.

Modood, Tariq. 1990. "Political Blackness and British Asians." *Sociology* 28 (3): 859–76.

Mohanty, Chandra, Ann Russo, and Lourdes Torres, eds. 1991. *Third World Women and the Politics of Feminism*. Bloomington, IN: Indiana University Press.

Ng, Roxana. 1993. "Sexism, Racism, Canadian Nationalism." In *Returning the Gaze: Essays on Racism, Feminism and Politics*, ed. Himani Bannerji, 223–241. Toronto: Sister Vision Press.

Parenti, Michael. 1996. *Dirty Truths*. San Francisco: City Lights Books.

Parmar, Pratibha. 1990. "Black Feminism: The Politics of Articulation." In *Identity, Community, Culture, Difference*, ed. Jonathan Rutherford, 101–126. London: Lawrence & Wishart.

Porter, John. 1965. *The Vertical Mosaic*. Toronto: University of Toronto Press.

Radcliffe-Brown, Alfred R. 1965. *Structure and Function in Primitive Society*. New York: The Free Press.

Roman, Leslie. 1993. "White is a Color! White Defensiveness, Postmodernism and Anti-Racist Pedagogy." In *Race, Identity and Representation in Education*, ed. Warren Crichlow and Cameron McCarthy, 71–88. New York, London: Routledge.

Sandoval, Chela. 1991. "U.S. Third World Feminism: The Theory and Method of Oppositional Consciousness in the Postmodern World." *Genders* 10:1–24.

Shivanandan, A. 1982. *A Different Hunger: Writings on Black Resistance*. London: Pluto Press.

Spelman, Elizabeth. 1988. *Inessential Woman: Problems of Exclusion in Feminist Thought*. Boston: Beacon Press.

Stoler, Ann Laura. 1995. *Race and the Education of Desire*. Durham, NC, London: Duke University Press.

Sudbury, Julia. 1998. *"Other Kinds of Dreams": Black Women's Organizations and the Politics of Transformation*. London, New York: Routledge.

Taylor, Charles. 1992. *Multiculturalism and "the Politics of Recognition."* Princeton, NJ: Princeton University Press.

Taylor, Charles. 1993. *Reconciling the Solitudes: Essays on Canadian Federalism and Nationalism*. Montreal: McGill-Queen's University Press.

Trudeau, Pierre. 1968. *Federalism and the French Canadians*. Trans. Patricia Claxton. Toronto: MacMillan.

Volpp, Leti. 1994. "Misidentifying Culture: Asian Women and the Cultural Defense." *Harvard Women's Law Journal* 17:57–101.

Wallace, Michelle. 1994. "The Search for the "Good Enough" Mammy: Multiculturalism, Popular Culture and Psychoanalysis." In *Multiculturalism: A Critical Reader*, ed. Theo Goldberg, 259–268. Oxford, UK: Blackwell.

10 "A Woman Out of Control": Deconstructing Sexism and Racism in the University[1]

ROXANA NG

At the conclusion of a course I taught on minority groups and race relations, a male student brought a complaint against me, charging that I used the class as a platform for feminism. He claimed that as a "white male" he felt completely marginalized. This incident is not unique. In the first year I taught, a male student circulated a petition complaining to the administration that half the materials in my course on "cross-cultural education" contained references to women and gender relations. I was pleased that I had unwittingly achieved a balanced curriculum, but the student and the administration disagreed that this was desirable, and I was asked to change the contents for the remainder of the course (Ng 1991). On at least two other occasions, complaining (male) students have physically threatened me. Indeed, complaints of this kind about my courses' contents and my pedagogical methods have recurred during my 10 years teaching in the university.

The advice administrators and colleagues have given me concerning these incidents generally revolves around contents and styles: perhaps I can tone down my lectures somewhat; change to less controversial materials; acquire more teaching techniques; prepare better. (With reference to the course on "cross-cultural education," the administration suggested I use videos and let the students draw their own conclusions.) As I continued to analyse how gender, race, and class relations operate dynamically in interactional settings, however, I realized that what I experienced has less to do with my competence as a teacher than with who I am.

I am a feminist and a member of a racial minority. My scholarly work focuses on integrating analyses of gender with those of race, and vice versa. My insistence on teaching ethnic and race relations with a feminist perspective, and on challenging Eurocentric assumptions in feminist theorizing, has consistently got me into trouble throughout my university teaching career.

Using a critical incident that occurred in one of the courses I taught, I want to draw attention, in this chapter, to how sexism and racism as power dynamics operate in everyday life to disempower feminist and other minority teachers. These dynamics, as we are discovering, affect how our formal authority is perceived and received by students, and, by extension, the degree to which we can be effective teachers, especially if our teaching challenges existing norms and forms of thinking and behaviour in the classroom, in the university, and in society (see, for example, in chronological order: Nielsen 1979; Heald 1989; Ng 1991, Hoodfar 1992).

In their introduction to a special issue of the *Canadian Journal of Education* on feminist pedagogy, Briskin and Coulter (1992) identified three power axes in the classroom: between teacher and students; between students and teacher, especially women and teachers who are women of colour; and among students (257). Here I examine an additional power axis: between the minority teacher and her/his colleague(s) in relation to the handling of student complaints. I show how gender and race relations interact to undermine the authority and credibility of minority[2] faculty members, and I deconstruct the complexity of sexism and racism as interlocking relations operating in a specific situation to maintain the subordination and marginalization of minority teachers. The complex and multifaceted character of the critical incident on which I base my analysis illustrates the pervasiveness of sexism and racism, and raises questions about the assumption of neutrality and fairness when university administrators and other staff members are asked to adjudicate complaints.

Although my discussion focuses on the teacher's experience, I suggest that other minority staff and students encounter similar situations, in which their experiences are frequently exacerbated because of their relative powerlessness in the university hierarchy. My discussion therefore raises issues about existing equity measures and about how to make the university more inclusive when people enter and participate in it as unequal subjects. In the conclusion, I propose an antisexist/antiracist approach to educational matters.

The Incident

Although I use one incident instead of a variety of examples, I am not treating it as typical or generalizable of similar types of situations. Following Dorothy Smith's (1987) method of problematizing the everyday world, my purpose here is to explicate the social organization that produced and reinforced my position as a gendered and racialized subject in the university. Here is how Smith puts it:

> If you've located an individual experience in the social relations which determine it, then although that individual experience might be idiosyncratic, the social relations are not idiosyncratic. [All experiences] are generated out of, and are aspects of the social relations of our time, of corporate capitalism. These social relations are discernible, although not fully present or explicable in the experiences of people whose lives, by reason of their membership in a capitalist society, are organized by capitalism. (quoted in Campbell n.d.)

The dynamics that partly shaped the interactions described in the incident involve relations of gender, race, and class. These relations, which I call "sexism" and "racism," are not peculiar to this incident but are rather relations that have developed over time in Canada and elsewhere as groups of people have interacted. They have become systemic; that is, they are taken for granted and not ordinarily open to interrogation. In examining the incident, my intention is not to attribute blame or to identify victims, but to explicate the systemic character of sexism and racism as they are manifested in interactional settings. I maintain that in so doing, we move away from treating these incidents as idiosyncratic, isolated "wrong doing" perpetrated by a few individuals with attitudinal problems. Instead, we aim at a fundamental re-examination of the structures and relations of universities, which have marginalized and excluded certain groups of people historically, and continue to do so despite equity measures implemented in the last 10 years or so.

In this particular incident, a student (who identified himself as a "white,"[3] immigrant male) brought a complaint against me regarding a course I taught on "minority groups and race relations," one of my primary teaching subjects in various universities since 1982.[4]

In this kind of course, I always include discussions of women as a minority group, and of race and gender dynamics. As I develop and refine these courses, I incorporate meditative and physical exercises, in addition to small group discussions, as a way to rupture standard modes of scholarly inquiry, which artificially separate body/soul and mind (Currie 1992). These courses are stimulating and contentious, and although most students seem to enjoy them, I receive complaints every time I teach them. What I report here, then, is not unusual. It signals and pinpoints how approaches that deviate from the perceived norm of teaching can be threatening to and are resisted by students.

Interestingly, the student complainant attended classes for the first four or five weeks, then was absent until the third-last class. During that class, he became very agitated when, in our discussion on antiracist education, we included women's experiences of discrimination. At one point he became extremely angry, interrupted the discussion, and insisted on talking about something else. I interceded and brought the discussion back on track. I also pointed out that this kind of interruption, and the ways male and female students reacted to it, illustrated the gender dynamics we had been discussing for the past couple of weeks.[5]

The student did not come to the last two classes, but complained to the administration about my teaching[6] – at a meeting I attended. During the meeting, he charged that the meditative and physical exercises I conducted (the reasons for which I had explained clearly) were completely inappropriate in a graduate class, and that my course outline did not specify my feminist perspective. He further complained that the reading materials, which he had to pay for, were exclusively on feminism and not on race relations (this was untrue). I refused to enter into a debate about the reading materials, and suggested that whether they were exclusively feminist was a matter open to examination. He then charged that I was using the course to advance a particular political agenda. He felt that in intercepting his disruption of the last class he attended, I had marginalized him as a "white male."

Three times in the meeting he told the administrator I was "a woman out of control." When I pointed out that my perspective was very clearly disclosed during the first two classes (indeed, I encouraged students who did not like my approach to withdraw from the course), he turned to the administrator and said, "But I thought it was a phase she was going through. I didn't think that she would keep on like this when I returned after a five-week absence." He finally threatened to take me and the department to court for "false advertising." He told us that his girlfriend, a lawyer, was waiting outside.

During the entire meeting, the administrator maintained a neutral stance. At the end of the student's complaint, he asked the student what would have constituted an acceptable approach, given that we obviously had different perceptions about the course and how he was handled. The student replied that at a minimum he would have expected me to state my perspective explicitly in the course outline. I interjected at this point that if I was to make my perspective explicit, I would expect all my colleagues to do the same. The student replied, "But I don't have problems with other courses! I only have problems with yours." He added that he would ask "a gay" to make his perspective explicit also.[7]

After the student left, the administrator expressed sympathy but suggested I seriously consider the student's request. Apparently the issue of legality (students are getting more militant about the products we claim to deliver and the products we actually deliver) had been raised at the senior level of the university administration. I declined consideration of the student's request about my course outline, and suggested the matter should be raised formally in a faculty meeting.

Sexism and Racism as Systemic

Much work combatting sexism and racism in the education system has emphasized attitudinal and curricular changes (for instance, prejudice awareness/reduction workshops; measures against sexual and racial harassment; introducing other cultures into the curriculum, especially under the rubric of multicultural education). These changes, important and necessary though they are, are based on what Mohanty (1990) has identified as a liberal pluralist conception of diversity. In her critique of what she calls "the race industry" and prejudice-reduction workshops in universities, Mohanty points out that they reduce historical and institutional inequality to an individualist and psychological level.

> In focusing on "the healing of past wounds" this approach also equates the positions of dominant and subordinate groups, erasing all power inequities and hierarchies ... [T]he location of the source of "oppression" and "change" in individuals suggests an elision between ideological and structural understandings of power and domination and individual, psychological understandings of power. (Mohanty 1990, 198)

Whereas the institution of women's studies has brought about a radical re-thinking of gender relations in society, especially in western societies, this cannot be said of curricular reform on race. Frequently, attempts in this area take an additive approach, adding an article (or two) to existing materials. There has been insufficient re-conceptualization of how race matters in the structuring of social experiences inside and outside the academy. More insidious and stifling, when racism is treated as an individualistic and attitudinal property, as Mohanty has pointed out, is that members of minority groups (both faculty and students) are tokenized. That is,

> specific "differences" (of personality, posture, behaviour, etc.) of one woman of colour stand in for the difference of the whole collective, and a collective voice is assumed in place of an individual voice. ... [T]his results in the reduction or averaging of Third World peoples [for example] in terms of individual personality characteristics. ... (Mohanty 1990, 194)

This approach overlooks the fact that power dynamics, based on one's race, gender, ability, and other characteristics, operate in mundane, taken-for-granted, and "common sense" ways. Thus, although attitudinal changes and multicultural education (e.g.) are necessary points of departure for creating an inclusive university, they do not address the embeddedness of sexism and racism as routine operation in the university.

I want to go beyond treating sexism and racism as if they reside only in certain individuals, by examining their systemic properties. I begin with the premise that sexism and racism are two systems of oppression and inequality based on the ideology of the superiority of one race and/or gender over others. Thus, "white" European men, especially those of British and sometimes French descent, will typically see themselves as superior to women and to people with other ethnic and racial origins. Systems of ideas and practices have been developed to justify and support this notion of superiority. In Canada these ideas and practices originate in colonization by the Anglo-Saxons and the French.[8] Over time, ideas about the superiority and inferiority of different groups become accepted ways of thinking and being. Certain behaviours and modes of operation are eventually taken for granted; they become ways of excluding those who do not belong to the dominant group(s).

This understanding is derived from Gramsci's analysis of ideology and of how certain ideas become hegemonic and "common sense" over time. Common-sense thinking is uncritical, episodic, and disjointed, but it is also powerful because it is taken for granted (Gramsci 1971, 321–343). Once an idea becomes common sense, it is no longer questioned. In applying Gramsci's historical discussion to racism in contemporary British society, Stuart Hall observes:

> [Ideologies] work most effectively when we are not aware that how we formulate and construct a statement about the world is underpinned by ideological premises; when our formulations seem to be simply descriptive statements about how things are (i.e. must be), or of what we can "take-for-granted." (Hall quoted in Lawrence 1982, 46)

Collin Leys[9] suggests that when an ideology becomes completely normalized, it is embedded in language. Some examples of common-sense statements are: "Blacks are good at sports but not at academic subjects"; "Women are nurturing"; "Unemployed people are lazy." Although these ideas may originally have been developed by the dominant group, they have become ways cohorts of individuals are "normally" thought of; they are popularly held beliefs.

These normalized ways of thinking (frequently referred to as "stereotyping") have real and profound consequences for people's lives. In her ethnographic research on how high school students are streamed into vocational programs, Jackson found that Chinese boys were advised to go into vocational-stream accounting courses which effectively curtailed their entrance into university. This advice was based on guidance counsellors' perception that these boys were good at maths, but not so good with language. Similarly, Chinese girls were routinely streamed into secretarial programs (Jackson 1987).

Let me give another example from my own research as illustration. My analysis (Ng 1992) of immigration policy reveals that when a household applies to Canada for landed immigrant status, usually only one member of the household is granted "independent" status; the other members are granted "family class" status. This classification system usually accords the man/husband, seen to be the household head, independent status, and designates the woman/wife and children "family class" immigrants. This system is based on the western notion of the "nuclear family" with the man/husband being the head of the household; it ignores the facts that other societies have different family structures, and that the wife and adult children make essential contributions to the household economy. Furthermore, since "family class" immigrants are seen as dependents, they are not eligible for state assistance (such as training subsidies) available to the household head. In an immigrant household, then, often the husband can receive such assistance, while the wife is ineligible by virtue of her classification, rendering her dependent on and subordinate to her husband. This is an instance of how sexism operates objectively and routinely in Canadian institutions, and illustrates what I mean by "systemic" sexism.

Sexism and racism are systemic in that, routinized in institutions, they have become ways of thinking about and treating groups of people unequally as if these ideas and treatments are "normal"; they are "common sense" and thus not open to interrogation. These ways of doing things keep certain individuals and groups in dominant and subordinate positions, producing the structural inequality we see both in the education system and in the workplace.

Sexism and racism are enacted in interactions. In the example of immigration policy above, when an immigration officer classifies people according to the law, s/he is implicated in the reinforcement of sexism in relation to the immigrant woman regardless of her/his attitude towards the person so classified. The way counsellors stream Chinese boys and girls into different programs is another case in point. Thus, acts of sexism and racism go beyond personal intentions and attitudes precisely because they are embedded in institutions and because individuals have different (and at times multiple and contradictory) locations within institutions. Sexism and racism are power relations that have crystallized in organizational actions in which we are implicated by virtue of our membership in institutions. We are not and cannot be exempted from them. To see sexism and racism as systemic, then, is to understand that power dynamics (including forms of inclusion and exclusion) permeate the settings in which we live and work. Knowing how these dynamics work is a first step in eradicating sexism and racism.

In analysing the incident, I want to draw attention to the interactional dimension of power relations operating as forms of exclusion and marginalization by recognizing that in addition to our structural positions as students, faculty, and staff in the academy, we are at the same time gendered and racialized subjects. Our race and gender, as well as other socially and ideologically constructed characteristics, shape how we see ourselves and how we are seen. They affect, enable, and disable how we negotiate our ways through the university system.

I use "socially and ideologically constructed" to refer to the identification of biological, sexual, and other characteristics as absolute differences. The term "races," for example, is used to denote the supposed differences, based on skin colour, brain size, and physical features, and so on, of groups of people. These differences, treated as "natural" and therefore immutable, are then used to justify the domination of one group over another. In fact, the construction of different groups as "races" varies historically and across societies (see Miles 1989; Ng 1989, 1993).

To see members of the university community as gendered and racialized subjects is to understand and acknowledge that we are not made equal. The social structure of inequality on the basis of class, gender, race, ability, and so on, which leaks into and becomes integral to the academy, means that we do not participate in the academy as equals. To make the university more inclusive, therefore, we must make special efforts to redress the unequal balance of power at every level.

Deconstructing the Incident

The incident cited above raises four central issues. First, it raises the issue of neutrality, objectivity, and fairness in adjudicating complaints about teaching that challenges societal norms. When dealing with these and other complaints, university administrators and staff frequently take a "neutral" and "objective" stance in the interest of "fairness." To be neutral is to adopt a disinterested position, to presume that people are equal or the same, and to overlook the inequalities that people embody as a result of their unique biographies. This stance is the cornerstone of the western intellectual tradition, established by men to engender and safeguard their privilege and institutionalized in the academy when the university was the exclusive domain of certain classes of men.

Feminist scholarship has challenged the notion of objectivity and demonstrated that so-called objective universal knowledge is constructed by men for men (see Smith 1974; Spender 1980). Adrienne Rich (1976) argues that the "detachment" and "disinterest" that constitutes objectivity in scientific inquiry are the terms men apply to their own subjectivity.[10] Mary O'Brien (1981) calls this "male-stream" thought. Susan Bordo (1987) argues that the exclusive preoccupation with Reason in scholarly pursuit is a product of Cartesian thinking, which creates an artificial dualism, separating the mind/intellect and the body/emotion. The idea that "truth" exists independent of the social and physical location of the knower is carried over to the adjudication of disputes in the university. As Martin and Mohanty (1986) point out,

> the claim to a lack of identity or positionality is itself based on privilege, on a refusal to accept responsibility for one's implication in actual historical or social relations, on a denial that positionalities exist or that they matter, the denial of one's own personal history and the claim to a total separation from it. (208)

It is interesting and revealing that, in spite of (or because of?) our unequal structural positions, the administrator attempted to treat the student's complaint on equal footing as my course design and pedagogical methods, that he did not see anything out of the ordinary about a student calling a faculty member "a woman out of control." (If he did think this was peculiar, he chose to ignore it, since he did not mention it either during or after the meeting.) This pretence of fairness was immensely disempowering to me as a minority teacher, especially since the student deliberately adopted a tone that denigrated me. As Patricia Williams (1991) says, "If faculty do not treat women as colleagues, then students will not treat women as members of the faculty" (63). This example shows precisely how sexism is normalized in men's, and frequently women's, collective consciousness. The attempt at fairness in this instance reveals how men collude with each other, intentionally or unwittingly, to restore the status quo of male dominance (see also Burstyn 1985).[11]

The second issue the incident raises is that of student resistance. This is a complex issue because students resist for different and contradictory reasons: they resist curriculum that challenges the status quo, especially if they identify with the status quo; they resist because certain materials make them realize and reflect on their own oppression; they resist because both the contents and the teacher represent authority in power structures that marginalize them (consider, for instance, the youths in Willis' [1977] and McClaren's [1989] studies); they resist for other social and psychological reasons (see Lewis 1990) too numerous to list here. Here I draw attention to the challenges we encounter in the classroom because of who we are as gendered and racialized subjects. Challenges to male teachers, as a colleague observed when I discussed the above incident in a faculty meeting, are frequently directed at course materials, and disagreements are played out in intellectual debates. In the case of a minority faculty member, both course materials and the person her/himself become targets. As a member of a racial minority and a woman, I have no authority despite my formal position. But it is not only my authority that is at stake here. The knowledge I embody and transmit is also suspect – I am a woman out of control. The sexism and racism in this case is based not only on the student's attitude towards minorities in general; it is also about minorities in positions of authority whose knowledge and expertise is dubious. In reflecting on her own teaching about women in the Third World, Hoodfar (1992) reports on similar experiences. In one course, she felt that her knowledge was finally accepted by the students only when it was corroborated by her white female colleague, who gave a guest lecture on the position of women in Uganda (313).

Third, this incident raises the issue of language. In his outbursts both in the class and in the meeting with the administrator, the student asserted that I was marginalizing him as a "white male." His language use is instructive: as marginalized groups are included and incorporated into the academy, the mainstream is appropriating and subverting feminist and other liberatory discourses for use against the very groups who developed these discourses in the first place. Statements such as "I don't feel safe [or comfortable]" and "I feel silenced [or marginalized]" are now widely used to describe individuals' experiences. This is another instance of the individualization and trivialization of collective experiences;[12] it erases the inequality among people due to race, gender, class, sexual preference, ability, and so on, and reduces systemic inequality to personal feelings. Liberatory language is thus normalized, so that the "white" male student, feeling threatened because his taken-for-granted way of thinking and acting is challenged, can assert that he is silenced or marginalized.

Finally, as universities are increasingly geared towards a consumer and corporate model (Newson & Buchbinder 1988), they have become marketplaces rather than places for people to interrogate existing knowledges and to create new ones. Although I believe that there must be accountability in teaching, and recognize that students can be and have been shortchanged, I also know, having taught in universities for the last 10 years, that student complaints are launched and threats of legal action are evoked in very specific situations: usually when a student is threatened by knowledges that rupture his/her common-sense understanding of the world. Threats of legality are intended to restore the status quo.[13] In the specific incident above, the legal threat was a tactically clever move on the part of the student, and it bared his class position and his recognition that what was at issue here was power, which he knew he had as a "white male" and which he intended to use. Raising the possible legal consequences of my pedagogy captured the administrator's attention, and summoned[14] him in his role as an administrator rather than as my colleague. That the student threatened legal action and that he received a neutral, if not sympathetic, hearing resulted from his subject position as a "white," articulate male who could invoke the law on his side.

Against the Grain: Combatting Sexism and Racism in the University

To conclude, I want to explore how we may begin to combat sexism and racism in the university in light of my preceding conceptualization and analysis. I recommend that we try to think and act "against the grain"[15] in handling various kinds of pedagogical situations. To act against the grain requires one first to recognize that routinized courses of action and interactions within the university are imbued with unequal power distributions which produce and reinforce various forms of marginalization and exclusion. Thus, a commitment to redress these power relations involves interventions and actions that may appear "counter-intuitive."[16] We need to rupture ways university business and interactions are "normally" conducted.

In introducing the notion of working "against the grain," obviously I am speaking not to those interested in preserving the status quo, but to the increasing numbers of groups and individuals who wish to make the university more inclusive of previously marginalized and disadvantaged groups (recognizing that they by no means represent a monolithic interest or position).

To work against the grain is to recognize that education is not neutral; it is contested. Mohanty (1990) puts it thus:

> [E]ducation represents both a struggle for meaning and a struggle over power relations. [It is] a central terrain where power and politics operate out of the lived culture of individuals and groups situated in asymmetrical social and political positions. (184)

We must develop a critical awareness of the power dynamics operating in institutional relations, and of the fact that people participate in institutions as unequal subjects. We must take an antisexist/antiracist approach to understanding and acting upon institutional relations, rather than overlooking the embeddedness of gender, race, class, and other forms of inequality that shape our interactions.

In her exploration of feminist pedagogy, Linda Briskin makes a clear distinction between non-sexist and antisexist education critical to our understanding here. She asserts that non-sexism is an approach which attempts to neutralize sexual inequality by pretending that gender can be made irrelevant in the classroom (Briskin 1990a, 1990b). Thus, for instance, neither asserting that male and female students should have equal time to speak nor giving them equal time adequately rectifies the endemic problem of sexism in the classroom. One of Briskin's students reported that in her political science tutorials, when a male student spoke, everyone paid attention, but when a female student spoke, the class acted as if no one was speaking (Briskin 1990a, 13). Neutrality conceals the unequal distribution of power.

An antisexist/antiracist approach would acknowledge explicitly that we are all gendered, racialized, and differently constructed subjects who do not interact as equals. This goes beyond formulating sexism and racism in individualist terms and treating them as personal attitudes. Terry Wolverton (1983) discovered the difference between non-racism and anti-racism in her consciousness-raising attempt:

> I had confused the act of trying to appear not to be racist with actively working to eliminate racism. Trying to appear not racist had made me deny my racism, and therefore exclude the possibility of change. (191)

Being antisexist/antiracist means seeing sexism and racism as systemic and interpersonal (rather than individual), and combatting sexism and racism collectively, not just personally (as if somehow a person could cleanse her/himself of sexism and racism).

The first thing we must do, regardless of whether we belong to minority groups, is to break the conspiracy of silence that has ensured the perpetuation of sexism, racism, and other forms of marginalization and exclusion in the university. Patricia Williams' closing remark in her article "Blockbusting the Canon" (1991) is worth quoting at length here:

> It's great to turn the other cheek in the face of fighting words; it's probably even wise to run. But it's not a great way to maintain authority in the classroom. ... "[J]ust ignoring" verbal challenges from my law students is a good way to deliver myself into the category of the utterly powerless. If, moreover, my white or male colleagues pursue the same path (student insult, embarrassed pause, the teacher keeps on teaching as though nothing had happened), we have collectively created that peculiar institutional silence that is known as a moral vacuum. (63)

Taking an antisexist/antiracist approach means we cannot be complacent as individual teachers or as members of the different collectivities to which we belong (for instance, on committees and in faculty associations). We must speak out against normalized courses of action that maintain existing inequality, although this may alienate us from those in power as well as those close to us. We must actively support our minority colleagues in their teaching, administrative, and other responsibilities, and consciously open up spaces for previously silenced or marginalized voices to be heard. We must create spaces for students to interrogate existing paradigms and to explore alternative ones, and support them in other endeavours. We must also constantly interrogate our own taken-for-granted ways of acting, thinking, and being in the world.

To explore what these principles may mean in concrete action, I return to the critical incident. I am not suggesting that administrators and staff handling and adjudicating disputes should categorically take the side of "the minority teacher/student." I am suggesting, however, that assessment of any situation should take account of people's varying subject positions within and outside the university. In this case, although the student's complaint was legitimate in that he felt uncomfortable with the materials and my instructions, his behaviour in class and in the meeting was not. It was explicitly sexist and implicitly racist; it was aimed at undermining my authority and expertise.

Administratively, to resolve such a dispute, the student could be advised to withdraw from courses with which he has problems rather than waiting until the end of the term. An appropriate administrative response could be to arrange for the student to withdraw from the course, even though the official deadline had passed (which was actually what this student wanted and proceeded to do).

Pedagogically, the student's complaint, with its sexist, racist, and homophobic subtext, presents an excellent opportunity for challenging the assumptions in his thinking, and for educating him about academic freedom. This kind of situation is a valuable pedagogical moment that can be used to engage students in what we teach in a formal classroom setting. To work against the grain as an educator is to close the perceived gap between the formal and the "hidden" curriculum, and to use any opportunity we can to challenge normalized and normalizing forms of behaviour and thinking.[17]

The concept of academic freedom could be deployed in this instance to educate the student about the nature of university education and about his consumer-oriented mentality towards university education; university education is intended to expose students to a range of perspectives and experiences, not to confirm and/or reinforce their limited views of the world. Taking Ferando's and his colleagues' (Fernando, Hartley, Nowak, & Swinehart 1990) definition of the role of an intellectual and an academic to be that of a social critic trained to challenge dogma and to express critical views (6), it can be argued that a fundamental aspect of our freedom and responsibility as academics is to expose the political and contested nature of education.[18]

Finally, I want briefly to take up the issue of safety and comfort, because these words have become currency in debates around discourses and practices that challenge existing modes of thinking and working. Understanding oppression and doing antiracist work is by definition unsafe and uncomfortable, because both involve a serious (and frequently threatening) effort to interrogate our privilege as well as our powerlessness.[19] To speak of safety and comfort is to speak from a position of privilege, relative though it may be. For those who have existed too long on the margins, life has never been safe or comfortable. Understanding and eliminating oppression and inequality oblige us to examine our relative privilege, to move out of our internalized positions as victims, to take control over our lives, and to take responsibility for change. Such an undertaking is by definition risky, and therefore requires commitment to a different vision of society than that which we now take for granted.

Teaching and learning against the grain is not easy, comfortable, or safe. It is protracted, difficult, uncomfortable, painful, and risky. It involves struggles with our colleagues and our students, as well as within ourselves. It is, in short, a challenge.

NOTES

1 This chapter is based on my presentation on a panel entitled "Racism, Sexism and Homophobia: Some Threats to Inclusivity and Academic Freedom in the University," at the OCUFA (Ontario Confederation of University Faculty Associations) Status of Women's Conference on Developing Strategies for the Inclusive University, 5–6 February 1993, in Toronto. The other panel members were Johann St. Lewis and David Rayside.

2 I use the term "minority" in the standard sociological sense to refer to people who are relatively powerless in a society. Thus, even though women are numerically the majority, they are a "minority" in terms of power and influence. Similarly, ethnic and racial minorities, especially non-whites, constitute a minority in this society. To avoid repetition, I use the term "minority" to refer to both women and ethnic/racial minorities.

3 I use the term "white" in quotation marks to emphasize that "white," similar to "coloured," is a socially and ideologically constructed term. Its designation changes historically according to the dominant-subordinate relations in a given society. I use "white" to refer to groups who have taken part in Canada's colonization and who are perceived to be or who perceive themselves to be part of the dominant groups. In this case, the student referred to himself as a "white male"; his original language, however, was not English. He also told the class he was an immigrant and had been discriminated against due to his legal status; but in the course he did not draw parallels between his own marginality as an immigrant and the experiences of other marginalized groups.

4 I am deliberately vague about details of the course to protect the identity of individuals involved. I want to emphasize that my intent is not to personalize the story, but to highlight the embeddedness of gender and racial dynamics in our experiences.

5 It was clear that this student had upset everyone in the class. Some students became angry. Some, especially the younger female students, immediately took on a nurturing role (see Lewis 1990), attempting to protect him from other students' anger and to painstakingly explain to him the parallels between women's subordination and the subordination of ethnic and racial minorities. When the only other male student in the class spoke up and confronted him about his sexism, he at last took notice, and, in my view, took on the male student as an equal (as opposed to as a bunch of hysterical women trying to overwhelm him). By this time the discussion had become a tennis match between the two men, so, using materials we read in the course, I pointed out the gender dynamics occurring in our midst.

6 In highlighting the focus of this article, I have to omit details that detract from the main theme(s). What brought this student's complaint to the administration was actually more complicated. Briefly, in addition to resenting what had occurred in the class he attended after being away, the student was upset that I had asked him to make up, by means of written work, the work the class had done in his absence (e.g., small group discussions, debates and writing exercises). He felt I was being unjust because his absence was due to medical reasons (which I accepted), but I insisted on his making up the work because of the length of his absence. He felt I was discriminating against him because I asked him to do "extra" work not mentioned in the course outline (which specifically stated that attendance, though ungraded, was required). This was unacceptable to him, hence his request for mediation. In the meeting, however, he completely bypassed the original issue and instead criticized the course.

7 This comment, made spontaneously, indicates the normalization of certain sexual practices and the overlapping character of forms of subordination.

8 This is a cursory and simplistic presentation of the complex history of Canada's colonial past. Space and time prevent a fuller exploration and explication of this topic, except to say that

although I recognize the subordination of French-speaking peoples, I want to note the two key colonizers of Canada.

9 Special lecture by Collin Leys organized by Tuula Lindholm for a Gramsci study group on 21 March 1993.

10 For an excellent discussion of objective versus subjective knowledge and the constitution of objectivity, see Currie (1992).

11 The myth of objectivity of school knowledge has also been challenged by those writing about the hidden curriculum. For an excellent summary, see Giroux (1981).

12 See also Mohanty (1990, 193–196). Mohanty raises an important critique of the use of "experience" in liberatory discourses which becomes individualized in the university.

13 I base this claim on my own experience and on informal conversations with minority faculty over the past ten years of my university teaching career. Given the corporatization and rise of politically correct movements in universities, I think this area is worthy of further investigation.

14 I borrow this term from Susan Heald's (1990) analysis of state formation (149). To summon is to call forth or to command a particular aspect of our multidimensional and contradictory identity.

15 Various writers have used this term-see Cochran-Smith (1991), Ng (1991), and Simon (1992). Although these authors attach slightly different significance and meaning to the term, it generally denotes educational practices aimed at instilling critical perspectives and consciousness in students in the classroom. I suggest it should be extended to our work in other settings.

16 The term "counter-intuitive" is borrowed from Linda Briskin, who used it in a workshop, "Negotiating Power in the Inclusive Classroom," we co-facilitated for the Toronto Board of Education on 21 January 1993. Similar to being "against the grain," to be counter-intuitive is to interrogate what we take for granted as the "natural" ways of doing things.

17 Realistically, of course, we cannot and do not seize every moment presented to us; however, critical pedagogical moments arise more often than we "normally" think of in our work, and they can be deployed as consciousness-raising opportunities for ourselves and others.

18 The meaning of academic freedom, like the role of education itself, is a topic of heated debates. I will not elaborate on this subject here except to say that the discussion in Fernando et al. (1990), together with the literature on critical pedagogy, can be used to re-conceptualize the academic freedom debate and related notions of "objectivity" and "fairness."

REFERENCES

Bordo, Susan R. 1987. *The Flight to Objectivity: Essays on Cartesianism and Culture*. New York: State University of New York Press.

Briskin, Linda. 1990a. *Feminist Pedagogy: Teaching and Learning Liberation (Feminist Perspectives, No. 19)*. Ottawa: Canadian Research Institute for the Advancement of Women.

Briskin, Linda. 1990b. "Gender in the Classroom." *CORE [Newsletter of the Centre for Support of Teaching*, York University] 1, no. 1: 2–3.

Briskin, Linda, and Rebecca P. Coulter. 1992. "Feminist Pedagogy: Challenging the Normative." *Canadian Journal of Education* 17 (3): 247–63. http://dx.doi.org/10.2307/1495295.

Burstyn, Varda. 1985. "Masculine Dominance and the State." In *Women, Class, Family and the State*, ed. V. Burstyn and D.E. Smith, 45–89. Toronto: Garamond Press.

Campbell, Marie. n.d. *An Experimental Research Practicum Based on the Wollstonecraft Research Group*. Unpublished Manuscript, Ontario Institute for Studies in Education, Department of Sociology, Toronto.

Cochran-Smith, Marilyn. 1991. "Learning to Teach Against the Grain." *Harvard Educational Review* 61 (3): 279–310. http://dx.doi.org/10.17763/haer.61.3.q671413614502746.

Currie, Dawn H. 1992. "Subject-Ivity in the Classroom: Feminism Meets Academe." *Canadian Journal of Education* 17 (3): 341–64. http://dx.doi.org/10.2307/1495300.

Fernando, Laksiri, Nigel Hartley, Manfred Nowak, and Theresa Swinehart. 1990. *Academic Freedom 1990: A Human Rights Report*. London: Zed Books, with World University Service, Geneva.

Giroux, Henry. 1981. "Schooling and the Myth of Objectivity: Stalking the Politics of the Hidden Curriculum." *McGill Journal of Education* 16:282–304.

Gramsci, Antonio. 1971. *Selections from the Prison Notebooks*. Ed. and trans. Q. Hoare and G. Nowell Smith. New York: International Publishers.

Heald, Susan. 1989. "The Madwoman Out of the Attic: Feminist Teaching in the Margin." *Resources for Feminist Research* 18 (4): 22–6.

Heald, Susan. 1990. "'Making Democracy Practical': Voluntarism and Job Creation." In *Community Organization and the Canadian State*, ed. R. Ng, G. Walker, and J. Muller, 147–64. Toronto: Garamond Press.

Hoodfar, Homa. 1992. "Feminist Anthropology and Critical Pedagogy: The Anthropology of Classrooms" Excluded Voices." *Canadian Journal of Education* 17 (3): 303–20. http://dx.doi.org/10.2307/1495298.

Jackson, Nancy. 1987. "Ethnicity and Vocational Choice." In *Breaking the Mosaic: Ethnic Identities in Canadian Schooling*, ed. J. Young, 165–82. Toronto: Garamond Press.

Lawrence, Errol. 1982. "Just Plain Common Sense: The "Roots" of Racism." In *The Empire Strikes Back: Race and Racism in 70s Britain*, 42–94. Birmingham: University of Birmingham, Centre for Contemporary Cultural Studies.

Lewis, Magda. 1990. "Interrupting Patriarchy: Politics, Resistance, and Transformation in the Feminist Classroom." *Harvard Educational Review* 60 (4): 467–89. http://dx.doi.org/10.17763/haer.60.4.w1r67q5135585122.

Martin, Biddy, and Chandra T. Mohanty. 1986. "Feminist Politics: What's Home Got to do with it?" In *Feminist Studies/Critical Studies*, ed. T. de Lauretis, 191–212. Bloomington: Indiana University Press. http://dx.doi.org/10.1007/978-1-349-18997-7_12.

McClaren, Peter. 1989. *Life in Schools*. Toronto: Irwin Publishing.

Miles, Robert. 1989. *Racism*. London: Routledge.

Mohanty, Chandra T. 1990. "On Race and Voice: Challenges for Liberal Education in the 1990s." *Cultural Critique* 14:179–208.

Newson, Janice, and Howard Buchbinder. 1988. *The University Means Business: Universities, Corporation and Academic Work*. Toronto: Garamond Press.

Nielsen, Linda L. 1979. "Sexism and Self-Healing in the University." *Harvard Educational Review* 49 (4): 467–76. http://dx.doi.org/10.17763/haer.49.4.j26488h507813014.

Ng, Roxanna. 1989. "Sexism, Racism, and Canadian Nationalism." In *Race, Class, Gender: Bonds and Barriers*, ed. J. Vorst et al., 10–25. Toronto: Between the Lines Press, with the Society for Socialist Studies.

Ng, Roxanna. 1991. "Teaching Against the Grain: Contradictions for the Minority Teacher." In *Women and Education*, 2nd ed., ed. J.S. Gaskell and A.T. McLaren, 99–115. Calgary: Detselig Enterprises.

Ng, Roxanna. 1992. "Managing Female Immigration: A Case of Institutional Sexism and Racism." *Canadian Women's Studies* 12:20–3.

Ng, Roxanna. 1993. "Racism, Sexism, and Nation Building in Canada." In *Race, Identity, and Representation in Education*, ed. C. McCarthy and W. Crichlow, 50–9. New York: Routledge.

O'Brien, Mary. 1981. *The Politics of Reproduction*. London: Routledge and Kegan Paul.

Rich, Adrienne. 1976. "Women's Studies: Renaissance or Revolution?" *Women's Studies* 3 (2): 35–47.

Simon, Roger L. 1992. *Teaching Against the Grain: Texts for a Pedagogy of Possibility*. Toronto: Ontario Institute for Studies in Education.

Smith, Dorothy E. 1974. "Women's Perspective as a Radical Critique of Sociology." *Sociological Inquiry* 44 (1): 7–13. http://dx.doi.org/10.1111/j.1475-682X.1974.tb00718.x.

Smith, Dorothy E. 1987. *The Everyday World as Problematic: A Feminist Sociology*. Toronto: University of Toronto Press.

Spender, Dale. 1980. *Man Made Language*. 2nd ed. London: Routledge & Kegan Paul.

Williams, Patricia J. 1991. "Blockbusting the Canon." *Ms* 11 (2): 59–63.

Willis, Paul E. 1977. *Learning to Labour: How Working Class Kids Get Working Class Jobs*. New York: Columbia University Press.

Wolverton, Terry. 1983. "Unlearning Complicity, Remembering Resistance: White Women's Anti-Racism Education." In *Learning Our Way: Essays in Feminist Education*, ed. C. Bunch and S. Pollack, 187–99. Trumansburg, NY: The Crossing Press.

11 Orientalizing "War Talk": Representations of the Gendered Muslim Body Post 9-11 in *The Montreal Gazette*

YASMIN JIWANI

> Imperial logic genders and separates subject peoples so that the men are the Other and the women are civilizable. To defend our universal civilization we must rescue the women. To rescue these women we must attack these men. These women will be rescued not because they are more "our" than "theirs" but rather because they will have become more "ours" through the rescue mission .... In the Islamic context, the negative stereotyping of the religion as inherently misogynist provides ammunition for the attack on the uncivilized brown men. (Cooke 2002, 468)

The ideological function of the news media as the bearer of "news," as a sentinel of warning, and as a purveyor of hegemonic views of the nation vis-à-vis the world, lends it a certain kind of influence and legitimacy (Gitlin 1979; Hall 1984, 1990; Hartley 1982; van Dijk 1991). The portrayal of the Orientalized, gendered body in the news media thus demands interrogation at various levels – in terms of its strategic use to define the boundaries of nation or imagined community (Anderson 1983), and as the contemporary signifier of an "other" who is considered to be the repository of all that is the antithesis or projection of the "self." The current and shifting nature of the news enables one to examine representations of an "other" from different historical vantage points. In other words, how are these representations being constructed at a given point in time in order to facilitate their consumption, and hence legitimization as part of common sense?[1] Furthermore, to what political ends are these representations being used?

In this chapter, I analyse *The Montreal Gazette's* coverage of the events following the destruction of the Twin Towers in New York on September 11, 2001. I contextualize this analysis within the framework of Orientalism as defined by Edward Said. In so doing, I explicate the links between colonial and post-colonial representations of the orientalized body. I pay particular attention to the ways in which the news media both construct a gendered interpretation of this orientalized body, and draw upon a cumulative stock of authoritative knowledge (Said 1978) to build upon and stabilize its materiality. Drawing on Yeğenoğlu (1998), my aim is to highlight the connections between the textually situated discourses that are present in *The Gazette*'s representations, with the sedimented or historically constituted materiality of the discourse of Orientalism. However, by drawing upon the discursive features used in the stories covered by *The Gazette*, I also highlight the nuances of contemporary representations; underscoring their fluidity, yet reflecting also on their deep-seated resonance with the collective stock of knowledge that informs Orientalist thought.

In the sections that follow, I present an analysis of 56 stories that included some mention of women in *The Montreal Gazette*. I describe the ways in which Muslim women and men are represented, and how these representations differ according to their location in the East or West. As well, I outline the ways in which stories concerning the threat of backlash as experienced by Muslims living in the West serve to reinforce the containment of Muslim women, as well as underscore the superiority of the West. Finally, I draw on excerpts from these stories to demonstrate the ways in which the discourse of backlash seeps into and is reinforced by the prevailing anti-immigrant sentiments of news media, and in particular of *The Gazette.*

The Gendered and Orientalized Body

Much has been written about the ways in which the binaries inherent in colonial discourses have feminized representations of subject nations, as well as their inhabitants (see for example, Fanon 1965; Huttenback 1976; Lazreg 1988; Stott 1989; Wyn Davies, Nandy, and Sardar 1993). The seepages of such representations into common sense thought through popular culture have also been documented in numerous instances (Greenberger 1969; Grewal 1996; Hall 1990; Isaacs 1958; Lalvani 1995; McBratney 1988, McClintock 1995; Schneider 1977; Shohat and Stam 1994; Stam and Spence 1985; Stott 1989). The continuity between past representations and contemporary portrayals has also been researched (van Dijk 1993).

Said (1978) has argued that the Orient has been conceptualized as feminized terrain, weak yet dangerous and ready to be subjugated/domesticated through the civilizing forces of the "progressive" West. Within this context, women are seen in terms of their role as signifiers of culture: the boundary markers between the "us" and "them" which underlie and structure the relationship of the dominant colonizers to the subordinated colonized (Fanon 1965; Lévi-Strauss 1966; Yeğenoğlu 1998). Thus, women's bodies have been used to solidify national boundaries, and/or to differentiate out-groups (Anthias and Yuval-Davis, in association with Cain 1992). The body of women as gendered beings then carries particular connotations and is located at multiple sites of discursive manipulation (Lalvani 1995). On the one hand, women are represented as the keepers of culture and the maintainers of tradition. On the other hand, they are represented as exchange commodities to be used to cement alliances, or to be used as sexual objects by occupying forces and indigenous patriarchal institutions.

The gendered discourse of power as underpinning colonialism and subsequently neo/post colonial relations is also evident in the ways in which the news media cover stories about "other" nations and "other" peoples. Existing studies point to the multiple ways in which "developing" nations are portrayed as backward, barbaric, traditional and "primitive" (Dahlgren with Chakrapani 1982; Hackett 1989). On the other hand, and in keeping with the Manichean allegories of colonial thought (JanMohamed 1985), the "natives" of these countries are also seen to be innocent, childlike and pure relics of a distant past (Wyn Davies et al. 1993). In the case of women, dominant representations tend to exoticize them, highlighting their perceived excessive sexuality, and representing them as dangerous and engulfing (Jiwani 1992; Lalvani 1995; Mohanty 1991). A critical feature of many of these representations is their inherent ambivalence (Bhabha 1990). As Stuart Hall (1990) has pointed out, if the representation of black women, for example, has centred on the magnetism of their perceived sexuality, this very sexuality is also seen as being threatening because of its "otherness" and its perceived potentiality to overcome and invade male psyche. Similarly, and in light of the ambivalence inherent in these stereotypes, the figure of the black woman is also contained through her depiction as the "mama" figure or the tragic mulatto.

Here, her transgressive potential is defused and evacuated through discursive and representational strategies of containment, trivialization, erasure or symbolic annihilation (in which she is completely denied any representation (Gross 1991). The containment of these representations is also evident in Hollywood's depictions of the gendered and orientalized body which range from the geisha girl or dragon lady, to the victimized and oppressed woman of colour.

Orientalism

Edward Said's (1978) significant contribution in defining the organizational features of Orientalism and examining it as a discursive regime has been critiqued by feminists on the grounds that it does not adequately address the issue of sexuality, and that it tends to be a totalizing discourse devoid of any spaces of resistance or counter discourses (Karim 2000; Lalvani 1995; Yeğenoğlu 1998). Nevertheless, Said's definition of Orientalism offers a useful point of departure for the present inquiry primarily because it highlights the existence of a repository of images from which the collective stock of knowledge – everyday common sense knowledge – continually draws upon to make sense of the world. The articulation of these images reveals a degree of fluidity based on the changing circumstances to which these images are called upon to respond. Nonetheless, as instantiations fashioned and wrought by contemporary events, as well as by the inherent constraints and enabling influences of various institutions and technologies, they tend to echo elements of that collective and cumulative reservoir of knowledge (Hall 1990). As Foucault would suggest, Orientalism constitutes a regime of truth based on an authoritative corpus of knowledge.

The discursive regime of Orientalism overlaps with and is derived from discourses of colonialism and imperialism. Hence, commonalities with these discursive traditions lie in the binary oppositions that form and inform the power coordinates of these "regimes of truth." These include a perception of cultural practices as indicative of inherent and innate traits, a collapsing of differences between subject peoples so that they appear as monoliths, and taxonomies of knowledge which situate subject peoples in particular relations of inferiority which are then naturalized. In terms of the tradition of Orientalism, then, the Orient is a place of mystery and danger; the Orientalized body discursively situated within this landscape serves to legitimize and naturalize unequal power relations. The Orientalized body becomes a projection of all that the West finds strange, alien and abhorrent, but simultaneously exotic, inviting and alluring. In short, the Orientalized body essentializes otherness (Lazreg 1988; Said 1981).

Methodology

Montreal has been described as "more like Europe" than other parts of Canada. Carrying a legacy of both French and English colonialism, the city is a remarkable site of uneasy coexistence between these two dominant cultures, with a medley of exoticized "other" cultures thrown into the mélange. The city has a significant Jewish population, as well as a growing number of diverse Middle Eastern communities.[2] As the only major English daily in Montreal, *The Gazette* is rather peculiarly situated. Owned by CanWest Global Communications Corporation (a corporation that also owns many of Canada's largest daily newspapers), it is obviously influenced by mainstream conservative political values of the dominant groups. However, in addition to serving the minority Anglophone community in Quebec, it is equally seen to represent the voice and interests of a significant number of English-speaking minority/immigrant communities. Hence, *The Gazette* is caught in the difficult position of trying to cater to both the traditional Anglophone and the more recently-arrived English-speaking immigrant communities, as well as adhere to the conservative bias of its owners.[3]

For the purposes of this analysis, daily editions of *The Gazette* over the two-week period following September 11, 2001 were scanned and inputted into FileMaker Pro database program.[4] A search using the keywords "women," "veil," and "burqa" was conducted. Out of a total of 449 articles dealing with the destruction of the Twin Towers and its immediate aftermath, only 56 articles either centred on women or made some mention of women. Of these, 29 primarily addressed Muslim women living in the West, 18 primarily addressed non-Muslim women living in the West, and 9 primarily addressed Muslim women in the East. The other 393 articles either explicitly mentioned men, or assumed an androcentric perspective.

The 56 articles containing references to women were examined using a combination of textual analysis and certain aspects of informal discourse analysis (van Dijk 1985, 1993). Central to the latter method are issues revolving around accessed voices (as in who gets to speak), types of description, semantic moves and discursive strategies. Signs were scrutinized in terms of their denotative and connotative meanings (Barthes 1957, 1973), as well as their resonance with Orientalism as defined by Said (1978). The combination of an informal discourse analysis with Said's epistemological perspective serves to delineate the various ways in which Orientalism is transformed at the level of *parole* – in terms of its instantiation within a particular news story – while at the same time, reproducing the larger discursive formation of Orientalism as *langue* (as defined in de Saussurean linguistics and explicated by Barthes (1964, 1973).[5]

In the analysis that follows, the major themes and signifiers to be found in these stories are detailed. No differentiation is made between stories filed by regular columnists, on-site reporters, the paper's editors, or informed citizens. While recognizing that there are important differences between these categories, the principal aim here was to examine all of the various representations that referenced the category "women." It should also be stressed that even though the articles selected were chosen because of their mention or inclusion of the keyword woman/women, the resulting analysis includes an examination of male representations in so far as these were portrayed in relation to women. The latter is predicated on the notion that gender is a relational category that derives its meanings from its contextual and social location vis-à-vis other categories.

Analysis and Discussion

In examining the coverage printed by *The Gazette*, it was apparent that descriptions regarding Muslim men far outweighed those pertaining to Muslim women. Of the total number of stories examined, 32 explicitly contained descriptions of Muslim men while only 23 referenced women or dealt specifically with Muslim women. The majority of these stories, especially those dealing with events related to Afghanistan, tended to utilize binary oppositions – pitting the oppressive, harsh, dictatorial and barbaric characteristics of the latter to the libertarian, democratic and superior character of the US. I will discuss this further in the section pertaining to the representations of Muslim men.

There were also significant differences in the ways in which Muslim women residing in Afghanistan, Pakistan or other parts of the Muslim world were represented, as compared to their counterparts living in Canada or the US. A significant corpus of stories pertaining to Muslims living in the US or Canada focused on the threat of backlash. Further, and in contrast to Muslim women living in Afghanistan, Pakistan or other parts of the Middle East, Muslim women living in the West tended to have a modicum of active representation in that they were interviewed, and their words were often quoted in print. However, whether the stories dealt with the threat of violence experienced by them here in the West or the conditions of patriarchal oppression confronting them in the East, Muslim women tended to be portrayed as victims.

Overall, however, it was difficult to separate out the representations of Muslim men from Muslim women given that the two were intertwined in the coverage, with the framing of one giving meaning to the framing of the other. Nonetheless, for analytical reasons I have separated out the main discursive themes used to represent women and men in the sections below. In addition, I outline the various ways in which the discursive constructions of Muslim women in the west, under the auspices of expressing concern for the backlash they might face as a result of their presence, in fact served to contain women in ways that converged with their containment in the East.

Muslim Women in the East

Of all the stories referencing Muslim women, orientalist themes were especially apparent in those that focused on Muslims living directly under Islamic rule. For example, several stories used the image of women veiled in burqas – appearing mute and fleetingly in the streets – as a backdrop against which the horrors and barbarism of the Taliban were more fully described. In a sense, there is nothing new here. In contemporary Western media, the veil remains a symbol of Muslim women and their oppression by tribal, primitive and conservative upholders of Islam (Ahmed 1992; Jafri 1998; Hoodfar 1993). As Anouar Majid (1998) remarks, "For the Western media, the picture of the veiled woman visually defines both the mystery of Islamic culture and its backwardness."[6] Yet, as Yeğenoğlu (1998) suggests, the veil also serves another function:

> The veil attracts the eye, and forces one to think, to speculate about what is behind it. It is often represented as some kind of a mask, hiding the woman. With the help of this opaque veil, the Oriental woman is considered as not yielding herself to the Western gaze and therefore imagined as hiding something behind the veil. It is through the inscription of the veil as a mask that the Oriental woman is turned into an enigma. Such a discursive construction incites the presumption that the real nature of these women is concealed, their truth is disguised and they appear in a false deceptive manner. They are therefore other than what they appear to be. (p. 44)

That said, in the corpus of the coverage examined, women's victimized and subordinate status was generally linked to the excessive patriarchal nature of Islam and of Afghan men by association. The following story underscores this kind of reporting:

> It's midday in Pakistan's deeply conservative northwest. Bearded men sit in small groups sipping sweet black tea. The rare woman hidden in an enveloping head-to-toe cloak called a burqa, scurries through the dusty market.
>
> The call to prayer sounds. The voice is soothing, almost mournful. Then the cleric begins to preach. His voice changes, suddenly shrill and angry and his message violent. Bellowing from

> a loudspeaker atop the mosque, the voice rails against internationally financed aid organizations and their promotion of women rights, girls' education and small home-based businesses. It hurls curses at the women who work for these groups, calling them evil handmaidens of a decadent West that wants to destroy traditions, culture and the Islamic religion. They should be punished, the voice says.
>
> Islamic clerics urge the faithful to shun women involved with such groups as prostitutes – or, alternatively, to kidnap them, force them into marriage and keep them locked away at home. "Don't allow these sinful women to enter our villages," roars Maulana Zia-ul Haq, a cleric in Banda, a village in the Dir district. "If you see any one of them, just take her home and forcibly marry her. If she is a foreigner, kill her." (Gannon, September 13, 2001, C7)

Entitled, "Where equality is 'obscene': Conservative Pakistani clerics vow to crush women's rights" and appearing just two days after the destruction in New York City, this article strategically brings together several orientalist tropes. For instance, orientalist imagery is evoked in the language used to describe the setting. The laziness of the "natives" comes through in the representation of men sitting around sipping tea while the women hurry about their business. Women are not to be seen or heard under Taliban rule (Franks 2003). Men, on the other hand, are charged with maintaining the patriarchal order as exemplified in the role of the clerics. The clerics then become the point men for the media, symbolizing fanaticism, ruthlessness, barbarity and excessive patriarchal violence. Lazreg notes that "[t]he fetishism of the concept, Islam, in particular, obscures the living reality of women and men subsumed under it" (1988, 95). Thus, Islam becomes the paradigm by which women and men's lives are understood as opposed to a force which emerges as a form of identification and mobilization as a response to external circumstances and conditions. Interestingly, news stories, such as the one above, conflate or collapse the differences between Palestinians and Afghanis, or Palestinians and Pakistanis, and reflect the tendency of dominant Western media to resort to homogeneous and totalizing representations (see also the Canadian Islamic Congress's evaluation of western media bias, 2002).

However, contradictions still abound. The voice of one of the clerics vowing to crush women's rights, for example, is described as "shrill and angry and his message [as] violent." This loaded description offers a view of the clerics as irrational and insane in their ultra-patriarchal insistence that women remains subjugated, but also as weak and feminized given that emotion is stereotypically considered to be the province of women. Similarly, the women who are interviewed are presented simultaneously as victims, and as active agents who, if somewhat deceptive by necessity, are resisting the patriarchal onslaught by organizing a shelter for women and setting up educational programs to make other women aware of their rights.

One of these "active" women, for instance, is described as "cover[ing] her head in a large sweeping shawl." Her victimization is made evident from the very inclusion of her experience of being in an abusive marriage with her first cousin whom she has not yet divorced. She is further described as being engaged in educational efforts to make other women aware of their rights. She adds: "Their self-esteem is not there. *They think of themselves as something akin to animals.*" (My emphasis.) The victimhood of Afghani women is thus rendered complete – as animals, they need to be saved.

Another young female worker at the shelter, Ruhi Tabassum, is also interviewed. "[S]miling beneath the shawl," as the reporter puts it, she is quoted as saying, "They [the men] know that if their women know their rights, they won't be able to control them."

The reporter's insertion of the smile is suggestive of Tabassum's duplicity. In other words, the overall portrayal of Afghani women in this article resonates with the colonial representation of women of colour as secretive, deceptive, and as appearing to be meek and submissive while plotting against their benevolent colonizers – or, for that matter, against their own men (Jiwani 1992).

This profile is carried over into a story about the necessity for increased security measures at airports (Smith and Philps, September 14, 2001, A4). Here, the traditional notion of Arab or Middle Eastern women as quintessential victims is shattered by the Israelis' contention that they have successfully identified Arab women travelling alone as constituting a high risk. In contrast, Israeli or Jewish women who know some Hebrew are considered to be low risks. Others who constitute a high risk include Arab males, priests, and individuals who purchase "their tickets at the last minute." By framing such travellers as hiding behind deceptive appearances, the article manages to justify racial profiling and to legitimize extensive state surveillance methods.

Again, this confusing and sometimes contradictory conflation of woman as helpless victim and manipulative activist is found in another article that contrasts the innocence of those female victims who turned up to work in the Twin Towers on that fateful day with the callous and uncanny behaviour of the Palestinian women in Ramallah who celebrated their demise by ululating in response to the tragic news (Schnurmacher, September 14, 2001, A19). Here, active agency in the form of militancy of the Palestinian women is presented in an extreme fashion by the writer who then goes on to make nebulous links between Palestinian women, their celebration, and their commitment to a cause beyond reason.

Such unquestioning and irrational commitment to a cause "beyond reason" is then harnessed to the female biological body by presenting Palestinian women as reproducers of terror – as mothers of suicide bombers. As this writer described it:

> [A] Canadian broadcast reporter whose coverage had always leaned strongly toward the Palestinian position recently became more even-handed after an encounter with the mother of a suicide bomber who told him she was happy with what her son had accomplished. Her only regret was she did not have other sons who could do the same thing. (Schnurmacher, September 16, 2001, A19)

The revulsion expressed towards Palestinian women who give birth to suicide bombers echoes the kinds of fears put forth in colonial literature around miscegenation. In this literature, colonial officers were advised not to consort with indigenous women because of the latter's perceived fecundity, and the fear that the growth of a mixed race population would lead to a weakening of the Empire's moral, political and economic strong hold over its colonies (McBratney 1988; Mohanty 1991).[7]

The same ambivalent framing of the victim/activist Muslim female is captured in a photograph and caption that accompanies a story on the US movement of arms to areas around Afghanistan. The photo shows women in burqa with guns protesting at a rally in Lahore. The caption reads: "Veiled women activists of a Pakistani religious-political party hold toy guns and the Koran as they chant anti-U.S. slogans at Lahore protest rally" (Blanchfield and MacKenzie, September 20, 2001a, A1). That women are actually actively engaged in protest as opposed to their usual stereotypical depiction as passive victims should, according to the gender liberation rhetoric of the West, suggest a disruption that is progressive. However, here, the very act of holding "toy guns" and copies of the "Koran" makes their action suspect and indicative of an emergent threat. In contrast, women educating other women and setting up shelters for their sisters – in short, women who behave like "us" – are acceptable. However, women who are militant "activists" are not (Thobani 2003).

In all these articles, Afghanistan and surrounding nations are also gendered. The latter are portrayed as "allies of convenience" that cannot be entirely trusted, given that they are also deceptive and motivated by their own agendas (Wallace, September 22, 2001: A13; Goldstein, September 29, 2001: B1). Images of failed states and primitive technologies and peoples come through in these stories. What is implicitly understood, and what is even sometimes explicitly stated, is that these countries have failed because of their own inherent shortcomings rather than because of any involvement by the Western or Soviet imperial powers (Friedman, September 14, 2001, B3). Thus, it is the "failure" of these countries that is deemed to be the motivating factor sparking resentment towards, and retaliation against, the West.

"Dependency" is another gendered term used to describe many of the countries surrounding Afghanistan, as well as the country itself. In the case of Afghanistan, this is the same country that the US bombed "up to the Stone Age" (Dowd, September 25, 2001, B3), a comment that implies that Afghanistan was even *more* primitive prior to US intervention.

Primitivism, then, becomes one of the discursive means by which to explain women's subordinate position (Bagnall, September 27, 2001: B3), the rejection of leisure through consumption (i.e., the banning of television sets, music, and even kites) (Dowd, September 25, 2001, B3), and the brutality of Afghani men (Gannon, September 13, 2001, C7). In contrast, America and Americans are represented as emblems of freedom, liberation and democracy. While they might have a few failings, these are not equivalent to the crimes committed by the Taliban. As one writer concludes:

> [B]efore September 11, it might have been possible to feel pity for the men who joined the Taliban, with their feelings of dislocation after 20 years of Soviet invasion and civil war, their poverty, their desire to make sense of their world. But not now. By now we know how they intend to order their world: women under house arrest; the rest of the world their enemy. (Bagnall, September 27, 2001, B3)

There is a complete erasure of history in the kinds of representations that are used to justify American intervention in Afghanistan. Moreover, the very notion of "pity" is suggestive of Western benevolence which, as Sherene Razack (1998a) insists, is the underside of Western racism.

Muslim Men in the East

The "lowness" of the Afghani men and the Taliban in particular (who are also Afghanis) comes through not only in the imagery of primitiveness, but also in descriptions of their brutality and zeal. Several stories underline this brutality by linking it to the treatment of women, and more importantly, to fanaticism. One mullah is described as "reputed to be so crazed that when shrapnel hit his eye in the battle with the Russians, he simply cut it out with a knife and kept going" (Dowd, September 25, 2001, B3). Another story discusses the attack on the World Trade Centre in 1993, concluding that "The mastermind, Ramzi Yousef, later boasted that he had hoped to kill 250,000" (Spector, September 12, 2001, B3).

Overall, the message is that primitivism leads to violent opposition of the West – an opposition which is irrational and grounded in a mixture of fear and resentment. Add poverty to this potent mix – a poverty which would seem, according to these stories, to be self-inflicted – and what we are left with is a confluence of factors that lends itself perfectly to the development of human weapons of mass destruction. These themes are exemplified in a story by a reporter who visits a Madrasa in Pakistan where orphan boys and refugee men are schooled in the practice and theological foundations of one particular interpretation of Islam. He calls it a "jihad factory" populated by "poor and impressionable boys who are kept entirely ignorant of the world and largely of all but one interpretation of Islam. They are the perfect jihad machines" (Goldberg, September 15, 2001, B1).

Nowhere in this article is there mention made of the fact that the type of Islam taught in this particular Madrasa is akin to the Islam practiced by the ruling elite in Saudi Arabia, a significant ally of the US, nor is there any mention of the diversity that exists within the Islamic world, the history of US involvement in the region. Nor why these young boys and men are orphans and refugees in the first place.

Another common trope in the coverage of Muslim men concerned their unwarranted envy of, and anger against, the West. As this writer argues:

> And this Third World War does not pit the U.S. against another superpower. It pits it – the world's only superpower and quintessential symbol of liberal, free-market, Western values – against all the super-empowered angry men and women out there. Many of these super-empowered angry people come from failing states in the Muslim and Third World. They do not share American values, they resent America's influence over their lives, politics and children, not to mention its support for Israel, and they often blame America for the failure of their societies to master modernity.
>
> What makes them super-empowered, though, is their genius at using the networked world, the Internet and the very high technology they hate to attack the United States. Think about it: they turned its most advanced civilian planes into human-directed, precision-guided cruise missiles – a diabolical melding of their fanaticism and American technology. Jihad Online. And think of what they hit: the World Trade Centre – the beacon of American-led capitalism that both tempts and repels them, and the Pentagon, the embodiment of American military superiority. (Friedman, September 14, 2001, B3)

The above excerpt from this article illustrates both the ambivalence inherent in these representations – the juxtapositioning of primitiveness with expertise in computer technology – and the strategic moves which underscore the differences between "us" versus "them." The latter includes those moves which minimize the grounds of "their" grievances. In other words, those grievances – regardless of how founded they might be – are simply translated into the emotions of anger, resentment and envy. "They" are thus rendered as undeserving "children" who have no legitimate basis for their anger. However, "their" anger, though illegitimate, is dangerous enough to signal the advent of a third world war. In addition, the excerpt illustrates the binary of the benevolent West which shares its technologies with the primitive East only to have the latter use it against their benefactors. The theme of betrayal is underscored in the above quote constructing the inhabitants of the "failed states" as beyond redemption and thus deserving of extreme retaliatory action.

The inferiorizing of Muslim men, then, is achieved through representing them as emotional, irrational, deceptive, resentful, untrustworthy, and above all, as child-like. This latter rendering serves to emasculate these men – reducing them to entities who are weak, vulnerable and conquerable. Another part of this strategy of emasculation is to render these men more feminine. The use of emotional descriptors serves this function as do other more explicit discursive devices. Witness for example, the following description of Osama bin Laden offered by one of the reporters:

> The image has flickered across North American television screens so many times in the last five days it will probably take years to fade – the liquid-eyed Osama bin Laden, almost girlishly pretty despite the breast-long beard, sits in the dust in flowing robes, firing an automatic weapon and smiling at the strength of its recoil. The film was shot years ago, but in the pictures, the charismatic gunman seems almost to be mocking the West and its grief. (Waters, September 15, 2001, B1)

The feminized portrayal of Osama bin Laden cited above coalesces a number of different signifiers and connotations, producing an overall picture of bin Laden as the beguiling yet ultimately menacing arch-villain who is cold, calculating, ruthless and sinister – all characteristics, incidentally, that are commonly associated with women of colour in colonial literature and popular culture (Jiwani 1992). A cartoon in the paper a week later also feminizes bin Laden, portraying him as a woman in a burqa. What is interesting about the cartoon and the above portrayal is its use of feminized terms such as "liquid-eyed," "girlishly pretty," "breast-long beard" combined with his representation in a burqa complaining about the heat generated by wearing such a garment.

At this point, it should be mentioned that, in the course of *The Gazette*'s post September 11, 2001 coverage, several reporters *do* attempt to explain Islam and its variegated nature to the Western audience, but all too often, dichotomous interpretations of Islam – as a religion of peace on the one hand and a religion advocating war on the other – are juxtaposed. These stories tend to draw heavily on the accessed voices of various elite Islamic scholars in the West and the East (Watanabe, September 27, 2001, B1). They also privilege a sense that the message of peace in Islam is particularly vulnerable to being hijacked, and that this very vulnerability is itself a function of the inherent flaws of Islam's religious structure. Thus, a structure which is perceived to be without a central authority, without policing mechanisms and with a kind of communal orientation is seen to lend itself to a collective ethos that then becomes the antithesis of Western capitalism with its hierarchal structures and its centralization of power. Within such a framing, even the intellectual tradition within Islam is seen to be at fault for encouraging this kind of hijacking. As one reporter puts it, "All of this flexibility and questioning mean that a clever leader or scholar with a bitter and often not very well-informed audience can twist Koranic ideas to his own ends. The jihad for example..." (Waters, September 15, 2001, B1). This statement follows that of a Muslim advocate in the West who counters the stereotypical view of Islam by emphasizing its intellectual tradition and its encouragement of questioning and internal search. That Christianity, as Karim Karim (2000) has suggested, has been similarly hijacked is an observation significantly missing from these articles.

"Backlash Stories"

A significant number of stories printed by *The Gazette* during this period cohered around the theme of "backlash," or the threat of backlash as experienced by Muslim communities in the US and Canada. What is interesting about these backlash stories is that they served a dual ideological function. On the one hand, they communicated to minority groups that their interests were considered important enough to garner press coverage – in other words, they counted. On the other hand, and from a somewhat cynical perspective, the inclusion of backlash stories served the strategic function of "balance". As Stuart Hall (1974) has argued, the codes of objectivity, balance and impartiality are critical to the ideological functioning of the news media with respect to their position as the "fourth estate" and their role in maintaining the hegemonic order. For the news media to appear to be partisan would not only detract from their credibility as the fourth estate and the voice of the "nation," but also make them vulnerable to boycotts, advertiser reprisals, charges of biased reporting and a disaffected audience.

Several interesting themes emerge in the stories concerning Muslim fears of a backlash. Of the 56 articles, 13 dealt specifically with the actual or potential threat of a backlash against the Muslim population living in the West. Of 10 such stories to appear in the first week following the event, two dealt with the Muslims in the US. Another concerned a personal account of a Pakistani woman and her experience of racism upon moving to a particular part of the province of Quebec many years ago. Two are editorials decrying the incidence of racist assaults and the targeting of Muslims in Montreal. One other story revolves around the reporter's overhearing of racist comments by non-Muslim women in the aftermath of the collapse of the Twin Towers. In many of these stories, incidents of assault – whether they are projected or fully realized – are noted. Most of these focus on women wearing the veil and their fears of doing so in the immediate aftermath of September 11.

In the single article that focuses on an actual assault of a young Saudi female resident at a local hospital, the reporter makes no mention of a veil or hijab, though the assault itself is graphically described. Further, there is no mention of how the attacker actually identified the woman as being Saudi or a Muslim (Macfarlane, September 18, 2001: B6). According to the report, the woman is "a fourth year resident in obstetrics and gynecology, described by her supervisors as a brilliant resident." Her dedication to her work is further emphasized by the mention that she stayed for most of her shift despite having being attacked and traumatized. While she is not interviewed, the Dean of McGill's Faculty of Medicine is quoted as saying that "female Muslim residents will not be on call during nights, effective immediately." What is striking about the Dean's response is that measures were not invoked to increase the protection of those who are rendered vulnerable to such assaults. Equally striking is that while the story appears to be sympathetic to the young woman and laudatory of her status, her own voice is erased.

In this story, as in the majority of the other backlash stories, the themes of fear and the possibility of retaliation emerge clearly. However, in most of them, it is the male authoritative figures (in general, key spokesmen or presidents of various organizations) who are interviewed or quoted extensively. Muslim women are directly interviewed in only three stories. An example of this trend is evident in the following story which appeared on September 13, 2001:

> In Canada, the backlash began Tuesday, said Shafiq Hudda, chairman of the Islamic Humanitarian Service, a national charitable organization based in Kitchener, Ont. "One of our lady volunteers was actually verbally assaulted on the highway," Hudda said.
>
> "Somebody called her an effing terrorist." Hudda said the woman, who is in her 50s and was wearing a head scarf, was shaken by the incident, which occurred near the downtown area of Kitchener.

> The Islamic Assembly of North America, which is based in the United States but also has an office in Quebec, is advising Muslims in both countries to stay home. "All Muslims in the U.S. and Canada must take precautions and care from the possibility of retaliatory attacks," said the group's Website. "Do not leave home unless absolutely necessary, especially women, who wear Muslim dress." (Richards 2001)

While the backlash stories serve the important function of highlighting the vulnerabilities of the Muslim population living in North America, their resulting message ends up reinforcing notions of the weakness and victim status of this particular group. This is especially evident in the references to women. The majority of the articles underline the view that women wearing the veil or the hijab are most vulnerable to attacks because they are easily identifiable (see, for instance, Fitterman, September 15, 2001a and September 21, 2001b). Male spokespeople for the various organizations that are interviewed all caution women who wear the hijab or veil to stay at home. One Muslim woman specifically mentions how her daughter was afraid of wearing her hijab to school and had to be accompanied by her brother to ensure her safety (Davenport, September 16, 2001, A3).

These words of caution, though well-intentioned, end up legitimizing Muslim women's containment in the private sphere of the home. That home might well be located in America or Canada, but the end result is a strategy of containment, ironically reminiscent of that which the Taliban in Afghanistan had been enforcing upon women. Gendering terror, then, becomes in part about the various ways in which the *threat* of violence and retaliation forces women and men to refrain from being seen, or from occupying space as legitimate citizens.

In yet another article, reference is made to a woman who now refrains from wearing the veil *precisely* because of this threat of backlash. In the same article, two female students recount their experiences of terror. One is told to "go home. You're just a terrorist." The other student states, "I do have a feeling of insecurity because of the looks I am getting of anger and suspicion" (Block, September 14, 2001: A17). In other words, fear, heightened security, and potential threats are all ways in which Muslim families and individuals are terrorized in to "going home" or staying at home.

In these latter stories, then, Muslim women are framed as victims who are acted upon by others rather than as active agents who are capable of determining their own course of safety or resistance to the perceived threat from the outside (see Franks 2003 for a more detailed discussion of this phenomenon). Such a framing accords with one of the main features of news reporting, namely, the tendency to create binaries between the victims and the perpetrators (Connell 1980). But interestingly, it also converges with the dominant ideology which, as evident from the controversial case of Émilie Ouimet who chose to wear the veil, suggests that symbols such as the veil communicate a reluctance to assimilate on the part of a minority group member and hence lead to their further marginalization. Thus, the victim of discrimination is blamed for "inciting" discriminatory attitudes by refusing to adhere to the dominant norms (Lenk 2000).

As for Muslim men living in the West, these backlash stories tend to depict them as authoritative, reasonable, compassionate and desperate to distance themselves from the acts of not only those who attacked the Twin Towers, but also from the more fundamentalist clerics who advocate a literal and conservative interpretation of Islam. Such a social distancing is symbolic of a retreat. By distancing themselves from those who attacked the Twin Towers and those who represent the Taliban and the Afghanis, Muslim men who were interviewed in many of *The Gazette* articles are, by their very geographic location, rendered more like "us." Such a sentiment is clearly articulated by one Muslim spokesperson – a professor at the University of Waterloo and president of the Canadian Islamic Congress – who is quoted as saying: "We are part of you and you are part of us" (Waters, September 15, 2001, B1).

The Gazette's representations also serve to reinforce the binary of East versus West, and tradition versus liberation. By locating these Muslim males in the West, the connotation is that these men are more "Westernized," and hence liberated. At the same time, the backlash experienced and articulated by these men serves to underline their subject position as members of weak and victimized minorities left to suffer the consequences of events far beyond their control. The terrorizing nature of the backlash becomes even more apparent with the subsequent forced incarceration of Muslim men in the US, and with the racial profiling of men who appear to be Muslim or of Arabic heritage. This subject position of Muslim men living in the West is also communicated in several stories through the juxtaposition of their voices against other white, authoritative experts who are renowned for their conservative perspectives on Islam (e.g. Professors Daniel Pipes and Samuel Huntington as quoted in Waters' above mentioned article).

However, despite the widespread publicity about unfair stereotyping, not to mention the stigmatizing of and threats of physical and psychological violence against, Muslim communities, there was virtually no mention in this coverage of an active or assertive involvement of state authorities, such as the police, in working with these communities to safeguard them from acts of violence. On the contrary, the coverage seemed at times to oscillate between the backlash and racial profiling discourses, with the latter seeping into the ever-present anti-immigration discourses extant in Canadian news coverage (Jiwani 1992; Mahtani 2001).

Harnessing the Fear to Support Anti-Immigrant Sentiments

This seepage between the two dominant discourses – the anti-immigrant discourse on the one hand, and the backlash discourse on the other – is evident in several cases. For example, in one of the few cases where a Muslim woman is interviewed, her interview is used to support the view that Canada's refugee system should be tightened to exclude "extremists and nationalists." She herself is described as a refugee from Kyrgyzstan, and as an Uzbek woman (Sevunts, September 14, 2001, A19). In the same story, the reporter interviews two other men, one of whose name sounds Muslim. In recounting these men's experiences, their observations regarding the vulnerabilities of the immigration system are emphasized:

> Bakhtiar said the Immigration and Refugee Board needs not to tighten the screws but train real professionals. "The sad truth that I learned while interacting with other refugees," Bakhtiar said, "is that a convincing liar can become a refugee because the tribunal members have no way of checking his story. But a real refugee who is so nervous that makes one mistake might be denied his claim."
>
> Another man who didn't want his name used said instead of tightening the refugee determination system Canada might want to invest more in its immigration screening process. "I know a thing or two about interrogation," the man said. "And I was appalled by the security screening interview I had." "The first thing the RCMP officer asked me was whether I had ever killed anybody. The second question was whether I belong to any terrorist organizations.

> As if I had been a terrorist and a killer I would have admitted to it." The whole interview lasted no more than 15 minutes, the man said. "No wonder they missed that Algerian terrorist and others like him. I'm sure they asked him the same questions and he said no. Now we all have to pay for it."

These men's accounts are then used to underscore the weakness of the current system which supposedly allows terrorists to enter the country undetected. Again, a forum intended for the open discussion of backlash stories is itself hijacked in order to reinforce the hegemonic interests of another dominant discourse.

Accessed Voices: Who Gets to Speak and Who Is Silenced

Throughout the two weeks of coverage that were analysed, the voices of authority accessed to make judgments and articulate a position on the issues at hand tended to be male. Furthermore, virtually all of these accessed voices belonged to men living in the West, and in only a minority of instances were these voices those of clerics in Pakistan. Where white male authoritative voices were accessed, they subordinated those of the Muslim spokespeople. The predominant pattern that emerged was that men spoke for women, and this was particularly true of Muslim men speaking on behalf of Muslim women living in the West.

Muslim or Middle-Eastern women who were directly quoted tended to be highly educated or enrolled as students in recognized institutions (e.g. at McGill University or Concordia University, or in one case, with a doctorate from the University of Western Ontario) (Block, September 14, 2001, A17; Fitterman, September 21, 2001, A13; Moore, September 24, 2001, A4). In only one instance was a Muslim woman living in the West quoted without these kinds of identifiers (Davenport, September 16, 2001, A3). The subtext seems to suggest that if these women are educated, then they are credible and their stories can be believed. They are, in other words, more like "us." On the other hand, no female activists in Afghanistan – for instance women representing organizations such as RAWA (the Revolutionary Association of Women in Afghanistan) – were cited or quoted despite the fact that they have long been advocating an end to the oppressive conditions imposed by both the Northern Alliance and the Taliban (Kolhatkar 2002; Moghadam 1999 and 2001).

Interestingly, this emphasis on citing Muslim women educated and sometimes born in the West seems to strategically underscore the West's representation of itself as the land of progress, gender equality and liberation for women. This sets the West ("us") apart from the Taliban ("them") which is, according to one reporter and several scholarly sources, specifically aiming their policies of containment at educated, middle and upper class urbanized Afghani women who they see as having been "contaminated" by Western notions of progress and liberation (Bagnall, September 27, 2001, B3; Moghadam 2001). That Afghani women are silenced in Afghanistan but allowed to speak in the West works ideologically to seal the dominant interpretation of the Western ethos of egalitarianism and its sense of superiority.

"Overcomplete" descriptions which are replete with unnecessary but identificatory details were also prevalent in the coverage of Muslim men and women living in the West. In one instance, a Muslim in Brooklyn was interviewed "as he stood behind a counter filled with incense sticks, surrounded by shelves of essential oils, trays of olives and jars of pistachios" (Richards September 13, 2001, B4). In another instance, a reporter talking to a Muslim man living in Montreal notes his grey hair and beard, as well as the fact that he is reclining on "deep red velvet cushions atop an ornate Afghan carpet in his sparsely furnished Longueil apartment" (Montgomery, September 18, 2001, B1). These descriptors are replete with signification about the Orient: its exotic lush colours and almost hedonistic lifestyle. In the same article, the reporter notes how this man's wife, Sabera, "laid out a plastic sheet on the floor, then proceeded to cover it with large pots full of rice, chicken stew, salad and plates of home-made flatbread." Here, the exoticization of the food and the simple manner of the serving style all work to underscore the otherness of this family, as well as its incongruous appearance in a Western milieu.

Conclusion

Within the context of post-September 11, 2001 news coverage, representations of the gendered Orientalized body did not depart from the existing pool of stereotypical images. The militant martyr or suicide bomber was a constant figure (perpetuated in part by the coverage of the situation in Palestine), as were hostage takings and violent upheavals. Likewise, the veiled woman received much media attention, depicted as being both oppressed by and subjugated under Islam, as well as unable to liberate herself without the help of Western powers (Hoodfar 1993; Jafri 1998; Lenk 2000; Todd 1998). As far as these stereotypical representations are concerned, *The Gazette* shared much in common with the dominant Western media, albeit with an interesting twist given the demographic it serves and Quebec's unique political and linguistic climate.

Nonetheless, the particular cluster of "backlash" stories examined also demonstrates ways in which the meta-narrative of Orientalism is not simply static but reproduced in a way that is responsive to contemporary circumstances. In the latter situation, the ethos motivating the coverage on backlash was likely mediated by the structural and institutional constraints of the print medium – the necessity to constantly provide fresh stories, continuity with previous stories, and the requirement for "balance" and impartiality. The latter factor is undoubtedly influenced by *The Gazette's* readership and the concentration of Muslims in the Montreal area, as well as the western tradition of liberalism. However, and despite the mitigating force potentially available to audiences, the fact that Muslim women and men in the East were represented in orientalized ways underscores how the media constantly shift our attention to the problems "out there" which are then presented as requiring our intervention "from here."[8]

These stories illustrate the imbricated nature of the gendered and orientalized discourse of the news media in their coverage the events following September 11. Further, they demonstrate the ways in which such imagery becomes common-place and commonsensical in the kinds of explanations being proffered. Woven throughout this gendered discourse are descriptive tropes that identify one side as being evil, manipulative and deceptive, while the other, notably the US, is presented as moral, open and explicit about its intentions. The ultimate rescue is then presented as the liberation of the oppressed by the "free world," and as the annihilation of evil by the powers of good: a belief reflected in the naming of the US intervention as "Operation Enduring Freedom," and grounded in the framework of Orientalism. In the final analysis, these news stories reinforce a sense of "nation-ness" – of "us" versus "them" – and analytically, offer insights into the ways in which contemporary forms of racism draw upon Orientalism but, in the process, reproduce it in ways that "make sense" of the contemporary political and social climate.

NOTES

1 I am using the term "common-sense" in the Gramscian sense of denoting the common stock of knowledge that is taken for granted, but that in itself, contains contradictory bits of information that are then selectively used to make sense of the world (see Hall 1979).
2 According to Statistics Canada (2001), 100,200 Muslims live in the Montreal area.
3 *The Gazette's* readership has been expanding after a decline over the last decade. Today, the paper has a readership of over half a million on the weekends, and between 360,000 – 380,000 during the weekdays.
4 This database was created by Ross Perigoe, Department of Journalism, Concordia University.
5 Barthes defines the difference between langue and parole as follows: "the systematized set of conventions necessary to communication, indifferent to the material of the signals which compose it, and which is a language (*langue*); as opposed to which speech (*parole*) covers the purely individual parts of language (phonation, application of the rules and contingent combinations of signs)" (1973, 13).
6 However, as she goes on to explain: Despite its close association with Islam, the veil is in fact an old eastern Mediterranean practice that was assimilated to Islam in its early stages of expansion. In the two suras in the Qur'an that refer to the veil, not only is there no specific mention of veiling the face but certain parts of the body in fact are assumed to be visible. Majid 1998, 334.
7 For more information on mixed race identities and the implications of multiculturalism, see Mahtani, 2002.
8 In this regard, see Razack 1998b in terms of her analysis of the use of "degenerate spaces" in Thailand in particular, as way to reinforce the legitimacy of the moral spaces of the West.

REFERENCES

Ahmed, Leila. 1992. *Women and Gender in Islam: Historical Roots of a Modern Debate.* New Haven: Yale University Press.

Anderson, Benedict. 1983. *Imagined Communities: Reflections on the Origin and Spread of Nationalism.* London: Verso.

Anthias, Floya, and Nira Yuval-Davis. in association with Harriet Cain. (1992). *Racialised Boundaries: Race, Nation, Gender, Colour and Class and the Anti-Racist Struggle.* London and New York: Routledge.

Bagnall, Janet. 27 September, 2001. "Tale of the Taliban: Once, You Could Feel Sorry for the Dispossessed Men, but no Longer." *Gazette*, p. B3.

Barthes, Roland. (Original work published 1957) 1973. *Mythologies.* Trans. Annette Lavers. London: Paladin.

Barthes, Roland. (Original work published 1964) 1973. *Elements of Semiology.* Trans. Annette Lavers and Colin Smith. New York: Hill and Wang.

Bhabha, Homi. 1990. "The Other Question: Difference, Discrimination and the Discourse of Colonialism." In *Out There: Marginalization and Contemporary Cultures.* Ed. Russell Ferguson, Martha Gever, Trinh T. Minh-ha, and Cornel West, 71–87. New York, Massachusetts: The New Museum of Contemporary Art and MIT Press.

Blanchfield, Mike, and Hilary Mackenzie. 20 September, 2001a. "U.S. Flexes Muscle: Warplanes Ordered to Gulf Bases; Bush to Address his Nation Tonight; Pakistan Tries to Defuse Unrest." *Gazette*, p. A1.

Blanchfield, Mike, and Hilary Mackenzie. 23 September, 2001b. "Saudis in a Squeeze: U.S. Bid for Air Base Runs Contrary to Policy, Sentiment." *Gazette*, p. A1.

Block, Irwin. 14 September, 2001. "City Muslims Appeal for Calm: 'We Thank God Until Now There is No Acceleration (of Violence) in the Montreal Area.'" *Gazette*, p. A17.

Canadian Islamic Congress. (2002). *Anti-Islam in the Media: Summary of the Fifth Annual Report*. Waterloo, Ontario, Canada. Retrieved May 28, 2003, from http://www.canadianislamiccongress.com/rr/rr_2002_1.php

Cooke, Miriam. 2002. "Saving Brown Women." *Signs (Chicago, Ill.)* 28 (1): 468–70. http://dx.doi.org/10.1086/340888.

Connell, Ian. (1980). "Television News and the Social Contract." In *Culture, Media, Language*, edited by Stuart Hall, Dorothy Hobson, Andrew Lowe, and Paul Willis, 139–56. Britain: Hutchinson in association with the Centre for Contemporary Cultural Studies, Birmingham.

Dahlgren, Peter, with Sumitra Chakrapani. (1982). "The Third World on TV News: Western Ways of Seeing the "Other."" In *Television Coverage of International Affairs*, edited by W.C. Adams, 45–65. Norwood, New Jersey: Ablex.

Davenport, Jane. 16 September, 2001. "Muslims Wary of Reprisals: 140 at Mosque Denounce Terror Attacks." *Gazette*, p. A3.

Dowd, Maureen. 25 September, 2001. "History Throws Knuckleball to Bush." *Gazette*, p. B3.

Fanon, Frantz. 1965. *Studies of a Dying Colonialism*. Trans. Haakon Chevalier. New York: Grove Press.

Fitterman, Lisa. 15 September, 2001a. "Hate Hits Canada: Muslims, Even Sikhs, Targets of Backlash." *Gazette*, p. A24.

Fitterman, Lisa. 21 September, 2001b. "Montreal's Pakistani Muslims Feel the Heat: 'We Are Here; We Are Not the Terrorists.'" *Gazette*, p. A13.

Franks, Mary Ann. 2003. "Obscene Undersides: Women and Evil Between the Taliban and the United States." *Hypatia: A Journal of Feminist Philosophy* 18 (1): 135–56. http://dx.doi.org/10.1111/j.1527-2001.2003.tb00783.x.

Friedman, Thomas L. 14 September, 2001. "It's World War III: America Will Have to Fight on Several Fronts, and Need All Its Will to Win." *Gazette*, p. B3.

Gannon, Kathy. 13 September, 2001. "Where Equality is 'Obscene': Conservative Pakistani Clerics Vow to Crush's Rights." *Gazette*, p. C7.

Gitlin, Todd. 1979. "News as Ideology and Contested Area: Toward a Theory of Hegemony, Crisis and Opposition." *Socialist Review* 9 (6): 11–54.

Goldberg, Jeffrey. 15 September, 2001. "Taking Courses at Jihad School: All-Islamic Classes." *Gazette*, p. B1.

Goldstein, Steve. 29 September, 2001. "Ex-Soviet States Will Be Key for U.S.: Most of the "Stans" have Muslim Majorities." *Gazette*, p. B1.

Greenberger, Allen J. 1969. *The British Image of India: A Study in the Literature of Imperialism, 1880–1960*. London: Oxford University Press.

Grewal, Inderpal. 1996. *Home and Harem: Nation, Gender, Empire, and the Cultures of Travel*. Durham, London: Duke University Press. http://dx.doi.org/10.1215/9780822382003.

Gross, Larry. 1991. "Out of the Mainstream: Sexual Minorities and the Mass Media." In *Gay People, Sex and the Media*, ed. Mitchelle A. Wolf and Alfred P. Kielwasser, 19–46. New York, London: Harrington Park Press. http://dx.doi.org/10.1300/J082v21n01_04.

Hackett, Robert. 1989. "Coups, Earthquakes and Hostages? Foreign News on Canadian Television." *Canadian Journal of Political Science* 22 (4): 809–25. http://dx.doi.org/10.1017/S0008423900020266.

Hall, Stuart. 1974. "Media Power: The Double Bind." *Journal of Communication* 24 (4): 19–26. http://dx.doi.org/10.1111/j.1460-2466.1974.tb00404.x.
Hall, Stuart. 1979. "Culture, the Media and the 'Ideological Effect.'" In *Mass Communication and Society*, ed. James Curran, Michael Gurevitch, and Janet Woollacott, 315–48. London: Sage Publications.
Hall, Stuart. 1984. "The Narrative Construction of Reality." *Southern Review (Baton Rouge, La.)* 17:1–17.
Hall, Stuart. 1990. "The Whites of Their Eyes." In *The Media Reader*, ed. Manuel Alvarado and John O. Thompson, 9–23. London: British Film Institute.
Hartley, John. 1982. *Understanding News*. London, New York: Methuen.
Hoodfar, Homa. 1993. "The Veil in Their Minds and On Our Heads: The Persistence of Colonial Images of Muslim Women." *Resources for Feminist Research* 22 (3/4): 5–18.
Huttenback, Robert A. 1976. *Racism and Empire: White Settler and Coloured Immigrants in the British Self-Governing Colonies, 1830–1910*. Ithaca, London: Cornell University Press.
Isaacs, Harold. 1958. *Scratches on Our Minds*. Connecticut: Greenwood Press.
Jafri, Gul Yoya. (1998). *The Portrayal of Muslim Women in Canadian Mainstream Media: A Community Based Analysis*. Afghan Women's Organization, Ontario, Canada.
JanMohamed, Abdul R., and the JanMohamed. 1985. "The Economy of Manichean Allegory: The Function of Racial Difference in Colonialist Literature." *Critical Inquiry* 12 (1): 59–87. http://dx.doi.org/10.1086/448321.
Jiwani, Yasmin. 1992. "The Exotic, the Erotic and the Dangerous: South Asian Women in Popular Film." *Canadian Women's Studies* 13 (1): 42–6.
Karim, H. Karim. 2000. *Islamic Peril*. Montreal, Quebec: Black Rose Books.
Kolhatkar, Sonali. 2002. "The Impact of US Intervention on Afghan Women's Rights." *Berkeley Women's Law Journal* 17:12–30.
Lalvani, Suren. 1995. "Consuming the Exotic Other." *Critical Studies in Mass Communication* 12 (3): 263–86. http://dx.doi.org/10.1080/15295039509366937.
Lazreg, Marnia. 1988. "Feminism and Difference: The Perils of Writing as a Woman on Women in Algeria." *Feminist Studies* 14 (1): 81–107. http://dx.doi.org/10.2307/3178000.
Lenk, Helle-Mai. (2000). "The Case of Emilie Ouimet, News Discourse on Hijab and the Construction of Quebecois National Identity/" In *Anti-Racist Feminism*, edited by Agnes Calliste and George J. Sefa Dei, 73–88. Halifax, NS: Fernwood.
Lévi-Strauss, Claude. 1966. *The Savage Mind*. Chicago: University of Chicago Press.
Macfarlane, John. 18 September, 2001. "Medical Resident Tells of Assault." *Gazette*, p. B6.
Majid, Anouar. 1998. "The Politics of Feminism in Islam." *Signs (Chicago, Ill.)* 23 (2): 321–61. http://dx.doi.org/10.1086/495253.
Mahtani, Minelle. 2001. "Representing Minorities: Canadian Media and Minority Identities." *Canadian Ethnic Studies* 33 (3): 99–133.
Mahtani, Minelle. 2002. "Interrogating the Hyphen-Nation: Canadian Multicultural Policy and 'Mixed Race' Identities." *Social Identities* 8 (1): 67–90. http://dx.doi.org/10.1080/13504630220132026.
McBratney, John. 1988. "Images of Indian Women in Rudyard Kipling: A Case of Doubling Discourse." *Inscriptions* 3 (4): 47–57.
McClintock, Anne. 1995. *Imperial Leather*. New York: Routledge.
Moghadam, Valentine M. 1999. "Revolution, Religion, and Gender Politics: Iran and Afghanistan Compared." *Journal of Women's History* 10 (4): 172–95. http://dx.doi.org/10.1353/jowh.2010.0536.
Moghadam, Valentine M. (2001). "Afghan Women and Transnational Feminism." *Middle East Women's Studies Review xvi*, no. 3/4.

Mohanty, Chandra Talpade. 1991. "Cartographies of Struggle: Third World Women and the Politics of Feminism." In *Third World Women and the Politics of Feminism*, ed. Chandra Talpade Mohanty, Ann Russo, and Lourdes Torres, 1–47. Bloomingdale, Indiana: Indiana University Press.

Montgomery, Sue. 18 September, 2001. "Loss Felt Among Local Afghans: Rights Activist Hopes Level Heads Will Prevail as U.S. Mulls Retaliation." *Gazette*, p. B1.

Moore, Lynn. 24 September, 2001. "Learning the Nature of True Islam: Mosques Educating Non-Muslims." *Gazette*, p. A4.

Razack, Sherene H. 1998a. *Looking White People in the Eye: Gender, Race, and Culture in Courtrooms and Classrooms*. Toronto: University of Toronto Press.

Razack, Sherene H. 1998b. "Race, Space, and Prostitution: The Making of the Bourgeois Subject." *Canadian Journal of Women and the Law* 10 (2): 338–76.

Richards, Sarah. 13 September, 2001. "Islam is Against This Kind of Act." *Gazette*, p. B4.

Said, Edward. 1978. *Orientalism*. New York: Random House.

Said, Edward. 1981. *Covering Islam*. New York: Pantheon Books.

Schneider, William. 1977. "Race and Empire: The Rise of Popular Ethnography in the Late Nineteenth Century." *Journal of Popular Culture* XI (1): 98–109. http://dx.doi.org/10.1111/j.0022-3840.1977.1101_98.x.

Schnurmacher, Tommy. 14 September, 2001. "Images of Celebration Tell the Story." *Gazette*, p. A19.

Sevunts, Levon. 14 September, 2001. "Refugees Fear Mood Change." *Gazette*, p. A19.

Shohat, Ella, and Robert Stam. 1994. *Unthinking Eurocentrism, Multiculturalism and the Media*. London, New York: Routledge.

Smith, Michael, and Alan Philps. 14 September, 2001. "Delta Force to Ride Planes: U.S. Anti-Terrorism Squad in New Role." *Gazette*, p. A4.

Spector, Norman. 12 September, 2001. "Deja Vu for Israelis: Scenes of Destruction and Pain Are Familiar to People Who Are Used to Being Attacked For Who They Are." *Gazette*, p. B3.

Stam, Robert, and Louise Spence. 1985. "Colonialism, Racism and Representation: An Introduction." In *Movies and Methods*, ed. Bill Nichols, 632–49. Berkeley: University of California Press.

Statistics Canada. 2001. Quebec: Largest Proportion of Catholics. Government of Canada, Ontario, Canada. Retrieved June 25 from http://www12.statcan.ca/english/census01/Products/Analytic/companion/rel/qc.cfm.

Stott, Rebecca. 1989. "The Dark Continent: Africa as Female Body in Haggard's Adventure Fiction." *Feminist Review* 32 (Summer): 68–89.

Thobani, Sunera. 2003. "War and the Politics of Truth-Making in Canada." *International Journal of Qualitative Studies in Education : QSE* 16 (3): 399–414. http://dx.doi.org/10.1080/0951839032000086754.

Todd, Sharon. 1998. "Veiling the "Other," Unveiling Our "Selves': Reading Media Images of the Hijab Psychoanalytically to Move Beyond Tolerance." *Canadian Journal of Education* 23 (4): 438–51. http://dx.doi.org/10.2307/1585757.

van Dijk, Teun, ed. (1985). *Discourse and Communication*. New York: de Gruyter. http://dx.doi.org/10.1515/9783110852141.

van Dijk, Teun. 1991. *Racism and the Press*. London: Routledge.

van Dijk, Teun. 1993. *Elite Discourse and Racism*. Thousand Oaks, CA: Sage. http://dx.doi.org/10.4135/9781483326184.

Wallace, Bruce. 22 September, 2001. "West Anxiously Courting a Willing Iran: With Its Leader's "Remarkable" Conversation, Islamic State Opens Door to a New Relationship." *Gazette*, p. A13.

Watanabe, Teresa. 27 September, 2001. "Extremists Distort Holy Tenets to Justify War." *Gazette*, p. B1.

Waters, Paul. 15 September, 2001. "Twisting the Faith: Islam is a Serene Religion, but can be Warped into a Form of Totalitarianism." *Gazette*, p. B1.

Wyn Davies, Merryl, Nandy, Ashis, and Sardar, Ziauddin. (1993). *Barbaric Others: A Manifesto on Western Racism*. London: Pluto Press.

Yeğenoğlu, Meyda. 1998. *Colonial Fantasies: Towards a Feminist Reading of Orientalism*. Cambridge, Melbourne: Cambridge University Press. http://dx.doi.org/10.1017/CBO9780511583445.

PART FOUR

Comparative Encounters

12 Decolonizasian: Reading Asian and First Nations Relations in Literature

RITA WONG

speak cree you're in canada now
speak siouan
speak salishan

– Rajinderpal S. Pal, "Collective Amnesia" (1998, 22)

At the minimal level, Aboriginal thought teaches that everyone and everything are part of a whole in which they are interdependent.

– Marie Battiste and Helen Semaganis (2002), "First Thoughts on First Nations Citizenship" (97)

Nestled intimately against the forces of citizenship that have propelled many an Asian Canadian subject to oversimplify herself by declaring "I am Canadian" are other possible configurations of imagined community. What happens if we position Indigenous people's struggles instead of normalized whiteness as the reference point through which we come to articulate our subjectivities? How would such a move radically transform our perceptions of the land on which we live? Scott McFarlane (1995) has suggested that in the Canada constructed through legislative mechanisms such as the Multiculturalism Act, "people of colour and First Nations people are figured outside the discourse as, for example, immigrants or nonpersons who become 'Canadian' through their relationship to whiteness, as opposed to 'the land'" (22). Oppositionality to whiteness – while logical in the face of racial oppression that was historically codified through instruments such as the Chinese Exclusion Act, the War Measures Act, and the Continuous Voyage Provision[1] – still directs energy towards whiteness without necessarily unpacking the specific problematics of racialized subjects who have inherited the violence of colonization. In particular, the challenging relationships between subjects positioned as "Asian Canadian" and "Indigenous" raise questions regarding immigrant complicity in the colonization of land as well as the possibility of making alliances towards decolonization. Turning the lens in this direction, we find ourselves in the realm of the partial, the fragmented, the ruptured, the torn. It is in our brokenness that we come to know the effects of our violent histories as they continue to exert force upon the present. The very language in which I articulate these thoughts, English, is weighted with a colonial history particular to the land called Canada, in contrast to the languages that I might desire to circulate this essay in, be they Cree, Siouan, Salishan, or Cantonese. Through legislation such as the Indian Act, the Immigration and Refugee Protection Act (IRPA), the Multiculturalism Act, and the Citizenship Act,[2] "we" have historically been managed, divided, and scripted into the Canadian nation-state.

Today ostensible security measures such as the Anti-Terrorism Act that passed in the wake of September 11th have given the state more power to criminalize Indigenous peoples, activists, and people of colour.[3] If, in a move towards both individual and collective survival, a subject decides to direct her allegiances towards Indigenous struggles for decolonization and sovereignty, she might consider the values described by filmmaker Loretta Todd:

> Our concept of ownership evolved independent of European concepts of ownership and it persists today. Without the sense of private property that ascended with European culture, we evolved concepts of property that recognized the interdependence of communities, families and nations and favoured the guardianship of the earth, as opposed to its conquest. There was a sense of ownership, but not one that pre-empted the rights and privileges of others or the rights of the earth and the life that it sustained. (1990, 26)

Critical engagement with Indigenous perspectives can be grounded in materially responsible and environmentally sustainable practices and models; the interdependency and land stewardship that Todd describes provide a focus for alliance building in the face of ongoing processes of racialization and class oppression.

Such alliance building must respect the values identified by thinkers such as Todd, so that the reaction against colonial frameworks is balanced with a generative vision of what one strives towards. Multiculturalism as government policy, while enabling in many regards, has also functioned to manage and contain difference. Although it is necessary to support multiculturalism in the face of white supremacist attacks, it is also important to understand the inadequacies of Canadian multiculturalism. As critics such as Himani Bannerji (2000) have pointed out, when multicultural policy was introduced in Canada in the 1970s,

> there were no strong multicultural demands on the part of third world immigrants themselves to force such a policy. The issues raised by them were about racism, legal discrimination involving immigration and family reunification, about job discrimination on the basis of Canadian experience, and various adjustment difficulties, mainly of child care and language. In short, they were difficulties that are endemic to migration, and especially that of people coming in to low income jobs or with few assets. Immigrant demands were not then, or even now, primarily cultural, nor was multiculturalism initially their formulation of the solution to their problems. It began as a state or an official/institutional discourse, and it involved the translation of issues of social and economic injustice into issues of culture. (44)

One of the challenges before contemporary cultural workers is to reappropriate "culture" in ways that lead the reader's gaze back to the social and economic injustices neglected and deflected when multiculturalism's lens becomes too narrow. Cultural labour has a role in fostering such a shift in values away from the economic violence and domination that our current neoliberal government normalizes through its submission to bodies such as the World Trade Organization, the World Bank, and the International Monetary Fund, bodies that arguably operate against the interests of the majority of the Earth's population (human and otherwise). An analysis that integrates considerations of planetary survival with local Indigenous struggles is consistent in the works of Indigenous thinkers such as Jeannette Armstrong (1996), Winona LaDuke (1999), and Loretta Todd (1990; 2001); this work signals a direction that those in Asian Canadian studies could benefit from. That is, where diasporic communities meet Indigenous communities, we encounter a process of contact and invention that deserves more attention than it has so far received.

As a writer and critic who lives on the unceded Coast Salish territory otherwise known as Vancouver, I am faced with the question of how to speak to and acknowledge debts and interdependencies that most of us were trained to ignore. Unfortunately, there are no guarantees that cultural representation does not repeat the violence that has already occurred. Yet, in those cases where silence also seems to be an equally and perhaps even more unsatisfying complicity with – and perpetuation of – this violence, tactics of troubled visibility provide an ethical line of engagement that holds promise. As the debates on cultural appropriation in the late 1980s and early to mid-1990s remind us, cultural representation is a fraught process, and the best of intentions can nonetheless have terrible effects.[4] However, we can still proceed carefully, humbly, open to dialogue, and attentive to how material conditions and existent power relations can shape the dynamics of whose cultural labour is validated, whose is disregarded, and how. Lee Maracle's warning bears remembering:

> If you conjure a character based on your in-fort stereotypes and trash my world, that's bad writing – racist literature – and I will take you on for it. If I tell you a story and you write it down and collect royal coinage from this story, that's stealing – appropriation of culture. But if you imagine a character who is from my world, attempting to deconstruct the attitudes of yours, while you may not be stealing, you still leave yourself open to criticism unless you do it well. (1992, 15)

In attempting to decolonize and deconstruct oppressive systems, writers racialized as Asian cannot avoid making reference to the First Nations of this land; at the same time, given the inheritance of racist, loaded discourses that have operated to dehumanize, commodify, and romanticize First Nations people, an immense challenge presents itself in terms of how to disrupt and derail these dominant discourses. The process of "doing it well" requires not only technical competency, however one might determine that, but also an understanding of how one is embedded within power relations that must be carefully negotiated. Scanning the textual horizon for novels, stories, and plays that address the complicated relationships between those who have been racialized as "Asian" and those who have been racialized as "Indigenous," I see some signs of life: SKY Lee's (1990) novel *Disappearing Moon Cafe*, Tamai Kobayashi's short stories in *Exile and the Heart*, Marie Clements's (2003) play *Burning Vision*, and Lee Maracle's (1998) story "Yin Chin" form part of a growing body of texts that discursively explores the possible relations between those racialized as "Asian" and "Indigenous" on that part of Turtle Island also known as Canada.[5]

I. Re-Viewing *Disappearing Moon Cafe*

> In my writing, I straddle the shifting locations of being Chinese, Canadian, contemporary, woman, and feminist of colour (etc.). Insider and outsider to my own culture, gender, history and so on. I am able to take risks and transgress the boundaries (of these social constructs) each category imposes.
>
> In *Disappearing Moon Cafe* (1990), the reader's gaze is never fixed due to these multiple locations, and travels through time and space. This is also a strategy of disrupting the conventional way texts are written and read so that the reader can be made more aware of her subject position. This awareness subverts the tendency toward passive consumption and the colonizing gaze. (Lee 1997, 12–13)

As many readers have noted, *Disappearing Moon Cafe* opens and closes with the relationship between Wong Gwei Chang, a Chinese man, and Kelora, a half-Native, half-Chinese woman of the Shi'atko clan. In so doing, it posits a potential alliance between two people who were both excluded by the Canadian nation in historically specific, racialized, gendered, and classed ways.[6] Gwei Chang's abandonment and betrayal of Kelora takes on both personal and social significance when we consider the role of cheap Chinese labour in facilitating the appropriation of Indigenous land by the Canadian government. The labour of Chinese railway workers supported not only their families but also a Canadian nation-building project based on the exclusion and exploitation of both First Nations and people of colour. The dynamite-blasting process of railway construction entailed both an immense human cost and environmental disfigurement: "[Gwei Chang] imagined the mountain shuddering, roaring out in pain, demanding human sacrifice for this profanity. And the real culprits held out blood-spattered chinamen in front of them like a protective talisman" (Lee 1990, 12–13). The "real culprits," the captains of industry behind the railway, remain outside the novel's realm, despite the impact of their decisions on both characters and readers. Gwei Chang's effort to retrieve the bones of the dead Chinese labourers depends greatly on Kelora's support in navigating unfamiliar land, for it is Kelora who leads Gwei Chang to safety when he is starving, "as if the barren wasteland around him had magically opened and allowed him admittance" (4). Where the Canadian nation would have refused a Chinese man entrance as a citizen with full rights, Kelora's act allows Gwei Chang admittance into her community as an equal. Kelora makes possible a relationship to the land that is not codified into the property laws of the nation: "she taught him to love the same mother earth and to see her sloping curves in the mountains. He forgot that he had once thought of them as barriers" (14–15). Having interviewed mixed-race families, Lee translates her research into a fictional frame that asserts what has been left out of official Canadian history. Examples of relationships between First Nations people and Chinese people, dating back at least to 1788,[7] are often marginalized in official historical narratives that privilege nation building premised on white dominance. The potential represented in the relationship between Gwei Chang and Kelora is not only based on desire and emotional connection but also shaped by the economic and political forces on their lives and by a respect for the land. Living with Kelora's people, Gwei Chang learns to appreciate the Native lifestyle before he rejects it for fear of poverty:

> The sight of all this good food being hauled in got Gwei Chang very excited. It made him feel good to learn the indian ways, because they made him think that he might never starve like a chinaman again.
>
> But Kelora told him that even with this abundance, her people faced famine later in the winter ...
>
> Gwei Chang had often looked into the sallow face of famine. He could see how famine was the one link that Kelora and he had in common, but for that instant, it made him recoil from her as surely as if he had touched a beggar's squalid sore. ...
>
> In the next instant, he looked at Kelora, and saw animal. (234)

Although famine is the one link that they share, the fear of this common threat is what drives Gwei Chang back to China to take a Chinese wife. This fear also drives him to dehumanize Kelora, to see her as "animal," in a way that echoes the first time they met, when he assumed that she was savage. Her elegant rebuke at that time, that "he has no manners" (3), surprises him in a way that makes him feel "uncivilized, uncouth; the very qualities he had assigned so thoughtlessly to her" (3–4). It is symptomatic of dominant power relations that Gwei Chang functions within what might be termed a sinocentric world view, one that eventually allows him upward mobility within the confines of the ethnic enclave of Chinatown. His trajectory can be read as a negotiation of survival tactics that drive an agent to form long-term relations of perceived racial cohesion rather than adhesion, with the attendant enabling and disabling limits of such moves.

In the context of Canada as a nation-state that historically excluded immigrants racialized as "nonwhite," the importance of organizing formations of Chinese community to offer assistance against the state's restrictions was compelling. In Lee's (1990) novel, it is clear that the closeness of the Chinese community formed in part as a survival mechanism against white supremacist hostility in everything from detaining new arrivals to racist legislation. At the same time, the limits and inadequacies of these formations are also signalled by the unhappiness of Gwei Chang at the end of the novel. As he says to Kelora, "I've lived a miserable life, grieving for your loss, bitterly paying" (235). His material wealth accumulated later in his life does not bring with it emotional fulfilment in that his marriage to Mui Lan is an unhappy one and his son Ting An rejects him once he realizes their biological relationship. The novel leaves us wondering what would have happened had Gwei Chang challenged ethnic containment and asserted solidarity with Kelora and her community. His failure to sustain such an alliance gestures not only to individual limits but also to the ways in which oppressive social norms and legislative measures – such as the Immigration Act and the Indian Act – have historically scripted and enforced divisions between First Nations and Asian people in Canada. A difficult question arises: how does one assess the ways in which Chinese people have been implicated, albeit inadvertently, in their own ethnic containment within a Canadian nation-state that is itself a violent imposition upon Indigenous land?

If, as Lee suggests at the beginning of this section, a subject is always multiply situated in terms of culture, gender, politics, and class, more comprehensive ways to articulate and understand such evolving, complicated, and often contradictory subject positions remain to be circulated more widely. One way of reading class mobility for immigrants within the Canadian nation-state has been through the filter of racialized categories rather than through the lens of immigrants' relations to Indigenous land. In Lee's novel, such categories are constantly troubled and unravelled. Gwei Chang occupies multiple class positions over the course of the novel, from a starving worker in the beginning to a bourgeois patriarch by the end. His upward mobility in the confines of Chinatown arguably depends on his rejection of Kelora and his disavowal of their mixed- race son, Ting An, whom almost everyone in Chinatown knows as an orphan benefiting from Gwei Chang's patronage rather than as his first son. Kelora's own economic status is complicated; Kelora has "no rank" in her community, although her mother's family is "very wealthy, old and well-respected," and her abilities are clearly valued, including her knowledge of how to survive based on the land's natural bounty. She arguably unsettles and disrupts hierarchies of class and race, as does her son Ting An. Within the heart of the novel's ostensibly "Chinese" space, there is racial and cultural hybridity; though Ting An is accepted as "Chinese," he is also part Native, as are his descendants, including the novel's narrator, Kae. As Kae points out, "People used to say that [Ting An] was half indian – his mother a savage. Before, Fong Mei used to search his face for traces of this, but she only saw a chiselled face, gracefully masculine, like a chínese from the north" (54). The problematic, dominant social scripts of racist othering ("savage") and assimilation ("like a chínese from the north") are inadequate to address the possibilities of mixed-race identifications. Ting An, in a sense the physical product of Gwei Chang and Kelora's relationship, is invited to live upriver with "a group of nlaka'pamux'sin people" but refuses because of his intuitive attachment to Gwei Chang (115). While Ting An is socially pulled into what turns out to be an unhappy life, the untaken alternatives that he has access to raise questions about what a shift in priorities would achieve. Such undeveloped alliances constitute the silences and empty centres upon which contemporary national formations continue to depend.

One could argue that, in *Disappearing Moon Cafe*, it is the hyperconspicuous absence of a Native woman, Kelora, that in a sense makes possible the novel's plot. First, this absence makes visible the uneven relations the "Asian" characters have with the Native peoples of this land, gestures towards the complicated histories between First Nations and Chinese people, and acknowledges the legacy of interracial relationships that have often been marginalized. Second, one might ask what kind of shift in social relations it would require to move from absence to presence(s). What is an ethical way to proceed on this difficult terrain? The figure of the writer, Kae, negotiates a complicated relation of proximity and distance to the figure of a Native woman. Historical distancing operates in the recognition of Kelora as an ancestor within the family tree at the beginning of *Disappearing Moon Cafe*, although this distance is then destabilized and undermined by Kae's retellings of family secrets as well as by Kelora's and Gwei Chang's interactions at the beginning and the end of the novel, putting the onus on the reader to imagine and build a present interracial alliance as compelling as the scene that closes the novel, "the heavy chant of the storyteller turning to mist" (237) in Gwei Chang's head. The question remains: what kinds of changes would enable such moments of looking "backward" to become a looking forward into First Nations and Asian relationships?

It is possible and indeed desirable to read *Disappearing Moon Cafe* into the context of a need to transform the social relations we currently know. The novel makes visible the importance of alliances along cross-racial, feminist, and anticapitalist lines, even though some of these alliances may not be directly achieved or successful in the novel's plot per se. The onus then shifts to the reader, for whom the mourning of lost possibilities frames the generations of turmoil represented in the novel's body. Within the novel, relations between Chinese and First Nations women are an uncharted territory. Although Kelora and Mui Lan are in a sense linked because of their relations to Gwei Chang, they never meet each other. At one point, Fong Mei states, "This was a land of fresh starts; I could have lived in the mountains like an indian woman legend" (188), suggesting that stories of Native women may be symbolic of freedom to her. It is more on the edges, the "outsides," of the novel that the potential of interracial relations is gestured to; on the dust jacket of the book's cover, blurbs by writers such as Joy Harjo and Audre Lorde signal a discursive community of politicized writers whose work has encouraged and inspired activists across North America. This political alignment also presents an obstruction to readings that would evacuate the novel of the resistant sensibilities out of which it partially arose.

Reading *Disappearing Moon Cafe* from this perspective only signals how much more there remains to do if cultural workers are to play a role in supporting alliance building to work towards decolonization. These temporary but strong affective bonds suggest that promise exists, even though it has not been fulfilled. Affective bonds do not necessarily translate into political solidarity, but effective political solidarity is also less likely to happen without a deeply felt understanding of each other's perspectives and the ways in which oppression is both common and different for people racialized as "First Nations" and

"Asian." Fiction offers a speculative space and challenges us to imagine the ways in which dialogue and interaction could spark deeper understanding of our interrelatedness.

II. Exile and the Heart

In an interview with Larissa Lai, Tamai Kobayashi states, "History trickles down into my work, sometimes it pours" (2000, 124). Questioning what constitutes "tradition," Kobayashi rejects conventional assumptions that position "the East" as the site of oppressed, submissive women and "the West" as somehow enlightened. She suggests that her "traditions" may be found in the writers who have influenced her, including Audre Lorde, Hisaye Yamamoto, Joy Harjo, James Tiptree Jr., Wilfred Owen, Octavia Butler, Rampo, and Eduardo Galeano. With regard to Harjo, Kobayashi notes that "the sheer beauty and hope of Joy Harjo's *She Had Some Horses*, how her experiences as a First Nations woman were reflected in her words, also had great impact" (122). As a politically active writer (a founding member of ALOT, Asian Lesbians of Toronto, among many other things), Kobayashi is conscious of how important it is to investigate interracial relationships that do not centre on whiteness:

> Race defines so much of you. I try to reveal this in my work, the quiet moments. Everything is contaminated by the way race has been constructed through history – this construction of people of colour by white people, by the structure of whiteness-as-the-ideal, whiteness-as-the-norm. I mean, think of how many times white people have been at the centre of stories, even if it's not supposed to be about them? *Come to the Paradise* was supposed to be about the internment but Dennis Quaid was the star; *Dances with Wolves* starred Kevin Costner; *Cry Freedom*, a film about Steven Biko, starred Kevin Kline. (124–25)

In her book of stories, *Exile and the Heart: Lesbian Fiction*, Kobayashi (1998) presents an everyday world where the interactions of Asian lesbians with other lesbians quietly take centre stage, deposing and dislocating whiteness, which still exerts pressure on the characters as a force but which is not the gaze through which perceptions come to form.

The relationship between Kathy Nakashima and Jan Lalonde in the story "Wind," which opens *Exile and the Heart*, draws together a Japanese Canadian woman who burns her family's redress letter of apology from Gerry Weiner and Brian Mulroney and a Metis woman with a "handful of Blackfoot and fistful of Cree" studying Land Claims in Canadian Law (Kobayashi 1998, 13–14). The lovers' road trip through the Albertan landscape takes them to the Old Man Dam, which the government built despite the protests of the Peigan: "They have passed through Blackfoot, Blood, Peigan, place names of Cypress Hills, Battleford and Buffalo Jump. What must it be like for her, Kathy wonders, these signposts, this road, that coulee, this river" (12). The narration does not give the reader access to what those place names signify for Jan Lalonde, but we do find out that this place was once hell for her (16). Portrayed as a blight on the land that will be useless in 10 years' time because of silt buildup (15), the dam marks an instance of colonial violence on Indigenous land.

While this awareness of colonial violation exists throughout the story, it does not allow the lovers' interactions to be defined or reduced to only reacting against colonization. The two characters continue to swim, to show each other affection, to go on relating to one another in subtle ways that affirm their connection. The poetic contemplativeness of the story ends abruptly with the violence of a gas station attendant who yells at Jan, "Get out of here and take your fucking squaw with you!" (16). In the face of the racist ignorance that would equate "squaw" with "Jap," the two women are positioned together, in rage against a common enemy. However, the characters do not stay fixed or united in reaction; their lives continue, and in a later story entitled "A Night at the Edge of the World" Kathy and Jan have broken up. Nonetheless, friendship remains, as Kathy and her current partner Gen host a farewell party for Jan, who is moving to British Columbia to look for her younger sister. Jan reappears in a later story, "Driftwood," seen from a distance in Oppenheimer Park by Kathy's mother, who observes a group of First Nations women tying memorial ribbons for 15 Native women murdered in Vancouver's Downtown Eastside (96). The possibility of relations that sustain and support one another without being tied to codified possession or ownership norms underlies Kobayashi's short, quietly intense stories, which evoke sensibilities and ways of thinking through a complicated, politically engaged, and emotionally deep lesbian-of-colour community. Here relationships are temporal, geographically situated on (de)colonized land, and open to negotiation and change.

III. Burning Vision

Awarded the 2004 Japan-Canada Literary Award, Marie Clements' play *Burning Vision* explores powerful connections between "Asian" and "First Nations" characters by following the trail of uranium as it was mined from Dene land and eventually detonated in atomic bombs over Japan.[8] Clements writes as a First Nations woman responding to the history of transnational economic relations that contributed to the devastation marking the end of World War II:

> In the 1940's uranium was mined from the Echo Bay Mine situated on the northeast corner of the Great Bear Lake in the Northwest Territories. The land it was mined from was on the Sahtu Dene territory. As a descendant of the Fort Norman Sahtu Dene Metis, [I have] always [found it] strange that the uranium that was used to build the first atomic bomb that was dropped on the Japanese in 1945 came from the land of my bones. ... In the 1990's Dene elders flew to Japan and met with Japanese survivors of the bombing. The story I'd like to trace is the uranium rock that landed inside us. The physical connection of land and features, of visions and machinery, of two worlds meeting over and under land and the burning noise that took the worlds' breath away. (cited in Greenaway 2002, 8)

In *Burning Vision*, narrative is in a sense torn apart and sundered by the nuclear detonations that begin and end the play, leaving shreds of interconnections and resonances between characters as diverse as Tokyo Rose,[9] a Native widow whose partner dies from mining uranium, a Japanese grandmother, a white woman poisoned from painting radium watch dials, a Dene elder who prophesied atomic destruction, the miners who "discovered" uranium on Dene land, and many others. As multiple worlds collide in dramatic tension and evocative imagery, the play's refusal of linear resolution speaks to the ongoing legacy of violence perpetuated through a process of colonization that encodes theft and violation as "discovery."

A number of relationships in the play enact moments of reciprocity and solidarity between racialized bodies. For instance, *Burning Vision* proposes a relationship between a Metis woman named Rose and a Japanese man named Koji that seems to be geographically impossible (given that he is frozen in Japan in the moment before the bomb drops) but is made spiritually possible through the chain of uranium that brings them together (and through the transformation and hope symbolized in the cherry tree where he waits for his grandmother). When Rose and the Widow talk about Koji, the Widow says of him, "Indian? He looks sorta like an Indian but there's something different going on."[10] Rose's response is that "He's Indian enough from the other side" (105), gesturing to the ways in which both the Japanese and the Indians have been slotted into the role of "the enemy." However, it is not being made the target of a common enemy that defines their relationship but what they produce out of these circumstances. In the collisions and devastations of a world shattered by the uranium that came from Rose's land, Koji and Rose somehow meet, comfort one another, and make a child. Rose asks Koji, "If you make me yours do we make a world with no enemies?" (95), and Koji reciprocates with "If we make a world, we will make one where there are no enemies?" (96). The mutuality implied by their parallel lines suggests that affiliation can be stronger than common enmity, though of course this possibility remains a question. Alongside the hope that their alliance brings is also the frighteningly faceless and ubiquitous threat to their environment caused by the radioactive mining by-products. Surrounded by the poisonous black uranium dust that the wind blows everywhere (103), even getting into the bread that she kneads, Rose's pregnancy is laden with both hope and danger (114).

In contrast to the tenderness between Rose and Koji, the (white) Fat Man, who finds Round Rose (an aged Iva Toguri, a.k.a. Tokyo Rose) and the (Native) Little Boy in his home, eventually throws them out after having initially accepted them in the subordinate roles of Asian wife and adopted Native child: "I want you two aliens to get the hell out of my living room. You hear me? I said I want you two ungrateful aliens to leave" (98). "Little Boy" and "Fat Man" are of course the names of the atomic bombs dropped on Hiroshima and Nagasaki on 6 and 9 August 1945, killing over 210,000 people by the end of 1945. While Fat Man functions as a historical reference to World War II, he arguably also embodies the War Measures Act, used against both Aboriginal people and Japanese Canadians.[11] While the character Fat Man soon shows remorse for his actions, actions that so perfectly replicate the colonization and appropriation of North America as a "white" home, Round Rose's words emphasize the inadequacy of remorse:

> You can't really be sorry for something you don't want to remember can you. Selective memory isn't it? Let's be honest, hell, you can't even apologize for the shit you did yesterday never mind 50 years ago. Indian residential schools, Japanese Internment camps, hell, and this is just in your neighborhood. But it's alright ... everybody's sorry these days. The politicians are sorry, the cops are sorry, the priests are sorry, the logging companies are sorry, mining companies, electric companies, water companies, wife beaters, serial rapists, child molesters, mommy and daddy. Everybody's sorry. Everybody's sorry they got caught sticking it to someone else ... that's what they are sorry about ... Getting caught. They could give a rat's ass about you, or me, or the people they are saying sorry to. Think about it ... Don't be a sorry ass, be sorry before you have to say you are sorry. Be sorry for even thinking about, bringing about something-sorry-filled. (100–1)

The connection of this neighbourhood to overseas neighbourhoods is in a sense configured through the Little Boy. A personification of the darkest uranium found at the centre of the Earth, he enters and leaves scenes through the television, embodying the technologies that materialize the human capacity for both creation and destruction. Aligned with Round Rose because they both face the violence of the Fat Man's gun pointed at them, the Little Boy is at once local (from Dene land) and global (beaming into and out of the television).

The complex relationships presented in Clements's visionary play interrogate the possibilities and limits of interracial affiliations.

The play's close, after the Japanese Grandmother has transformed into the Dene Widow (120), creates an overlap between two previously separate relationships. Koji's ongoing comments to his grandmother, and the Widow's ongoing talk to her dead husband, merge, so that the Widow's Words to Koji bring together a number of previously fragmented relationships. The Widow states, "You are my special grandson. My small man now. My small man that survived. Tough like hope. If we listen we can hear them [their loved ones] too" (121). Although the term "small man" might, in another context, be taken to emasculate the Asian male, here it alludes to and transforms "little boy," positing Koji as a hope that loving affiliations might grow out of surviving historic violence and destruction. The play ends with Koji's words – "They [the Japanese and Dene loved ones] hear us, and they are talking back in hope over time" (122) – and images that merge Dene and Japanese references: "Glowing herds of caribou move in unison over the vast empty landscape as cherry blossoms fall till they fill the stage" (122). What brings the characters together is not only shared suffering but also the one Earth on which they all live.

In a question-and-answer period following her reading at the Emily Carr Institute of Art + Design on 4 November 2004, Clements (2005) stated that her writing process begins with the land. The land presents itself to her, and then the characters follow, like a musical score. As such, a discussion of the characters' interracial relationships needs to be framed within the structure of the play, which consists of four movements that begin with the fiery explosion and then pass through the four elements: "the frequency of discovery," "rare earth elements," "waterways," and "radar echoes." The context of people belonging to the land, rather than the land belonging to people, suggests that people are but one element in a larger view of the world that respects all nonhuman forms of life as well. Thus, the context that matters for the "small man" at the end of the play is the immensity of the planet itself, the land as the main reference point, not a white masculinity that belittles or emasculates the Asian male. The way in which the play is shaped in movements, not acts (which harken back to human activity), pushes towards a paradigm where land, not people, are the central focus. Thus, the "characters," in their fragmentation and symbolic weight, are not only people but also material signs of how the land has been disrupted and changed by human activity.

IV. "Yin Chin'

Dedicated to SKY Lee and Jim Wong-Chu, "Yin Chin," by First Nations writer Lee Maracle, offers a number of insights into the realm of Native Asian relations, naming both the distances and the moments of camaraderie between communities. Published in Maracle's 1990 collection of short stories, *Sojourner's Truth*, "Yin Chin" bravely questions the narrator's own humanity (291) by admitting the insidious effects of racial categorization upon her interactions with other people. While the First Nations narrator is a little scared by how she has "lived in this city in the same neighbourhood as Chinese people for twenty-two years now and [doesn't] know a single Chinese person" (291), she is also aware of the political urgency that links her own struggle against oppression to that of other peoples. A recent memory describes the common recognition of the importance of fighting imperialism among writers from subordinated cultures:

> Last Saturday (seems like a hundred years later) was different. The tableload of people was Asian/Native. We laughed at ourselves and spoke very seriously about our writing. We really believe we are writers, someone had said, and the room shook with the hysteria of it all. We ran on and on about our growth and development and not once did the white man ever enter the room. It just seemed all too incredible that a dozen Hans and Natives could sit and discuss all things under heaven, including racism, and not talk about white people. It only took a half-dozen revolutions in the Third World, seventeen riots in America, one hundred demonstrations against racism in Canada, and thirty-seven dead Native youth in my life to become. ... We had crossed a millennium of bridges the rivers of which were swollen with the floodwaters of dark humanity's tenacious struggle to extricate themselves from oppression and we knew it.
>
> We were born during the first sword wound that the Third World swung at imperialism. We were children of that wound, invincible, conscious, and movin' on up. We could laugh because we were no longer a joke. But somewhere along the line we forgot to tell the others, the thousands of our folks that still tell their kids about old chinamen. (291–92)

How many more sword wounds must follow this first one? There is still a need to share this consciousness of a common struggle against oppression in the face of educational systems and media structures that are not designed for this, that arguably operate to produce docile citizen subjects who do not question the arbitrary borders we inhabit and carry within ourselves.[12] In the space of a few pages, Maracle juxtaposes this larger picture against the daily and often overlooked incidents that materialize internalized oppressions. In particular, she interweaves two anecdotes into "Yin Chin." First, there is her contemporary experience of driving around Chinatown and seeing a Native man bully and harass an old Chinese woman. The narrator assists the old woman by beating the man off. Second, while she listens to the old woman's anger that none of the Chinese men around her had intervened, the narrator recalls a childhood experience with the Chinese storekeeper, Mad Sam.[13]

Having absorbed "the words of the world ... [words such as] 'don't wander off or the ol' chinamen will get you and eat you'," the narrator-as child's internalized racism quietly manifests in her monthly vigil of watching old Chinese men to make sure they don't grab children (293). One might consider how laws forbidding Chinese immigration, which made family reunification impossible for decades, might have contributed to such racist myths. Her internalized racism then flares up with a scream when a Chinese man looks through Sam's store window at her. The narrator's childhood response, "The chinaman was looking at me," shames her mother and hurts Sam. Her description of Sam's injured look as "the kind of hurt you can sometimes see in the eyes of people who have been cheated" (294) suggests that racism has systemically devalued people like Sam, who are viewed as dangerous by small children like the narrator through no fault or action of their own. That the child narrator eventually grows to have an analysis of imperialism's effects on racialized peoples requires that she grapple with the contradictions of small, everyday moments such as that brief encounter in Sam's discount food store.

When the old woman is done expressing her frustration, the narrator states, "How unkind of the world to school us in ignorance," and gets back into her car (294). The narrator's words allude to both her childhood anecdote and the contemporary experience of comforting an old woman (who might or might not have an analysis of colonization's effects on First Nations people) and beating off a Native man (whose violence refuses any affiliations that could be made along racial or gender or class lines). The differences in scale between individual and mass change are made concrete by Maracle's stories embedded within stories, memories within memories.

V. Not a Closing but a Reopening

In an ongoing movement between fictional investigations and the social text, I would like to juxtapose a couple of instances from contemporary society against this discussion of fiction to speculate upon what further associations might be made. In *All Our Relations: Native Struggles for Land and Life*, Winona LaDuke describes the struggle against General Motors's PCB contamination in the reservation of Akwesasne, where about eight thousand Mohawk people live. This 25-square-mile reservation spans the St. Lawrence River and the international border between Canada and the United States, Quebec and New York. It is grandmothers such as Katsi Cook (who jokes, "if you want something done, get a Mohawk to do it") who are leading this struggle for a healthy community. In Vancouver, I had heard of Akwesasne because an article by Peter Cheney and Miro Cernetig (1999) in the *Globe and Mail* mentions the smuggling of Chinese migrants through Akwesasne. Straddling the border, the reserve is a hot spot, a place both vulnerable to corporate and governmental threats but also strategically located to challenge the state's authority over national borders. Akwesasne exists concurrently with and alternatively to the nation-state's uneasy partnership with corporate hegemony. That some Mohawks have chosen to assist Chinese migrants – whether for political, economic, or other reasons, in effect putting themselves at risk of police retribution – can have the effect of asserting their independence as well as political solidarity with the imagined Third World.[14]

There is a growing awareness among people concerned about social justice that those who live in this space we call Canada need to educate ourselves about what First Nations people are doing and how we might act in solidarity with them.[15] As Loretta Todd suggests, First Nations land claims should take precedence over international trade mechanisms such as NAFTA, for the preservation of First Nations land rights is in the long term interests of everyone living on this land, not only First Nations people:

> What could happen is aboriginal title could supersede the Free Trade Agreement, because [the courts] could say that aboriginal title to the water is more fundamental than the Free Trade Agreement. As a consequence, we could potentially have some say over how the water is used. So when we talk about the whole land claim issue, we're really talking about restoring the health of the land so that there can be co-existence and co-management of all the people but also of all the animals and resources on the land. (2001, 83)

As the discourse of corporate globalization threatens to recolonize our imaginations, alongside the material takeover of natural resources, I see it as a matter of not just principle but also survival to strive for an international network of locally based alliances challenging the transnational corporate hegemony that is protected and reinforced by neoliberal states.

With British Columbia's referendum on the treaty process in 2002, a dubious, poorly executed referendum that intensified racist violence against First Nations people,[16] globalization returned with a vengeance to questions of local land claims. One of the referendum questions asked people to say yes or no to the following statement: "The terms and conditions of leases and licenses should be respected; fair compensation for unavoidable disruption of commercial interests should be ensured." It can be argued that this clause dovetails with Chapter 11 of NAFTA,[17] which allows private companies to sue states for perceived losses of profits and limits the ability of governments to safeguard environmental, health, and various social values when there are conflicting commercial interests, to prepare the government to further renege on its fiduciary responsibilities to the public, which includes First Nations people. While this might initially seem to be far away from my concerns about cultural production, I would argue that this sets the stage for the destruction of local communities and of course the cultures produced in and by these communities. As such, cultural workers do not have the luxury of ignoring these urgent matters; rather, they need to work with others to strengthen engagement with concepts of Aboriginal title as taking precedence over neoliberal trade agreements such as NAFTA.[18]

By way of concluding my speculations, I would like to turn to the warnings and possibilities raised in the novel *The Kappa Child* by Hiromi Goto (2001), wherein we find a childhood friendship between Gerald, a mixed-race Japanese and Blood boy, and the narrator, who is of Japanese descent. The fluid process of the social construction of racial and gender identity is emphasized in a telling moment when Gerald asks the narrator "You a boy or a girl?" and the narrator asks him back "You Blood or Japanese?" (168). The novel operates in a realm where it is possible to answer "both," thus rejecting the binary divisions that have historically been deployed to systemic, oppressive effect.[19] At the same time that the possibility for better forms of coexistence hovers, terrible mistakes can also happen. In particular, the narrator, in a moment of weakness and confusion, lashes out at Gerald when he tries to physically comfort her by calling him a sissy boy: "This hateful coil of ugliness twisting in my gut, the words stinging something inside me, but unable to stop" (200). After wrecking her childhood friendship with Gerald, the narrator is given a second chance towards the end of the novel when she encounters him as an adult. What happens next remains outside the text, for the reader to imagine and perhaps enact. The fragile, incomplete, and fraught relationship in *The Kappa Child* –like the broken and dynamic interracial relationships in *Disappearing Moon Cafe*, *Exile and the Heart*, *Burning Vision*, and "Yin Chin" – gestures towards how much remains to be addressed and worked through in the process of decolonization. At both the level of individual interactions and the level of larger socioeconomic frameworks, building alliances that respect First Nations values of interdependency and land stewardship is an urgent focus if we are to foster ethical ways of long term survival on this Earth.

NOTES

1 The Continuous Voyage Provision, enacted in 1908, in effect encoded the exclusion of people from India to Canada. The War Measures Act, in place from 1914 until it was repealed in 1985 (and replaced in 1988 by the Emergencies Act), was used to detain people on the basis of their ethnicity. This power included confiscating Indian reserves from Aboriginal people and the internment of Japanese Canadians during World War II (see Sunahara 1996). More commonly known as the Chinese Exclusion Act, the misleadingly named Chinese Immigration Act barred almost all Chinese people from immigrating to Canada between 1923 and 1947. Prior to that, from 1885 to 1923, Chinese immigrants were the only people charged a head tax ($50 in 1885, $100 in 1900, and $500 from 1903 to 1923) to enter Canada. Due to this racist policy, the Canadian government collected about $23 million from 81,000 Chinese immigrants. Today the so-called right of landing fee, which subsequently became

the Right of Permanent Residence Fee, is a contemporary head tax that continues to effectively discriminate along class lines that disproportionately affect many people of colour. While the 2006 apology from the Canadian Government for the head tax was an important step in acknowledging the few surviving head tax payers, it did not redress their families. The Chinese Canadian National Council continues its efforts to get redress for the head tax payers' immediate families. As Charlie Quan, who paid the head tax in 1923, stated at a press conference at Strathcona Community Centre in Vancouver on 7 April 2002, it took him about ten years of hard labour seven days a week to pay off the debt he owed for his $500 head tax. See Chan 1983; Li 1988; and Wickberg 1982 for more information about the history of Chinese in Canada.

2 McFarlane points out that the "exclusion of the Yukon and Northwest Territories as well as First Nations and band councils from the [Multiculturalism] Act (Section 2) suggests a crisis of representation with respect to aboriginality. It is through these exclusions that the Act perpetuates two myths of Eurocentrism, providing a rationale for the operation of the liberal nation while at the same time obscuring a colonialist history of violence" (22). For a thoughtful discussion of the tensions between Canadian citizenship and Aboriginality, see Battiste and Semaganis. They note that "the federal Indian Act created new categories and definitions of Aboriginal peoples. Under the policy of divide and conquer, the federal government defined 'Indians' in order to destroy communities by arbitrary criteria of residency, marriage, employability, education, and military service. These definitions, conceived without consent of the Aboriginal peoples, segmented Aboriginal societies into categories of status and non-status, treaty and non-treaty, urban and reserve, and enfranchised and disenfranchised Indians" (105). Given this history, Battiste and Semaganis argue that "current issues in citizenship in Canada ... drive ... First Nations relationships, treaties, and self-determination to a bias towards Eurocentric perceptions of citizenship and governance" (93). Immigration legislation further reinforces Eurocentric systems that structurally disadvantage people racialized as nonwhite. For example, with post-9/11 changes, Canada's mechanisms for the already fragile "protection" of refugees have rapidly deteriorated, weakening the "refugee protection" aspect of IRPA. In December 2003, immigration enforcement activities were transferred from Citizenship and Immigration Canada to the newly created Canada Border Services Agency. The transfer of these powers to an agency that reports to the deputy prime minister and the minister of public safety and emergency preparedness has the effect of further associating refugee claimants with criminality. See the Canadian Council of Refugees website at < http://ccrweb.ca/.

3 An example of antiterrorism legislation being used against First Nations activists occurred on 21 September 2002 when INSET (the Integrated National Security Enforcement Team) raided the home of John Rampanen, Nitanis Desjarlais, and their children, finding no weapons but effectively intimidating and threatening the family. Rampanen is a member of the West Coast Warriors Society who has been active in supporting Indigenous fishing rights. See http://www.turtleisland.org/news/news-wcwarriors.htm. As Zygmunt Bauman 2003 suggests, "Terrorists are the least likely casualties of territorial wars: the self-proclaimed 'anti-terrorist wars' destroy well-nigh everything except the terrorism, their declared targets. Having torn or frayed the web of social bonds supporting life routines, such wars make the assaulted territory more hospitable to terrorists than ever before" (6). In 2004, the Immigration and Refugee Protection Act also provided for the usage of "security certificates" to detain at least five Muslim men without charge or bail on secret evidence that they are not allowed to see (http://www.homesnotbombs.ca/secrettrials.htm).

4 One could trace artists' and writers' concerns about cultural appropriation through a number of articles that appeared in Fuse from about 1989 to 1993, including Joane Cardinal- Shubert's "In the Red," Lee Maracle's "Native Myths: Trickster Alive and Crowing," Janisse Browning's "Self-Determination and Cultural Appropriation," as well as most of the summer 1993 issue of *Fuse*, which includes Richard Fung's "Working through Cultural Appropriation," Marwan Hassan's "words and sWord: An Anagram of Appropriation," Ardith Walkem's "Stories and Voices," Rozena Maart's "Cultural Appropriation: Historicizing Individuality, Consciousness, and Actions," and more.

5 In a longer article, novels such as Richard Van Camp's *Blanket of Butterflies*, Joy Kogawa's *Obasan* and *Itsuka* and Kevin Chong's *Baroque-a-Nova* would also deserve discussion, as would instances of racial misrecognition that have been noted in *Calendar Boy* by Andy Quan and *Scared Texts* by Jam Ismail (1991). Films such as *A Tribe of One* (2002) also explore the relationships between Asian and Native peoples. *A Tribe of One* tells the story of the Larabees, a half-Native and half-Chinese family that survived the residential schools and Chinatown in the 1930s and 1940s in part by denying their Aboriginal background. Directed by Eunhee Cha, the film follows the discovery of a woman raised in Vancouver's Chinatown, Rhonda Larabee. Her mother, Marie Lee, was born into the New Westminster Band, the Qayqayat First Nation. When smallpox reduced the band to fewer than one hundred members, the federal government closed the reservation and effectively wiped out the band. Larabee's efforts to re-establish the New Westminster Band led to her becoming its chief in 1993. Also see Brandy Lien Worrall's 2007 anthology, *Eating Stories: A Chinese Canadian and Aboriginal Potluck*, and Marie Lo's 2008 article "Model Minorities, Models of Resistance: Native Figures in Asian Canadian Literature."

6 Scott Kerwin (1999) points out in his essay "The Janet Smith Bill of 1924 and the Language of Race and Nation in British Columbia" that very different racist tropes were deployed against the "Oriental menace" and the "vanishing" Indian in the 1920s: "Using the metaphors of the day, the Aboriginal population could easily be "absorbed" into the bloodstream of British Columbia without "imperiling" the "original type." The dominant stereotype of the Asian population as the "Yellow Peril" was the polar opposite of the metaphor of the "Vanishing [Native] American." British Columbia's white elite feared that a massive influx of Asian immigrants would "dilute the bloodstream of the body politic and literally change the face of the nation" (107).

7 See, for instance Wong-Chu and Tzang (2001), which mentions the arrival of fifty to seventy Chinese artisans at Nootka Sound on the west coast of Vancouver Island on a ship captained by John Meares in 1788 as well as a ship called the *Pallas*, which left a crew of thirty-two Indians and three Chinese seamen stranded in Baltimore in 1785.

8 This play was first performed in Vancouver's Firehall Theatre from 23 April to 11 May 2002.

9 Although Tokyo Rose was a generic name under which a series of women worked, Iva Toguri d'Aquino was singled out as "Tokyo Rose," scapegoated, arrested in Tokyo, flown to San Francisco in 1948, and tried for eight counts of treason. In *Betrayal and Other Acts of Subversion: Feminism, Sexual Politics, Asian American Women's Literature*, Leslie Bow 2001 looks at how the examples of "traitors" such as Yoko Ono and Iva Toguri d'Aquino speak to "a belief in the power of sexual alliances to disrupt other collective alliances, specifically, loyalty to nation and comrades-in-arms." The accusation of "betrayal" then "deauthenticates some affiliations while reconsolidating others" (7).

10 A number of writers have made fun of the ways in which Asians get misrecognized in all sorts of ways, including as First Nations people. Jam Ismail's *Scared Texts* comes quickly to mind: "young ban yen had been thought Italian in kathmandu, filipina in hong kong, eurasian in kyoto, Japanese in anchorage, dismal in london england, hindu in edmonton, generic oriental

in Calgary, western Canadian in Ottawa, anglophone in montreal, metis in jasper, eskimo at hudson's bay department store, Vietnamese in Chinatown, tibetan in Vancouver, commie at the u.s. border, on the whole very asian" (128).

11 See Sunahara 1996 for more detail regarding how the War Measures Act was used to confiscate Indian reserves during World War I. Use of the act to intern Japanese Canadians has also been well documented. See, for example, Miki 2004.

12 Maracle has also written a play called *If We'd Met*; which, through its spirited dialogue between multiracial characters, including Native and Asian women, enacts a process of decolonization through, among other tactics, decentering whiteness.

13 Note that "the mad was intended for the low prices and the crowds in his little store, not him" (292).

14 One must look carefully at who is doing this work and why. Despite the possibilities of political solidarity, there are also problems with the violence that some smugglers have perpetrated on migrating people. What gets interpreted as "crime" is often the effect of poor-bashing systems but can also be considered an unregulated branch of the private sector, as Dara Culhane (2002) points out. See also the 2008 film *Frozen River*.

15 For example, Habacon (2002) states, "We owe much to those who have taken great risks ahead of us to make their voices and histories heard, who have resisted homogenization and being forgotten about and silenced; we are indebted to those who have made efforts to demonstrate the complex diversity of Canadian culture. I am especially inspired by Loretta Todd's film *Forgotten Warriors* (NFB, 1996), which reminds me that ours is not the only worthy cause; that there exists an even greater framework of resistance and cultural identity. I have to acknowledge that any equality I experience – as an artist of color in Canada – is to some degree the product of the First Nations' resistance against the loss of their history, heritage and uniqueness of ethnic experience as well as their desire to be acknowledged by participating in Canadian culture. In gazing deeply upon ourselves, may we not neglect to consider where it is we are, and with whom we share this space: our context." While I am heartened to see Asian Canadian spaces such as *RicePaper* recognize our dependence on First Nations resistance, I am also troubled by how phrases such as "participating in Canadian culture" and "ethnic experience" encode what might otherwise be respectively described as "self-determination" and "survival of ongoing colonization." In the same issue, the relation of "First Nations" to "Canada" also requires more unpacking in Adrienne Wong's (2002) article, which discusses the lack of roles for Asian Canadian actors in Vancouver theatre. Wong states, "We need to work ... together as Asian Canadians – no – as Canadians. We need to form communities and support networks so that promising, exciting artists don't get discouraged and drop out. And we need to start writing and producing plays that specify Canadian culture as multiracial and multicultural. Our society and country are built on the experiences of immigrants and the First Nations populations they stole from" (15).

16 For example, on 12 April 2002, CBC Radio reported that a white supremacist group in Kelowna named B.C. White Pride was conducting a door-to-door leaflet campaign urging people to support the referendum to make British Columbia "a better place for white families." For more information regarding the referendum, see http://www.cbc.ca/news2/background/aboriginals/bc_treaty_referendum.html.

17 NAFTA is available online at http://www.naftanow.org/default_en.asp.

18 Article 1 of the International Covenant on Economic, Social, and Cultural Rights, of which Canada is a signatory, states that "All peoples have the right of self-determination. By virtue of that right they freely determine their political status and freely pursue their economic, social, and cultural development." First Nations organizations have at times referred to this international covenant in their struggles for self-determination.

19 Dorothy Christian (2000), a filmmaker who is exploring what she calls her "Chindian" (Chinese and Indian) background, also asks how to live in a way that honours and respects both cultures rather than being forced to choose one over the other (29). Christian was raised as an Okanagan-Shuswap Indian, and for most of her life having a Chinese father was shameful, although this has changed in more recent times.

REFERENCES

Armstrong, Jeannette. 1996. "Sharing One Skin: Okanagan Community." In *The Case Against the Global Economy*, ed. Jerry Mander and Edward Goldsmith, 160–70. San Francisco: Sierra.

Bannerji, Himani. 2000. *The Dark Side of the Nation: Essays on Multiculturalism, Nationalism, and Gender*. Toronto: Canadian Scholars' Press.

Battiste, Marie, and Helen Semaganis. 2002. "First Thoughts on First Nations Citizenship: Issues in Education." In *Citizenship in Transformation in Canada*, ed. Yvonne Hébert, 93–111. Toronto: University of Toronto Press.

Bauman, Zygmunt. 2003. Interview with Christian Holler. "Global China Shop Part 1." *Springer* in 2. 20 Jan. 2004. <http://www.springerin.at/en/>.

Bow, Leslie. 2001. *Betrayal and Other Acts of Subversion: Feminism, Sexual Politics, Asian American Women's Literature*. Princeton: Princeton University Press. http://dx.doi.org/10.1515/9781400824144.

Chan, Anthony. 1983. *Gold Mountain: The Chinese in the New World*. Vancouver: New Star.

Cheney, Peter, and Miro Cernetig. 1999. "Chinese Gangs Flood Canada with Lucrative Human Cargo." *Globe and Mail*, Feb. 2: A1.

Christian, Dorothy. 2000. "Articulating the Silence." *RicePaper* 9 (3): 22–31.

Clements, Marie. 2003. *Burning Vision*. Vancouver: Talonbooks.

Clements, Marie.2005. *Reading and Talk Emily Carr Institute*. Vancouver, BC. Nov. 4.

Culhane, Dara. 2002. Conversation with Rita Wong. Aug. 2.

Fung, Richard. 1993. "Working through Cultural Appropriation." *Fuse* 16 (5–6): 16–24.

Goto, Hiromi. 2001. *The Kappa Child*. Calgary: Red Deer.

Greenaway, John Endo. 2002. "Fire in the Sky." *Bulletin [Burnaby, BC]* 44 (4): 8–9.

Habacon, Alden. 2002. "Editor's Note." *RicePaper* 7 (4): 5.

Ismail, Jam. 1991. "From Scared Texts." In *Many-Mouthed Birds: Contemporary Writing by Chinese Canadians*, ed. Bennett Lee and Jim Wong-Chu, 124–35. Vancouver: Douglas and Mclntyre.

Kerwin, Scott. 1999. "The Janet Smith, Bill of 1924 and the Language of Race and Nation in British Columbia." *BC Studies* 121:83–114.

Kobayashi, Tamai. 1998. *Exile and the Heart: Lesbian Fiction*. Toronto: Women's Press.

Kobayashi, Tamai. 2000. "Interview with Larissa Lai." *West Coast Line* 33 (3): 121–6.

Laduke, Winona. 1999. *All Our Relations: Native Struggles for Land and Life*. Cambridge, MA: South End.

Lee, S.K.Y. 1990. *Disappearing Moon Cafe*. Vancouver: Douglas and Mclntyre.

Lee, S.K.Y. 1997. "*Disappearing Moon Cafe* and the Cultural Politics of Writing in Canada." In *Millennium Messages*, edited by Kenda Gee and Wei Wong, 10–13. Edmonton: Asian Canadian Writers Workshop Society of Edmonton.

Li, Peter. 1988. *The Chinese in Canada*. Toronto: Oxford University Press.

Lo, Marie. 2008. "Model Minorities, Models of Resistance: Native Figures in Asian Canadian Literature." *Canadian Literature* 196:96–114.

Maracle, Lee. 1992. "The "Post-Colonial" Imagination." *Fuse* 16 (1): 12–15.
Maracle, Lee. 1998. "Yin Chin." In *An Anthology of Canadian Native Literature in English*, ed. Daniel David Moses and Terry Goldie, 290–4. Toronto: Oxford University Press.
McFarlane, Scott. 1995. "The Haunt of Race: Canada's Multiculturalism Act, the Politics of Incorporation, and Writing Thru Race." *Fuse* 18 (3): 18–30.
Miki, Roy. 2004. *Redress: Inside the Japanese Canadian Call for Justice*. Vancouver: Raincoast.
National Film Board. 1996. *Forgotten Warriors*. Directed by Loretta Todd. Montreal: National Film Board.
Pal, Rajinderpal S. 1998. "Collective Amnesia." In *Pappaji Wrote Poetry in a Language I Cannot Read*, 20–3. Toronto: TSAR.
Sunahara, Ann. 1996. "Legislative Roots of Injustice." In *Justice: Canada, Minorities, and Human Rights*, ed. Roy Miki and Scott McFarlane, 7–22. Winnipeg: National Association of Japanese Canadians.
Todd, Loretta. 1990. "Notes on Appropriation." *Parallelogramme* 16 (1): 24–33.
Todd, Loretta. 2001. "On Redress for Aboriginal People." In *Across Currents: Canada-Japan Minority Forum*, edited by Roy Miki and Rita Wong, 72–83. Vancouver: JC.
A Tribe of One. 2002. Directed by Eunhee Cha. National Film Board.
Wickberg, Edgar, ed. Con, Henry, Con, Ronald J., Johnson, Graham, Wickberg, and Willmott, William, E. 1982. *From China to Canada: A History of the Chinese Communities in Canada*. Toronto: McClelland & Stewart.
Wong, Adrienne. 2002. "Restless Nights: Race and Representation on Vancouver Stages." *RicePaper* 7 (4): 13–15.
Wong-Chu, Jim, and Linda Tzang. 2001. *A Brief History of Asian North America*. Vancouver: Vancouver Asian Heritage Month Society.
Worrall, Brandy Lien, ed. 2007. *Eating Stories: A Chinese Canadian and Aboriginal Potluck*. Vancouver: Chinese Canadian Historical Society of British Columbia.

13 Marginalized and Dissident Non-Citizens: Foreign Domestic Workers[1]

DAIVA K. STASIULIS AND ABIGAIL B. BAKAN

The systemic reproduction of migrant domestics as non-citizens within the countries where they work and reside renders them in a meaningful sense stateless, as far as access to state protection of their rights is concerned. This is despite the formal retention of legal citizenship status accorded by their home country, and, often, the legal entry as non-citizen migrant workers in the host country. Elsewhere, we have identified how the construction of non-citizenship is central to maintaining the vulnerability of foreign domestic workers in Canada. In this chapter, we consider the lived experiences of domestic workers themselves, based largely on a survey of foreign domestic workers living in Toronto. This chapter offers a comparative analysis of the experiences of two groups of women of colour, those of West Indian and Filipino origin, working in the homes of upper-middle- and upper-class Canadian families resident in Toronto, Ontario in the mid-1990s.

The limited literature on foreign domestic workers in Canada indicates patterns of structural discrimination, ranging from overt physical abuse, to denial of privacy rights, to denial of fair wages and adequate benefits. Our study attempts to identify both common and differential patterns of discrimination among foreign domestic workers originating from the two main regions of the English speaking Caribbean and the Philippines.

Our findings suggest that there are notable differences between West Indian and Filipino domestic workers in terms of immigration status, with a higher concentration of illegal migrants among the former than the latter. The recent pattern of discrimination against the legal entry to Canada of West Indian domestic workers, indicated in the previous chapter, is expressed in this finding. Illegal immigration status among a notable portion of West Indian domestic workers interviewed was indicated in the survey not only in response to directed questions, but also in terms of the impact of such status on working conditions and access to benefits that would otherwise accrue to workers who have legal means of access. Our survey findings suggest further, that upon securing live-in, domestic work with a Canadian family in Toronto, Ontario, there are great discrepancies between employment situations regarding wages, general working conditions, and parameters of employee bargaining rights. However, while certain discrepancies based on immigration status were clear, the findings suggest that other aspects of domestic work bear greater commonality based on similar workplace conditions and systemic structures that favour Canadian citizen employers over their non-citizen employees. The variability of conditions that was discernible in the survey results is reflective of the absence of standards of employment and mechanisms to enforce the labour rights of foreign domestic workers upon their arrival in Canada. The capricious control of private employers explains many aspects of the work experiences of foreign domestic workers, rather than the place of origin of the domestic workers. The commonalities in the overall experiences of these two groups of domestic workers from the West Indies and the Philippines are greater than the differences: both groups are seriously underpaid, over-worked and treated with minimal-trust or respect for privacy by their employers.

In sum, we were able to identify two main lines of demarcation revealed in the study. The first is determined by the gatekeeping mechanisms. The changes in immigration policy since the 1980s have tended to disfavour West Indian domestic workers and promote a patronizing racialized favour towards Filipinas that has directly impacted on the workplace experiences of these two groups of workers. However, the more profound line of demarcation appears to be not between the conditions and experiences of West Indian versus Filipino domestic workers, but between the employers on one side, and West Indian and Filipino workers collectively on the other. Racialized relations of exploitation within the private home are expressed in a hierarchy of class and citizenship, reinforced by the gatekeeping structures which overwhelmingly favour citizen/employers over non-citizen/employees. Even in a province such as Ontario, where certain legal rights have been won by domestic workers, the lack of enforcement mechanisms ensures relations of continued discrimination. The exercise of legal rights for domestic workers is dependent upon the registration of a formal complaint; such complaints, raised individually, are assessed by the domestic worker as a calculated risk. Any given complaint may lead to an improvement in the working conditions of the live-in, temporary status, female foreign domestic worker, but it alternatively may lead to a decline in conditions, as in the event of the complaint resulting in the dismissal and loss of job and domicile for the worker. Moreover, the restrictions associated with the FDM and the LCP, federal immigration policies, are not mitigated by labour legislation that resides in the jurisdiction of the provincial state.

Our findings suggest that various negotiating strategies among immigrant women seeking employment in Canada lead them to adopt various paths that culminate in live-in employment in private domestic service. Upon taking up residence and work in the homes of wealthy Canadian citizen employers, common structural conditions that promote systemic exploitation and racialization come into play. Here class exploitation is amplified by racial discrimination, and both of these hierarchical relationships are enforced by systemic patterns across the citizenship/non-citizenship divide.

A note on the survey methodology is in order. The data is drawn from 50 questionnaires, 25 from interviews conducted with live-in domestics from the West Indies, and 25 from those originating from the Philippines.[2] Country of origin was determined by birthplace. The interviews were conducted by female research assistants of the same regional or national origins as the interviewees. They were conducted face-to-face, or in the rare cases when respondents were unable to meet, by telephone. In all cases, individual interviews were about 90 minutes long, and followed a questionnaire guideline. The sample was selected through a snowball approach of community contacts. No more than three names were suggested from each interviewee, among whom no more than one name was subsequently interviewed. Interviewees were asked to respond to all questions, though it was not uncommon for some questions to be declined a response.[3]

Because the study is numerically small, it is of qualitative rather than quantitative significance. However, the Caribbean and the Philippines are not arbitrary reference points in terms of the general experience of Third World migration.[4] Data of this nature is based on generalizing collective patterns of work and living experiences and upon the assumption of social patterns of negotiation. While the size of the sample is small in regard to statistical trends, it is substantially larger than an approach based on individual life histories. The study effectively highlights the working and living conditions of women workers treated as temporary visitors who are compelled to live with their employers and who perform duties of private domestic service. Though they provide labour in serious demand, employers and the Canadian state designate them as menial servants. These findings are explored in more detail below, according to a series of specific topics, notably: immigration status; the live-in requirement and accommodation; working conditions, wages and benefits; and remittances and family support.

Immigration Status

Faced with the threat of deportation for non-fulfilment of duties, domestic workers who live with their employers work long hours for low pay in very isolated and highly regulated conditions. Regarding their immigration experience and status, however, there was a divergence of experience between the two groups of women interviewed in this study. Among the West Indian women, 20 out of 25 responded to a question about place of work immediately prior to working as a domestic in Canada (Q7).[5] Of these, all but two (who had worked in Europe) had worked in the West Indies immediately before coming to Canada. Among the Filipinas, 23 responded to this question; only 11 of these came directly from the Philippines. Others had worked in the Middle East, Asia and Europe, immediately prior to coming to Canada to work.

This finding reflects divergent patterns of migration for the two groups of women, and distinct strategies for negotiating the global restrictions they face. The migration of West Indian domestics to Canada reflects historical and imperial country/region to country ties. In contrast, Philippine migration indicates the aggressive marketing of labour for export on the part of various Philippine governments. The latter process has had the unintentional effect of rendering unskilled or deskilled Filipino women experienced international migrants.[6]

We have demonstrated that negotiating citizenship involves navigating the selection processes of various gatekeepers. There is a preference among domestic placement agencies in Canada to recruit Filipinas from outside Manila; moreover, the experience requirement of the LCP in Canada has tended to favour those who had previously served as household workers in other countries. This trend is reflected in the survey findings, especially notable given the small size of the sample. In contrast, West Indian women in search of domestic service as a means of emigrating are no longer readily welcomed in Canada. Among the West Indian domestics in our study, 10 entered Canada as domestic workers on either the FDM or the LCP, and therefore were legally admitted as foreign live-in domestic workers; 14 entered Canada as visitors, and one claimed asylum as a refugee (Q15). It is illegal to work in Canada while on a visitor visa, and refugee status is almost never granted to those who claim the need for asylum from the West Indies. Refugee claimants can only work with a separately issued work permit. Therefore, the majority of the West Indian respondents entered domestic service in Canada as undocumented migrant workers. Among the Filipinas, 23 had entered Canada on the FDM or LCP program as foreign domestic workers, while only two entered as visitors.

The divergent patterns of entry into Canada and the subsequent differences in migration status for the two groups indicate the relatively more restrictive access for West Indian women compared with Filipinas. The relatively high proportion of undocumented workers among West Indian women reflects the effectiveness of gatekeepers in Canada in limiting the legal access of these applicants. However, evidence suggests that neither the numbers seeking work as domestics in Canada, nor the demand for live-in domestic service, have declined. Such racialized bias compels more and more West Indian women to enter the country as visitors and work without any formal status in the country. This pattern of increasing numbers in undocumented personal service is widespread in other countries such as the United States and Italy.[7] Despite a general trend towards increasing restrictions regarding the numbers of domestic workers admitted on the LCP, Filipino applicants are currently considered in a racist stereotype to be "good servants," and therefore some continue to find it possible to pass through Canada's closely guarded gates. This legal passage is conditional, however, on their willingness to work as maids and nannies, to arrive on temporary visas and to live with their employers.

In response to another question regarding current immigration status within Canada, the picture changed somewhat (Q16). Among both groups of women workers, several had obtained landed, or permanent resident status, yet continued to work as live-in domestic workers. Among the West Indian domestic workers, 16 had temporary or unidentified status within Canada at the time of the interview, whereas nine had obtained landed immigrant status or actual legal citizenship. Among the Filipino domestic workers, 19 were legal temporary workers, whereas six had obtained landed immigrant status.

The notable feature here is that historically it has been unusual for any worker to accept live-in domestic service in Canada unless they are temporary workers. The implication is that the economy in Canada today is so restrictive for "unskilled" immigrant workers of colour that even those who are legally eligible to leave live-in domestic service are faced with few or no other options. At least some West Indian workers, and the more recently arrived Filipino workers, continued to work at least partially as live-in domestic servants despite having obtained landed immigrant or citizenship status. This is an unusual phenomenon within the postwar Canadian workforce, and one that has not been formally recognized by the Canadian government.

Regarding immigration status, then, our findings reveal two patterns. First, there are apparently more illegal or undocumented domestic workers among the West Indian sample. Second, the findings suggest that both West Indian women and Filipinas who have the right to work legally in occupations other than domestic service are compelled to remain working as domestics. This second pattern runs counter to the thesis of "ethnic succession" whereby only the most recent of immigrant groups are to be found in the most exploited ("dirty, dangerous and difficult") jobs.

Live-in Requirement and Accommodation

These findings have implications for the live-in requirement of the LCP. The LCP obliges foreign domestics to work and live in their employers' home for two years within a three-year period if they are to be eligible to apply for permanent residence in Canada. Domestic workers will commonly share an apartment for weekend use in order to obtain some privacy and time away from what are often 24 hour on-call obligations. Such arrangements are not incorporated into the LCP, and employers and immigration authorities can challenge caregivers for doing so without their permission.[8]

Those who are illegal, however, and have no hopes of obtaining permanent legal status, would feel no obligation to live in their employers' homes to meet the FDM/LCP regulation.

Yet workers with undocumented status are also at greater risk of deportation as they have no legal claim to residence within Canada. Therefore, there is likely more, rather than less, obligation among undocumented workers to live in the employers' home if this is established as a condition of employment. Those who are landed immigrants or citizens, however, would be released from the live-in requirement and would normally seek alternative employment other than domestic service.

Domestic workers interviewed for this study were all "officially" live-in domestic workers: this was a precondition of qualification in the study. However, the respondents indicated that the "live-in" feature for domestic service occupational status did not necessarily mean living with one's employer all week long; and in some cases, officially designated "live-in" workers, actually lived out. In such a case this likely meant that they not only had a residence in the employer's home, but also maintained their own private or shared residence. Among the West Indian domestics, of the 24 who responded to this question, only four lived with their employer during the entire seven-day week (Q28). Thirteen lived with their employer during the five- or six-day working week only; five lived-out; and two had "other" living arrangements that were not specified. Among the Filipinas, of the 24 who responded, only six lived with their employer all week. Sixteen lived with their employer during the working week only; and two lived out.

Regarding the live-in requirement of the FDM/LCP, the survey findings suggest that both employers and domestics are inclined to bend the full time live-in rule. This represents an important finding in the collective negotiating strategies of foreign domestic workers. The live-in requirement has been identified as one of the most oppressive features of the regulated policy in Canada.[9] Research internationally and over historical time has found that the single most important element in domestic workers' ability to negotiate or bargain for improvements in conditions of domestic service is the ability to live out, away from the dictates of the employing family.[10] Among both the Caribbean and Filipino domestic workers, the attraction to obtaining private, part-time residence away from the employer is clear. In addition to the restrictions and limitations associated with living with one's employer, who is also responsible for managing access to residence and work in Canada, the live-in requirement assumes that the employee has no family or personal life of her own. In spite of the potential risk of dire consequences, including termination and deportation, the rate of success in obtaining some degree of live-out arrangement apparent in our findings represents a significant accomplishment in negotiating citizenship rights for this non-citizen population. It may, however, also intersect with the desire on the part of the employer to not want the domestic worker in the home in all instances and to negotiate some "family time" or "personal time" away from the domestic employee.

The quality of accommodation reported by the domestic workers from both groups suggests another reason why attempting to live-out for at least part of the week is attractive. Among the West Indian domestics, 11 of 25 who responded reported that their room in their employers' house was in the basement (Q29); only seven of 25 had their own telephone (Q30D); 10 of 24 who responded had no lock on their door (Q30E). Among the Filipino domestics, 16 of 24 who responded had a basement room; 16 of 23 had their own telephone; and fully 18 of 25 had no lock on their door.

While the quality of accommodation varies markedly, the living space for the majority of live-in domestics in Canadian middle-class homes is not designed to provide privacy and separation for live-in workers from employer's families. The resulting lack of privacy and constant employer (and employing family members') surveillance – whether by design or by default – inhibits domestic workers from having any private life of their own. The potential restrictions include barring intimate friendships and familial and sexual relationships, creating conditions that are in direct contradiction with the ideals of autonomous adulthood, so-called "family values" and personal freedom in Canadian society. When asked what changes they would like to see in the LCP (Q36F), 18 of 25 West Indian domestics, and 16 of 23 Filipinas who responded said they favoured changes in the live-in requirement. The commonality of this response among both groups of workers in the interview sample is notable. Upon entering the country and experiencing the pressures of living with one's employer, both groups of foreign domestic workers in Canada encounter a commonly oppressive set of circumstances.

The live-in requirement has been identified in Canadian government policy circles as an essential feature of the foreign domestic worker program. According to government explanations, the LCP exists due to a chronic shortage of labour from within the Canadian citizen employment market who are willing to provide live-in domestic service.[11] The LCP was enacted in 1992, following the earlier FDM policy of 1981, to address the purported need to recruit workers from out of the country for the sole purpose of filling this niche in the labour market.[12]

Our findings, however, suggest a different interpretation. From the standpoint of the employers, demand for live-in service is generally assumed to be high among those with small children, or in some cases elderly parents, who require care during all hours of the day and night. In the context of declining real incomes for the majority of income-earners, however, employers may in fact be more concerned to hire domestic workers who are willing to work for low wages and are subject to minimal regulation – whether they live in or live out. The purpose of recruiting foreign domestic workers may be motivated less by the necessity to compel an indentured, live-in labour force, as government policy has assumed, than to recruit a labour force kept in a sufficiently vulnerable position to compel them to accept low wages and poor working conditions. Our findings suggest that the compulsory live-in requirement is not as obvious a demand factor as government policies have earlier suggested. In either case, it is the interests of employer/citizens rather than those of employee/non-citizens that are considered as central to the policy. In sum, our findings indicate that among both West Indian and Filipino foreign domestic workers, arrangements for partially mitigating the live-in requirement through additional or alternative accommodation for one or more days per week appears to be far more common than acknowledged. Employers may be either compelled or willing to accept such a limitation to the live-in requirement even though this practice runs contrary to the terms and conditions of the LCP.[13]

Working Conditions, Wages and Benefits

We have identified the temporary immigration status of foreign domestic workers in Canada, combined with the compulsory live-in requirement, as the main conditions that render them vulnerable to the arbitrary designs of their employers. These conditions are heightened by the personalistic nature of the employer/employee relationship characteristic of domestic service, and the differential impact of class, race and citizenship status. Among both West Indian and Filipino domestic workers, a substantial majority of respondents surveyed indicated that the two main areas of responsibility associated with their employment were caring for the employers' children, and cleaning the employers' house. For West Indian domestic workers, 22 of 24 respondents who answered this question identified care for the employers' children as part of their current job; among Filipinas, the 24 out of 25 who responded to this question all identified childcare.[14] Moreover, when asked to identify the frequency with which such care was provided (Q4A2A2), all 21 West Indian domestics who responded to this question answered seven days per week; all 24 Filipinas who responded offered the same frequency rate.

This is particularly interesting given the responses to the questions regarding accommodation. Though all of those who answered this question indicated they were expected to care for children seven days per week, a majority of respondents did not actually live in the employers' homes throughout the entire week. This suggests that employers' expectations were for the provision of care every day, every week; however, by arranging to live out for part of the week, workers were able to get some time off away from their childcare responsibilities.

The LCP is designed to provide affordable and flexible care for children, disabled persons and seniors for upper-middle-class and wealthy families. In order to employ a worker through the program, the provision of personal care, rather than only the performance of other household duties such as house cleaning or gardening for example, must be part of the duties of the migrant worker. Thus, it is not surprising that virtually all Filipinos (most of whom entered through the program) were engaged in childcare. What is more notable, is that all of the West Indians, most of whom did not enter through a government program, were also engaged in childcare.

Not surprisingly, cleaning house was another major area of work responsibility characterizing the employment situation of West Indian and Filipino domestic workers (Q4A2C1).[15] For the former, the response rate of those who identified housework was 21 of 25; for the latter, 21 of 24. Other common tasks, indicated by at least 18 affirmative responses from both the West Indian and the Filipino respondents, were: serving guests (Q4A2K1); shovelling snow in the winter (Q4A2J1) and gardening (Q4A2L1). Thus, it was common for both Filipino and West Indian workers, hired as nannies, also to be expected to work simultaneously as housekeepers. This is consistent with the association of household labour with "women's work," and defined as combining child care and housekeeping as part of the same job description. It also indicates the tendency for women of colour to be expected to perform the duties of the employing "woman of the house" in a gendered, hierarchical, heterosexual, nuclear family structure. When paid female domestic labour is employed in the private Canadian home, gendered divisions become altered by class divisions within the home. Women of means employ poor women to perform the domestic duties associated with women's labour; in the process a clear line of demarcation according to class and enforced by citizenship and race come into play. This pattern was common in the study whether the foreign domestic workers came to Canada from the West Indies or the Philippines.

The general expression of the citizenship divide within the household was notably uniform. However, when it came to breaking down the specific tasks involved in performing the duties associated with household labour, and the frequency with which they were executed, the responses became more varied, among both West Indian and Filipino domestic workers. For example, among West Indian respondents, 11 of 20 who answered this question (Q4A2C2) cleaned house once per week; eight did so every day of the week, and one only once per month. Eleven of 25 were involved in menu preparation (Q4A2D1), and the same number did so daily (Q4A2D2). Twelve of 14 who responded cooked meals for the children only (Q4A2E1), while 10 of 25 who responded to a separate question (Q4A2F1) stated that they cooked meals for the household as a whole.

When we turn to the Filipino domestic workers, we see a pattern of responses that is equally diverse. Among 20 respondents for the question regarding frequency of cleaning house (Q4A2C2), 12 identified once per week, while eight noted that they cleaned the employer's house on a daily basis. Sixteen of 23 Filipinas who responded stated that their jobs included menu preparation; 10 of 13 Filipinas who answered a separate question indicated that they prepared menus for meals every day of the week, while three did so once per week. Twelve of 22 Filipino domestic workers who responded indicated that they cooked meals for the children only, while 12 of 23 who responded to this question cooked meals for the entire household.

Doing the laundry appeared in the findings to be a task more universally included in the "house cleaning" job description. Among West Indian domestic workers, 21 of 25 who answered this question (Q4A2G1) did the laundry; for Filipinas, the response rate was 22 of 24. Even here, however, when the question of frequency was asked, variations emerged again. Fourteen of 21 West Indian domestic workers who responded (QA2G2) did the laundry once per week; seven did the laundry on a daily basis. Among Filipinas, of 15 who responded, 10 did the laundry once per week, while five did laundry daily. When a question was asked about ironing (Q4A2H1), all 25 of the West Indian domestics who were interviewed responded, among whom 13 indicated this task was part of their job description, performed once a week. For Filipino domestic workers surveyed, again there was a response rate of 100 per cent regarding the task of ironing: 22 indicated that ironing was a regular part of their expected duties. Sixteen of 18 Filipinas who responded indicated that they did the ironing once per week; one ironed every day; and one ironed only once per month.

What is most clearly indicated by these findings is the variation in the job descriptions and frequency of performing specific tasks associated with full time, live-in domestic labour. Not only are there great variations in the work performed – a characteristic in general of women's work in the home – but also in the frequency of the performance of those tasks within any given time period, and the hours of work in any given week.

Caring for and raising young children, maintaining the complex series of duties associated with household cleaning and maintenance, and serving the personal needs of adults in the private home, are forms of work notoriously invisible in modern capitalist societies. Household workers are often expected to perform several of these tasks simultaneously, even though performing one of these duties makes it difficult or indeed impossible to perform another. The expectations associated with the performance of these tasks are often unclear to the employee, as is the order of priority.

The characteristics of migrant domestic work that emerged in the findings of this survey are reflective of migrant domestic work in general, not only in Canada but internationally.[16] The absence of transparent standards according to which of these tasks are performed indicates the lack of clarity associated with the replacement of paid for unpaid household work in the family unit. What is clear, however, is that such an absence of standardization supports the arbitrary, nearly accidental, norms of work imposed on paid live-in domestics. Work performed as personal service in the home is subject almost entirely to the discretion of the employing adult or adults, and usually the adult woman. The employing adults who own the home, hire the employee and supervise the performance of duties expect such work to be "natural" for foreign domestic workers, and commonly communicate expectations in vague, inconsistent and personal terms. In addition, vulnerable immigration status and the live-in requirement associated with Canadian foreign domestic worker policy exacerbate exploitative conditions of work and the risk of abuse. For the employee to ask questions of clarification may be taken as a sign of incompetence or confusion; workers are more likely simply to perform the duties requested with minimal instruction, simply hoping to "please" the employer.

Another feature of live-in domestic work is the spatially restrictive nature of the arrangement, where the employer is not only one's boss but also one's landlord. When the landlord is responsible for determining access not only to private residence but also to permanent residence in the country, the regulatory power of the employing family is augmented even further. Employers determine not only what the domestic worker is expected to do, but also what she is expected not to do, or denied access to do at all.

One finding that emerged in the survey data related to job description was conspicuous in this negative sense. A clear majority of respondents indicated that they were *not* expected to perform one duty commonly associated with household labour: grocery shopping (Q4A2I1). Among the West Indian domestic workers, of 25 who answered this question, 21 stated they did not do the grocery shopping; among Filipinas, of 24 who answered this question, 21 had the same response.

We believe this finding is suggestive of a pattern worthy of further exploration among foreign domestic live-in workers. Grocery shopping is unquestionably a task associated with household labour and with meal planning. However, given that there is no obvious correlation between the numbers of respondents responsible for menu preparation and the numbers who do the grocery shopping, this factor alone does not explain the high negative response rate. The survey does not suggest that domestic workers were not asked to plan the meals; what is indicated in the findings is only that they were not asked or expected to buy the groceries for the meals.

Alternatively, we suggest an interpretation of the labour of grocery shopping in relation to the household as a work site. Grocery shopping for a family on a regular basis suggests several forms of behaviour that may be considered distinct from other household duties. It compels fairly autonomous activity outside of the household. It requires transportation, in a car or taxi that would logically be paid for by the employer, and assumes responsibility in managing this transportation to and from the household work site. It is also dependent upon financial exchange; sometimes in considerable amounts measured over a period of time, both for transportation and especially the purchase of the groceries. Indeed, the grocery bill for an employing family with two or more children, which is typical of employers of foreign domestic workers, may exceed the wages paid to live-in household workers. Given that most of the domestic workers cared for young children, it would also likely require that the children accompany the domestic worker in the activity, where responsibility on the part of the employee is increased. Moreover, as live-in domestics are expected to pay for their board out of wages paid them by the employer, the live-in domestic worker who buys groceries for her own consumption would, in a sense, be paying her own wages from the employer's funds. Grocery shopping is a duty that demands considerable individual discretion – choosing the best products, managing variation in price options, and so on. We believe that it is precisely because grocery shopping encouraged these features of autonomy, increased responsibility, physical distance from the household as a work site, control of family finances, and individual, mature discretion, that domestic workers tended not to be asked to perform this duty. Despite the small size of the interview sample, the uniformity of the responses among both West Indian and Filipino domestic workers is suggestive of the need for further investigation of this dimension of live-in domestic service.

Another set of survey questions regarding working conditions focused on the number of hours worked and the payment of wages. West Indian domestic workers interviewed worked an average of 51.3 hours per week; Filipinas worked an average of 49.2 hours per week. According to Ontario labour legislation, any work performed over 44 hours within a given week is overtime. Overtime pay for domestic workers is expected to be at the rate of 1½ the hourly rate, and time off in lieu is required to be at the rate of one and one-half hours per hour of overtime worked.[17] In response to a question about payment for overtime, however, among 25 West Indian workers who answered this question, 10 received overtime compensation, while 15 did not. Among Filipino domestic workers, of 22 responses, 16 received overtime compensation, while six did not.

There is sufficient discrepancy here to suggest a possible variation between the two groups, indicating that West Indian workers surveyed, who work an average of 2.1 hours more per week, are also less likely to receive overtime pay or time off in lieu for the work they perform. We interpret the discrepancy in overtime pay combined with the longer average work week to have resulted from the absence of security among these workers in demanding adequate compensation from their employers. The larger number of undocumented workers among the West Indian workers surveyed would suggest greater vulnerability in the workplace, and less bargaining power to enforce compensation for overtime. However, the fact that six of 22 respondents among the Filipino workers indicate lack of compensation for overtime pay is significant insofar as this national group of domestics is predominantly here under the LCP. Our survey indicates that both West Indian and Filipino domestic workers are vulnerable to extreme discrepancies in pay, in part due to the long hours of work associated with private service employment and the difficulty of enforcement of overtime compensation. The more vulnerable the immigration status of the worker, the more likely she is to be unfairly compensated, and the greater the margin of discrimination she is likely to suffer.

The measurement of hours of paid work in the home has long been a contentious and hard-fought issue among domestic advocacy organizations in Canada. In 1987, overtime pay or time off in lieu for domestic workers was recognized in Ontario law, a direct response to domestic workers' demands.[18] Subsequent studies indicate, however, that while a majority of domestic workers routinely work overtime, only a minority receive fair compensation for overtime work performed.[19] For the live-in domestic worker, enforcement of such a provision is dependent upon a separation of work performance in the home as a worksite, from time off while resident in the same home as a site of respite from work. Our findings reflect this pattern of contestation surrounding hours of labour performed, a pattern suggested in the findings for both West Indian and Filipino workers.

We can now turn from number of hours worked, to hourly rates of pay. Here, again, there was considerable discrepancy, but the variations in pay were characteristic of both West Indian and Filipino domestic workers. There was wide variation in frequency of pay, with a majority expecting to receive a cheque every two weeks (Q4A122B); 12 West Indians and 14 Filipinas. Others expected to be paid monthly (Q4A12C): four among the West Indian domestic workers and eight among those from the Philippines. Still others expected to be paid weekly (Q4A12A): six in the West Indian group, three among the Filipinas.

While the frequency of pay is variable, this factor taken in isolation is not significant. However, when we combined information from responses regarding frequency of pay with hours of work per week and pay rates, we were able to approximate the hourly wages of West Indian and Filipino domestics in the survey.[20] Accordingly, West Indian workers were paid on average $4.53 per hour; Filipino workers in the survey were paid an average of

$4.73 per hour. The 20 cent per hour discrepancy is a relatively small margin of difference given the number of undocumented workers among the West Indian group. What is more noteworthy is the fact that both the West Indian and Filipino workers received hourly wages considerably below the legal minimum wage in Ontario at the time ($5.40–$6.85 per hour).[21] Not only is the average earned demonstrably low, but it is also merely a statistical average. Among West Indian workers, the pay scale went as low as $2.14 per hour; for Filipino workers, the low end of the hourly pay rate was $1.91 per hour.

Our findings confirm and expose the highly unregulated employment standards applicable to foreign domestic workers in Canada, reflected in arbitrary and unaccountable rates of pay. Since 1987 full-time live-in domestic workers have been entitled to receive at least the minimum wage. Employers are allowed to deduct the costs of room and board, within standards provided in federal guidelines; however, the parameters for arbitrary pay rates are greatly increased by the live-in requirement of the FDM and LCP. The discrepancy in pay demonstrates the unregulated control placed in the hands of employers of live-in domestic workers in Canada. Moreover, the employee does not necessarily retain a formal record of payment for work performed. When asked if a pay slip was received with payment (Q4B4), among the 12 West Indian respondents who answered this question, only one received a pay slip with every payment; three received a pay slip once per year; and seven stated that they never received a pay slip. Among the Filipino workers, 14 responded to this question; three received a pay slip with every payment; 11 never received one. These findings are significant given that under the conditions of the LCP, the "employer is required to include a statement of earning with [each] paycheque."[22] Such a record of employment is necessary should the worker apply for employment insurance benefits, and as proof that the employee has worked the necessary length of time as set out in the federal regulations.[23] Our findings suggest that there is systematic non-compliance of employers with this pay slip requirement.

The survey investigated not only amounts and frequency of pay, but also workplace benefits. While the general conditions of work among the West Indian and Filipino domestic workers in the survey were similar, or similarly varied, certain benefits indicated a different pattern. Live-in domestics in Ontario are entitled to equal pay for equal work, pregnancy leave, paid public holidays, parental leave, regular payment of wages, vacation time, free periods away from work at designated intervals, termination notice and work details in writing.[24] They are also, like all Ontario workers, eligible for health care coverage, workers' compensation, certain tax benefits based on pay scale and employment insurance (formerly referred to as "unemployment insurance" in federal legislation).

West Indian domestic workers were less likely to be guaranteed receipt of these benefits than Filipinas. Regarding health care benefits, among West Indian workers, of 25 respondents who answered this question (Q4A8A), 13 stated that they did receive benefits, eight did not, and four did not know. Among the Filipino workers, among 24 who answered this question, all received health care benefits. Regarding pension benefits (Q48B), of 24 West Indian respondents, four received benefits, 11 did not, while nine did not know. For the Filipino domestic workers, among 22 respondents, 20 did receive pension benefits and two did not. Turning to unemployment insurance (Q4A8D), of 23 West Indian domestic workers who answered this question, three received benefits, 17 did not, and three did not know. Among the Filipinas, of 22 respondents, 20 received unemployment insurance benefits while two did not. Finally, regarding the benefit of receiving a tax refund (Q4A8C), of 24 West Indian domestic workers who answered this question, 12 stated that they did,

11 did not and one did not know. For the Filipino domestic workers, of 22 respondents, 19 stated that they did receive a tax refund while one did not and two did not know.

Despite the small size of this study, these findings fall sufficiently along the lines of nationality to suggest further exploration. These benefits, when received, accrue to the employees from the government, whereas the necessary paperwork and ensuring receipt of benefits rests with the employer. Unlike the payment of wages, there is not necessarily a direct cost to the employers in allowing these benefits to be accessed by the employees.[25] However, there are costs involved for the employer in the regularization of the employee/employer relationship, including paying the employer's contributions to various government funds. Given that we discovered that a significant number of the West Indian domestics interviewed had no documented migration status, one of the indicated effects is the inability to access benefits to which legal foreign domestic workers are entitled.[26] Despite the illegality of employing and harbouring an undocumented worker, the lack of regulation of the work process means that the employer gains even greater control and more work for fewer costs. It is likely that the significant gap in the access to employee benefits revealed in the findings is a feature of the undocumented status of many of the West Indian respondents.

Remittances and Family Support

Our survey also investigated the role of female domestic workers as the economic supporters of their own families. Immigration to Canada as a means to acquire remittances to support family members "back home" for both groups of workers was a key issue of exploration. This is an important element of the negotiating strategy of migrant communities, particularly of women for whom compensatory paid work sufficient to support their families is limited relative to men in virtually every country in the world. The interviewees were asked to rank the importance – on a five-point scale with "very important" at one end, ranging through "important," "neutral" and "not very important," and with "not important at all" at the other end of the scale – of a number of factors considered in their decision to come to Canada as a domestic worker. Each question was ranked separately.

For a significant number of women workers, among both the West Indian and Filipino groups, the decision to come to Canada was largely linked to their family's financial and social welfare. Among the West Indian domestic workers, of 25 who responded to the statement "I wanted to immigrate to Canada," 24 ranked this as either important or very important (Q12A). Among 25 Filipino workers who responded, 20 ranked this statement in these categories. When asked to rank the statement, "I wanted to bring over my family or certain family members to Canada" among 25 West Indian respondents, 15 placed this reason as important or very important; and among 25 Filipinos who responded to this question, 18 placed this statement in these categories (Q12B). When asked to rank the statement, "I wanted to be able to earn money to send back home," 24 West Indian and 25 Filipino workers responded to this question. Among the West Indian workers, 17 placed this statement as important or very important, as did 19 Filipinas (Q12H).

Another question, this one open ended, asked "What are the major things you have gained, or hope to gain, in becoming a live-in domestic worker in Canada?" (Q31). Here, there was a differentiated emphasis between the West Indian and Filipino workers. The former stressed personal achievements associated with raising their standard of living, while the latter emphasized the importance of remittances. The largest number of West Indian domestics first mentioned furthering their education (10 of 25 who responded); the second most common answer was about integrating with others or getting to know Canada (eight responses); and the remaining responses were about raising their standard of living, acquiring landed immigrant status or bringing their family to Canada. The Filipino responses were different. Here, sending money home was the most common goal mentioned first (10 of 20 who responded); after this, the most common answers focused on bringing their family to Canada (six responses); and the remaining answers were scattered among educating their children, improving their standard of living and gaining a better job.

The role of remittances figures more highly in the concerns of the Filipina domestics interviewed than among the West Indians. In both cases, remittances are important, but the relative weight is different. When asked to rank their response to the question directly posed, "For your family back home, how important do you feel it is that you send them money from your work in Canada?" (Q25), among 21 West Indians responding, 14 stated very important or important. Out of 25 Filipinas who answered this question, 19 stated very important or important.

This variation in emphasis may in part be reflective of the more recent migration flow of Filipinos to Canada, with more dependents remaining back home in need of overseas support. Around 15 per cent of households in the Philippines receive income from their relatives deployed abroad.[27] Further, the Philippine state is highly dependent upon overseas remittances as the main source of foreign currency, and for this reason often refers to its exploited female migrants abroad as national "heroines." There is a massive network of state and private interests encouraging overseas work for this purpose.[28] The West Indies are, however, also dependent upon overseas remittances. However, the culture of praising immigrants for sending back funds is not as pronounced as in the Philippine case. Another feature in explaining the difference in emphasis is the number of undocumented workers among the West Indian interviewees. Sending money to another country that has been earned under the table is not only challenging, but highly risky to those both at the sending and receiving ends of the funds.

Despite the differences, an interesting similarity regarding remittance payments was also indicated in the survey. A majority in both the West Indian and Filipino groups did not send their remittance cheques to their husbands/partners back home, but to their mothers or other relatives. In answer to the question, "To whom do you generally send remittance cheques?" (Q24), among 20 West Indian respondents, only three stated that money was sent to their husbands. Other responses included their mother (nine); combinations of relatives (six); or another relative or person (two). Among the 23 Filipino respondents who answered this question, only six stated that they sent money to their husbands. Other responses were their mother (nine); combinations of relatives (three); another relative or person (three); and eldest daughter (two).

Of note is the fact that among both groups of women, a greater number directed their remittance cheques to their mothers than to their husbands/partners, and to other relatives in general than to their husbands/partners. This is despite quite divergent marital patterns between the two samples (Q18). Of 25 West Indian domestics who answered a question about marital status, only three were in the category of married/partner prior to arrival in Canada; one described herself in the category of separated/divorced/widowed; and 21 stated that they had never married. Among the 25 Filipinas who responded, roughly half (12) identified themselves as married/partner; two in the separated/divorced/widowed category; and 11 stated that they had never married. Therefore, there were a larger number of married/partnered Filipinas compared with the West Indian women.

This is a finding consistent with the divergent cultural norms related to the institution of marriage. In the Philippines, the majority of the population are practising Catholics and formal legal marriage is commonly expected of young women. In the West Indies, on the other hand, there is a common tradition of unions without formal marriage, and single-parent families headed by women are far from unusual.[29] In both groups, however, husbands were notably not the principle recipients of the remittance cheques.

This cross-cultural similarity in remittance patterns conforms to worldwide observations that women tend to work to support the basic needs of their families rather than for personal consumption. Moreover, it implies that there should be no automatic presumption that male partners or spouses are part of the familial picture; and if they are, there should be no automatic assumption that they are trusted to distribute the family earnings in accordance with the wishes of the women migrant wage-earners. As a strategy for negotiating citizenship, the financial independence of women workers is therefore an important factor in the process. This finding adds emphasis to the case for considering female migration patterns distinctly from male migration patterns and marital relations, even when considerations of family support as a motivation for immigration are highlighted.[30]

Conclusion

Despite the small size of this survey sample, certain discernible patterns are revealed in the findings. The citizenship divide on a global scale, enforced by gate keeping mechanisms, is expressed within the private homes of Canadian families. Facing profound obstacles, women workers from the West Indies and the Philippines have negotiated strategies motivated overwhelmingly by the basic desire to support themselves and their families. Our study indicates that the restricted immigration status of both West Indian and Filipino domestic workers has a profound impact on their working and living conditions in Canada. More specifically, the greater the restriction faced at the border, the greater the risk of intense exploitation and discrimination. Our research suggests that the increased restrictions against West Indian workers has only served to increase the likelihood of illegal employment, without leading to any concomitant improvement in domestic service working or living conditions for those of Filipino origin. On the contrary, employers of domestic service continue to be subject to minimal regulation that might ensure a transparent standard of work expectation and enforcement of mechanisms to guarantee workers' legal rights.

The identification of the particular matrix of citizenship, class, race and gendered relations among foreign domestic workers in Canada that we suggest to be evidenced by our study is to our knowledge unique. While several studies have identified patterns of abuse, racism and exploitation, these have either traced general trends, or focused largely on a single racial/citizenship group. Rina Cohen has identified a more instrumental connection between race and job performance, tracing a pattern within domestic service where lighter-skinned workers were nannies, and darker-skinned workers were cleaners and cooks.[31] Our study indicates, alternatively, that there are indeed dramatic variations in the job descriptions and levels of compensation among domestic workers, but these variations are within a general spectrum of exploitation not directly reducible to the country of origin or racial identity of the domestic workforce. Instead, the sharp demarcation in class and citizenship status between the employers and migrant employees, supported by systemic factors in Canada and the world system fundamentally shape the relations of paid domestic labour. As Brigitte Young has aptly summarized:

> The flexibility of the labour market has produced greater equality between educated middle-class women and men while creating greater inequality among women. High value is placed on the integration of professional women into the formal economy while the "paid" reproductive work of women in the informal economy (the household) continues to be undervalued; women's "paid" work outside the home is not equal to women's "paid" work inside it ... These changes have produced two categories of women within the household: professional women and maids.[32]

Our findings revealed the complexity of paid reproductive work performed by live-in household workers. Placed in the wider context of the global political economy, West Indian and Filipino women workers are part of a system that Parrenas refers to as the "international transfer of caretaking." In such a system, women from the Third World care for the children of wealthy women in the First World, and in turn support through their labour and remittances the provision of care for their own children back home.

NOTES

1 Sections of this chapter are drawn from Stasiulis and Bakan 1997.

2 The 50 interviews took place between 1994 and 1995, after the new LCP legislation was enacted. Some of the interviewees arrived in Canada under the previous FDM and others by means elaborated further in the chapter.

3 For purposes of security and confidentiality we did not interview the employers of the domestic workers in this survey, upon whom the interviewees depended for their very livelihood and residence in Canada.

4 Respondents identified Trinidad and Tobago, Jamaica, Barbados and Guyana as the countries of origin among West Indian domestic workers participating in the survey.

5 The reference "Q" followed by a number refers to the question number of the interview schedule. This chapter is an interpretation of selected findings, relevant to the wider analysis of negotiating citizenship rights. The survey questionnaire is available on request from the authors.

6 See Bakan 1987.

7 See Parrenas 2001.

8 According to the Department of Citizenship and Immigration Canada (CIC): "An important requirement of the Programme is that employees must live in the employer's home. The Live-in Caregiver Program exists only because there is a shortage of Canadians to fill the need for live-in care work. There is no shortage of Canadian workers available for caregiving positions where there is no live-in requirement" (1999).

9 See e.g., Arat-Koç and Villasin 2001.

10 See Romero 2002; Chang 2000; Bunster and Chaney 1989 and Heyzer, Nijeholt and Weerakoon 1995.

11 LCP Employment and Immigration Canada 1992.

12 See Department of CIC 1999.

13 According to the CIC: "Any live-in caregiver who decides to live out, or who accepts any other type of employment, can be disqualified from the Program." However, during time off from work, CIC also states that: "Off-duty time is yours to spend as you wish: your employer cannot insist that you spend your own time in his or her house" (1999).

14 Question 4A2A1.

15 The CIC guidelines are silent in regard to house cleaning. However, there is the recommendation of a written contract between the employee and the employer upon acceptance of a job in Canada on the LCP, with the proviso that the federal government has no authority for enforcement and that labour standards vary across the provinces. In the CIC's Sample Contract, "Housekeeping Responsibilities" are, however, listed under the heading of "Care Responsibilities/ Duties," and accompanied by two boxes, "Yes" and "No." Then there is room in the sample contract under the heading "Describe," to explain the specific duties expected. See CIC 1999.
16 See e.g., Chang 2000.
17 The Ontario Employment Standards Act was amended in 2000, but it continues to permit employers the option to give workers time off in lieu of pay for overtime worked. The law specifies that such an arrangement must be agreed upon by the employee and must be met within 12 weeks after the pay is earned. Ontario 2001.
18 See Fudge 1997.
19 INTERCEDE conducted a study in 1989 of live-in domestic workers, which revealed that fully 65 per cent of the 576 workers surveyed, reported they were regularly required to work overtime, but only 33 per cent who were so required received the legal compensation; 43.7 per cent of those required to work overtime received no compensation whatever (Arat-Koç and Villasin, 1990, 5–7).
20 This was based on results from Q4A12A, Q4A12B and Q4A12C, where respondents paid weekly, bi-weekly or monthly, respectively, provided their regular earnings over the appropriate time period. These figures were averaged according to the number of respondents, and divided into hourly units according to the average working week for West Indian and Filipino workers.
21 The Ontario NDP government raised the minimum wage from $5.40 per hour to $6.85 per hour on January 1, 1995. Interviews were conducted both before and after this date.
22 CIC 1999, 5.
23 CIC 1999; Minister of Supply and Services, Canada, 1992, 7.
24 Ontario 2001.
25 In some provinces and territories, the employer is required to pay the cost of belonging to Canada's national health insurance system, while in others the worker is responsible for paying these costs. See CIC 1999, 4.
26 For instance, the Immigration booklet for the Live-in Caregiver lists employment standards that "may" be accessible to domestic workers, depending on provincial/territorial standards as including days off, vacation time with pay, paid public holidays, overtime pay, minimum wage, equal pay, equal benefits, pregnancy leave and notice of employment termination, employment insurance, Canada pension plan and old age security. See CIC, 1999, 4.
27 Stalker 1994, 126.
28 See Heyzer, Nijeholt and Weerakoon1995.
29 See e.g., Eviota 1992; Momsen 1993.
30 Mattei 1996.
31 See Cohen 1987.
32 Young 2000, 315–16.

REFERENCES

Arat-Koç, Sedef, and Fely Villasin. 2001. *Caregivers Break the Silence: A Participatory Action Research on the Abuse and Violence, Including the Impact of Family Separation Experienced by Women in the Live-in Caregiver Program.* Toronto: INTERCEDE.

Arat-Koç, Sedef, and Fely Villasin. 1990. *Report and Recommendations on the Foreign Domestic Movement Program.* INTERCEDE report for submission to the Ministry of Employment and Immigration.

Bakan, Abigail B. 1987. "'The International Market for Female Labour and Individual Deskilling: West Indian Women Workers in Toronto." *Canadian Journal of Latin American and Caribbean Studies* 12 (24): 69–85. http://dx.doi.org/10.1080/08263663.1987.10816594.

Bunster, Ximena, and Elsa M. Chaney. 1989. *Sellers and Servants: Working Women in Lima Peru.* Granby, Mass.: Bergin and Garvey.

Chang, Grace. 2000. *Disposable Domestics: Immigrant Women in the Global Economy.* Cambridge, Mass.: South End Press.

Cohen, Rina. 1987. "The Work Conditions of Immigrant Women Live-in Domestics: Racism, Sexual Abuse, and Invisibility." *Resources for Feminist Research* 16 (1): 36–8.

Department of Citizenship and Immigration Canada (CIC). 1999. "The Live-in Caregiver Program: Information for Employers and Live-in Caregivers from Abroad." Ottawa, February.

Eviota, Elizabeth Uy. 1992. *The Political Economy of Gender: Women and the Sexual Division of Labour in the Philippines.* New Jersey: Zed Books.

Fudge, Judy. 1997. "Little Victories and Big Defeats: The Rise and Fall of Collective Bargaining Rights for Domestic Workers in Ontario." In *Making the Match: Domestic Placement Agencies and the Racialization of Women's Household Work*, ed. Abigail Bakan and Daiva Stasiulis, 119–45. Toronto: University of Toronto Press.

Heyzer, Noeleen, Geertje Lycklama à Nijeholt and Nedra Weerakoon, eds. 1995. *The Trade in Domestic Workers*, vol. 1. London: Zed Books.

L.C.P. Employment and Immigration Canada. 1992. "Operations Memorandum" (Draft). April 23.

Mattei, Linda Miller. 1996. "Gender and International Labor Migration: A Networks Approach." *Social Justice (San Francisco, Calif.)* 23 (3): 38–54.

Minister of Supply and Services, Canada. 1992. 7.

Momsen, Janet, ed. 1993. *Women and Change in the Caribbean.* Bloomington: Indiana University Press.

Ontario. 2001. *Employment Standards - Fuel Sheet: "Domestic Workers'.* http://www.gov.on.ca/LAB/es/dome.htm.

Parrenas, Rhacel. 2001. *Servants of Globalization: Women, Migration, and Domestic Work.* Stanford, CA: Stanford University Press.

Romero, Mary. 2002. *Maid in the USA.* New York: Routledge.

Stalker, Peter. 1994. *Tile Work of Strangers.* Geneva: International Labour Organisation.

Stasiulis, Daiva, and Abigail B. Bakan. 1997. "Negotiating Citizenship Globally: Migrant Domestic Workers as a Case Study." *Feminist Review* 57:112–39. http://dx.doi.org/10.1080/014177897339687.

Young, Brigitte. 2000. "The 'Mistress' and the 'Maid' in the Globalized Economy." In *Socialist Register 2001,* edited by Leo Panitch and Colin Leys, 315–16. Pontypool: Merlin Press.

14 Residential Segregation of Visible Minority Groups in Toronto

ERIC FONG

Racial and ethnic residential integration has been viewed as an indicator of group relations in any society. It is a basic form of association that provides the mechanisms and occasions for intergroup interaction. Intergroup contact in neighbourhoods is unique because it is informal and not competitive (Park 1967; White 1987). Thus it fosters intergroup friendships and corrects misunderstandings among groups (Jackman and Crane 1986; Sigelman, Bledsoe, Welch, and Combs 1996).

Racial and ethnic residential segregation is perceived as a barrier that minority groups must overcome in order to achieve full integration with the larger society (Massey and Mullan 1984). Massey and Mullan contend that assimilation cannot occur in a vacuum. Most interactions occur in a physical environment. Thus the residential integration of minority groups facilitates other types of assimilation, such as labour force participation (Massey and Shibuya 1995) and educational achievement (Kasarda 1989; Wilson 1987).

In explaining residential segregation patterns, Park suggested that "physical and sentimental distances reinforce each other, and the influences of local distribution of the population participate with the influences of class and race in the evolution of the social organization" (1967, 10). Later work delineated three main complementary, albeit sometimes competing, explanations for residential segregation patterns.

The first explanation is that racial and ethnic residential segregation is a reflection of group desirability (Clark 1986; Farley et al. 1978; Massey and Denton 1993). The hypothesis is that every group has neighbourhood preferences in terms of racial and ethnic composition. The racial preferences in the neighbourhood reflect the social distance of various groups (Fong 1997a). A group not welcomed in the neighbourhood is seen as having a greater social distance from other groups.

The racial and ethnic preferences of a neighbourhood affect the residential mobility of minority groups in two ways. First, institutionalized discrimination in the housing market arises to minimize the chances of the unwanted group moving into certain neighbourhoods (Massey and Denton 1993). Through a variety of discriminatory mechanisms, entry by the undesirable group is blocked by local residents. Sometimes the unwanted group must pay higher prices than other groups to move into the same neighbourhoods (Fong 1997b; Massey and Fong 1990). Moreover, some groups go to any lengths to avoid living in the same neighbourhoods as undesirable groups, even if it means paying to move away (Clark 1991; Schelling 1971). Thus when members of an unwelcome group do move into a neighbourhood, rapid residential turnover often follows. Studies have suggested that minority groups are more likely to be treated as undesirable. It has been shown that in the United States and Canada, blacks pay higher prices to move into certain neighbourhoods (Fong 1997b;

Massey and Fong 1990). "White flight" from American urban neighbourhoods because of an increase in black residents has been well documented (Massey and Denton 1993; Farley et al. 1978).

The second explanation for residential patterns was offered by Burgess (1967) in his classic study of the growth of Chicago. Burgess linked residential patterns to the integration processes of immigrants. He elegantly demonstrated how residence in neighbourhoods changes and evolves according to the integration process. He observed that recently arrived immigrants usually cluster in areas next to the central business district, mainly because of lower housing costs. As they stay longer and become socially mobile, they move out of these areas and into better-quality neighbourhoods.

Studies of ethnic communities provide explanations for the residential segregation pattern described by Burgess. When immigrants first settle in a new country, they stay close to their compatriots in order to ease the adjustment process (Piore 1979; Portes and Sensenbrenner 1993). Strong ethnic networks can provide financial, social, and emotional support. As immigrants stay in the country longer, they establish their own networks. At the same time, their attachment to their ethnic group may decrease. At that point they feel less need to stay in the established ethnic community and have more motivation to move out (Alba et al. 1997).

The third explanation for racial and ethnic residential segregation patterns suggests that these patterns reflect differences in the socioeconomic resources of groups (Clark 1986; Massey 1981). Because residential locations are associated with a variety of resources, such as schools, housing, services, and job opportunities, they differentiate the life chances of the groups. Thus once families improve their socioeconomic situation, they seek neighbourhoods with better qualities. Yet in any society, for various sociohistorical reasons, different groups have different socio-economic resources. Groups with fewer socio-economic resources are less competitive in the housing market. Thus when other groups move into neighbourhoods with better qualities, they are left behind. They are less able to move into and share the more desirable neighbourhoods with the other groups (Fong 1997b).

Given that the residential segregation patterns of racial and ethnic groups reflect various aspects of race and ethnic relations, I will discuss the residential segregation of visible minority groups in Toronto. I will focus on visible minority groups because their populations have been growing rapidly as Toronto has become increasingly diversified racially and ethnically. There is extensive literature on racial residential patterns, yet there have been only a few analyses of the racial residential patterns of visible minorities in Toronto, and all of these have been descriptive in nature.

Residential Segregation in Toronto

As Toronto increased its population size and its racial and ethnic diversity at in the beginning of the twentieth century, its segregation levels also rose (Herberg 1989). These levels have become relatively high compared to other Canadian cities. For instance, using the 1981 census data, Balakrishnan and Selvanathan (1990) have documented that Toronto has the second-highest mean segregation scores for all major racial and ethnic groups among the major Canadian census metropolitan areas (CMAs).

Research has also found that segregation levels among racial and ethnic groups in Toronto vary substantially. Until recently, most studies focused on the segregation patterns of European groups before 1980. Visible minorities represented a small proportion of the population, and information about their segregation patterns was limited. Recent studies are beginning to include visible minority groups such as Asians and blacks (Balakrishnan 1976, 1982; Balakrishnan and Selvanathan 1990; Fong 1996, 1997a, 1997b). The results in general show that both these groups experience higher levels of residential segregation from the Charter groups than do other European groups. South Asians in particular usually experience high levels of segregation, similar to those of blacks.

Most studies that explain the differences in residential segregation patterns do not focus on Toronto but explore general patterns of major Canadian cities. Thus, Balakrishnan (1982) posited the importance of social distance among groups. He compared the segregation levels of groups in various Canadian cities and identified persistent residential segregation patterns among groups that corresponded closely to their social distance. Since visible minority groups are at the bottom of the social hierarchy and the Charter groups are at the top, their residential segregation levels are high. In recent studies using the 1991 census (Fong 1997b) found that blacks and South and Southeast Asians have lower levels of spatial contact with the Charter groups, controlling for socio-economic and demographic variables. Similarly, Fong and Gulia (1997, 1999) found that these two groups must pay higher prices than whites to live in neighbourhoods with similar amenities. Fong and his colleagues suggested some possible effects of social distance among groups on the attainment of neighbourhood qualities. However, these studies did not directly or explicitly explore how social distance affects the segregation patterns of visible minority groups.

Another account of the residential segregation patterns of minority groups focused on levels of social integration, which usually are measured by nativity or the length of time since immigration. Fong (1997b) showed that the proportion of immigrants in a group substantially affects the group's spatial contact with Charter groups. Even among minority groups, members who have been in the country for a longer time usually encounter lower levels of segregation from other groups. However, a detailed multivariate study by Fong and Wilkes (1999) showed that among blacks, the effects of length of time in the country on the improvement of neighbourhood qualities become insignificant when other factors are controlled. In addition, Kalbach (1990) obtained mixed results when he compared the segregation levels of major ethnic groups across generations. He found a gradual decline in segregation levels for successive generations of older European immigrant groups (i.e., the Charter groups, northern Europeans, and southern Europeans). However, this general pattern of decline did not apply to recent European immigrants (such as southern and eastern Europeans) or to visible minority groups. Taken as a whole, the empirical evidence suggests that the effects of social integration may apply more to Charter groups and older immigrant groups than to others.

Studies in the United States have identified the importance of a group's socio-economic resources in determining its residential segregation level; however, the impact is not as significant for residential patterns in major Canadian cities (Fong 1996). An early study by Darroch and Marston (1971), based on the 1961 census, showed that the education, occupations, and income of groups explained only very small proportions of residential segregation among groups. In a series of studies based on unique data from the 1986 and 1991 censuses, Fong and his colleagues developed causal models to disentangle the residential segregation patterns of major racial and ethnic groups (Fong 1996; Fong and Gulia 1994, 1997, 1999). They found repeatedly that the effects of socio-economic resources on residential patterns in Canadian cities are insignificant for all groups, including visible minority groups. However, studies by Balakrishnan (1982) and Balakrishnan and Selvanathan (1990) offered a different picture. They discovered a consistent effect of socio-economic resources on residential segregation patterns between 1961 and 1981. Comparing the dissimilarity indexes of census tracts with different socio-economic status, they found segregation levels to be lower in tracts with higher socio-economic status.

It is in this context of mixed research findings and scant information about the residential segregation of visible minority groups in Toronto that I examine the patterns and test the effects of social distance, social integration, and social mobility on the residential segregation patterns of these groups.

Data and Methods

Data for this study were obtained from specially requested tables of the 1996 Canadian census (Statistics Canada 1998). These tables provide detailed socio-economic and demographic information about major racial and ethnic groups. The central purpose of this paper is to compare the residential patterns of these groups. To do so, I have used the census tract as the unit of analysis. Tracts are small areas with an average of four thousand residents. They are drawn to maximize socio-economic homogeneity and are the closest approximation to "neighbourhoods."

The major racial and ethnic groups included in the study are British, French, northern European, western European, eastern European, southern European, East and Southeast Asian, South Asian, and black. Among all these groups, special attention will be given to visible minority groups, including East and Southeast Asians, South Asians, and blacks. Asians are treated as two separate groups because of their different social and cultural backgrounds. For all groups except British and French, I use broad categories (such as East and Southeast Asians) rather than specific ethnic groups (such as Koreans) because using broad geographic locations minimizes the likelihood of suppression due to confidentiality. Statistics Canada requires the suppression of all information about groups in a geographic unit if their number is smaller than 50. I am confident about using the broader geographic designations because past studies have shown that the housing experiences of specific ethnic groups from the same geographic locations are similar (Balakrishnan 1982; Balakrishnan and Selvanathan 1990).

To measure the level of residential segregation, I used the index of dissimilarity, which measures the uneven distribution of two groups. Despite some reviews which have identified limitations of the index, it has been widely used for the last several decades (Pielou 1977; Zoloth 1976). One major advantage is that the index is easy to interpret (White 1986). In addition, the dissimilarity index allows the results obtained from this study to be directly compared with the results obtained from previous studies using the same index.

The index is calculated as,

$$D = \frac{1}{2}\sum_{i=1}^{n}\left|\frac{X_i}{X} - \frac{Y_i}{Y}\right|$$

where X_i and Y_i are the populations of group X and Y in tract i. X and Y are the total populations of group X and Y in the city. The value of the index indicates the percentage of a group that would have to relocate to achieve the same percentage as its distribution in the city. The

Table 14.1 Residential Segregation of Major Racial and Ethnic Groups in Toronto, 1996

	British	French	Northern Europeans	Western Europeans	Eastern Europeans	Southern Europeans	East & Southeast Asians	South Asians	Blacks
British		13.1	33.3	16.6	38.3	47.8	52.5	55.7	52.2
French			35.2	20.9	37.5	46.2	50.0	53.8	50.0
Northern Europeans				35.0	47.0	56.4	54.9	61.7	59.1
Western Europeans					38.7	47.0	53.0	56.5	53.5
Eastern Europeans						45.0	49.9	54.7	52.1
Southern Europeans							48.6	48.7	45.0
East & Southeast Asians								41.8	43.4
South Asians									30.4

Source: 1996 Canadian Census Specially Requested Table

index ranges from 0 to 100. Total segregation is reflected in the maximum value (i.e., 100); a completely unsegregated situation yields a value of 0.

Results

Table 14.1 presents the dissimilarity index for major racial and ethnic groups in Toronto. Although these statistics represent the residential segregation patterns of visible minorities in the city, our discussion focuses on the residential patterns of these groups. The table reveals two interesting findings. First, there are pronounced residential segregation levels between visible minority groups and the Charter groups and northern Europeans and western Europeans. The lowest segregation level between visible minority groups and any of these groups is 50 (French vs blacks; French vs East and Southeast Asians); the highest is 62. Second, the results also show that the segregation levels of eastern and southern Europeans from Asians and blacks are all above 45 – slightly lower than those of the Charter groups and northern and western Europeans. Although the periods of arrival of these groups (eastern Europeans, southern Europeans, Asians, and blacks) were close, they have still experienced high levels of residential segregation along racial lines.

Although our study is about the residential segregation of visible minority groups, I would like to point out a few important patterns among European groups that provide a context for understanding the patterns of visible minority groups. Segregation levels among the Charter groups and northern and western Europeans are low, ranging from 13 to 35. In addition, there are moderate levels of residential segregation of the Charter groups and northern and western Europeans from eastern and southern Europeans. Among these groups, the lowest value of the segregation index is 37.5 (eastern Europeans vs French), and the highest reaches 56.4 (southern vs northern Europeans). The results suggest that northern and western Europeans share similar residential patterns but also that their residential patterns are different from those of southern and eastern Europeans.

It is reasonable to suspect that these patterns indicate the effects of the groups' social integration. Asians and blacks are the most recently arrived groups, followed by southern and eastern Europeans. The average years of arrival among members of the Charter groups and northern and western Europeans were earlier than for any other group. The results closely correspond to length of time in Canada: for Asians and blacks, segregation levels are high with the earlier groups, moderate with southern and eastern Europeans. However, one can argue against this hypothesis about the effects of social integration on residential segregation patterns because the close arrival periods of southern and eastern Europeans vis-a-vis Asians and blacks should not result in their high levels of segregation from one another. The patterns may equally well reflect the socio-economic resources of groups. The relatively lower socio-economic resources of blacks and Asians may affect their ability to move into neighbourhoods with the Charter groups and northern and western Europeans. The patterns may also reflect a stable hierarchy of social distance among groups. According to past studies, visible minorities (Asians and blacks) are at the bottom of the social hierarchy, followed by southern and eastern Europeans (Pineo 1977). The Charter groups and northern and western Europeans are at the top.

The Prevalence of Residential Segregation Among Visible Minorities

The first table documents consistently higher levels of residential segregation of visible minority groups (Asians and blacks) from the Charter groups and other European groups. To further assess the prevalence of residential segregation among visible minority groups in Toronto, I report the proportion of visible minorities living in neighbourhoods with different concentration levels (more than 30, 50 and 70 per cent) of non-visible minority groups. To simplify the presentation, I have combined the Charter groups and all European groups into one category labelled "whites." I have then created two subcategories: "old European immigrant groups" are the two Charter groups and northern and western Europeans, whereas "new European immigrant groups" include southern and eastern Europeans. These two categories reflect the results of Table 14.1: the two Charter groups and northern and western Europeans share similar residential patterns that are uniquely different from those of eastern and southern Europeans. The last two columns in the table show the percentage of visible minorities living in old and new European immigrant neighbourhoods. I define neighbourhoods as old European immigrant neighbourhoods when the concentration of old immigrant groups in the tract is more than half their percentage in the city. The same criterion was used to define new European immigrant neighbourhoods.

The second to fourth columns in Table 14.2 give the average percentages of the three visible minority groups in neighbourhoods with different percentages of whites. The results show a very clear picture. As the percentage of whites living in neighbourhoods rises, the percentages of visible minorities drastically shrink. For example, in neighbourhoods where whites are more than 30 per cent, the average percentage of South Asians is 6 per cent. The percentage drops to 1 per cent in neighbourhoods where whites are more than 70 per cent – a reduction of 75 per cent. Similarly, the presence of blacks decreases from 5 per cent in neighbourhoods with more than 30 per cent white population to1 per cent in neighbourhoods with more than 70 per cent white population. Given the difficulties visible minorities have in gaining access to predominantly white neighbourhoods, it is not surprising to find other research in Canada which shows that visible minorities must pay high prices to live in neighbourhoods with higher proportions of whites (Fong 1997a).

Table 14.2 Distribution of visible minority groups in neighbourhoods by percentages of White in Toronto, 1996

	Average	White > 30%	White > 50%	White > 70%	Old European Immigrant Groups	New European Immigrant Groups
East & Southeast Asians	11.7	8.8	5.9	3.0	10.8	13.6
South Asians	6.8	5.5	3.1	1.4	5.6	8.6
Blacks	5.9	5.1	3.3	1.3	4.9	7.9

Source: 1996 Canadian Census Specially Requested Table

The last two columns break the white population into old and new European immigrant groups. The results show that lower percentages of Asians and blacks live in neighbourhoods with predominantly old European immigrant groups than in neighbourhoods with new European immigrant groups. When we fold these findings into the results reported in Table 14.1, we see that even when visible minority groups share neighbourhoods with whites, a smaller proportion of them live in neighbourhoods with the old European immigrant groups that have been in Canada for a longer time and that are socially and culturally established. This segregation between old immigrant groups and visible minority groups in the city suggests that it may be difficult for visible minority groups to achieve full participation in the larger society and to share neighbourhoods with the more established groups in Canada.

Distribution of Visible Minorities in Toronto

Our analyses so far only show the levels of residential segregation; they do not reveal the geographic distribution or the locations where the racial and ethnic groups reside. This information is important because it provides a glimpse of the desirability and accessibility of the locations where groups reside. In the following discussion I present two series of maps. The first shows the distribution of groups in the city of Toronto and neighbouring suburbs. The second displays the distribution of groups in the Toronto CMA designated by Statistics Canada. The area covered is much larger since it includes the outer suburbs of Toronto. To facilitate this discussion, I have classified census tracts into three types: a particular group's population in the tract is either 4 per cent above its city distribution, or 0 to 4 per cent above its city distribution, or below its city distribution. These classifications can be interpreted as high, moderate, and low concentrations of a group in the tract.

Figure 14.1 shows the distribution of East and Southeast Asians in the city of Toronto and neighbouring suburbs. Most East and Southeast Asians live in middle-class suburbs such as Markham and Scarborough or near the downtown area of Toronto. Those living in the middle-class suburbs may represent recent immigrants from Hong Kong, Taiwan, and Korea who have financial resources. East and Southeast Asians are highly concentrated in a few locations. About 177 of the 633 census tracts have a proportion of East and Southeast Asians that is 4 per cent or more than their city proportion. The number of such tracts is much higher for other groups. Most South Asians, as shown in Figure 14.2, live in middle-class suburbs such as Mississauga; however, a closer look suggests that most of them live in relatively poorer areas of these suburbs, such as southern Scarborough. This suggests that their socioeconomic resources may be limited. Figures 14.3 and 14.4 show clearly that both Asian groups are underrepresented in the outer suburbs.

Figures 14.5 and 14.6 show the distribution of blacks. Figure 14.5 shows that blacks are scattered in diverse areas of Toronto. These areas are always associated with poorer

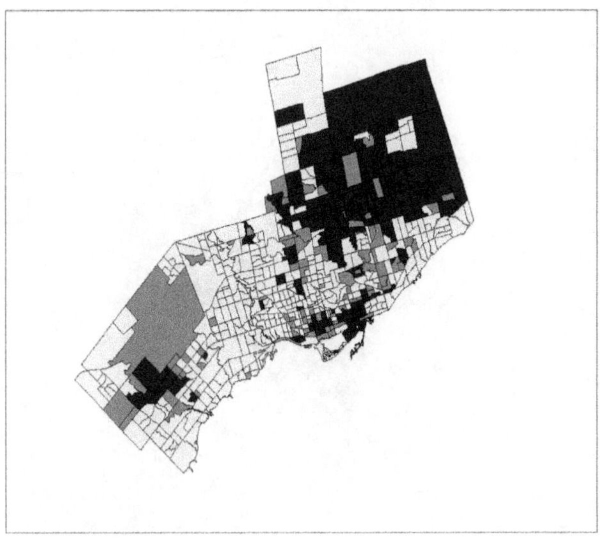

Figure 14.1 Distribution of East and Southeast Asians in the City of Toronto and neighbouring suburbs, 1996

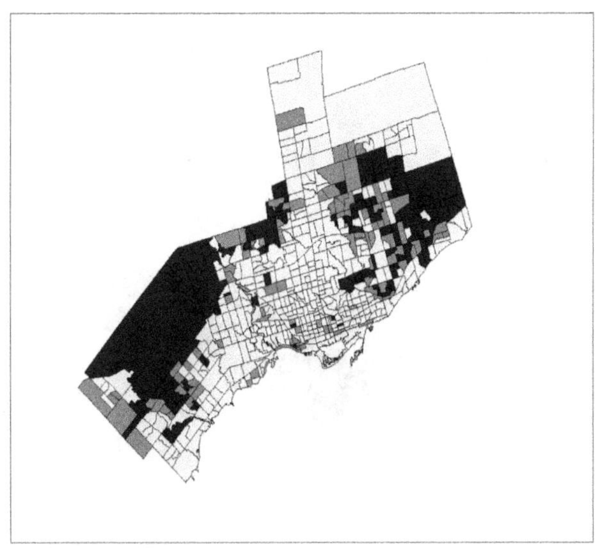

Figure 14.2 Distribution of South Asians in City of Toronto and neighbouring suburbs, 1996

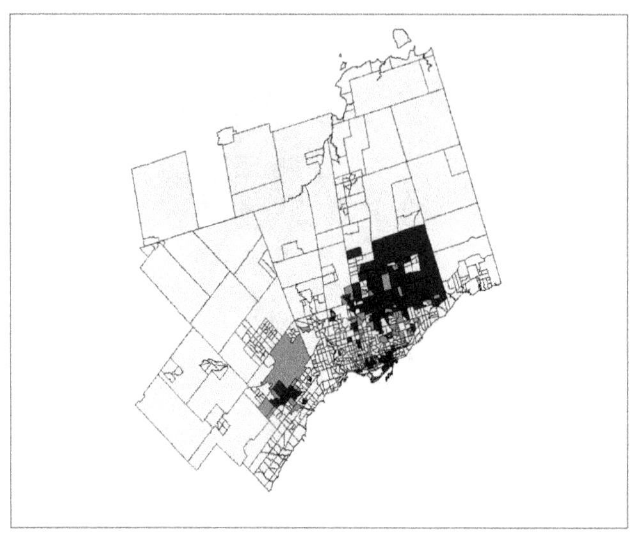

Source: 1996 Census Specially Requested Table

Deviation of Group % in Tract
from Group % in the City

■ 4% and above (177)
■ 0% - 4% (92)
□ 0% (544)

Figure 14.3 Distribution of East and Southeast Asians in Toronto Metropolitan Area, 1996

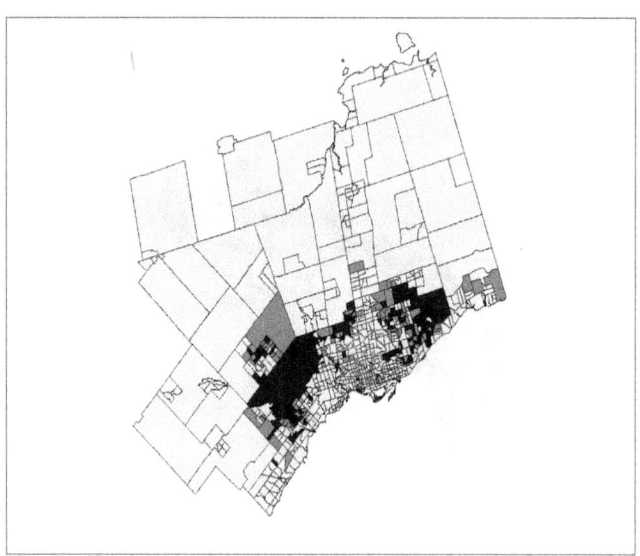

Source: 1996 Census Specially Requested Table

Deviation of Group % in Tract
from Group % in the City

■ 4% and above (140)
■ 0% - 4% (119)
□ 0% (554)

Figure 14.4 Distribution of South Asians in Toronto CMA, 1996

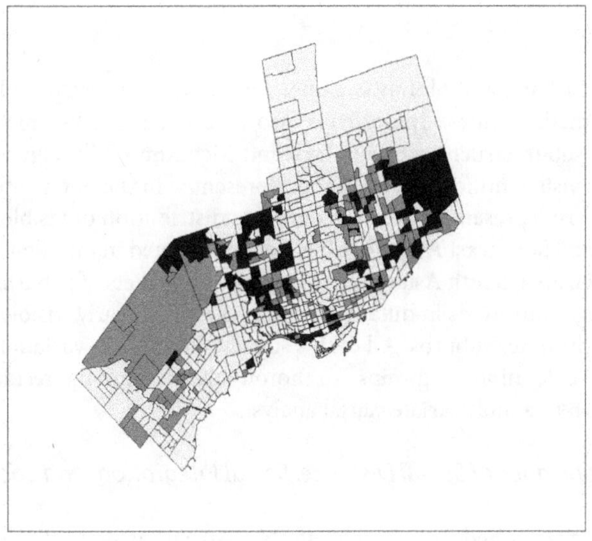

Source: 1996 Census Specially Requested Table

Deviation of Group % in Tract
from Group % in the City

- 4% and above (118)
- 0% - 4% (124)
- 0% (391)

Figure 14.5 Distribution of Blacks in City of Toronto and neighbouring suburbs, 1996

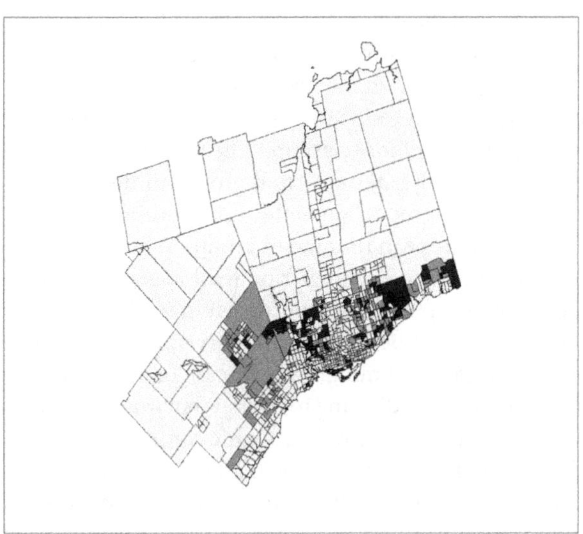

Source: 1996 Census Specially Requested Table

Deviation of Group % in Tract
from Group % in the City

- 4% and above (125)
- 0% - 4% (152)
- less than 0% (536)

Figure 14.6 Distribution of Blacks in Toronto CMA, 1996

amenities, echoing Fong and Shibuya's earlier finding (2000) that poor blacks are highly segregated in Canadian cities. These maps also reveal that blacks are underrepresented in more affluent suburbs such as North York and Richmond Hill. Figure 14.6 shows that blacks, like other visible minorities, are underrepresented in the outer suburbs.

In sum, these maps present a diverse geographic distribution of visible minority groups in Toronto. East and Southeast Asians are highly concentrated in middle-class communities and the downtown area; South Asians are living in poor pockets of suburbs; blacks are scattered in poor neighbourhoods in different parts of the city. Clearly, visible minority groups are not living in the outer suburbs. All of this suggests significant variations in the residential patterns of visible minority groups. To thoroughly examine the residential patterns of groups, I now turn to a multivariate causal analysis.

The Relative Importance of Social Distance, Social Integration, and Social Mobility

Past analyses have suggested the possible effects of social integration, social distance, and social mobility on the residential patterns of visible minority groups in Toronto. However, the relative importance of these factors has yet to be determined. In this section I develop causal models to compare their relevance.

I compare the effects of the three possible factors on the residential segregation levels of visible minority groups. The dependent variables are the proportion of whites, older European immigrant groups, and new European immigrant groups. I have included three sets of independent variables in order to capture the possible effects of social integration, social mobility, and social distance. The first set of variables is intended to measure the social integration of visible minority groups. They are the proportion of minority groups in the tract who are immigrants and the proportion who do not know either official language (i.e., English or French). The immigrant population of the visible minority groups is further differentiated into the proportion who arrived after 1992. According to the discussion of the effects of social integration on residential segregation, one would expect a larger immigrant proportion of the visible minority group to be associated with a smaller proportion of whites and old and new European immigrant groups in the tracts. I further expect the effects of the recent immigrant proportion of the visible minority groups on the proportion of whites and old and new European immigrant groups to be stronger because immigrants who have been in the country for a short period tend to stay with members of their own ethnic groups. In addition, I expect a higher proportion of visible minority individuals not knowing any official language to be related to a lower proportion of whites and old and new European immigrant groups. Immigrants who are unable to speak either official language face enormous obstacles in adjusting to the new environment, so they have a stronger incentive to maintain social contact with their ethnic community.

The social mobility hypothesis argues that higher levels of socioeconomic status are associated with lower levels of residential segregation for visible minority groups. In this study, socio-economic status is measured by the median household income of the minority groups in the tract and by the proportion of members who completed university education. A higher median income and a larger proportion of members with university education are expected to be related to lower levels of residential segregation. More group socio-economic resources would imply that members have more choices in residential location.

Finally, the social distance between groups is indicated by the intercept of the model. Once we control for social integration levels and for the socio-economic status of the visible

Table 14.3 Estimated coefficients for selective variables on proportion of whites, old European immigrant groups, and new European immigrant groups in Toronto neighbourhoods, 1996

	Proportion of Whites	Proportion of Old European Immigrant Groups	Proportion of New European Immigrant Groups
East and Southeast Asians			
Median Education	0.121*	0.255**	−0.147**
Median Income	0.002	0.027	0.001
Prop. not knowing English./French	−0.173**	−0.190**	0.024
Prop. Immigrants	−0.318**	−0.433**	0.123*
Prop. Recent Immigrants (arrived after 1992)	−0.259**	−0.145**	−0.111*
Intercept	0.736**	0.561**	0.160**
R^2	0.214	0.314	0.022
N	733	733	733
South Asians			
Median Education	0.097**	0.175**	−0.078*
Median Income	−0.003	−0.001	−0.000
Prop. not knowing English./French	−0.039	−0.177*	−0.177*
Prop. Immigrants	−0.111**	−0.086*	−0.025
Prop. Recent Immigrants (arrived after 1992)	−0.154**	−0.138**	−0.016**
Intercept	0.586**	0.346**	0.306**
R^2	0.059	0.114	0.019
N	733	733	733
Blacks			
Median Education	0.138**	0.178**	−0.036
Median Income	−0.008**	0.002	−0.040
Prop. not knowing English./French	−0.755*	−0.953**	0.198
Prop. Immigrants	−0.116**	−0.172**	0.056
Prop. Recent Immigrants (arrived after 1992)	0.004	−0.244**	0.248**
Intercept	0.572**	0.399**	0.173**
R^2	0.043	0.135	0.065
N	733	733	733

Note: p** < 0.05; p* < 0.1
Source: 1996 Canadian Census Specially Requested Table

minority groups, we can interpret the intercept as the initial level of residential segregation of the visible minority group. By comparing the intercepts of the models for different groups, we will be able to see the relative distance of each visible minority group with whites, older European immigrant groups, and newer European immigrant groups.

In Table 14.3 I present the results of a set of regression equations that estimate the effects of the three proposed factors (social integration, socio-economic status, and social distance) on the proportion of whites, the proportion of old European immigrant groups, and the proportion of newer European immigrant groups in the neighbourhoods. I ran separate models for each visible minority group. The results can be used to compare the possibly different effects of social integration, socio-economic status, and social distance on the residential patterns of visible minority groups.

The first column delineates the results of the models for the proportion of whites. There is strong and significant support of the social integration hypothesis for East and Southeast Asians. For those two groups, all three variables intended to capture the effects of social integration (proportion of group members not knowing any official language, proportion of immigrants, and proportion of recent immigrants) are negatively related to the proportion of whites. For the two other groups – South Asians and blacks – not all three variables are related to the proportion of whites. However, the effects of any of the social integration variables that are related to the proportion of whites are markedly strong. Although the literature suggests that income and education should be positively related to the proportion of whites in the neighbourhood, results show that for all three visible minority groups, only education is significant (moderately) to the proportion of whites in the neighbourhood.

Since the intercept of the model can be interpreted as the beginning segregation level of the visible minority group, the comparison of intercepts among models identifies the relative social distance of the three visible minority groups from whites. The results of this analysis correspond to the relative social distances of the three visible minority groups documented in other studies: both South Asians and blacks have distinctively disadvantaged beginning levels compared to East and Southeast Asians.

In columns 2 and 3, I further compare the effects of social integration, socio-economic status, and social distance at the spatial contact level with old and newer European immigrant groups. The comparison shows the relative importance of the three proposed factors on residential patterns for visible minority groups with whites who arrived in different time periods.

In general, the results in column 2 reflect a consistently strong effect of social integration and a moderate effect of socio-economic resources on the spatial contact between older immigrant groups and visible minorities. All visible minority groups with higher levels of education, lower proportions of members not knowing any official language, lower proportions of immigrants, and lower proportions of recent immigrants have increased levels of spatial contact with older European immigrant groups. A closer look suggests that most of the effects of socio-economic variables on the proportion of old European immigrant groups are consistently stronger when compared with the previous models. When the intercepts of all three visible minority groups are compared, the results show a similar picture: both South Asians and blacks are at more disadvantaged beginning levels of spatial contact with older European immigrant groups than are East and Southeast Asians.

Column 3 shows a different picture. The level of social integration is not always related to the proportion of new European immigrant groups in the neighbourhoods. A higher proportion of immigrants and a higher proportion of recent immigrants – if the effects are statistically significant – are not always related to lower proportions of new European immigrant groups. Similar patterns are also found with the socioeconomic variables. Even when socio-economic variables are related to the proportion of newer European immigrant groups, they are not in the expected direction.

Taken together, the results show a clear picture. Groups with higher socio-economic status and integration levels are associated with higher proportions of whites in the neighbourhoods. In other words, the socioeconomic and social integration levels of a visible minority group explain its residential patterns. Some visible minority groups face disadvantaged beginning positions in improving their residential integration with whites; this corresponds to their social distance from whites in society. However, when the analysis further compares the old and newer European immigrant groups, the results reveal that these relationships only apply to the older groups. The findings regarding spatial contact between new European immigrant groups and visible minority groups give another picture: Socioeconomic status is not necessarily related to the proportion of new European immigrants, and a higher proportion of immigrants in the visible minority group is related to a higher proportion of newer European immigrant groups in the neighbourhoods.

Conclusion

This chapter documented the residential segregation levels of visible minority groups, the fastest-growing and newest immigrant groups in Toronto. Based on the 1996 census data, results show that the residential segregation levels of visible minority groups are higher with the older European immigrant groups than with recent European immigrant groups. The extent of segregation in the city between the old immigrant groups and visible minority groups suggests that it may be difficult for visible minority groups to achieve full participation in the larger society and to share neighbourhoods with the more established groups in Canada. The results also suggest significant variations in the geographic distribution of the visible minority groups. East and Southeast Asians are highly concentrated in middle-class communities and the downtown area; South Asians are living in poor pockets of suburbs; blacks are scattered in different parts of the city where poor neighbourhoods are usually found. Visible minority groups clearly are not living in the outer suburbs. The information suggests substantial differences in the residential patterns of visible minority groups.

To disentangle the factors affecting the residential segregation levels of visible minority groups, I examined their social integration levels, socio-economic status, and social distance from other groups. The data indicate that all three processes are operating. First, the effects of social integration on the residential segregation of visible minority groups are strong and consistent. The results suggest that as visible minority groups – especially old European groups – stay in the country longer, their residential segregation levels from European groups decline. However, this optimistic picture is blurred by another major finding in the study – the social distances among groups also play a significant role in the residential patterns of visible minority groups. South Asians and blacks at the bottom of the social hierarchy are in a more disadvantaged position in the beginning process of residential integration. Finally, the results show that socio-economic resources affect the residential segregation levels of visible minority groups. However, this effect is more applicable in relation to old European immigrant groups than to new European immigrant groups.

The data form a complex picture. On the one hand, as visible minority groups stay in the country longer, their residential segregation levels from European groups decline. On the other hand, the spatial integration processes for some visible minority groups are hampered by their social distance from European groups. The evidence suggests that the spatial integration processes of visible minority groups do not rely solely on their ability to integrate and their socio-economic achievements, but rather depend on other factors – such as social distance from other groups – that are beyond their control.

REFERENCES

Alba, Richard D., John R. Logan, and Kyle Crowder. 1997. "White Ethnic Neighborhoods and Assimilation: The Greater New York Region, 1980-1990." *Social Forces* 75 (3): 883–912. http://dx.doi.org/10.1093/sf/75.3.883.

Balakrishnan, T.R. 1982. "Changing Patterns of Ethnic Residential Segregation in the Metropolitan Areas of Canada." *Canadian Review of Sociology and Anthropology. La Revue Canadienne de Sociologie et d'Anthropologie* 19 (1): 92–110. http://dx.doi.org/10.1111/j.1755-618X.1982.tb01323.x.

Balakrishnan, T.R. 1976. "Ethnic Residential Segregation in the Metropolitan Areas of Canada." *Canadian Journal of Sociology* 1 (4): 481–98. http://dx.doi.org/10.2307/3339757.

Balakrishnan, T.R., and K. Selvanathan. 1990. "Ethnic Residential Segregation in Metropolitan Canada." In *Ethnic Demography*, ed. Shiver S. Halli, Frank Trovato, and Leo Driedger, 393–413. Ottawa: Carleton University Press.

Burgess, Ernest W. 1967. "The Growth of the City: An Introduction to a Research Project." In *The City*, ed. Robert E. Park, Ernest W. Burgess, and Roderick D. McKenzie, 47–62. Chicago, IL: University of Chicago Press.

Clark, William A.V. 1991. "Residential Preferences and Neighborhood Racial Segregation: A Test of the Schelling Segregation Model." *Demography* 28 (1): 1–20. http://dx.doi.org/10.2307/2061333.

Clark, William A.V. 1986. "Residential Segregation in American Cities: A Review and Interpretation." *Population Research and Policy Review* 5 (2): 95–127. http://dx.doi.org/10.1007/BF00137176.

Darroch, Gordon A., and Wilfred G. Marston. 1971. "The Social Class Basis of Ethnic Residential Segregation: The Canadian Case." *American Journal of Sociology* 77 (3): 491–510. http://dx.doi.org/10.1086/225160.

Farley, Reynolds, Howard Schuman, Suzanne Bianchi, Diane Colasanto, and Shirley Hatchett. 1978. "Chocolate City, Vanilla Suburbs: Will the Trend Toward Racially Separate Communities Continue?" *Social Science Research* 7 (4): 319–44. http://dx.doi.org/10.1016/0049-089X(78)90017-0.

Fong, Eric. 1997a. "A Systemic Approach to Racial Residential Patterns." *Social Science Research* 26 (4): 465–86. http://dx.doi.org/10.1006/ssre.1997.0605.

Fong, Eric. 1997b. "Residential Proximity with the Charter Groups in Canada." *Canadian Studies in Population* 24 (2): 103–24.

Fong, Eric. 1996. "A Comparative Perspective of Racial Residential Segregation: American and Canadian Experiences." *Sociological Quarterly* 37 (2): 199–226. http://dx.doi.org/10.1111/j.1533-8525.1996.tb01746.x.

Fong, Eric, and Milena Gulia. 1999. "Differences in Neighborhood Qualities among Major Racial and Ethnic Groups in Canada." *Sociological Inquiry* 69 (4): 575–98. http://dx.doi.org/10.1111/j.1475-682X.1999.tb00887.x.

Fong, Eric, and Milena Gulia. 1997. "The Effects of Group Characteristics and City Contexts on Neighborhood Qualities of Racial and Ethnic Groups." *Canadian Studies in Population* 24:45–66.

Fong, Eric, and Milena Gulia. 1994. "Residential Proximity among Racial Groups in U.S. and Canadian Neighborhoods." *Urban Affairs Quarterly* 30 (2): 285–97. http://dx.doi.org/10.1177/004208169403000206.

Fong, Eric, and Kumiko Shibuya. 2000. "Spatial Separation of the Poor in Canadian Cities." *Demography* 37 (4): 449–59. http://dx.doi.org/10.1353/dem.2000.0003.

Fong, Eric, and Rima Wilkes. 1999. "An Examination of Spatial Assimilation Model." *International Migration Review* 33:594–620. http://dx.doi.org/10.2307/2547527.

Herberg, Edward N. 1989. *Ethnic Groups in Canada: Adaptations and Transitions*. Scarborough, ON: Nelson Canada.

Jackman, Mary R., and Marie Crane. 1986. "'Some of my best friends are black ...': Interracial Friendship and Whites' Racial Attitudes." *Public Opinion Quarterly* 50 (4): 459–86. http://dx.doi.org/10.1086/268998.

Kalbach, Warren E. 1990. "Ethnic Residential Segregation and Its Significance for the Individual in an Urban Setting." In *Ethnic Identity and Inequality*, ed. Raymond Breton, Wsevolod W. Isajiew, Warren E. Kalbach, and Jeffrey G. Reitz, 92–134. Toronto: University of Toronto Press.

Kasarda, John D. 1989. "Urban Industrial Transition and the Underclass." *American Academy of Political and Social Science* 501 (1): 26–47. http://dx.doi.org/10.1177/0002716289501001002.

Massey, Douglas S. 1981. "Social Class and Ethnic Segregation: A Reconsideration of Methods and Conclusions." *American Sociological Review* 46 (5): 641–50. http://dx.doi.org/10.2307/2094945.

Massey, Douglas S., and Nancy A. Denton. 1993. *American Apartheid: Segregation and the Making of the Underclass*. Cambridge, MA: Harvard University Press.

Massey, Douglas S., and Eric Fong. 1990. "Segregation and Neighborhood Quality: Blacks, Hispanics, and Asians in the San Francisco Metropolitan Area." *Social Forces* 69 (1): 15–32. http://dx.doi.org/10.1093/sf/69.1.15.

Massey, Douglas S., and Brendan P. Mullan. 1984. "Processes of Hispanic and Black Spatial Assimilation." *American Journal of Sociology* 89 (4): 836–73. http://dx.doi.org/10.1086/227946.

Massey, Douglas S., and Kumiko Shibuya. 1995. "Unraveling the Tangle of Pathology: The Effect of Spatially Concentrated Joblessness on the Well-Being of African Americans." *Social Science Research* 24 (4): 352–66. http://dx.doi.org/10.1006/ssre.1995.1014.

Park, Robert E. 1967. "The City: Suggestions for the Investigation of Human Behavior in the Urban Environment." In *The City*, ed. Robert E. Park, Ernest W. Burgess, and Roderick D. McKenzie, 1–46. Chicago: University of Chicago Press.

Pielou, E.G. 1977. *Mathematical Ecology*. New York: Wiley.

Pineo, Peter C. 1977. "The Social Standing of Ethnic and Racial Groupings." *Canadian Review of Sociology and Anthropology. La Revue Canadienne de Sociologie et d'Anthropologie* 14 (2): 147–57. http://dx.doi.org/10.1111/j.1755-618X.1977.tb00338.x.

Piore, Michael. 1979. *Birds of Passage: Migrant Labor and Industrial Societies*. New York: Cambridge University Press. http://dx.doi.org/10.1017/CBO9780511572210.

Portes, Alejandro, and Julia Sensenbrenner. 1993. "Embeddedness and Immigration: Notes on the Social Determinants of Economic Action." *American Journal of Sociology* 98 (6): 1320–50. http://dx.doi.org/10.1086/230191.

Sigelman, Lee, Timothy Bledsoe, Susan Welch, and Michael W. Combs. 1996. "Making Contact? Black-White Social Interaction in an Urban Setting." *American Journal of Sociology* 101 (5): 1306–32. http://dx.doi.org/10.1086/230824.

Schelling, T. 1971. "Dynamic Models of Segregation." *Journal of Mathematical Sociology* 1 (2): 143–86. http://dx.doi.org/10.1080/0022250X.1971.9989794.

Statistics Canada. 1998. *1996 Census Custom Data - Job E00352*. Toronto: Statistics Canada.

White, Michael. 1987. *American Neighborhoods and Residential Differentiation*. New York: Russell Sage Foundation.

White, Michael. 1986. "Segregation and Diversity Measures in Population Distribution." *Population Index* 52 (2): 198–221. http://dx.doi.org/10.2307/3644339.

Wilson, William Julius. 1987. *The Truly Disadvantaged*. Chicago: University of Chicago Press.

Zoloth, B.S. 1976. "Alternative Measures of School Segregation." *Land Economics* 52 (3): 278–98. http://dx.doi.org/10.2307/3145527.

PART FIVE

Transnational Encounters

15 Sweet and Sour: Historical Presence and Diasporic Agency

LILY CHO

Sweet and sour pork is one thing in English. In Cantonese it tells a very different story. This chapter is a meditation on the significance of that difference. Thinking about the story of the naming of sweet and sour pork in Cantonese I came to questions about the relationship between postcolonial and diaspora studies, and the question of agency. These questions brought me to another story of food and naming that is set in nineteenth-century Hong Kong. Through two stories of food and rumour, this chapter is concerned with the problem of reading for agency not just in the slenderness of historical narrative, but also in the precariousness of migrancy.

I will begin in Hong Kong and close somewhere in small town Canada. It is also a trajectory that moves from the postcolonial to the diasporic. I am aware that this chapter seems to move from the specificity of Hong Kong and postcoloniality into the vagueness of an un-named small town somewhere in the vastness of the Canadian landscape and the quality of dispersion that characterizes diaspora. It is not that the space of diaspora is necessarily so vague, but rather, as I will show, that it is marked by a precariousness that flourishes in dispersion.

Let me turn then to the first meal: Hong Kong, 1857.

At the time, many Hong Kong Europeans bought fresh bread daily from the E Sing Bakery belonging to a Chinese man, Cheong Ah Lum. On 15 January 1857, large numbers of that European community became violently ill. The colonial police were called in; the investigation was immediate; and it was soon discovered that the cause of the January 15th illness was this: arsenic in the morning loaves. Fortunately, for the colonialists, the arsenic had been added to the loaves in such large quantities that most of the poisoned Europeans vomited at once and thus ejected most of the poison from their systems. Although Ah Lum, the owner of the bakery, had left that same morning to Macau with his family, they soon tracked him down. At the trial, he claimed to have known nothing of the incident and that his own family had also been violently ill that day. The real crisis began when Ah Lum was acquitted at the trial. Fifty-two of his workers were jailed and 10 were tried. It was eventually decided that the Chinese government in Canton probably incited the poisoning, but no proof was ever found. Mass arrests followed the poisoning and thousands of Chinese were deported. Ultimately, 26,000 Chinese people left Hong Kong that year.[1]

In the Ah Lum affair, as it came to be known, we are confronted with a colonial dynamic where anti-colonial political agency is, at best, dispersed. There is a massive overdetermination. It brings the colonial government to the vexing problem of an obvious occasion of criminality where there is no clear single agent. Fifty-two workers were arrested. Ten were tried. But Ah Lum himself, the man whose name became synonymous with the entire incident, was acquitted. And there were no answers. Despite the attempts of the colonial government to bring justice to the colony, the discourse of rumour and panic amplified the incident; very quickly, the poisoning moved beyond Ah Lum, beyond the 52 incarcerated workers, beyond 10 convicted felons: it amounted to mass arrests and mass deportations. The Ah Lum affair touched the skittish nerve of the British community.

In the introduction to *Elementary Aspects of Peasant Insurgency in Colonial India*, Ranajit Guha offers a way of reading for peasant insurgency despite the paucity of non-elite, non-colonial primary historical materials. Examining colonial documents, Guha suggests that the colonial archive betrays itself. In the uncertainty, the gaps of that archive, there is the possibility of reading for a peasant rebel consciousness.

> For counter-insurgency, which derives directly from insurgency and is determined by the latter in all that is essential to its form and articulation, can hardly afford a discourse that is not fully and compulsively involved with the rebel and his activities. It is of course true that the reports, despatches, minutes, judgments, laws, letters, etc. in which policemen, soldiers, bureaucrats, landlords, usurers and others hostile to insurgency register their sentiments, amount to a representation of their will. But these documents do not get their content from that will alone, for the latter is predicated on another will – that of the insurgent. (Guha 1983, 15)

In the spirit of Guha's project, we can read in the colonial archive of the letters, dispatches, and laws for the history of anti-British Chinese insurgency.

Sir John Bowring, then governor of Hong Kong, communicated the news of the poisoning to Her Majesty's Government in Britain in a letter that is itself a performance of a futile attempt to contain the fear and panic that gripped the colony. Writing on the morning of the poisoning, Bowring details the increase of various security measures and begs twice "to impress [upon] Her Majesty's Government the urgent necessity of sending at once, from India if possible, a Force of not less than 5000 men" (Hong Kong Public Records Office, CO, 129–62, at 95). The letter begins with references to a series of previous despatches of previous ordinances concerning the security of the colony. Bowring refers only ambiguously to the poisoning: "I now forward copies of four Government modifications, issued in connection with that Ordinance and *the existing condition of things*" (93, emphasis added). Bowring's letter attempts to maintain the formality of official correspondence. It outlines the official response to the crisis in the form of the actions they have taken: the appointment of a new assistant to the superintendent of police; the increase of the police force itself by one hundred men, 50 English and 50 Indian; the hiring of a merchant steamer to patrol the waters in the bays and creeks surrounding Hong Kong until English gun boats arrive. Bowring only gestures to the poisoning. His letter suppresses the news of the poisoning until it explodes at the end of the letter into a full-out admission of panic. It is not until close to the end of the letter that Bowring describes the events that lead to these new security measures:

> Incendiarism was the only subject of our apprehension till this morning when a diabolical attempt was made to poison the foreign community by putting arsenic in the bread supplied by the Esing [*sic*] Bakery and largely used in the town. The principal, one Alum [*sic*] is said to have absconded to Macao, and I have this instant written to the Governor of that Settlement desiring assistance in his apprehension. (94)

After detailing the news of the poisoning itself, Bowring closes the letter with his second entreaty for military reinforcement and declares that "these may be necessary for the defence of the Colony, and certainly are for the assertion of our Treaty Rights, the security of our Trade, and the very maintenance of our position in China" (95). It is finally only in the postscript that Bowring permits himself the admission of a moment of personal panic. Scrawled at the end of the letter, Bowring adds: "PS I beg to apologize if anything should have been forgotten at this last moment – I am shaken by the effects of poison, *every member* of my family being at this moment suffering from this new attempt upon our lives" (94). Only after five pages of official reporting does Bowring finally arrive at an explanation for the actions he has taken. His emotional anxiety only resurfaces all the more powerfully in the postscript – the attempt to script the poisoning after the fact of its occurrence.

In "The Prose of Counter-Insurgency," Guha (1988) notes that there is a quality of raw, instantaneousness that accompanies primary historical documents written first-hand by those who had the most to fear from anti-colonial resistance. It is a quality that is suppressed, contained, and controlled in secondary and tertiary historical treatments. In the case of Bowring's first letter reporting the poisoning, Bowring's own attempt to suppress the rawness of his fear makes the tenor of his panic all the more vociferous.

In the panic of Hong Kong, January 1857, I cannot help but hear the echo of Meerut, May 1857 – the beginning of the so-called Indian Mutiny or Sepoy Rebellion. Word had reached the British that chapatis were being passed, from hand to hand, in the villages surrounded by the British military cantonments. Homi Bhabha's essay "By Bread Alone" suggests that we might read the agency of the chapati not in the ambiguity of the content of the message embedded in the chapati, but rather in the productivity of rumour, the contagion of panic. Moreover, the chapati frustrates the colonial desire for a single agent of history. Bhabha's conclusion is in part that the power of the chapati narrative lies precisely in the failure of colonial authority to pin it down to a single agent, to secure it by naming it.

Even when colonial authority has named its agent, it still cannot secure it. One of the problems for colonial authority that emerges throughout the archive lies in the simple problem of finding a name for the man they had deemed to be guilty of the poisoning. Ah Lum's name is spelled differently, ranging from Alum to Allum to Ah Lum and so on, in almost every letter referring to the incident.[2] There is no stability to his identity from a colonial referent point. In that first report of the poisoning, Bowring's letter reveals its anxieties around the problem of naming in the marginalia. In his naming of Ah Lum as the primary culprit, Bowring admits his own ignorance of the baker's identity. Next to the sentence "The principal, one Alum is said to have absconded to Macao" Bowring writes in the margin, "*merely a mythical name*" (PRO, CO, 129–62, at 94, emphasis added). Despite Bowring's desire to fix Ah Lum as the principal perpetrator, his own marginalia transport Ah Lum into the larger collective space of myth. Not only is his identity unfixable in the language of the colonial, but, despite the colonial desire for a single agent, Ah Lum's identity emerges into something larger.

The naming of the entire affair also reveals the way in which Ah Lum came to stand in for something larger than himself. The bakery poisoning in 1857 became known in the English-language newspapers in Hong Kong at the time as the Ah Lum Affair. In other words, the man who was deemed by the British court to be innocent of any knowledge of the poisoning nevertheless became synonymous with the poisoning. Why, in the popular colonial imaginary, did the event not become known as the E Sing Affair? How is it that Cheong Ah Lum comes to occupy a central place in the incident? Subsequent events suggest one answer. Taking the indignation of the English community upon himself, William Tarrant, the editor of one of the major papers at the time, the *Friend of China and Hong Kong*

Gazette, sued Cheong Ah Lum for damages. Tarrant was awarded $1010, but Ah Lum left the colony before he could collect.[3] The judgment of the colonial court failed to converge with a decision that the English community had already made: that Ah Lum was the central agent in the poisoning. Tarrant's actions articulate the lingering accusation, the persistent desire for identifying, securing, and incarcerating a single agent. The naming of the affair exposes the colonial authorial desire for a single agent of history.

Long before Tarrant's actions, the Hong Kong attorney general's letter to the Colonial Secretary already exposes the failings of colonial governance. In a letter dated 20 January 1857, only five days after the poisoning, the attorney general, T. Chisholm Anstey, reveals the fissures that had begun to emerge within the colonial bureaucracy itself. He writes to W.T. Mercer, the Colonial Secretary:

> At a private conversation with His Excellency to which I understood myself to be invited, I had also this morning informed him that since last evening I have had cause to apprehend a failure of justice in the event of the poisoners being tried in the Criminal Court. The common jurors of Hong Kong are not generally men of affluent circumstances, and it is believed that most of the houses of business are in debt to their own Compradors or Shroffs. These latter again are strongly of the party, or under the influence of the miscreant Allum [*sic*], a man of wealth and, of course, a moneylender. Placards having been posted everywhere calling *his friends* to his assistance, the Compradors and Shroffs have – generally responded to the call, and they are going about to the European houses asserting violently *his* innocence, and the duty of the Court to set him free. One European so influenced may defeat the course of justice by simply becoming a juror, should chance so determine.
>
> I simply informed His Excellency: I did not advise him: I continued of the opinion expressed in my letter of Sunday last the 18th instant that it was not for me to advise whether a Court Martial should be appointed to try cases of this kind during the present crisis: eminently desirable as many think it, and much as the general enforcement of Martial Law is unquestionably required.
>
> I shall however obey His Excellency's desire that no information be laid before him that is not reduced to writing and addressed to the Colonial Secretary; although I cannot help fearing that the present awful crisis will not be best provided for by a general adherence to His Excellency's wishes in that respect, on the part of persons, like myself, who are anxious not to lose time in communicating the intelligence of the hour. (PRO, CO, 129, at 112–14)

While Bowring and Mercer held to the importance of a considered administration of justice, missives such as Anstey's reveal the shortcomings of adhering to process and protocol. The urgency of Anstey's letter and his impatience with the Colonial Secretary's insistence upon due process exposes the colony's own lack of faith in the process of colonial governance in a moment of crisis.

For the attorney general, the miscarriage of justice was preferable to an appearance of governmental weakness. Anstey felt that Ah Lum's acquittal would not only cause a lack of faith among the colonial community but would also produce contempt in the Chinese community. As Norton-Kyshe notes, Anstey regretted that the case ever went to trial at all because he was fully aware of the inadequacy of the evidence against Ah Lum. To the jurors, Anstey said,

> We have rather hastily apprehended these men; we found no evidence that would have justified a Magistrate to commit them, so we manage to waive that process; and now that we have rather forced a trial, you must give us a conviction to save our character. *Better to hang the wrong men*

than confess that British sagacity and activity have failed to discover the real criminals. (Norton-Kyshe 1970, 1: 417, emphasis added)

The attorney general's fears pushed the alibi of empire to its limit. The resulting five to one majority vote acquitting Ah Lum becomes a testimony to both a faith in the power of colonial governance on the part of the jurors, and failure of that colonial governance as an expression of the popular colonial belief that Ah Lum really was the culprit.

Anstey's letter also divulges a kind of second level of poisoning. The average jurors of Hong Kong, he notes, are generally compromised by their debts to Chinese merchants. "One European so influenced may defeat the course of justice by simply becoming a juror, should chance so determine" (PRO, CO, 129, at 114). Only one compromised juror, Anstey suggests, poisoned by his relationship to the moneylenders of the colony, could annul the entire judicial process. Of course, what was so offensive about Ah Lum was not just that he owned a bakery that had, until that point, supplied all the bread for the colony, but that he was also a Shroff. The *Oxford English Dictionary* defines a Shroff as "[a] banker or money-changer in the East; in the Far East, a native expert employed to detect bad coin." In other words, according to Anstey, Ah Lum is also a principal in the economy of the counterfeit. Members of the colony are indebted to him and to his friends not only for capital, but also for the entire process of the *exchange* of capital. Moreover, trade in the colony is an exercise in capitalist exchange, as well as an exchange that occurs in translation. Colonial traders depended upon local intelligence to differentiate between good and bad coin, real and counterfeit currency. The very notion of shroffing depends upon and implies the pre-existence of an economy of the counterfeit, a place where distrust, suspicion, and anxiety already run rampant. In this sense, Ah Lum's culpability lies not only in the possibility of his role in the bread poisoning, but also in the way his role as a moneylender exposed the weaknesses of trade in the colony and the dependence of the British upon those whom they colonize. This dependency had poisoned the judicial process before it was ever put into action against Ah Lum.

The Ah Lum affair epitomizes the failure of languages of colonial management. At the moment when Ah Lum, the perceived principal actor in the incident, was acquitted, when no clear enemy could be established, the whispers of conspiracy and insurgency became rampant shouts of alarm. If the alibi of empire is the rule of law, the Ah Lum affair exposed its paucity. When the British colonial government officially claimed Hong Kong, it dealt with the existing population of about five thousand Chinese inhabitants of the island by declaring them subjects of the Queen of England. On 1 February 1841, Captain Elliot issued the following proclamation:

TO THE CHINESE INHABITANTS OF HONG KONG PROCLAMATION

Bremer, Commander-in-Chief, and Elliot, Plenipotentiary, etc., etc., by this proclamation make known to the inhabitants of the island of Hongkong [*sic*], that that island has now become part of the dominions of the Queen of England by clear public agreement between the High Offices of the Celestial and British Courts; and all native persons residing therein must understand that they are now subjects of the Queen of England, and to whom and to whose officers they must pay duty and obedience.

The inhabitants are hereby promised protection, in Her Majesty's gracious name, against all enemies whatever; and they are further secured in the free exercise of their religious rites,

> ceremonies, and social customs, and in the enjoyment of their lawful private property and interests. They will be governed, pending Her Majesty's further pleasure, according to the laws customs and usages of the Chinese (every description of torture excepted) and by elders of villages, subject to the control of a British magistrate; and any person, having complaint to prefer of ill-usage or injustice against any Englishman or foreigner, will quietly make report to the nearest officer, to the end that full justice may be done. Chinese ships and merchants, resorting to the port of Hongkong [*sic*] for the purposes of trade, are hereby exempted, in the name of the Queen of England, from charge or duty of any kind to the British government. The pleasure of the government will be declared from time to time by further proclamation: and all heads of villages are held responsible that the commands are duly respected and observed. (Norton-Kyshe 1970, 5–6)

The proclamation is in itself a rich text for the study of colonial rhetoric. The language of justice, protection and fairness recurs throughout this foundational text of colonial administration. If the British traders justified their presence on the island because of the enlightened juridical and legal management they brought to it, then the failure of this colonial management in the face of an unmanageable inscrutability represents a moment in the failure of empire.

Here we come to the course of expulsion. Could the colonial administration of Hong Kong deport thousands of people on the suspicion of criminality that could not be proved? More specifically, could they deport thousands of people on a suspicion of criminality that had no other grounding than that of race?[4] In the quasi-juridical response to the Ah Lum affair, we can see the beginnings of a discursive moment of criminal typing that begins with containment and ends with expulsion. This is the trajectory of the colonial response to the poisoning – deploying a notion of agency in its singularity in an attempt to arrest the rampant rumour of insurgency and the contagion of panic.

In my consideration of a postcolonial model of agency, I have drawn largely from the work of the Subaltern Studies group because they articulate an understanding of agency that is not based in the individual, autonomous subject of history. Instead, they propose the possibility of thinking about agency across collectivities. Ranajit Guha's discussion of rumour and the circulation of the chapati in 1857 Meerut, the belief in Thakur during the Santal Rebellion of 1855, and Dipesh Chakrabarty's insistence upon the existence of precapitalist working-class consciousness in the jute mills of colonial India all suggest models of agency that do not depend upon single agents of history.[5] As Gayatri Spivak (1988) notes, "Subaltern consciousness as emergent *collective* consciousness is one of the main themes" of the work of the Subaltern Studies group (14).

I understand this collectivity within Spivak's (1988) contention that the group's assertion of subaltern consciousness is a *strategic* one: "Although the group does not wittingly engage with the post-structuralist understanding of 'consciousness,' our own transactional reading of them is enhanced if we see them as *strategically* adhering to the essentialist notion of consciousness" (15). Spivak's deconstruction of "the opposition between the [Subaltern Studies] collective and their object of investigation – the subaltern – on the one hand; and … the seeming continuity between them and their anti-humanist models on the other" (20), enables an understanding of subaltern collectivity that is not simply the work of restoring subaltern subjectivity. I will take up Spivak's deconstruction with particular attention to her discussion of rumour later in this chapter.

Like the chapati, the bread from the E Sing bakery transforms an old and familiar symbol into a performative sign of conspiracy and insurgency; the bread of the E Sing bakery circulates as the sign of contagion, conspiracy and violence:

> The semiotic condition of uncertainty and panic is generated when an old and familiar symbol (chapati) develops an unfamiliar social significance as sign through a transformation of the temporality of its representation. The performative time of the chapati's signification, its circulation as "conspiracy" and/or "insurgency," turns from the customary and commonplace to the archaic, awesome, terrifying. (Bhabha 1994, 202)

The colonial archive of the bread poisoning reveals yet another attempt to return this sign of violence and conspiracy to the register of the familiar and sensible. The chemist's report attempts to re-situate the terrifying sign of the poisoned bread into a narrative of the rational. The chemist of the War Department, F.A. Abel, examined four specimens of bread and reported that "each of the specimens of bread was found to contain arsenic, which was proved to have been introduced in the form of arsenious acid (white acid of commerce)" (PRO, CO, 129, at 285). After a breakdown of the amount of arsenic found in each specimen, the chemist concludes the following: "It may be observed that the quantity of arsenious acid contained in four ounces of the specimen of toast (no. 1) about 2½ grains has frequently been known to produce death when taken into the system" (285). But an entire colonial community, including Bowring's wife and family, consumed this same bread and no one was killed. The result of the poisoning contradicts the chemist's own analysis. He fails to mention in his report that this may have actually been a case of excess, of too much poison to kill. Abel's scientific conclusion suggests an overreaching or overwhelming desire to name guilt and culpability despite the contradictions of the evidence at hand.

Although the chapati and the white bread of E Sing may not be historically contiguous, Bhabha's work offers a way of reading postcolonial agency in the Ah Lum affair. The poisoning of the E Sing Bakery bread occurred on the eve of the second Opium War. For a colony established on poison (opium), the valency of an act of rebellion that injects poison back into the daily bread of the colonizer must not be overlooked. It becomes a fitting metaphor for the eruption of otherness into the space of white domesticity. Attempting to contain the contagion of panic, the body politic of colonial Hong Kong convulsively expelled its foreign hosts. And yet, in that expulsion, there is a residual apprehension. Cheong Ah Lum's freedom functions as a conspicuous example of the inability of colonial symbolic management to safeguard the colonial community from the possibility of future contamination and malignancy. Despite the horrors of a day of endless retching, the body was unable to purge itself of all the arsenic. Despite the upheavals of mass deportations, the body politic of colonial Hong Kong could not purge itself of all its poisoning agents.

The white bread of colonial Hong Kong undergoes a violent reinscription and is transformed from an object of ordinary nourishment into one of poison and danger. In *Dissemination*, Jacques Derrida (1981) notes that this story of the origin of writing has been fundamentally misread because it relies on a translation of the word "*pharmakon*" that occludes the ambivalence of its meaning. Prior to Derrida's intervention, *pharmakon* had been translated as "remedy." Derrida argues that this "translation by 'remedy' can thus be neither accepted nor simply rejected … Writing is no more valuable, says Plato, as a remedy than as a poison … There is no such thing as a harmless remedy. The *pharmakon* can never be simply beneficial" (99). Thus, every antidote must contain within it another kind of poison. The power of the signs of insurgency lies in the understanding that nothing is safe from the violence of reinscription – at any moment, the potentially curative may emerge as poisonous and vice versa.

Understanding the sign of the poisoned bread through Derrida's (1981) reading of the *pharmakon* makes possible a reading of anti-colonial insurgency that is not mired in a positivist notion of agency. The "victory" does not lie in the poisoning, but in the effects of ambivalence unleashed by this reinscription of the ordinary, of daily bread. In her reading of Guha's work on rumour in "Subaltern Studies," Spivak (1988) argues that rumour can be most usefully understood as a form of "illegitimate writing rather than the authoritative writing of the law" (23). By the writing of the law, Spivak recalls for us Plato's association between "speech and law, *logos* and *nomos*. Laws speak" (23). For Spivak, "rumour is a relay of something always assumed to be pre-existent. In fact the mistake of the colonial authorities was to take rumour for speech, to impose the requirements of speech in the narrow sense upon something that draws its strength from participation in writing in the general sense" (24). Sidestepping the phonocentrism of taking rumour for speech and thus attributing to it an authority which it cannot have, and which it thrives without – "rumour" is not error but primordially (originally) errant, always in circulation with no assignable source" (23) – Spivak illuminates rumour as *pharmakon*. Understanding the power of subaltern reinscriptions thus demands attending to the poisonous as well as the curative effects of writing.

Let me turn then to another rumour, another inscription. The second meal: a Chinese Canadian restaurant today. Stepping through the doors, you will sit down at one of the booths. Opening the menu, you will come to sweet and sour pork.

The origins of the Cantonese name for sweet and sour pork, a staple of Chinese-Canadian restaurant menus, bear the slivers of a textual, nominal resistance. The real sweet and sour dish is all about bones, drenched in honey and vinegar and succulently crisp. When Chinese cooks on the railway made this dish for Europeans, one version of the story goes, they were chastised for stealing the meat and serving their superiors only the bones. The cooks then left the meat on the bones and renamed the dish *goo lo yok* in the village dialect, *gwei lo yok* in Cantonese, or, in a repetition of that now familiar derogatory term for white people, "ghost man meat" in English. It was a little culinary joke with a rebellion in the ribs. On Chinese restaurant menus today, the words *goo lo yok* have no literal meaning but are a phonetic approximation of the village dialect – the original slur phonetically translated and defamiliarized in translation. This nominal resistance, this moment of postcolonial ribbing, has become so standardized that contemporary consumers of Chinese food never realize they are ingesting chunks of sly civility with every sweetly sour mouthful.

It is in this second meal that I want to look now at the residual of resistance in diaspora. What happens when the eruption of otherness occurs in the space of migrancy, when the native at home is transported and becomes the migrant, the diasporic subject? How do you read for postcolonial agency not just in the slenderness of historical narrative, as Bhabha asks, but also in the precariousness of migrancy? In Hong Kong, 1857, we have a narrative of containment and expulsion; in the narrative of sweet and sour pork, we have a semiotic virus that cannot be contained. Unlike the Ah Lum affair, where the lingering suspicions – the residual – followed the subjects of resistance, in sweet and sour pork the residual follows the object. Raymond Williams writes that

> the residual, by definition, has been effectively formed in the past, but it is still active in the cultural processes, not only and often not at all as an element of the past, but as an effective

> element of the present. Thus certain experiences, meanings, and values which cannot be expressed or substantially verified in terms of the dominant culture, are nevertheless lived and practised on the basis of the residue. (Williams 1977, 122)

Williams distinguishes the residual from the archaic, noting that the archaic is "that which is wholly recognized as an element of the past, to be observed, to be examined, or even on occasion to be consciously 'revived'" (122). This understanding of the residual is one that recognizes explicitly its potential as "alternative or even oppositional ... to the dominant culture" (122). The residue of sweet and sour pork opens up a reading of white anxiety that is not unrelated to the histories of Chinese migration. Following the object, sweet and sour pork, we can track the lingering unease of white authority and the incorporation of a nominal resistance that has spread throughout the Canadian cultural reality in the menus of the ubiquitous Chinese diner.

The story of sweet and sour pork shares with rumour some defining features. It has no basis in fact. It would be wrong to read it in any literal sense as a history of the evolution of a particular dish on the contemporary menu. It is not an unearthed artefact of food history, brushed off and translated. Its status as true or false is irrelevant, because the narrative's currency lies not in any claim it might have to historical truth value but in its circulation. The narrative's value lies in a retelling that suggests the existence of another register of emplacement, another temporality of enunciation. As Bhabha (1994) notes of the chapati, "Whether we take the chapatis as historical 'myth' or treat them as rumour, they represent the emergence of a form of social temporality that is iterative and indeterminate" (200).

The difference between the story of the poisoned bread of 1857 and the story of sweet and sour pork lies in their circulation. In the case of the latter, it is a myth or rumour that circulates in limited form – only among the Chinese-speaking diasporic community. This is a story that is twice-buried under the cover of another language, Toisanese under Cantonese under English. It does not circulate among settler colonialists and so its effects unfold differently than those of the poisoned bread. There is no contagious panic through which we might look for the agency of the Chinese subject. From the perspective of agency as a sign of resistance circulating through panic and rumour in the colonial community, the story of sweet and sour pork seems to have had no effect at all. A dead letter gathering dust, the sly civility of sweet and sour pork seems to have missed its destination. Its potential for agency seems to be annulled by the mistake of its address. This is not just the problem of language. In 1857 the problem of language was equally present. This is about a process of submersion that happens through incorporation.

As Williams (1977) notes, dominant culture deals with residual elements through incorporation. While "a residual cultural element is usually at some distance from the effective dominant culture ... some part of it, some version of it ... will in most cases have had to be incorporated if the effective dominant culture is to make sense in these areas" (123). The narrative of sweet and sour pork suggests the possibility of a model of agency that does not effect expulsion but consumption and incorporation. Current models of postcolonial agency ultimately dwell upon the agency of the native. They do not translate entirely in the space of diaspora. Here, we are really talking about the migrant. And so I come to the meal that is leftover and the incorporation of the residual. However, incorporation is not without its risks.

Relating the circulation of the chapati in colonial history to the Freudian totem meal, Bhabha (1994) notes that "it is the indeterminacy of meaning, unleashed by the contingent chapati that becomes the totem meal for historians of the Mutiny. They bite the greased bullet and circulate the myth of the chapatti" (202). While Bhabha reads a totemic value in the chapati, a place that the narrative of colonial history must return to again and again for its own legitimating mythology, Diana Fuss (1995) observes that the narrative of the totem meal has a specifically colonial history. The subtitle of Freud's *Totem and Taboo*, "Some Points of Agreement Between the Mental Lives of Savages and Neurotics," functions as a reminder that, as Freud's own preface to the book notes, the essays in the book "represent a first attempt ... at applying the point of view and the findings of psycho-analysis to some unsolved problems of social psychology [*Völkerpsychologie*]" (Freud 1950, xiii).[6] The story of the totem meal is first and foremost the story of identification with otherness through violent incorporation.

Situating the story of sweet and sour pork within an understanding of the problem of identification gives new meaning to the idea of "eating Chinese." In the Freudian story of the totem meal, the brothers of a clan contend with their fear and jealousy of the totem (who is the substitute for the father) by killing and consuming it. In so doing, the "clansmen acquire sanctity by consuming the totem: they reinforce their identification with it and with one another" (Freud 1950, 140). Afterwards, the brothers feel guilt and remorse and hold a memorial festival to allay their guilt. Fuss argues that there is an intimate relationship between cannibalism and identification where she "uncovers the *violence* at the heart of identification. All active identifications, including positive ones, are monstrous assassinations: the Other is murdered and orally incorporated before being entombed inside the subject" (34). Although Fuss's interpretation is very compelling, the violence of identification would be more poignantly understood if we complicate her reading of the cannibalistic moment of identification. Fuss is a little misleading in suggesting that all acts of identification are monstrous assassinations. Freud's totem meal is not only about the repetition of the actual act of violence, the murder of the father, but is also the repetition that represses and preserves the desire for violence. In this sense, it is at once an enactment and a disavowal. This understanding of the double-edged nature of identification explains more satisfactorily how it works within the heart of a liberal project of the incorporation of otherness. The cannibalism that girds Freud's totem meal is more than a transparent "colonialist construction of the Other as primitive, bestial, and predatory" (Fuss 1995, 36). It is also a clue to the desire for and repression of otherness in modern liberal states. In Hong Kong, 1857, the government could and did attempt to simply deport thousands of native Hong Kong inhabitants from the colony. In contemporary Canada, the repression and preservation of the desire for violence mediates the problem of the incorporation of otherness. The violence of identification is then more than just "the primary means of gaining control over the objects outside itself; identification is a form of mastery modeled directly on the nutritional instinct" (Fuss 1995, 35). The incorporation of otherness enacts the cannibalistic scene while also simultaneously disavowing it.

In the context of identification, the idea of eating Chinese takes on the significance of a moment of violent incorporation with all of the cannibalistic connotations that accompany that moment of consumption.[7] However, eating Chinese in Canada is not simply a mastery of Chinese otherness driven by the nutritional instinct. It is a repetition of the cannibalistic scene where the desire for violence is both preserved and repressed. It is at once an enactment and disavowal of violence, achieved through the positivism of embracing otherness.

And yet this form of mastery depends upon a stabilized otherness. Keeping in mind that Freud's project in this meditation on the lives of "these poor naked cannibals" is one of understanding the less well-developed members of his own contemporary society, the dependence of the totem meal, the scene of cannibalism crossed with parricide, on an absolute primitive other becomes especially paramount (Freud 1950, 2). As Fuss notes, Freud's account depends upon an understanding of the savage as being suspended in the timelessness of perpetual otherness: "Freud relies upon the signifier of temporality to construct the racial Other in culturally ethnocentric terms, reading in the unconscious life of 'primitives'" the preservation of "the primeval past in a petrified form" (Fuss 1995, 35). This construction of otherness as without a history, as perpetually caught in an evolutionary stage prior to that of the European, is a familiar one in postcolonial theory. As Bhabha's work on the colonial stereotype in "The Other Question" makes clear, stereotype depends upon a fetishized fixing of the racialized subject. Similarly, as documents such as the 1885 *Report of the Royal Commission on Chinese Immigration* reveal, there is a kind of timelessness, a perpetual sameness, read onto Chineseness in Canada.[8] The Chinese subject has always been, and will always be, Chinese. Sweet and sour pork has always been on the menu. It has always tasted like this. It always will.

The story of sweet and sour pork poses a challenge to the narrative of the primitive and unchanging ethnic other. Its nominal resistance suggests that Chineseness in Canada, the construction of Chineseness in migrancy, has not only a history, but a genealogy: "The totem meal, which is perhaps mankind's earliest festival, would thus be a repetition and a commemoration of this memorable and criminal deed, which was the beginning of so many things – of social organization, of moral restrictions and religion" (Freud 1950, 142). We can understand the story of sweet and sour pork as having a kind of counter-totemic value. The story functions as one of the genesis of fake Chinese food. It would be the story of the creation of a Chineseness specifically for Western consumption and this Chineseness comes to stand in for Chineseness in general in Canadian culture. The story of sweet and sour pork suggests the creation and circulation of a Chineseness that is a substitute for the authentic, timeless, and unchanging other of settler colonial consuming desires. In this story of creation, the Chinese immigrant denies the white settler colonial subject the moment of identification, of violent incorporation, while appearing to provide it. The story suggests that the idea of "eating Chinese," with all the violence of appropriation and incorporation that accompanies it, is not quite eating Chinese at all. In thinking that he is eating Chinese, the settler colonialist will actually consume *goo lo yok*, white man meat, a version of himself, and will engage in a moment of symbolic self-cannibalism. Serving back to the settler colonialist his own excessive desires, the story deflects the violence of colonial identification and incorporation away from the Chinese subject and back towards the settler colonial one. This narrative suggests a way in which the Chinese migrant escapes the dialectic of self-otherness. Chinese migrants did not need whiteness or Europeanness to define themselves. Right from the beginning, there was another register of emplacement.

In the space between *goo lo yok* and sweet and sour pork, we can hear the doubled discourse of diasporic resistances. The doubled process of naming extends to the doubled language of the menu itself. The ambivalence of European authority surfaces in suspicions around the doubleness of the menu. Not only is there a Chinese chop suey menu juxtaposed with the Western one of hamburgers and milkshakes, but there is also always a lingering sense that the menu doesn't tell the whole story. Somewhere, past the swinging doors dividing those in the diner from those in the kitchen, there is the suspicion that there are dishes that are simply not on the menu. We've all heard the urban myth about how Chinese restaurants have one menu for white people and another for Chinese people. What the menu makes manifest is the latent suspicion that all is not self-evident. What is maddening about the menu is that it is at once explicitly readable and equivocally illegible. Along the margins of the menu lies the possibility of conspiracy, of another language, of a second menu.

Let us return to the materiality of sweet and sour pork. Imagine it – gooey, unnaturally red-orange, shiny with an aura of plasticity that could come only from that special combination of vegetable oil, rice wine vinegar, and a lingering sense of its inauthenticity. After all, we all know that this isn't *real* Chinese food. It is Chinese and not Chinese, at once impossibly full of ethnic meaning and yet strangely meaningless in that excess. In this materially ambivalent plasticity, let me explore further the relationship between rumour and history.

Describing the way in which rumour can bend and change according to the subjectivity of its transmitter, Guha proposes that

> rumour functions as a free form liable to a considerable degree of improvisation as it leaps from tongue to tongue. The aperture which it has built into it by virtue of anonymity permits its message to be contaminated by the subjectivity of each of its speakers and modified as often as any of them would want to embellish or amend it in the course of transmission. The outcome of all this is a *plasticity* that enables it to undergo transformations. (Guha 1983, 261, emphasis added)

In this plastic quality of rumour, in the way it changes shape while still retaining the trace of its original form, there is a sense of the materiality of rumour's memory – a sense of its materials memory. Borrowing the phrase from materials engineering, Richard Terdiman suggests that signs carry within them a quality not unlike that of the crease in a pair of Perma-press slacks. Bend them, fold them, and they will still retain the trace of their original shape. Terdiman notes that

> certain products and materials resume their shape after they have been deformed ... This property is termed "materials memory." It seems a process without a subject: it just happens. This may be a useful notion for understanding the conservative character built into social existence and practice by the sorts of mechanisms Marx and Freud – among many other – have sought to account for. Such a concept would allow us to argue that the knowledge of social process does not disappear, but (like the productivity of the worker reified in the tool) rather it seems to migrate to a different place, into a text different from the one we carry in our recollection. Such a memory forcefully produces the past in the present. (Terdiman 1993, 35)

In the aura of plasticity that attends the materiality of sweet and sour pork with all of its shiny red-orange artificiality, we might read for the production of the past in the present. In the lingering sense of its inauthenticity lies precisely the moment of the echo, of the materials memory of a sign that carries with it the memory of its production. The plasticity of sweet and sour pork carries within it an echo of an earlier resistance. Knowledge of that social process does not disappear and resistance does not simply end with the deportations and failed judicial processes. Rather, it resonates through history into a different text.

The story of sweet and sour pork destabilizes Chineseness in a nominal resistance that forces into the present the history of its production. Terdiman (1993) argues that "[w]e are not free to keep the past *past* – it colonizes our present whether or not we realize its encroachment" (46). The past of language continually infects its present, bouncing back through the memory of the production of its significations. The past of sweet and sour pork inexorably seeps into the present of its consumption; the history of coolie labour echoes in the plasticity of its red-orange sauce and colonizes the present of its consumption.

Signs carry within them the capacity for rememoration. It is not that the bread of the Ah Lum affair and the sweet and sour pork of contemporary menus are historically contiguous or causal, but that they offer one way of reading both the affinities and the distinctions between resistances in different historical moments and in different nation spaces. As Terdiman points out, the process of inscription and reinscription is one that is necessarily about history, about the contagious process of citation and re-citation. The poisoning of the bread in 1857 emerges as a violent reinscription of the ordinary into a sign of danger and insurgency. The story of sweet and sour pork embeds within its nourishing exterior a barb, a serving back to Europe-in-Canada a sign of its own excessive desire. As Derrida's theory of the *pharmakon* suggests, writing, or inscription, always carries within it the potential to be both poisonous and curative. Every remedy carries within it the potential for violent reinscription, for poison. In sweet and sour pork, the residue of arsenic remains in the story of its production. Guha's thinking on rumour anticipates the way in which agency thrives on continual citation. "The additions, cuts and twists introduced into a rumour in the course of its circulation transform its message (often just minimally) by such degrees as to adjust it to the variations within a given ideology or mode of popular expression and by doing so broaden the range of its address" (Guha 1983, 261). The agency of Guha's text thrives on contamination. In the story of sweet and sour pork, we can locate a citation that thrives on the traces of old poisonings.

In both colonial Hong Kong and the Chinese diaspora in Canada, we have an example of agency without a singular agent of history. The affinity between subjects of colonial Hong Kong and diasporic subjects in Canada lies precisely in the frustration of the colonial and settler colonial desire for identifiable and knowable agents. However, these two subjectivities diverge when we give full recognition to the different material circumstances that contour their daily existence. There is a difference between resistance under a colonial regime, wherein the entire colonial community can be poisoned with a single batch of morning bread, and resistance under a liberal state as a migrant subject. Within the difference between a colonial regime's response to the unknowability of anti-colonial agency and Europe-in-Canada's response to diasporic agency lies the difference between expulsion and incorporation. In the diaspora, the precariousness of migrancy forces a different kind of engagement with power than that of anti-colonial resistance.

Unlike in colonial India, in diaspora, there are not always rebellions or other large, identifiable acts of resistance to which we can point. Part of the work of this chapter is to explore the possibilities of collective forms of agency within small acts, those acts that may have quietly become a part of our everyday lives while still retaining the traces of oppositionality. Robin Kelley's (1994) reading of black resistance on public transit in post-Second World War Birmingham, Alabama, offers one way of reading for agency within the everyday. Noting that most black working-class resistance "has remained unorganized, clandestine and evasive," Kelley suggests that "examples of black working-class resistance in public spaces offer some of the richest insights into how race, gender, class, space, time and collective memory shape both domination and resistance" (56). Kelley examines a range of tactics, from using the bus as a "moving theatre" (72) to blaming the "unreliability of public transportation" as "a plausible excuse for absenteeism, for stealing a few extra hours of sleep, for attending to problems or running errands – all of which were standard resistance strategies, or purely strategies for making ends meet, waged by household workers" (70). This attention to the small resistances that take place in public spaces suggests one way of reading for agency in diaspora.[9]

Tracking the residuum of sweet and sour, we find that there is another language of emplacement – that of the migrant. The agency of sweet and sour pork cannot be symbolically managed, not only because it occurs in a foreign language, but also because it asserts a different register of emplacement altogether. In delivering back to Europe-in-Canada a sign of its own excess, Chinese cooks on the railway also produced a narrative of resistance that would circulate throughout the Canadian culinary landscape; it is a resistance that becomes a part of the Canadian body politic in the meal that is consumed and incorporated.

In the final part of this chapter, I will consider more closely the connections between the agency of the poisoned loaves of the E Sing bakery and that of the naming of *goo lo yok*. There has been a slippage between the postcolonial and the diasporic that is a symptom of something more than just a categorical confusion. It is a symptom of postcolonialism's ongoing concern with what Stuart Hall (1996), echoing Ella Shohat, has marked as the productive tension of the "post" in postcolonialism. That is, the tension between a postcolonialism that is the study of the aftermath of colonialism, and one that focuses on going beyond colonialism in terms of a theoretical and epistemic shift. Within the productivity of this tension, the diasporic subject emerges. At postcolonialism's limit, which Hall presciently notes as a process wherein the postcolonial is always under erasure, where its very undecidability must be read as the strength of its interventionary work, diaspora emerges as one way of understanding the subjects of colonial displacement.

Postcolonialism's repeated turn to the diasporic subject is an expression of its desire to follow the subjects of colonialism's oppressive histories outside of the space of European colonialism and into the sphere of its aftermath. Some of postcolonialism's harshest critics have focused on the breadth of its embrace. It has been accused of being its own colonizing force in terms of First World theoretical work mining the raw materials of Third World literature, of having no historical specificity, of being opaque and disconnected from true subjects of oppression, and of being too ambivalent about the terms of its own debate.[10] In some ways, post-colonialism could be seen as travelling too easily without the specificity of local referents. But it travels because it is concerned with following the subjects of colonial oppression after the ostensible end of that oppression – both in the sense of aftermath, and in the sense of going beyond. Postcolonialism travels into the space of diaspora because colonialism is a dislocating force.

While it seems more obvious to understand Chineseness in terms of diasporic formation, it is equally important to think through the relationship between Chineseness and postcolonialism. In the postscript to the chapter "Against the Lures of Diaspora" in *Writing Diaspora*, Rey Chow (1993) addresses the problem of thinking of Chinese identity within a postcolonial frame. For Chow, this problem is one of the situation of Chinese intellectuals in the West as well as that of the limitations of postcolonial theory. Pointing to the experiences of peoples living in Hong Kong, Macau, and Taiwan, Chow notes that China "was never completely 'colonized' over a long period by anyone foreign power, even though the cultural effects of imperialism are as strong as in other formerly colonized countries in Asia, Africa, and Latin America" (118). Although Chow is preoccupied here with the responsibility of Chinese intellectuals abroad to those in China, this chapter also, while incidentally foreshadowing the increased interest in diaspora studies to come, gestures to the gap in theorizing the politics of dislocation that diaspora studies can mediate. Chow's warning against diaspora is more precisely a warning against the desire of "third world" intellectuals in the West to claim minority positions while masking their own "hegemony ... over those who are stuck at home" (118). However, if we shift our understanding of Chinese diasporic subjectivity away from that of Chinese intellectuals in the West and towards those who are stranded in the West with none of the privileges with which the intellectual arrives, the space of critical diaspora studies might be something to explore rather than avoid.

In exploring these two stories of food, rumour, and resistance, I suggest that there is something to be said for embracing the lures of diaspora and understanding diasporic subjects as those who have been displaced by the effects of colonial oppression. This is not a preoccupation with victimhood. Rather, it is a recognition of the inescapable histories of traumatic dislocation from which modern diasporas have emerged. Colonialism and imperialism in their direct form have been responsible for the vast majority of nineteenth- and twentieth-century displacements of peoples from the south to the north, from the postcolony to the metropole.[11] I acknowledge Stuart Hall's (1996) important observation about the kind of presumptuousness that lies at the heart of assuming that all diasporic trajectories are uni-directional: "The notion that only the multi-cultural cities of the First World are diaspora-ised" is a fantasy which can only be sustained by those who have never lived in the hybridized spaces of a Third World, so-called "colonial city" (250). However, I want to dwell on the problem of diaspora as one of the limits of postcolonial and minority discourse theory. Because the term diaspora must retain its resonances with the dislocations of oppression, we must untangle it from the concerns of transnational migrancy in general.

The recent resurgence of the term diaspora in the Western academy has arisen out of a profound perplexity around the cultural spaces and products of peoples who have been displaced by oppression and violence. If the term diaspora is to retain its potential as a space of powerful critique, it cannot float away from the constitutive sorrows of dislocation. Reading for agency in the precariousness of migrancy, I want to highlight the ways in which the state of migrancy is framed by social and political precariousness. It is not that all migrants exist in a precarious state, but rather that migrancy carries within it the potential for precariousness. This is a precariousness marked by race, gender, sexuality, and class. What stands out for me in this marking is the way in which the words "Go home" resonate more for some communities than for others. For some, the injunction to go home carries with it a profoundly different capacity for pain, humiliation, and political disempowerment than it does for others. In the context of the Chinese diaspora, I am focusing on a diaspora marked most explicitly by race but inescapably defined by issues of sexuality, class, and gender. As the history of race riots and race-based legislation such as the head tax illustrates, the Chinese Canadian community has been attacked primarily on the basis of its Chineseness, even though issues of sexuality, class, and gender – especially evident in the promulgation of the perception of a degenerate bachelor society that has taken jobs away from upstanding and hardworking white men – are crucially imbricated in the targeting of Chinese immigrants.[12] Writing of the way in which racism perpetuates the exclusivism of racialized diasporic communities, Vijay Mishra (1996) notes in "The Diasporic Imaginary" that "as long as there is a fascist fringe always willing to find racial scapegoats for the nation's own shortcomings and to chant 'Go home', the autochthonous pressures towards diasporic racial exclusivism will remain" (426). Mishra describes the sense of "familiar temporariness" that marks what he has called the old Indian diaspora, the diasporic community that is the legacy of indentured labour in the West Indies (426). In this idea of a familiar temporariness we can begin to read for the kind of precariousness that lies within racially marked diasporic communities.

A fourth- or fifth-generation Chinese Canadian might still be asked to "go home" in a way that the fourth- or fifth-generation white Canadian will never be.

In the story of sweet and sour pork, I established a reading for agency where success is measured not so much in capital accumulation but in the challenges posed to colonialism. Rather than reading for agency within the terms of success defined by contemporary global capitalism, Chinese diaspora studies need to read for resistances that upset the colonial order and its legacy. A study of the Chinese diaspora with a more rigorous assessment of the relationships between colonialism, postcolonialism, and the diasporic community foregrounds the history of diasporic trajectories and offers a way of reading for the agency of the dispossessed in dislocation.

As a brief history of migration in the case of the Chinese diaspora community in Canada shows, immigration to Canada is marked by the effects of European colonialism as well as relations with Japan and Russia, most significantly due to the Opium Wars and the series of unequal treaties that China was forced to sign as a result of the wars. Between 1838 and 1900, China was in unequal trading relations with Britain, France, Germany, Austria, Japan, the United States, Italy, and Russia. The penetration of foreign capitalism undermined China's own economic integrity and accelerated its breakdown. The enormous taxation pressures brought about by the unequal treaties, in combination with poor harvest yields and an increase in popular unrest, led to a number of rebellions in China – including the Taiping Rebellion of 1850–64 and the Boxer Rebellion of 1900. These instabilities and hardships were, at least in part, triggered by colonialism. Moreover, Canada's desperate shortage of cheap labour led to an indenture system that was responsible for the vast majority of Chinese immigration to Canada in the late nineteenth and early twentieth centuries.[13] Of course, Canada was not the only destination for Chinese indentured labourers. Slavery was abolished and banned in British colonies in 1834. As a result, indenture was the next solution to labour shortages in the British empire. While the ship the *Caribbean* landed in Victoria with three hundred contract Chinese labourers in 1858, yet other ships were crossing the Pacific and the Atlantic carrying indentured labourers from Asia (mainly China and India) to sugar plantations in the West Indies, railroad work all along the western coast of both the Americas, farms in Australia, and mines in South Africa.[14]

The history of Chinese diasporic trajectories is thus intimately linked to the history of colonialism. As Jenny Sharpe (1995) notes, "The designation of postcolonial as an umbrella term for diaspora and minority communities is derived in part from an understanding of decolonization as the beginning of an unprecedented migration from the former colonies to advanced industrialist centers" (182). However, as the trajectory of Chinese indenture labour shows, diaspora begins not only with the end of colonialism but also with its instigation. The nineteenth and twentieth centuries marked the mass exodus of dispossessed communities who were bound by indenture. In "Diasporas Old and New" Gayatri Spivak argues that diasporic scholarship must continue to be vigilantly attentive to the old diasporas of indenture and slavery and seek out their connections with contemporary diasporas of the dispossessed rather than simply celebrate the achievements of the new diasporas of savvy transnational capitalists. At issue in separating the old from the new is not only the futility of forgetting, but also a denial of the constitutive effects of colonial traumas.

The public space of the small town Chinese restaurant opens up the possibilities of resistances that may not have a record in the colonial or settler colonial archive, but that are nevertheless present. This chapter suggests that postcolonial models of agency enable a reading of diasporic agency that is dispersed, without a single agent, hero(ine), or authorial presence. I have also argued that reading for diasporic agency demands a different, altered model than that of postcolonial theory. The postcolonial model of agency offered by Bhabha and connected to the work of Ranajit Guha does not entirely translate to the space of the diaspora. Agency looks different depending on whether you are a native or a migrant. In both the narrative of sweet and sour pork and the story of the poisoned loaves in Hong Kong, 1857, agency is dispersed. There is no single historical agent who poisoned the loaves at the E Sing bakery; there is no single historical agent who renamed sweet and sour pork. And yet, the migrant agency that emerges in the story of sweet and sour takes a different form. In that form, I come to what is left over: the meal that is incorporated. I suggest that in diasporic space, the model of agency functions less on panic than on the incorporation of the residual. Nevertheless, the relationship between the postcolonial and the diasporic is an intimate one. The challenge of a diasporic reading of agency lies in looking for the productivity of that intimacy. The diasporic cannot forget the history of colonial displacements. From the acerbity of rice wine vinegar, I hope our tongues have found their way to honeyed ginger, to the culinary joke in the nominal resistance of eating Chinese in diaspora.

NOTES

1 This a brief summary of the poisoning. Accounts of the event appear in a number of histories of Hong Kong, including Nigel Cameron's (1978) *Hong Kong: The Cultured Pearl* and G.B. Endacott's *A History of Hong Kong* (1973, 44–60, 93–4). In popular history, the story has been retold by Jan Morris in *Hong Kong* (1997, 42–3). Each of these accounts names Cheong Ah Lum as the principal perpetrator. The most thorough account of the specifics of Ah Lum's trial can be found in James William Norton-Kyshe's *The History of the Laws and Courts of Hong Kong* (1970, 414–18).

2 In *The Potlatch Papers*, Christopher Bracken (1997) makes a similar point regarding the multiple spellings of the "potlatch" in the settler colonial archive.

3 The main currency at this time was the silver dollar. The problem of currency has been a constant factor of doing business in Hong Kong, where transactions were often transnational. Endacott (1973) notes that a May 1845 proclamation set a number of coins as legal tender in addition to sterling and British coins: "the East India Company's gold mohur at 29s. and 2d.; the rupee at 1s. 10d. and the half, quarter, and one-eighth rupees, pro rata; the dollar of Spain, Mexico and any South American state at 4s. 2d. and the Chinese copper cash at 288 for one shilling" (76–7). These equivalents remained in force until the growth of trade and forgery prompted then governor Sir Hercules Robinson to insist on a series of new coins for Hong Kong and the declaration of silver Spanish, Mexican and South American dollars to be legal tender in the colony (117). The use of these particular currencies makes an interesting comment on early Pacific Rim trade and the intersection between British and Spanish imperial interests.

4 From the beginning, the Hong Kong legal system differentiated its subjects on the basis of race. The problem of finding an appropriate legal system of governance for the colony haunted the Hong Kong administrators for decades. As the proclamation declaring Chinese inhabitants to be subjects of the Queen of England makes clear, Hong Kong began with a dual system – British settlers would be governed by English law and Chinese inhabitants would be governed by Chinese law. However, despite a series of subsequent ordinances, there were still a number of problems with this system. As Endacott (1973) notes, "The official attitude towards the Chinese was liberal enough in theory, but much of the legislation providing for law and order

discriminated against them" (70). Endacott's discussion of early Hong Kong governance, particularly under Sir John Davies, highlights many of the problems that the colonial administration encountered in their attempts to apply English law in the colony. Peter Wesley-Smith's (1994) chapter "Statutory Provisions Importing English Law" in *The Sources of Hong Kong Law* discusses these issues in some depth.

5 See Guha 1988, 78–84; 1983, 251–77; and Chakrabarty 1988, 225–30.

6 A.A. Brill's 1918 translation of *Totem and Taboo* highlights the text's preoccupation with race more explicitly than does James Strachey's subsequent translation in the Standard Edition (Freud 1918, 1950). Brill's translation of the same line from the preface suggests that the essays in the book "represent [Freud's] first efforts to apply view-points and results of psychoanalysis to unexplained problems of *racial psychology*" (ix, emphasis added). Strachey's translation of the term *Völkerpsychologie* suppresses the racial undertones of the text. However, neither the Strachey nor the Brill translation is satisfying. Both seem anachronistic in their readings of the compound adjective *Völkerpsychologie.* This instability around the translating of *Völkerpsychoiogie* itself points to a larger issue in the text around the situating of cultural others.

7 Nunes (1994) also writes of the relationship between race, cannibalism, and the problem of the residual or what is left over. While my argument has taken a detour through the issue of identification and Freud's totem meal, Nunes's analysis focuses more specifically on the problem of race in Brazil and a reading of Brazilian modernism. Nunes focuses on the Brazilian modernist movement's emphasis on cultural cannibalism articulated in texts such as Oswald be Andrade's *Omanifesto pau Brazil* (The brazilwood manifesto) and *Omanifesto antropofago* (The cannibalist manifesto). Writing of the Brazilian modernist movement's approach to cultural mixing and miscegenation through the cannibalist method, Nunes notes that the desire to consume and absorb what is useful in a culture and excrete the rest fails to recognize the exclusions inherent in excretion: "The law of assimilation is that there must always be a remainder, a residue – something (someone) that has resisted or escaped incorporation, even when the nation produces narratives of racial democracy to mask this tradition of resistance" (125). For Nunes, the remainder constitutes a problem for the state.

Gunew (1999) also discusses the idea of cannibalism in relation to multiculturalism, specifically that of multicultural food festivals. Through the work of Julia Kristeva, Gunew argues that "while food signifies actual bodies it also stands in for ... language itself. Thus, the dominant 'culture engages with multicultural cuisine as a way of not acknowledging multicultural words'" (147). Gunew explores mother-daughter relationships in a number of Australian minority writers and charts some of the ways in which food replaces language and, in the sense of Deleuze and Guattari's work on Kafka, "deterritorializes the language from within" (155).

8 In "Rereading Chinese Head Tax Racism" I explore the discursive production of Chinese as a legal category in the 1885 *Report of the Royal Commission on Chinese Immigration.*

9 For an account of "everyday resistance" as it has been theorized in postcolonial studies, see Jefferess (2008). Of particular relevance to the present discussion is his account of "resistance as subversion," which "constitutes the disruption or modification of colonial modes of knowledge and authority" (20).

10 These criticisms are most cogently argued in texts such as Ahmad (2008) and Dirlik (1998).

11 In *Postcolonialism*, Robert Young (2001) traces the history of the deployment of the idea of imperialism and differentiates imperialism in its direct form (conquest) from indirect forms such as political or economic influence, which functions as an effective domination (27). Also, see pp. 15–43 for an excellent discussion of the historical emergences of colonialism and imperialism and the distinction between the two.

12 There have been a series of race riots targeting Chinese immigrants in Canadian history, including the 1907 Vancouver riot that caused enough concern at both a local and a national level that then-prime minister Wilfrid Laurier stepped in to police the situation. For detailed discussions of anti-Chinese riots and anti-Chinese legislation (the two often went hand in hand) see Li (1998), Roy (1989), Ward (1978), and Wickberg (1982).

13 See Li (1998) and Wickberg (1982) for excellent historical surveys of some of the "push" and "pull" factors that mark early-nineteenth- and late-twentieth-century Chinese emigration to Canada.

14 For detailed discussions of the trajectories and histories of Chinese indentured labour, see Look Lai (1993); Lal, Munro, and Beechart (1993); Jung (2006); and Saunders (1984).

REFERENCES

Ahmad, Aijaz. 2008. *In Theory: Classes, Nations, Literatures*. London, New York: Verso.

Bhabha, Homi. 1994. *The Location of Culture*. London, New York: Routledge.

Bracken, Christopher. 1997. *The Potlatch Papers: A Colonial Case History*. Chicago: University of Chicago Press.

Cameron, Nigel. 1978. *Hong Kong: The Cultured Pearl*. Hong Kong: Oxford University Press.

Chakrabarty, Dipesh. 1988. "Conditions for Knowledge of Working-Class Conditions." In *Selected Subaltern Studies*, ed. Ranajit Guha and Gayatri Chakravorty Spivak, 179–232. London, New York: Oxford University Press.

Chow, Rey. 1993. *Writing Diaspora: Tactics of Intervention in Contemporary Cultural Studies*. Bloomington: Indiana University Press.

Derrida, Jacques. 1981. *Dissemination*. Trans. Barbara Johnson. Chicago: University of Chicago Press.

Dirlik, Arif. 1998. *The Postcolonial Aura: Third World Criticism in the Age of Global Capital*. Boulder, CO: Westview Press.

Endacott, G.B. 1973. *A History of Hong Kong*. 2nd ed. Hong Kong: Oxford University Press.

Freud, Sigmund. 1918. *Totem and Taboo*. Trans. A.A. Brill. New York: Moffat, Yard & Co.

Freud, Sigmund. 1950. "Totem and Taboo." In *Standard Edition,* vol. 13. Translated by James Strachey, vii–162. London: Hogarth Press.

Fuss, Diana. 1995. *Identification Papers*. London, New York: Routledge.

Guha, Ranajit. 1983. *Elementary Aspects of Peasant Insurgency in Colonial India*. Delhi: Oxford University Press.

Guha, Ranajit. 1988. "The Prose of Counter-Insurgency." In *Selected Subaltern Studies*, ed. Ranajit Guha and Gayatri Spivak, 45–88. New York, Oxford: Oxford University Press.

Gunew, Sneja. 1999. "The Melting Pot of Assimilation: Cannibalizing the Multicultural Body." In *Transnational Asia Pacific: Gender, Culture, and the Public Sphere,* ed. Shirley Geok-Lin Lim, Larry E. Smith, and Wi mal Dissanayake, 145–58. Urbana: University of Illinois Press.

Hall, Stuart. 1996. "When was 'the Post-Colonial'? Thinking at the Limit." In *The Post-Colonial Question: Common Skies, Divided Horizons*, ed. Iaian Chambers and Lidia Curti, 242–60. London, New York: Routledge.

Jefferess, David. 2008. *Postcolonial Resistance: Culture, Liberation, and Transformation*. Toronto: University of Toronto Press.

Jung, Moon-ho. 2006. *Coolies and Cane: Race, Labor and Sugar in the Age of Emancipation*. Baltimore: Johns Hopkins University Press.

Kelley, Robin. 1994. *Race Rebels: Culture, Politics, and the Black Working Class*. New York: Free Press.
Lal, Brij, Doug Munro, and Edward Beechart, eds. 1993. *Plantation Workers: Resistance and Accommodation*. Honolulu: University of Hawaii Press.
Li, Peter. 1998. *The Chinese in Canada*. 2nd ed. Toronto, Oxford: Oxford University Press.
Look Lai, Walter. 1993. *Indentured Labor, Caribbean Sugar: Chinese and Indian Migrants to the British West Indies*, 1838–1918. Baltimore: Johns Hopkins University Press.
Mishra, Vijay. 1996. "The Diasporic Imaginary: Theorizing the Indian Diaspora." *Textual Practice* 10 (3): 421–47. http://dx.doi.org/10.1080/09502369608582254.
Morris, Jan. 1997. *Hong Kong: Epilogue to an Empire*. London: Penguin Books.
Norton-Kyshe, James William. 1970. *The History of the Laws and Courts of Hong Kong: From the Earliest Period to 1898*. 2 vols. Hong Kong: Vetch and Lee.
Nunes, Zita. 1994. "Anthropology and Race in Brazilian Modernism." In *Colonial Discourse/Postcolonial Theory*, ed. F. Barke, P. Hulme, and M. Iverson, 115–25. Manchester: Manchester University Press.
Roy, Patricia E. 1989. *A White Man's Province: British Columbia Politicians and Chinese and Japanese Immigrants 1858–1914*. Vancouver: University of British Columbia Press.
Saunders, Kay. 1984. *Indentured Labor in the British Empire, 1834–1920*. London: Croom Helm.
Sharpe, Jenny. 1995. "Is the United States Postcolonial?" *Diaspora* 4 (2): 181–99. http://dx.doi.org/10.1353/dsp.1995.0004.
Spivak, Gayatri Chakravorty. 1988. "Introduction: Subaltern Studies: Deconstructing Historiography." In *Selected Subaltern Studies*, ed. Ranajit Guha and Gayatri Chakravorty Spivak, 3–34. London, New York: Oxford University Press.
Terdiman, Richard. 1993. *Present Past: Modernity and the Memory Crisis*. Ithaca, London: Cornell University Press.
Ward, W. Peter. 1978. *White Canada Forever: Popular Attitudes and Public Policy toward Orientals in British Columbia*. Montreal: McGill-Queen's University Press.
Wesley-Smith, Peter. 1994. *The Sources of Hong Kong Law*. Hong Kong: Hong Kong University Press.
Wickberg, Edgar, ed. Henry Con, Ronald J. Con, Graham Johnson, Edgar Wickberg, and William E. Willmott. 1982. *From China to Canada: A History of the Chinese Communities in Canada*. Toronto: McClelland & Stewart.
Williams, Raymond. 1977. *Marxism and Literature*. Oxford: Oxford University Press.
Young, Robert. 2001. *Postcolonialism: An Historical Introduction*. London: Blackwell.

16 Altered States: Global Currents, the Spectral Nation, and the Production of "Asian Canadian"

ROY MIKI

Prologue: Arrivals and Departures

"I see some lights," said Jonathan. "They're coming."

The "coming" is a story told by Steve Chao (2000), a reporter for Vancouver Television. His eyewitness account of the moment of encountering appears in an alternate magazine of Asian Canadian locations, Rice Paper, *curiously distant from the other more powerful news outlets. "The Backlash Against Chinese Migrants: One Reporter's Perspective" positions the I of the writer/witness as a signifier in the unfolding drama, a fold in the textual performance of the contemporary crisis of an arrival of the other as one's own.*

The "aliens" are on their way, and Steve Chao is summoned by his superior to act as reporter/translator – he speaks "their" language – after all, he is Chinese, or Asian, and they have crossed the oceanic divide. But he is also one of four Canadians who have waited "under a pier in the dead of night" in a skimpy aluminum boat – "two cameramen, a cook, and myself." Sighting the ship, they move out to sea, and then Chao recalls, a mere 12 hours before he had been in Vancouver "covering a protest," an event that becomes strange to itself, just as his own Chinese Canadian cultural identity begins to oscillate in his memory.

He had always wanted to be a voice for Chinese Canadians, "fiercely proud of where I came from," but he does not say whether the "where" is a cultural matrix, a hyphenated community within the nation, or a country of origin. The ambiguity, however, is constitutive and unfolds in and through the estrangement that descends on him as he finds himself drawn into and then immersed in the "Fujian migrant" crisis – a crisis of global proportions that would destabilize his own imagined history as a Chinese Canadian.

From Ottawa, where he was getting ready to go backpacking, when he accepted an offer from Vancouver Television to help explain Chinese Canadians to viewers, to the seas off Campbell River to cover the "arrival," and then to China: September 1999, he is given the task of investigating the local determinants that produced the migrants. There he collects knowledge of the parasitic underside of global capitalism – what's not told in the Nike ads with the suave and smiling Michael Jordan. As Masao Miyoshi writes, "In Indonesia, [Nike contractors] pay young girls $1.35 for sewing shoes all day. Overtime is often mandatory. There are no union protections. A pair of Nike shoes sells in the United States for between $45 and $80 but costs only $5.60 to produce. Michael Jordan's reported $20 million fee for promoting the brand was more than Nike's entire payroll of these young workers in its six factories in 1992" (Miyoshi 1995, 61). The necessity of exploitable labour to run the new economy of transnational corporations *on the hunt for any means to proliferate capital produces the conditions for the emergence of "snakeheads," or smugglers. These are the brokers who deliver up labouring bodies to sites of mass production. They feed on the class fantasies of the poor and desperate, who are willing to indenture themselves for the fleeting opportunity to move into the future time of corporate capitalism's mediated representations of plenitude. "Snakeheads," Chao learns, "charge anywhere between $35,000 to $38,000 US for the journey." Since few can afford that exorbitant amount, they are forced into years of slave labour in restaurants and sweatshops, and "women are forced to sacrifice their bodies in massage parlours and brothels." A prime destination is New York, where "it's estimated there are more than a half a million Fujinese." The snakeheads have extensive global connections and flourish on the culture of commodification that requires large pools of labouring bodies.*

Chao also discovers that some Chinese Canadians are connected to the snakeheads in this global traffic of bodies. But this was not as traumatic as the defensiveness – the lack of empathy – demonstrated by many Chinese Canadians. "'Send them back to where they came from'" has been the typical sentiment," he writes, confirmed by a poll "that showed more than 80 per cent supported the government's lock up of migrants and a 'get-tough' policy."

The backlash against the Fujian migrants, a group Chao came to see as an extension of his own, exploded the trajectory of his own identity formation, so the article concludes, "I wanted to be the voice for the Chinese community in Canada. Now, I'm not so sure I want to anymore."

It may be easy to dismiss Chao's reporter's perspective as merely personal – but then the personal itself, to draw from Michel de Certeau (1988), "is a locus in which an incoherent (and often contradictory) plurality of ... relational determinations interact" (xi). His entry into the efficacy of global currents in making the nation strange to itself, even transforming its once-model minority community into the voice of xenophobia, brings the crisis of time into all the rivulets of our social and cultural relations. Steve Chao, then, is one of "us" in his estrangement – an estrangement bringing back home the awareness that racialization can no longer be read as out there – it never was – and that the arrival of the global/local throws all subject positions and all values into altered states. "Meanwhile," to appropriate a linguistic prop of fictional time, the re-articulation of the nation not only becomes possible, but is also necessitated in the moment of arrival.

So let's return to the movement out at sea. The camera lights go on, and as Chao's gaze is directed at the "listing" ship with its hull eaten away by rust, he confronts the appearance of "the ghostly faces of more than 150 weak and frightened men and women [who] stared hauntingly at us. Many looked gaunt, clothes hanging off them as if draped on clothes racks. It was evident they had endured a hellish voyage." What to say?

I asked in Mandarin where they were from.

One woman replied, "Zhong guo." China.

Arrivals as departures. Where are you we us from?

We live in a globalized world where imperialist and national structures, differences between the tangible and the intangible, the monumental and the everyday, and even the very notion of humanity are no longer the same as our characterizations of them twenty years ago.

Néstor García Canclini (2000, 38)

A Crisis in Time

Do we not now live in our various national enclaves, or seem to, on the cusp of a present evanescing even as it supposedly materializes before our very eyes? Is there not now a race for knowledge that can forestall the inevitable unravelling of social and cultural formations and that makes us yearn for the stability of "identities" to close the gaps? Do we not sense that even as we produce a proliferation of commodities that we are accomplices in transactions with their seductive discourses that make us yearn for a future language of brands and marks to subsume the nation? How can we – or can we? – resist or otherwise negotiate the undercurrents to the crisscrossing of borders in the modus operandi of a now-dominant globalization process that makes us aware (and wary) of the prominence accorded the figurative and literal passports that delimit our movements?

Such speculative questions suggest that the now-familiar adoption of the prefix *post* to point towards new temporal conditions, as in the postmodern, post-national, and postcolonial, is less a sign of progress and more a sign of a crisis of time – with the arrival of globalization as a term that portrays as well as produces a move away from the modern, the national, and the colonial as an extension of the linear and progressive (hence empty) time of imperial and colonial expansion. In Canada, for instance, the notion of the modern as a movement beyond the colonial functioned to produce the time of the nation that subsumed the time of colonial invasion, and therefore the time of the aboriginal presence that was appropriated. Anne McClintock's (1994) critique of the term postcolonialism in "The Angel of Progress" still rings true. Seeing it as simultaneously an effect of colonialism and the sign of a crisis, she writes, "the almost ritualistic ubiquity of 'post-' words in current culture (post-colonialism, post-modernism, post-structuralism, post-cold war, post-marxism, post-apartheid, post-Soviet, post-Ford, post-feminism, post-national, post-historic, even post-contemporary) signals, I believe, a widespread, epochal crisis in the idea of linear, historical 'progress'" (292). In Canadian terms, the crisis in the time of the nation is manifest as a decreasing capacity to conjure the present, hence what we inhabit, as presence. The recourse to *post* when no other term appears appropriate gestures towards the beyond or the future as fraught with uncertainty and the anxiety of irresolution.

The crisis brings in its wake the unease of "a world without meaning," to borrow a phrase from the title of Zaki Laidi's (1998) study of the impact of globalization. Laidi argues that the Cold War era was the last one to play out the legacy of a European-produced enlightenment, with its universalizing discourses of meaning that naturalized assumptions about progress, rationality, and collectivity. Paradoxically, the imagined end of the Cold War was to be the moment of fulfilment, the moment when the forces of liberalism would bring about a new global order. But when one of the most monumental material symbols of the era, the Berlin Wall, was dismantled in November 1989, there was no triumph of liberation. Life simply went on, in more disarray than ever, and the lack of allegorical completion brought onto the stage a social and cultural emptiness – a temporal vacancy.

The vertigo effects of the emptiness – into which commodity culture is filtered – takes on the aura of an altered state, a condition that embodies the instability of a kind of double-or-nothing end: the end of the boundaries governing Cold War nation time and also the end of the nation-based social and historical identities that had been mediated, scripted, or otherwise mapped as the measure of the dominant. These ends produce the effect of the temporal as a dislocation. It is in this nexus of incompatible projections that the normalized coordinates of space and time – geography and history – appear dislodged from the linear assumptions of progress and are cast into an unfolding but nebulous and seemingly boundless global future that is paradoxically more and more the limit against which the present – and hence the past – performs variations on a vanishing act. Future time, in the operative language of global capitalism, always beckons with the rainbow fantasy of a pot of golden commodities that vanquishes time.

As removed as English studies may seem to be from the mass culture of commodification, it nevertheless occupies a zone of intersections within institutional domains where knowledge production is invested. No longer conceived as its own end – the arc is now from the lab to the marketplace – knowledge as such has also taken on the identity of commodities, accommodating itself to the logic of capitalization. No one is immune from this rush towards an "end" that must forever await the advent of technologies to produce new and newer formations. In the "practice of everyday life," to draw from de Certeau (1988), our subjectivities become a variation of the un-settled, a variation of transient formations that are increasingly sutured into the time of global capitalism's networks of contingencies whose infrastructures remain beyond apprehension. And as the consumers who are so necessary to capital's expansionary processes, we are washed in the proliferation of images that present the dissemination of newly forming subjects in global scenarios, of bodies undergoing forced movements and expulsions as refugees in flight from homelands, and of migrants whose displacements and passages across borders have become central narratives of our time. From the position on the raft, the shore seems forever out of reach.

As we learned in the opening story of Steve Chao (2000), a local manifestation of the altered state of Canadian social consciousness involved the "sudden arrival" of unidentified but Asian-identified figures in rundown ships, some of them emerging in the nation's space from the confines of cargo containers. Dubbed, first, as the "boat people" – a phrase linking them discursively to the Vietnamese refugees who arrived in the late 1970s – and later simply as "migrants," these figures entering the Canadian mediascape in the summer of 1999 were instantly enmeshed in representations that occluded their visibility as contiguous with a global capitalist economy in which bodies – often Asian-identified bodies – are reduced to labour machines. In the logic of capital, in other words, their arrival was already conjured across the oceanic divide to serve corporate agendas – agendas that bring economic and ideological benefits to Canadians. The reaction of the media and some vocal Canadians, including some Chinese Canadians, who accused the would-be refugees of the impropriety of queue jumping, disguised the more violent desire to demonize the figures and to expel them from the territorial and symbolic boundaries of the Canadian nation. Already exhausted from the long and terrifying ordeal of travelling across an ocean, "a voyage during which two people from the second ship died" (Direct Action Against Refugee Exploitation 2001, 10),[1] these figures turned out to be economically deprived individuals from the Fujian region of China who desperately wanted to find a safe haven in what they imagined as a bountiful Canadian nation.

But what was the identity of the nation that was being defended? What substance in its precious and reified border justified the line drawn between alien and normal? When those who called for expulsion – in the familiar "send them back where they came from!" or "Go Home," to cite one newspaper headline – and who found no difficulty in disregarding the refugee policy set up to counter such xenophobia, in what manner did they imagine the national inside that needed to be shielded from the aliens knocking at their door?

Effects of Globalization on the State of the Nation

The processes of economic globalization are producing contradictory and unpredictable effects in nation-state formations including those of Canada. Here, for instance, the social and cultural mechanisms that stabilized national identity around a centre have been compromised and even undermined by global forces that Jan Penrose has described as "suprastate economic networks and systems" and "multi-state organizations" (29) that promote the removal of barriers and that arrest the ability of nation-states to control their own affairs – in Canada the Free Trade Agreement (FTA) and the North American Free Trade Agreement (NAFTA), both of which paved the way for transnational corporations to challenge state powers.[2] At the same time, or in the same flows, the nation becomes a conduit for the influx of global capital, trading off its controls for a share of the market pie, hence its complicity with the corporate agendas that give rise to the flow of migrant bodies while simultaneously shoring up its territorial borders to prevent those bodies – all too often racialized – from becoming citizens.

The speculation, then, is that the discrepancies generated by – and indeed sustained for the sake of – global capitalism bring with them the losses and gains that propel the normalizing language of its market economy. The loss of state control over structures of social cohesion is not simply a determinism, though it may be named as such by corporate interests and by politicians who mime these interests; rather it offers the often-enormous financial gains made possible through the strategic deployment of political mechanisms that facilitate the entrance of multinational corporations (mostly US corporations in Canadian contexts)[3] into its national spaces. The compromised role of nation-states in capital expansion results in a dissolving language of cultural nationalism which, in its unravelling process, makes the nation – as if suddenly – strange to itself. Social life takes on a spectral quality, an altered state, as national borders are perceived as being open to threat by alien forces that can no longer be normalized through its historically constituted codes of racialization and differential relations of subject positioning.

In this altered state, the future begins to loom as a vacant elsewhere, and social, cultural, and political formations are no longer reliable measures of meaning, but become more uncertain and unpredictable. It is into such a void that the fantastic images of capitalist commodity culture bringing in their wake a host of material and intellectual commodities that have the power to mediate the loss of meaning and to generate and placate the desire of their consumers. Who needs the identity of the nation's time, their voices say, when there are commodities about to be born with the potential to remake the very boundaries of the human. We read in the local newspaper, the *Vancouver Sun*, that Jeremy Rifken (author of *The Biotech Century*) believes we can look forward to biotechnological wizardry to increase the intelligence of newborns. The merging of the discourses of biology and consumer capitalism looks towards future generations of so-called designer babies in which national allegiances with its ties of lineage, ethnicity, and citizenship will survive only in archives: "In the future the parent becomes an architect and each child becomes the ultimate shopping experience" (Urquhart 2000). The ultimate fantasy in this biotechnological venture perhaps resides in the not-so-bizarre image of the deceased body held in a cryonic suspension, awaiting the moment of its arrival on wholly other shores in a post-ethnic, post-historical, post-contemporary, post-future, post-whatever time – but if only the forces of capitalism are obeyed. So is this, then, the rub? Who can know who is drugged or who is on the placebo? And what may be your preference?

Against this soporific temptation of the atemporal, the migrancy of altered states, in a transformative iteration, turns and re-turns the affects of what Bhabha (1997) calls the "unhomely" (445) that marks the arrival of the postcolonial. The unhomely is the event of a disjuncture, a crisis in spatialized time, between here and there, near and far, one's own and one's alien, internal and external; the I doubled up, subject and object, in the alterior spaces between shifting formations. When the influx of globalization makes the nation strange to itself, the present takes on the face of the uncanny and what was (now previously) in place is set adrift – to encounter the spectres of estrangement, loss, nostalgia, and liminality.

From a position of critique, the effects of destabilization make visible the borders of nation-based formations, bringing into relief the constructedness of the norms in a process of "articulation" (Stuart Hall's term) through which the coherence of historical narratives are enabled. As Hall explains in an interview with Lawrence Grossberg, "the so-called 'unity' of a discourse [and by extension a formation] is really the articulation of different, distinct elements which can be re-articulated in different ways because they have no necessary 'belongingness'" (Grossberg 1996, 141). Articulation has to do with a "connection" or "linkage" made "under certain historical conditions" in a formation that is "not necessary, determined, absolute and essential for all time" (Grossberg 1996, 141), but provisional and always subject to change.

Hall's notion of articulation helps to expose Canadian nation-formation and the identity discourses it produces as not "natural,"[4] that is, as givens that both precede and supersede its individuated subjects, but an articulation of historical trajectories through which its subjects were marked and translated – in certain ways – from the signs of colonial invasion and territorialization into the abstract language of citizenship. Hall's "theory of articulation asks how an ideology discovers its subject rather than how the subject thinks the necessary and inevitable thoughts which belong to it" (Grossberg 1996, 142). The question of how – by what kind and manner of discourses – the Canadian nation-state has been articulated in the twentieth century thus contains within it the prospect of a re-articulation that can negotiate the ambivalent ends of its current altered state.

There is some advantage, then, in imagining that the global currents making the Canadian nation strange to itself expose its interior as an articulation linked to the colonial moment of invasion and the subsequent forging of a national unity. As the post-Cold War national formations unravel, so does the nation's unity that has been shaped, on the one hand, by ethnocentric and racialized social and cultural hierarchies and, on the other, by state mechanisms that would ensure the ascendancy of ruling groups whose colonial backgrounds would constitute the norms of the new nation. The translation process has been complex and always adjusting to shifting conditions, but it has worked most effectively through the discursive apparatus of identity-making (which is to say, difference-making), most evident, for instance, in such state discourses as the Indian Act which produced what Marcia Crosby (1991) has aptly identified as the "imaginary Indian"[5] and the complex weave of immigration and citizenship regulations that produced a nation in which privilege and positioning were determined through the normalization of the differences through race, gender, ethnicity, and class. In this historical formation, the minoritization of women, non-whites, and gays and lesbians in the history of citizenship has worked to occlude the racialized privileges accorded to white, male, heterosexual norms, thus placing the burden on them to erase, remake, or otherwise elide their differences in order to gain access to its spaces – in effect, to camouflage themselves as transparent to these norms. Or, to see it from a more tactical perspective, they have had to don what Stacy Takacs (1999) describes as a "prosthetic" (596) identity that disguises their marked status as minorities, in this sense undergoing an assimilation process through which they have been able to occupy dominant positions through mimicry (and learning ways to inhabit contradictory subjectivities) or, in more compliant terms, have accepted positions prescribed for them.

While the state has worked to naturalize the differences that constitute its minority subjects, it has been at the point of entrance – the point of arrival at the borders of the nation-state – that the most intense beams of racialization have shone. The question of marking legitimate from illegitimate bodies is not a recent phenomenon, but a preoccupation that has played itself out in its immigration regulations. As several cultural historians[6] have noted, the discourses of immigration – of who gets in and who does not fit – come alive as the site of a social engineering process in the service of the dominant groups. "Nation-building," then, "is a dual process, entailing the management of populations and the creation of national identity" (Mackey 1999, 23). Nothing has been more indispensable for shaping the racialized body of Canada's identity than the legalization of policies that would support the eugenic agenda of the dominant Anglocentric group at the turn of the nineteenth century. The territories that were secured by invasion, colonization, and the authority of the British North America Act (1867) that created Canada as a state could not be properly occupied without the formation of a collective identity, a nation that would protect the "white settler societies" (the English and the French) from the influx of otherness.

The construction of a nation-state, Penrose (1997) reminds us, "frequently bears a remarkable likeness to the self-image and aspirations of those who have power to forge it" (27). The dominant group or groups, as in the case of the English and French colonialisms in Canada, will act in their own best interests and, in conditions of challenge to their control, will devise accommodations (think here of the discourse of multiculturalism)[7] in order to maintain their founding status. In describing the "vision of [English] Canada which emerges from its history of nation-building," Penrose sets out the now-familiar determining profile, crucial for constituting the normative discourse of the Canadian imaginary: "The hegemonic ideal prescribed that, in customs, Canadians would be British; they would speak the English language (though some French had to be tolerated, temporarily at least); they would hold to the Christian faith (preferably Protestant); and, incontrovertibly, they would be white" (27).[8]

At the outset of the century the "color-line," announced by US writer W.E.B. DuBois (1994) in *The Souls of Black Folk* as "the problem of the Twentieth Century" (v), had to be drawn in shaping the Canadian nation-state. And it was accomplished by discursive means through the valorization of the desirable subjects over those who were racialized as the "undesirable," a category that made its first appearance in the 1906 Immigration Act, was reinforced in its 1909 version, and then assumed as state policy in the decades ahead. These acts were articulated during another moment of crisis in nation making, in another period of capitalist expansion (c. 1896–1914) when the Canadian economy, stimulated by an unprecedented growth of a more diverse population of immigrants, entered a global market hungry for its natural resources. With cheap labour in high demand, Canadian capitalists welcomed an exploitable pool of Asian bodies to provide the labour for nation building – the thousands of Chinese railway workers among them. While their bodies crossed over state borders, their subject status was monitored through policies that named them as outside the nation then in formation, as the "undesirables,"[9] who threatened the purity of a "white Canada forever" (to cite Peter Ward's [1990] study of anti-Asian racism in the history of British Columbia).

These externalized "undesirables" within would translate over time into Asian Canadians who would not receive the franchise until the late 1940s. Even then, and more likely to placate his dominant white constituencies, Prime Minister Mackenzie King could dip into the inkwell of racialized immigration policy to reassure his fellow Canadians that his government had subdued the monstrous menace of "yellow peril":

> The policy of the Government is to foster the growth of the population of Canada by the encouragement of immigration. The government will seek ... to ensure the careful selection and permanent settlement of such numbers of immigrants as can advantageously be absorbed in our national economy ... I wish to make it quite clear that Canada is perfectly within her rights in selecting the persons whom we regard as *desirable* [emphasis added] future citizens. It is not a "fundamental human right" of any alien to enter Canada. It is a privilege. It is a matter of domestic policy ... The people of Canada do not wish, as a result of mass immigration, to make a fundamental alteration in the character of our population. Any considerable Oriental immigration would ... be certain to give rise to social and economic problems ... (House of Commons, May 1, 1947; qtd. in Kelley and Trebilcock 1998, 312)

For the Asian migrants who arrived at the borders of this colonial-cum-national-cum-state articulation in the transitional years between the late nineteenth and early twentieth century, the language of racialization would produce them as the "strangers within our gates," to invoke the title of J.S. Woodsworth's 1909 book that addressed the coming of Asians into Canada. Woodsworth's book came on the heels of the infamous 1907 riot in Vancouver's Chinatown and Japantown, a riot that was instigated by the Asiatic Exclusion League, a broad coalition of influential white-identified organizations that sought to expel or otherwise exclude Asian immigrants. These "strangers" would also face a complex of now-well-known legislated terms to curtail and expunge their presence in the developing Canadian nation. There was the head tax levied on Chinese immigrants, which started at $10 in 1884, rose to $50 in 1885, to $100 in 1900, and to an exorbitant $500 in 1903. When even these measures did not stop immigration, the federal government in 1923 passed the Chinese Immigration Act (aka the Exclusion Act), an act that banned those identified as Chinese from Canadian territories, in effect until 1947. There was also the so-called Gentleman's Agreement, made with Japan by Minister of Labour Rodolphe Lemieux in 1907, which limited emigration to 400 per year and drastically cut the flow of Japanese into Canada. Then came the Continuous Journey policy, which required that Asians could enter Canada only through a continuous route directly from their ascribed country of origin, even if they did not reside there. With the absence of regular steamship lines coming directly from India, this policy, in addition to successively higher landing fees, severely reduced the numbers of Indians entering Canada. As Kelley and Trebilcock (1998) write, "The number of East Indian immigrants fell from 2,623 in 1908 to 6 the following year. It rose to 10 persons in 1910, and fell again the next year to 5. Between 1908 and 1915, slightly more than 100 East Indians were admitted to Canada" (149).

Those already within the nation, moreover, had to contend with a barrage of policies and laws of disenfranchisement, such as the notorious Provincial Elections Act of BC, which stipulated: "No Chinaman, Japanese or Indian shall have his name placed on the Register of Voters for any Electoral District, or be entitled to vote in any election." By preventing those signified as "Japs," "Chinese," and "Hindoos" from placing their names on the voters' list, this legislation in effect barred them from participation in the democratic process until

1947 for South Asians and Chinese Canadians and 1949 for Japanese Canadians. As a rule, restrictive policies that affected capital expansion (e.g., outright exclusion of Asians, which was proposed many times by the BC legislature) were denied by the federal government and those that affected identity formation (e.g., gaining the right to vote) and therefore the right to belong to the nation were upheld. The cultural legacy of this history, of course, reaches into our own time.[10]

On the other hand, when the norms of a "hegemonic ideal" undergo a sea change, as they have in the large-scale demographic shifts of Asian Canadians since the late 1960s, the white founding settler identities – despite retaining their institutionalized powers through entrenched historical precedents – lose the substance of their authority in the heterogeneity of the contemporary. The nation has already moved elsewhere, and in its displacement there are signs of an "alien-nation," a formation that Takacs (1999) says marks "both the sense of psychic alienation experienced by the majority population when faced with the prospect that they will no longer compose a majority by the year 2050, and the sense that the root cause of this alienation is, literally, the presence of aliens (both legal and illegal) within the nation" (612).

Are those strange glances from across the lane the isolated optics of individual estrangements, or can the social be reconceived as a web of incommensurate subjectivities prompted to navigate the elsewhere in the alien-nation? Can this be the premonition of an alter-nation beyond the hierarchic frames of difference making – of social positionings modelled on migratory intersections rather than centralist settlement?

Re-Situating Asian Canadian as a Critical Formation

The re-articulation of the past to account for the emergence of alterior narratives of the nation opens the possibility that Asian Canadian, as one site of visibility, can be read into the moment of alteration. As a formation linked to the nation and simultaneously in excess of its borders, it is marked by the "processes of globalization, and their impacts," which "cannot be fully understood without reference to attendant processes of fragmentation" (Penrose 1997, 45). It is these processes of fragmentation that initially instil a sense of estrangement in nation-based contexts, as those who have been subjectivated – Judith Butler's (1997) paradoxical term, from Michel Foucault, which "denotes both the becoming of the subject and the process of subjection" (83) – disarticulate themselves from their variously compromised positions to produce the vertigo effect of the same as suddenly "alien." This condition then becomes a crisis that could stimulate xenophobic responses of defensiveness, scapegoating, and othering, recalling the formative phase of nation-state construction, but at the same time – and this is the direction I hope critical thought can pursue – be read as a field of transitions in which, and through which, attentive vocabularies of resistance can begin to create alternate forms of collectivity.

From this critical location, the very contradictions inherent in Asian Canadian begin to suggest its social and cultural value in the crisis of the *post*, the crisis of what might be understood as the nation's constructed time. This is the time that unfolds in its narrative of progress from its colonial moment to its maturation as a modern liberal nation. Asian Canadian, when dislodged from the foreclosure of such a narrative, becomes a revolving sign that re-articulates and thus exposes discourses of both globalization (i.e., towards Asian markets and economies) and a reactionary nationalism (i.e., as a "yellow peril" that is asianizing white Canada). Asian Canadian then becomes both a localized subject – of research, cultural production, interrogation – but also a double-edged site: where relations of dominance can be remobilized (more of the same), *or* where critiques of the nation can posit future methodologies of resistance and collective formations.

Thought of in a provisional manner, globalization as such need not be conceived as a monolithic force. While its economic power to level local cultural specificities and to reduce everything to a standardized mass culture should never be underestimated, it also has its limits. The subjects of global mass mediation, while formed by the influx of so-called information technologies, are never passive recipients but always engaged in re-inscriptions, some of which reproduce normative assumptions but some of which challenge and undermine these assumptions through the production of cultural contradictions and even deformations that elicit unpredictable performances. There is, despite the hollowed out language of determinism, always the potential for new collectivities to form in response to dominant representational systems. According to Roland Axtmann (1997), for instance, "The social groups and collectives that are the recipients of the 'global message' interpret, or bestow meaning upon, these messages on the basis of their own specific experience and memories as they grew out of their own particular histories and cultures; they creatively modify 'messages' and cultural products in light of their own local needs and requirements" (37).

What I want to propose, then, is that the fragmentation of formerly (more or less) coherent public spheres can provide the motivation for practices of critique, counter moves, and alliances. These practices have the capacity to enable a rethinking of *nation* as a complex of heterogeneous global/local formations, not constituted solely as enclaves of identification but more generatively produced by or through negotiations across and within temporalities and boundaries. The time of the nation needs to be reconceived as non-synchronous – in contradistinction to the linear and totalizing time of imperialism and colonization – so that texts, and especially racialized texts, can have the mobility to open cultural transactions that encourage the re-articulation of a more radical democratic system of values. This would be a move beyond a hierarchy of "differences from" a normative centre to a more limited field of indeterminacies where social subjects assume responsibility for the production of meanings tied to the range of positions they occupy – positions that are themselves the local sites which set limits on what can or cannot be enunciated.

Reading Beyond?: The Local and the Postcolonial

The contemporary interest in Asian Canadian texts may be, in part, the consequence of an ethnocentric nationalism achieving obsolescence, in stages, during the period from the early 1970s to the late 1980s. The phenomenon, if it can be characterized as such, hinges on a contradiction that is both aside from and tied to the affects initiated by these texts in more localized contexts, arriving perhaps as representational compensation for absences in dominant cultural institutions. Their presence has been conceived in the critical narrative of an emergent minority literature, a narrative that has covered over the externalization of Asian Canadians in the overall construction of the modern Canadian nation-state from the late nineteenth century to the present.

What is important to recognize, however, is that the so-called minority spaces that would come to visibility during the 1970s and 1980s simultaneously produced and were produced by a largely unstructured network of racialized writers and artists who initially identified themselves through the marks of hyphenation – for instance, Japanese Canadian and Chinese Canadian. These marks, in turn, would call for an acknowledgment of linkages, not through some prior cultural homogeneity, but in the warp and weave of the nation's formation – a condition that attests to the burden of representation in such a term as Asian Canadian. While such naming establishes limits that can be used in coercive practices, it can also function as the horizon towards which cultural processes can project the situated imagination of writers and artists. It is in the material expression of their imagination – in literary texts, for instance – that the internal seams of the nation's contradictions, ambivalences, inequities, traumas, and conflicted loyalties find themselves localized as inscriptions that run counter to dominant Canadian literary formations. And they do so no longer as other, but as cultural signs that can be approached as a localism that exceeds the nation, even as they inscribe its internally constituted differentiations.

In its specificities, this localism would then both remember and inscribe the legacy of racialization and externalization wherein the traumatic comes to embody the effects of the inner violence used to establish and maintain the state's centrality, the very violence that has been covered over to give a benign face to the nation's liberal values. This conceptualization of the contradictory social and cultural zones in which the term Asian has circulated does not diminish in any way the subjective instances of cultural resistance, community activism, and creative agency that have been enacted by individuals and collectivities formed under its signs; instead, it proposes that the term operates as an interface in its always shifting and shifty negotiations with the term *Canadian*. However imagined, the existence of Asian in Canadian has always been a disturbance – a disarticulation that had to be managed as the "Asiatic," as the "Oriental," and subsequently as a sign of the multicultural, as the "Visible Minority," in order to sustain the figure of the citizen as the end of assimilation – rather than a subject position vested with privileged differences based on racialization (white), ethnicity (Anglo/European), sexual orientation (hetero), and gender (male).

The tension between inscription and excess in Asian Canadian cultural production is aligned to unpredictable and potentially volatile public spheres of social and institutional interventions, ranging from compliance to complicity to resistance to defiance – which is to say, risk is always an omnipresent critical variable. There is, for instance, the internal temptation of a nation strange to itself – and I include its institutions – to retreat into a defensive posture, unleashing the politics of backlash and blame. Or there might be an attempt to overcome estrangement through reversions to remodelled colonial tactics of appropriation, containment, and management, translating what is alterior into an extension of its "own" on the liberal assumption of a minority desire to be incorporated or, worse, to become a site of desire in and for dominant cultural formations. As colourized versions of CanLit, then, texts such as Joy Kogawa's *Obasan* (1981), SKY Lee's *Disappearing Moon Cafe* (1990), Hiromi Goto's *Chorus of Mushrooms* (1994), Larissa Lai's *When Fox Is a Thousand* (1995), Fred Wah's *Diamond Grill* (1996), Ashok Mathur's *Once Upon an Elephant* (1998), Kerri Sakamoto's *The Electrical Field* (1998) can be read into – rather than as critiques of – a nation articulated through racialized cultural codes. Moreover, such a reading into a national formation that is all but spent implicates the more ambivalent desire of a salvage operation: a reconstituted – even "improved" – Canadian can be retrieved through minority subjects who are supposedly connected to vital cultural networks with the resources to rejuvenate a nation that, by implication, has made them possible. Such a reification process, in turn, could inflict a form of critical and institutional branding that replays the function of the brand name in commodity capitalism – the curious inversion of a branding through a re-racialization process. We are here returned to the site of the transaction – i.e., of readers and texts – and the already-instrumental role of the discourse of commodification in corporate modes of production.

Consider, for instance, the escalation of the brand name into the status of creator in mass culture (largely US-controlled, of course). The Gap brand is only one of a complex of commodities incarnated through an aesthetics that was previously the domain of art culture, and thus, in a free trade mode, it elides the boundary between the economic and the creative. The brand name announces the rebirth of the author function, producing a line of postmodern commodities in which form is the content. The consumer, not unlike a reader, inhabits a style, deriving pleasure in performing the product, literally wearing it on the body. The power of this cult of commodification is so pervasive that cultural producers – of the biological sort – are themselves re-presented in its discourses as authors who strive to become brand names – packaged identities that accrue cultural and economic capital according to the market logic of mass consumption and distribution. This is why the practice of creative enactments, especially those once thought to be counter-narratives of national exclusions (i.e., those exemplified in the 1980s through the institutionalization of Kogawa's *Obasan*), cannot be repeated with the same effects. In the new commodification of identities, authorial signs are much more malleable and thus open to appropriation and invention, so that the so-called repressed of the era of nation-state stability may emerge in the new faces of born-again difference in the liberal culture of capitalism.

Thus, if we were to speculate that the heightened visibility of Asian Canadian texts is part of a compensatory response to the collapse of once normalized nation-based cultural representations, a potentially troubling question is the extent to which this process interacts with, or otherwise conditions, the desires of writers who set out to produce creative texts. Or, approached from another angle, when the nation turns spectral, the figure of the Asian Canadian in that nation is then dislodged from its minoritized state. But what would/does a post-Asian Canadian look like? How would/does it write? As it encounters the global currents that unravel its former nation-based identity, can it be immune from the realm of the spectral? Is there that moment when the transformation of Asian Canadian releases the ghosts in the system that only existed as nominations? Who, in this instance, was then the Asian in Canadian? How are we to read the future in the past?

In any case, the baseline of global capitalism, informing as well its discourse of liberalism and individualism, is the maximization of profit – no surprises there. Its reductive powers have meant that the market economy has come to be more the common denominator than ever before, leaving less provisionality for cultural works that undermine, or even refuse, the model of consumption that underwrites its anticipations. The textual productions that circulate as Asian Canadian cannot in themselves withstand the aesthetic and social expectations of market constraints – constraints whose reach extends to the currently fashionable commodification of difference as pleasure, the exotic consumed as versions of cultural enhancement. The resistance to modes of reading as ingestion alone has to be articulated through critical interventions that continually negotiate and navigate the locations of production, addressing, in highly site-specific fields of attention, the nexus of power relations out of which differential subject positions are formed. Even though a term such as post-colonial has been contested as inadequate to deal with the consequences of colonial violence[11] – and I am mindful of the charge that it may itself be read as an effect of "global capitalism" (see Dirlik 1998, 517) – its advantage, specifically in this moment of altered states, may reside in its undecidability. The mobility of its articulations and re-articulations may then offer a critical potential to expose and unravel homogeneities – of culture, identities, discourses – which cover over global/local indeterminacies in the production of aesthetic forms. The arrival of what I have suggested is the elsewhere of the spectral nation is not to be understood only as a periodization, i.e., as a *post* that argues a liberation from the colonial, but more as a lateral move that undercuts and refuses the binaries (centre/margin, self/other, white/visible, we/they) of the now-obsolescent nation formations. What comes to appearance in this lateral move are the more specific and singular inflections of the local as a mobile configuration of global/local relations. Not as a territory possessed and named as property – but the local as simultaneously the site and cite of enunciation. The subjects of the local then come to formation, as texts do, "out of a specific history, out of a specific set of power relationships" (Hall 1997, 185). For cultural creators such as writers and artists, the local may then be considered the nexus of historical, social, cultural, and economic variables that situate the boundaries of subjectivity, but which are always appearing in the signs of relationships – including provisional collectivities – that are underwritten by the power dynamics of what comes to be taken as normative in given public spheres.

While a postcolonial frame may itself be both a symptom and product of the crisis in the nation's time, and this is my suggestion, it may also function as a transitional point of transference. In this instance, as terminology itself undergoes severe semantic indeterminacies, it offers at the very least a discursive screen to project and thus reflect on the fragmentation of subject positions and the figures of alterity that continue to haunt the social and cultural parameters of nation-based representations. For Stuart Hall the "concept *may* help us ... to describe or characterise the shift in global relations" and "help us (though here its value is more gestural) to identify what are the new relations and dispositions of power which are emerging in the new conjuncture" (Hall 1996, 246).

I would like to imagine, then, that the social intersections of the global/local in our midst, even as they dissolve old terminologies in a relentless process of obsolescence, also harbour the ingredients for the emergence of critical reading practices to address and account for the complicities of subject positionings that both produce and are produced in relations of power. This always open-ended and site-specific dynamic cannot be sustained without the nuanced ethics of critical discourses – the very ethics that is at issue in the reading practices we bring to cultural texts. These texts, and especially those issuing from Asian Canadian and other comparable locations, provide the occasions for reading processes that bring into play a complex of subject positions, often contradictory and conflicted but also in correspondences, which call for ongoing negotiation and reflexivity. Against the teleology of consumerist intake, such a critical reading practice would out-take the discursive positions that make meaning possible; in effect, it would break the gaze of subject-object relations and allow cultural texts to become signs of contestation, incommensurability, and singularity. An ethics of reading would seek to perform those social spaces that refuse the exertion of power over subjects and instead speculate on what we might call the postcolonial imaginary of an alternate nation beyond the spectral. But more than this, these texts also offer the possibility of an aesthetics that can locate the reading act in the present – a present that Homi Bhabha (1997) writes "is not a transcendental passage but a moment of 'transit', a form of temporality that is open to disjunction and discontinuity and that sees the process of history engaged, rather like art, in a negotiation of the framing and naming of social reality – not what lies inside or outside reality, but where to draw (or inscribe) the 'meaningful' line between them" (448). If we can call this line the moment of the postcolonial, then the term can be read as an acknowledgment of the non-totalizable temporalities coexisting in the nation. It would then provide a hinge for critical vocabularies to generate those readers who are themselves the evidence of alternate histories.

NOTES

1 In Vancouver, the arrival of Chinese migrant labourers from the Fujian province elicited the interventionist activism of a new organization called DAARE (Direct Action Against Refugee Exploitation 2001), "formed by a group of women in Vancouver to support the rights of the people – especially the women – from China seeking refuge in Canada" (from a pamphlet). DAARE has been instrumental in speaking back to media misrepresentations and in assisting those seeking refugee status. Their educational work brought to the public's attention the complicit relations between Canada's global capitalist agenda and the exploitation of Asian labour – a reinscription of the brutal exploitation of racialized Chinese railway workers in the nineteenth century.

2 In addition to Penrose's (1997) essay, the following resources have been helpful in providing a basis for this discussion: Ann Cvetkovich and Douglas Kellner's (1997) *Articulating the Global and the Local*; Anthony D. King's (1997) *Culture, Globalization and the World-System*; Fredric Jameson and Masao Miyoshi's (1998) *The Cultures of Globalization*; and Rob Wilson and Wimal Dissanayake's (1996) *Global/Local*. Along with Penrose, theorists such as Miyoshi (1995) and Dirlik (1998) also point to the emergent power of the transnational corporation in displacing the concentration of capital within the nation's boundaries and its dispersal across borders in networks that begin to supersede the control of specific nation-states.

3 This is not the occasion to address the specific impact of US control of media representations in Canada as a form of cultural imperialism, except to agree with Fredric Jameson (1998) that unequal relations of power underscore the ubiquitous "Americanization" process that is carried out under the auspices of economic trade. As he says, "American mass culture, associated as it is with money and commodities, enjoys a prestige that is perilous for most forms of domestic cultural production" (59) – Canada, for instance – and it is all the more reductive and standardizing as it brings in its folds, to undermine the cultural specificities of local conditions, the figure of the consumer as a kind of cultural patron and the goods s/he consumes as a form of cultural performance.

4 For a critique of the "natural" as constructed, see Stacy Takacs (1999).

5 See Marcia Crosby (1991), as well as work by Roxana Ng (1993) and Daniel Francis (1992). Regarding various mechanisms used by the Canadian state to construct a nation, Jan Penrose (1997) points to the use of education to get subjects to identity with the "nation" through constructed narratives of "historical and contemporary events and, perhaps most importantly of all, for standardizing language" (23). The dramatic instance still remains the so-called "Residential Schools" through which First Nations children were deracinated with the intent to re-make them as colonial subjects through the medium of Christian discourses. The state also makes use of national media (print, radio, and television) "for promulgating hegemonic views of what the Canadian nation was or ought to be" (24).

6 See, for instance, Eva Mackey (1999), Veronica Strong-Boag et al. (1998), Daiva Stasiulis and Radha Jhappan (1995), Ninette Kelley and Michael Trebilcock (1998), and Jonathan Kertzer (1998).

7 The critique of multiculturalism is voluminous, and beyond the specific focus of this paper, but Katharyne Mitchell's (1996) essay, "In Whose Interest?", focusing on Vancouver, offers a

compelling argument for the caution that cultural theorists and activists need to exercise in reading new cultural productions by minoritized artists and writers through the discourse of multiculturalism as developed in Canadian contexts. What is interpreted as progressive or inclusionary, e.g., new texts by Asian Canadian writers, may be seen as such through its complicity with the expansion of transnational Asian capital that requires the language of multiculturalism as a means of covering over, or even mediating, the continuing racialization of Asian Canadians.

8 It is also important to note that "whiteness," as itself a shifting and malleable category, has historically adjusted its exclusionary borders to maintain its normative conditions. Hence "Ukrainians," for instance, as well as East Europeans, initially considered non-white – by the largely Anglo-Saxon majority – were eventually incorporated into the sphere of an expanded whiteness, in contrast to "Asians," "Aboriginals," and "Blacks" who have consistently been constituted through variations on their projected otherness.

9 For a fascinating, and meticulous, examination of the effects of legalized racialization on the local conditions of Chinese Canadian subjects in Saskatchewan in the early part of this century, see Constance Backhouse's (1996, 1999) excellent legal "narrative" (her term) on two trials set in Moose Jaw, Saskatchewan, in May 1912. Two "Chinese" men, Quong Wing and Quong Sing, had been charged with a recently passed provincial statute – the "first of its kind in Canada" (315) – that made it an offence for "Chinese" to hire "white women" in their businesses.

10 For further discussion of this early history, see Patricia Roy (1989), Kay Anderson (1991), and Ken Adachi (1976).

11 See, for instance, the complicated debates that have formed around the term in books by Anne McClintock, Aamir Mufti, and Ella Shohat (1997); Iain Chambers and Lidia Curti (1996); and Patrick Williams and Laura Chrisman (1994). Its Canadian variations can be found in *Past the Last Post,* edited by Ian Adam and Helen Tiffin (1991); and the special issues, *Testing the Limits,* edited by Diana Brydon (1995), and *Postcolonialism and Its Discontents,* edited by Pamela McCallum, Stephen Slemon, and Aruna Srivastava (1995).

REFERENCES

Adachi, Ken. 1976. *The Enemy That Never Was: A History of the Japanese Canadians.* Toronto: McClelland and Stewart.

Adam, Ian, and Helen Tiffin, eds. 1991. *Past the Last Post: Theorizing Post-Colonialism and Post-Modernism.* New York: Harvester Wheatsheaf.

Anderson, Kay. 1991. *Vancouver's Chinatown: Racial Discourse in Canada, 1875–1980.* Montreal: McGill-Queen's University Press.

Axtmann, Roland. 1997. "Collective Identity and the Democratic Nation-State in the Age of Globalization." In *Articulating the Global and the Local: Globalization and Cultural Studies*, ed. Ann Cvetkovich and Douglas Kellner, 33–54. Boulder, Colorado: Westview Press.

Backhouse, Constance. Fall 1996. "The White Women's Labor Laws: Anti-Chinese Racism in Early Twentieth-Century Canada." *Law and History Review* 14 (2): 315–68. http://dx.doi.org/10.2307/743786.

Backhouse, Constance. 1999. "White Female Help and Chinese-Canadian Employers: Race, Class, Gender, and Law in the Case of Yee Clun." In *Law in Society: Canadian Readings*, ed. Nick Larsen and Brian Burtch, 3–22. Toronto: Harcourt Brace & Company.

Bhabha, Homi K. 1997. "The World and the Home." In *Dangerous Liaisons: Gender, Nation, and Postcolonial Perspectives*, ed. Anne McClintock, Aamir Mufti, and Ella Shohat, 445–455. Minneapolis: University of Minneapolis Press.

British North American Act. 1867. http://www.justice.gc.ca/eng/re-pr/csj-sjc/constitution/lawreg-loireg/p1t11.html.
Brydon, Diana, ed. 1995. *Testing the Limits: Postcolonial Theories and Canadian Literature. Essays on Canadian Writing* 56 (Fall).
Butler, Judith. 1997. *The Psychic Life of Power: Theories in Subjection*. Stanford: Stanford University Press.
Canclini, Néstor García. 2000. "The State of War and the State of Hybridization." In *Without Guarantees: In Honour of Stuart Hall*, ed. Paul Gilroy, Lawrence Grossberg, and Angela McRobbie, 38–52. London: Verso.
Chambers, Iain, and Lidia Curti, eds. 1996. *The Post-Colonial Question: Common Skies, Divided Horizons*. London, New York: Routledge. http://dx.doi.org/10.4324/9780203297865.
Chao, Steve. 2000. "The Backlash Against Chinese Migrants: One Reporter's Perspective." *Rice Paper* 5 (4): 20–21.
Crosby, Marcia. 1991. "Construction of the Imaginary Indian." In *Vancouver Anthology: The Institutional Politics of Art*, ed. Stan Douglas, 267–290. Vancouver: Talonbooks.
Cvetkovich, Ann, and Douglas Kellner, eds. 1997. *Articulating the Global and the Local: Globalization and Cultural Studies*. Boulder, Colorado: Westview Press.
de Certeau, Michel. 1988. *The Practice of Everyday Life*. Trans. Steven Rendall. Berkeley: University of California Press.
Dirlik, Arif. 1998. "The Postcolonial Aura: Third World Criticism in the Age of Capitalism." In *Dangerous Liaisons: Gender, Nation, and Postcolonial Perspectives*, ed. Anne McClintock, Aamir Mufti, and Ella Shohat, 501–528. Minneapolis: University of Minnesota Press.
Direct Action Against Refugee Exploitation. 2001. *Movement Across Borders: Chinese Women Migrants in Canada*. Vancouver: DAARE.
DuBois, W.E.B. 1994. *The Souls of Black Folk*. New York: Dover.
Francis, Daniel. 1992. *The Imaginary Indian: The Image of the Indian in Canadian Culture*. Vancouver: Arsenal Pulp.
Goto, Hiromi. 1994. *Chorus of Mushrooms*. Edmonton: NeWest.
Grossberg, Lawrence. 1996. "On Postmodernism and Articulation: An Interview with Stuart Hall." In *Stuart Hall: Critical Dialogues in Cultural Studies*, ed. David Morley and Kuan-Hsing Chen, 131–150. New York, London: Routledge.
Hall, Stuart. 1996. "When Was 'The Post-Colonial'?: Thinking at the Limit." In *The Post-Colonial Question*, ed. Ian Chambers and Lidia Curti, 242–260. London, New York: Routledge.
Hall, Stuart. 1997. "The Local and the Global: Globalization and Ethnicity." In *Dangerous Liaisons: Gender, Nation, and Postcolonial Perspectives*, ed. Anne McClintock, Aamir Mufti, and Ella Shohat, 173–187. Minneapolis: University of Minnesota Press.
Jameson, Fredric, and Masao Miyoshi, eds. 1998. *The Cultures of Globalization*. Durham, London: Duke University Press.
Jameson, Fredric. 1998. "Notes on Globalization as a Philosophical Issue." In *The Cultures of Globalization*, ed. Fredric Jameson and Masao Miyoshi, 54–77. Durham, London: Duke University Press. http://dx.doi.org/10.1215/9780822378426-003.
Kertzer, Jonathan. 1998. *Worrying the Nation: Imagining a National Literature in English Canada*. Toronto: University of Toronto Press.
Kelley, Ninette, and Michael Trebilcock. 1998. *The Making of the Mosaic: A History of Canadian Immigration Policy*. Toronto: University of Toronto Press.
King, Anthony D., ed. 1997. *Culture, Globalization and the World-System: Contemporary Conditions for the Representation of Identity*. Minneapolis: University of Minnesota Press.

Kogawa, Joy. 1981. *Obasan*. Toronto: Penguin.
Lai, Larissa. 1995. *When Fox Is a Thousand*. Vancouver: Press Gang.
Laidi, Zaki. 1998. *A World Without Meaning: The Crisis of Meaning in International Politics*. Trans. June Burnham and Jenny Coulon. London, New York: Routledge.
Lee, S.K.Y. 1990. *Disappearing Moon Cafe*. Vancouver: Douglas and McIntyre.
Mackey, Eva. 1999. *The House of Difference: Cultural Politics and National Identity in Canada*. London, New York: Routledge.
Mathur, Ashok. 1998. *Once Upon an Elephant*. Vancouver: Arsenal Pulp Press.
McCallum, Pamela, Stephen Slemon, and Aruna Srivastava. 1995. "Postcolonialism and Its Discontents." *ariel* 26 (1).
McClintock, Anne. 1994. "'The Angel of Progress': Pitfalls of the Term 'Post-colonialism.'" In *Colonial Discourse and Post-Colonial Theory: A Reader*, ed. Patrick Williams and Laura Chrisman, 291–304. New York: Columbia University Press.
McClintock, Anne, Aamir Mufti, and Ella Shohat, eds. 1997. *Dangerous Liaisons: Gender, Nation, and Postcolonial Perspectives*. Minneapolis: University of Minnesota Press.
Mitchell, Katharyne. 1996. *Whose Interest?: Transnational Capital and the Production of Multiculturalism in Canada." In Global/Local*, ed. Rob Wilson and Wimal Dissanayake, 219–251. Durham: Duke University Press.
Miyoshi, Masao. 1995. "Sites of Resistance in the Global Economy." *Boundary 2* 22 (1): 61–84. http://dx.doi.org/10.2307/303662.
Ng, Roxana. 1993. "Racism, Sexism, and Nation Building in Canada." In *Race, Identity and Representation in Education*, ed. Cameron McCarthy and Warren Crichlow, 50–59. New York, London: Routledge.
Penrose, Jan. 1997. "Construction, De(con)struction and Reconstruction: The Impact of Globalization and Fragmentation on the Canadian Nation-State." *International Journal of Canadian Studies* 16 (Fall):15–49.
Roy, Patricia. 1989. *A White Man's Province: British Columbia Politicians and Chinese and Japanese Immigrants, 1858–1914*. Vancouver: University of British Columbia Press.
Sakamoto, Kerri. 1998. *The Electrical Field*. Vintage.
Stasiulis, Daiva, and Radha Jhappan. 1995. "The Fractious Politics of a Settler Society: Canada." In *Unsettling Settler Societies: Articulations of Gender, Race, Ethnicity and Class*, ed. Daiva Stasiulis and Nira Yuval-Davis, 95–131. London: Sage. http://dx.doi.org/10.4135/9781446222225.n4.
Strong-Boag, Veronica, Sherrill Grace, Avigail Eisenberg, and Joan Anderson, eds. 1998. *Painting the Maple: Essays on Race, Gender, and the Construction of Canada*. Vancouver: University of British Columbia Press.
Takacs, Stacy. 1999. "Alien-Nation: Immigration, National Identity and Transnationalism." *Cultural Studies* 13 (4): 591–620. http://dx.doi.org/10.1080/095023899335068.
Urquhart, Conal. 2000. "US Scientists 'Close' to Identifying Genius Genes." *Vancouver Sun* (August): 10.
Wah, Fred. 1996. *Diamond Grill*. Edmonton: NeWest Press.
Ward, Peter W. 1990. *White Canada Forever: Popular Attitudes and Public Policy Toward Orientals in British Columbia*. Montreal: McGill-Queen's University Press.
Williams, Patrick, and Laura Chrisman, eds. 1994. *Colonial Discourse and Post-Colonial Theory: A Reader*. New York: Columbia University Press.
Wilson, Rob, and Wimal Dissanayake, eds. 1996. *Global/Local: Cultural Production and the Transnational Imaginary*. Durham, London: Duke University Press. http://dx.doi.org/10.1215/9780822381990.
Woodsworth, J.S. 1909. *Strangers Within Our Gates: Or, Coming Canadians*. Toronto: F.C. Stephenson.

17 Whose Transnationalism? Canada, "Clash of Civilizations" Discourse and Arab and Muslim Canadians

SEDEF ARAT-KOÇ

In this chapter, I look at Arab and Muslim communities in Canada as communities under siege. The reality of siege has implications not just for the ability of individuals and groups to safely *cross* borders, but also for their ability to live in safety and as equal citizens *within* borders. The specific context in which the paper is being written necessitates that we pose a set of critical questions as to *what* gets to be studied as transnationalism and *how*; what kind of questions get to be asked, about *whom*; and what does *not* get to be asked. In the environments of racism, anti-immigration and anti-multiculturalism, which prevail in many western states today, the transnational identities of many ethnic minorities get discussed as a way to interrogate and question their "loyalties" to the nation-state they are living in. In the political environment that prevails post 9/11, identities and loyalties of Arabs and Muslims are especially suspect. What are rarely, if ever, interrogated in this context are the "loyalties" as well as the various material transnational connections – economic, cultural, political and even military – of dominant groups and of the state.

In Canada, since the 1990s, but more specifically since September 11, 2001, we are in a period of retreat from multiculturalism and a politics of inclusion. This is a period when racism is not only intensified but also, and more importantly, legitimated through public discourse and mainstream institutions. Precisely at this historical moment, it may be useful, as Enakshi Dua has suggested, to ask "what it means to recodify immigrants and some ethnic and racialized groups as 'transnationals'"; to question "whether the concept itself does not contribute to the *dis*location of immigrants from the nation in new ways"[1]. Like the popular – and even most academic – uses of the term "ethnic group", which is implicitly or explicitly juxtaposed to the "real Canadians" who are assumed to have no ethnicity, there is the danger that the common use of the term "transnational" will be used to apply almost exclusively to racialized groups to, once again, question their belonging, and even their loyalty. In Canada, it has been only after long struggles by people of colour, that the concept of "Canada" or "Canadian nation" has, since the 1960s, started to include the histories and present experiences of many peoples that make up this nation. It is only recently that "immigrants" – used, almost exclusively to refer to ethnic and racialized minorities – have become a part of the concept of the nation. This inclusion, however, has been of a very fragile and tentative nature. Conception – and isolation – of immigrants and most racialized groups as transnational subjects makes their inclusion even more fragile. Their membership in the nation can be more readily questioned and even their deportation can be more easily legitimated as it may appear to be ethically unproblematic.[2]

The post September 2001 moment in Canada is one where we are witnessing renewal of nationalism in Canada. As I will elaborate below, this is nationalism of a transnational kind, a white nationalism confirming *some* Canadians' belonging in "the Western civilization." In Canada – as well as Europe and the United States – this new, reconfigured notion of the nation – based on a "clash of civilizations" perspective – serves to practically jettison those of Arab and Muslim background out of belonging in Western nations and "Western civilization" altogether.

As we contemplate the nature and significance of transnationalism as a phenomenon, it is important that we do not – naively – approach or celebrate transnationalism as a free movement of people around the world. As Ong has pointed out, it is essential to remember the continuing role of the state "to define, discipline, control, and regulate all kinds of populations, whether in movement or in residence" (Ong 1999, 15). Since 9/11, the national security states we are living with have increased and intensified such disciplinary and regulatory roles of the state. In addition to intensification at the local and national levels, there is also a reconfiguration of regulatory regimes at the transnational level through cooperation on "anti-terror" legislation, intelligence and border control.

In Saskia Sassen's frequently cited words, economic globalization is "*denationaliz(ing)* national economies", whereas immigration is "*renationalizing* politics" (Sassen 1996, 59, emphases mine). If borders were already important – with "Fortress Europe", and changes in immigration and border policies in Europe and in countries such as Australia, Canada and the US – when Sassen wrote these words, they have gained more significance – and one, also defined by security – in the post September 11, 2001 world.

For vast majority of people, borders were already far less permeable than what optimistic theoreticians of transnationalism might have assumed. They are even less permeable today. We are living at a time when transnational ties for Muslims and Arabs – whether they are social and familial ones; financial ones involving remittances or charity donations; political ones; or simply ties that shape a general sense of identity – are perceived as suspect, if or when they are not directly criminalized. While transnational ties of some groups may be increasing, those of Arabs and Muslims are subject to intense forms of surveillance.

There are empirical as well as ethical difficulties of doing research in communities under siege. Rather than keeping "the gaze" on diasporic Arab and Muslim "community" or "communities" in the post 9/11 period, the paper returns "the gaze" and raises questions about the often unscrutinized and unnamed dominant transnationalisms in Canada, transnationalisms which are not just reconfiguring Canadian national identity and its boundaries but also changing "national" institutions like borders, immigration, justice and the military. I start the paper with a description of the siege that has gripped Arabs and Muslim Canadians post 9/11 and the effects this has on their identities and transnational connections. I then focus on the nature of the dominant transnationalisms that create and reproduce the siege. I end with a discussion of "alternative transnationalisms", trans-ethnic and non-ethnic solidarities that are developing to challenge the current national and transnational order.

A clarification about the category "Arab and Muslim": The category is problematic as it often does not recognize the complexity and the heterogeneity of the categories "Arab" or "Muslim" themselves. It is also problematic as it conflates "Arabs" and "Muslims." As Suad Joseph argues, there are multiple conflations that underpin representations of Arabs, Muslims and Middle Easterners. Even though there are some overlaps between the categories, the conflated category makes the diversity of Arabs invisible. Arabs are not just Muslims, but also Christians and Jews. In popular representations in Western countries, "Arab" may be used to include other ethnic groups such as Turks, Armenians Persians or gypsies, groups with different languages, ethnic or national identifications, who do not identify as

Arab. Conflations overlook the fact that the category "Muslim" encompasses many ethnocultural and linguistic groups the majority of whom are neither Arab nor Middle Eastern, but are Indonesian, Malaysian, Filipino, Sudanese, Indian or Chinese. Joseph argues that in the US context the inaccurate conflations *erase* difference, to "serve the *creation* of another difference: the difference between the free, white, male American citizen and this constructed Arab" (Joseph 1999, 260).

Despite the inaccuracy of the conflations, and their racist connotations, however, I will make references to the category "Arabs and Muslims." I will do so as the category has become "real" socially and politically, in making references to racialization of a specific kind. Discourses on "Arabs and Muslims" – as inaccurate and ideologically biased the uses of the term might be – have become "real" in the subjectification of a category of people to specific forms of racialization and *political* designation in North America. The category has been politicized with Palestinian resistance to Israeli occupation since 1967; and gained special significance in the 1990s, during and after the Gulf War and in the post-Cold War political discourses in search of a new enemy of "the West" or globalizing capitalism. Following the attacks of September 11, 2001, the category has been raised to the status of "common sense" in depictions of "the enemy." So inaccurate, confused and ambiguous the category continues to be that since September 11, 2001, as a concept of racialization, it has resulted in attacks on many non-Arab and non-Muslim people, often of South Asian background, who are thought to "look like Muslims."

Transnationalism and Identity for Arab and Muslim Canadians

Heterogeneity and complexity of the categories "Arab" and "Muslim" – separately and as conflated – suggest that it is impossible to make a simple set of assumptions about a type of identity among Arabs and Muslims. There are further complications in conceptualizing identity of Arabs and Muslims in Canada as the already existing diversity in people's backgrounds multiplies with different experiences and modes of adaptation to living in diaspora. The current climate of intensified racialization and vilification in post 9/11 also yields different types of responses from people and different ways of *being* Arab and Muslim in Canada.

Different authors have articulated why it is analytically essential to use a transnational perspective on immigrants. Spivak points out the shortcomings of "focusing on the migrant as an effectively historyless object of intellectual and political activism" (Spivak 2000, 354). She argues that one could not simply treat the postcolonial migrant as a "blank slate", pretending that she could be analysed simply within a class-gender-race calculus that begins and ends in the first world metropolis. While I agree with Spivak that the migrant is not a blank slate, I also think that it is important to conceptualize the history and connectedness of the migrant in non-essentialist ways. When Ong argues that identities are "constituted through transnational systems", she also offers an approach to identity "as a politics rather than as an inheritance ... as fluidity rather than fixity, as based in mobility rather than locality, and as the playing out of these oppositions across the world" (Ong 1999, 327).

In the context of the post 9/11 environment, it is safe to say that for the majority of people, it is racialization rather than a common national or religious identity that is creating the basis for identification and organizing.

> For me, my whole life is now demarcated by 9/11. It is now pre-9/11 and post-9/11. ... The attacks were a break with our past as Muslims. Sept. 11, 2001 is not a defining moment

> in the history of North American Muslims but *the* defining moment. (ARM cited in Safieddine 2003, B2)

As Du Bois brilliantly argued, race operates both to assign and deny people their identity (cited in Winant 1997). Hours after the horrific events of September 11, 2001, Arab and Muslim Canadians found themselves racialized in new ways. No longer considered just "exotic" subjects or bearers of irrational traditional cultures, they were now "the enemy" The words of a New York lawyer summarizes how many Arab and Muslim Canadians also felt like:

> Before last week, I had thought of myself as a lawyer, a feminist, a wife, a sister, a friend, a woman on the street. Now I begin to see myself as a brown woman who bears a vague resemblance to the images of terrorists we see on television ... As I become identified as someone outside the New York community, I feel myself losing the power to define myself. (AR cited in Deaux 2001)

In an environment where Islam became loaded with – almost exclusively negative – political connotations, people of a Muslim background who had never seen religion as a central part of their identity, suddenly found others imposing this identity on them:

> For me, Islam was not a factor in structuring my identity at an early age. My parents were both secularists. I wasn't brought up according to Islamic tradition ...
>
> Sept. 11, 2001 all of a sudden changed that. People started to identify me as a Muslim. They would ask: You are from the Middle East, are you Muslim?
>
> For a while, it was incredibly confusing. It was not a question that I could answer simply. It needed a lot of qualification that people did not have the patience for ...
>
> It was as if I woke up one day to find that a special type of a Muslim identity was imposed on me. (HL cited in Safieddine 2003, B3)

Racialization is not a recent phenomenon for Arab and Muslim Canadians. In certain periods, however, such as the Gulf war, they have experienced an intensification of the white gaze and criminalization of their communities as the "enemy within." There were several prevailing racist discourses in Canada prior to 9/11 – some used for Arabs and Muslims, some not – such as immigrants "taking advantage of Canada" as "bogus refugees" or immigrants or people of colour being "welfare cheats." According to Sunera Thobani, after 9/11, discourse of security became *the* racist discourse (Thobani 2004b). Since security is an issue that concerns everyone, it makes the new racist discourse an especially powerful one.

What is new for Arab and Muslim Canadians post September 11, 2001, is not the experience of racism, but its growing public legitimacy and spread to and mainstreaming in all major institutions from the media to law and policy. Overt acts of violence and expressions of hatred from the civil society in the aftermath of September 11 were soon followed by "security" measures by the government which not only justify but also further fuel racialization and an environment of suspicion which surrounded most Muslim and Arab Canadians. Once considered an illegitimate practice, racial profiling has not only become de facto policy but also gained significant popular legitimacy. A recent survey by Ekos Poll revealed that as many as 48%, close to half of Canadians find it acceptable that "security officials give special attention to individuals of Arabic origin" (Alghabra 2003).

While negative and politically loaded portrayal of Arabs and Muslims in the media were by no means new or rare, they have since September 11, 2001, been defined as the "enemy within." George Jonas of the *National Post*, for example, fanned the flames of hatred that were rapidly gaining force. "[N]ot all the terrorist caves are in Afghanistan ... some are in Quebec and Ontario" he argued (cited in Kutty and Yousuf 2002). After September 11, the view that Arabs and Muslims belong to a radically different civilization – or perhaps even a different species! – with a very different set of values than those of "Canadians" became the basis news stories and commentaries were framed. In the media – juxtaposed to the self-portrayal of white Canadians as rational, civilized, liberal, democratic and peaceful – depictions of Muslims and Arabs as "extreme, vengeful, irrational, suicidal and fanatical people pathologically predisposed to violence with an incorrigible mindset" (Alghabra 2003) became regular fare.

Immediately following September 11, 2001 were countless cases of harassment, intimidation and violence that were directed at Arabs, Muslims and those who were thought to "look like Muslim." Arson at mosques and Sikh temples were accompanied by physical and verbal attacks, or dirty looks directed at Muslims, Arabs, Sikhs and Hindus. Darker people and those with visible signs of religion or ethnicity – such as women wearing the hijab – bore the brunt of attacks. The Canadian Islamic Congress advised Muslims to stay home from school and work to avoid harassment. It also urged Muslims to avoid crowded areas "where a mob mentality m[ight] develop" (Small and DeMara 2001, A2). As disturbing as, or perhaps even more disturbing, than the actual harassment, intimidation and violence that took place was that many people who experienced these were so distressed and insecure about their place in Canada that they did not report them to the police (Khouri, interview).

In addition to blatant attacks on their physical safety, Muslim and Arab Canadians faced a number of different pressures. Some business owners and corporate employees were pressured to change their Arab names to more non-Arab or "Anglo-sounding" names (Jamal 2002: 46; Khouri, interview). In one case, a business owner, decided not to personally conduct the more public aspects of his business, and instead sent a "white Canadian" to meet with his clients (Jamal 2002, 46).

While some political leaders made political statements appealing to "Canadians" – a category which did not seem to include Arab and Muslim Canadians – to stop the violence and harassment, they seemed to be giving double and conflicting messages as they themselves were participating in a discourse of clashing civilizations and moving rapidly towards legitimization of racism through institutionalization of racial profiling and new anti-terrorism, immigration and border policies.

A recent survey conducted by the Canadian Arab Federation in the Arab-Canadian community paints an unsettling picture of where Arabs see themselves in the larger Canadian society. According to the survey, 41.3% of the respondents believe that Canadians "don't like Muslims"; and 84% believe that Canadians think Muslims and Arabs are violent (Canadian Arab Federation 2002, 17). While these responses are subjective, they clearly raise questions about the sense of reception and belonging in Canada. The respondents to the survey almost unanimously agreed that "in general Canadians know very little about Arab culture" and that "what Canadians know about Arab culture stems from negative stereotypes and myths" (2002, 17). 38% of the respondents said they were made uncomfortable by the way white Canadians look at them and almost half said they encountered racism in daily interactions (2002, 18).

In addition to perceptions of racism in the media and experiences of racism in schools[3] and workplaces, 28.1% of respondents mentioned institutional racism as a problem. The examples they gave were of a wide range: post September 11 detentions; interrogations by CSIS; Bill 36, the Anti-Terrorism bill; the Immigration Department; employment in the public sector, etc. (2002, 18). 73.9% % of the respondents strongly or somewhat disagreed with the statement that "the Canadian government is concerned with what Canadian Arabs want from it." The level of dissatisfaction was particularly high for the federal government and on foreign policy (2002, 21).

These responses are especially ironic when juxtaposed to the responses immigrant respondents gave about why they chose Canada as their immigration destination: 71.9% of the respondents said it was for Canada's Human rights and freedoms, and 51.5% said it was for its multiculturalism (2002, 13). Given the perceptions of and expectations from Canada Arab and Muslim immigrants had, it is not surprising that the intensified racialization and demonization that followed September 11 attacks were a shock: "Anxiety, fear, alienation, marginalization, betrayal and disillusionment: This is how Sept. 11, 2001 and its aftermath have left Arab and Muslim Canadians feeling – indeed reeling" (Khouri 2003).

The implications of the whole-scale racialization and victimization of Arabs and Muslims are very serious not just for members of the communities, but also for Canadian society in general. Reflecting on the implications of these developments for Canadian multiculturalism, the current national president of the Canadian Arab Federation, Raja Khouri is grim:

> Our country has effectively engaged in an exercise of self-mutilation: stripping away civil liberties it holds dear, trampling in citizens' rights it had foresworn to protect, and tearing away at its multicultural fabric with recklessness.
>
> Arab Canadians are today convinced that there is a bigger threat to our way of life from the security agenda than there is from terrorism itself.
>
> The question that remains is: Given that multiculturalism is premised on the equal treatment and respect of all citizens, will multiculturalism survive the security agenda? (Khouri 2003)

Recent research shows that even though children of Arab Canadians born in Canada were "Americanized, ... their Arab identity has been raised as a result of these events [9/11]" (Jamal 2002, 47). I will suggest that for Arabs and Muslims in the diaspora the post 9/11 environment has created a specific *positionality*, but not necessarily an *identity* with specific outcomes. The positionality is created in an environment of intensified racism which holds every Arab and Muslim guilty by association; and with the commonly used discourse of "the clash of civilizations", increased sense of exclusion from mainstream notions of what/who constitutes "Canada." The discourse and logic of "clash of civilizations" constructs a monolithic conception of both "the West" and of some of the communities that live within it. The implications of such monolithic conceptions and of the notion of a naturalized, inevitable "clash" are catastrophic for some diasporic communities who suddenly find themselves outside the borders of what is conceived as "the West."

Despite the powerful forces intensified racialization and exclusion create in developing a sense of "we" – forcefully and/or voluntarily – among Arab and Muslim Canadians, this positionality could not and did not automatically translate into an identity. Rather, we can argue that different identities have been in the process of forming from this positionality. For some, a process of intense racialization led to identification with those from the same ethnic or religious background with whom one might not have had much in common before:

> Prior to 9/11, I never identified with women who wear the veil …
>
> But all of a sudden, I take the public transportation in the week following the attacks, and the driver allows me in but closes the door in the face of a veiled woman waiting at the bus stop. This happened a number of times. At a certain point I started thinking it could have been my cousin or a member of my family, some of whom cover their hair with a scarf. (HL cited in Safieddine 2003, B3)

For others, the connotations of the category "Arab and Muslim" were too painful to lead to identification with the racialized co-ethnics. Some Arabs interviewed by Jamal regrettably observed that "misunderstanding of [their] culture and prevalent stereotypes have led to a confused Arab identity. Fear has led to people suppressing their Arab identity" (cited in Jamal 2002, 49). Instead of identifying, some, especially those who could "pass" due to social class, looks, accent or level of assimilation, attempted to distance themselves from ethnic identity and community. Some Christian Arabs tried to distance themselves from the vilified Muslim co-ethnics. One way to do this was by wearing large, visible crosses to emphasize non-Muslim identity (Khouri, interview).

> … some … retract and retrench from society while others throw away their Arab culture and become fully "Canadian" by changing their names, habits, and values to the extreme – and neither is happy. (cited in Jamal 2002, 49)

While some continued to nurture multiple identities and multiple connections to different communities, for some, intensified racialization and othering led to a rigidification of and defensiveness around essential identities. Those who were religious Muslims found themselves especially isolated. Demonization of their religion was particularly painful as religion was a central part of their identity.

Many Muslims in the diaspora, especially refugees, who are survivors of fundamentalist regimes, find themselves in a specifically difficult position. They try to continue to articulate a critique of fundamentalism when they also find themselves under a new type of attack by racism and Islamophobia in Canadian society (Tahmasebi 2004).

> What became clearer to me post-Sept. 11 is that everyone should be against hatred, whatever it is, if it is happening from the pulpit or from the government or from ordinary people on the street. (AM cited in Safieddine 2003, B2)

The environment of suspicion that surrounded Muslim and Arab Canadians post 9/11, served to create a climate of intimidation and fear. Several members of the communities have made references to internment, to describe what this environment felt like: "Ghettoization since 9/11 became clear. In reality we could have been physically interned. Instead we have been interned by fear – psychological internment" (cited in Jamal 2002, 48).

Intimidation based on racialization and demonization led to different responses by individuals in Muslim and Arab Canadian communities. For some, intimidation led to de-politicization. They found security in the image of the "good Muslim" and "good immigrant" which came to be defined in this context as someone who makes generalized negative statements – approaching racism – about Islam and Arabs, gives unconditional support to everything the Canadian government does and is forever grateful to Canada.

Despite the environment of vilification and intimidation, many Canadian Muslims and Arabs felt compelled to express their disagreement with the war on Afghanistan, which Canada participated in. Jehad Aliweiwi, the executive director of the Canadian Arab Federation, observed an intense scrutiny of the loyalties, actions and the beliefs of Arab and Muslim Canadians in the post 9/11 environment as amounting to "a new form of internment." He described the costs of dissent for people from communities already for suspicion of disloyalty: "We're perceived as the enemy and as responsible collectively ... And now, we're seen as guilty because we don't support the bombings. It's a frightening position to be in" (quoted in Mitchell 2001). Despite the intimidation, some people interpreted their duties as Canadian citizens as the duty to express what they saw as the truth, even if it was risky to do so. As Mohamed Elmasry, the national president of the Canadian Islamic Congress stated: "Some people feel it may be time to have a low profile and just support the government, no matter what ... Others feel it is their duty to be a good citizen and voice their opinion" (quoted in Mitchell 2001).

Transnationalism of Communities Under Siege

Discussing translocal or transnational character of Islam, we come across wide discrepancies between representation and reality. On the one hand, both the media as well as much of the academic literature is saturated with claims on the cultural exceptionality of Islam as a uniquely reactionary and violent religion and one that is relatively unchanging over time. On the other hand, there is the reality of a very complex and diverse "Muslim world" with a multiplicity of interpretations and expressions of what it means to be Muslim. In addition to the heterogeneity of its local forms Islam is diverse as it "travels." As Mandaville (2001) argues in his research on transnational Muslim politics, Islam is no more or less fixed, monolithic or fluid in its transnational forms than its religious or cultural counterparts. Even though Mandaville limits his analysis to "individuals whose self descriptions and identities ... involve ... Islam as a key ... component" and excludes those who do not but are of a "Muslim background" (Mandaville 2001, 111), he still finds Islam to be widely plural in its historical and spatial practices, as well as variable and changing as it moves into new locations in the diaspora.

In discussing transnationalism of diasporic subjects, it is important to see class differences in the amount of freedom and mobility different transnational subjects enjoy (Ong 1999). It is also important not to exaggerate the deterritorialization of the state and to recognize the monopoly states enjoy over exercise of legitimate force within their borders. Depending on their class or race or political status, bi-national subjects "... may be doubly empowered or doubly subordinated, depending on historically-specific local circumstances" (Guarnizo and Smith 1998, 9).

For many ethnic groups, transnational affiliations cannot be interpreted as voluntary and politically neutral results of globalization and travel. They rather need to be seen in their political contexts. Sometimes, the context is a hostile one of racism, exclusion, discrimination and even criminalization. In an environment of racism, isolation and exclusion combined with hostile or at least insensitive foreign policy towards the peoples in the lands of origin, transnational identifications with the "homeland", or with people of shared ethnic or religious background seems to be of significance for Arabs and Muslims. Kabbani writes in the British context:

> We still read our old countries' papers. We were ravaged by news from Bosnia, Iraq, Kashmir or Palestine and increasingly infuriated by Britain's hostile policies on these matters of grave import to 2 million of its citizens. The umbilical cord with home had not been cut and there was no soothing local midwife to help. (Kabbani 2002)

In the US context, Cainkar mentions that since the Gulf War in 1991, exclusion of Arabs from American civil society and government led Arabs towards "transnational affiliations, rather than the affiliations sought by minorities able to participate in democracy." As a result, there was "a major shift in identification, affiliation and behaviour ... among a significant proportion of Arab Muslims ... Their primary affiliation changed from secular to religious" (Cainkar 2002, 26).

When we talk about transnationalism, it is useful to distinguish between transnational identification and practical transnational ties. While the "civic exclusion, political voicelessness and popular denigration" of Arabs in the US have pushed them towards transnational affiliations, Cainkar predicts that "these homeland ties – return travel, family visits, foreign students, family reunification, remittances and charitable donations – are likely to drop significantly due to changes in policies, the social climate and Arab-American fears after September 11" (2002, 26). Although we have no research confirming it, it is reasonable to expect that for Canadian Arabs and Muslims, a practical transnationalism might also be in decline due to the intimidation intense surveillance creates over return travel, charitable donations and even sending of remittances (Khouri, interview).

Limitations to travel occurs not just at the individual level, but sometimes at a larger scale. Just before Air Canada was about to launch direct flights between Montreal and Beirut – a route the airline had thought would be popular and profitable – in summer of 2003, it learned that the Canadian Transportation Agency had cancelled the flights. Arab Canadians interpreted the decision as one imposed by the US. They also saw it as sending yet another message about Arabs as dangerous and violent (see Jamal 2003).

Transnationalism is not just restricted to connections between the home country and the new home. Many Arab and Muslim Canadians have also found since September 11, 2001 that their travels to the United States is limited with intense questioning and harassment at the border. This is something which not only affects people's ties with family and relatives in the US, but also, potentially their employment security:

> I am worried that these new measures adopted by the American authorities are going to create a new culture in corporate Canada. A lot of Arab-Canadians cross the border frequently ...
>
> Once corporate Canada begins to realize that Arab-Canadians create a hassle for them when they cross the border, next time they hire somebody who needs to be traveling to the U.S., inadvertently or not, they may prefer to hire a non-Arab. (OA cited in Safieddine 2003, B1)

Dominant Transnationalisms: Transnational Identity of the Canadian State and "Ordinary Canadians"

> It is a banal fact of contemporary existence that economic forces, communication systems, military interventions, and ecological disasters continually transcend nation-state boundaries, yet state authorities remain deeply suspicious of all international movements, loyalties, and relationships they cannot regulate. (Asad 2009, 266)

There is an irony in the political discourses that have dominated the mainstream since September 11, 2001. While there has been an inflation in nationalist discourses interrogating the belonging and loyalties of suspect "ethnics", mainstream "Canadian identity" is more than ever defined in transnational terms and specifically in relation to the US. The disproportionate focus of the transnationalism literature on the transnationalism of – often racialized – minorities is misguided. This focus tends to ignore or make invisible the transnationalism of the dominant racial/ethnic groups as well as the transnationalism of the state. The latter is particularly important in the post September 11, 2001 context in Canada, as the already close ties with the United States –in terms of trade, culture, tourism, etc. – have not only solidified but also reconfigured to redefine a number of other areas, such as national identity and harmonization and integration of military policy, security legislation and immigration and border controls. I would like to start by focusing on the redefinition and reconfiguration of Canadian identity as belonging in "the West." These changes in Canadian identity, constantly fed and refueled by mainstream media, are very significant in making racialization and othering of Arab and Muslim Canadians possible. Also, and more importantly, however, they continue to legitimize institutional racism.

"Canadian Identity" as "Western" Identity

Even though President Bush in the US and Prime Minister Jean Chretien in Canada both declared that Islam was not the enemy, the mainstream media in both countries continued to write as if it was. In specifically targeting not just Arabs and Muslims externally but also in the diaspora, security policies in both countries also strengthened the idea that this image corresponded to reality. The entire discursive framing of the attacks of September 11, 2001 was based on the notion of a "clash of civilizations." After the attacks of September 11, 2001, Samuel Huntington's book with this name was praised as visionary, ingenious and brilliant. Five years after its publication in 1996, it rose to the bestsellers list. Its thesis was taken up wholeheartedly by the media and it came to be used as the common sense explanation for what had happened.

With the end of the Cold War at the end of the 1980s, some US intellectuals deeply embedded with the state started actively redrawing maps of international conflict and identifying who the new enemy would be in the new world order being created. The concept of a "clash of civilizations" was first used by Bernard Lewis to explain what he saw as the conflict between political Islam and "the West" (Lewis 1990). It was then taken up by Samuel Huntington – a long-time Cold-War warrior – who used the term with a question mark in the title of an article (Huntington 1993). Huntington expanded the concept into a universal thesis on the state of the world after the end of the Cold War. In a book that he wrote in 1996 with the same title, Huntington got rid of the question mark and suggested that the world was now divided on *civilizational* lines – as opposed to ideological ones of the Cold War – based on ethnic, cultural and religious differences. Defining seven or eight major civilizations in the world today – in Huntington's words, "Western, Confucian, Japanese, Islamic, Hindu, Slavic-Orthodox, Latin American, and possibly African" – Huntington highlighted the increased significance of ethnic identifications in the post-Cold War world and expressed his expectation that the most serious threats to "the West" would come from the "Islamic" and Chinese civilizations. Huntington articulated the nature of civilizational conflict in this new era in military and potentially catastrophic terms: "In a world where culture counts, the platoons are tribes and ethnic groups, the regiments are nations, and the armies are civilizations" (Huntington 1996, 128).

Huntington's book has been criticized from a number of angles. The bold strokes he paints the world with, the sweeping generalizations he makes are not based on a good knowledge or understanding of the "civilizations" he talks about. He uses a very monolithic conception of culture and "civilization identity", not paying any attention to their diversity, internal contradictions or their historical variability. He conceptualizes cultures and civilizations as sealed-off, isolated entities, whose historical relationship to each other consists of wars and conflict, instead of exchange, interaction and cross-fertilization. This perspective on cultures denies the significance of a shared history between cultures, even ignoring the recent interconnections through colonization, imperialism and globalization. Huntington's simplified and monolithic perspective on cultures leads to an exaggeration, absolutization and mystification of cultural differences. Exaggeration of cultural differences implies that – at least some – cultural differences are irreconcilable, leading Huntington to naturalize conflict (Arat-Koç 2002b).

It is interesting to observe how rapidly the notion of culture – or civilizational – clash became the dominant framework in which political leaders and the media interpreted the developments of and after September 11, 2001. Columnists in mainstream media made constant references to how "they" – used in a very slippery way to sometimes refer to the terrorists, sometimes to the culture they belonged – hated "our" freedoms, democracy, human rights and women's rights. In the article "Why Do They Hate Us So Much?" in the *Globe and Mail*, columnist Margaret Wente represents a discourse that was – and to this day, still is – very common in the media. Wente rejects any reflection on "root causes" from a history of the relations between countries. Opting instead for the essentialism of the cultural clash perspective, she writes – with the confidence of those who think they speak the common sense – how "we" in "the West" have "a culture of peace", while "theirs" is "a culture of violence." Referring to suicide bombers, she declares: "The poison that runs through the veins of the suicide bombers does not come from America. It comes from their culture, not ours. The root causes are in their history, not ours" (Wente 2001). By the end of October 2001, some columnists were predicting that the war against Afghanistan would only be an "opening battle" in a long war that would "spread and engulf a number of countries in conflicts of varying intensity." They declared that this war would "resemble the clash of civilizations everyone had hoped to avoid" (Kristol and Kagan, cited in Alam 2003).

The Canadian media played a very significant role in creating, not just an imaginary conception of the nation, but also of trans-national alliances (Thobani 2002). As the "clash of civilizations" thesis began to be employed daily to define "us" and "them", definitions of "Canada" and Canadian identity rapidly evolved to a transnational one, as part of "the Western civilization" (Arat-Koç 2002a, 2003; Thobani 2002, 2004a). It is important to stress here that the notion of "the West" that was used was one which not only excluded other civilizations, but also the histories and cultures of "non-Western" diasporas living in "the West." Thus, in effect, the redefinition of Canadian identity as part of "the West" implied a re-whitening of Canadian identity after decades of multiculturalism. In Canada, with its geography and its history, belonging to "the West" also came to mean strong identification with the US in particular. The repeated statement "we are all Americans now" did not just represent an expression of a temporary solidarity with what was perceived as a victimized, terrorized neighbour, but rather an identification with the white imperial power the US state epitomised.

The new borders of Canadian identity were so rigidly drawn that in the immediate aftermath of September 11, 2001, there was no tolerance among the new "ordinary Canadians" for dissent against strong identification and unquestioning cooperation with the US. In this environment, Sunera Thobani, the former president of the National Action Committee on the Status of Women, was demonized for her remarks that the US, through its foreign policy, had blood in its hands and that we needed to be able to extend the same sympathy we've had for the victims of the terrorist attacks of 9/11 towards victims of US aggression in many different parts of the world. Not even some "mainstream Canadians" were necessarily spared the questioning of their belonging in this newly defined national identity. A letter to the editor, for example, called Alexa McDonough, then the leader of the New Democratic Party, "un-Canadian" for her opposition to Canada's participation in the war against Afghanistan (Lafond 2001).

Institutionalization of "Western" Identity

> If some "ethnics" were showing the sort of loyalty to another country as Canadian right-wingers are to the United States, they would have been branded traitors to Canada. (Siddiqui 2003)

A significant section of Canada's business, political and media elite have been pushing very hard since 9/11 towards an integration of Canada's military, borders and policies with those of the United States. In addition to the active role they have been playing in redefining Canadian identity in transnational terms, therefore, this elite is actively pursuing a materialization of this new identity in concrete institutions[4]. While I call the constitution and institutionalization of this identity "transnational", it is important to recognize that this is not a transnationalism of equal partners. It is rather based on an agenda defined specifically by the US and it defines a union in which Canada is erased. This is a reality even the proponents of this integration recognize:

> ... our condition of virtual sovereignty is like that of all the member states of the European Union. With one difference. The political construct that is developing here isn't a comparable North American union. It's just an American union. (Gwyn 2001b, A13)

The discourses used to justify the desire for integration with the US often articulate business interests with concerns about "security" (see Canadian Council of Chief Executives 2004). State discourses explaining new forms of integration with the United States also accept and naturalize this articulation by speaking about trade and security in one breath. For example, the Smart Border Declaration that was signed on December 12, 2001, states:

> The terrorist actions of September 11 were an attack on our common commitment to democracy, rule of law and a free and open economy. They highlighted a threat to our public and economic security ...
>
> Public security and economic security are mutually reinforcing. By working together to develop a zone of confidence against terrorist activity, we create a unique opportunity to build a smart border for the 21st century; a border that securely facilitates the free flow of people and commerce; a border that reflects the largest trading relationship in the world. (Government of Canada 2002)

A) MILITARY ALLIANCE OR INTEGRATION?

Just a few days after the attacks of September 11, 2001, columnists in the mainstream Canadian media starting giving – or rather advocating – a fatalistic picture of Canada's "inevitable" integration with the US:

> On the anti-terrorist war… it goes without saying that the U.S. will take for granted our full political and diplomatic support, as well as, of course, military and intelligence. We will have to operate on the assumption that the U.S. will simply not accept, and at best angrily reject, any criticisms we might make about its excessive use of force or about actions it engages in that cause "collateral damage" to innocent bystanders.
>
> At least for the time being, and probably for some time to come, those terrorists have fused the U.S. and Canada together. (Gwyn 2001a, A1, A10)

When Canada participated in the war on Afghanistan, Canadian troops went under the operational control of the US army. Even though Canada did not directly participate in the subsequent war and invasion of Iraq, Canadian navy went to and stayed in the Gulf in the initial stages of the war to provide "protection" for the US army.

The nature of transnational military cooperation that Canada has participated in has serious implications for the citizenship and belonging of Arab and Muslim Canadians. In his discussion of the Australian participation in the Gulf War and the implications of this for Arab-Australians, Hage (2002) elaborates on the meaning of *belonging*. In emphasizing the need to go beyond a rights-based conception of citizenship, he introduces the concept of *honourability:* "belonging is not about citizenship as rights but about citizenship as 'holding your head high'" (Hage 2002, 2). Reflecting on the rapidity of the decision of the Australian government to participate in the Gulf War, Hage suggests that in today's world where most nations are multicultural in their composition, war-making does not fit the model of distinct ethno-national states, as "it is very hard to have an enemy that is totally 'not us'":

> Because there will always be cultural groups of citizens who will be personally in a state of trauma as a result of a decision to go to war, the government of a multicultural country ought to always "pause" and "reflect" a bit more than others before going to war. (Hage 2002, 10)

Hage argues that the heritage of a multicultural nation extends beyond the national territory. It therefore involves a recognition of the worthiness of a migrant culture beyond the borders of the nation-state (2002, 11–12).

B) ANTI-TERRORISM LEGISLATION

In the days and weeks following 9/11, Canada was under immense pressure from the United States to develop tough new measures in legislation and in policy to demonstrate that "it was doing all it can" in the "war against terrorism." One of the significant measures came in the form of C-36, the Anti-Terrorism Act that was hastily passed even though it posed major challenges to basic civil liberties and would probably never pass the test of constitutionality if it is ever challenged.

Although the proponents of the bill argued that it was "necessary" in this time of crisis, the bill was not a response to a national crisis or tragedy. In fact, as Audrey Macklin ironically recalls, Canada had experienced the deadliest terrorist attack in aviation prior to

9/11 – the Air India tragedy of 1985 which involved a Canadian departure point and whose victims were almost all Canadian citizens and permanent residents – and had yet never treated it as "a fundamental assault on our nation, our values, our people" (Macklin 2001, 399). Proponents of the bill did not demonstrate that Canada specifically was under an imminent terrorist threat. Rather, it was complete identification with the US and the logic of "civilizational clash" which convinced people that as part of "the West", Canada was a potential target. Even the factsheet the Department of Justice produced on the proposed bill failed to make nationally specific arguments about the necessity or the constitutionality of the bill. The factsheet was titled: Canada's Proposed Anti-Terrorism Act: *Working with Our International Partners* (emphasis mine) (Department of Justice 2001).

During the very short time the bill was proposed and passed, critics insisted – unsuccessfully – that "Canada must reflect on its specific needs and legal structure" and that it should move with "caution and calm deliberation" (Canadian Arab Federation 2001). According to Amina Sherazee, Bill C-36 was the most controversial legislation in the history of Canada and yet it passed in less than a month. Even legislators who voted for the bill were reading about its implications from the newspapers after the bill had already passed and getting surprised about its implications (Sherazee 2004).

C-36 uses a very broad definition of "terrorism", implicating a number of basic rights and liberties defined by the Canadian Charter of Rights and Freedoms, such as freedom of expression, freedom of association, the right to be secure against unreasonable search and seizure, the right not to be arbitrarily detained or imprisoned and the right to a fair trial. At the same time, however, it uses a very selective definition of "terrorism." Anti-terrorism legislations are framed in civilizational and racialized terms. While the definition can be interpreted to include civil disobedience or even boycotting of products, it explicitly excludes state terrorism (Sherazee 2004). The simultaneous broadness of the definition, on the one hand, and its selectiveness, on the other, lead many people question exactly *what* and *who* the legislation targets.

While the effectiveness of the legislation in terms of actually preventing terrorism is questionable, one of its unquestionable consequences is intimidation and silencing of critical and oppositional voices. The Anti-Terrorism Act gives the police, the RCMP and CSIS new powers for increased surveillance of persons; increased suppression of protests; increased monitoring of email and listservers; and increased spying on protestors and political activists during rallies, meetings and conferences (Sherazee 2002). One of the most significant implications of this legislation has been "criminalization of dissent", "the creation of a climate in which even those who are not specifically targeted are still affected and are either silenced or silence themselves" (Sherazee 2002, 20).

Another aspect of the legislation is that it criminalizes transnational fundraising or humanitarian aid for organizations or groups which are or may become designated in a list of terrorists. Some groups have argued that creating such a list is inherently discriminatory as such "blacklisting" is always open to the government's "discretion to determine, depending on its own changing foreign policy needs, which groups are legitimate and which are not" (Canadian Arab Federation 2001, 10).

There is widespread belief among Arab and Muslim Canadians that Bill C-36, despite its universal language, specifically targets their communities. One of the things that Bill C-36 does is to give extraordinary discretion to police and to immigration officers. In a period of intensified racialization and demonization of Arab, Muslim and South-Asian Canadians, it is not surprising that they are the people who get targeted for "random checks" or treated as suspect by law enforcement and intelligence agencies (Canadian Race Relations Foundation n.d.; Macklin 2001, 395).

Even though Bill C-36 and similar measures are generally defended as "a small inconvenience" or "a small price to pay in exchange for security", people in targeted communities are questioning who is inconvenienced and who is paying the price for "security." Many Arab and Muslim Canadians believe, there would have been widespread opposition and the bill would not have passed if it did not target specific communities (Jamal 2002, 48). Given the history in Canada of targeting specific communities for an abstract "security" of "Canadians" in general, Audrey Macklin cautions about the implications of this bill: "... while many look to the criminal law to protect us from the enemy within, I urge us to attend to the law's role in *producing* the alien within" (emphasis mine) (Macklin 2001, 398).

C) TRANSNATIONALIZATION OF JUSTICE OR TRANSNATIONALIZATION OF TORTURE?

As the well-publicized Maher Arar case demonstrates, it appears that in situations when the Canadian intelligence agencies find the task of preparing a case against suspected terrorists under the Anti-Terrorism legislation cumbersome, they may be downloading the work of detention and questioning to foreign governments. In what some are calling "torture by proxy" (Kutty 2004), Canadian intelligence agencies are accused of passing erroneous information to the US authorities about Arar; and the US government is accused of Arar's rendition to Syria where he was tortured. In a more recent case, another Canadian citizen, Dr. Khawaja, has argued that he was detained – but not tortured – by Saudi authorities at the request of Canadians. Dr. Khawaja also argues that the Canadian authorities asked his interrogators to ensure that he would not be able to contact the Canadian Consulate in Riyadh (Kutty 2004).

The Arar and Khawaja cases have received some attention in the media as both are Canadian citizens. As Cynthia Wright argues (2003, 2004), much less known and less controversial are the cases of non-citizens, including those with no legal status in Canada. So far, there are at least five known cases of non-citizens detained indefinitely without charge on security certificates. As they are held with secret evidence, their lawyers have no access to the evidence against them, and therefore no effective way to prepare a defence. There is also the case of more than 20 young Pakistani and Indian nationals arrested in August 2003 under Project Thread. Even though there has been no case for charges, they have been detained until most have been deported.[5] The question some ask in these cases is: "If there is evidence then why not charge, arrest and prosecute them in Canada to the full extent of the law?" (Kutty 2004). Audrey Macklin may have the answer. She predicted at the time of the introduction of C-36 that criminal prosecution under the anti-terrorism law would be difficult. She thought, therefore, that for non-citizens the state would use the investigative powers allowed under C-36, but then issue security certificates under the Immigration and Refugee Protection Act, as it would be "easier to deport than to imprison" (Macklin 2001, 397).

D) TRANSNATIONALIZATION OF IMMIGRATION AND BORDER ISSUES

Within just weeks after the September 11 attacks, the Canadian government moved rapidly towards harmonization of immigration and border issues with the United States and creating a "security parameter" which would encompass Canada and the United States. On December 12, 2001, the Canadian foreign minister and US. Homeland Security director signed a Canada-US. Smart Border Declaration.

As the notion as well as the specifics of the "security parameter" were clearly dictated and defined by the US, proponents of the "security perimeter" were aware of the implications of this in terms of Canadian sovereignty. This did not, however, prevent "a coterie of Canadian media commentators and right-wing politicians [from] tripp[ing] over each other in the rush to blame Canada's allegedly lax refugee policies for September 11 in particular and global terrorism in general" (Macklin 2001, 388). Some openly acknowledged the sovereignty issue, and yet defended it, as "inevitable" and as the only significant contribution Canada could make to the "war on terrorism" – given its weak military capacity:

> ... the Chretien government's decision this week to adopt a common North American perimeter – U.S. standards applying everywhere, that's to say – for security and intelligence, for immigration and for our refugee systems represents one of the most significant abandonments of our sovereignty in our history.
>
> Abandonment is the wrong term. Accepting the inevitable would be the right way to put it ...
>
> A common North American security perimeter is the single substantial contribution we can make to the war against terrorism. (Gwyn 2001b, A13)

As I have argued above, the notion of a "smart border" is based on an articulation of "security" in terms of business concerns. The declaration outlines a 30-point action plan to "secure" flow of people as well as a flow of goods. It establishes "border cooperation" in a number of areas including immigration, crime and security as well as transportation and customs. The plans involve reviewing and working towards harmonization of several policies and procedures, such as refugee/asylum processing, visa policy, issuing of identity cards for permanent residents, development of joint immigration databases, common border policing and common standards for biometrics to be used on identity cards.

Sharryn Aiken argues that a "security parameter" would "give primacy to the unfettered movement of goods and investment capital," but lead to a situation where "the border intrudes into everyday life of all non-citizens and the periphery is mapped by high fences in the name of safeguarding those on the inside from dangerous foreigners" (Aiken 2001, A17). Aiken draws analogies between policies today and harmonization of policies with the United States regarding treatment of Japanese Canadians after the attacks on Pearl Harbor.

> ... an inclination to get closer to America in this time of crisis merely exposes Canadians to greater risk. We will come to regret reflexive policy responses, just as we did, eventually, of our wartime policies in the wake of Pearl Harbor. (Aiken 2001)

The move towards a North American perimeter, introduced as an anti-terrorism measure, is based on the notion that immigrants and refugees are the problem. It is not an accident that the introduction of a discourse of a "common security parameter" corresponded to the hasty passing of Bill C-11, the Immigration and Refugee Protection Act, which was based on the same assumption that immigrants and refugees are security threats.

Alternative Transnationalisms?: Transethnic and Non-Ethnic Identifications and Solidarity

> we are not lumps of clay, and what is important is not what people make of us but what we ourselves make of what they have made of us. (Jean Paul Sartre, *Saint Genet*)

In a world that is increasingly multicultural and transnational, an approach by the state and dominant ethno-cultural groups to diversity as a "clash of civilizations" – a la Huntington – would have catastrophic consequences. Such an approach could, in the least, be used to justify deportations, exclusion and criminalization, and potentially lead all the way to an all-out holocaust to exterminate those identified as the civilizational others. In this section, I will argue that while such apocalyptic possibilities are not inconceivable, there have been significant developments in Canada and abroad of a positive kind that constitute a resistance and challenge to the dominant transnationalisms I have mentioned in the previous section. I will suggest that the kind of transnational, trans-ethnic and non-ethnic bonds of solidarity established in response to a climate of war, hatred and racism promise to subvert the logic of a "clash of civilizations" discourse.

In the last decade, several important concepts have been developed to deal with the complexity of identities produced in transnationality. Two of these concepts are hybridity and diaspora. Even though these concepts represent important attempts to complicate and de-essentialize identity, however, they do not go far enough in doing so, as they continue to privilege "culture" as the central element in defining identity and community (Anthias 2001, 2002). In conceptualizations of identity and community, the concept of diaspora privileges a notion of "origin." As such, it "fails to pay adequate attention to *transethnic*, rather than transnational, processes" (Anthias 2002, 37). I would add to Anthias' argument and suggest that we look into *nonethnic*, as well as transethnic processes in making sense of the new identities that emerge.

While an atmosphere of racism, and specifically a discourse of "clash of civilizations" attempts to fix racial, religious, national and civilizational identities, a politics of solidarity (organized around principles of anti-racism, anti-colonialism, anti-imperialism, peace, or civil rights) has the potential to counter this fixing of identities and lead to the emergence of new democratic subjects.

In a post 9/11 world shaped by the discourse of a "clash of civilizations", there are enormous pressures towards a fundamentalism of identities, not just on the part of minorities but also for the dominant ethnic group. As Ella Shohat succinctly puts it "war is the friend of binarisms, leaving little place for complex identities" (Shohat 2006, 217). There is the danger, therefore, that the widespread acceptance of the "clash of civilizations" discourse by "ordinary Canadians" and its internalization by isolated and alienated Arab and Muslim Canadians can turn the discourse into a self-fulfilling prophecy through the mutual distrust and mutual isolation it may create in different communities.

As some "ordinary Canadians" started seeing their neighbours with suspicion and fear, there has also been a great sense of disappointment and betrayal among Arab and Muslim Canadians who previously enjoyed a sense of belonging in the professed Canadian ideals of multiculturalism and democracy:

> Our failure as a society in this regard was in not sending a clear signal to the contrary – society did not come to the aid of this maligned minority …
>
> … by and large, Arab and Muslim Canadians were left on their own, having to explain themselves and prove their loyalty; defend their religion and demonstrate its goodness; and at times hide their ethnicity and deny their heritage in a bid to escape scrutiny.
>
> The effect on our communities is that, like our Japanese-Canadian counterparts during World War II, we, too, have become victims of psychological internment. In the meantime, our mainstream institutions, including governments, simply looked the other way. (Khouri 2003)

Despite the sense of disappointment and betrayal in the community, however, there were unprecedented levels of mobilization among Arab and Muslim Canadians. According to Raja Khouri of the Canadian Arab Federation, marginalization forced some people in the community to be more politicized and, in an ironic way, led them to be more integrated politically. Activism among Arab Canadians increased substantially. In addition to participating in interfaith activities, working in civil rights, anti-war, anti-racist coalitions with other groups, some Arab Canadians also started to work towards developing a voice in some of the political parties in Canada (Khouri, interview).

There is an indeterminacy about the transnational politics of ethnic groups and their implications for the larger society. Analysing the conflicts surrounding the Rushdie affair and the (first) Gulf war in Britain, Pnina Werbner observes that:

> far from revealing ambiguous loyalties or unbridgeable cultural chasms, British Muslim transnational loyalties have challenged the national polity ... to explore new forms of multiculturalism and to work for new global human rights causes. (Werbner 2000, 309)

Reeling after the demonization and attacks in the aftermath of September 11th and during the bombing of Afghanistan, Arab and Muslim Canadians braced themselves once again in the period preceding the Iraq War. Some Iraqi Canadians even feared internment if Canada participated in the war. There was a huge relief in the community when the Canadian government decided against participation. As important as the decision of the government was the sense of solidarity that developed through the anti-war demonstrations in Canada and worldwide. During the heavily attended anti-war demonstrations in Canada, Arab and Muslim Canadians felt a sense of belonging, for the first time after 9/11 (Khouri, interview). The enormous diversity of groups – including ethnic organizations, church groups, labour, anti-poverty, women's groups, etc. – in demonstrations, teach-ins and various kinds of meetings meant that rather than clashing as expected, as essentialized civilizational subjects, participants were learning from each other, making connections between the various issues different groups were concerned with, and developing new political subjectivities. In a sense, the emerging picture looked more like a multiculturalism based on intercommunal coalitions – rather than monoculturalist identities – which Ella Shohat proposes:

> Rather than ask who can speak, ... we should ask how we can speak together... How can diverse communities speak in concert? ... In this sense, it might be worthwhile to focus less on identity as something one "has", than one identification one "does." (Shohat 1995, 177)

Worldwide demonstrations that involved a total of 12 million people against the Iraq War on February 15, 2003, represented a historic moment of transnational solidarity. Subverting the very logic of the discourse of civilizational conflict, these demonstrations were a show of solidarity against imperial power gone out of control and accountability.[6]

In the widespread violence and harassment of Muslims and Arabs that followed 9/11, there were many expressions of support and solidarity from interfaith groups. Some church groups even offered to protect mosques. While organizations such as the Canadian Muslim Civil Liberties association received many hate e-mail messages, they received five to six times more in messages of support (Kutty and Yousuf 2002). Several groups expressed desire and support for notions of a Canadian nation that are different from those based on a supposed "clash of civilizations." As early as October 2001, observing blaming and victimization of Arab and Muslim Canadians for terrorism, the Canadian Federation of Nurses Unions expressed its solidarity with the declaration "we are all Muslim Canadians until this crisis is over":

> Nurses have traditionally been advocates for those who are vulnerable. ... Caring for the community is what trade union activism is all about.
>
> From this perspective, I say that this hatred, this harassment is wrong and it's anti-Canadian. We are a multi-cultural society made up of people from all over the world. And no one ... no hate is going to take this from us ...
>
> There are 300,000 people in Canada of Muslim faith. I represent 120,000 nurses and we say, we are all Muslim Canadians until this crisis is over – all 420,000 of us. (Connors 2001)

Experiences of racial profiling are sometimes bringing different ethnic and racialized communities together. In the US, soon after September 11, 2001, to demonstrate solidarity against the racial profiling they predicted would follow, the National Asian Pacific American Legal Consortium invited Arab Americans to join them at the National Japanese American Memorial (Stein 2003). In Canada, on the issue of racial profiling, there have been some attempts to express mutual solidarity and establish transethnic ties between black communities and Arab and Muslim groups.

Writing a few weeks after the September 11 attacks, Avtar Brah makes some observations about what she sees as the emergence of a novel transnational political subject. Listing a very diverse range of organizations which participated on 29 September in rallies for the "International Day Against War and Racism" held in San Francisco and Washington DC – including Women for Afghan Women, Mexican Support Network, Collective for Lesbian, Gay, Bisexual and Trans-Gender Rights, Pastors for Peace, Action for Community and Ecology, Black Voices for Peace, Healthcare Now Coalition and AFSCME, part of the labour movement – Brah sees "a new collective subject being constituted as speaker after speaker made connections across many different experiences, forms of differentiation and social divisions." Finding this political subject "simultaneously diasporized and localized", Brah suggests that the current conjuncture allows for a space to "imagin(e) and negotiat(e) alternative transnational conceptions of the person as 'holder of rights' that are distinct from the current notions of citizenship" (Brah 2002, 41–42).

Even though many acts of resistance and demonstrations of solidarity have not necessarily been long-lasting so far, what might be emerging post 9/11, out of the worst of fear, suspicion and hatred, in Canada and in other locations might be a loose but strong anti-racist, anti-imperialist, pro-democracy movement and a new political subject in the making.

NOTES

1 Dr. Enakshi Dua, York University, in personal conversation, April 2004.

2 As recent calls – April 2004 – for the deportation of or denial of citizenship rights to members of the Khadr family demonstrate, despite the existing legal status of citizenship in Canada, even the membership of some citizens can be open to questioning.

3 11.8% of parents mentioned teasing and name-calling by fellow students; 13.2% indicated differential treatment by teachers or school administrators. Examples given for the survey included one case where a teacher called a child "a little terrorist" (Canadian Arab Federation 2002, 18).

4 At the time of the writing of this essay, Canadian Prime Minister Paul Martin was planning a trip to the U.S. A few weeks before the P.M.'s visit, the Canadian Council of Chief Executives, a group made up of the leaders of Canada's biggest corporations, released a "discussion paper" and headed to Washington for a discussion of their vision of the "Canada-United States Partnership" with some high level American politicians and bureaucrats. The Council proposes a "partnership" with the U.S. that includes "a common security agenda, joint military institutions, an integrated energy market and harmonized tariffs and regulations" (Goar 2004, A18; Canadian Council of Chief Executives 2004).

5 See the following website for information on Project Threadbare, a group formed in response to the arrest and detention of the South Asian men: https://canadiandimension.com/articles/view/inventing-enemies-project-thread-canadian-security.

6 There are numerous examples for this kind of organizing which brought very diverse groups together. For example, the groups which starting to organize a protest against a planned visit by George W. Bush to Ottawa in May 2003 – a visit which was subsequently cancelled – were the Anti-Capitalist Community Action and the Committee for Peace in Iraq, groups which themselves were very diverse internally.

REFERENCES

Aiken, Sharryn. 2001. "The Enemy Within." *Globe and Mail*, October 24: A17.

Alam, M. Shahid. 2003. "Is This a Clash of Civilizations?" *Counterpunch*, February 28. http://www.counterpunch.or/alam02282003.html.

Alghabra, Omar. 2003. "A Chance to Lift the Veil of Ignorance About Arabs." *Toronto Star*, October 17: A24.

Anthias, Floya. 2001. "New Hybridities, Old Concepts: The Limits of 'Culture.'" *Ethnic and Racial Studies* 24 (4): 619–641. http://dx.doi.org/10.1080/01419870120049815.

Anthias, Floya. 2002. "Diasporic Hybridity and Transcending Racisms." In *Rethinking Anti-Racisms: From Theory to Practice*, ed. Floya Anthias and Cathie Lloyd, 22–43. New York: Routledge.

Arat-Koç, Sedef. 2003. "Tolerated Citizens or Imperial Subjects?: Muslim Canadians and Multicultural Citizenship in Canada Post 9/11." Paper presented in the session on Citizenship and the Politics of Subjectification, at the *2003 Annual Meeting of Canadian Sociology and Anthropology Association, Learned Societies Conference*, Halifax, Nova Scotia, June 1–4.

Arat-Koç, Sedef. 2002a. "Clash of Civilizations?: Anti-Racist, Multicultural Feminism and Diasporic Middle Eastern Identities Post September 11th." Paper presented at the *Unsettling Imagi(nations): Towards Re-Configuring B/orders Conference*, Vancouver, March 22–24.

Arat-Koç, Sedef. 2002b. "Orientalism and the Cages of Civilizations: Re-Articulations of Nation, Race and Culture in Canada, Post September 11th." Paper presented at the *Critical Race Scholarship and the University Conference*, Toronto, April 25–27.

Asad, Talal. 2009. *Genealogies of Religion*. Baltimore, Maryland: Johns Hopkins University Press.

Brah, Avtar. 2002. "Global Mobilities, Local Predicaments: Globalization and the Critical Imagination." *Feminist Review* 70 (1): 30–45. http://dx.doi.org/10.1057/palgrave/fr/9400008.

Cainkar, Louise. 2002. "No Longer Invisible: Arab and Muslim Exclusion After September 11." *Middle East Report* 224: 22–29.

Canadian Arab Federation. 2001. "Submission to the Standing Committee on Justice and Human rights on the Proposed Bill C-36: Anti-Terrorism Act." (Prepared by Amina Sherazee), November 6.

Canadian Arab Federation. 2002. "Arabs in Canada: Proudly Canadian and Marginalized." Report, April.

Canadian Council of Chief Executives. 2004. "New Frontiers: Building a 21st Century Canada-United States Partnership in North America." (Discussion Paper). http://www.ceocouncil.ca.
Canadian Race Relations Foundation. n.d. *Racial Profiling: Information Sheet.* (Pamphlet).
Connors, Kathleen. 2001. "Canadian Nurses: 'Until this Crisis is Over, We are All Muslims.'" Retrieved May 27. http://www.labornotes.org/archives/2001/1001/1001f.html.
Deaux, Kay. 2001. "Negotiating Identity and Community After September 11." Retrieved April 23. http://www.ssrc.org/sept11/essays/deaux.htm.
Department of Justice. 2001. "Canada's Proposed Anti-Terrorism Act: Working with Our International Partners." (Factsheet), October.
Goar, Carol. 2004. "Odd Way to Build a Consensus." *Toronto Star*, April 12: A18.
Guarnizo, Luis Eduardo, and Michael Peter Smith. 1998. "The Locations of Transnationalism." In *Transnationalism from Below*, ed. Michael Peter Smith and Luis Eduardo Guarnizo, 3–34. New Brunswick, New Jersey: Transaction Publications.
Gwyn, Richard. 2001a. "Canada Will Have to Go Ahead With Whatever U.S. Does Next." *Toronto Star*, September 14: A1, A10.
Gwyn, Richard. 2001b. "We Must Accept the Inevitable." *Toronto Star*, September 30: A13.
Hage, Ghassan. 2002. "Citizenship and Honourability: Belonging to Australia Today." In *Arab-Australians Today: Citizenship and Belonging*, ed. Ghassan Hage, 1–15. Melbourne: Melbourne University Press.
Huntington, Samuel P. 1993. "The Clash of Civilizations?" *Foreign Affairs* 72 (3): 22–49. http://dx.doi.org/10.2307/20045621.
Huntington, Samuel. 1996. *The Clash of Civilizations and the Remaking of World Order*. New York: Simon and Schuster.
Jamal, Audrey. 2002. *Arab-Canadians: The "Other" Within*. M.A. thesis in Conflict Analysis and Management, Royal Roads University.
Jamal, Audrey. 2003. "Anti-Arab Prejudice Flies Again." (Comment). *Globe and Mail*, June 4: A15.
Joseph, Suad. 1999. "Against the Grain of the Nation—the Arab." In *Arabs in America*, ed. Michael W. Suleiman, 257–271. Philadelphia: Temple University Press.
Kabbani, Rana. 2002. "Dislocation and Neglect in Muslim Britain's Ghettos." *Guardian*, June 16.
Khouri, Raja. 2003. "Can Multiculturalism Survive Security Agenda." *Toronto Star*, March 9.
Kutty, Faisal. 2004. "Globalizing the Harassment of Muslims: The Dirty Work of Canadian Intelligence." April 28. http://www.counterpunch.org/kutty04282004.html.
Kutty, Faisal, and Bushra Yousuf. 2002. "Climate of Distrust Threatens Our Basic Values." *The Hamilton Spectator*, September 11.
Lafond, Richard. 2001. "Alexa's View Un-Canadian." (Letter to the Editor). *Toronto Star*, October 16: A25.
Lewis, Bernard. 1990. "The Roots of Muslim Rage." *Atlantic Monthly* (September): 47–60.
Macklin, Audrey. 2001. "Borderline Security." In *The Security of Freedom: Essays on Canada's Anti-Terrorism Bill*, ed. Ronald J. Daniels, Patrick Macklem, and Kent Roach, 383–404. Toronto: University of Toronto Press.
Mandaville, Peter. 2001. *Transnational Muslim Politics: Re-Imagining the Umma*. London: Routledge. http://dx.doi.org/10.4324/9780203453155.
Mitchell, Alanna. 2001. "Canadian Muslims, Arabs Anxious." *Globe and Mail*, October 12. http://www.arts.ualberta.ca/peace/articles/alanna_mitchell_oct_12.htm.
Ong, Aihwa. 1999. *Flexible Citizenship: The Cultural Logics of Transnationality*. Durham, London: Duke University Press.

Safieddine, Hicham. 2003. "One Religion, 12 Voices: Interviews (with Omar Alghabra)." *Toronto Star*, September 11.

Sassen, Saskia. 1996. *Losing Control?: Sovereignty in an Age of Globalization*. New York: Columbia University Press.

Sherazee, Amina. 2002. "Criminalization of Dissent." *Fireweed* 77.

Sherazee, Amina. 2004. "Criminalizing Dissent: Secret Trials, Racial Profiling and the Enemy Within." Paper presented at *Race, Racism and Empire: The Local and the Global Conference*, Toronto: York University, April 29–May 1.

Shohat, Ella. 1995. "The Struggle Over Representation: Casting, Coalitions and the Politics of Identification." In *Late Imperial Culture*, edited by Roman de la Campa, E. Ann Kaplan, and Michael Sprinker, 166–178. New York: Verso.

Shohat, Ella. 2006. "Dislocated Identities: Reflections of an Arab Jew."In *Beyond Borders: Thinking Critically about Global Issues*, edited by Paula S. Rothenberg, 216–220. New York: Worth Publishers.

Siddiqui, Haroon. 2003. "Siding with the U.S. Against Canada." *Toronto Star*, April 6: F1.

Small, Peter, and Bruce DeMara. 2001. "Canadian Muslims Feel Under Siege." *Toronto Star*, September 14.

Spivak, Gayatri Chakravorty. 2000. "Thinking Cultural Questions in 'Pure' Literary Terms." In *Without Guarantees: In Honour of Stuart Hall*, edited by Paul Gilroy, Lawrence Grossberg, and Angela McRobbie, 335–357. London: Verso.

Stein, Eleanor. 2003. "Construction of an Enemy." *Monthly Review* 55 (3): 125–129. http://dx.doi.org/10.14452/MR-055-03-2003-07_12.

Tahmasebi, Victoria. 2004. "Islamic Identity and Secular, Progressive Voices of Iranian Women in the Diaspora: Problems and Dilemmas." Presentation at the Women's Voices from the Middle East symposium, York University, March 11.

Thobani, Sunera. 2002. "Racism and Canadian Democracy in Times of War." Paper presented at the *Racism and National Consciousness Conference*. Toronto: University of Toronto, October 26.

Thobani, Sunera. 2004a. "Contesting Empire: A Case for Anti-Racist Feminism." Paper presented at *Race, Racism and Empire: The Local and the Global Conference*, Toronto: York University, April 29–May 1.

Thobani, Sunera. 2004b. "Imperial Longings, Multicultural Belongings." Paper presented at *Race, Racism and Empire: The Local and the Global Conference*, Toronto: York University, April 29–May 1.

Wente, Margaret. 2001. "Why Do They Hate Us So Much?" *Globe and Mail*, September 22: A13.

Werbner, Pnina. 2000. "Divided Loyalties, Empowered Citizenship?: Muslims in Britain." *Citizenship Studies* 4 (3): 307–324. http://dx.doi.org/10.1080/713658798.

Winant, Howard. 1997. "Behind Blue Eyes: Contemporary White Racial Politics." *New Left Review* 225 (September/October).

Wright, Cynthia. 2003. "Moments of Emergence: Organizing by and with Undocumented and Non-Citizen People in Canada after September 11." *Refuge: Canada's Periodical on Refugees* 21 (3): 5–15.

Wright, Cynthia. 2004. "The Nationalization of Maher Arar." Paper presented at the *Acts of Citizenship Symposium*. Toronto: York University, March 25–27.

PART SIX

After Encounters

18 Global Migrants and the New Pacific Canada

HENRY YU

The New Canada

In the last quarter of a century, a wholesale shift of immigration patterns from transatlantic to trans-Pacific flows has created a new Canada. The changes were quiet at first, beginning after the creation of a the new "points system" for immigration in 1967, but rising in volume during the 1980s so that increasingly the voices of the "new Canada" are spoken in various Asian languages, a powerful new blend of multilingual Canadians that has created a globally connected Pacific Canada in the last 25 years. We have become a new nation that remains in conversation with the dominant Anglo-French society of the mid-20th century, but our future no longer makes sense as a bilingual dialogue solely between English and French. Our national past, built on the outer edges of British imperial settlement that displaced societies already existing in North America, is at the present moment a complicated global conversation in multiple languages, and if we are to embrace a future that builds upon the strength and diversity of this new Canada rather than silencing the great potential we now possess, we must recognize what we have become and reconcile with a colonial past that continues to haunt us.

What is the demographic reality of the new Canada? The top 10 places of birth for immigrants who arrived in Canada between 2001 and 2006 included only two European countries: Romania, at number seven, was the origin of just over 28,000 immigrants; the United Kingdom, which was the dominant sending nation for the first century of Canadian history, was even lower on the list at number nine, sending just over 25,000 new immigrants. In contrast, six of the top 10 countries were in Asia, and the top four on the list alone – the People's Republic of China, India, the Philippines, and Pakistan, accounted for two-thirds of all new migrants to Canada in that period. China sent over 155,000; India over 129,000; the Philippines over 77,000; and Pakistan over 57,000 (Statistics Canada 2007).

In 2006, 83.9 per cent of all new immigrants to Canada came from regions outside of Europe, and the very moniker "visible minority" to designate nonwhite Canadians had become a questionable descriptor of Canada's urban populations. Over 96 per cent of Canada's "visible minorities" live in metropolitan regions. Two main groups – south Asians and self-identified ethnic Chinese – accounted for half of all visible minorities in Canada, with each accounting for roughly a quarter of the total. Ethnic Chinese and south Asians account for eight per cent of Canada's total population, but because they have settled overwhelmingly in either the metropolitan regions of Toronto or Vancouver, they have transformed those cities. Between 1980 and 2001, for instance, the largest proportion of new migrants to

Canada were ethnic Chinese who came from various locations in Southeast Asia (including Hong Kong), along with migrants born in the People's Republic of China. These various ethnic Chinese migrants went overwhelmingly (87 per cent) to the five largest cities in Canada, with 41 per cent going to Toronto and 31 per cent to Vancouver alone (Guo and DeVoretz 2005). Chinese Canada is not homogenous, with a range of linguistic and social variation reflecting diverse origins not only in Asia, but from around the globe. The same can be said of south Asians, who, like ethnic Chinese, often come to Canada as part of global diasporas that emanated from home villages decades and even centuries earlier, bringing with them a wide array of family journeys and complicated histories from around the world and over many generations. By 2006, south Asians had slightly surpassed ethnic Chinese as the largest group of "visible minorities" in Canada, but both are categories that envelop a complex spectrum of family and personal histories that cannot be reduced to simple ethnocultural or racial categorizations.

What is clear, however, is that trans-Pacific migration from Asia has transformed Canada in the last 25 years. Toronto and Vancouver have become the urban capitals of Pacific Canada, and Vancouver in particular has become a city in which the term "visible minority" to describe Asians makes no sense. In 2006, four out of 10 Vancouverites were immigrants, and five out of 10 were of Asian ancestry. Richmond and Burnaby, suburbs of metropolitan Vancouver, were 65 per cent and 55 per cent visible minority, and 50 per cent of Richmond's population is ethnic Chinese: in Vancouver, Canada's third largest city, the visible minority is white.

If the new Canada can be understood by looking at the changed face of Canada's cities in the present, so too can the future be seen in the young faces of the largely Asian, nonwhite Canada of visible minorities. Visible minorities in Canada are the face of tomorrow: their median age in 2006 was 33, versus an average age of 39 for the population as a whole. The demographic future of Canada will continue to shift towards a world derived from and oriented towards the Pacific world.

The New Pacific Canada and the Old Pacific Canada

What is meant by using the phrase "Pacific Canada"? Clearly, Pacific Canada is not just a new term for "western Canada," since the changes that trans-Pacific migration has wrought in the last 40 years extend across the nation, from Victoria to Halifax, and every small town in Canada has seen a local manifestation of the new demographic shifts. Toronto, the largest city in Canada and the financial hub of the nation's economy, has received the largest trans-Pacific migration in absolute numbers, so it is clearly not a phenomenon restricted to the west coast or western Canada. Rather than a geographical description, Pacific Canada refers to a perspective on Canada's past, present, and future that highlights the ways in which the nation has been and increasingly will be shaped by its engagement with the Pacific rather than the Atlantic world. More than just immigration flows and networks of migration between Canada and Asia, Pacific Canada also refers to economic linkages and trade flows, as well as social, cultural, and political connections. Whether in the form of goods manufactured in China dominating the store shelves in the smallest Canadian town, or in the shifts of manufacturing jobs from North America across the Pacific, the role of Asia in our national future cannot be measured strictly in population flows or even balance-of-trade figures. Whether we like it or not, China has become a dominant player in the global economy, and our future is tied to its future.

Ironically, the new Pacific Canada is also a return to an old Pacific Canada, a world in which migration networks and trade flows connected the new nation of Canada to Asia and the Pacific region. In the late 19th century, both before and after Confederation, British Columbia was engaged with a Pacific world through its dominant migration patterns and trade connections. It is often seen as a matter of ethnic trivia that "the Chinese built the railroad," but the fact that trans-Pacific migrants from China built the Pacific portions of every major transcontinental railroad in the late 19th century is a significant indication of a growing Pacific world of migration and trade that had been developing throughout the century. It was much easier for migrants to the western coasts of North America to arrive by trans-Pacific shipping than it was for migrants to come from the Atlantic coast. In 1789, when the expedition of Captain John Meares arrived to trade with the Nu-chul-nath peoples, on board were 29 Chinese who helped build the fort and who likely intermarried with local First Nations peoples after the trading post failed. In 1858, when the colony of Victoria was established as the first British colony on the Pacific coast, Chinese merchants and labourers arrived at the same time as British migrants. The 15,000 or so Chinese workers who built the western portion of the Canadian Pacific Railway in the 1880s did so because it was possible to bring them in large numbers to British Columbia by water from China and from California. It should also be noted that the British capital that funded the building of the CPR would find a return on its investment from the creation of a more rapid means of transporting the luxury goods of Asia across the land barrier of North America, avoiding the difficult sea journey around either the Cape of Good Hope in Africa or Cape Horn at the tip of South America. Silk and other trade goods from Asia were rapidly unloaded in Vancouver and rushed across Canada on express trains before being loaded onto waiting ships in Halifax for the journey to European markets.

The irony is that the Chinese built the very means of transportation that allowed large numbers of migrants from the Atlantic coast to come to British Columbia and to begin displacing them and First Nations peoples. It is no coincidence that the 1885 Chinese head tax, designed to curb Chinese immigration to Canada, was passed at exactly the moment that the Chinese finished building the transcontinental railroad that brought workers in large numbers from the east coast. What these newly arriving Atlantic migrants in the late 19th and early 20th century saw when they stepped off the train in Vancouver was a province that already had Chinese migrants engaging in marriage alliances and trade relations all across British Columbia. Even with the passage of the discriminatory head tax (which charged only Chinese migrants a tax equivalent to over a year's salary upon arrival in Canada), over 96,000 Chinese arrived between 1885 and 1923 (when an almost complete ban on Chinese immigration was passed under the euphemistically named "Chinese immigration act"). These Chinese migrants travelled across the country eastwards on the same railroad that transatlantic migrants used to move westwards, passing them going the other way to deposit them in every small town and city across the Prairies and all the way to Nova Scotia and Newfoundland.

Pacific Canada, therefore, also refers to this earlier world of trans-Pacific and transatlantic migrants engaging with First Nations peoples, a world that was eclipsed by white supremacy as a nation-building tool in the late 19th and early 20th centuries. The growing numbers of European migrants to British Columbia, stepping off the railroad built by the Chinese, organized around the banner of a "White Canada Forever" (a popular bar-room song and political rallying cry). Depriving both aboriginal peoples and Asian migrants of the vote, the increasing numbers of transatlantic migrants pushed for aggressive legislation designed to clear aboriginal peoples from their lands and strict anti-Asian immigration laws that curtailed further trans-Pacific migration to Canada.

Between the 1920s and the 1960s, Canada was a forbidding and hostile place to Asian migrants. Those who were descended from the early trans-Pacific migrants of the late 19th and early 20th century faced racism and legislated discrimination in multiple forms, including disenfranchisement and legal segregation in housing and employment. White supremacy in Canada was universal and racial apartheid akin to the forms in other British settler colonies such as Australia, New Zealand, and South Africa – enshrined in laws in areas as disparate as voting rights through housing titles and labour relations. Not until the Canada Citizenship Act of 1947 did Canadians of Asian ancestry begin to receive voting rights, and immigration laws did not formally remove racial preferences until 1967.

A post-1967 Canada echoes the incipient Pacific Canada that was developing in British Columbia before white supremacy took hold. For instance, the proportion of British Columbia's total population that was Chinese in 1901 was roughly 10 per cent (14,885 of 149,709). It took a full century before that proportion was reached again in 2001 (373,830 of 3,698,850). In 1881, before the imposition of the head tax, Chinese made up almost 20 per cent of British Columbia's non-aboriginal population and an even greater proportion of its workforce. Chinese, Japanese, south Asian, and aboriginal workers in lumber, mining, fishing, and agriculture dominated early industrial development, and well into the latter part of the 20th-century Chinese-Canadian farmers in Vancouver's lower mainland region were an integral part of the agricultural industry – growing, distributing, and selling produce in a vertically integrated network that connected farms on the Fraser River with grocery stores in every urban neighbourhood and small town throughout British Columbia. Chinese-Canadian family-owned import/export firms moved millions of dollars of goods back and forth across the Pacific, creating global connections that are often overlooked even though they created many of the trans-Pacific networks of business linkages that created the base for the flows of capital from Hong Kong and other parts of southeast Asia to Canada in the 1980s and 1990s.

If we consider the half century of "white Canada" between the 1920s and 1960s as an aberration, then the return to a Pacific Canada over the last four decades requires new engagements between First Nations peoples and migrants from both the Atlantic and Pacific worlds on terms other than those of white supremacy. For all of Canada, not just the western regions, the increasing importance of Asia and the Pacific world for the future involves more than just lip service to the existence of Asian migrants as marginal figures of our past and claims that we have left all vestiges of our white supremacist past behind. We must remember that the Pacific Canada in which we will live in the future is also a return to a world ended prematurely in our past (Yu 2007–8).

Trends from the Last 25 Years

Looking back on the transformations that new trans-Pacific migration patterns wrought in Canada, several trends stand out. The first was the increasing prevalence of global migration flows that are circular, with frequent travel back and forth between two or more locations on both sides of the Pacific, rather than the one-way immigration flows from sending country to receiving country that had been the hallmark assumption of most immigration policy during the 20th century. The second trend was the creation of a distinct set of highly mobile migrants who were the most visible in exhibiting these forms of circular migration.

These migrants tended to be well educated and strategic in their migrations, encouraged to move to Canada by new immigration laws designed to attract highly educated and financially secure migrants, and seeing in Canada a safe and relatively accessible place for their children's education. Split families became a significant phenomenon, with children going to school in Canada, often with wives or grandparents accompanying them, while fathers or parents continued to work in Asia. A third trend has been the rapid growth in linguistic diversity among Canadian immigrants and their children, in particular in a range of Asian languages, and a subsequent increase in the ability of Canadians to engage across the Pacific in cultural and commercial exchange. All three trends are in fact not entirely new, with each having antecedents in the trans-Pacific migrations of a century before. What is distinctly new, however, is the volume and impact of these trends and their capacity to shape our collective future.

Migration Rather Than Immigration

One of the signature observations of the new scholarship that has grown in the last two decades to study and understand the new immigration to Canada has been to note that the term "migration" – denoting the movements of people in multiple directions and with multiple journeys throughout a person's life – is a much more useful framework than the term "immigration" for analysing the way that people move. Immigration was a term that captured the one-way journeys of so many migrants from the British Isles and Europe who came to Canada in the 20th century as settlers and as refugees from war. But just as the period between 1920 and 1960 was aberrational because of the dominance of white supremacy in immigration policy, it was also atypical in terms of how migrants overwhelmingly moved in a single direction, usually within the British empire from Britain to colonial settlements such as Canada and Australia, but also in the great refugee migrations spurred by the Second World War and the Cold War from Europe to North America. Within the great labour migrations of the late 19th and early 20th centuries, trans-Pacific migrants such as the Chinese and transatlantic migrants such as Italians tended to follow highly circular paths of migration, with young men leaving to make their fortunes around the world and often planning to return home to buy land and raise a family.

In the last decades of the 19th century, and again in the last decades of the 20th century, Canada was often one site among many for a significant portion of migrants (Ley and Kobayashi 2005). The term "astronaut" arose to describe fathers who jetted back and forth across the expanse of the Pacific Ocean to visit family in Canada while continuing to work in Asia. "Parachute children" came to be used as a description for those kids who came to, or were left in, Canada to go to high school or university while parents continued to work in other parts of the world. Although always a minority of the total migrants who came to Canada in the last 25 years, the significance of circular migrations increasingly became a focus of interest for research projects such as the "research on immigration and integration in the metropolis" project in Canada. Studies showed that not only were migrants often highly strategic in thinking about when they should live in Canada and when it was more advantageous to live or work somewhere else in the world, but native-born Canadians also saw Canada as only one site among many to live and work. Locations in Canada were understood within a life process of aspirations, often as a good place to go to school or to live out retirement in comfort and leisure, but a much less ideal place to work during the prime wage earning years at mid-life. Kenny Zhang (2008) of the Asia Pacific Foundation has estimated that there were over 2.7 million Canadians living outside Canada, and findings from surveys reveal that those in the age range of 30–44 were most likely to be somewhere else, with the most popular reason by far being job-career opportunities.

The presence of Canadian citizens outside of Canada, living and working for decades, became an increasingly noted phenomenon in scholarly studies and the popular media. In the first decade of the 21st century, it became widely known that there were 250,000 Canadian citizens living and working in Hong Kong. To put this in perspective, more Canadians lived in the city of Hong Kong than in either Saskatoon or Regina, and if the Canadians in Hong Kong were counted as a city in Canada, it would have been in the top 20 in size.

Switzerland of the Pacific?

One of the most remarkable trends in the last quarter century has been the increased targeting of a particular set of immigrants who carry with them substantial financial resources. The business migration program was revamped in the 1980s to specifically target investors and entrepreneurs who could commit to a certain level of investment in Canada (beginning with $250,000 at the start of the program and rising eventually to a minimum of $400,000 as the program became successful) or to the creation of a set number of jobs. The targeting of wealthy migrants was not new for Canadian immigration policy – even anti-Chinese legislation such as the 1885 Chinese head tax and the exclusionary 1923 Chinese immigration act both contained exemptions for merchants. The novelty of this new program lay in the explicit description of the exact amount of financial commitment that migrants needed to make in order to be given fast- track immigration status, and how aggressive provincial and federal governments in Canada were in setting up recruitment stations in Asia, in particular in Hong Kong before the 1997 reversion of political control from Britain to China.

The strategic targeting of wealthy migrants was enormously successful, with ethnic Chinese from all around Southeast Asia making up the majority of those who responded to the call. In some ways, acquiring Canadian citizenship and a Canadian passport became a form of security guaranteeing high mobility, an exit visa out of any location (such as Hong Kong post-1997) that might prove difficult to leave with another form of citizenship. The investments made in Canada could be considered a transaction cost for the acquisition of this form of secure mobility, but access to Canada itself became a commodity because other nations such as Australia and the United States also began to pass immigration legislation targeting the same set of financially successful migrants. As the most sought-after migrants began to consider an array of choices for migration, comparisons between cities such as Toronto, Vancouver, San Francisco, and Sydney were made strategically by would-be migrants.

The desirability of Canadian citizenship from the point of view of these highly mobile migrants increasingly centred upon factors such as quality of life (air and water quality, availability of good food, health care, accessibility by air to Asia for commuting), and most commonly the accessibility and cost of higher education for children. Vancouver-based architect Bing Thorn made an off-hand observation in 2003 that Vancouver had become the "Switzerland of the Pacific" – offering a safe haven for wealth for the elite of the Pacific world, just as Swiss banks did in Europe, and providing a handy location for the same families to send their children for schooling, just as Swiss boarding schools provided in Europe.

Educational mobility – the strategic migration of young students around the Pacific region – became a noticeable trend that had particular impact on the major universities in the Vancouver and Toronto metropolitan region, as well as in the rapid growth of small private schools and colleges in those cities designed to prepare students from Asia (in particular South Korea, China, and Taiwan) for entrance into Canadian universities. By 2008, for instance, roughly 15 per cent of the undergraduate population of the University of British Columbia were foreign students paying non-resident tuition rates that were four times the tuition for Canadian residents; however, it is likely that one third of the students were born outside of Canada and had become Canadian citizens sometime before their entrance into UBC. Forty-four per cent of UBCs incoming class in 2005, for instance, listed English as a second language, an approximation of the migrant origins of either themselves or their parents. As one of Canada's most Asian-Pacific universities in both composition and orientation, the University of British Columbia (and Vancouver's other major institution, Simon Fraser University) are perhaps the clearest examples of how the composition of Canada's future educated elite is global in origin, with a particular weighting towards Asia. In terms of ethno-racial makeup alone, with no differentiation in terms of native-born versus immigrant origins, UBC also reflects perhaps the most significant example of how the demographic trends in Canada towards an Asian-Pacific future are more marked among the educated and the young than for Canada's population as a whole. In 2005, 53 per cent of the incoming class at UBC self-identified as Asian, compared with the 33.5 per cent self-identifying as white. Students identifying themselves as Chinese were roughly 37 per cent of the incoming class.[1]

Clearly, Canada has become a desirable destination in terms of educational mobility for migrants in the Asia Pacific region, just as it has for wealthy migrants planning to safely secure their holdings in the ever-rising real estate market that Canadian cities such as Vancouver and Toronto have enjoyed in the last 25 years. A safe and secure location to deposit both capital and school-age children, Canada did begin to acquire a role in the Pacific world akin to Switzerland in the Atlantic region. Because the sale of primary residences in Canada was not subject to capital gains taxes, the high rate of return for investments in the housing market was in practice a tax-free investment instrument. Located in the secure and stable financial environment of Canada, such investments seemed as safe as a Swiss bank account.

The Infusion of Linguistic Capital

Perhaps the most significant trend in the last quarter of a century has been the rapid expansion of linguistic diversity in Canada in terms of Asian language usage. In British Columbia, the second most used language other than English was Chinese in one form or another. In Vancouver, for instance, the 2006 census counted nearly 117,000 residents who spoke Punjabi as their first language. At the same time, almost 129,000 residents who counted Cantonese as their mother tongue, along with roughly 115,000 who spoke Mandarin, nearly 69,000 who spoke Taiwanese, and another 120,000 who just listed Chinese rather than a specific dialect as their mother tongue. This meant that 20 per cent of metropolitan Vancouver's residents reported some form of Chinese as their first language. In comparison, out of the 537,000 self-reported ethnic Chinese in Toronto, 403,700 reported some form of Chinese as their mother tongue, roughly eight per cent of Toronto's residents. Although Toronto in absolute numbers contains more Canadians who speak some form of Chinese than Vancouver does, the proportion of Chinese-speaking residents among the total number of residents of Toronto is smaller. This does not mean, however, that the impact of Chinese and other Asian Canadians has been any less. For instance, suburban regions of

Toronto such as Markham, Scarborough, and Richmond Hill have been transformed by Asian migration, and the presence of young south Asian Canadians and Chinese Canadians in Toronto reflects a city that counts 50 per cent of its total population as having been born outside Canada.

Within a business environment in Canada and across the Pacific where transactions often take place as easily in Cantonese, Mandarin, Gujarati, or Punjabi as they do in English, such linguistic diversity has become a form of human capital with global ramifications for Canada. Multilingual migrants who can move with ease across the Pacific to conduct business and to engage in social and cultural exchange in Asian languages have created the potential for a globally engaged Canada that can leverage such human capital.

Unfortunately, Canada at present continues to waste such capital because of language policies that place little or no emphasis upon retaining such language ability in children. Other than a highly successful kindergarten-through-grade-12 bilingual Mandarin-English program in Edmonton, Alberta, that has been in place for 25 years and has expanded to 13 public schools, there are virtually no examples of public school education that helps either teach or maintain Asian language use. Children of immigrants are more likely to retain the use as adults of their parents' language if they arrive later in their lives rather than earlier, since public schooling in Canada is designed around either English or French. In terms of the retention and maintenance of linguistic capital among Canada's youth, a Canadian is better off coming to Canada as a 10-year-old than being born in Canada, since the likelihood of them growing up to have multiple language use is much better if they are not native-born.

The Impact on Civil Society

For most of Canadian history, nonwhites were disenfranchised and excluded from political life because of the formal implementation of white supremacy. Most Asian Canadians were granted citizenship and the vote in 1947 (Japanese Canadians, who were still interned despite the end of the Second World War, did not receive the vote until several years later). However, Asian Canadians remained in practice second-class citizens well into the 1960s because of the long-term legacies of legislated and formal racial discrimination. It is perhaps no surprise, then, that the delayed entry of Asian Canadians into formal electoral politics in Canada might have profound consequences for their political engagement. With the recent demographic transformations towards a Pacific Canada, what has been the impact on the political life of the nation?

If the effects of mass migration to Canada from the Asia Pacific region are measured only in terms of formal electoral politics, their impact on political life in Canada seems at first glance limited. The number of elected officials at the federal and provincial levels is at a lower proportion than that of Asian Canadians to the general population. Because of the concentration of Asian Pacific migrants in urban areas, their impact on municipal politics has been much greater than at the provincial and federal levels, and yet even at the municipal level the number of elected officials who are Asian Canadian has remained limited. Both Toronto and Vancouver now have significant enough voting populations of south Asians, southeast Asians, Chinese, and Filipinos that the promise of "ethnic voting" trends might prove decisive in elections. However, Asian Canadians have tended to vote in just as diverse and sophisticated a manner as other Canadians, belying assumptions of simplistic ethnic block voting for ethnic candidates. In Vancouver, three of the 10 elected councillors in 2009 were Chinese Canadian, roughly mirroring the overall percentage of ethnic Chinese in the city. However, any simplistic analyses that assume a correlation between ethnic voting and elected officials at the municipal level would be wrong. Each of the three city councillors in Vancouver who are Chinese Canadian – George Chow, Kerry Jang, and Raymond Louie – came into civic politics from very different backgrounds and varying constituencies that were not limited to ethnic Chinese voters.

In Toronto, the proportion of city councillors who are of Asian-Canadian background is well below their overall percentage of the city's population (in 2009, only two of the city's 44 councillors were Asian Canadian, or 4.5 per cent, despite the fact that the city of Toronto is over 30 per cent Asian Canadian). Toronto, which switched to a ward system in 2000, shows a very different spatial distribution of Asian-Canadian communities than Vancouver, with many new Asian migrants clustering in particular neighbourhoods, whereas in Vancouver, ethnic Chinese in particular are much more evenly distributed throughout the city. For instance, Toronto city Councillor Raymond Cho, first elected in 1991, represents at the present moment ward 42 of Scarborough-Rouge River, an incredibly diverse area that contains 88.7 per cent visible minorities, with 39.8 per cent south Asian, 17.6 per cent black, 10.7 per cent Chinese, and 10 per cent Filipino. In terms of migration status, nearly 80 per cent of those over 15 years of age in ward 42 were first-generation Canadians who had arrived from elsewhere, and only 6.2 per cent were third-generation Canadians. It is interesting to note, however, that this district contains almost four times as many residents of south Asian origin than Chinese, again belying simplistic correlations between ethnic block voting within Asian-Canadian communities for co-ethnic candidates.

If civil society and political life are conceived in broad terms, with politics including networks of economic and social participation as well as influence in informal political processes (beyond voter turnout numbers and the fielding of "ethnic" candidates), then the demographic shift towards a Pacific Canada is more significant and argues for broader ways of understanding political life.

Since the overwhelming majority of migrants from the Asia Pacific region to Canada have arrived within the last three decades, it is perhaps no surprise that the impact of these newer migrants upon electoral politics may still be delayed. But how can the underrepresentation of Asian Canadians in electoral politics be explained, beyond a time lag because of recent arrival? Theories about whether migrants from Asia come from places with underdeveloped democratic practices have been propounded, often based upon abstract analyses that misapprehend the depth of political practices that exist in places of origin. Migrants from Hong Kong from the 1970s through the early 1990s, for instance, were coming from a colonial city where the British did not allow open democratic elections until just before they lost political control. Political culture under British rule evolved not around electoral politics but elite networks that reflected economic and social status to influence policy, as well as the use of nongovernmental organizations and grass-roots mobilization to enact political change.

Many Hong Kong migrants to Canada brought sophisticated knowledge of how to create organizations that could engage with political institutions. SUCCESS, an immigrant service agency founded in 1973, was the creation of the early Hong Kong migrants who came to Canada after immigration policy reform in 1967 removed racial barriers. Growing from a small network of social welfare professionals trained in Hong Kong who recognized the need for helping newly arrived ethnic Chinese into a large organization providing a wide spectrum of social services to immigrants of all ethnicities, SUCCESS is an example of how civil society can be profoundly changed through processes beyond formal electoral politics. Several of the organization's founders went on to serve in municipal political office in Vancouver and yet the political impact of the organization should be measured in how it transformed civil society.

In contrast, south Asian migrants from India over the last few decades came from a nation with a well-developed representative democracy and sophisticated voting practices that dated from the end of British colonial rule in 1947. South Asian-Canadian politicians have been able to win election by representing districts with heavy concentrations of south Asian voters, in particular in suburban and semirural areas such as Surrey in the lower mainland of BC. The first nonwhite premier of a Canadian province, Ujjal Dosanjh, was an Indo-Canadian whose provincial riding had a significant Punjabi Sikh community. And yet the impact of south Asian migration upon civil society in Canada goes beyond these elected officials. For instance, in terms not of legislative governance but in the ways by which law governs the practices of daily life, Punjabi Sikh migration has transformed the face of policing in Canada. The metropolitan police forces of all the major cities, as well as the RCMP, the national police force of Canada, have seen significant growth in Punjabi Sikh officers. Indeed, the most potent symbol of the shift from a nation founded upon white supremacy towards the new Pacific Canada might have been symbolized by the successful fight of Baltej Singh Dhillon in 1990 to wear his turban as an RCMP officer. The symbolism of seeing the iconic symbol of the Canadian Mounties now wearing a Sikh turban was a watershed moment in understanding how a legal regime in Canada that for most of its history had undergirded the politics of white supremacy now had a new face.

If the political life of Canada is defined in broad terms, then the transformation of civil society has seen deep changes that are rooted in local neighbourhood transitions. There continues to be a lag in how formal electoral politics reflects such shifts in civil society and local politics, in particular at the higher levels of provincial and federal politics, but the future will undoubtedly be shaped by these profound changes.

The Future of Pacific Canada?

What the next 25 years brings is uncertain, but if the current immigration policy remains the same, and the dominant trends in trans-Pacific migration continue to transform our future into one heavily infused with the voices of Asian migrants, then Canadian cities such as Toronto and Vancouver will enter the realm of global cities such as Singapore, Sydney, San Francisco, and Los Angeles, where significant populations with Asian ancestry have created connections and networks that span the Pacific. However, state educational policies in almost all of those cities have yet to recognize the potential of these new demographic admixtures. Singapore has adopted language education policies that are designed to promote the use of English and one Asian language in all of its youth. Canada has yet to make a similar investment in the linguistic potential of its younger generations, and as of now the retention of valuable Asian language skills varies greatly, depending upon the individual circumstances of each family.

What will be the future of Pacific Canada? It is highly unlikely that its development will be prematurely clipped as it was 100 years ago. But if we have returned to an engagement in Canada with the Asian-Pacific world, and our migration networks and the linguistic background of our immigrant population create an enormous potential for linkages and connections across the Pacific, the question remains whether our state policies at the local, regional, and national levels recognize and leverage such potential. The answer to this question will greatly determine whether Canada will look back in 25 years and judge our success or failure in capitalizing on this transformative moment in our nation's history.

NOTE

1 Figures for University of British Columbia's incoming class in 2005 are care of Walter Sudmant, derived from a survey conducted of undergraduate students.

REFERENCES

Guo, Shibao, and DeVoretz, Don. 2005. *The Changing Face of Chinese Immigrants in Canada*, Research on Immigration and Integration in the Metropolis, Vancouver Centre, no. 05-08, February.

Ley, David, and Audrey Kobayashi. 2005. "Back to Hong Kong: Return Migration or Transnational Sojourn?" *Global Networks* 5 (2): 111-27. http://dx.doi.org/10.1111/j.1471-0374.2005.00110.x.

Statistics Canada. 2007. "*World: Place of Birth of New Immigrants to Canada, 2006*," *2006 Census*. Geography Division.

Yu, Henry. 2007-2008. "Refracting Pacific Canada: Seeing Our Uncommon Past." *BC Studies* 156, Winter, 5-10.

Zhang, Kenny. 2008. "Global Canadians: Scale, Profile, and Impact." *Asia Pacific Foundation* 13-14, December.

19 Asian Canada: Undone

LAURA J. KWAK

Murasaki: Obachan, everyone wants to hear stories. And I can't finish them. They scatter like sheep. Like dust.

Naoe: No need to tie them up. There is always room for beginnings.

(Goto 1994, 63)

Becoming

The whimsical imagery that animates Hiromi Goto's 1994 novel *Chorus of Mushrooms* illustrates, for me, the current juncture of Asian Canadian Studies (ACS). In telling the story of Murasaki and the loss of her Obachan, Goto focuses our attention on the place of wounds and fracturedness in order to open up a new field of meaning. In their world, memories are textual, inherited and often they scatter. Unbound by strict borders, their conversations illuminate the fecund in the transient. The two characters speak to one another across the line that distinguishes the living from the dead, enabling them to enter into vast depths of their interiority. And by joining them, we find ourselves turning inward as well, sifting our own memories, and watching the dust whirl, settle and then scatter again. We are not quite sure when one story ends and another begins, which can leave us frustrated like Murasaki. Yet, Naoe's suggestive advice might be taken as a lesson for ACS as well. She says there is no need to master the stories, to tie them up and finish them. Staying with the unruly and the impermanent ends up being incredibly meaningful for them both. From them, we can derive a methodology for Asian Canadian Studies; one that is as fecund as it is unruly. For both Murasaki and for ACS, this is an incredibly generative place to find ourselves.

Over the past several decades, a considerable body of Asian Canadian scholarship has been published in both the humanities and social sciences (Chang 2007; Li 2007; Miki 2011; Thobani and Hellwig 2006; Ty and Goellnicht 2004; Roy 2003; Ujimoto and Hirabayashi 1980). Yet one question continues to plague us again and again: *What exactly is Asian Canadian Studies?* Also, who counts as Asian Canadian? Is there, and should there be, a single theoretical framework and methodology for scholars identified with this field? Numerous edited volumes, monographs, essays, exhibitions and creative works have been dedicated to addressing these questions. These many projects demonstrate not only that Asian Canadian Studies does exist but also that it is robust and wide-ranging. Yet, the persistence of *the question* seems to beg for a stable and definitive answer to organize the heterogeneous, sometimes contradictory, stories and to discipline them into a field of knowledge. Of course, the urgency of an institutionalizing project is reasonable given the constraining hold that the neoliberalized academy has over our labour. Space, funds, and support are vital to continue apace in our scholarly endeavours. A simultaneous concern, however, is what effect the constitution of the field, as it is folded into the Academy, will have on the ethos of Asian Canadian Studies questions moving forward.

"Being included" has had a catalogued record of narrowing, rather than opening up space, where a select few scholars become "enough" to carry the burden of representation and diversity (Ahmed 2012). Delineating a single theoretical framework and methodology for ACS is as equally pernicious. The most politically emboldening works in Asian Canadian Studies, to date, have written against this disciplinary grain as they address "... permissions and prohibitions, presence and absence ..." (Gordon 2008, 17). Engaging in Asian Canadian Studies is, in many ways, an attempt to make sense of intense ambivalences and contradictions. There are tensions left to explore, ghosts left lingering, and absences left to address, which demand interdisciplinary analyses. For instance, what are the historical and contemporary relations within the broad category of Asian (West/ South/ East/ South-East) as non-preferred settlers in Canada? How might our scholarly and political questions seriously address settler colonialism? What is the political and communal salience of the term "Asian Canadian"? These questions are meant to suggest that a collection such as *Asian Canadian Studies Reader* does not imply a comprehensive and fixed impression of the borders of Asian Canada nor of the theoretical and methodological approaches exclusively assumed in Asian Canadian Studies. Rather, the volume encompasses key readings, which are not often read together and against each other. It presents scholarly, political, and methodological interventions by scholars of varying disciplines from Comparative Literature to Sociology to Gender Studies, marking ACS as an interdisciplinary endeavour. It broadly addresses Asian Canada including the national and transnational experiences of South-Asians, East-Asians, West-Asians, and South-East Asians in Canada, thus interrogating the common and widespread understanding of Asian as simply East Asian. Asian Canadian Studies is also located on a continuum of arrivals and departures or a larger interconnected axis of Asian Canadian scholarly and political work (Miki 2000).

Simple and static answers to *the question* are insufficient because both "Asian" and "Canadian" represent terms fraught with contestation. It also suggests that the future direction of the field is also fraught and contested. In the future of Asian Canada, which research questions will be asked and prioritized, of and by which communities, and which issues will be taken up as Asian Canadian issues? These futures are mediated by which stories have been told, not told, and unheard about Asian Canada. A long and ongoing history of anti-Asian racism in Canada has been documented, including the 1907 race riots in Vancouver, BC, the 1924 Chinese Exclusion Act, the Japanese Internment initiated in 1941, the 1914 *Komagata Maru* incident, the 1992 Live-in Caregiver Program, and (trans)national security policies that racially profile Arab and South Asian men post-9/11. These defining events are not only important to Asians in Canada but they also constitute the ongoing legacy of Canadian nation building. Yet these histories are often un-contextualized and relegated to a Canadian past that has supposedly since been absolved. While anti-Asian racism gets trivialized, the racial profiling of particular Asian Canadian groups is an ongoing and increasingly systemized project, in the name of national securitization in the post-9/11 era. While concepts such as diversity, equality and tolerance have been scripted in multicultural policies, racist logics continue to operate through the seemingly neutral language of Canadian values. Racial discrimination is then contained as historical transgressions that have been resolved and privatized as matters that occur between individuals, thereby foreclosing meaningful public conversations. Thus, one of ACS's political objectives should be to address these foreclosures and work to open up spaces for meaningful public debates about social justice.

In what follows, I highlight four interrelated research interventions that I hope will animate the scholarly and political futures of Asian Canadian Studies: (1) Relational Racialization, (2) Confronting Settler-Colonialism, (3) Asian Canadian politics, and (4) Asian Canadian feminisms. These four interventions certainly overlap and are meant to serve as frameworks to facilitate meaningful public debate. For instance, the recognition of relational racialization within Asian Canadian communities and intersections of gender, sexuality, ability and class are necessary in imagining interracial and Pan-Asian coalitional politics and activism. Asian Canada, as a category of non-preferred settlers has emerged in relationship to white preferred-settlers and Indigenous people. This trichotomous power relationship is central to ACS research questions that deal with human rights, citizenship, and redress in the Canadian context.

Relational Racialization

Various Asian diasporas exist in relation to each other in Canada; each has different historical trajectories of arrival and relationship to the Canadian nation-state, mediated through different categories of labour. Within each of these diasporas, there are further heterogeneities and multiple identifications, maps of desire and attachments. People in movement include students, specialists, entrepreneurs, refugees, sponsored family members, and labour migrants, both documented and undocumented. Examining Asian Canadian diasporas necessarily involves the historicization of these multiple trajectories, arrivals, departures, and settlements and also take up their relationality across the social, economic, and political. While national borders and borders between various groups under the category "Asian Canadian" are political constructs, there are material consequences to these demarcations as they determine peoples' mobility, access, and political inclusion. Racial categorizations enforced by the state determine how one's geographic and communal space comes to articulate different histories, simultaneously spaces of safety and trauma, or contested spaces. Avtar Brah asks:

> How and in what ways do these journeys conclude, and intersect in specific places, specific spaces, and specific historical conjunctures? How and in what ways is a group inserted within the social relations of class, gender, racism, sexuality, or other axes of differentiation in the country to which it migrates? The manner in which a group comes to be "situated" in and through a wide variety of discourses, economic processes, state policies and institutional practices is critical to its future. (Brah 1996, 179)

Brah raises important questions that pertain to the intersection of experiences, space, and histories. The category of Asian Canadian broadly encompasses a wide range of migrants coming from continental Asia and Pacific Islands as well as from other diasporas around the world such as the Caribbean, Africa, and South America. The ways in which the Canadian state has racially and ethnically classified Asian Canadians through census and surveys over time, while arbitrary, have been historically and materially generative (Day 2008). How have Asian Canadians been sorted out along racial and ethnic lines and for what political purpose? How have these categorizations reinforced the pitting of immigrant communities against each other? Brah notes how axes of differentiation along gender, class, race, and sexuality determine processes and experiences of migration and migrant lives. This is significant to the theorization of Asian Canada as it situates migrants as imbricated in a set of discourses, economies, policies and institutions, which are racialized, gendered, and classed. In this way, relational racialization has always been part and parcel of the Canadian nation-building project.

The history of Asian inclusion in Canada has entailed continuities as well as ruptures. Identity politics as informed by race and ethnicity have created important political activist communities but this should not foreclose debates about how *exclusion operates through inclusion* (Dua 2007). There is a great risk of depoliticizing and dehistoricizing patterns of racial profiling when racialization is not conceptualized as systemic. More importantly, racialization must be understood as a set of social and political processes constructed relationally. Within the broad category of Asian Canada, West Asians, South Asians, Southeast Asians, and East Asians have been racialized very differently from and against each other and non-Asian raced people and communities. Based on the ways in which various Asian communities have been racialized and stereotyped within Canada, it is clear that within the large category of Asian Canadian, there are preferred and non-preferred groups. For instance, while some Asians have been stereotyped as industrious and elite, particularly since the 1967 Points System was introduced, other Asians have been racialized as perilous or imperiled as a result of post-9/11 "security" measures that work to legitimize increased racially profiling. Simultaneously, Southeast Asians, specifically Filipina women, are invoked in the Canadian imaginary as caretakers since the Temporary Foreign Worker Program (TFWP) introduced the 1992 Live-In Caregiver Program (LCP). These seemingly neutral state programs are clearly gendered and racialized and over-determine access to resources, mobility, and citizenship. This sort of racial discrimination homogenizes communities and steamrolls over differences within; differences, which also sustain power asymmetries and determine who gets to speak for whom. For instance, Asian Canadian feminists have demonstrated how elite male leaders often claim to represent entire ethnic communities (Ng 1991). Also, while Asian elites are able to migrate and fluidly travel back and forth between home- and host-nations, others may not have such access. Similarly, while elite women are able to hire live-in caregivers as they pursue their careers, this does not dismantle gendered and racialized labour inequalities. The concept of relational racialization thus reveals how the conditions that sustain differing access to resources, space, and citizenship are structurally reproduced. Thinking through relational racialization should enable an understanding of our multiple and synchronous positions at once victims of and complicit in ongoing structures of inequality. We must be attentive to the ways in which racialization is indeed flexible especially as evidenced by the language of liberalism, which has sustained gendered and racialized inequalities. In theorizing the contested sites of diasporas, Brah suggests,

> It is important, therefore, to be attentive to the nature and type of processes in and through which the collective "we" is constituted. Who is empowered and who is disempowered in a specific construction of the "we"? What is the relationship of this "we" to its "others"? Who are these others? (Brah 1996, 181)

That is, how do Asian Canadians experience and negotiate the condition of being and of not being of the nation according to the ways they have been racialized? How does relational racialization operate in the (re)construction of nation? Deliberating these questions is critical to providing counter-discourses and counter-publics of being and relating. So long as belonging and citizenship are only imagined through the dominant coded relationship of "self versus other", struggles for recognition, redress, and community formation culminate in the reconsolidation of variations of this coded relationship. What happens when the marginal moves closer to the centre, becoming recognizable and palatable? Should our struggles end with inclusion?

In *Melancholy of Race*, Cheng suggests that "... attachment to progress and healing, eagerly anticipating a colorblind society, sidesteps the important examination of racialization: How is a racial identity secured? How does it continue to generate its seduction for both the dominant and the marginalized?" (Cheng 2001, 7). Here, Cheng asks us not to underestimate the power of race as a structure of feeling. Community-organized protests of Canada's long history of anti-Asian exclusion eventually resulted in enfranchisement for Chinese, Sikh, and Japanese Canadians between 1947 and 1949. Activists also fought for official state apologies for Chinese exclusion (2006) and the Japanese internment (1988). While these are important dates in Canadian history, claims making processes for political inclusion should not foreclose the space to critique inequalities sustained by the same legal system. For instance, the argument that racism and sexism lie in the resolved past has always been central to liberal racial projects.

I began this afterword amidst a flurry of debate about a *Maclean's* article called "Too Asian" in November 2010, where it is argued that elite universities around Canada are overflowing with Asian students (read: Asian as Chinese). The arguments made in "Too Asian" echo the 1979 W5 piece "Campus Giveaway," which argued that Canadian universities were being overstocked with Asian students (again, referring to East Asians). The article describes Asian students as a homogeneous mass thereby ignoring differences among the multiple, hybrid, and heterogeneous subjectivities within the category of Asian and subsequently steamrolls over different experiences of migrations to Canada that have informed their varying degrees of access to citizenship and education. Narratives like the ones documented by *Maclean's* can be located in a long history of racial anxiety that re-erases Indigenous populations and Black Canadians and re-stigmatizes Asians as non-preferred settlers. The "Too Asian" case exemplifies that "... racist institutions in fact often do not want to fully expel the racial other; instead, they wish to maintain that other within existing structures" (Cheng, 12). This is an effective example of how Asians in Canada are depicted as abject in the nation's imaginaries: at once essential to Canada's economic futures and yet at the same time, undesirable and perpetually foreign.

The article itself and responses to it illustrate how race is sustained relationally. First, focusing on the white student informants that expressed anti-Asian racism against their peers individualizes the legacy of Canadian racism, thereby depoliticizing the issue. Second, many responses that countered the racist *Maclean's* article did so through the language of liberal meritocracy, which argues that Asian students work hard and thus are deserving of their places in Canadian universities. The narrative is that many of us are also Canadian-born and therefore have earned the right to take our place in elite universities. This makes sense, yet, the discourse around meritocracy does not address those vital questions that Cheng posed: how is racial identity secured? How does it generate seduction for both the dominant and the marginalized? The liberal language of meritocracy underestimates the deeply structural racial logics that sustain the conditions under which anti-Asian articles, like "Too Asian," circulate as legitimate, un-racist journalism in a nation that prides itself on being officially multicultural.

It is not paradoxical that "Too Asian" was published at an historical juncture where East Asians have increasingly experienced class privileges that are not afforded to Indigenous peoples, Black Canadians, West Asians, South Asians, and Southeast Asians. For instance, it is not often taken seriously that non-preferred Asians including Filipino, Cambodian, Thai, Malaysian, and Tamil youth are underrepresented at elite universities and in professional occupations in Canada. The language of meritocracy does not sufficiently address the severe underrepresentation of Southeast Asian and other racialized students who also work hard, have the grades, and deserve their places in universities. The seemingly paradoxical and contradictory elements around "Too Asian" demonstrate that race, as a floating signifier, has always been flexible. Such ambiguities and contradictions are commensurate with racial projects like official multiculturalism that position non-preferred settlers as both victims of and complicit in ongoing nation-building projects. Relational racialization also challenges us to work through issues of Asian Canada through an approach to research and political work that any singular identitarian politic would not facilitate. It pushes us to move towards what Sedef Arat-Koç calls "transethnic and non-ethnic identifications and solidarity" (Arat-Koç 2006). Relational racialization as a conceptual frame can then help us to read events like "Too Asian" as part of larger socio-political matrix where racial logics are sustained through their disavowal.

Confronting Settler-Colonialism

A marginal discourse, the story of how the real story has emerged, consistently shadows and threatens to subvert the very authority that establishes disciplinary order. (Gordon, 26)

In this section I identify the significance of confronting settler-colonialism on Asian Canadian identities, communities, and political mobilization. For instance, how might we consider the ways in which the histories of Indigenous people provide alternative ways of conceptualizing, politicizing, and knowing our place in Canada? Goto illustrates the diasporic subject as a two-headed mushroom:

> somewhere, somehow, two spores must have melded together, because there is a huge bulge on the main body of the stem, a two-headed mushroom with two possible umbrellas filled with gills of tiny spores. I hold the mushroom in my crack-lined palms and breathe in deep, the smell of growing. (Goto 1994, 74)

Not only is the metaphor of the two-headed mushroom reflective of Asian Canadianness as hyphenated and multiple but also it is important to note on what soil the mushrooms are planted. Murasaki wanders through her family's mushroom farm in Alberta, Canada and notes the smell of growing, which illustrates the emergence of Asian Canada in relation to Native land.

Canadian history has characteristically been presented as a story of the arrival of Europeans to a virgin, uninscribed and "uninhabited" land. Aboriginal people at this time were (and to a large extent still are) depicted as savage, uncivilized, and child-like. After the Royal Proclamation in 1763, which set the foundation for a Nation-Nation relationship between Aboriginal peoples and the Crown, original goals for the "protection" of Aboriginal lands changed into notions of assimilation and oppression via a dominating ethnocentric world view. The Indian Act, a federal statute enacted in 1876 was originated with the

Constitution Act (1867), by assigning Parliament the legislative jurisdiction over "Indians and lands reserved for the Indians." This statute essentially turned the Indigenous (First Nations, Métis, and Inuit) populations of Canada into state wards and contained stipulations focused on assimilation as well as political and economic control. It remains a violent racial tool that legalized racism in our country. The Indian Act has forced the appropriation of colonialist systems of patriarchy, domination and knowledge onto Indigenous peoples, as well as institutionalized racial hierarchies, and sanctioned the condemnation of Indigenous bodies onto unhealthy spaces such as reserves and residential schools. It is an administrative means of domination and oppression, dehumanizing Indigenous peoples, creating categories of exclusion, especially for Native women, and limiting agency through the bureaucratic control of human rights and education. Bonita Lawrence writes:

> In order to maintain Canadians' self-image as a fundamentally "decent" people innocent of any wrongdoing, the historical record of how the land was acquired – the forcible and relentless dispossession of indigenous peoples, the theft of their territories, and the implementation of legislation and policies designed to effect their total disappearance as peoples must also be erased. It has therefore been crucial that the survivors of this process be silenced – that Native people be deliberately denied a voice within national discourse. (Lawrence 2002, 23–4)

As Lawrence stresses, there is great importance in documenting processes and effects of colonization from the perspective of those who were colonized especially when resistances that Indigenous communities manifested against colonization are silenced from Canadian history and are often met with state violence.

Drawing from Rita Wong's (2008) work that reflects upon meaningful and ethical engagement with Indigenous people and their histories of resistance, I urge future interventions in ACS to shift the understanding of relationship to land from a colonial one of the Canadian nation-state towards paradigms that Indigenous peoples have offered. This shift necessarily involves challenging ongoing colonization, one in which we confront the abuse of natural resources and conceptualizations of property through privatization, not as an attempt to absolve settler-coloniality but rather to learn and work ethically for a place in Canada that is mindful of inaugural and ongoing systemic colonization. So long as humanity is imagined through the lens of Modernity, then we will continue to subjugate bodies, land, raw materials, and reinforce the colonial project. Since the Asian Canadian diaspora and the Canadian nation are simultaneously and continuously *becoming* it is possible to make such interventions. A reflection on the processes of becoming is then necessarily a reflection on the making of histories, in this case, Asian Canadian histories. I suggest that there is a concurrent dynamism and nihilism in the act of writing or making history as "a labor of death and a labor against death" (de Certeau 1988, 5), or become present through that which is absent. In the passage above, Avery Gordon gestures to the possibility of a marginal discourse as a tool of subversion against the dominant discourse. By challenging the ways in which the dominant story has emerged, this marginal discourse is a consistent challenge to the order of things and life as we know it. The marginal discourse as organized by those who have been deemed external to the centre (state, community, body) has the potential to overturn the status quo and write humanity into stories that have otherwise been unrecognized. In this way, re-historicization becomes the archive of spaces of belonging or declaring presence out of absence through further absence-making. It remains the scriptural invention of history, space, subjects and its Others. Thus, it is crucial to unpack the discursive and material effects of claiming space and citizenship as non-preferred settlers in Canada as well as the occlusions that it enables, as emerging from historical, spatial, psychic sites of racist colonial trauma. Part of that unpacking is to excavate entwining histories and resist situating ourselves as Canadian through the erasure of Indigenous people, land, history and knowledges or the exaltation of the living through the disparagement of others as always already dying.

Asian Canadian Politics

Presently, very little is known about the voting patterns and political beliefs and values of Canada's largest visible minority group. Asian Canadians have been held up as models for change as well as for moderation, as hyper-political and apolitical, as isolated or over-communal and too individualistic, and as super-threatening and super-loyal. The study of Asian Canadian politics must involve careful attention to the racial logics that shaped the history of legal exclusion and later, inclusion as voters and as political candidates. The legacies of this history continue to shape debates around citizenship, immigration, multiculturalism, and employment equity today. Future research might address gender and politics, political interest and knowledge of electoral process, membership and involvement in ethnic community organization, and mobilization by political parties. Questions should draw attention to the limits of Asian Canadian political inclusion as merely statistical demographic representation and fight for more substantial representations that are committed to social justice. In this way, Asian Canadian political studies might meaningfully engage with intra- and inter-ethnic and racial political divergences in order to shape a more substantial political diversity.

There has also been a sizeable gap in the study of elected and appointed government officials even though Asian leaders have emerged and played key governmental roles in Canada since the late 1950s. For instance, Douglas Jung, a Progressive Conservative in British Columbia, became the first Asian Canadian Member of Parliament serving from 1957 to 1962 and since Jung, many more Asian Canadians across the political spectrum have been elected to the House of Commons. While it is obviously important for ACS to acknowledge such political inclusion, it is equally important to recognize that struggles for social justice are not resolved especially when "the national subject remain[s] empowered by displacing the patterns of discrimination and racial hatred onto the now disclaimed past" (Thobani 2007 154). Rather, ACS should heed what British cultural theorist, Stuart Hall calls a "politics without guarantees" (Hall 1997). Hall cautions us to work against fixed biological and historical notions of race that map sets of guarantees onto racialized bodies as representative of entire groups. Social justice as a political objective is an ongoing practice; one that does not simply end with select Asian Canadians being elected into parliament.

My focus on the realm of formal politics is not to suggest that this is the only site, or even most effective site, through which Asian Canada does political work. In fact, because of formal exclusions, Asian Canadian political histories are often found in grassroots community organizations as well as in literary works, film, and other visual arts. A robust archive exists of scholars, artists, and activists that have used art and literature to talk back to politics and have theorized diaspora as a site of memory and attachments as well as working through trauma, uprootings, regroundings, loss, and migrations. These artefacts can help to articulate the diasporic experience of unsettled-ness and illuminate the everyday experiences of the lived diaspora, which would otherwise fall into the crevices of history. For instance

Larissa Lai's (2002) *Salt Fish Girl*, Hiromi Goto's (1994) *The Chorus of Mushrooms*, and SKY Lee's (1991) *Disappearing Moon Café*, among many other Asian Canadian literary works, underscore the significance of story-telling, memory, recollection, and the archaeological project of diasporic subjects in the construction of both personal and collective narratives. Memory work becomes a vehicle through which diasporic subjects are able to revisit the past and present and work through those pains, individually and collectively. In this way, this process of mourning becomes an important political project locally, globally, and pan-historically. The work of mourning might address the ongoing maps of desire, attachment, and relationship between diasporas, host-nations, and home-nations, while challenging the notion of authenticity between race and nation, identity and place, origins, and belonging. It also involves addressing heterogeneities within and along lines of race, gender, class, sexualities, and abilities. Thus, theorizing Asian Canada necessary involves expanding notions of the political.

Asian Canadian Feminisms

What are Asian Canadian feminisms (ACF)? What are the limitations and possibilities of feminisms for Asian Canada? How have Asian women and men in Canada resisted racism, sexism, homophobia, and economic oppression? What are the global and transnational dimensions of Asian feminisms? Asian Canadian Studies must critically explore the various (re)constructions, (re)negotiations, and transformations of gender identities; revealing the many layers and meanings of diasporic identities and communities. Heteronormative and patriarchal methods of arranging societies cut across national borders and as Huang, Teo, and Yeoh have argued, it is necessary "to counter such male-centered discourses on diaspora and to keep the ambivalent gender politics of diaspora in view" (Huang, Teo & Yeoh 2000, 393). In theorizing diaspora, the stories and experiences of men have tended to be normalized. Rather than relying on patriarchal perspectives that centre themselves as the norm, feminist epistemologies can offer a more generative framework to research diasporas. This means that rather than thinking of gender and sexualities as additive variables to our research, critical feminist analysis should be foundational to thinking about ACS research questions.

The 2006 edited volume *Asian Women: Interconnections* explored some of the issues at stake in constituting Asian-Canadian feminisms and what it means as a political constituency for subject formation and community building. Other important collections have been published since, for example, *Han kŭt* (Korean Canadian Women's Anthology Collective 2007); *Active Geographies: Women and Struggles on the Left Coast*, a special issue of West Coast Line (Lee & Wong 2008) and *Voices Rising: Asian Canadian Cultural Activism* (Li 2007). Contributors to these anthologies issued an urgent call to self-identified Asian Canadian feminists to create space to learn, share, and support each other in struggles for justice and equality. In order to continue these conversations, a group of Asian Canadian feminist scholars organized a participatory roundtable called *W(h)ither Asian Canadian Feminisms in Theory and Practice?* for the 2010 Canadian Women's Studies Association annual meeting. This session explored the idea of ACF as a terrain on which the scholarly and the political are permeable.

The panel agreed that documenting and understanding Asian women's history as immigrants, migrant worker, refugees, and settlers on their own terms and in relation to the dominant groups and other Others has only just begun. But the politics of cultural nationalism, of restoring historical memory, claiming and enacting rights of full citizenship, and advancing recognition and redistribution within the nation-state as racialized ethnic minority women, cannot be privileged as ACF's primary political agenda. Just as Asian Canadian Studies should not be shaped through the politics of identity, Asian Canadian feminisms cannot be sustained simply by mobilizing around any singular identitarian politic. The diversity of being and becoming Asian Canadian and feminist undermines the use of identity and experience as the basis for producing knowledge or adjudicating competing claims for ACF. By working through an analysis of relational racialization and settler-colonialism as central to Asian Canadian experiences, it will be possible to explore shared ethics and values necessary for common political agenda and unified political action. By expanding notions of political work as entwined survival and negotiated citizenship and belonging, ACF might begin to work through various politics and constituencies among Asian Canadian communities and with other racialized groups resulting from different historical trajectories, social networks, and relations of trust.

Dissolving

It is the nature of words to change with the telling. They are changing in your mind even as I speak. (Goto 1994, 32)

In this chapter, I have outlined four scholarly and political interventions that can further push Asian Canadian studies and serve as directions for future research: (1) Relational Racialization, (2) Confronting Settler-Colonialism, (3) Asian Canadian politics, and (4) Asian Canadian feminisms. These are by no means the only important areas of research but together they provide a critical lens for the future of ACS. What these suggestions should facilitate is a reassessment and departure from comfortable and familiar political and intellectual investments. This is particularly important in efforts to institutionalize ACS within academia. It is significant in the project of institutionalization and disciplining that research frameworks and methodologies do not become increasingly static and settled. As many of the chapters in this edited volume suggest, Asian Canadians occupy a particular space in Canada, as at once desirable and undesirable, as at once victimized and complicit. From this location of ambivalence and contradiction, it is important to address concerns about cooptation and appropriation of Asian Canadian politics and scholarship into celebratory multiculturalism that often homogenizes Asians and depoliticizes ongoing violence.

Relational racialization, settler-colonialism, Asian Canadian politics, and Asian Canadian feminisms are conceptual frameworks rather than additive variables or sub-categorical areas of research. It is my hope that they will help to illicit critical, even unruly, research questions that will push the borders of Canadian studies. Accordingly, I hope they will allow us to imagine the field as "in the process of becoming and yet again also in the process of dissolving" (Cho 2007, 16). By keeping the field of meaning open or undone, it is my hope that scholarly and political endeavours in Asian Canadian Studies will continue to explore divergent histories that converge in the present.

REFERENCES

Ahmed, Sarah. 2012. *On Being Included: Racism and Diversity in Institutional Life*. Durham: Duke University Press. http://dx.doi.org/10.1215/9780822395324.

Arat-Koç, Sedef. 2006. "Whose Transnationalism?: Canada, 'Clash of Civilizations' Discourse, and Arab and Muslim Canadians." In *Transnational Identities and Practices in Canada*, ed. Lloyd Wong and Vic Satzewich, 216–40. Vancouver: University of British Columbia Press.
Brah, Avtar. 1996. *Cartographies of Diaspora: Contesting Identities*. New York: Routledge.
Chang, Elaine. 2007. *Reel Asian: Asian Canada on Screen*. Toronto: Coach House Books.
Cheng, Anne Anlin. 2001. "The Melancholy of Race." In *The Melancholy of Race: Psychoanalysis, Assimilation and Hidden Grief*, 3–30. New York: Oxford University Press.
Cho, Lily. 2007. "The Turn to Diaspora." *Topia* 17:11–30.
Day, Iyko. 2008. "Must All Asianness Be American? The Census, Racial Classification, and Asian Canadian Emergence." *Canadian Literature Issue* 199:45–73.
de Certeau, Michel. 1988. *The Writing of History*. Trans. Tom Conley. New York: Columbia University Press.
Dua, Enakshi. 2007. "Exclusion Through Inclusion: Female Asian Migration in the Making of Canada as a White Settler Nation." *Gender, Place and Culture* 14 (4): 445–66. http://dx.doi.org/10.1080/09663690701439751.
Gordon, Avery. 2008. *Ghostly Matters: Haunting and the Sociological Imagination*. Minneapolis: University of Minnesota Press.
Goto, Hiromi. 1994. *Chorus of Mushrooms*. Edmonton: NeWest Press.
Hall, Stuart. 1997. *Race, the Floating Signifier*. Directed by Sut Jally. Media Education Foundation.
Huang, Shirlena, Peggy Teo, and Brenda S.A. Yeoh. 2000. "Diasporic Subjects and Identity Negotiations: Women in and from Asia." *Women's Studies International Forum* 23 (4): 391–8. http://dx.doi.org/10.1016/S0277-5395(00)00103-5.
Korean Canadian Women's Anthology Collective, ed. 2007. *Han Kŭt: Critical Art and Writing by Korean Canadian Women*. Toronto: Inanna.
Lai, Larissa. 2002. *Salt Fish Girl*. Toronto: Thomas Allen Publishers.
Lawrence, Bonita. 2002. "Rewriting Histories of the Land: Colonization and Indigenous Resistance in Eastern Canada." In *Race, Space, and the Law: Unmapping a White Settler Society*, ed. Sherene Razack, 21–46. Toronto: Between the Lines.
Lee, S.K.Y. 1991. *Disappearing Moon Café*. Vancouver: Douglas & McIntyre.
Lee, Jo-Anne, and Rita Wong, eds. 2008. Special Issue: "Active Geographies: Women and Struggles on the Left Coast." *West Coast Line* 58 (42).
Li, Xiaoping. 2007. *Voices Rising: Asian Canadian Cultural Activism*. Vancouver: University of British Columbia Press.
Miki, Roy. 2011. *In Flux: Transnational Shifts in Asian Canadian Writing*. Edmonton: NeWest Press.
Miki, Roy. 2000. "Altered States: Global Currents, the Spectral Nation, and the Production of "Asian Canadian."" *Journal of Canadian Studies / Revue d'Etudes Canadiennes* 35 (3): 43–72.
Ng, Roxana. 1991. "Sexism, Racism and Canadian Nationalism." In *Race, Class, Gender: Bonds and Barriers*, ed. J. Vorst, 10–25. Toronto: Garamond Press.
Thobani, Sunera. 2007. *Exalted Subjects: Studies in the Making of Race and Nation in Canada*. Toronto: University of Toronto Press.
Thobani, Sunera, and Tineke Hellwig, eds. 2006. *Asian Women: Interconnections*. Toronto: Women's Press.
Roy, Patricia. 2003. *The Oriental Question: Consolidating a White Man's Province, 1914–1941*. Vancouver: University of British Columbia Press.
Ty, Eleanor, and Donald Goellnicht. 2004. *Asian North American Identities: Beyond the Hyphen*. Bloomington: Indiana University Press.
Ujimoto, K. Victor, and Gordon Hirabayashi, eds. 1980. *Visible Minorities and Multiculturalism: Asians in Canada*. Toronto: Butterworths & Co.
Wong, Rita. 2008. "Decolonizasian: Reading Asian and First Nations Relations in Literature." *Canadian Literature* 199:158–80.

20 "Too Asian?": On Racism, Paradox, and Ethno-nationalism

ROLAND SINTOS COLOMA

In November 2010, Canada's premiere weekly newsmagazine, *Maclean's*, published an article titled "Too Asian?" that outraged and galvanized Asian Canadians and other communities across the country (Findlay & Köhler 2010).[1] Considered "one of the shabbiest and laziest pieces in the history of Canadian magazine journalism" (Mallick 2012), the article was widely reviled for depicting Asian Canadian students in racially stereotypical ways and generating a binary "us" versus "them" distinction between the presumptively normal Whites and the academically focused and socially insulated Asians in institutions of higher education. Concerned students and community advocates claimed that the article could end up inciting racial antipathy and division in universities and society at large, instead of fostering a constructive dialogue on social diversity and cohesion (Coloma & Lee 2010).

Consequently, many Asian Canadians demanded that *Maclean's* ought to issue a public apology and to establish anti-racist editorial and employment policies. Some called for the boycott of *Maclean's* parent company, the media conglomerate Rogers Communications, while others lobbied local and federal politicians to condemn the article and stop the $1.5 million in public funding subsidy that the magazine regularly received. Ultimately, the *Maclean's* "Too Asian?" article brought into public discourse the paradoxical position of Asians in Canada as an un/wanted racialized minority group. Simultaneously, it also marked the emergence of ethno-nationalism as a disturbing development in anti-racist resistance by Asian Canadians in response to their paradoxical subjectivity in the Canadian nation-state.

This article contributes to critical examinations of education, race, and racism by focusing on Asians, who constitute the largest racialized minority group in Canada (Statistics Canada 2010).[2] Asians in Canada are generally perceived as model minority that has overcome racial discrimination in education and society and has integrated into the country's neoliberal, multicultural mosaic (Maclear 1994; Pon 2000). Yet the *Maclean's* article brought into sharp relief the paradoxical position of Asians as a racialized minority: they are needed and rejected at the same time, desired and undesirable for inclusion and integration in educational and social institutions. Such a paradoxical position has historical antecedents since the mid-1800s when Asians migrated to Canada to work in the gold and coal mines, railway and road construction, and the agricultural, fishing, and lumber industries (Adachi 1976; Buchignani, Indra, & Srivastava 1985; Lai 1988). Asians – more specifically, the Chinese, Indians, and Japanese – were welcomed for their labouring bodies in service of the economic development and prosperity of Canada, which became a confederated dominion in 1867. However, when Asians were viewed as threats to White labour and the social moral order of "White Canada forever," their immigration was restricted and then terminated, and their civil rights were severely curtailed (Ward 2002). In other words, Asians' economic usefulness was their key to enter Canada's racialized gates of labour, migration, and eventual citizenship.

This article also addresses the edge of race within the relatively contemporary contexts of putatively race-neutral immigration and diversity-welcoming multicultural policies. Prior to the 1970s, Canada pursued and maintained a staunch white supremacist ideology in its political, economic, and social policies that exalted Western Europeans, especially the British and the French, as the preferred immigrants, settlers, and citizens of the nation-state (Thobani 2007). However, the Immigration Act of 1976 moved away from national and racial origins, and instead stressed educational and occupational skills as major selection criteria for admitting immigrants (Li 2003). The introduction of the Multiculturalism Policy in 1971 and the passage of the Multiculturalism Act of 1988, which recognized minority groups' cultural heritages, religions, and languages, has been regarded as a significant milestone in Canadian history of race and race relations and a global model for intercultural pluralism and governance (Kymlicka 1996). With these policy changes, one might suggest that Asians as a group, overall, have benefited and thrived. Immigrants from the Asia Pacific region constituted approximately half of the total immigrants to Canada from 2007 to 2011. During the same time period, the top three source countries of immigrants to Canada were from Asia – the Philippines, China, and India (Asia Pacific Foundation of Canada 2012a, 2012b). Moreover, individuals of Asian ancestry now occupy high-profile positions in Canadian government, arts, media, sports, and education, such as Governor General Adrienne Clarkson, writers Joy Kogawa, Michael Ondaatje, and Madeleine Thien, film director Deepa Mehta, actress Sandra Oh, figure skater Patrick Chan, scientist David Suzuki, and Donna Quan, former director of Toronto District School Board, the largest school board in the country.

The increased immigration from Asia and the ensuing changing racial demographics in educational and social spaces serve as a crucial backdrop in the controversy over the *Maclean's* "Too Asian?" article. Many critics contended that the article was offensive and divisive by promoting anti-Asian racism and xenophobia (Coloma & Lee 2010; Heer 2010; Mahtani 2010; Yu 2010a). Since the article did not depict Asians as "real" Canadians, critics disputed such misrepresentation by asserting the subjectivity of Asian Canadians as "real" Canadians, albeit of the hyphenated kind of a racialized minority, who rightfully belong in elite educational institutions. The assertion of Asian Canadians' genuine Canadianness marks what I am calling the discursive enactment of "ethno-nationalism" by racialized minority individuals and groups. I construe ethno-nationalism as a form of identification and resistance by racialized minorities who contest and work to redress their marginalized status and conditions in White-dominant nation-states by appropriating and associating themselves with national citizenship in order to be regarded as full-fledged members of the civil society. For Asians who have been excluded from the rites and rights of White-dominant countries like Canada, a powerful strategic recourse for inclusion and integration into the nation-state has been to claim and declare their ethno-national belonging as genuine Canadians. Yet what I find troubling in the enactment of ethno-nationalism by Asian Canadians is the assertion and privileging of their Canadianness, while simultaneously distancing themselves from and rejecting their Asianness.

As a researcher, educator, and activist who was involved in the political organizing related to the "Too Asian?" controversy, I considered writing this chapter as an opportunity to reflect on what happened in 2010 and afterwards. My scholarly inclination as a historian pushed me to understand and situate the events within the broader vista of continuities and changes over time. It compelled me to document and make sense of the events as they occurred with a historical view in mind. Meanwhile, the educator and activist within me considered writing this chapter as a teachable moment for myself and others to self-reflexively examine our organizing praxis, its possibilities as enactments of resistance, and its limitations for social justice solidarity and coalition building. This chapter, consequently, will unfold as a mixture of multiple yet converging designs. The first section will examine the *Maclean's* "Too Asian?" article, and will outline the issues raised by its critics. The second section will frame the article's depiction of Asian Canadians within a broader historical context that will delineate their paradoxical subject position as an un/wanted racialized minority group. The third section will track the organizing efforts related to the "Too Asian?" article, and will raise concerns regarding the deployment of ethno-nationalism as a form of resistance to racism.

Throughout this chapter, I will include the perspectives of fellow critics and activists to affirm and honour their incisive analyses of the "Too Asian?" article and the status of Asians in Canada. I will also insert myself, hopefully appropriately, in my narration of events to dispel the usual academic stance of a disinterested scholar and locate my multiple engagements.[3] At stake are two separate yet interconnected issues: first, the production of a sharper analytical grammar of race to unpack the dynamics of social relations in liberal multicultural societies; and second, the enactment of a more inclusive political praxis for pan-Asian solidarity and for coalition building among racialized minority and immigrant communities in the context of White-dominant nation-states. My case study on media and higher education, with a focus on Asians in Canada, will aim to contribute to these intellectual, political, and pedagogical endeavours.

Maclean's "Too Asian?"

On 10 November 2010, I began receiving emails and phone calls from students, faculty colleagues, and community activists about the *Maclean's* "Too Asian?" article, which appeared in its popular annual University Rankings issue. The initial online version of the article was titled "Too Asian: Some frosh don't want to study at an Asian university." It was changed to "Too Asian?" with a question mark which, according to the publisher, was

> a direct quote from the title of a panel discussion at the 2006 meeting of the National Association for College Admission Counseling where experts examined the growing tendency among US university admission officers to view Asian applicants as a homogenous group. (*Maclean's* 2010)

Then, in response to the deluge of critical comments, the final online title became "The enrollment controversy: Worries that efforts in the US to limit enrollment of Asian students in top universities may migrate to Canada." What is confusing and frustrating about these title changes is that the hard-copy printed version, which was published on 22 November 2010, had different titles, as well. In the magazine's table of contents, the article was called "Asian advantage? Some frosh don't want to study at an 'Asian' university," which was similar to the initial online versions with the exception of the use of the phrase "Asian advantage?" instead of "Too Asian" (with or without the question mark) and the use of scare quotes around the word "Asian" in the subtitle. Yet, the article inside bore a different title:

> "Too Asian?" A term used in the US to talk about racial imbalance at Ivy league schools is now being whispered on Canadian campuses–by everyone but the students themselves, who speak out loud and clear. (Findlay & Köhler 2010, 77)

What's an "Asian university" or a university that is "Too Asian"? According to the article authors Stephanie Findlay and Nicholas Köhler (2010), "an 'Asian' school has come to mean one that is so academically focused that some students feel they can no longer compete or have fun" (77). The term "too Asian," Findlay and Köhler point out, is

> used in some US academic circles to describe a phenomenon that's become such a cause for concern to university admissions officers and high school guidance counsellors that several elite universities to the south have faced scandals in recent years over limiting Asian applicants and keeping the numbers of white students artificially high. (77)

And which Canadian universities are considered "Too Asian"? These are "top-tier post-secondary institutions with international profiles specializing in math, science and business: U of T [University of Toronto], UBC [University of British Columbia] and the University of Waterloo" (78). According to "Alexandra" (pseudonym), a graduate of an all-girls private school in Toronto, "The only people from our school who went to U of T were Asian ... All the white kids go to Queen's, Western and McGill" (77).

So, what's the problem with a university being "Too Asian'? My analysis of the article reveals that there seem to be three problems. First, for many White students, like "Alexandra" who was interviewed for the article, they believe that

> competing with Asians – both Asian Canadians and international students – requires a sacrifice of time and freedom they're not willing to make. They complain that they can't compete for spots in the best schools and can't party as much as they'd like. (77–8)

Second, for institutions of higher education, their commitment to "pure" meritocratic admissions has "many in the education community worried that universities risk becoming too skewed one way" (78). Even though the phrase "too skewed one way" is not explained in the article, it signals what is perceived to be an overabundance of Asian Canadian and international students on campus. This problem "puts Canadian universities in a quandary [because if] they openly address the issue of race they expose themselves to criticisms that they are profiling and committing an injustice," but if they do not address it, they are accused of being "too Asian."

Third, for the general populace, even though racial diversity has enriched Canadian universities, "it has also put them at risk of being increasingly fractured along ethnic lines. It's a superficial form of multiculturalism that is expressed in the main through segregated, self-selecting, discrete communities" (81). For instance, "there is little Asian representation on student government, campus newspapers or college radio stations" (80). The authors also indicate that, although Asian Canadian students may not be involved in mainstream organizations, they actively participate in ethnic cultural groups. Hence, instead of universities functioning as "oases of dialogue, mutual understanding and diversity" for the society at large, they "risk becoming places of many solitudes, deserts of non-communication" (78).

The vast majority of the emails, phone calls, and personal conversations that I had on November 10 and afterwards were overwhelmingly disapproving of the *Maclean's* article.

The critiques included the *normalization of whiteness* by presuming the experiences of economically privileged, White students as the universal standard against which others' educational and social conditions are assessed; the *illusion of meritocracy* through universities' failure to account for the history and legacy of White preferential treatment, and the continuous systemic oppression of Aboriginal peoples and racialized minorities; *race baiting* through the seemingly purposeful use of a controversial title to attract public attention and boost magazine sales; and *irresponsible journalism* by not disclosing the real identities of their main interview subjects for verification and by misrepresenting the purpose of the article when discussing it with other key informants.

Other critics openly shared their concerns in mainstream and alternative media outlets. For instance, Minelle Mahtani (2010), a professor of geography and journalism at the University of Toronto, indicated that the *Maclean's* article "reveal[ed] a growing crisis in news and current affairs storytelling ... [when stories] reflect a pervasive pattern of racism and stereotyping." To reverse this pattern, she called for "ethical journalism" that "honours the profession's commitment to truth, accuracy and balanced reporting. It means finding the untold stories about immigration, diversity and race and covering the undercovered." York University doctoral student and journalist Jeet Heer (2010) listed three key offences of the article's "bad aftertaste": its monolithic homogenization of "Asians" by disregarding their diversity based on ancestral, national, and economic backgrounds; its stereotypical portrayals of White students as "privileged preppies who are more interested in partying and drinking than studying" and Asian students as "socially dysfunctional nerds who lack any sense of fun, virtual robots who are programmed by their parents to study"; and its miscasting of the "problem as one that is caused by the mere presence of 'Asians' on campus, rather than by the social and cultural barriers that divide students." Finally, Henry Yu (2010b), a history professor at the University of British Columbia, provided a genealogy of "yellow peril" and "model minority" in order to claim that "when the *Maclean's* writers and editors trafficked in this image, they invested in their article the values of a century-and-a-half of white supremacy."

Building on the insightful commentaries offered by Mahtani, Heer, Yu, and other critics, I will analyse the *Maclean's* article by drawing attention to the paradoxical position of Asians in Canada as an un/wanted racialized minority in historical and contemporary contexts. Using Yu's genealogical move as a point of departure, I will situate the racialization of Asians in Canada in relation to broader economic, political, and socio-cultural dynamics, and will track their status of being wanted and unwanted within a historical pattern.

Paradox of Being Un/wanted

From the mid- to the late 1800s, Asians were actively recruited to help develop Canada's nascent agricultural, fishing, lumber, mining, and transportation industries. They were considered ideal labourers by economic elites and industrial capitalists who wanted a working force that was cheap, diligent, docile, and expendable (Goutor 2007). Matthew Begbie, the first Chief Justice of British Columbia, stated, "I do not see how people would get on here at all without Chinamen. They do, and do well, what white women cannot do, and do what white men will not do" (Li 1998, 29). The use and ubiquity of Asians in many labour-intensive industries can lead one to suggest that they were vital to the establishment and prosperity of Canada as a newly formed nation-state. However, their contributions were often minimized, if not erased altogether. For instance, the image of the "Last

Spike," considered "possibly the best-known Canadian photograph," captures the completion of Canada's transcontinental railway in 1885 (Brown 2007, 363). It shows well-dressed White men, including prominent railway financiers and officials, surrounded by a crowd of White male workers. Missing in this photograph are the Chinese workers whose labour was instrumental in the construction of the railway, which facilitated communication, trade, travel, and settlement across the country. Unfortunately, the erasure of their contributions continues in recent renditions. Library and Archives Canada's (2012) video titled "Driving the Nation: The Last Spike and the Faces of the CPR" only highlights the White men in the photograph. Not once does the video mention or show the existence and labour of Asian workers in constructing the transcontinental railway.

During periods of financial boon and stability, the presence of Asians in Canada was tolerated and drew minimal attention from the general White populace. However, their continued migration and settlement, especially during periods of economic recession, raised nativist alarm. Asians were seen as ruthless competition for jobs and dangerous threats to the social moral order (Goutor 2007; Lai 1988). Racial antipathy became intricately linked to labour anxiety in White-dominant countries under the industrial capitalist system. White public and working labourers' sentiments against Asians were reflected and reinforced by elected politicians, who marshalled the state's institutional power to discriminate (Ward 2002). Anti-Asian laws and regulations focused on restricting Asian immigration to Canada, such as the Immigration Act of 1885, which levied a head tax on the Chinese; the Continuous Journey Regulation of 1908, which posed a migration barrier for Indians by requiring all immigrants to travel uninterrupted from their point of origin to Canada; and the Hayashi-Lemieux Agreement of 1908, which limited Japanese immigration to 400 individuals per year. When Chinese immigration did not abate in spite of increasing head tax payments from $50 to $100 and then to $500, the Immigration Act of 1923 banned Chinese immigration to Canada, with the exception of diplomats, merchants, and students.

Asians in Canada lived in an openly racist and hostile environment from the late 1800s and throughout the first half of the 1900s (Adachi 1976; Buchignani, Indra, & Srivastava 1985; Lai 1988; Ward 2002). Additional legislative controls were passed in order to severely curtail their political, economic, and social rights. The first bill to disenfranchise Chinese was passed in British Columbia in 1872, and was subsequently extended to Indians and Japanese. Seventy-six years later in 1948, when the last disenfranchisement statute was repealed, Asian Canadians were finally granted the right to vote. Along with losing their right of suffrage, Asian Canadians were excluded from running for political office, thereby shutting them out of political self-representation and determination. It was only in 1957 that the first Asian Canadian, Douglas Jung, was elected to a political office. Other laws prohibited Asian Canadians from owning Crown lands, getting hired in public works or underground mines, and holding licences for liquor or logging enterprises. They were also barred from white-collar professions such as law and pharmacy, from night work in laundries, and from employing White females (Li 1998; Mar 2010; Mawani 2010).

Denying Asian Canadians their citizenship and civil rights was emblematic of White nativism and patriotism, and fortified the former group's status as an unwanted racialized minority. In addition to anti-Asian laws and regulations, they were subjected to frequent racial attacks and hostilities, led prominently by the Asiatic Exclusion League under the auspices of the Trades and Labour Council. For instance, Asian Canadians suffered tremendous property damage, not to mention intense psychological affliction, during the 1887 and 1907 riots in Vancouver (Ward 2002). Anti-Asian racism culminated in the mid-1900s with the internment of 22,000 Japanese Canadians during the Second World War, two-thirds of whom were Canadian-born citizens (Miki 2005; Oikawa 2012). In the name of national safety and security, the Canadian government mobilized the War Measures Act to incarcerate, dispossess, deport, and disperse Canadians of Japanese ancestry. No evidence has been found that indicates Japanese Canadians' complicity in the Pearl Harbor bombing, in speculations of sabotage or espionage, or as actual threats to Canadian national well-being.

Given these explicit anti-Asian hostilities and regulations, it is no wonder the general public would view the period from the 1970s onward as a positive transformation in Canadian racial attitudes and race relations. The legislative passage, in particular, of the Immigration Act of 1976 and the Multiculturalism Act of 1988 signalled the dawn of Canada's era of liberal multiculturalism. According to philosopher Will Kymlicka (1996), for minorities to acquire and benefit from full citizenship, "a comprehensive theory of justice in a multicultural state will include both universal rights, assigned to individuals regardless of group membership, and certain group-differentiated rights or 'special status' for minority cultures" (6). Kymlicka's notion of justice is premised on a liberal-democratic theory that is "grounded in a commitment to freedom of choice and … personal autonomy" (7). Hence, on the one hand, the revised Immigration Act may be interpreted as representing a universal right since the policy no longer privileges immigrants from Europe. Instead, presumably race-neutral criteria, such as educational and employment backgrounds, have become the main filters for admitting immigrants. On the other hand, the Multiculturalism Act may be understood as forwarding a group-differentiated right since it enables minorities to preserve and celebrate their distinct cultures. Combined, these two legislations have become hallmarks of the Canadian brand of liberal multiculturalism.

The publication of the *Maclean's* "Too Asian?" article came at a time when Canada is turning to immigrants to bolster the country's economic development. Canada set a record in 2010 when it allowed the highest number of immigrants in more than fifty years (Citizenship and Immigration Canada 2011). Jason Kenny, minister of Citizenship, Immigration and Multiculturalism, stated,

> As we recover from the recession, increasing economic immigration will help ensure employers have the workers they need to supplement our domestic labour supply … Canada [also] needs investor immigrants … to keep Canada competitive with other countries, and keep pace with the changing economy. (Citizenship and Immigration Canada 2010)

Economic immigrants include individuals who qualify under the federal skilled worker category of "in-demand occupations," such as architects, dentists, medical doctors, nurses, scientists, and skilled trades workers. They also include individuals who qualify under the immigrant investor program, which targets "experienced business people" with a personal net worth of at least $1.6 million who can make a minimum investment of $800,000 for economic development and job creation initiatives. These selective government priorities have generated an immigration stream from Asia that has privileged and benefited those with economic capital, white-collar professions, and flexible mobility. In 2010, more than half of all immigrants to Canada from Asia were economic immigrants and their dependants. A year after, the number of economic immigrants and their dependants increased to two-thirds of all Asian immigrants (Asia Pacific Foundation of Canada 2012c).[4]

For its future prosperity, Canada is building capacity for the "Great Brain Race" by aiming to attract top global talent and turning to international education (Wildavsky 2010).

Right before the publication of the "Too Asian?" article, a couple of high-profile Canadian visits to Asia were intended to build greater cooperation and partnership in education. The Council of Ministers of Education, Canada, held a consultation meeting in China in September 2010, while the Association of Universities and Colleges of Canada organized the largest delegation of Canadian university presidents to India in November 2010. Then, a couple of months after the article's release, University of British Columbia president Stephen Toope appeared in a three-part video titled "The Battle for Brains," where he discussed "how international students change Canadian schools," "why we need to assert our stake in the global brain race," and "how universities can help Canada become a global leader" (Toope 2011). A year later, a federal advisory panel, led by Western University president and former University of Waterloo provost Amit Chakma, released a report titled "International Education: A Key Driver of Canada's Future Prosperity" (Foreign Affairs and International Trade Canada 2012). The panel's first recommendation is to double the number of international students coming to Canada to more than 450,000 by the year 2022 in order to raise the country's "international mind share" (i). The report specifically identifies "priority markets" with the "greatest growth potential," such as China, India, and Vietnam (alongside Brazil, Mexico, the Middle East, and North Africa), and "mature markets," such as South Korea (alongside the United States, France, and the United Kingdom), to tap into for "innovation, trade, human capital development and the labour market" (viii, xiv).

Since the 1970s, the government's immigration and multiculturalism policies have facilitated the migration and settlement of Asians in Canada and, consequently, the development of Asian Canadian families and communities. According to population projections by Statistics Canada (2010), released a few months before the *Maclean's* article, racialized minorities will double by 2031, and will be the numerical majority in urban metropolitan centres like Toronto and Vancouver, with South Asians and Chinese continuing as the largest non-White groups. Canada's political, business, and educational leaders have turned to Asian immigrants, investors, and international students in order to capitalize on their labour, economic, and educational strengths as Canada shores up its national prosperity and global competitiveness in the twenty-first century. Similar to their counterparts in the mid- to late 1800s, today's elites have welcomed immigrants, especially from Asia, when they serve the economic imperatives of the nation-state as workers and, in recent times, as investors and students. In the era of liberal multiculturalism, Asians from privileged economic and educational backgrounds have become Canada's preferred immigrants and desired racialized minority group.

However, traces of contemporary anti-immigration sentiments and movements are emerging. Politically conservative and nativist organizations, such as the Fraser Institute and Immigration Watch Canada, have published research reports, held conferences and community meetings, and used mainstream and social media to convey their alarmist message on immigration. Moreover, a public opinion poll in 2010 reveals that "more Canadians are questioning the benefits of immigration" (AngusReid 2010). Out of "a representative sample" of 1,007 Canadians who responded to an online survey, 46% believe that immigration has a "negative effect in Canada," 34% indicate that it has a "positive effect," and 20% are "not sure" of its effect. A national poll of 2,926 Canadians in 2011 indicates that

> Canadians are somewhat conflicted about Asia and Canada's relations with the region. While the results over time show that Canadians increasingly view Asia as critically important

> economically and politically, we do not seem to be fully embracing Asia's rise. Indeed, the number of Canadians who perceive China and India's growing economic power as more of an opportunity than a threat has been declining over the past few years. These divergent trend lines suggest that Canadians may be growing uneasy about this historic shift and, unsure of how to engage with Asia, they seem to be reflexively turning inward. (Asia Pacific Foundation of Canada 2011)

Canadians' uneasiness over immigration in general and over Asia's rising economic power can be gleaned in their social anxieties as they turn reflexively inward and examine the increasing presence of Asians and the consequent changes in social spaces and institutions. For instance, in the mid-1990s, long-time residents of suburban Toronto expressed tremendous concern over the construction of a large Asian-themed mall catering to the growing concentration of Asians moving to and settling in the area (Preston & Lo 2000). The increase of immigrants to the area was "due mainly to political events in East Asia coinciding with legislative change in Canada" including the transfer of sovereignty over Hong Kong from the United Kingdom to China; the Tiananmen Square Incident and the suppression of the student pro-democracy movement in China; and the establishment of the business immigrant program in Canada (183). The residents' struggle over land use and cultural space was triggered by the influx of Asian immigrants who, in their view, were not conforming to established norms and built environments and, instead, were asserting their own identities and preferences in the local geography.

My historical delineation demonstrates that Asians occupy a paradoxical subject position as an un/wanted racialized minority population in Canada. On the one hand, they are recruited and welcomed as workers, investors, and students, and become wanted as desirable immigrants and citizens when they serve the economic priorities and objectives of the nation-state. On the other hand, they become unwanted when they are perceived as threats to the normalized sociocultural order and take away positions and resources from "rightful" Canadians. In the *Maclean's* article, an Asian Canadian student states, "At graduation a Canadian – i.e., 'white' – mother told me that I'm the reason her son didn't get a space in university and that all the immigrants in the country are taking up university spots" (Findlay & Köhler 2010, 78). The White mother's anti-Asian resentment echoes the general attitude in the late 1800s and early 1900s when legislations and regulations transformed public prejudice into institutionalized forms of racism and discrimination against Asians. In the past, political, social, and capitalist elites were initially in favour of Asian immigration since they served the country's economic interests. But they ended up expressing anti-Asian rhetoric and joining the ranks of the masses when the racial tide turned. History often has a way of repeating itself, and only time will tell how the current traces of anti-immigration and anti-Asian sentiments will materialize.

Ethno-nationalism as Resistance and Its Limits

On 15 November 2010, a few days after the online release of the *Maclean's* "Too Asian?" article, I convened a public meeting at University of Toronto to provide a public space for collective dialogue and organizing. Over 120 students, educators, and community members came to share their perspectives and discuss potential plans of action.[5] Victor Wong of the Chinese Canadian National Council (CCNC) compared the *Maclean's* "Too Asian?" article to the 1979 *W5* television episode "Campus Giveaway" by CTV, Canada's largest private broadcaster:

> Over footage of Asian-looking faces in a pharmacy class at the University of Toronto, the show declared that "foreign" students were invading Canadian universities, and that the federal government was subsidizing their education and denying Canadian students the opportunity of higher education. (Asia/Canada n.d.)

Reminiscent of the *W5* program from over 30 years ago, the *Maclean's* article recycled the racist and xenophobic discourse of Asian Canadians as perpetual foreigners who took educational spots away from allegedly real Canadians. Wong shared the Chinese Canadian community's successful strategy of obtaining its central goal – a public apology from CTV – by raising awareness in both ethnic and mainstream groups, outreaching and building cross-cultural coalitions, and staging public protests. With key leaders from CCNC National and the CCNC Toronto Chapter, Wong met with the publisher and editors of *Maclean's* to demand an apology.

From the 15 November meeting, the idea of an Open Letter to *Maclean's* was hatched. Community historian and former journalist Brad Lee and I drafted the letter, with invaluable input from organizer Karen Sun, and circulated it to various individuals and groups across the country for feedback and support. The letter, titled "A call to eliminate anti-Asian racism," generated over 100 organizational signatories from race/ethnic, labour, feminist, migrant, and student sectors, including the National Anti-Racism Council of Canada, Asian Canadian Labour Alliance, CCNC Toronto, Council of Agencies Serving South Asians, National Association of Japanese Canadians, Philippine Women Centre of Ontario, Raging Asian Women, Ontario Council of Agencies Serving Immigrants, and Canadian Federation of Students, Ontario. The letter also called for "a comprehensive and unqualified public apology to Asian Canadians," and pressed for institutional changes including the need to "engage in public consultation to address racial profiling and stereotyping via their media outlets," to "implement measurable corporate and editorial anti-racism policies in consultation with relevant community constituents," and to "implement employment equity programs to diversify their corporate and editorial boards and frontline personnel" (Coloma & Lee 2010). Moreover, it considered the institutional contexts of higher education, and demanded that universities and colleges

> must develop academic programs and courses that explicitly address racism in Canada and the historical and contemporary experiences, representations, and contributions of Asian Canadians; must undertake and publish campus climate surveys of racialized students, staff, and faculty; and, must establish advocacy and support offices for racialized students, staff, and faculty. (Coloma & Lee 2010)

From the discussions, planning, and organizing that transpired in the Toronto area, the Solidarity Committee Against Anti-Asian Racism was established as a network of activists committed to racial justice, multi-sectoral collaborations, and grassroots organizing.[6]

When *Maclean's* refused to apologize and respond to the Open Letter demands, organizers understood the need to raise awareness and mobilize the public to obtain support and mount pressure on the media corporation. Education campaigns included holding discussion forums in universities and community gatherings; sharing views through social media, such as Facebook, Twitter, and YouTube; and writing opinion pieces and letters to the editor in mainstream, ethnic, and other alternative media outlets. Ken Noma of the National Association of Japanese Canadians (NAJC) made important historical connections at the public teach-in held at the University of Toronto. He reiterated these linkages in his own open letter to *Maclean's* magazine in the NAJC website, where he wrote:

> racist stereotyping is a very disturbing reminder for Japanese Canadians of the time before and after World War II when the Government of Canada summarily condemned all Japanese Canadians living in [British Columbia] as "enemy aliens," without a shred of evidence to support such slander ... The *Maclean's* article constitutes a serious setback in creating a truly free and equitable society, leaving many sadly wondering whether the media as represented by *Maclean's* have learned nothing about the insidious nature of racism in all its evil manifestations and effects. (Noma 2010)

Asian Canadians enacted various forms of activism as cultural and political resistance to racism.[7] Students and community members lobbied politicians to take a public position on the issue. As a result, the city councils of Victoria and Vancouver in British Columbia, and Toronto, Richmond Hill, and Markham in Ontario issued official statements condemning the "Too Asian?" article and insisting on a formal public apology from the magazine. Member of Parliament Olivia Chow raised the issue in the federal legislature, while Senator Vivienne Poy asked James Moore, the minister of Canadian Heritage and Official Languages, to "consider reviewing the allocation of $1.5 million in public funding to *Maclean's*" (Poy 2010). Poy pointed out a criterion in the ministry's Canadian Periodical Fund indicating that periodicals with "offensive content (defined as 'material that is denigrating to an identifiable group')" can be considered ineligible for federal support. The undergraduate student council at the University of Victoria voted to boycott the sales of *Maclean's* magazine on campus. Inspired by the student boycott, many community members cancelled their magazine subscriptions and their Rogers communications services.

The educational and mobilization campaigns of Asian Canadian advocates and allies generated intense public discussions and grassroots organizing that were centred on the discursive representation and political status of Asians in Canada. I was, and continue to be, in agreement with the issues raised and strategies enacted by fellow critics and organizers. In fact, I was deeply involved in various campaigns denouncing *Maclean's* magazine and Rogers Communications. What I found troubling in our political analysis and organizing, however, was the enactment of what I am calling an "ethno-nationalism" that asserted and privileged one's Canadianness, or rightful belonging to Canada, albeit from the vantage point of a racialized minority, while simultaneously distancing oneself from and rejecting one's Asian-ness. Put differently, my problem with those who take up the "ethno-national" as a discourse and a subject position is their alignment and identification with the "dominant-national" while simultaneously disavowing and rejecting the "foreign-national." In this configuration, the modifier "dominant-" signifies White, while the modifiers "ethno-" and "foreign-" denote Asian. These modifiers are linked and related to the main word "national," which, in this case, means Canadian. For ethno-nationals, their Asianness is secondary to their Canadianness; hence, ethno-nationals are Canadians who *happen to be* of Asian ancestry. However, for foreign-nationals, their Asianness primarily defines their juridical and sociocultural relationship to Canada; hence, foreign-nationals are Asians who *do not belong* to Canada due to their foreignness. In other words, Asian Canadians who assert ethno-nationalism are keen to claim their Canadianness and quick to dismiss their Asianness, especially when certain traits might relegate them as "too Asian" who are "too foreign." In my view, the move of hyphenated "ethno-national" minorities to identify *with* the "dominant-national" and identify *against* the "foreign-national" is a dubious form of resistance that is based on disavowing an-Other in order to assert and situate one's Self in the hegemonic national order.

My theorizing of ethno-nationalism is quite different from how it has been conventionally used. It is not the same as political scientist Walker Connor's (1993) notion of ethno-nationalism, which focuses on the emotional bond or sentient identification of groups related to "two loyalties – loyalty to the nation and loyalty to the state" (Connor 1993, 81). Connor examines separatist movements during the second half of the twentieth century as instances "when the two loyalties are seen as being in irreconcilable conflict, [and] loyalty to the state loses out." However, for groups that are "so dominant within a multinational state as to perceive the state as essentially their nation's state ... the two loyalties become an indistinguishable, reinforcing blur" (81). My work differs from Connor's in two significant ways: first, I focus on the dynamics of racialized minorities in White-dominant nation-states, which Connor does not address; and second, I examine the strategic identification by a marginalized minority group with the nation-state, which his theory does not account for.

My work on ethno-nationalism is more akin to queer theorist Jasbir Puar's (2007) concept of homonationalism, which manifests in the convergence of three factors: "sexual exceptionalism, queer as regulatory, and the ascendancy of whiteness" (2). Puar draws from Lisa Duggan's notion of homonormativity as a "new neo-liberal sexual politics" that "does not contest dominant heteronormative forms but upholds and sustains them," and mobilizes homonationalism "to mark arrangements of US sexual exceptionalism explicitly in relation to the nation" (38–9). The assertion of homonationalism by White lesbian, gay, bisexual, and transgender (LGBT) people is a "discursive tactic" that distinguishes and distances themselves from "racial and sexual others, foregrounding a collusion between homosexuality and American nationalism that is generated both by national rhetorics of patriotic inclusion and by queer subjects themselves" (39). As an example of "the dual movement in which certain homosexual constituencies have embraced US nationalist agendas and have also been embraced by nationalist agendas" (xxiv), Puar cites the post-9/11 patriotism expressed by many White LGBT individuals through their support of the War on Terror, within the historical context of governmental affirmation of same-sex marriage and the legal overturning of sodomy regulations. Among Puar's analytical interventions to studies of race, sexuality, nation, and violence, I find two aspects particularly useful for my work: first, she reverses the conventional notion of queers as always resistant and oppositional, and instead locates their complicity as a (sexual) minority group to a hegemonic political and sociocultural order; and second, she tracks the inclusion of a marginalized community into the folds of the nation-state by rejecting and distinguishing themselves from an-Other constituency.

Vestiges of ethno-nationalism can be gleaned in some of the critical writings on the *Maclean's* article. For instance, Jeet Heer, one of the book co-editors that used the "Too Asian?" controversy to address race and representation in Canadian higher education (Gilmour, Bhandar, Heer, & Ma 2012), states that

> the "Asian campus" is only a problem if you believe that Asian-Canadians are not real Canadians ... [It creates a] distinction between Canadians whose presence in universities is natural and those Canadians who, even if they were born in Canada, are seen as alien intruders. (Heer 2010)

Henry Yu (2010a), a University of British Columbia professor, also asks,

> Have we not advanced enough to recognize that people with black hair who do not look like their families came from Europe can still be "Canadian," rather than harbouring the assumption of the writers that "Asian" is the opposite of "born in Canada"?

Both Heer and Yu, alongside many Asian Canadian activists and organizers whom I worked with, are making an important political point that Asian Canadians are "real Canadians" and not opposite of Whites "born in Canada." Yet in their articulation to equate Asian Canadians *as Canadians*, they also indicate that Asian Canadians are *not Asians*. In short, ethno-national Asian Canadians are Canadians who happen to have Asian ancestry, but are not Asians.

The Asian Canadian ethno-national move to distance themselves from the Asian foreign-national is evident in the *Maclean's* article. Describing the social dynamics at University of Waterloo, one of the institutions considered "too Asian," the article indicates that students call the mathematics and computer buildings on campus "mainland China" and "downtown China," where students "can go for days without speaking English" (Findlay & Köhler 2010, 80). The Asian Canadian students interviewed in the article highlight some of the tensions between them and Asian international students. An Asian Canadian student finds that "The mainland China group tends to stick together," while another states that "We can talk to them, but we don't mingle." At various community and organizing discussions that I attended and participated in, a major point of contention for many Asian Canadians is *Maclean's* visual use of two university-aged Asian men carrying the flag of the People's Republic of China as the opening photograph for the article. They claimed that the magazine was reinforcing the stereotypes of Asian Canadians as having primary affinity and affiliation with Asia (with China, in this case) and of Asian Canadians as perpetual foreigners in Canada. Underpinning such differentiations is the growing tension between the Canada-born or -raised Asian Canadians and the Asia-born and -raised Asians, an issue that has been openly and often heatedly discussed in social co-ethnic circles, yet has received relatively little scholarly attention.

My intellectual and political concern with ethno-nationalism derives partly from my own autobiography. As someone who was born in the Philippines, yet raised and educated in the United States, and moved to Canada a couple of years prior to the "Too Asian?" controversy, I felt uneasy with what I perceived to be an ardent assertion of Canadianness by Asian Canadian friends and colleagues during the campaign. As someone who did not identify as an Asian Canadian, much less as a Canadian, I felt excluded at certain moments of our organizing, and began to wonder the limits of the political strategy in claiming Canadianness for pan-Asian solidarity and for coalition building among racialized minority and diasporic groups. However, given my previous experiences of anti-racist and pro-immigration advocacy in the United States, I understand and have enacted similar moves to assert allegiance and claim belonging to the dominant-national. To me, ethnonationalism is a strategic form of identification and resistance by racialized minorities who contest and redress their marginalized conditions by appropriating and associating with the White-dominant nation-state to gain status and recognition as rightful citizens. Therefore, my disapproval of ethno-nationalism is an intimate and self-reflexive critique, one that is pointed towards fellow racialized minority scholars, educators, and activists and towards myself who have mobilized it even in the name of social justice.

The seduction of ethno-nationalism for racialized minorities is the promise of inclusion in a hegemonic nation-state that dangles the affective rites of belonging and the juridical rights of citizenship. Its appeal can be quite considerable given the history and continuation of racist exclusion and oppression at both individual and institutional levels. Ethno-nationalism coincides with liberal multiculturalism that is premised on universal and group-differentiated rights. Ethno-national Asian Canadians can claim their universal Canadianness and their differentiated Asianness, so long as their Asianness remains subsumed under the dominant sociocultural order. In other words, their Asian ethno-racial background primarily functions as a modifier to their Canadian national subject position. Hence, ethno-national Asian Canadians are Canadians who happen to have Asian ancestry, but are not Asians. The ethno-national disavows the foreign-national – in this case, the Asian foreign-national – since that figure symbolizes what is deemed as too foreign, the opposite of the dominant-national or White-Canadian. The political bargain struck by the ethno-national is their strategic alignment and identification with the dominant-national, and the rejection of the foreign-national, in order to assert what they deem as their rightful place in the nation-state.

Conclusion

The educational and political organizing around the *Maclean's* "Too Asian?" article produced a mixture of results. *Maclean's* did not apologize, thereby dismissing the central demand of the campaign. On 25 November 2010, it published an official statement to the critical public commentaries, which ended with:

> Although the phrase "Too Asian?" was a question and, again, a quotation from an authoritative source, it upset many people. We expected that it would be provocative, but we did not intend to cause offence. (*Maclean's* 2010)

On the following day, the Chinese Canadian National Council–Toronto Chapter received a letter from *Maclean's* legal counsel in response to the delivered Open Letter, of which CCNC Toronto was one of over 100 organizational signatories. The letter from lawyer Julian Porter indicated that "My client objects to your deliberate and obscene misrepresentation of *Maclean's* journalism and in particular your attribution to *Maclean's* of the phrase 'yellow and brown perils.'" It considered the Open Letter's attribution of this phrase to the magazine as "objectionable" and "defamatory." It culminated with a "demand that you withdraw the letter immediately and publicly acknowledge that *Maclean's* never made such a statement, and apologize to *Maclean's* for the misquotation and the imputation of racist views suggested by the phrase." Then, a year later, on 14 December 2011, the Solidarity Committee Against Anti-Asian Racism received a written reply from the Ministry of Canadian Heritage and Official Languages in response to our petition campaign for the federal agency to stop subsidizing the magazine, based on the research by Anna Liu of Asian Canadian Labour Alliance. Minister James Moore stated that

> Freedom of expression is a concept that is constitutionally enshrined in Canada and one of the cornerstones of our democracy. Our Government supports a free and independent press, and we are committed to making responsible choices in implementing public funds.

In sum, *Maclean's* non-apology response, its legal retribution, and the government's invocation of freedom of expression were three solid strikes against the campaign.

However, these strikes did not deter the educational and political work of Asian Canadian activists and allies. In spite of *Maclean's* refusal, organizers continued to lobby politicians to condemn the "Too Asian?" article and demand a public apology from the magazine. In spite of the legal threat, the Solidarity Committee Against Anti-Asian Racism did not withdraw the Open Letter, did not apologize to *Maclean's*, and instead used their newly developed network list of over 100 organizational partners across the country to share information and coordinate actions. In spite of the federal minister's response, activists asserted their support of freedom of expression, but continued to question the government's failure to enforce its own rule regarding withdrawal of public funding from periodicals with offensive content. Moreover, Asian Canadians and allies deployed conventional and new tactics of outreaching, raising awareness, and working with racialized minority communities and the general public. They used mainstream, ethnic, and social media to share critical perspectives, report on events, and announce public forums. Organized discussions on race, media, and higher education proliferated in many universities and community centers across the country. The Solidarity Committee Against Anti-Asian Racism has convened two "anniversary" conferences in order to continue the difficult yet necessary conversations on race and anti-racism.[8] When I asked fellow activists about the significance of the "Too Asian?" controversy, they shared two important positive effects: it produced local and national coalitions for anti-racist, pan-Asian, and cross-cultural organizing; and it generated much-needed critical discussions on race and racism, especially in relation to Asians in Canada.

Even though Asians constitute the largest racialized minority population in Canada, their subject position as a racial collective entity has received relatively little theoretical and empirical analysis. I am mindful of the tremendous diversity within this group in relation to ancestral and national backgrounds, migration and generational patterns, socio-economic status, genders, sexual orientations, and religious and spiritual beliefs, among other markers of difference. For instance, the conditions and trajectories of those who came as investor or business immigrants from Hong Kong in the mid-1990s are vastly different from those who arrived from the Philippines as live-in caregivers in the same time period (Coloma et al. 2012). It is also problematic to homogenize the experiences of those from the same ethnic/regional background. For example, Punjabi Sikhs composed the overwhelming majority of South Asian immigration in the early 1900s. Now they are joined by individuals and families from other parts of India, by those of Indian ancestry but are from the Caribbean, Africa, and Europe, and by those from other countries in the subcontinent, such as Bangladesh, Pakistan, and Sri Lanka (Buchignani et al. 1985). Yet, in spite of such diversity, people of Asian descent are generally construed as Canada's model minority and the main beneficiaries of liberal multiculturalism and immigration policies. They are perceived to be diligent, docile, and self-sufficient, traits that are positively regarded and that derive putatively from their cultural traditions and filial obligations (Maclear 1994; Pon 2000). These traits were valued by financial elites and industrial capitalists in the past when Canada was establishing itself as a nation-state. They are similarly valued by today's economic, political, and educational elites as Canada continues to build its capacity for national prosperity and global competitiveness in the twenty-first century.

In this chapter, my central objective has been to produce a sharper analytical grammar of race, especially in relation to Asians as a racialized minority group in White-dominant, multicultural nation-states like Canada. Instead of reinforcing the model minority thesis,

I consider the racial subject position of Asian Canadians as an un/wanted minority from a broader historical vantage point. The paradoxical subjectivity of Asian Canadians as wanted and unwanted, as desired and undesirable, for inclusion and integration in the nation-state was and continues to be shaped by economic, political, and sociocultural conditions locally, nationally, and globally. To resolve this paradox, many Asian Canadians claim their affective belonging and assert their juridical citizenship to the nation-state as genuine Canadians. They do so in order to strategically work through and against the violence inflicted on them. These violent acts can range from seemingly mundane micro-aggressions, such being repeatedly asked "Where are you from?" to blatant violations of their human rights during times of war in the name of national security.

The discursive tactic of ethno-nationalism, therefore, can be understood as a form of resistance by racialized minorities in general and by Asian Canadians in particular to address and redress racist exclusion and oppression in White-dominant contexts. Ethno-nationalism enables Asian Canadians to identify and associate with the nation-state, which desires and disavows them. It facilitates their claim to belonging and citizenship in spite or, perhaps, because of persistent efforts to reject and marginalize them. In the current moment, Asian Canadians have embraced Canadian ideals of nationalism, infused with social multiculturalism, economic neo-liberalism, and political democracy.

Simultaneously, the Canadian nation-state has embraced Asian Canadians for their financial, labour, and educational capital. Working alongside Jasbir Puar's (2007) concept of homonationalism, I suggest that ethno-nationalism takes place within contexts of a dual movement in which certain racialized minority groups have embraced White-dominant nationalist agendas and have also been embraced by these nationalist agendas. In the case of Asian Canadians, their ethno-nationalist move occurs in their simultaneous assertion of Canadianness and rejection of Asianness. While such a move may seem strategic in order to lay political claim to a White-dominant nation-state, the consequences for pan-Asian solidarity and for community building across racialized minority and diasporic communities are profound. In particular, foreign-nationals who already have limited juridical and tenuous sociocultural relationships to the White-dominant nation-state will become disregarded even further. In the end, our task as critical scholars of race and anti-racism is to formulate and enact an educational and political praxis in which the advancement of a racialized minority group does not occur at the expense of another group in the margins.[9]

NOTES

1 I employ the categorical term "Asian" to designate the heterogeneous, dynamic, and socio-politically constructed grouping of peoples, cultures, materials, and ideas that derive from East Asian, South Asian, Southeast Asian, and West Asian backgrounds. It is, admittedly, geographically regional and broadly continental in its articulation. It is attentive to the local and global histories, legacies, and continuations of imperialisms, colonialisms, wars, and conflicts over sovereignties, nationalisms, and territorialities. My use of the term "Asian," especially in the Canadian context, moves away from the dominant emphasis on East Asia and on the peoples and cultures of Chinese, Japanese, and Korean ancestry. Its conventional use often excludes other Asian ethnic groups, such as Indians and Filipina/os (e.g., Coloma et al. 2012). *Maclean's* reinforces the East Asian emphasis in the article by focusing on "Asian" individuals and organizations that,

in actuality, are primarily of Chinese ancestry. Hence, as a discursive intervention, I mobilize the term "Asian" to address the broader and more inclusive grouping, and name particular ethnic groups in reference to regulations and events that specifically focus on them.

2 According to Canada's Employment Equity Act (S.C. 1995, c. 44), "members of visible minorities means persons, other than aboriginal peoples, who are non-Caucasian in race or non-white in colour" (http://laws-lois.justice.gc.ca/eng/acts/E-5.401/page-1.html). I prefer to use the term "racialized minority" instead of "visible minority" since, following Block and Galabuzi (2011),

> the term racialized is used to acknowledge "race" as a social construct and a way of describing a group of people. Racialization is the process through which groups come to be designated as different and on that basis subjected to differential and unequal treatment. (19)

Building on my deployment of the term "Asian" and tracking the racialization of Asians in Canada as an un/wanted minority group, I explicate and expand on an insight made by cultural critic Roy Miki (2000): "these 'undesirables' would translate over time into 'Asian Canadians'" (50).

3 I learn from and work alongside anti-racist feminists who refuse to compartmentalize the intellectual and activist, the personal and political, the private and public (e.g., Ng, Staton & Scane 1995; Razack, Smith & Thobani 2010).

4 Unfortunately, many economic immigrants experience deprofessionalization, deskilling, and downward mobility when they arrive and settle in Canada. Even though the immigration system privileges those with educational, occupational, and financial capital, they confront considerable institutionalized barriers, especially in the realm of employment. For instance, their academic and professional credentials are not recognized as on par by Canadian universities and accreditation agencies; they are required to have Canadian work experience; and when employed, they face racial, gendered, and linguistic/accent discrimination (e.g., Block & Galabuzi 2011; Coloma et al. 2012; Razack et al. 2010).

5 At this meeting, educator Maria Yau, who convened a community conference titled "East Asian Parents: Multiple Pathways to Success," connected the *Maclean's* "Too Asian?" article to the *Toronto Star* newspaper article on her conference, both of which were published at the same time. She indicated that these media outlets practised sensationalized journalism by stereotyping Asian parents as academically obsessed tyrants who were "pushing their children into university programs for which many have no real interest or talent and often quit in distress" (Brown 2010).

6 The Solidarity Committee Against Anti-Asian Racism was, and continues to be, pivotal in my political education and organizing in Toronto.

7 Other activist and organizing acts included wearing "Too Asian for *Maclean's*" buttons; writing letters and postcards to *Maclean's* parent company, Rogers Communications; staging a flash mob at a Rogers store in a busy Toronto shopping mall, led by the Youth Coalition co-chairs Florence Li and Chase Lo; and creating a satirical YouTube video on multi-racial harmony through a parody of the "We Are the World" song by Tetsuro Shigematsu and his collaborators at University of British Columbia.

8 The 2012 "anniversary" conference was convened at Ryerson University in Toronto, spearheaded by Gordon Pon and May Lui of CCNC Toronto, in conjunction with a simultaneous gathering at University of British Columbia, led by Ray Hsu of the Asian Canadian Writers' Workshop. Moreover, Neethan Shan of the Council of Agencies Serving South Asians featured the youth and community organizing on the "Too Asian?" issue in its Racism Free Ontario campaign, and Estella Muyinda of the National Anti-Racism Council of Canada highlighted the issue at one of its annual events for the International Day for the Elimination of Racial Discrimination.

REFERENCES

Adachi, Ken. 1976. *The Enemy that Never Was: A History of the Japanese Canadians*. Toronto: McClelland and Stewart.

AngusReid. 2010. "More Canadians are Questioning the Benefits of Immigration." 10 September. Retrieved 27 March 2013. http://angusreid.org/more_canadians_are_questioning_the_benefits_of_immigration/.

Asia/Canada. n.d. "Too Asian?" Retrieved 3 December 2012. http://asia-canada.ca/new-attitudes/continuing-tensions/too-asian.

Asia Pacific Foundation of Canada. 2011. *2011 National Opinion Poll: Canadian Views on Asia*. Vancouver, BC: APFC.

Asia Pacific Foundation of Canada. 2012a. "Immigrants by Category—All Categories." Retrieved 20 January 2013. http://www.asiapacific.ca/statistics/immigration/arrivals/immigration-category-all-categories.

Asia Pacific Foundation of Canada. 2012b. "Immigrants by Regional Source as Percentage of Total Immigration." Retrieved 20 January 2013. http://www.asiapacific.ca/statistics/immigration/arrivals/immigrants-regional-source-percentage-total-immigration.

Asia Pacific Foundation of Canada. 2012c. "Immigration by Category – Economic Immigrants." Retrieved 20 January 2013. http://www.asiapacific.ca/statistics/immigration/arrivals/immigration-category-economic-immigrants.

Block, Sheila, and Grace-Edward Galabuzi. 2011. *Canada's Colour Coded Labour Market: The Gap for Racialized Workers*. Ottawa: Canadian Centre for Policy Alternatives.

Brown, Craig. 2007. *The Illustrated History of Canada*. Toronto: Key Porter.

Brown, Louise. 2010. "Educators Encourage Parents of Asian Background to Let Their Children Study Trades and Arts." *Toronto Star*. 10 November. Retrieved 3 December 2012. https://www.thestar.com/life/parent/2010/11/10/educators_encourage_parents_of_asian_background_to_let_their_children_study_trades_and_arts.html.

Buchignani, Norman, Doreen M. Indra, and Ram Srivastava. 1985. *Continuous Journey: A Social History of South Asians in Canada*. Toronto: McClelland and Stewart.

Citizenship and Immigration Canada. 2010. "Government of Canada Will Welcome More Economic Immigrants in 2010." 26 June. Retrieved 27 March 2013. http://news.gc.ca/web/article-en.do?nid=543279.

Citizenship and Immigration Canada. 2011. "Canada Welcomes Highest Number of Legal Immigrants in 50 Years While Taking Action to Maintain the Integrity of Canada's Immigration System." 13 February. Retrieved 27 March 2013. http://news.gc.ca/web/article-en.do?nid=588879.

Coloma, Roland Sintos, and Brad Lee. 2010. "Open Letter: A Call to Eliminate Anti-Asian Racism." 23 November. Retrieved 3 December 2012. http://asiancanadianstudies.ca/node/31.

Coloma, Roland Sintos, Bonnie McElhinny, Ethel Tungohan, John Paul Catungal, and Lisa M. Davidson, eds. 2012. *Filipinos in Canada: Disturbing Invisibility*. Toronto: University of Toronto Press.

Connor, Walker. 1993. *Ethnonationalism: The Quest for Understanding*. Princeton, NJ: Princeton University Press.

Findlay, Stephanie, and Nicholas Köhler. 2010. "'Too Asian?' A Term Used in the US to Talk About Racial Imbalance at Ivy League Schools is Now Being Whispered on Canadian Campuses–By Everyone but the Students Themselves, Who Speak out Loud and Clear." *Maclean's* 123, no. 45: 76–81.

Foreign Affairs and International Trade Canada. 2012. "International Education: A Key Driver of Canada's Future Prosperity." Retrieved 27 March 2013. http://www.international.gc.ca/education/assets/pdfs/ies_report_rapport_sei-eng.pdf.

Gilmour, R.J., Davina Bhandar, Jeet Heer, and Michael C.K. Ma, eds. 2012. *"Too Asian?" Racism, Privilege, and Post-Secondary Education*. Toronto: Between the Lines.

Goutor, David. 2007. "Constructing the "Great Menace': Canadian Labour's Opposition to Asian Immigration, 1880–1911." *Canadian Historical Review* 88 (4): 549–76.

Heer, Jeet. 2010. "Too Brazen: *Maclean's*, Margaret Wente, and the Canadian Media's Inarticulacy About Race." *The Walrus*. 24 November. Retrieved 3 December 2012. https://restructure.wordpress.com/2010/11/26/criticism-of-macleans-too-asian-by-jeet-heer/.

Kymlicka, Will. 1996. *Multicultural Citizenship: A Liberal Theory of Minority Rights*. Oxford, New York: Oxford University Press. http://dx.doi.org/10.1093/0198290918.001.0001.

Lai, David C. 1988. *Chinatowns: Towns within Cities in Canada*. Vancouver: University of British Columbia Press.

Li, Peter S. 1998. *The Chinese in Canada*. 2nd ed. Toronto: Oxford University Press.

Li, Peter S. 2003. *Destination Canada: Immigration Debates and Issues*. Don Mills, ON: Oxford University Press.

Library and Archives Canada. 2012. "Driving the Nation: The Last Spike and the Faces of CPR." March 14. Retrieved 30 January 2013. https://www.youtube.com/watch?v=sQcm4RYrpjw.

Maclean's. 2010. "Merit: The Best and Only way to Decide who gets into University." 25 November. Retrieved 3 December 2012. http://www.macleans.ca/2010/11/25/who-gets-into-university/.

Maclear, Kyo. 1994. "The Myth of the 'Model Minority': Re-Thinking the Education of Asian Canadians." *Our Schools/Our Selves* 5, no. 3: 54–76.

Mahtani, Minelle. 2010. "Canadian Media: It's Time to Cover the Undercovered." *Globe and Mail*. 19 November. Retrieved 3 December 2012. http://www.theglobeandmail.com/opinion/canadian-media-its-time-to-cover-the-undercovered/article1314521/.

Mallick, Heather. 2012. "Review of the Book '*Too Asian?*' by R.J. Gilmour, D. Bhandar, J. Heer, & M.C.K. Ma." Retrieved 3 December 2012.https://www.btlbooks.com/othertextinfo.php?index=861.

Mar, Lisa R. 2010. *Brokering Belonging: Chinese in Canada's Exclusion Era, 1885–1945*. Toronto: Oxford University Press. http://dx.doi.org/10.1093/acprof:oso/9780199733132.001.0001.

Mawani, Renisa. 2010. *Colonial Proximities: Crossracial Encounters and Juridical Truths in British Columbia, 1871–1921*. Vancouver: University of British Columbia Press.

Miki, Roy. 2000. "Altered States: Global Currents, the Spectral Nation, and the Production of 'Asian Canadian.'" *Journal of Canadian Studies/Revue d'études canadiennes* 35 (3): 43–72.

Miki, Roy. 2005. *Redress: Inside the Japanese Canadian Call for Justice*. Vancouver: Raincoast.

Ng, Roxana, Pat Staton, and Joyce Scane, eds. 1995. *Anti-Racism, Feminism, and Critical Approaches to Education*. Westport, CT: Praeger.

Noma, Ken. 2010. "Letter to *Maclean's* re: 'Too Asian.'" 28 November 28. Retrieved 20 January 2013. http://www.najc.ca/human-rights-committee-action/letter-to-mcleans-re- "too-asian"/.

Oikawa, Mona. 2012. *Cartographies of Violence: Japanese Canadian Women, Memory, and the Subjects of the Internment*. Toronto: University of Toronto Press.

Pon, Gordon. 2000. "Importing the Asian 'Model Minority' Discourse into Canada: Implications for Social Work and Education." *Canadian Social Work Review* 17 (2): 277–91.

Poy, Vivienne. 2010. "Letter to the Honourable James Moore." 16 December. Retrieved 20 January 2013. http://www.viviennepoy.ca/english/speeches/2010Speeches/Moore,J_161210(2).pdf.

Preston, Valerie, and Lucia Lo. 2000. "'Asian Theme' Malls in Suburban Toronto: Land Use Conflict in Richmond Hill." *Canadian Geographer/Géographe canadien* 44 (2): 182–90. http://dx.doi.org/10.1111/j.1541-0064.2000.tb00701.x.

Puar, Jasbir. 2007. *Terrorist Assemblages: Homonationalism in Queer Times*. Durham, NC: Duke University Press. http://dx.doi.org/10.1215/9780822390442.

Razack, Sherene, Malinda Smith, and Sunera Thobani, eds. 2010. *States of Race: Critical Race Feminism for the 21st Century*. Toronto: Between the Lines.

Statistics Canada. 2010. "Study: Projections of the Diversity of the Canadian Population." Retrieved 3 December 2012. http://www.statcan.gc.ca/daily-quotidien/100309/dq100309a-eng.htm.

Thobani, Sunera. 2007. *Exalted Subjects: Studies in the Making of Race and Nation in Canada*. Toronto: University of Toronto Press.

Toope, Stephen. 2011. "The Battle for Brains." *Globe and Mail*. 26 January. Retrieved 20 January 2013. http://www.theglobeandmail.com/opinion/stephen-toope-how-international-students-change-canadian-schools/article602521/?from=4480232.

Ward, Peter M. 2002. *White Canada Forever: Popular Attitudes and Public Policy Toward Orientals in British Columbia*. 3rd ed. Montreal and Kingston: McGill-Queen's University Press.

Wildavsky, Ben. 2010. *The Great Brain Race: How Global Universities are Reshaping the World*. Princeton, NJ: Princeton University Press.

Yu, Henry. 2010a. "Why *Maclean's* and Racism Should No Longer Define Canada." *Georgia Straight*. 16 November. Retrieved 3 December 2012. http://www.straight.com/article-358546/vancouver/henry-yu-why-macleans-and-racism-should-no-longer-define-canada.

Yu, Henry. 2010b. "*Maclean's* Must Answer for Racial Profiling: Asian-Canadians Aren't Just Being Too Sensitive. There's a History Behind their Reaction to the Magazine's 'Too Asian?' Article." *Vancouver Sun*. 27 November. Retrieved 3 December 2012. http://henryyu.blogspot.com/2010/11/sorry-is-not-enough.html.

Contributors

Sedef Arat-Koç is Associate Professor in the Department of Politics and Public Administration and in the graduate program of Immigration and Settlement Studies at Ryerson University in Toronto. Her research focuses on Canada and the Middle East. In the Canadian context, her work addresses immigration policy and citizenship, especially their impact on immigrant women, and the racialization of Muslims in the post-9/11 period. In relation to the Middle East, she is interested in the politics of imperialism and the reconfiguration of social and political identities in the context of neo-liberalism and post–Cold War geopolitics in Turkey. Her research has examined "white Turkishness" and the influence of "neo-Ottomanism" on Turkish foreign policy and internal politics.

Abigail B. Bakan is Professor and Chair of the Department of Social Justice Education at the Ontario Institute for Studies in Education (OISE) of the University of Toronto. Her publications include *Theorizing Anti-Racism: Linkages in Marxism and Critical Race Theories* (edited with Enakshi Dua); *Negotiating Citizenship: Migrant Women in Canada and the Global System* (with Daiva Stasiulis); *Critical Political Studies: Debates and Dialogues from the Left* (edited with Eleanor MacDonald); and *Employment Equity Policy in Canada: An Interprovincial Comparison* (with Audrey Kobayashi). With Yasmeen Abu-Laban, she is conducting research on the United Nations World Conferences against Racism and the processes of racialization in the context of Israel/Palestine. Her articles have appeared in *Race and Class, Social Identities, Rethinking Marxism, Politikon, Socialist Studies, Atlantis, Signs, Canadian Journal of Law and Society*, and *Studies in Political Economy.*

Himani Bannerji is Professor of Sociology at York University in Toronto. Her research and writing life extends between Canada and India. Her interests encompass anti-racist feminism, Marxism, critical cultural theories, and historical sociology. On India, she has written *The Mirror of Class: Essays on Bengali Theatre* (1998), *Inventing Subjects: Studies in Hegemony, Patriarchy and Colonialism* (2001), and *Demography and Democracy: Essays on Nationalism, Gender and Ideology* (2011). On Canada, she is the author of *The Writing on the Wall: Essays of Feminism, Marxism and Anti-Racism* (1995) and *The Dark Side of the Nation: Essays on Multiculturalism, Nationalism and Racism* (2000), and the editor of *Retuning Gaze: Essays on Gender, Race and Class by Non-White Women* (1993). Her current research is on the social thought of Rabindranath Tagore.

Lily Cho is Associate Professor of English at York University in Toronto. Her book, *Eating Chinese: Culture on the Menu in Small Town Canada* (2010), examines the relationship between Chinese restaurants and Canadian culture. She is a member of the Toronto Photography Seminar. Her essays have been published in journals such as *Interventions*, *Canadian Literature*, and *Photography and Culture*. She is currently conducting research on two projects. *Mass Capture: Chinese Head Tax and the Making of Non-Citizens in Canada* examines the relationship between surveillance and citizenship. *Asian Values: Fictions of Finance and Beautiful Money* explores diasporic movement and theories of value in post-colonial Asia.

Roland Sintos Coloma is Professor of Cultural Studies in Education and Chair of the Department of Teacher Education at Northern Kentucky University (USA). Previously he was a faculty member in the Department of Social Justice Education at the Ontario Institute for Studies in Education (OISE) of the University of Toronto, where he taught the first courses on Asian Canadian History and Theorizing Asian Canada at the university. His research interests include history and cultural studies; race, gender, and sexuality; curriculum, policy, and teacher education; and Filipina/o and Asian diasporas. He is the lead editor of *Filipinos in Canada: Disturbing Invisibility* (2012), editor of *Postcolonial Challenges in Education* (2009), and editor of the *Educational Studies* journal. He is completing a book manuscript on a history of colonial education in the Philippines under United States rule in the early 1900s.

Eric Fong is Professor and Chair of the Department of Sociology at the Chinese University of Hong Kong. He is also Director of the university's Centre of Migration and Mobility. Previously he was a Professor of Sociology at the University of Toronto. He served as President of the North American Chinese Sociologists Association, President of the Canadian Population Society, and Chair of the International Migration Section of the American Sociological Association. Fong has published widely in the areas of immigration and Asians in Canada. His forthcoming book, *Immigration and City*, will be published by Polity.

Richard Fung is Professor in the Faculty of Art at OCAD University. He is a video artist and writer, born in Trinidad and based in Toronto. His documentaries and experimental videos include *Orientations: Lesbian and Gay Asians* (1984) and its redux *Re:Orientations* (2016), *My Mother's Place* (1990), *Sea in the Blood* (2000), and *Rex vs. Singh* (2008), co-directed with John Greyson and Ali Kazimi. His essays have been published in numerous journals and anthologies, and he is the co-author with Monika Kin Gagnon of *13: Conversations on Art and Cultural Race Politics*. Among other honours, Richard is the recipient of the 2000 Bell Canada Award for outstanding achievement in video art, the 2001 Toronto Arts Award for Media Art, and the 2015 Kessler Award for significant contribution to LGBTQ Studies.

Kenneth Huynh is a PhD candidate in the Department of Social Justice Education at the Ontario Institute for Studies in Education (OISE) of the University of Toronto. His SSHRC-funded dissertation, *Model Re-Framings: Asian Canadian Cultural Poetics and Racial Politics*, utilizes theories of race, representation, and affect to explore how Asian Canadian artists engage in politicized cultural work in the context of state-led multiculturalism. He has presented his research at the Canadian Ethnic Studies Association and the Association for Asian American Studies conferences. His article with Benjamin Woo entitled "Asian Fail: Chinese Canadian Men Talk About Race, Masculinity, and the Nerd Stereotype" (2015) appeared in *Social Identities*. He is currently a Visiting Fellow in the Department of English at City University of Hong Kong.

Alice Ming Wai Jim is Associate Professor of Contemporary Art at Concordia University in Montreal. She teaches contemporary art, media arts, ethnocultural and global art histories (with a focus on contemporary Asian and Asian Canadian art), international art exhibitions, and curatorial studies. She is founding co-editor of the scholarly journal *Asian Diasporic Visual Cultures and the Americas*, and is the 2015 recipient of the *Centre de documentation d'Artexte* Award for Research in Contemporary Art. From 2003 to 2006, she was curator of the Vancouver International Centre for Contemporary Asia Art (Centre A). Recent publications include contributions to *Third Text, Journal of Curatorial Studies, Journal of Visual Culture, Triennial City: Localising Asian Art* (2014), *Negotiations in a Vacant Lot: Studying the Visual in Canada* (2014), *Human Rights and the Arts: Perspectives from Global Asia* (2014), and *Mass Effect: Art and the Internet in the 21st Century* (2015).

Yasmin Jiwani is Professor in the Department of Communication Studies at Concordia University in Montreal. Her research interests include mediations of race, gender, and violence in the context of war stories; press reporting of sexual violence and femicide; and representations of women of colour in popular television programs. She is the author of *Discourses of Denial: Mediations of Race, Gender and Violence* (2006), lead editor of *Girlhood: Redefining the Limits* (2006), and co-editor of *Faces of Violence in the Lives of Girls* (2014). Currently she is working on a manuscript focusing on representations of race and gender in Canadian media.

Laura J. Kwak is a PhD graduate of the Department of Social Justice Education at the University of Toronto. Her thesis, "Asian Conservatives in Canada's Parliament: A Study in Race and Governmentality" (2016), challenges the supposed incommensurability of racialized identity and conservative politics by examining Asian politicians who have served as Members of Parliament in Canada's conservative parties. Contributing to research on political representation, racial governmentality, and critical race theory, the study investigates how politicians of colour are vital to the state's narrative of post-racialism as a way to sustain the social order.

Peter S. Li is Professor Emeritus of Sociology at the University of Saskatchewan. He has published about 100 academic papers and 11 books, including *The Chinese in Canada*. He served as president of the Canadian Sociology Association and as editor of the *Journal of International Migration and Integration*. He has received several awards, including the Outstanding Contribution Award (2002) from the Canadian Sociology Association, the Earned Doctor of Letters (2011) from the University of Saskatchewan, and the Queen Elizabeth II Diamond Jubilee Medal (2012) from the Governor General of Canada. He is a fellow of the Royal Society of Canada, and was appointed to the Order of Canada in 2016.

Roy Miki is Professor Emeritus of English at Simon Fraser University in Vancouver. He has published widely on Canadian literature and on Japanese Canadian concerns. He is the author of *Redress: Inside the Japanese Canadian Call for Justice* (2004) and five books of poems. His third book of poems, *Surrender* (2001), received the Governor General's Award for Poetry. He has contributed to many collections of critical essays, including *Speaking*

My Truth: Reflections on Reconciliation and Residential School (2012); *Reconciling Canada: Critical Perspectives on the Culture of Redress* (2013); and *Critical Collaborations: Indigeneity, Diaspora, and Ecology in Canadian Literary Studies* (2014). His recent books are *Mannequin Rising* (2011), a series of poems and photo collages; *In Flux: Transnational Shifts in Asian Canadian Writing* (2011), an essay collection; and *Dolphin SOS* (2014), a children's book co-written with his wife Slavia Miki, which received the 2015 Christie Harris Illustrated Children's Literature Prize.

Roxana Ng was Professor in the Adult Education and Community Development program and Director of the Centre for Women's Studies in Education at the Ontario Institute for Studies in Education (OISE) of the University of Toronto. Her research analysed the experiences of immigrant women, including the experience of exclusion in the labour market; the lives of garment workers in Canada; race, gender, and class; and embodied learning and decolonizing pedagogy. A pioneer and leading figure in the fields of immigration and Asian Canadian studies, she died of cancer in 2013.

Mona Oikawa is Associate Professor in the Department of Equity Studies at York University in Toronto, where she teaches critical race and anti-colonial studies. She is the author of *Cartographies of Violence: Japanese Canadian Women, Memory, and the Subjects of the Internment* (2012). Her current research examines the National Association of Japanese Canadians' relationship to Indigenous peoples and Canadian settler colonialism.

Gordon Pon is Associate Professor in the School of Social Work at Ryerson University in Toronto. His research interests include anti-racism, anti-colonialism, child welfare, and the racialization of Chinese Canadians. Prior to joining Ryerson, he was a frontline worker in child welfare. His research in child welfare examines the experiences of racialized workers and how anti-Black racism and colonialism are implicated in the over-representation of Black children in the care of child welfare authorities.

Geraldine Pratt is Professor of Geography and Canada Research Chair in Transnationalism and Precarious Labour at the University of British Columbia. She has worked in collaboration with the Philippine Women Centre of British Columbia (PWC of BC), Filipino Canadian Youth Alliance, and Migrante. She is the author of *Working Feminism* (2004) and *Families Apart: Migrant Mothers and the Conflicts of Labor and Love* (2012), co-author of *Gender, Work and Space* (1995) and *Film and Urban Space: Critical Possibilities* (2014), and co-editor of *The Global and the Intimate: Feminism in Our Time* (2012). With Caleb Johnston and in collaboration with PWC of BC, she co-authored *Nanay*, a testimonial play that premiered at Vancouver's PuSh Festival (2009), and toured in Berlin (2009), Edinburgh (2012), Whitehorse (2015), and Metro Manila (2013, 2015). Working with the Conversation Collective in Whitehorse Yukon, she was involved in the development and staging of *Tlingipino Bingo!* in 2016.

Sherene H. Razack is the Penney Kanner Endowed Chair in Women's Studies in the Department of Gender Studies at the University of California–Los Angeles (USA). Her recent publications include *Dying from Improvement: Inquests and Inquiries into Indigenous Deaths in Custody* (2015), *At the Limits of Justice: Women of Colour on Terror* (edited with

Suvendrini Perera, 2014), and *Casting Out: The Eviction of Muslims from Western Law and Politics* (2008).

Daiva Stasiulis is Professor of Sociology at Carleton University in Ottawa. Growing up in an immigrant household of parents who arrived as "displaced persons" from the Baltic Republics had a profound effect in shaping her research interests. Her publications explore Canada's white settler colonial and migration history, multiculturalism, citizenship and statelessness, anti-racist feminism, and intersectionality. She has worked with domestic worker associations, and served as Chair of the United Nations Expert Group Meeting on Violence Against Female Migrant Workers. With co-author Abigail Bakan, she was awarded the 2007 Canadian Women's Studies Association annual book prize for *Negotiating Citizenship: Migrant Women in Canada and the Global System* (2005). Her most recent book, co-edited with Amanda Gouws, is *Gender and Multiculturalism: North-South Perspectives* (2014). She is the 2016 recipient of the Marston Lafrance Award, and is completing a book manuscript on *The Emotional Cartographies of Dual Citizenship: The Lebanese Diaspora in the Shadow of War.*

Sunera Thobani is Associate Professor in the Institute for Gender, Race, Sexuality, and Social Justice at the University of British Columbia. Her scholarship focuses on critical race, postcolonial, and feminist theories; globalization, citizenship, and migration; and Muslim women, the War on Terror, and media. She served as Director of the Race, Autobiography, Gender, and Age Centre at UBC; as Ruth Wynn Woodward Endowed Chair in Women's Studies at Simon Fraser University in Vancouver; as President of the National Action Committee on the Status of Women; and as founding member of Researchers and Academics of Colour for Equity. She is the author of *Exalted Subjects: Studies in the Making of Race and Nation in Canada* (2007), and co-editor of *Asian Women: Interconnections* (2005) and *States of Race: Critical Race Feminist Theory for the 21st Century* (2010). Her research has been published in peer-reviewed journals including *Borderlands*, *Feminist Theory*, *International Journal of Communication*, and *Race & Class.*

Rita Wong is Associate Professor in Critical + Cultural Studies at the Emily Carr University of Art + Design in Vancouver. She is the author of four books of poetry: *undercurrent* (2015), *sybil unrest* (with Larissa Lai, 2008), *forage* (2007), and *monkeypuzzle* (1998). *forage* won Canada Reads Poetry in 2011. With Cindy Mochizuki, Wong co-authored *perpetual* (2015), a collection of graphic essays. She received the Emerging Writer Award from the Asian Canadian Writers Workshop in 1997 and the Dorothy Livesay Poetry Prize in 2008. Her work investigates the relationships among contemporary poetics, social justice, ecology, and decolonization. She has developed a humanities course focused on water, for which she received a fellowship from the Center for Contemplative Mind in Society. She and Dorothy Christian co-edited a collection of essays entitled *Downstream: Reimagining Water* (2016).

Henry Yu is Principal of St John's College at the University of British Columbia. His research and teaching involve collaborations with local communities, and he served as Co-Chair of the Anniversaries of Change Committee that oversaw a year of cultural events, art exhibits, and civic dialogues marking the 100th anniversary of the anti-Asian riots in Vancouver in 1907. In 2010–12, he was Co-Chair of the City of Vancouver's

Dialogues between First Nations, Urban Aboriginal, and Immigrant Communities project, and the Project Lead for the *Chinese Canadian Stories* public education project. In 2015, Yu was appointed Co-Chair for the Legacy Initiatives Advisory Council following the province's apology in 2014 for BC's historic anti-Chinese legislation. He has received the Queen Elizabeth II Diamond Jubilee Medal and the BC Multicultural Award in recognition of his community-based research and leadership.